Change/Education

Change/ Education

Issues in Perspective
SECOND EDITION

EDITED BY

Glenn Smith
Elice Rogers
Richard Tapia
Linda O'Neill
Tony Porter
Carmen A. Cruz
Norma Salazar
Alejandro Sentis
Bruce Woll
Marge Tye Zuba
Fred M. Schied

LEPS Press, Northern Illinois University
DeKalb, Illinois 60115

Cover Design: Katrina Elisa Davis-Salazar

Art: Richard Tapia
         Guang Li Zhang

Managing Editor: Caryn Rudy

Distributed by LEPS Press

Library of Congress Catalog-in-Publication
Change/education: issues in perspective / edited by Glenn Smith ... [et al.]. — 2nd ed.
        p.   cm.
    Includes bibliographical references and index.
    ISBN 1-879528-12-6
    1. Multicultural education—United States. 2. Education, Bilingual—United States.
3. Minorities—Education—United States. 4. Discrimination in education—United States. I. Smith,
Glenn, 1939
    LC1099.3.C48   1995   94-44349
    370.19'6—dc20   CIP

Contents

Contents

Contents

Contents

Preface

Glenn Smith

Each academic year more than 1200 students at Northern Illinois University enroll in a course entitled "Education as a Agent for Change."

The course encourages students to examine their inherited presuppositions, to be open to understanding life from perspectives quite different from those of their own families.

The editors and their confreres have chosen the material contained in this book because it illustrates important issues around the three themes of education, change, and agency. The selections in the first edition were a result of many hours of intense discussion. In the second edition, 25 percent of the material is new. The items retained from the first edition have all provoked animated discussions.

We do not expect everyone to reach a common opinion as a result of these readings. The editors themselves disagree about many issues. We all agree on one point: Dialog is important in learning and each participant is ultimately responsible for her or his own part of the conversation—and for his or her own conclusions.

We hope students who read this book will enter into dialog with each author, with each other, and with their co-learner/instructors about the issues.

We hope readers will experience a heightened sense of their own identities, become critically informed about multiculturalism, and gain a platform for thinking about and planning for the future.

Acknowledgements

Many people contributed to this volume. We want to thank the authors and publishers of the articles for permission to reprint them. And special thanks go to all those who offered their critical insights growing out of using the first edition in their classes.

Thanks to Katrina Elisa Davis-Salazar, Richard Tapia, and Guang Li Zhang for providing art.

Thanks to Amelia Gould, Lydia Larson, Geri Heberlie, Guang Li Zhang, for all their help.

Caryn Rudy managed the production process, set type, designed layout, and performed many other essential tasks with an impossible time schedule—all with her usual grace and enthusiasm.

Introduction: Mixed-Blood Nation

Jack Weatherford

Lower Fort Garry overlooks Manitoba's Red River, which flows north to form the broad Lake Winnipeg. The fort rises up on a lonely, quiet stretch of the river, not too far from the geographical center of the North American continent. If one drew a large X on a map of North America, running one line from northern Quebec to Baja California in Mexico, and the other from Florida to the northwestern tip of Alaska, the lines would intersect in southern Manitoba, near Lower Fort Garry.

At only a little over fifty degrees north of the equator, Lower Fort Garry lies only a few hundred miles north of the halfway point between the equator and the North Pole. Despite this equidistance, the climate of the area seems markedly more regulated by the Arctic than the tropics. This part of Canada feels the full blast of the winter winds that blow in from the north and make the area a zone of transition between the agricultural prairie of southern Canada and the northern tundra.

Trees grow in this area, but they are small, stunted things, barely higher than the single-story houses that dot the fields. Few of them grow large enough for a person to wrap both hands around the trunk without being able to touch fingers.

In most years, ice still covers parts of Lake Winnipeg in May.

The creamy limestone walls of the fort form a nearly perfect square, and the bastions built at each corner make it look, in fact, like a military fort. But since construction began on the fort in 1846, it always served as a trading fort of the Hudson's Bay Company in what the traders then called Rupert's Land. The bastion that seems to protect the fort actually served as washrooms, cookhouses, and storerooms rather than as shelters for cannons or sentries.

Because the fort occupies a high river bluff near a good limestone source, the typical visitor might assume that the builders of Lower Fort Garry had a major military, political, or perhaps economic reason for building it where they did. The fort seems to be the type that would protect the intersection of two great rivers, guard the crossing point of a traditional Indian trail, or serve as a northern boundary against attack.

Any of these could have been the reason, but cursory inspection dispels them all. The fort does not lie at the confluence of rivers or on the intersection of trails. It does not straddle an important boundary, and seems merely to divide one stretch of flat plain from another.

An older fort, the original Fort Garry, occupied a much better spot to the south at the confluence of the Assiniboine and Red rivers in the heart of what became the city of Winnipeg. Old Fort Garry to the south, and not Lower Fort Garry to the north, served as the crossing point of major trails and offered easier connection down to Lake of the Woods on the United States border, and from there into the Great Lakes and the cities of Ottawa and Montreal.

To find the reason why Governor George Simpson of the Hudson's Bay Company built Lower Fort Garry in 1839, we need to look beyond colonial policy, corporate interests, and economic accounts to Simpson's sex life. He built it because he had married a respectable white woman, his eighteen-year-old cousin Frances Simpson, and he wanted the fort to protect her. He did not need to protect her from the Indians or from the savage Americans to the south or the French to the east. Simpson built Lower Fort Garry to protect his new bride from having to socialize with his Indian wives and children, who lived at *Old Fort Garry*.

Like virtually all the men who worked for the Hudson's Bay Company, Simpson had a succession of Indian wives. Unlike most of these men, who acknowledged Indian women as their "country wives" for at least a few years, and in some cases for life, Simpson led a debauched life with a succession of women whom he acknowledged as merely mistresses and "bits of brown." At least four Indian and mixed-blood women bore Simpson five children, in addition to two illegitimate daughters born of two white women before he emigrated from Britain (Newman, p. 260). Some estimates of the number of Simpson's illegitimate children have been as high as seventy, which led to his being called, insightfully, "the father of the fur trade."

To accommodate the flow of women in and out of his bedroom, Simpson insisted on a private entrance to his rooms. He dismissed these short liaisons curtly. Even Simpson's country wives who lived with him a long time and bore his children received scantily better treatment than the women hustled in and out of his special love door.

Simpson deserted one of his country wives pregnant and under the charge of his associate with the instruction to "keep an Eye on the commodity and if she bring forth anything in proper time and of the right color let them be taken care of but if any thing be amiss let the whole be bundled about their business." At another time Simpson gave the same associate instructions about another of his Indian women: "If you can dispose of the Lady it will be satisfactory as she is an unnecessary and expensive appendage . . . but if she is unmarketable I have no wish that she should be a general accommodation shop to all the young bucks at the Factory." If the wife could not be disposed of, Simpson instructed his associate that she be padlocked into a chastity belt to

keep her from cavorting with men of lower class (Newman, p. 260).

By keeping his new white wife at Lower Fort Garry, Simpson sought to protect her from association with the racially mixed couples and their mixed-blood offspring who lived at Old Fort Garry and the nearby community of St. Boniface. The children of Indian women and Scottish or English men became known as half-breeds The even more numerous offspring of French Indian alliances became known as Métis, from the French word for "mixed." The French colonial government of Canada never succeeded in stimulating massive immigration of French settlers to America the way the British did in the South. From earliest colonial times the French government and religious hierarchy encouraged intermarriage of French soldiers and traders with Indian women as a way of bringing the Indians into the power of the French state and the Catholic Church. As early as 1628, the charter of the New French Company, issued by Cardinal Richelieu, provided that any Indians who converted to Christianity "shall be held to be native Frenchmen." This enabled them to "inherit and accept gifts and bequests in the same way as subjects born in the realm and native Frenchmen" (Borah, p. 718). This acceptance of Indians as Frenchmen according to their religion (or culture) rather than a mythical or quasi-scientific notion of "blood" made the French much more accepting of intermarriage with Native Americans.

The contrast between French and British policy appeared clearly in early travel commentaries, such as that of Thomas Forsyth, who visited North America in 1818. Ac-

cording to him, the French Canadian men within one year of arriving in America "will eat, drink, sleep and be hail fellow well met with the Indians, will learn in the course of a few months the Indian language by which means the Indians become attached to the Frenchmen." He wrote further that most of the French villages consisted of men "who were married to Indian women and followed a life similar to that of the Indian themselves such as hunting, fishing & by which means the Frenchman's children were related to both parties." (Forsyth, p. 210).

The intermarriage of Frenchmen with Indians continued after Canada passed to British control. Britain encouraged Scottish immigration to America, and the Scots also intermarried frequently with Indians, although the English did so only rarely. Following American independence from Britain, many of the loyalist Scots from the south moved north, and they added to the number of mixed marriages in Canada.

With the shortage of white women in the western and northern British colonies in Canada, men practiced a lively commerce in female Indian slaves. Although not legally recognized by the government, men bought and sold women, or even leased them for a certain number of years. They trafficked in Indian and mixedblood women for cash, to repay gambling debts, and in trade for horses and rum. They auctioned women to the highest bidder much the way Africans were sold at public auctions for Southern plantations. Sometimes Indian or mixed girls as young as nine or ten years of age were sold in this trade (Newman, p. 21).

After such extensive interbreeding through marriage, slavery, or casual relations, a large mixed-blood population emerged in western Canada. In the nineteenth century the Métis people formed a distinct ethnic group centered on the site of modern Winnipeg. They spoke Michif, a Cree-French creole, and adhered to a mixture of Catholicism and native spiritual belief. For subsistence they depended on the buffalo, which they hunted in annual maneuvers that approached the scale of a military operation complete with ranks and officers. The Métis formed annual caravans of two-wheeled ox-drawn carts that ventured south to St. Paul on the Mississippi River for supplies, which they hauled to Manitoba.

Métis culture combined elements of both Woodland and Plains Indian culture with European heritage. The men wore a bright red sash that readily identified them as Métis, and both men and women wore elaborate beaded patterns on their clothes. Because of their extensive use of floral motifs in their beadwork, the Dakota called the Métis "the flower beadwork people" (McMillan, p. 279).

While the Métis (Indian-French) controlled the buffalo hunt, the half-breeds (Indian-English and Indian-Scottish) worked as laborers for the Hudson's Bay Company and as small farmers along the Red River. They grew vegetables, potatoes, and grains for the local trade forts and for York Factory on Hudson Bay, where the growing season was too short even for garden crops.

This complex cultural and economic system of commerce and ethnic relations had been well established in the area for generations when Simpson arrived, but attitudes were changing. The new Victorian era of the nineteenth century looked with increasingly diminished tolerance on the interbreeding of whites with native peoples. New and supposedly scientific theories predicted dire Consequences from race mixing: at best it led to criminal behavior and sexual wantonness; at worst it threatened to corrupt and eventually destroy the white European race and thus bring down the British Empire.

Because of Governor George Simpson's disregard for his own Indian wives, he broke up the traditional system of Hudson Bay men and their country wives. When he brought his white wife Frances to the Red River, he started a new tradition of higherclass men bringing white wives out to the Canadian west. For the first time in that area, men could no longer bring their country wives out in public. He forbade his men to bring their mixedblood wives even to visit the new fort, much less to meet or in any other way interact with the minute collection of white women housed there.

As early as 1806, the North West Company, the fur-trading rival of the Hudson's Bay Company, tried unsuccessfully to stop intermarriages between its employees and Indian women by levying a fine of one hundred pounds for engaging in such unions (Newman, p. 23). As the century progressed, the pressures against mixed marriages increased across North America. Traders, officers, and men who had the slightest claim to being part of educated or polite society followed Simpson's example and yielded to social pressure and the newly stringent Victorian morals to withdraw from their Indian families. Three centuries of racial mixing in North America suddenly became shameful, unhygienic, unpatriotic, immoral, and in many places illegal.

The history of America is a history of racial and ethnic mixtures from the earliest contacts, and that mixture predates the arrival of European settlers. The Pilgrims, the first Europeans to make permanent settlements in New England, arrived in Massachusetts in 1620, but they found that other whites had already been there. They discovered this inadvertently while robbing Indian graves in search of goods they might use or trade. They were startled by one grave, which contained, in addition to all of the usual Indian goods next to the skeleton of a small child, the skeleton of a man with "fine yellow hair." This blond-haired man had many typical Indian possessions, but he also had some of the clothing and accoutrements of a European sailor (Cronon, p. 84). No one knew whether the sailor had been involuntarily Cast up on the shore or whether he had voluntarily sought refuge among these people, but the grave made it apparent that he had lived among them for some time. It would be mere guesswork to speculate whether or not this particular blond man sired Indian children who lived, but such unions were common.

White settlers frequently deserted their own communities to live in the civilization of the Indians. White captives who lived among the Indians often refused to return to their own people, preferring to live among the Indians and raise their mixed children as Indians. This reluctance of whites to return created great theological and cultural problems for the settlers, who could not understand how a "civilized" Christian could possibly adopt the life and beliefs of "uncivilized savages." To combat such losses to the Indians, several colonies passed laws forbidding "Indianizing."

To help people resist the temptation to join the natives, colonial writers began a wholly new, American genre of literature in their "captive accounts" that depicted Indian capture of settlers in horrifying detail. These tales induced fear of Indians in the reader, but also helped serve as a guide and supposedly as Christian inspiration to the reader who might one day become a captive.

Despite the horrors described in captive accounts, a white trader among the Indians might find that his business thrived if he married an Indian woman. She gave him a status within the kinship organization of the tribe, and her relatives gave him a network of trading partners and helpers. Throughout North America we see evidence of such unions, and the children often attained positions of great respect within the native nations. Alexander McGillivray, the son of a Scottish trader and a Creek mother, became the Emperor of the Creeks in the southeastern United States. The Scottish Ross family produced many generations of leaders among the Cherokee nation.

Even within the white American elite, some important cases of intermarriage with Indians occurred, particularly during the early and crucial years of colonization. After the Virginia settler John Rolfe married Pocahontas, they had a son, Thomas Rolfe, whom Pocahontas bore in England. After his mother's death he returned to his maternal homeland, where he became a scion of the great families of Virginia including the Randolphs and Bollings (Robert, p. 9).

Ely S. Parker and his brother, Nicholson Parker, both married white women of prominent families. In 1867, Ely Parker married Minnie Orton Sackett, the daughter of a fellow general in the army. She was a popular socialite in Washington, and General Ulysses S. Grant gave her away at her wedding in the place of her deceased father.

In Alaska, unions of Russian men and native women produced many offspring to whom the Russians usually gave equal rights as Russian citizens and subjects of the czar. When the United States acquired these territories, however, officials sought to deny the mixed-bloods recognition as whites, and to force them into the ranks of Indians.

Some of the Founding Fathers openly encouraged such mixtures. Patrick Henry proposed to the Virginia House of Delegates that the state promote Indian-white marriages by exempting such couples from taxes. He further proposed that the state subsidize Indian-white marriages by offering money as an incentive for mixed couples and to supplement that marriage fee with additional gifts of money at the birth of each mixed-blood child (Johansen and Grinde, pp. 7, 10).

The bill failed to pass, but a similar sentiment was expressed in less monetary though far more ideal terms by Thomas Jefferson at a presidential reception for "Delawares, Mohicons, and Munries" in 1802 when he invited the assembled Indians to mix with the white settlers in every way. In a paternalistic manner he addressed them as his children and said that if they agreed to live under American law and understand private ownership of property, they would join white society.

Jefferson said, rather overoptimistically, "you will unite yourselves with us, join in our great councils and form one people with us, and we shall all be Americans; you will mix with us by marriage, your blood will mix with ours, and will spread, with ours, over this great island" (Padover, p. 503).

From the time of De Soto's arrival in Florida, Africans found refuge from European slavery by fleeing to Indian communities. Three of De Soto's slaves, two Africans and a Moor, became so enchanted with the land of the Lady of Cutifachiqui that they escaped from De Soto and found refuge with the Indians. They stayed on in Cutifachiqui, and according to one narrative account, one of the escaped slaves became the husband of the famed Lady of Cutifachiqui. Throughout De Soto's rampage from modern South Carolina to the Mississippi River, slaves of African descent escaped and intermarried with the local Indians, making these escaped slaves the first Old World settlers throughout much of the Southeast and the Gulf Coast.

Over the next three centuries, Indian groups throughout the Southeast provided a sanctuary for escaped slaves from the plantations. Some groups, such as the Choctaw and the Seminole, took in large numbers of slaves with ease. Other groups sometimes enslaved the runaways in imitation of colonial practices, but even in these cases the Indians often allowed the slaves to marry and become members of the tribe. The Seminole leader Osceola himself married an African-American woman of slave descent.

Indians and Africans also intermarried on the Southern plantations where both groups were enslaved. The slaveowners cared little which dark-skinned slave married which other dark-skinned slave. It quickly became difficult to tell Indian from African slaves, as is evidenced in many of the newspaper advertisements for runaway slaves. In New Jersey, a 1747 advertisement for a fifty-three-year-old man named Cohansie describes him as having "some Indian blood in him," and accompanied by an adolescent boy, Sam, who "was born of an Indian woman, and looks like an Indian." The advertisement continues to say that "they both talk Indian very well, and it is likely they have dressed themselves in the Indian dress and gone to Carolina (Forbes, p. 87).

Many of the African-Indians appear to us in history only in these rather anonymous forms. We have reports of them, but we do not know them by name or by any other information. One of the first African-Indians whose name was recorded in history was Cripus Attucks, who fell in the Boston Massacre of March 5, 1770, and thus became known as the first patriot to die in the struggle for American independence.

Although little is known about Attucks, he was probably in his early thirties when he died, and was of mixed parentage. He may have been an escaped slave from Framingham, Massachusetts. His Indian heritage is usually cited as Natick, but he is frequently called a mulatto in the historical literature. Attucks was described as a "stout" young man who carried "a large cord-wood stick" at the front of a crowd protesting on the Boston public square against British colonial policy. When the British soldiers fired on the crowd, Attucks dropped after the first volley, with two musket balls lodged in him. He died immediately, as did three other men. Of the eight other men wounded, two subsequently died as well. In the words of the poet John Boyle O'Reilly, published in 1889 to honor the men who fell in the Boston Massacre, Attucks had been "the first to defy, and the first die" (Quarles, p. 4).

People of African descent found their way into many groups of Indians in some of the most distant parts of the continent. When Henry Rowe Schoolcraft visited the Fond du Lac Ojibwa community near the eastern shore of Lake Superior on one of his early trips of "discovery" in 1820, he found that an African-Canadian had already found them. Bungo, a free African, had traveled through Canada with the British army in the War of 1812, and had married an Ojibwa woman with whom he reared four children at Fond du Lac before Schoolcraft ever arrived.

In colonial North America, intermarriage among Europeans and Indians occurred most frequently in Spanish-controlled lands, including Mexico, Florida, the Caribbean, and the western half of the United States. Like the French, the Spanish government sent soldiers to settle in America, but did relatively little to stimulate the emigration of women. Without European women around them, the soldiers married Indian women. The resulting mestizo class gradually became a majority of the population throughout most of the Spanish areas of North America.

Persistent prejudice in the Spanish colonies against Indian blood caused most people to obscure their Indian heritage and emphasize their Spanish blood. In this way, everyone strove to move up in the racial hierarchy. Indians who could speak Spanish and who wore Mexican clothing became known as mestizos, while many mestizos became white. The eighteenth-century Spanish colonial government sold "certificates of whiteness" to Indians who had mastered Spanish language and culture sufficiently to make enough money to buy such a certificate. Obviously white people, of course, needed no such document to vouch for their Europeanness.

In North America during the nineteenth century, the new social order of the modern industrial and scientific world had no room for mixed-blood and Métis. Excluded from Canadian society and losing their economic position, the Métis began to push for their own land. As pressures increased against them, and as the railroads simultaneously threatened their former livelihood, the Métis began to advocate independence from Britain. Because they were the New People born of both Indians and Europeans, they wanted to create a New Nation on the Red River with its capital at Winnipeg.

The quest for independence became even greater in 1869 when the Hudson's Bay Company gave its past North American holdings to newly emerging Canada. Known as Rupert's Land, this region included vast tracts of Indian territory. Under the Montreal-educated Métis Louis Riel, the Métis seized Fort Garry in revolt. The rebels established a provisional government in

Winnipeg, and petitioned for admission to Canada as a new province. Even though supported by full-blood Indians and by many of the Anglophone mixed-bloods, Louis Riel and his New Nation failed. By 1870, British authorities had crushed their New Nation.

After the failure of his rebellion, Louis Riel fled to the United States while many of his followers dispersed through Manitoba and Saskatchewan, as far from colonial authorities as possible. Many other Métis also found refuge in Montana as well as North Dakota and Minnesota, but they did not surrender the dream of a new, mixed-blood nation that would include all Americans. Meanwhile, the Canadian government admitted Manitoba as a new, but non-Indian, province, whereupon the Métis repeatedly elected Riel to represent them in the Canadian parliament. But he was never seated.

It was a difficult time for Indians, but it was also a time for exaggerated hopes. The Sioux defeated Custer and his Crow allies at the Battle of the Little Bighorn in 1876, and this victory excited many Indian people with new hope for freedom and independence. Like the newly emerging Balkan nations, which had managed to throw off the yoke of Ottoman government, and like many European ethnic groups experiencing a growing sense of nationalism, the American Indians began to see themselves as a united group deserving better treatment.

When deprived of any hope of economic or political solutions to their problems, oppressed people often search for salvation in the spiritual realm. Just as the French had followed the mystic Joan of Arc in their struggle against English oc-

cupation, and just as the Spanish had liberated themselves from Muslim occupation by a fanatical Catholicism, Indian leaders in the nineteenth century often turned to spirituality as a means to redress their subjugation. In the United States, the Shawnee prophet Tecumseh led a religious and political movement. In the Southern states, the Red Sticks rose in rebellion under Chief Red Eagle. In the Yucatan, the Maya revolted while following a blend of traditional and Christian beliefs known as the Talking Cross.

Louis Riel also had a religious vision that he hoped would help his people to find salvation. Like many Catholics of the time, he resented the 1870 declaration of the Church proclaiming the infallibility of the Pope. He felt that the European Church, like the European governments, was out of touch with America. He favored a new religion for the New World, one that would be free of the Pope and would unite American Catholics and Protestants. Like the traditional Indians of his area, the new religion would allow polygamy, but it gave new rights to women, who would always be allowed to select their own mates and not be compelled by a father or anyone else to marry.

Riel showed a scholarly awareness of the hundreds of religious movements across North America during his time, and he borrowed or considered ideas from a variety of them. He thought of celebrating the Sabbath on Saturday as the Jews and the Seventh Day Adventists did. He accepted the Mormon teaching that the Indians of America were related to the Jews. He also supported the creation in Poland of a Zionist homeland for Jews that

would be like the new Indian and mixed-blood homeland he wanted to create in America.

Riel wanted to create a pan-Indian confederacy, including all of the Indians and mixed-bloods of the central part of North America. This new nation would offer refuge to all the oppressed of the world, particularly to groups such as the Irish, who had suffered so severely under the British in much the same way that the Indians had suffered under British colonial rule. Riel's ideal Indian nation would also have close ties with the Indian peoples of Mexico and South America. He wanted to make St. Boniface in Manitoba an educational center that would teach children from throughout Latin America as well as Canada and the United States.

Although Riel hoped for assistance from the American government and repeatedly petitioned President Grant for support, he hoped to position his new nation as a counterweight to the United States, because it would keep the United States from dominating all of North America. Prophetically, he foresaw that Britain needed North America more than America needed Britain; he even predicted that Britain would need help in future wars with Germany (Flanagan, p. 169).

Riel traveled extensively throughout the United States and returned secretly to parts of Canada in pursuit of his mission. On one of his trips back into Canada, the Canadian authorities seized and imprisoned him in a Quebec insane asylum at St.-Jean-deDieu, outside of Montreal. In a preview of twentieth-century treatment of political dissidents, the forces of medical science and the newly emerging field of psychiatry were marshaled against Riel, and he was diagnosed as suffering from delusions of grandeur (Flanagan, p. 57). He spent much of his time in solitary confinement, tied by modern restraining devices. The authorities released Riel after he recanted his heretical political and religious beliefs.

In 1885 the Métis once again called on Riel for help, but this time the struggle erupted farther west, in Saskatchewan, rather than in Manitoba. The Métis had once taken arms against white settlers who wanted to take over the new farms the Métis had scratched out on the Saskatchewan plains after fleeing the Red River Valley in Manitoba. Knowing the importance of public and world opinion, Riel drew up petitions and wrote defenses of the creation of his new nation. He sought to solve the problem through diplomatic and political means rather than military ones, but that was not to be. This new revolt failed even more quickly than the first. Government forces rushed into Saskatchewan, dismantled the provisional government established by the Métis, and captured and imprisoned Riel. Despite the jury's plea for mercy toward Riel, the government hanged him on November 16, 1885, in Regina, the new city named for Queen Victoria and her new age of enlightenment and science.

After their crushing defeat, the Métis went through a long period of decline during which most of them had to choose between being Indian or white. Many joined their Indian relatives as Cree or Ojibwa around the western Great Lakes and central plains of Canada and the United States. Many of the Métis families, especially those headed by French-speaking men, settled down to become farmers. They joined the white settlers moving in from Scotland and Eastern Europe. Other Métis moved east, where they joined French-speaking communities in Quebec, Vermont, and Maine.

The nineteenth century proved a hard epoch for North American Indians. In some ways it was the hardest of all since the Europeans had first arrived in America. During that century, white society tried in many ways to bar Indians and mixed-bloods from membership in the greater society; academic, government, and religious leaders tried to purge the white race and to undo three hundred years of race mixing.

Today the body of Louis Riel lies in a simple graveyard in St. Boniface, on the banks of the Red River, across from modern downtown Winnipeg. He lies in the graveyard of what was the Basilica of St. Boniface, but today the building is only a hulking shell, gutted by fire in 1968. The massive neo-classical facade stands hollow, deserted, and naked. The giant hole in the front left by the shattered stained-glass rose window stares out at the river like the blind eye of a giant cyclops. It seems ironically fitting that Riel should be buried before a destroyed church, since he spent so much time trying to rip the American church out of European hands.

Riel remains today as controversial a figure in Manitoba and Saskatchewan politics as he was in his own lifetime. Graffiti on odd walls around Winnipeg glorify or vilify him, and on radio stations the visitor can still hear songs dedicated to him. Riel symbolizes the rich mixture of cultures, genes, and ideas that created the modern population of North America. He also symbolizes the independent-minded people of the West who sought control over their own communities against the political, religious, and financial powers of the East.

English, native, and French musicians composed ballads, reels, and jigs in English and in French dedicated to Louis Riel and his quest for a totally new nation for the new mixed-blood culture that arose in North America. One such ballad, commonly available on cassette tape throughout Indian lands in the Canadian west, poses the question of who Louis Riel was, and answers that Louis Riel lives in all North Americans. The mixed-blood singers repeatedly emphasize their loud refrain, "It is we who are Louis Riel."

References

Borah, Woodrow. "The Mixing of Populations." In *First Images of America*, vol. 2, edited by Fredi Chiappelli. Berkeley: University of California Press, 1976.

Cronon, William. *Changes in the Land: Indians, Colonists, and the Ecology of New England.* New York: Hill and Wang, 1983.

Flanagan, Thomas. *Louis "David" Riel: "Prophet of the New World."*

Toronto: University of Toronto Press, 1979.

Forbes, Jack D. *Black Africans and Native Americans.* Oxford: Basic Blackwell, 1988.

Forsyth, Thomas. "The French, British and Spanish Methods of Treating Indians." *Ethnohistory* 4(2), Spring 1957.

Johansen, Bruce E., and Donald A. Grinde, Jr. *Exemplar of Liberty: Native America and the Evolution of Democracy.* Unpublished manuscript.

McMillan, Alan D. *Native Peoples and Cultures of Canada.* Vancouver: Douglas & McIntyre, 1988.

Newman, Peter C. *Caesars of the Wilderness.* Markham, Ontario: Viking, 1987.

Padover, Saul K. *The Complete Jefferson.* New York: Duell, Sloan & Pearce, 1943.

Quarles, Benjamin. *The Negro in the American Revolution.* Chapel Hill: University of North Carolina Press, 1961.

Robert, Joseph C. *The Story of Tobacco in America.* New York: Knopf, 1952.

Section One

Who Am I?/
How Have I Become Who I Am?

G. ZHANG 1994

Each group we belong to has its own identity/culture. This article deals with college campuses and the cultures they have represented over time.

The Changing Student Culture: A Retrospective

Helen Lefkowitz Horowitz

As freshmen arrived on campus this September, they stepped into a new and bewildering world. Bulletin board posters vied for attention, calling first-year students to Know Your Library, Join Crew, Go Phi Delt, Learn About AIDS, and Find Your Support Services. Just as dramatically, if not quite so explicitly, upper-class students were drawing them into alternative student cultures.

On each campus exists a social order that has persisted from an earlier time—the undergraduate cultures that today's students inherit have traditions dating from the late eighteenth century.

Led by the wealthier and worldlier students, college life was born in the violent revolts of the eighteenth and early nineteenth centuries. Pleasure-seeking young men who valued style and openly pursued ambition rioted against college presidents and faculty. When these revolts were forcibly suppressed, the conflict went underground and collegians turned to covert forms of expression. They forged a peer con-

sciousness sharply at odds with that of the faculty and serious students, and gave it institutional expression in the fraternity and club system.

College life as it emerged in the male college of the nineteenth century was altogether agreeable to affluent male adolescents. In a competitive world of peers, *college men* fought for position on the playing field and in the newsroom, and learned the manly arts of capitalism. As they did so, they indulged their love of rowdiness and good times in ritualized violence and sanctioned drinking. Classes and books existed as the price one had to pay for enjoying college life. *College men* disparaged the especially diligent student as a "grind." They saw themselves at war with faculty, and if cheating were needed to win the battle, no shame inhered in the act. No *real college men* ever expected to learn in the classroom, at least not the kind of knowledge that bore any relation to his future life.

But college life always had to contend with a significant number of students who have wanted no part

of it—the *outsiders*. The initial *outsiders* were those for whom higher education originally was intended: those studying for the ministry. Future ministers avoided the hedonism and violence of their undisciplined classmates. Studious, polite, and respectful of authority, these hard-working students sought the approval of their teachers, not of their peers. When fraternities were formed, these students stood outside. For them, college was not a time of fun, but of preparing for a profession. Achievement in the future would compensate for the work of the present.

Beginning in the mid-nineteenth century, other *outsiders* took the pastors' places: ambitious youth from all over rural America: the first college women; immigrants, especially Jews; and then blacks; World War II veterans; and commuters.

Beginning in 1910, college *rebels* emerged and directly challenged traditional college life, calling it false and exclusive. They claimed both the politics of the broader society and the intellectual commitment of the faculty. Excited by ideas, college *rebels* could be as cavalier about grades or as hedonistic as *college men*, for they did not see their college years as instrumental to future success. Starting in the 1920s, college *rebels* divided into two groups. Some students of an independent cast withdrew from political discourse to struggle for inner freedom; others continued their openly political fights to link questions on campus to broader national issues.

The first women to go to college were as serious and aspiring as any male *outsider*. Although many had only the vague wish to continue study, others sought to become teachers. At the all-female schools, they had a chance to define themselves on their own terms. The more outgoing created a robust college life. Although independent and hedonistic, they did not incorporate the *college men's* hostility to the faculty or their disinterest in study. Within a community of women, *college women* learned new skills that took them beyond the traditional range of feminine behavior.

In co-educational institutions, women began as *outsiders*, but the second generation of coeds at the end of the nineteenth century were both more affluent and more conventional. They found a way to get partly inside: they created the sorority world that allied them with male power on campus. Conservative and cautious, sororities insisted on social distinctions and feminine behavior. Less affluent women, or those with intellectual ambitions, remained *outsiders*. The more freewheeling joined male *rebels* and entered the political fray.

Nothing ever hit the college world so hard as the cumulative events of the 1960s. In 1959 a student who entered college normally fit into one of the pre-established grooves. A decade later, amid student strikes and demonstrations, those categories seemed anachronistic. Of course, they were not—the continuities between the 1960s and earlier periods have become clearer in retrospect, and successive student generations gradually have recreated many of the institutions of traditional college life. But the impact of the 1960s is still felt. *College men* and *women*, *outsiders*, and *rebels* exist today: but they are different from their counterparts in the first half of the twentieth century, and that difference is attributable to the 1960s.

In the 1960s, cultural currents strong enough to feel like a revolution in consciousness opened new ways of thinking and behaving and caused many students to question the nature and goals of higher education. At that time, economic changes firmly linked higher education to the increasing importance of the professions and to technical training. Grades, once of significance only to *outsiders*, were now inextricably bound to the guarantors of material success—jobs and careers. Even relatively affluent students felt new pressures to earn high marks in order to get into law school. Some of them complied willingly, but others resented being told to give up the pleasures and freedom their fathers had enjoyed.

By 1960, mentors such as Paul Goodman and C. Wright Mills told them they should not have to. Influenced by these critiques and by those of iconoclastic professors, college *rebels* began to challenge not

just football and fraternities, but the curriculum as well. They fought against the notion that college was a factory to turn out intelligent, efficient products; they demanded intellectual challenge and growth.

External forces spurred these changes. The moral legitimacy of the emerging Civil Rights movement was overwhelming, and the 1960 sit-ins involved direct action by students themselves. The early battles over segregation moved rebellious college students into politics, taught them techniques of nonviolent protest, and gave them a complicated but exhilarating education about American society. As they returned from summers in the South, some felt eager to move beyond the particular issues of their campuses to develop theoretical and collective approaches.

In the early 1960s, a small group of late 1950s *rebels* and younger recruits reinvigorated the Student League for Industrial Democracy and renamed it Students for a Democratic Society (SDS). SDS's emerging ideology galvanized questioning college youth. With black groups, especially the Student Non-Violent Coordinating Committee (SNCC), and a constellation of other student organizations, the loosely controlled SDS helped create the New Left or, more familiarly, the Movement.

It changed the nature of campus rebellion. In contrast to the 1950s isolation of traditional college *rebels* and their search for personal solutions, the Movement provided a sense of common ground, political explanations for student discontent, and a program for action. Unlike the *rebels* of the past, members of the New Left did not intend to educate fellow students with words.

They engaged in direct action to build a moral society.

In the 1960s, campus *rebels* not only became radical; they became numerous. The emerging counter-culture created new bonds between once-divided students. Style, sexual openness, music, and drugs flaunted adult authority and drove a wedge between generations. Confronting a hostile world, young people lowered the barriers among themselves.

As the Vietnam War escalated, a growing number of students turned against their government: the war changed the complexion of authority. College youth saw the U.S. administration as waging an evil war paid with the lives of young men. As each young man confronted his future, what might have remained distantly "out there" became immediate and intensely personal. The numbers of students opposed to the war swelled.

The first collective expression of the changing consciousness of college students came a Berkeley in 1964, but, while political groups demonstrated on many campuses in the mid-1960s, widespread strikes came only after the violent 1968 conflict at Columbia University. The 1969-70 academic year brought 9,408 student outbreaks, 731 of which led to police intervention. Radicalism proved attractive to a significant segment of the under-graduate community; the numbers of self-identified *radicals* grew. In 1968, 5 percent of college youth surveyed by Daniel Yankelovich "strongly agreed" on thee need for a "mass revolutionary party," and 14 percent agreed "partially."

The degree of student radicalism, as measured by membership in organizations or by participation in demonstrations, was actually less than in the 1930s, but it carried new power. Especially at the smaller, elite liberal arts colleges and the great research universities, *radicals* became the catalytic force that drew new adherents and great numbers of sympathizers from among affluent college youth. Lacking the borders that had divided *rebels* from traditional *college men* and *women*, students identified with their peers and rallied to their defense. Striking students often included the best and the brightest—those who in earlier decades would have been the mainstays of the Greek System.

With the killings at Kent and Jackson State and the winding down of the war, college protest at some places suddenly stopped. Observers who had anticipated an ever-growing radical movement among college youth were caught off guard. In the early 1970s, calm—unnatural calm—descended. The formerly secure place of the college *rebel* seemed in jeopardy. But the 1950s had not returned. Although fraternity and sorority appeal widened throughout the decade, the Greek system's power on campus was gone.

What was left? With both *rebels* and *college men* and *women* subdued, what triumphed in the 1970s was the world of the *outsider*. Long scorned as "grinds" who worked for themselves, not for the college, *outsiders* came into their own. Their pursuit of their futures through correct public behavior and hard work became the dominant mode in colleges and universities across the country.

In the 1970s, the imperatives of a bureaucratic and technologic order, visible since the turn of the century, came home to a majority of students. Undergraduates responded with a vengeance to the message that they make high grades for medical and law school. These students now included young women who read the 1970s message of feminism in a limited, narrow way: simply as a call to enter the professions. College students wondered if there was anything for them either in campus high jinks, or in political action groups. The corrosive effect of this question decimated the ranks of the *rebels* and the *college men* and *women*.

Unlike earlier *outsiders*, those in the 1970s did not come from the upwardly mobile elements of society who sought college in anticipation of the promise of American life. Rather, the *new outsiders* of the 1970s were prosperous collegians, terrified that they might fail to attain the material well-being of their affluent parents. They had, like their rebellious 1960s predecessors, grown up in suburban enclaves. But their aspirations centered on their desire to return to that privileged world, not escape from it. *Outsiders* behavior—once permeated with optimism—took on a new, sour quality, as the nation's privileged children adopted it in an era permeated by a conviction of economic and political failure. This explains the ugly mood that descended on campus in the 1970s. As the *new outsiders* brought to the campus their conservatism, sense of entitlement, and hostility to classmates vying for places in the economic and social order, they helped create the harsh college world that students in the 1980s have inherited.

By 1989, changes in the economy, voices calling for service, and sheer human decency have moderated somewhat the strident selfishness of the *new outsider*. Many campuses also have seen a return of both college life and rebellion, contemporary style.

Those today who choose to become *college men* and *women* share much of the culture of the *new outsider*. The Greek system is attracting more takers, offering in many places the pleasures of an established group, social exclusiveness, and a place to drink alcohol. Hedonism is no longer the preserve of *college men*, but many fraternities continue to support cheating, violence, and rape. Elitism and conformity do not set sorority women apart from independents, but nonetheless can be located in their more vicious forms in the houses. At a time when the consciousness of the *new outsider* pervades the campus, fraternities and sororities have added the rhetoric of academic excellence and future connections to their credos.

Collegiate rebellion has returned in its more politicized forms to campus. As the children of the 1960s *rebels* enter college, they are bringing to campus both their assertive independence and their heightened sense of conscience. Feminist, African-American students, and gay and lesbian activists have found their voices. Rebellious students have made alliances with faculty and administration members transformed by the 1960s. Thus, campuses may see increased political activity in the immediate future. Perhaps more important at present, however, is a rebellion that questions rather than attacks. The en-

emy of many *rebels* today is not college life, but the ethos of the *new outsider*. These *rebels* distance themselves from careerism and grade-grubbing. Many of these undergraduates outwardly conform as they struggle to frame an independent course, to mediate the pressures of parents, professors, and peers. Their independent consciousness may now be emerging as a distinct modality.

On many of today's campuses, the old *outsider* again has become the primary component of the student body. As new immigrants seek to gain their place in American society, as older students return to campus, as the economy and consumerism cause many students to concentrate on their off-campus jobs, and as the number of commuting students grows, higher education becomes increasingly valued for the technical competence and certification it can impart. That undergraduate years can be a transforming experience, a radicalizing force, or just plain fun is beyond the ken of such students.

Predictions about college students invariably miss the mark. In 1970, the cultural revolution and widening protest appeared to signal the dawning of the post-industrial world of heightened individuality. Today, the twentieth century's insistence upon disciplined professional training seems likely to persist. But we ought to know better.

Part of the difficulty in imagining undergraduate futures has been the monolithic way in which students have been perceived. In any decade

since 1920, single images of collegians have dominated public consciousness. Undergraduates, however, are divided into contending cultures. In any one era, one of these appears to be dominant and catches the public eye. Other student worlds, less visible or less interesting to reporters, do not vanish. The 1960s ended both the hegemony of the *college man* and the sharp boundaries between campus cultures, intensifying the impact of the *new outsiders* in the 1970s. Their assertion, however, did not end college life or rebellion. Thus, whatever imperatives underlie the ethos of the *new outsider*, it seems likely that it will come under attack by the resurgence of college life, rebellion, the new independent consciousness, or the sheer number of old *outsiders*.

Finally, new forms of campus life may appear. Nothing ordains that existing divisions contain the only possibilities. Within the varied mix of campus life today, students are quietly—or perhaps noisily—shaping a future we cannot yet imagine.

This article has been adapted from the author's Campus Life: Undergraduate Cultures from the End of the Eighteenth Century to the Present. (New York: Alfred A. Knopf, Inc., 1987; Chicago: University of Chicago Press, 1988, paperback) which provides full documentation.

Helen Lefkowitz Horowitz is a professor of history at Smith College.

© 1989 American Council on Education. Reprinted by permission.

Barnes provides a universal definition for the ideas of multicultural education. It provides a perspective into the questioning of reform that sometimes dismisses the miniority intellectual as racist or fanatical. "There are no blaspheming beasts to be silenced, only colleagues to be listened to."

Blaspheming Like Brute Beasts: Multiculturalism From an Historical Perspective

A. E. Barnes

> Certain persons who know nothing are trying as hard as they can to imagine the study of philosophy. . . . They blaspheme like brute beast against things of which they know nothing.
> Albertus Magnus.[1]

There is a great deal of contention about the subject of multiculturalism these days, and I believe that the positions maintained by those who seek to reform existing curricula are being misrepresented by those who want to maintain the status quo. Arrayed against the latter are neither barbarians, nihilists, nor perverters of the minds of the next generation of students, but men and women equally within what has been labeled the Western intellectual tradition. The arguments put forward by both those for and those against educational reform have roots that go back at a minimum to the late European Middle Ages. At least since then a cultural dynamic has been in operation in which groups that identify themselves as intellectually mature have dismissed the efforts at intellectual self-assertion by other groups as juvenile. The former's dismissal has never stopped the latter's growth, though it has had a negative impact on the directions of that growth. Relating this point to the present debate, the question I have pondered is whether the attacks on the integrity of minority intellectuals are not in fact creating the hatred and animosity these intellectuals have been accused of preaching. If this is the case, then a halt in such attacks might help get the reform of education past the present impasse.

Multiculturalism is a term that has come to serve as shorthand for a host of different and not necessarily related cultural and educational issues. Arguments relating to gender studies, ethnic and racial studies, affirmative action, freedom of speech on campus, compromise and corruption among educational administrators have all been aired under the title, multiculturalism. Based on the amount of attention each issue had attracted, though, it seems fair to say that at the center of the debate have been questions about racial and ethnic studies and how they are to be incorporated into the education received by minority students in particular, and the majority of other students in general. Although gender issues have often been an independent source of contention, at present the greatest amount of misunderstanding occurs in commentaries concerning ethnic and racial studies and the threat they pose to the "canon" of humanistic studies. Concentrating on the conflict within these commentaries is the way I hope to advance the debate.

Minority educators, even when their intellectual integrity has not been questioned, have found their ideas for reform dismissed as racist or fanatical. At the base of this misinterpretation is a reading of the actions of minorities as reflecting an intellectual predisposition deemed to civilization by Academy liberals. In fact, the dangers attached to acknowledgement of minority demands for cultural self-assertion are not widespread. There are no blaspheming beasts to be silenced, only colleagues to be listened to.

My argument is mostly framed as a response to Diane Ravitch's essay, "Multiculturalism: E Pluribus Plures," published in the Summer 1990 issue of The American Scholar, but I also take issue with points raised by other commentators, especially John Scarle in his review article "Storm Over the University," in the December 6, 1990 issue of the New York Review of Books. Let me say at the onset that I share many of the concerns and convictions of Professors Ravitch and Searle, but I think that both have failed to organize the linkage of the arguments they condemn. Especially in the case of Ravitch, the failure to recognize the historical context in which the assault by minority intellectuals on the existing curriculum of humanistic studies

has to be placed has led to some unnecessary and unproductive conclusions about the threat posed by this assault.

Ravitch begins her essay with a brief survey of recent progressive changes in American education from which she concludes:

As a result of the political and social changes of recent decades, cultural pluralism is now generally recognized as an organizing principle of this society. In contrast to the idea of the melting pot, which promised to erase ethnic and group differences, children now learn that variety is the spice of life. They learn that America has provided a haven for many different groups and has allowed them to maintain their cultural heritage or to assimilate, or—as often the case—to do both; the choice is theirs, not the state's. They learn that cultural pluralism is . . . a national resource rather than a problem to be solved. Indeed, the unique feature of the United States is that its common culture has been formed by the interaction of its subsidiary cultures. It is a culture that has been influenced over time by immigrants, American Indians, Africans (slave and free), and by their descendants. American music, art, literature, language, food, clothing, sports, holidays, and customs all show the effects of the commingling of diverse cultures in one nation. Paradoxical though it may seem, the United States has a common culture that is multicultural.[2]

This new common culture which she fables "pluralistic multicultururalism" is being threatened by a

"particularist multiculturalism." Particularist multiculturalism is both "filiopietistic" and "deterministic," i.e.,

. . . it teaches children that their identity is determined by their "cultural genes." That something in their blood or their race memory or their cultural DNA defines who they are and what they may achieve.[3]

Such particularist arguments ultimately conclude by denying that any common culture exists or could exist.

Ravitch singles out for condemnation the work of the Temple University Professor Molefi Kete Asante, who argues in his book *Afrocentricity* that African Americans must seek to develop an "Afrocentric" as opposed to a "Eurocentric" sense of culture, one which rejects the classicism of composers such as Beethoven and Bach in favor of this quality in the works of Coltrane and Ellington. Asante rejects the universalism Ravitch sees promoted by the new pluralistic multiculturalism. As Ravitch notes, he views universality as a form of "Eurocentric arrogance."[4] For Asante, there is no common culture, but only a collection of ethnocentric experience, a position which, as Ravitch observes, leads to the conclusion that "children can only learn from people of the same race."[5]

Ravitch likewise dismisses as "cultural baggage from our own society" both the efforts of the Senegalese scholar Chick Amadow Diop to show the African nature of Egyptian civilization, and those of Martin Bernal to demonstrate the "Afro-Asialic roots" of Greek culture.[6] Her point is that the effort to identify the racial orgins of past cultural achievements cannot be pursued with any objectivity. In fact the effort itself is pointless because "cultures are constantly influencing one another, exchanging ideas about art and technology, and the exchange usually is enriching, not depleting."[7]

Ravitch limits her distinction between particularistic and pluralistic multiculuralism to supposed policy positions concerning grade school curricula. An attempt to place this distinction in a broader historical context is useful. In his *Victorian Anthropology*, George Stocking argues that by the 19th century Anglo-French intellectuals had developed the concept of civilization as a generic term to describe "both the overall process of human progress and its cumulative achievement in every area of human activity."[8] In response, German intellectuals redefined civilization to mean the "universal *external* phenomena of material progress," a concept which could then be contrasted to the idea of culture, which involved the "varied *inward* moral and aesthetic manifestation of the human spirit"[9] or as Stocking also described it, "the positive evaluation of *mythopoetic mentality*." This idea of culture, to his mind, allowed for the glorification of the presumed characteristics of a self-defined human group. Over the nineteenth century it diffused from Germany to England where it modified the notion of civilization in such a way that the latter became synonymous with the concrete expression of the mythopoetic expression of a given folk. Thus by the end of the 19th century it was possible to speak about "Anglo-Saxon Civilization."

I would suggest that Ravitch uses the term "universalism" much in the same way early nineteenth century English and French writers used the term "civilization," i.e., as representing "cumulative achievement in every area of human activity." It is in this sense that she quotes the Roman playwright Terence, "I am a man; nothing human is alien to me."[10] Her pluralistic common culture contains all that is identifiably the best from every human culture—though it is not exactly clear who is doing the identifying.

Likewise, her notion of particularism is in essence the mental expression of the German idea of culture (Kultar), the "inward moral and aesthetic manifestation of the human spirit" of a given group. Her argument is that ethnocentrism glorifies the "mythopoetic mentality" of a group to the detriment of some universal notion of common culture.

To the extent her distinction fits larger notions of the basic dichotomy in the Western intellectual perspective, I agree with her, I question, however, whether the pluralistic multiculturalism she assumes now exists in the United States has been as freed of its Eurocentricity, or to use her term, "filiopielism," as she concludes. John Searle, in attacking the "Cultural Left," ponders why the controversy over the curriculum has centered in literacy studies. As he observes, in history of philosophy courses:

> there is little or no objection to the fact the great philosophers taught in these courses are mostly white Western males, from Socrates, Plato, and Aristotle through Frege, Russell, and Wittgenstein.[11]

As to the fact that Frege, Russell and Wittgenstein are "white Western males" I cannot but agree. But Socrates, Plato and Aristotle represent a parentage only claimed, but not proven, as "white, Western." Several civilizations, removed from each other in space and time, have found intellectual values in the teachings of the three ancient Athenians. Whether the teachings of the three twentieth century northern Europeans chosen by Searle will someday be perceived as being of equal value is for future generations to say.

Something more is going on here than mere chauvinism. Searle's premature granting of immortality to Frege, Russell, and Wittgenstein is an act of cultural imperialism on at least two levels. Not only is he claiming the legacy of the ancient Mediterranean as validation of the cultural achievement of modern Germanic peoples, he is denying claim to it to any other people, culture, or region. Behind Searle's granting of honorary white status to the great minds of the past is a particularism which insists that every intellectual achievement of significance must be the result of some north European cultural gene.

The instinct toward identifying human consciousness in terms of how it was assumed to have evolved in northern Europe remains prevalent within the scholarly community. Perhaps it is to be expected that European Americans attempt to explain the world from their own perspective. If so, then it should be equally expected that Americans who trace their ancestry to other parts of the globe find nothing of universal application in these explanations. The starting point of

Ravitch's argument is wrong. As yet there is no pluralistic multiculturalism in this society. European American scholars continue to argue for cultural continuity between the civilizations of the ancient Mediterranean and contemporary European intellectual achievement. Based on this supposed connection, they continue to argue that the contributions of European intellectuals have a value and validity above and beyond that of intellectuals from other regions of the world. One does not take anything away from the value of Russell, Frege and Willgenstein to European intellectuals in saying that the value of the ideas of these three men to non-European intellectuals is something that has to be demonstrated, not assumed. Granting them the pedigree Searle claims for them only highlights the kind of European presumption to which minority intellectuals must take exception.

There are a host of reasons why the supposed connection between the cultures of the ancient Mediterranean and those of the modern North Atlantic should be looked upon with suspicion, not the least being the fact that more than one thousand years elapsed between the decline of Roman civilization in the western Mediterranean and the emergence of an intellectual culture of more than local repute in the North Atlantic. Given the centrality of the connection to contemporary claims of European cultural superiority, it cannot be that surprising that intellectuals with origins elsewhere seek not only to deny it to Europeans, but to claim it for themselves. And whatever one thinks of their effort, they cannot be accused of attempting to destroy Western civilization or even the supposed canon of that civilization's greatest literary works.

I think Ravitch is right in arguing that school curricula are far less Eurocentric than in the past. But that is not to say that they have ceased to be Eurocentric, or, more importantly, that they have begun to offer any idea of common culture appealing to people not of European descent. It is really not for any group of scholars or educators to determine whether or not a common culture has been created in American schools. That determination rests in the minds of African, Asian, European and Hispanic Americans, and will come when these people see in the idea of America being promoted through the schools an idea that counts them in.

Meanwhile, it is to be expected that minority intellectuals will fight European-American cultural imperialism by protesting the arrogance of its claims and by asserting the value of their own cultural experience at least for their own people. Condemning these intellectuals as filiopietistic is much like the pot calling the kettle black. Such accusations can only reinforce minority perceptions of majority hypocrisy.

The present instance is not the only occasion in the history of Western civilization when claims of universality have been met with accusations of self-interest. It can be argued, in fact, that the cultural transformations accepted in the United States as the origins of the modern intellectual tradition emerged out of a similar set of claims. It was only toward the beginning of the fourteenth century that Western Europeans gained sufficient intellectual self-confidence to claim their homelands the best on earth and themselves the best of all

peoples.[12] Even then, however, self-awareness by one group served as inducement to categorize others as barbarians. It was also during the first half of the fourteenth century that Italian commentators first began to question the intellectual capacities of their northern neighbors and former overlords in the Holy Roman Empire. Why is not exactly clear. Certainly, intellectual culture in the region which would become modern Germany was far less developed than in Italy. But such was the case everywhere in Europe except France. Probably centuries of German military predations had created sufficient resentment among Italians that they responded favorably to any accusation leveled against Germans. Whatever the case, Petrarch has been credited with being the first explicitly to make the charge. According to Alexander Murray, however, "statesmen who saw the world with Italian eyes" had by that time long "called the Germans barbarian."[13]

Of interest here are German responses to such claims, which first begin to appear toward the end of the 15th century. As the young humanist Franz Freidlieb (Irenicus) explained in his *Exegesis Germaniae* (1518):

> According to the Greek use of the word "barbarian," only those who cannot speak Greek fluently and well should be called by that name . . . After the Trojan war the term was used only to describe non-Greek peoples. The early Romans were called barbarians . . . But once Rome had gained the imperium, Italians and Latins tended to be exempted from the applications of the word. Following the birth of

Christ, a barbarian was one who was neither Greek, nor Roman, nor Hebrew. More recently, the name has been given to all those people not subject to the Roman empire. . . .

Italians to this day speak of Germans as an unformed and rude people, an opinion they could only have derived from writers altogether ignorant of German society. They call us rough and uncultivated; see, for example, the remarks of Hermolaus Barbarus in a letter to Pico della Mirandula. Hermolaus writes: "Among Latin writers I do not number the Germans, whose works do not survive nor, indeed, did they ever live, or, if they live, they live in contempt. The whole world calls them uncouth, rude, uncivilized barbarians." Upon what other nation, besides the German, does Hermolaus heap such abuse? This man, who traveled in Germany and wrote on German affairs, goes out of his way to say unpleasant things about us. Joannes Campanus brands us with similar words, claiming that we all, without exception, are uncultured barbarians; indeed, there is no subject in Campanus' letters which seems so to engage his interest and talents as the depreciation of the name and glory of our German people . . .[14]

I have quoted Irenicus at length to illustrate the similarity of the alienation felt by a marginalized intellectual of the European late middle ages to that of marginalized intellectuals of the present, and to point out the preconditions to the emergence of what might be labeled the first era of European multiculturalism.

Irenicus published his text the year after Martin Luther nailed his 95 theses on the cathedral door in Wittenberg, and two years before, in his *Appeal to the German Nobility*, Luther explicitly invited the German elite to step in and correct the abuses Italian self-interest had allowed to creep into the institutions of the Christian church. One of those abuses was the low esteem in which Italians still held German intellectual abilities, an important concern since German thinkers continued to look to Rome for validation of their ideas. To free the German mind from the "halfman, halfchild" status in which Italian insisted it be placed was part of the motivation behind Luther's decision to make the Bible available to literate Germans in their own language. And to insure the supply of literate Germans, he helped pioneer one of the first generalized programs of primary education. Luther's actions initiated a period of cultural reform during which the type of changes he introduced into Christian worship in Germany were implemented by other reformers in every territory christianized through Rome. A century after the publication of his 95 theses, all of Protestant Europe was divided into territorial churches. And even within Catholicism the old idea of a universal church under the guidance of the Roman pontiff, now labeled *ultramontism*, was losing the battle against the new idea of territorially based churches.

In characterizing the Reformation era as the first era of multiculturalism, I do not deny the religious and political motivations behind the events which took place in the 16th and 17th centuries. All I want to do is call attention to the opportunity these events presented for the amelioration of the intellectual alienation expressed above. Before the Reformation there was little opportunity for literate articulation of Stocking's mythopoetic mentality. After the appearance of Luther's 95 theses, this mentality gradually began to dominate European intellectual life. Luther's translation of the Bible into German was only the first of a host of vernacular translation. His break with Rome was likewise the stimulus for a flood of catechisms and devotional works, most aimed at the students fitting the new parochially based schools, all published in newly crafted written versions of regional dialects. These new books were written, these new educational programs were taught by local clerics, who for the first time found themselves at the center of the intellectual world as opposed to its margins.

We should keep in mind that, beneath the Latin-reading network of prelates and clerks who tied the national church to the international religious establishment, the devotional practices of ordinary folk continued to be ritualistic and locally oriented.[15]

The breakup of medieval Christiandom into regionalized churches under localized control could have reinforced local religious custom and ritual. The English could have centered their devotional life even more around pilgrimage to Canterbury, the Spanish even more around the shrine to Compostella. The breakup instead helped give rise to regional literate cultures, which indicated the degree to which it was exploited by local intelligentsius as a pathway to employment and social status, and also to how the common international intellectual culture of medieval Christendom gave way to nationalized cultures of the same sort during the post-Reformation era.

The problem of intellectual continuity was also conceptualized by early Protestant thinkers. Luther's case was not that Roman Christianity had to be jettisoned, but that it had to be reformed, that is, taken back to its original purity. To follow recent interpretation, Luther was far more interested in making a German claim for the spiritual inheritance of the ancient world than he was in attacking the universalist claims put forward by Rome.[16] Behind this claim was a confidence that in their struggles against Italian chauvinism, Germans had gained the higher ground. As he proclaimed in a treatise addressed *To the Burgomeisters and Counsellors (1524)*:

Dear Germans, take advantage, because our moment has come. Gather in, while it still shines and is good weather. Use God's grace and Word while they are still present. For you should know that God's Word and grace are a traveling object that rains blessings. It does not return to where it has once been. It was with the Jews, but away it went and now they have nothing. Paul brought it to Greece. But again it went away through neglect, and Greece now has Turks, Rome and the Latin lands have also had it, but away it goes and now they have the pope. And you Germans are not allowed to think that you will have it forever, because it cannot be retained by those who show ingratitude and contempt. Grasp it and retain it, whoever can.[17]

Luther saw the movement of God's grace as granting Germans their moment at the center of the world's mind. During this moment he expected the Germans to free themselves from Roman control.

To help the Germans realize this goal Luther made the case for a stolen legacy, most forcefully in his "On the Babylonian Captivity of the Church," in which he empowers German princes to recapture it. Thus, in his attack on the sacrament of ordination, he traces the Catholic justification for withholding communion in both kinds from the laity to an erroneous reading of the statement, "Do this in remembrance of me" made by Christ at the Last Supper.

There are a host of examples of attacks on European claims of cultural superiority which follow the line pioneered by Luther in his attack on Rome. I will illustrate only one in detail. Murray argues that part of the cause for the development of a faith in reason in the European West was the emergence of what he calls an "arithmetical mentality," by which he means a consciousness of the comparative efficiency of quantitative analysis in comprehending phenomena.[18] Some might wonder whether Murray is not creating an ancestor to a particular modern sensibility, especially in light of the numerous examples of faith in very irrational numbers available for both the medieval and early modern period. A consciousness of the evaluative quality of numbers had to be wed with a philosophical belief in empiricism before his "arithmetical mentality" could emerge. But I think he is right in perceiving that, as the growing study of artificial intelligence demonstrates, the twentieth century European certitude that mathematical logic lies at the heart of human consciousness is so complete, the conviction must have fairly deep roots in the Western psyche. Many whites have assumed or argued that non-whites are less open to mathematics.

These two points help explain why Diop, without doubt the most influential promoter of an Afrocentric view of the origins of Western civilization, made mathematics the core of his argument for the stolen legacy of ancient Egypt. Most readers of Diop stop with his case for the racial Africanness of the ancient Egyptians. If they read further, they would see that this argument connects to a second one having to do with the Egyptian discovery of most of the principles of mathematics up through geometry. If they read still further, they would appreciate that these two arguments culminate in one that the mentality that produced these discoveries was diffused at least across the latitude of Africa. It is, he says, Africans who are truly mathematically minded.[19]

For most of the last two centuries European science has stressed the biological source of much cultural behavior. Diop adopted the same approach, looked back at ancient Egypt, and laid claim for Africa in the one trait most precious to modern Western thought, a sense for numbers. Diop's case was that the

European celebration of the Greeks as the first collective expositors of this trait signaled a theft from Egyptian Africans, a theft the latter's modern-day heirs must reclaim. Just as Luther's case for a stolen legacy was an invitation for German intellectuals to seize the day, so Diop's had behind it a desire for African intellectuals to reclaim a birthright. This reclamation was not in order to justify African cultural ascendancy, but to be a source of confidence for the African prepared to participate in an emerging world civilization:

> The African who has understood us is the one who, after the reading of our works, would have felt a birth in himself, of another person, impelled by an historical conscience, a true creator, a Promethean carrier of a new civilization and perfectly aware of what the whole Earth owes his ancestral genius in all the domains of science, culture, and religion.

> Today each group of people, armed with its rediscovered or reinforced cultural identity, has arrived at the threshold of the postindustrial era. An atavistic, but vigilant African optimism inclines us to wish that all nations would join hands in order to build a planetary civilization instead of sinking down to barbarism.[20]

Like mainstream Protestant reformers, Diop and those who follow him presume the existence of a universal culture which, once reoriented, can serve their own ends. Black separatist groups such as the original Nation of Islam, as did Protestant radicals before them, reject the possibility that the culture of the larger community can aid in their self-development. None of the academic intellectuals accused of "particularism," however, has taken their arguments to the extreme of separatism. Ravitch rightly attacks Asante for offering a concept of culture so narrow that it excludes much of the cultural interests expressed by the majority of African Americans. She misses the degree to which even for Asante his concept of culture is idealized. Few black intellectuals want to destroy Western civilization. The more quietest among these writers, like Asante, attempt to limit the intellectual compromise of living within this civilization. The more ludacious, like the many followers of Diop, press the claim that this civilization first belonged to them.

In *Black Athena* Martin Bernal also makes the case for a stolen legacy, in this instance concerning the way in which modern European scholars have systematically erased the contributions to the development of Western civilization of the Phoenicians, a Semitic people of the ancient Mediterranean. Bernal takes the arguments advanced by Diop relating to the Egyptian origins of mathematical and religious ideas and goes off with them in a completely different direction. For Bernal, intellectual Romanticism and racism were the primary forces behind the refusal of European intellectuals to accept that Indo-European or Aryan Greeks could have learned anything of lasting intellectual significance from Semites of Africans.[21]

While accepting his assessment of the end result, I would make race less, Romanticism (ideology) more of a factor in how it came about. German writers never did get over the sting of Italian dismissal of the German capacity for cultural enlightenment. When, during the 18th century, Protestants and *philosophies* began to search for a past for the regionally based cultures they had created, they found the path back to the ancient world already congested with "Romanists." The idea about culture upon which most of the above debate is premised, i.e., that culture is a legacy of ideas and values bequeathed by a people to posterity, could not be maintained by Catholic intellectuals. Thus, in order to establish pedigrees for the cultures they had developed, northern intellectuals were constrained to identify a connection to the ancient world which did not go through Rome, and which did not depend upon any notion of cultural diffusion.[22]

The resulting "Aryan model"—as Berat labels it, explains ancient Mediterranean history as the results of wave upon wave of Aryan warriors sweeping down, enslaving the inferior native stock, and then, based upon their brains, and the latter's labor, building great civilizations. The model makes culture completely a function of what we today would call genetic make-up. As such, civilization does not move from people to people. Rather, it emerges through the collective efforts of a given group, and then evolves through the actions of the progeny of that group.

The appeal of this argument to the expansionistic societies of the North Atlantic should be obvious. In conquering and exploiting the peoples of the world they were simply following in their forefathers' footsteps. But the appeal went deeper. The Aryan model evolved in Germany, but like the Reformation three centuries before, it soon attracted interest across northern Europe, where it became the basis of what were then seen as "progressive" curricular reforms. The certainty with which the intelligentsias of the European North accepted the inherent racial superiority their Teutonic ancestry granted them provided the first point of consensus between these groups in centuries. The first era of multiculturalism came to a conclusion with the acknowledgement across northern Europe of the new universal: not only was race in terms of cultural expression everything; but everything great in terms of cultural expression came from the European (Aryan) race. The idea was so self-gratifying that the so-called science community committed itself to finding corroborating evidence. It was so captivating that even Mediterranean intelligentsias, patriarchs of the old universal, sought to live their lives by it.

As Bernat discusses, the possibility that Asian and African peoples might have had ideas worth sharing with other peoples was simply dismissed. The real questions were whether Semitic people had made any contributions to the civilization which now dominated the globe, whether or not they even belong with the European races. By the end of the nineteenth century the answer to both questions was no.

Although twentieth century scholars no longer hold to the notion that Indo-Europeans were culturally superior to the people they conquered, some of the racist legacy of the nineteenth century theory remains. Many of the criticisms of Bernal ignore or downplay his important investigation of the evolu-

tion of European cultural racism and concentrate on his linguistic and other arguments regarding the Greeks' debt to Egypt. The tragedy of this development is that it yanks from public view, at a time when it is sorely needed, what I suspect was an inadvertent, but still exceptional case study of how the Romantic mind works. Such studies are hard to come by in these days when European consciousness is assumed to have always been rationalistic in its essence and when past expressions of the Romantic temperament in Europe are written off as fanaticism or juvenile angst.

It can be argued, though, that what has changed since the Middle Ages is that Romanticism has ceased to be explicitly religious, that intellectual developments in the eighteenth and nineteenth century European North allowed the romantic goal of the salvation of humankind to be replaced by the salvation of the folk, folk being understood as a human population with sufficient biological affinity that members of the population recognize some shared consciousness.

What has also changed since the Middle Ages is that groups outside the European upper classes have come to condemn the bourgeois enclave from which technology rules as the source of all social ills. Within a generation of acquisition of skills in European languages native intelligentsias were rejecting in print the justifications offered for the plunder of their lands and peoples. In the United States, even before Emancipation, African Americans were rejecting supremacist rationalizations for slavery. Initially in the United States, because of the romantic mystique which surrounded plantation slavery, the aris-

tocratic principle was associated with racial exploitation. The rest of the world, however, saw racial exploitation at the end of an umbilical cord of steamships. For them the bourgeois rationalist principle was the cause of their suffering. Eventually in the U.S. this conclusion has also come to rule. It is the connection between rationalism and oppression which often leads non-European Romanticism to appear in the guise of Marxism, as opposed to the more regular association of the latter with the rationalist critique of capitalism in the European context. The most astonishing thing about the condemnations by whites of victimization arguments is the ignorance these condemnations reveal about what minorities mean by the term victim. That which has been taken has been lost forever, therefore the arguments are not presented as part of a case for reparations. The complaint is about the loss of purity and therefore the loss of consciousness of one's true former self. The expectation really is that whites confirm their oppressor status and thus verify the victim's awareness of the distance he or she still must travel to his or her destiny. Alone than anything else, victimization arguments reflect a romantic mindset.

Searle sees the Left's willingness to grant victim status to any and all corners as an instinct toward nihilism. Actually, it represents the successful reintroduction of the earlier hierarchical relationship between dominant and dominated intellegentsias which had existed between missionaries and their proselytes. Since the time of Franz Boaz, academic anthropology has repudiated the notion that western intellectual culture stood at the apex of world civilizations, though without replacing it with a notion equally attractive to European American intellectuals. Under the rubric of victimizer and victim the Left has brought the hierarchy back, this time with the academy taking on the challenge of freeing the victims from their alienated selves.[23]

Searle doesn't perceive the inclusivist motivations behind the Left's incorporation of minority voices. One listens to victims in order to help them cease to be victims, that status to be realized, according to Leftist eschalology, in some raceless, classless, genderless future. In the here and now, the one difference between the former victim's progress toward a healthy consciousness and the former heathen's progress toward Christian enlightenment is that the former victim gets an office and status within the contemporary version of the missionary compound. The task of the two intellectuals is the same—to provide a barometer of the "humanity" of European-American society. The pay scale, however, has improved immensely.

But the issue is not money, but recognition. If you develop a curriculum which withholds recognition for intellectual merit from certain groups, it has to be expected that intellectuals from those groups will press for recognition based on merit denied. The Left's willingness to provide minority intellectuals with a forum has been known since the days of Claude McKay, West Indian, fellow traveler of John Reed, and composer of "If We Must Die," the one poem of defiance every black school child learned in the sixties. Minority awareness of the price tag for this recognition has been evident since the work of

Ralph Ellison. Though they are aware that the Left's greatest goal is to use their intellectual privation to flagellate the conservative majority which dominates the Academy, minority intellectuals still turn toward the Left for an audience. More than anything else, this decision should be read as a measure of minority perception of the close-mindedness of the mainstream intellectual establishment.

My point in this section has been more than that the two lendencies in recent African American thought which frighten those like Ravitch— the argument of a stolen legacy as advanced by Diop, and the argument for a particularist culture advanced by Asante, have long ancestries within European culture. At the base of Ravitch's essay is a misconception about the cultural process the debate about multiculturalism reflects. She insists on reading the assertion of a self by minority intellectuals as a "bad idea whose time has come," as the advent of a new dark age. More accurately this assertion should be read as a rationale for the appropriation of center stage in modern cultural life by ethnic intelligentsias previously marginalized. Far from questioning the values of European society, these efforts to claim part of the center have followed the lines of argument established by European intellectuals themselves. Black intellectuals, at least, might be accused of being more conscious of themselves as intellectuals than as blacks, since coming up with arguments to refute European intellectuals is not the same as coming up with arguments to inspire the black masses. Whatever one feels about what they argue and with whom they converse, it is unfair to treat

them as Cossacks primed to rampage through the village. Neither does it serve any useful purpose to lecture them like a set of particularly juvenile graduate students. It would be more helpful to treat them as intellectuals who, no matter what their predisposition, remain convinced that in their confrontation with European chauvinism they now hold the high ground.

The past few years for most thinkers of European descent in the nations bordering the North Atlantic have been a period of exaltation because of the fall of centrally planned economies in the U.S.S.R. and its satellites. The failure of Marxist-inspired totalitarianism has been read as a final, negative verdict on Marxism, a philosophy which gathered force among European intellectuals in the late 19th and early 20th centuries because it provided a rational explanation of social inequality. For most of that period Marxism competed for attention with another explanation of social inequality which also might be called rational, Social Darwinism. In its twentieth-century garb of scientific racism it, likewise, has recently lost its powers to persuade subjected peoples, though this latter revolution of consciousness has elicited far less acclaim from white intellectuals.

It is not clear exactly what sort of attitudes are to be expected of intelligentsias recovering from systematic bombardment by the notion that they do not exist. One thing should be self-evident. Peoples who have had to survive several centuries on a spiritually based idea of their own self worth, are not going to give up that idea easily. Even if they were not, in their victory over scientific racism, celebrating a victory over Romanticism masquerading a Science, minority intellectuals might be expected to see this triumph as one of the spirit. That liberal minority intellectuals who believe that exteral criteria of merit do exist are in such short supply simply cannot be that shocking. It is a bit foolish to expect a type of mentality rejected by both sides in a debate to thrive.

The supply of liberals being so low, it is pertinent to ask what input should be given the ideas of minority Romantics in a time when consensus on the reforms to be made to the school curriculum is desperately needed. From her study Ravitch concludes that there is a danger of retrogression if minorities gain too much influence. She accuses the Manchester University scholar George Joseph of advocating the teaching of a form of ethnomathematics for complaining in his book, *Race and Color*, that the contribution of "Egypt, Babylonia, Mesopotamia and India" to the history of mathematics has been "distorted by racist Europeans who wanted to establish the dominance of European forms of knowledge."[24] Reform of the curriculum in such a way that minority students would be made systematically aware of his point would result in "ancient mathematics (being) taught mainly to minority children," which in turn would mean that "the gap between them and middle class white children is apt to grow."[25] Neither Joseph nor any of the other authors cited by Ravitch justify this absurd, alarmist conclusion. But the underlying argument she is putting forward, that people whom we have identified as Romantics have traditionally stood outside of any inclusivist idea of civilization, and thus

can be expected to wreck any effort at creating a common culture, is worth addressing.

Merit-denied arguments, such as Irenicus leveled against the Italians, appeal to intelligentsia who feel their worth being slighted. It is the one type of argument which attracts both Rationalists and Romantics, the former because it explains their lack of reputation outside their group, the latter because it provides a measure of the magnitude of their suffering. Stolen legacy arguments are a sub-category of the genre. Few Romantics would ever make the case that the legacy stolen from their people, was mathematics. It is a fairly safe bet, then, that any intellectual who makes a play for his ancestors' authorship of the first treatises on mathematics, as did Diop, is a Rationalist. One response to Ravitch is that many she would identify as Romantics are actually Rationalists yearning for acknowledgement. Give the latter group an audience, and they will be most eager to show how much they really want to share.

"Particularism has its intellectual roots in the ideology of ethnic separatism and in the black nationalist movement," according to Ravitch.[26] Actually those roots go much further back, into intellectual stances which made their first appearance in the lecture halls of medieval European universities. While on the surface Ravitch ignores the historical roots to the present debate over multiculturalism, on a deeper level the clinching argument to her brief has to do with a hindsighted apprehension that the retreat of Liberalism before the forces of European Romanticism which culminated in the rise of fascism, Nazism and the senseless death of millions,

had its beginnings in the capture of influence over educational reform by Romantic nationalist movements in the nineteenth century. We can see, in retrospect, the consequences of allowing particularism to triumph over universalism. In permitting American minorities the right to seek some sort of ethnic satisfaction through the curriculum, is not the Academy allowing the horror to begin again?

The first problem with her concern is that it presumes a Herrenvolk (Master race) mentality on the part of each and every group that is adamant about self-expression. Not every group of people wants to rule the world. Proclaiming yourself and your ancestors unique does not necessarily lead to the conviction that every other group must become your servants. Master race beliefs are quite dangerous and should be suppressed. Few minority educators, if any, subscribe to them.

The second fault with Ravitch's fears is that they tie the relationship between the Romantic mentality and political authority too narrowly to one set of historical experiences. What happened in mid-twentieth century Europe is not looming in late twentieth America. However, obnoxious individual minority reformers may be, none can be compared to Hitler and Mussolini without trivializing the latter. As Fritz Stern demonstrated, late nineteenth century and early twentieth century European Romantics believed that if Technology (Science) could be destroyed, it was still possible to return to the pure like of the folk. In German thinking, Technology became embodied in a group of people, the Jews, whose eradication would bring back the pre-industrial world.[27] Few minority intellectuals hold such views either about Technology or its embodiment in a given group of people. Ravitch presents the example of the conflict over reform of the New York State history curriculum as an example of minority educators making scapegoats out of respected authorities in pursuit of group self-aggrandizement.[28] If she could only free herself from the model she has in her head she might appreciate that from the perspective of minority reformers even the reformed curriculum may still remain too Eurocentric, and that the educational establishment's acknowledgment of this fact does not represent appeasement of the forces of evil.

Ravitch's case is that there are too few minority educators who accept the idea of civilization as an external, transferable thing, for the present effort at developing a pluralistic multiculturalism to have any success. As I have tried to show, there are many more minority Rationalists out there than she recognizes; they just need to be provided with a set of options more rationalistic than the ones they are dealing with at present. But I would agree with the idea that a greater supply of minorities with a liberal bent would help the process along. The recruitment of the latter would not be as difficult as many keep insisting. After all, the cry which emerges from the inner city along with the proclamation of the African origins of mathematics is not one for a return to some pristine African past, but one for more computers and mathematics education.

Since the Middle Ages schools have been the place where spiritual values were instilled in the intelligentsia. The spirit behind the values has changed several times, but the process of conditioning the next generation to die for (in) that spirit has gone on. Disregarding the exaggerations of Dinesh D'Souza, the problem with serious liberal criticism of minority insistence on specific acknowledgement in the curriculum is that it ignores or remains ignorant of the degree to which European Romanticism still permeates the course of study in American schools.[29] Indeed it goes so deep that it can still pass itself off as Rationalism. Thus Searle boasts, specifically about women, but in general about all marginalized intelligentsias:

> Even if the canon is opened up, even if membership in the club is thrown open to all corners, even after you have admitted every first rate woman writer from Sappho to Elizabeth Bishop, the various groups that feel that they have been excluded are still going to feel excluded, or marginalized. At present there are still going to be many Western white males.[30]

What free market certified this conclusion? And if the ideas of Western white males are this competitive, why is it necessary to maintain a canon, a form of intellectual protectionism? The music critic Edward Ruthstein has recently complained that without much greater subsidization, the preservation of Western classical music will be seriously jeopardized, the victim of audience desertion to other "world" musics.[31] At least in the Conservatory, where the market does intrude, it is possible to measure the true appeal of the ideas and creations officially recognized as the products of Western civilization. In the Academy, people who call themselves liberal vehemently reject the possibility that in free competition the values they identify as essential for the continuation of Western society might be discerned more thoroughly in the writings of thinkers whose names they have never bothered to learn. And then they are shocked when minorities or women perceive them as chauvinists.

It is because I believe that the enfranchisement of the ideas of minority Rationalists would be more effective in getting curriculum reform past the present impasse than would the suppression of those of minority Romantics that I have spent so much time identifying the antecedents to each position. Acknowledgement of these lineages may not bring an end to the trench warfare now sapping the energy for the movement toward educational reform, but at least it should align the combatants on the same battle field. I remain hopeful though, in good Rationalist fashion, that once the name calling is put aside, and the conflict over the curriculum recognized as having settled down to an ages old debate among intellectuals, progress can be made.

Notes

1. Quoted in Alexander Murray, *Reason and Society in the Middle Ages* (New York: Oxford University Press, 1978), p. 236.

2. Diane Ravitch, "Multiculturalism: E Pluribus Plures," *The American Scholar*, 59 (Summer 1990): 339.

3. Ravitch, 341.

4. Ravitch, 342.

5. Ravitch, 343.

6. Ravitch, 347-8.

7. Ravitch, 347.

8. George W. Stocking, Jr., *Victorian Anthropology* (New York: The Free Press, 1987), p. 11.

9. Stocking, 20.

10. Ravitch, 342.

11. John Searle, "Storm Over the University," *New York Review of Ranks*, 37 (December 6, 1990): 36.

12. Murray, 252-3.

13. Murray, 257.

14. Taken from Gerald Strauss, *Manifestations of Discontent in Germany on the Eve of the Reformation* (Bloomington: Indiana University Press, 1971), pp. 73-74.

15. William Christian, *Local Religion in Sixteenth Century Spain* (Princeton: Princeton University Press, 1981).

16. Heiko Oberman, *Luther: Man between God and the Devil* (New Haven: Yale University Press, 1989), pp. 40-49.

17. John M. Headley, *Luther's View of Church History* (New Haven: Yale University Press, 1963), p. 242.

18. Murray, *Reason and Society*, 162-188.

19. Cheikli Anta Diop, *Civilization or Barbarism. An Authentic Anthropology*, trans. Yna-Lengi Meema Ngemi, eds. Harold J. Salemson and Jargolijn de Jager (Brooklyn: Lawrence Hill Books, 1991).

20. Diop, 6-7

21. Martin Bernal, *Black Athena: The Afroasiatic Roots of Classical Civilization*, vol. I, "The Fabrication of Ancient Greece 1785-1985," (New Brunswick, NJ: Rutgers University Press, 1987).

22. See E. M. Butler, *The Tyranny of Greece Over Germany. A study of the influence exercised by Greek art and poetry over the great German writers of the eighteenth, nineteenth and twentieth centuries*, (Boston: Beacon Press, 1958).

23. See George W. Stocking, Jr., *Race, Culture and Evolution. Essays in the History of Anthropology*, (New York: Free Press, 1968).

24. Ravitch, "Multiculturalism," 345.

25. Ravitch, 345.

26. Ravitch, 342.

27. Fritz Stern, *The Politics of Cultural Despair. A Study in the Rise of the Germanic Ideology*, (Berkeley: University of California Press, 1961).

28. Ravitch, 349-51.

29. See Dinesh D'Souza, "Illiberal Education," *The Atlantic*, 267, 3 (March 1991).

30. Searle, 35.

31. Edward Rothstein, "Roll Over Beethoven: The new musical correctness and its mistakes," *The New Republic*, 204, 5 (February 4, 1991).

Reprinted by permission from Debates in Society, Culture, & Science Spring, 1992, 38-57.

Each of us is a product of a culture, a family, and of unique individual experiences. Also, in the United States many people experience more than one cultural/linguistic tradition. In addition to discomfort, diverse experiences can lead to growth and understanding.

Reflections on a Career in Education: A Puertorriqueña Looks Back

Carmen A. Cruz

History is the memory of human group experience. If it is forgotten or ignored, we cease in that measure to be human. Without history, we have no knowledge of who we are or how we came to be, like victims of collective amnesia groping in the dark for our identity.[1]

I am a nomad, a marginal person. I have always felt as if I stand on the outside looking in, never really fitting anywhere. I have always felt left out. The focus of this paper is my own experience in the American education system. My larger quest will be to identify key American figures who throughout the history of education in Puerto Rico have made so many Puerto Ricans feel marginalized as I do. I want to understand the relationship between these feelings of marginality and the way Americans dispense education. Why do these feelings exist? How far in history must I explore to get at the root cause?

On an island 500 years ago, the Arawak Indians of Puerto Rico felt the trade winds caress their bodies. They stood in watch of their mortal enemies, the Caribs. Yet their many battles were not about superiority in intelligence. Genetic inferiority was not in question. They battled to see who was the most able warrior. After the battle, warriors departed without having played mind games. They fought; they won; they lost; but they were one with their tropical homeland, Borinquen (Puerto Rico).

Christopher Columbus disembarked upon the shores of Puerto Rico in 1493. "All of these islands are very handsome and very good earth, but this one seemed to everybody the best," he wrote of Puerto Rico. Columbus was greeted by the Taino Indians, a sub-tribe of the Arawak. The Taino were a kind and peace-loving people. When Columbus first met them, he wrote, "They go quite naked as their mothers bore them." He continued, "They are so ingenious and free with all they have, that no one would believe it who has not seen it. Of anything they possess, if it be asked of them,

---

1 Robert V. Daniels, *Studying History–How and Why* (New Jersey: Prentice-Hall, 1966), 3.

they never say no."[2] Estimates of the numbers of these native peoples at the time of Columbus range from two to three million on all the islands and thirty thousand on the island of Puerto Rico. What happened to them? Some were killed by the Carib raids. Spanish domination of the natives brought extensive race fusion, blending Indian, Spanish, and later African. The Spanish also brought countless deadly European diseases which killed many more of the Arawak.

By the end of the seventeenth century, all of the arable coastal land was under the control of the aristocratic Spanish sugar planation owners. African slaves were brought to the island to work on these plantations. Many slaves ran for freedom and safety to the mountains. The large sugar plantations also forced the native Puerto Ricans who wanted to farm to move inland. Thus when the coffee growers planted their first beans it was in the rich hilly soil of the West. This occurred over a century after sugar cane first covered the coast.

Coffee growers did not become Europeanized. Rather, they grew apart from the San Juan latifundia (large sugar estates) Spaniards and developed a mountain culture. The same was true for the subsistence and semi-subsistence level farmers known as the Jibaros. These Jibaros lived inland, independent from the Europeanized coastal cultures. Their jaunty self-sufficiency came to symbolize the indigenous Puerto Rican. "No importa cuanto trate un jibaro de quitarse su mancha de platano, esta siempre le acompañara. (It does not matter how

hard a Jibaro tries to get rid of his plantin stains, these stains will always accompany him.)"[3]

The Jibaro symbolized the true Puerto Rican, with straw hat and plantain-stained hands. The Jibaros were subsistence farmers, growing what they needed and living off the land. The Jibaros developed their style of country music and other forms of entertainment: cockfighting, dancing, singing, and sleeping in a hammock under the trees. They were culturally self-sufficient.

Life on the Island

My father comes from this background. He was a typical Jibaro to some degree. Yet he was not resigned to that way of life. He eventually moved our family from the rural area to the city. As a young man, not satisfied with what he had (nothing!), he tried getting a job; but his third grade education soon put a stop to his endeavors. Seeing no way out, he finally joined the army and served during World War II. When the war was over, he returned to Puerto Rico and married my mother.

As a young married man, my father picked coffee beans in the huge plantations of Puerto Rico. The work was hard, the hours were long, and the pay was minimal. He was no Juan Valdez happily picking only the finest coffee beans. I remember living in a shack, which my mother kept spotless by scrubbing with water that my sister and I (the two Jitas, as we were nicknamed) carried from the stream in buckets balanced on our heads. I remember playing in the scrub water as my

mother swept it out the door. Our meals consisted of rice and beans with an occasional tortilla (in Puerto Rico, an egg omelet). We could not afford meat.

By then my mother had five children, four girls and one boy. My brother was my father's pride and joy. My father was always tired, worried, and resentful. He could never make enough money to provide for all the needs in our home. He finally allowed my mother to take a job that she could do at home. She embroidered beautiful flowers on white gloves. I remember her working late into the night, straining her eyes by candle light to finish the required number of gloves. Sometimes she would make a special lace edging for the gloves. Many nights, I would wake up to the glow of her candle. So much time, so much work for so little pay. With the few cents she earned, she would buy material to make our clothes. The material was inexpensive, but her crafting was superb.

My father heard of all the great job opportunities in America. Jobs could be had by all who were willing to work. He could not take poverty any more. He started saving for his fare to the United States. Way into the night my parents discussed their plans. Dad would go first and find a job. He would work for a year and send for us.

Once in the United States and working, my Dad did send money home every week. Mom kept her piece work job. Dad's family and Mom's brothers watched over us.

---

2   Roberta A. Johnson, *Puerto Rico: Commonwealth or Colony?* (New York: Praeger, 1980), 3.
3   Ibid., 110.

The Land of Opportunity

With my father gone, I found myself spending much time alone, playing on the hillsides, running barefoot through the stream, eating canapas (a sweet fruit) under the hot sun, and sleeping under tropical breezes that cooled the night. One day when it seemed like Dad would never send for us, we received a letter. We were all caught up in the excitement, the frantic packing, and the tearful goodbyes of our final departure from our beloved Puerto Rico.

The most vivid memories of my trip to Chicago are of terror. I remember boarding a huge monstrous thing. The monster turned out to be just an airplane. That airplane represented my journey into the unknown. Anxiety about the unknown became a major theme with me. This trip was my introduction to the fears that would shape my life. The noise, movement, and mayhem of this first airplane ride tossed me into world of fear. I remember thinking to myself, "I am going to die because I am in Heaven!"

After many hours of fear and confusion, I remember feeling some type of downward movement. Once the plane landed, I stepped into a totally alien world.

The cold Chicago wind whipped through the thin material of "mi trajecito que mamita me hizo" (the little dress my mother had sewn for me). What was this white stuff that was falling from the sky? Nieve (snow), mamita explained to me. We must hurry, papi is waiting for us. The change was extraordinary; not only did we have to learn to cope with the chill of the northern winds, but we had to learn to live in the coldness accorded us by these strange Americanos.

Schooling in Chicago

I started the first phase of my journey into the social and educational system of the United States. My first experience in school was to stand in line . . . terrified! Strange noises surrounded me. I did not understand them! No one spoke my language, no one wanted to learn it. What was I supposed to do? Pay attention? Watch? Do what others did? Somehow, I made it through my first year in a Chicago public school. There was no bilingual program for this child. I was shy and quiet and this experience took its toll. I was taught at an early age to keep my mouth shut. Teachers did not want to be bothered by a child who didn't speak English. "They" didn't have the time to decipher what I was trying to say in my broken English. So I learned—the English language, English history, and the English way. I did what it took to survive in a harsh and strange world.

To make it, I had to learn the history of the American people and forget the history of my people. A person must know some history to begin to understand the world or to act with any wisdom and perspective.[4] As children in school, we were told that we must study the history of this country because we must learn to be good Americans. We were told that history is the record of all experiences. However, I now know that a school child is exposed to a history which consists of the selected experiences of a given group of people, usually the dominant group in that society. Those experiences are not only preselected for children, but they are also given interpretations by the dominant group.

In Chicago, I attended eight grammar schools and two high schools. This constant moving took place because my family had grown so large (twelve children plus my mother and father) that we weren't welcomed in any one place for too long. Through these years of perpetual movement from school to school, I developed a tremendous fear of speaking up in class. Being shy and withdrawn to begin with, I never made many friends. I was always one of the "new kids" in the classroom. My parents didn't allow us to go outside much, so I didn't have opportunities to make friends around the neighborhood either.

Grammar school had one good memory for me. I learned to read well enough to be able to read fairy tales. So I had one thing to look forward to in each new school: a new set of fairy tale books. I graduated from grammar school, a nice student with good grades. I don't think half my teachers knew who I was. I remember always trying to hide in the back, so the teachers would not call on me and the students would not pick on me.

High school turned out to be another nightmare. The first day I spent most of my time lost in the corridors of a huge and impersonal building. My fear of speaking in front of groups kept me full of anxiety most of the time. I went to classes and straight home to help my mother with the younger children.

One day I heard that the after school program was hiring students to help as teacher's aides. Because I would be bringing home a little extra money, my parents allowed me to apply for the job. I was hired. I now got paid for what I had been doing for free all my life—taking care of kids. Through that job I met Mrs. Evachinko. She gave me the confidence I needed to apply for the scholarships and grants that got me through college. Mrs. Evachinko was a wonderful, kind person who kept telling me what a good teacher I would make.

College Life

History never repeats itself exactly. No historical situation is the same as any other. History teaches us that nothing ever stays the same. "You cannot step twice into the same river," said the Greek philosopher Heraclitus, "for fresh waters are ever flowing in upon you." The only unchanging focus in human affairs is the constancy of change itself.

But, as I find myself in yet another situation, I again experience feelings of inadequacy. I continue to feel the loneliness of always feeling left out. I want to question our great philosophers and historians for it seems to me, that within my lifetime, history is repeating itself. As a rational being, I know this is not true. My first experiences in the Chicago public schools which caused me so much anguish, were interpretations of events from a child's perspective. Now that I am an adult, I can control the situation, manipulate the events, and interpret these occurrences in my life as I wish. If history teaches us judg-

ment by supplying us with acknowledgeable background, and if history trains us in the technique of criticism and reasoned conclusion, then I see no other route for myself except to study the history of education.

My initiation into college life followed that same old pattern of anxiety and fear of the unknown. Yet I was more determined than ever to succeed. First I had to overcome the objections of my father. I had to convince him that he did not have to pay for any of my schooling. Then I had to convince him that I would be safe away from home. It took a lot of talking, but he finally allowed me to go. I remember having no clothes for college. My mother gave me some of her old skirts and blouses. I was probably the worst dressed student at the University of Illinois in Champaign-Urbana.

I remember the first day in my dorm room. My roommate was complaining about how terrible it was to have to share a room. I couldn't understand why she was complaining. There were two people in a room with two beds. I was accustomed to four people in one room in one bed. I felt like I was in heaven! What in the world was this girl complaining about?

The academic part of college life was not so bad after all. Most of my classes were huge lecture sections, where I was lost among the other three hundred or so students attending. In those classes, I did not have to worry about being called on or having to make any presentations. When I did have to make presentations I managed somehow with the help of a few friends I made in college.

My first taste of freedom away from home was great! I worked

hard, studied hard, and played hard. My college years were the best of my life.

Working for my People and for Myself

I went to college to become a teacher. As soon as I graduated, I got a job in Chicago. I wanted to make enough money to buy my mother a house. The year I started working, however, she died. My new job helped me get over my mother's death. I loved working with kids. My classes were wonderful. I felt like I was really accomplishing what I had set out to do.

Six years after I started teaching, I went back to school to get my masters. In the meantime, I got pregnant and decided to have my child. Two years later, I had a beautiful one-year-old son, Michael Christian, and a new master's degree from National College of Education now called National-Lewis University. I told myself this was enough schooling for me.

Oh! But, life is strange. Ten years later, a friend told me about a doctoral program being offered at Northern Illinois University. I went to the first meeting as a joke, because I knew I could never make it in such a program. Well, the joke was on me, because not only was I accepted, but I have received straight A's in all my courses and I am at the dissertation stage of the program.

Now I find myself doing historical research to complete my degree, and I go back to the same question: Why? Why history? I believe I have turned to history because history teaches us to ask questions. Only history can satisfy my curiosity or my quest for truth and knowledge. History has a subjective side that makes room for opinion, values, and imagination. Finally, I am able to truly understand that the only unchanging paradigm in my life is constancy of change. Through the study of history, I am learning to feel comfortable with change.

If the study of history of education has taught me anything, it has taught me to value my opinion. I have learned to base my opinion on data and knowledge, and I am ready to revise it when new knowledge makes that necessary. History has given me opportunities and skills to enhance my ability to think. History is cultivating my general powers of intellect. My work in history is always personal and a never-ending intellectual venture into the unknown.

The history of colonialism and its effects on the educational system in Puerto Rico has provided me with rewarding and enlightening insights. Because this type of intellectual outlook is abstract, I first found it hard to grasp. As a neophyte in the study of history, I have used concepts of "colonialism" and "hegemony" as a basis for interpretation.

Yet this historical research into the concepts of colonialism and its effects on the Puerto Rican educational system has shown me how facts and ideas must be used together. Ideas developed from knowledge of the facts must constantly be weighed against each other. These facts and ideas shape our interpretation of history, the history that defines who I am and who you are. As I understand how American colonial policies affected those Puerto Ricans of long ago, I am understanding a little more why I feel the way I do.

Through history, I am trying to understand the experiences of the Puerto Rican people. I don't want their experiences forgotten or ignored. These experiences are of enormous value to me because they help me to understand myself. But these experiences are of value to others because they bring knowledge and understanding of another group of human beings within our society.

The study of history is helping me finally to understand who I am, where I came from, and where I am going. History expresses the emotions, values, and ideals of my people, the Puerto Ricans. If at times, I still feel like I am on the outside looking in, I can at least understand why I am feeling that way. History of education is helping me define my place in education as well as in life.

Carmen Aida Cruz has had nineteen years of experience in the Chicago Public School system. Her work in bilingual education and bilingual special education has led to her involvement in multicultural education and minority issues in higher education. Ms. Cruz's dissertation is tentatively entitled, "The Intent and Effects of American Policies on the Educational System of Puerto Rico between 1898-1903: A Study in Colonialism."

Cruz, Carmen. "Reflections on a Career in Education." Vitae Scholasticae 11 (Fall/Spring 1992). Reprinted by permission.

Carmen Cruz's experiences
as a Spanish speaking
five-year-old in Chicago
frightened and challenged
her. Norma Salazar came to
the United States after
attending school for six years
in Mexico. She, too, mastered
cultural and personal
challenges in this
multicultural society.

Hasta Que Levanto la Cabeza: Self-discovery in the Search for Sor Juana Inés de la Cruz

History, in effect, results in the principal formula of self-discovery; its object, to clarify the enigma that man [woman] is, to try to get to him [her] through the only accessible route we know, which is precisely that, history.[1]

Introduction

Why does an elementary teacher decide to do historical research? I have asked myself this question several times in the past two years. I certainly know now how difficult historical research is, especially for someone without a history background. Nevertheless, I have forged ahead in this endeavor, sometimes blindly, sometimes intuitively, because I know I'm on the road to self-discovery.

I was sixteen years old when I came across the poem "Satira Filosofica" ("Philosophical Satire") better known as "Hombres Necios" ("Foolish Men"). A friend who knew my interest in poetry gave me an anthology that included works of well-known Latin American poets— *100 Poesias Escogidas*.[2] The poem was written by Sor Juana Inés de la Cruz, a sixteenth century nun, poet, feminist, and educator. At the time I was not completely aware of who she was. I was more interested in the content of the poem, so much so that I memorized the following four verses:

Foolish men, you who blame
women without cause;
you, promoting the very flaws
to which you give women fame.

If to hopeless evil you belong;
within them wickedness incite,
why do you wish them to do right
if you encourage them to do wrong?

You fight their resistance with haste
and then, with such appalled gravity,
you say it was their own levity,
that brought them immoral disgrace.

---

1   Josefina Zoraida Vazquez, *Historia de la historiografia* (Mexico: Ediciones Ateneo, S.A., 1985), 10.
2   Heraclides D'Acosta, *100 Poesias escogidas* (Mexico: El Libro Espanol, 1960), 93.

Your boldness wrapped in "pure"
  white sheet
hides seemingly unaware;
in closet as a ghost: beware;
it will frighten you when you meet.[3]

Why would I be interested in this type of poem? More importantly why have I chosen this woman as the topic of my current research?

There are things I have discovered about myself in doing my research. Sor Juana's poem dealt with a serious issue I was dealing with even though I was very young. In retrospect, I remember noticing injustice and unfairness when I compared how differently men and women were raised.

Autobiographical Background

Family

My family comes from Mexico. My mother was born in Tantoyuca, Veracruz. She came from a wealthy family. My father was born near San Antonio, Texas, but moved to Mexico when he was a young man. I don't know much about his family.

My parents lived in Barco y Periquillo, an oil camp in the state of Veracruz. My father was in charge of the camp. My mother told me she paid the employees with gold pieces. She helped with payroll even though she was considered just a "housewife"—a label she never internalized. Looking back, my mother was the one who was always in charge. She never played the submissive role that Mexican culture had assigned her.

At this time in their lives, my parents had five children. They had servants and nannies for my two brothers and three sisters, who went to private schools in Tampico, Tamaulipas. They lived there with my paternal grandmother. Out of eight children, I was the only one born in Tampico. My brothers and sisters were all born in Barco y Periquillo, but would not acknowledge that. They were embarrassed to say they were born in a rural area instead of the metropolis.

My parents also owned a ranch (there may have been two). They had cattle which provided them with meat and dairy products. Food was sent to Tampico where the main house was located and where my brothers and sisters lived.

I was barely three months old when my father left for the United States. He had lost his job during the oil expropriation of 1938 and was too proud to ask Mexico for another job. I remember my mother telling me that she had written to the president requesting a job for my father. My father was reinstated; but he still decided to leave, stating that he was not going to settle for handouts from Mexico.

Thinking back, I realize that it was just the excuse my father needed to abandon his parental responsibilities. He left my mother with eight children to raise. Lacking the skills to support all of us, she had to be inventive. As a child she had sewn for her dolls. She continued her sewing when she had her family. Sewing was a lifelong activity for her, one that later provided her with the skills to support herself and eight children.

Soon after my father left for Chicago, we moved to Nuevo Laredo, Tamaulipas. We lived there for nine years before emigrating to the United States.

Childhood

Life in Nuevo Laredo was a lonely experience for me. My mother worked all day in a shirt factory. My brothers and sisters were either in school or at work. I was the first one home from school. It seemed as if I waited an eternity for my mother to get home. Looking back, what I remember most of all is being lonely and hungry. There was never anything to eat in the house when I got home, but I knew my mother always brought something for us. So, I waited every day.

It was in Nuevo Laredo where I began to notice a double standard between women and men. It didn't seem right that my sisters went to work and then were expected to do household chores; this was not expected of my brothers. Many times the household chores became my responsibility. They told me that since I didn't work, I should at least clean the house. My going to school was not considered work. Yet, my brothers were not expected to do any housework. On the contrary, we (the women) were expected to tend to their needs. Somehow all this seemed unfair, but I didn't know why.

The irony was that my mother was teaching us to play a submissive role when she herself never did. In fact, she would get upset when the woman next door was beaten. Her husband thrashed her about two or three times a week. My mother always would ask, "When is that woman going to lift her head?" ("¿Cuando va a levantar la cabeza esa mujer?"). That woman never

3   Author's translation.

did. She was trapped. She was part of the socialization process that gave men power.

I was about five years old and I still had no memory of my father. I remember some of our neighbors asking me where my father was. I always replied that he was working in Chicago. I added that we were going to see him soon. This is what my mother had explained to me. I repeated it verbatim.

When I was five my mother and I did make our first trip to Chicago so I could meet my father. We arrived at the rooming house where he lived, and she sent me up the stairs first. Obviously she wanted to surprise him. She pointed to him and said, "That's your father." He was coming down with a friend. She told me to walk past him. As I did, I remember my father saying to his companion, "See that little girl; I have a daughter that looks just like her." I kept walking up the stairs and wondered why my own father had not recognized me. The little girl he was referring to was my older sister. We looked so much alike that when we were older, people thought we were twins.

My mother and I enjoyed a short visit with my father, and then I didn't see him again until I was twelve years old.

I was in fifth grade when my mother informed me that we were finally going to be reunited with my father. Evidently the paper work from the immigration office had come through and we were going to move again. Except that this time it was just my mother and I. Three of my sisters were married, one was already in Chicago with my father, and my brother was going to Mexico City to the university. To prepare for our move my mother en-

rolled me in an English academy. I attended for two years, during my fifth and sixth grade. It was a night school from 7:00 P.M. to 9:00 P.M.

First School Experience in the United States

The idea of moving to Chicago filled me with excitement, but also anxiety. I was truly excited that we were finally going to be united as a family. At the same time, I was anxious because I was going to attend a new school in a new country. We arrived in Chicago on 2 August 1955.

I will never forget my first school experience in the United States. I'm specifically referring to my first day in school. My sister was not able to go with me because she had to leave early for work. My mother didn't speak English. Therefore, my father walked with me and dropped me off at the door. It was a parochial school—Maternity of the Blessed Virgin Mary school, also called MBVM.

Not knowing the language, I stood outside and kept to myself, just observing and listening to all the student laughter. I felt alone again. It was a familiar feeling from many times in Nuevo Laredo.

Soon the bell rang and everybody formed lines outside the church entrance. That told me to get in line, but I didn't know where I belonged. I looked to see who was my height and I got in line with them. Nobody talked or paid attention to me. It was as if I were invisible.

Once inside, everybody seemed to know where to go. They were walking into classrooms. The nuns received the students with a smile and then closed the door after the last student had entered. When it came to the group I was in, the nun

stopped me by putting her hand on my shoulder. She obviously said I didn't belong there because she closed the door behind her, leaving me outside. I tried another door; the same thing happened. The teacher motioned with her hand to go away. I tried one more classroom door and this teacher did not claim me as her student either. I was left in the hall all alone. I remember looking down at the shiny floor.

I started walking very fast toward the stairs. I wanted to go home. By the time I reached the streets, I was running. As I walked into my house, I started crying inconsolably. My sister was irate. She could not believe my father had left me at school to find the classroom by myself. Evidently she could have taken me, but she was allowing my father to assume a role he could not. I didn't know how a father was supposed to be. All I knew was that he had forgotten how to be a father.

Adolescence

Moving to Chicago did not improve family closeness. The way I perceived our relationship with my father was that we—my sister, my mother, and I—remained close. My father just happened to live with us. He was more like a roomer in our house. I still answered to my mother. I still slept with her as I had since my father had left us.

Living with my father did not improve feelings of double standards either; rather it reinforced them. I watched my sister doing things for my father. My brother would periodically live with us and my mother took care of his needs. I was going to school and the rest were working. Yet, the females continued existing in a subordinate role.

There were restrictions put on us, the women in the family, and none on the men. I was not allowed to go out by myself. If I did go out, it was with my sister (eight years older) or in a group. Being the youngest, I was disciplined by everybody. I was specifically required to listen to my father and my brothers.

I was a teenager when I first began rebelling. I refused to go on an outing with my mother and sister. They were going to Wisconsin for the day. I thought it would be boring for me. They insisted. My mother finally ordered me. I still refused to go with them. They did not want to leave me alone in the house, even though I was fifteen years old. I locked myself in the bathroom. My father was called to make me go. I did not open the door for him either. I sensed his anger building up as he told me to come out. I was determined to stay home. No one was going to force me to go. No one did, but I had no idea what was in store for me.

I stayed in the bathroom until my mother and sister had left. I was relieved because I thought the incident was all over. I went to the basement to wash clothes. I didn't realize my father was still angry and waiting for me to come out of the bathroom. He followed me to the basement. I can still see his silhouette standing in front of me. The basement was dark because I had not turned the lights on. I just left the door open to allow some daylight to come into the room. He took his belt off and beat me with it. I remember feeling helpless. I didn't make a sound. I didn't run, which is what I normally did when I knew I was going to get a beating. I was just frightened. Everything

happened so fast that I was actually confused, until I saw my arm begin to swell into a huge black welt. I didn't know how to react to this. I hardly knew this man who was my father; and yet he felt he had the right to beat me.

My mother taught us to be strong by her example. On the other hand, she also taught us how to act "appropriately," meaning submissive and polite. The proof is that she approved of the beating I got. I disobeyed her; therefore, I must be punished.

Marriage

My mother sent a constant double message. She wanted me to be strong, independent, and self sufficient. Yet all the time she was telling me to take care of myself, she was also telling me that I needed a man. I should get married and have someone to take care of me. My relatives in Mexico were already thinking I was an "old maid" because I was nineteen years old and still not married. I knew this worried my mother.

I replicated the double standard situation by getting married, being submissive, and relying on my husband. I did what I was expected to do. My husband-to-be asked for my hand in marriage. It was the appropriate thing to do according to the Mexican culture. He told my mother that he wanted to marry me and that he would take care of me. My mother agreed. I was also sitting at the dinner table. Why did I feel I was watching a business transaction?

Educational Aspirations

I had been married about ten years when I decided to go to school. I was getting restless. I needed to do something meaning-

ful for myself. I saw an ad in our local newspaper for a new program (early childhood education) through the human resources department at College of DuPage. It caught my eye because it had a picture of a little Hispanic girl. One of the courses was Street Spanish.

I attended the College of DuPage on a part-time basis. I scheduled my classes carefully because I wanted to be home when my daughters came home for lunch and in the afternoon when they were dismissed from school.

I enrolled in basic courses such as psychology and English, under the guidance of a wonderful advisor who became my friend. She had developed and was the director of the program in which I enrolled. Her name was Dulce. She also introduced me to existentialism. I read Kierkegaard and Unamuno.

The first book I read—for a sociology class—was *Blaming the Victim*. I read and reread every paragraph in the book to make sure I understood it completely. I was convinced that I lacked the skills of a "good student." For that reason, I had to study twice as hard.

I soon found out that learning was freedom. I found myself wanting more. I have never approached anything with as much tenacity as I have approached my education. It could be that watching my mother attend evening school for ten years set the example. That's how long she lived in the United States. I don't think she ever missed one class. She used to tell me how much she wanted to go to school when she was a young girl. She told me she only had a second grade education. To get an education she would have needed to go to Mexico City.

Relatives in Mexico City had wanted my mother to live with them so she could continue her education. Her father refused, she confided in me. He told her that it wasn't necessary for her to have an education since she was going to get married. According to my grandfather, all girls needed to get married.

My mother's example has certainly affected my life decisions, especially concerning education. Sometimes I wonder whether I was simply influenced by her example and advice or whether I also wanted her to fulfill all her dreams through me.

I had accumulated thirty-five semester hours at the College of Du-Page when I saw another ad in our local newspaper. A nearby school district was looking for a bilingual aide. I applied. A week later I started my career in education. The youngest of my daughters had recently started kindergarten. To lessen the guilt of leaving my daughters, I sent a lunch and paid a neighbor to supervise them after school. The internal stress I felt was intense, but I continued with the new position.

My new job was challenging. The concept of bilingual education was new in this particular district. Bilingual teachers were scarce. I was there alone for weeks before the district found a bilingual teacher. The person they finally hired spoke little Spanish. Therefore, I found myself in the position of teacher, mother, and social worker. I read everything about bilingual education I could find. I was determined to do the right thing for these students. The students and I became close. I was their link to the school because they and their parents did not speak English.

I worked as an aide for two years. By the middle of the second year, I was extremely frustrated. I knew that as an aide I had no authority to make decisions concerning the students. I only made suggestions. It finally occurred to me that the only way to get rid of my frustration was to go back to school and get a degree in teaching.

I decided that if I were going back to school it would be full time. I wanted to finish as soon as possible. This would mean a lot of time away from my household duties. I didn't know how my family was going to take change in their lives. I didn't even know if I was intellectually able to do it, yet I was determined.

I remember asking my daughters to come into the kitchen. The whole family was present, including my husband. They were not receptive when I told them that I wanted to be a full time student. My oldest daughter asked who was going to bake cookies. Later I bought her a children's cookbook and taught her how to bake cookies. That satisfied her.

I chose to go to Northeastern Illinois University because it offered a bilingual education major. Tuition was economical, but I had to travel fifty miles every day. Before I could do that, I had to learn how to drive. I remember my husband drove in the car with me the first time I had to go to class. He always showed me how to get to my destinations. He was happy as long as I was dependent on him.

I had to ask for a loan, which I had no trouble getting. My husband and I had three daughters and he was the only one working outside of the home.

I signed up for a full load of courses in the first semester. It was

frightening carrying four courses. I was afraid of failing. After the first semester, I carried over loads. I was getting good grades, mostly A's. I attended in the summer sessions also. My daughters were usually involved with my education. They helped me develop "learning center activities" required of elementary education majors. My husband helped build math counters and number lines out of wood.

It was lonely on campus. I sometimes spent the whole day reading and studying without speaking to anyone while I waited for my next class. I didn't make many friends. Most of the students were younger. I tried to schedule all my classes in two or three days so I wouldn't have to drive to the university every day. I was so exhausted; I told myself that as soon as I finished this degree I would never take another course.

Teaching

The need for bilingual teachers was so intense that, when I graduated from Northeastern, I already had two teaching job offers. I began working in a small district that had a large language minority population. The district had been cited by the state for not complying with bilingual rules and regulations. Evidently they were running an English as a Second Language program, which they thought was the same as bilingual education. They were counting on me to make the bilingual program comply with state rules.

Because it was a small district, I was involved in setting up entry and exit criteria, including testing. I assisted the Bilingual Coordinator in writing the yearly funding proposal. Much of the work was not my responsibility, but I did it anyway because I wanted to learn and understand all facets of the bilingual program.

I had been teaching for two years when I heard about a new master's degree program at National College of Education, now National-Louis University. The program appealed to me because it met once a week and it was geared for working people. Evidently, I forgot I had sworn I would never take another course because in 1984 I applied to National College and began my weekly trips to Evanston. It took me an hour to drive to Evanston. I usually got home about ten in the evening. I graduated in the summer of 1986.

I continued to expand my knowledge on the topic of bilingual education, taking courses related to language acquisition, the whole language approach to reading, and assessment of language minority students. Much controversy surrounded bilingual education. Opponents were trying to prove it ineffective. Proponents attacked negative studies as flawed. I concluded that the best way to help my students was by learning as much as I could about bilingual education.

Teaching was and is rewarding for me. There was a satisfaction in knowing that I had broken the barriers of traditional schooling when I saw my students learn. I felt I had created an accepting environment for them. Once I did this, all my students were able to learn—in their own ways, at their own paces.

I was happy with teaching, but I was not happy with administrator and school board indifference toward the program and the students. I needed to move into a different position to effect the changes I believed needed to happen. Students lacking English skills were usually labeled Limited English Proficient (LEP) Students. I thought more positive terms were needed, something like PEPS, Potentially English Proficient students. The best way to effect change was to move into the administrative end of public education. A colleague informed me that Northern Illinois University was organizing a doctoral cohort that would include an administration component. She invited me to a meeting in Chicago at a place called El Valor. In 1988 I began the course work for the doctorate. My goal was to obtain an Illinois Type 75 certificate and go into school administration.

I was finishing my doctoral course work when I decided I was not interested in school administration. As I reflected, I realized that the only courses I had not enjoyed were the ones dealing with administration. It was a painful recognition because I found myself without direction when I abandoned my program in administration.

Then an opportunity opened up at Northern Illinois University, and I applied for a temporary teaching position. I thought it would be a way to find out whether I liked teaching at the university level. I was not surprised. I thoroughly enjoyed the first class I taught and the rest that followed.

I knew then I would pursue the professorate in education. My goal was still to effect changes. What better place than the place where future teachers are trained. I felt that they needed to become aware of our present diverse student population. If they did not, they would be excluding many students in their classrooms. I was back on track—with a new direction.

Choosing a Dissertation Topic

I finished all my course work and I was in the process of choosing a dissertation topic. I was certain that my topic would be in some area of bilingual education. I began keeping a journal. Looking back at my entries, I noticed that I changed topics three times. I was still not excited about any of the three. Some of my colleagues in the cohort were well launched on their topics while I continued to search.

One afternoon I was looking for a book and I came across my old anthology of poems. The first poem I thought of before I even opened the book was Sor Juana's "Hombres Necios" or "Foolish Men." The book also contained a short biography. I immediately thought of using Sor Juana as my subject. There was excitement in thinking I could research a topic that dealt with Mexican culture. My interest in history had begun and I didn't even know it.

Sor Juana Inés de la Cruz was an outstanding literary figure in seventeenth century Mexico. In doing my research I have found several similarities between her life and mine. Her father abandoned her and her family. She had an intense desire to learn. And she rebelled against social injustices imposed on women. Sor Juana finally lifted her head when she stood up to her superiors, specifically her Jesuit confessor.[4]

---

4   Norma Salazar Davis, "Sor Juana Inés de la Cruz, Feminist, Educator," *Journal of the Midwest History of Education Society* 19 (1991): 35.

Juana wanted to go to Mexico city to study. She pleaded with her mother to let her dress in men's clothes so she could attend the university, an exclusively male privilege. This incident reminds me of my mother's wish to study in Mexico City.

Archival Research

How does an education major begin to do historical research? "Where do I begin?" I asked myself. With the guidance of a caring advisor, I searched for archives in Mexico and Spain. I located Archivo General de la Nacion de Mexico, Archivo General de Indias in Seville, and Biblioteca Nacional de Madrid.

I found doing historical research difficult. My first experience was in Mexico City. I felt like a detective, looking everywhere for clues. I began by getting acquainted with Eutequio Franco, the archivist, hoping he would give me direction. He showed me the layout of the building. The archivo had been a prison at one time—la Carcel Lecumberri. Each wing or sala housed manuscripts from different colonial periods. I worked mostly in sala four and six—viceroys, archbishops, and Jesuits. It was not uncommon to find discrepancies in the cataloguing system, so I learned to look wherever my intuition led me.

I spent several lonely weeks in Mexico City. This was the first time I had been on my own. Before I got married, there was my mother to

take care of me. After I got married, my husband assumed the caretaker role. The nights were especially difficult because I was unable to sleep. I left the television on until all stations were off the air. I was in constant fear that someone might break into my room. I did not trust anyone.

Daytime was more bearable and time went faster. I established a routine. In the morning, I had breakfast at the restaurant in the hotel. Then I took the Metro to the Archivo General. It was odd. Every day I passed hundreds of people and talked to no one. Once again, I felt invisible.

I spent most of the day sifting through dusty boxes, marvelling at the casual way the clerks handled sixteenth century documents. I was terribly excited when I came across a name related to my topic, and doubly excited when it was usable information.

Conclusion

It is just recently that I have come to a clear understanding of my educational quest. In the process of looking into the past, I have come to know the present. In searching for Sor Juana's past, I encountered my own.

Throughout history, women's education has been based on men's needs. I now understand why a mind like my mother's was wasted. She was strong, independent, and resourceful. Yet, she went along with a patriarchal system that kept

her subjugated. This explains her acceptance of a double standard that still exists in Mexican culture, and the double message she sent me.

I strongly believe I have fulfilled my mother's dream. As I walked through the streets in Mexico City, suddenly I no longer felt alone. She was with me.

I must continue my educational quest alone, because I have yet to fulfill my own dream. I am at peace with myself because I have come in touch with the past. History has helped me notice why I am the way I am. My youngest daughter has learned who she is at a much younger age. Recently she wrote in her diary:

> I never realized how Mexican I was until I was submerged in a white middle class farm town. I'm not glad. I'm not sad. It's just a fact. I no longer want to be Mexican. I just am.

I will probably continue teaching at the university level. I will incorporate more and more history in my teaching. Hasta que levante la cabeza. I have lifted my head.

Norma Salazar is on faculty at Chicago State University. Dr. Salazar is the author of Foolish Men! Sor Juana Inés de la Cruz as Spiritual Protagonist, Educational Prism, and Symbol for Women (DeKalb, IL: LEPS Press, 1994).

Salazar, Norma. "Hasta Que Levanto La Cabeza." Vitae Scholasticae 11 (Fall/Spring 1992). Used by permission.

In the process of studying the history of radical German workers in nineteenth-century Chicago, Fred Schied reflects upon his own working class connections.

"Most Uncommon Common Men:" The Working Class and Nineteenth Century Educational History—A Personal Odyssey

Fred M. Schied

We are systematically separated from our past/our history. We are taught to understand ourselves through the distorting filters of a falsified, censored version of our history. This denial of opportunity to know as much as possible about the historical bases of our experiences (and thereby the possibility of change) is one of the fundamental mechanisms underlying the reproduction of daily life in capitalist society.
—Karl Klaren

A passionate interest in history is not all that common in the United States, notable for its emphasis on the present. Moreover, the study of history, at least at the pre-university level, is notoriously un-popular. Students in the United States consistently rate history as one of the two or three most un-popular subjects in their academic careers. This lack of interest often has to do with a sense that history somehow happens "outside" one's own experiences. This kind of ahis-torical perspective was demon-strated to me when, at a relatively young age, I attempted to explain to my American playmates that I was born in a refugee camp in post-World War II Austria, and had im-migrated with my family to the United States. My new American friends asked if I had played with kangaroos and koala bears. They mistook "refugee camp" and "Aus-tria" for "reservation" and "Austra-lia." This can be dismissed as the mere ignorance of small children, if it had not happened on more than one occasion and with older indi-viduals as well.

In my neighborhood in Chi-cago—a city with strong immigrant history—my background and knowl-edge of what I thought were bare essentials of history made me ex-otic. History, for me, never was a subject to be studied or something that happened in a vague undefined past. For me it was always a *lived* experience. From my status as a refugee in Austria, to my family's displaced persons status in the United States, I was always con-scious that I lived in an historical present. That is, the present is not only shaped by history, but the past is always present in everyday life. For me to be interested in history was as natural as breathing.

As an immigrant, I naturally have some personal experiences with the way in which immigrants interact with the larger society. Moreover, I believe my perspective is typical. That is, immigrants view the American society from the perspective of the ethnic group of which they are a part. They filter American society through the values, traditions, and viewpoints of that ethnic group. For immigrants, growing up in and adopting the values of American society rarely leads to a feeling of being completely part of the mainstream. The memories, if not the actuality, of the ethnic values and traditions remain. In some important emotional and intellectual ways I remain an immigrant.

My work has focused on understanding education within a German-American workers' community. I have tried to examine how this community came to be, what values and educational traditions it brought with it, and how it functioned within the larger society. My emphasis has not been primarily on the impact that American society had on German-Americans. Rather, I have looked at how radical Germans came to make sense of American society and how the German working class has helped shape a distinctly American working class. Such a perspective, I believe, turns the table on those who view immigrants in terms of assimilation and adjustment and instead asks how American society came to adopt some of the values and traditions of the immigrants themselves.

Obviously, my personal experiences within an immigrant community made me aware of the links to the rich traditions of the German community life, a tradition going back more than two hundred years. In Chicago, a city at one time filled with German immigrants, how could a German-speaking immigrant not see the remnants of the once-thriving ethnic community?

But understanding and coming to terms with one's ethnicity is not enough. Growing up in Chicago in the 1950s and 1960s brought me face-to-face with the great unspoken fact of life in the United States: social class. As the grandson, son, and nephew of immigrant janitors and cleaning women, it soon became clear to me that there were class divisions in this officially classless society. And these divisions . . . both included and transcended ethnicity. Moreover, the school more than any other aspect of experience devalued my own and my family's working class background. It was the school that denied me my heritage, and it was the school that attempted to channel my intellectual development into ways "appropriate" to the son of working class parents. The way to the middle class was open through the door of education, but only at the cost of my ethnic and working class heritage.

Education, however, is both a controlling and liberating force. In college I became aware of a history previously hidden from me: the rich radical, working class traditions in Chicago and the role German socialists had played in creating the labor movement. Furthermore, events in Chicago in the late 1960s—especially the destruction of the monument dedicated to the police "victims" of Haymarket (the statue was blown up by an unknown group in 1969)—made me aware not only of Haymarket, but of the German working class traditions which had led to Haymarket. Graduate study in European history also convinced me that, contrary to the then prevailing interpretations, strong connections existed between radical traditions in Europe and America. . . .

Education and History

My immigrant background and my discovery, on both a personal and intellectual level, of the consequences of social class in the United States help explain my interest in history, but they do not explain my interest in educational history.

Unlike many of my colleagues, I do not come to education from a background of public school teaching. Nor, quite frankly, do I have a strong interest in the history of the public schools, though I do recognize the historical significance of schooling.

I have long thought that some of the most exciting and stimulating learning takes place in contexts far removed from schools and institutions officially dedicated to education. Why this is so has little to do with the insights of those educational historians such as Lawrence Cremin and Bernard Bailyn who expanded the definition of education beyond schooling. It has much to do with my own experiences.

That education and schooling were not synonymous became obvious to me at a relatively early age. While I was at school, the subtle (and not so subtle) message was that one needed an education and the way to get an education was to stay in school. The obvious conclusion was that more years of schooling meant a more educated person. Yet my experience outside the school contradicted this. My father, despite his lack of schooling, seemed to me intelligent and well-educated. He certainly knew world history and world politics, not having been subjected to the pablum we were being fed by teachers in school.

Moreover, my family's relatives and friends—mostly steelworkers, janitors, housewives, and semiskilled factory workers—were intelligent and seemed educated. They struck me as being very intelligent men (this being the 1950s, "serious" discussions were thought to be an exclusively male province), able to fix anything that was broken or didn't work. They discussed world politics and history much more fully and in a more interesting fashion than anything that we heard or read in school.

I looked forward to attending union meetings with my father. The members of the Flat Janitors Union, Local 1 seemed so interesting and well-informed. I could always count on one of the old-timers who had been around when the union was organized in the 1930s to tell stories of how they shut down a non-union building or "encouraged" (through physical intimidation), a non-union janitor to join the union. The local's vice president, a man who had walked the picket lines as a seven-year-old with his father in the 1930s and now ran the monthly union meetings, was a hero to me. Although I didn't use or even know the word, I saw this vice president as an intellectual. His way of speaking, of knowing everything that was going on in the city, of analyzing the local political scene, of explaining who labor was supporting in the next election—all these abilities impressed me. His stories of labor organizing in the early days made a deep impression on me. I thought him the most intelligent man I had ever heard.

At the same time my own education (more accurately my schooling) was, for the most part, a disaster. Always among the poorer students, I managed to fail the third grade entirely and came perilously close to repeating several other grades. By

the time I was a sophomore in high school, I was quite comfortable being in the bottom third of my class. I began to show some improvement academically in my junior year. By the time I was a senior, I had achieved the impossible—a B average in my final year. I wish I could say that my improvement was due to some brilliant teacher who saw my potential and changed my life through dedication and pedagogical skill. Unfortunately, though I did have a few good teachers, there was no inspirational one. My academic turnaround had more to do with my father convincing me that unless I continued my schooling I would be doomed to the same life of hard labor that he had. He drilled home his point by forcing me to accompany him while he demonstrated how tedious, dirty, and nasty his work was. To reinforce his point, he took me on tours of what seemed to be every dirty, overheated coal-bin and sweat shop on the North Side of Chicago. His plan worked.

I entered university study in one of those experimental programs popular in the United States of the 1960s that (according to the neo-conservatives of the 1980s) began the decline of academic standards. I was the second most surprised person in the building in which we lived. The most surprised was my former eighth grade teacher who had recently (to my horror) moved into our building. She confided to my father that she never thought I would make it past my second year in high school. She still had her doubts whether I would graduate from college.

The program under which I was admitted opened the university's doors for thousands of so-called un-

derachieving, mostly working-class students. Yet it threw those working class students into a highly competitive, unfamiliar environment with little support. Not surprisingly, just as cynics had predicted, three-quarters of those admitted under this special program flunked out or were on academic probation after one year. Conservatives could nod their heads approvingly; the barbarians had been turned back at the gates and academic standards had once again been upheld.

I not only survived, I thrived. Driven by fear and anger—fear that if I didn't succeed I would be doomed to my father's life and anger at those teachers who would have condemned me to his life—I became an academic success.

The more successful I became at school, however, the less educated my parents and their friends seemed. Learning, real learning, took place in classrooms among intellectual peers, I decided.

My father's union, though still important in some abstract way, seemed increasingly irrelevant to me personally. Now, on those rare occasions when I went to the monthly meetings, I was struck by the pettiness of the arguments and the graft that seemed to pervade the union. The vice-president I had admired so much owned a local hardware store where he "suggested" that all janitors make their purchases of supplies and tools. Increasingly, I began to get comments from my father's friends about the length of my hair and my style of clothes. Some of the younger union members were just a few years older than I was, yet I could see little that we had in common. Increasingly I believed that the university was where I belonged.

Even though (or maybe because) I participated in radical student politics in the late 1960s and early 1970s, I became less engaged in the world of my parents and their working class community and more involved in university life. It wasn't until the mid-1970s that I began to see what I had lost by removing myself from my working class roots.

My work for a community mental health center in the Uptown area of Chicago, one of the poorest, most ethnically diverse, and economically depressed areas in the city, brought me back in contact with a world I had partly forgotten. I began teaching English as a second language to recently arrived immigrants. At first I found this disconcerting. It brought back strong memories of the times when my parents attended similar English language classes. My parents and I had attended classes quite similar to the ones I was now teaching. I recalled the intense feelings of pride and shame I felt when I knew answers to teacher's questions before my parents did: pride that any child feels at knowing something his parents don't, shame that one's parents could be so ignorant. It was strange to look in my students' eyes and realize that they looked at me in the same way that twenty years earlier my parents and I had looked at our English teacher.

Working in Uptown also brought me in contact with community organizations and the public schools. Once again, I realized that some of the most interesting and influential people in Uptown seemed highly educated, although

they had little schooling. They had a sophisticated understanding of the world; it was, however, different from an academic view. At the same time, I began working with so-called drop-outs from the public schools. Old feelings about school resurfaced. Schooling, I saw once more, had little to do with education and a lot to do with social control.

I found the Uptown community organizations and community cultural groups much more interesting. Unlike the schools, these groups were exciting and, if somewhat chaotic, at least they were alive. Uptown in the 1970s was both very familiar and very strange to me.

I gradually realized the source of these ambivalent feelings: I no longer truly belonged to a community like Uptown. Nor, if I was honest, did I totally want to. The university and university life had some appeal to me. I had become, at best, a middle class activist, an intellectual with working class roots.

Largely because of my work in the Uptown area of Chicago and my basic antipathy toward schooling, I entered the doctoral program in adult education at Northern Illinois University. It seemed to be a good fit. Adult education, with its emphasis on learning outside the school, and its seemingly close connection with community development, provided an attractive alternative for someone like me who, as one commentator noted, "greatly admires the laboring man but does not seek to do his labor."

My experience and my interest in history led me to a different view of

educational history. It is a view that, I believe, provides some insight into the social construction of knowledge, and the assumptions that educators have about education.

Most Uncommon Common Men: History, Education and Knowledge

The labor historian Bryan Palmer has traced the life of a nineteenth century German-American printer named Karl Ungling. Ungling lead an eventful life. He participated in the 1848 uprising in Baden, Germany, travelled to the United States where he fought in the Mexican-American War, moved from Maine to Louisiana, established a German newspaper in San Francisco, and started a theatrical company in Cincinnati. At his death a friend said of Ungling: "He could spin a yarn, write a poem, make a speech, sing a song, bring a melody from a guitar, or tip a glass of lager bier with unequalled spirit and cosmopolitan politeness." He was, in Palmer's words, a most "uncommon common man."[1] In fact, Ungling's life was typical of many nineteenth century artisans. Movement (or tramping as it was called), political activism, and education were central features of artisan life. What is striking about Ungling is the fact that he was so highly *educated*. In fact, as numerous historians have discussed, it was the artisans—that is, the shoemakers, printers, cobblers, cigarmakers, etc.—who were often the most educated members of their communities.[2]

---

1   Bryan D. Palmer, "Most Uncommon Common Men: Craft and Culture in Historical Perspective," *Labour/Le Travailler* 1 (1976): 5.
2   See Herbert Gutman's classic study, "Work, Culture and Society in Industrializing America, 1815-1919," *American Historical Review* 78 (June 1973): 531-88.

If we are to understand the educational traditions of these artisans, especially during the time of rapid industrialization when they lived, we need to think of education differently than we have typically done. Richard Johnson has suggested that the informal nature of much of working class education, especially its more radical manifestations, is crucial to understanding working class education.[3] Johnson argues that during the nineteenth century there were four main aspects to radical education. First, radical education provided a critique of the present educational enterprise. In other words, it had a tradition of opposition to established forms of education. Moreover, this opposition was not exclusively limited to educational institutions, but it was understood that education was involved in a much broader cultural and ideological struggle. Second, radical education developed alternative educational goals. These goals embraced an alternative (often utopian) future with its own sense of what was really important to know. Third, radical education was concerned with education and politics—knowledge and power. Knowledge was a right and a natural good. Educating oneself was an important step in changing the world. Fourth, radical educators developed a "various and vigorous educational practice of their own."[4] The emphasis was on providing adults with a mature understanding of the means available for producing a more just social order.[5]

The most important feature of this radical education was its *informality*. Educational functions were not separated from other functions and education did not necessarily take place in premises specifically designed for educational activity. Education was subsumed within related activities, often on a temporary basis. To concentrate only on educational institutions, even when those institutions were in opposition to the dominant society, runs the risk of creating a "mirror image" of orthodox schooling. Education is reduced to telling the story of schooling—an alternative schooling of radical pedagogy and radical teachers and students, but schooling nonetheless. As Johnson has noted, "educational pursuits were not separated out and labelled schooling."[6] Education did not usually take place in places given over for one purpose. Rather it happened within the framework of cultural activities, events, and non-educational institutions. This education was not "rationally" designed with specific objectives and measurable outcomes but was often temporary and sometimes haphazard.

Education, in this sense, occurred within the neighborhood, family, places of work, and processes of socialization. Thus, education was expressed through distinct working class cultural practices.

Education took place in the various types of workers' clubs, reading rooms, discussion and debate societies, through the reading of radical newspapers available in saloons, and through attending lectures provided by the numerous associations and organizations of the community. Moreover, these forms of education were part of a broader radical working class culture that had its own entertainment, traditions, and festivals rooted in European traditions and adapted to American conditions. It is within this cultural milieu that German-American working class education took place. In order to understand this informal educational process, I looked at the places in which informal education happened: saloons, *Turnvereine*, singing societies, reading clubs, and local newspapers and numerous informal gatherings.

Reflecting on my research now that it is complete, it becomes obvious to me why it took the direction it did. To cite E. H. Carr again:

What the historian catches will depend partly on chance, but mainly on what part of the ocean he chooses to fish in and what tackle he chooses to use. These two factors being, of course, determined by the kind of fish he wants to catch. By and large, the historian will get the kind of facts he wants. History means interpretation.[7]

---

3   See Richard Johnson, "'Really Useful Knowledge': Radical Education and Working-Class Culture, 1790-1848," in *Working-Class Culture: Studies in History and Theory*, ed. John Clarke et al. (London: Hutchinson, 1979), 75-103; Idem., "'Really Useful Knowledge' 1790-1850: Memories of Education for in the 1980s," in *Radical Approaches to Adult Education: A Reader*, ed. Tom Lovett (London: Routledge, 1988), 3-34.

4   Johnson, "Memories of Education," 5.

5   Johnson, "Radical Education," 77.

6   Johnson, "Radical Education," 79.

7   E.H. Carr, *What is History?* (New York: Vintage Books, 1961), 26.

In my case the "ocean" was *informal* education, education not usually studied because it occurs outside of schools and classrooms. But the reasons I decided to fish in this ocean and the tackle I brought with me were shaped by my own experiences. I have stated that in some ways the subject chose me as much as I chose it. I don't mean this deterministically but rather in the sense that my experiences, and my reflection on those experiences, led me to my subject and also suggested the approach. Carr also stated that "history cannot be written unless the historian can achieve some kind of contact with the mind of those about whom he is writing."[8] It is impossible, of course, to completely understand the minds of any people, not to mention people who lived nearly one hundred years ago. But I believe that in a small way I was able to achieve some contact with the radical German workers in nineteenth century Chicago. In the process, I came to know a little more about myself.

Fred M. Schied received his Ed.D. in Adult Education from Northern Illinois University. Previous to joining Penn State in the fall of 1992 as Assistant Professor, he was Assistant Professor in the Leadership and Educational Policy Studies department at Northern Illinois University. He has served as an Assistant Dean of Adult Education at a large metropolitan community college in the Chicago area, conference planner for a national non-profit organization, and was a staff member of university-based community adult education classes as well as adult basic education and English-as-a-second language class-es in community settings. His recently published book, Learning in Social Context: Workers and Adult Education in Nineteenth Century Chicago (DeKalb, IL: LEPS Press, Northern Illinois University 1993), won the Houle Award.

Adopted and reprinted from Vitae Scholasticae 11 (Spring/Fall 1992), reprinted by permission.

Schied, Fred. "Most Uncommon Common Men." Vitae Scholasticae 11 (Fall/Spring 1992). Reprinted with permission.

---

8   Carr, *What is History?* 27.

Rogers demonstrates how experiences in family shape who we are, what we are, and our attitudes about education and learning. She shows the importance of historical and ideological influences on four generations of an African-American family.

Mirror of Opportunity: Reflection of Struggle

Elice E. Rogers

History is the memory of human group experience. If it is forgotten or ignored we cease . . . to be human. Without history, we have no knowledge of who we are or how we came to be, like victims of collective amnesia groping in the dark for identity. It is the events that are recorded in history that have generated all the emotions, the values, the ideas that have given men [and women] something to live for, struggle, and die for. (Daniels, 1966)

As a voice representing the fifth generation of Rogers, I have found that experiences acquired within the context of my family were influential in shaping who I am, what I am, and my perspectives about education and learning. I find

it difficult to debate about the impact education and learning has had upon my life without acknowledging a companion.

This companion, known as "struggle," can best be described as lack of sufficient resources to fulfill one's daily needs or provide an investment for self and family. "Struggle" has been an integral part of my academic pursuits as well as permeating my entire life experience.

I can articulate my "struggle" only by acknowledging the historical influences of race, class, and gender and their impact upon my family.

In this paper I (1) highlight the importance of social family history as a tool for understanding the "self" in an everchanging society (Zinn & Eitzen, 1993); (2) demonstrate how social class and other forces affect family and how my family responded to these forces; and (3) I examine how experiences within my family influenced me as

an educator and learner. My construction and interpretation is based upon stories I heard in my family.

The Rogers Family Narrative: Late 1800s-Middle 1920s

My father's grandfather, Nim Rogers (1890-1943), was a descendant of Josh Rogers, who lived in the slavery era. Nim claimed to be of Creole descent, migrating with his mother as a small child from Louisiana to Arkansas. Nim married Ann (1892-1968), a woman who was fair in appearance due to her mixture of African American and Native American blood. From this union the couple had five children, R.C., Elton, Nettie, Richard Mickey (my grandfather), and Blanche. The stable presence of Nim and Ann Rogers contradicts the popular notion of a matriarchal unit headed by a powerful female with an absentee father (Zinn & Eitzen, 1993). Moreover, the presence of both male and female within the family is consistent with an organized family life (Gutman, 1976).

My grandparents and great-cousin described life for Nim and Ann Rogers as simple but often dangerous. Part of the danger can be attributed to the personality of Nim Rogers. A man of dark appearance, Nim reportedly had a ruthless personality, carrying two guns at all times. These guns were in Nim's possession when he attended church and when he went to the cotton fields. Both Blacks and Whites respected his forceful personality. Nim was also eccentric. He rarely left home to visit others, trusted no one outside of his family, and kept his guns close, even when he slept. Nim was a well groomed man who had a fondness for outstanding clothing; Members of the family who knew him remarked on his elaborate hats.

Ann's temper was comparable to that of her husband's. "Big Ma," as I called her, was a stern woman with whom one seldom joked. Ann's aura indicated at all times that she meant business.

Typical of most African Americans of their time, neither Nim nor Ann had land or money. Their occupation was sharecropping, a system of tenant farming where the owner had few obligations to those who worked the land. In return for their labor, sharecroppers kept either half or three fourths of money from selling the crops.

Nim sharecropped on the half which meant that he had to submit half of his crops to the landowner. Nim would have provided only a quarter of his profits had he and Ann possessed their own equipment (a team of horses and wagon).

As a result of the sharecropping system, roles within the family were defined by each person's ability to work. Children were essential for their labor. The more children one had, the more valuable the sharecropping activity, and thus the greater a family's value to the landowner.

Nim was skilled in most matters relating to farm life, and he transmitted to his sons and daughters the importance of land, nature, farm life, and farm activities.

Ann's role within her family included work in the fields as well as within the home. She managed the family budget, quilted, manufactured and mended clothes by hand, and cooked and served meals. She quickly acquired budgeting and management skills when she discovered that Nim could not read. (She had learned prior to marriage while working as a domestic servant.)

Although Ann managed the family budget, only males frequented the general store. All of Ann Rogers' public activities were confined within the boundaries of the church.

Despite the rigid demeanor of Ann and Nim's personalities, they were praised and respected by children and adult members of the African American community.

Their children were Nim and Ann's special joy and sustained them in the face of frequent adversity. Nim liked to play with his children and grandchildren, even following a full day of work in the fields. Outside of these special play times, the general rule was that children should be seen and not heard. Children who exhibited negative behavior or violated family rules received severe punishment. During this time, young women stayed with their families until finding husbands. Single women rarely lived alone. Unmarried women who remained with their families contributed increased revenue to the family and received protection in return. Nim's household consisted of his children and grandchildren as well as fictive kin who often frequented the Rogers' home.

My great-grandmother was known as a visionary, meaning she saw visions or auras about people, events, and that she had a particular way of understanding unusual situations. "Big Ma" would often sit near the fire on a chilly night and would inform her children, grandchildren, and great-grandchildren about the wrath of God, her understanding of spirits, and her theory of interpreting watchful eyes.

Strong community support was a general characteristic of "Big Ma's" time. She often assisted other families by sending potatoes or other supplies. Nim was known for helping widows in the name of service and good Christian principles.

All the children in my family regularly attended church with their parents. Each acknowledged his or her belief in God around age twelve.

Nim died of typhoid fever in 1943 at age fifty-three. Even though he had labored hard during his adult life, the nature of the sharecropping system precluded his accumulating anything to pass on to his wife and children. Following Nim's death, Ann packed what little she had and moved in with her son, Richard Mickey (my grandfather). She remained with Richard Mickey and his wife Carrie until her death at age ninety in 1968.

1920s-1961

Richard Mickey, Nim and Ann's fourth child (b. 1915), married Carrie (b. 1913). (Carrie, a woman of creole descent, moved with her parents and brother from Louisiana to Arkansas when she was a child. Carrie's parents abandoned their family when she was about twelve. As a result, Carries assumed responsibility for herself and her brother.) My grandparents had three children, my father Richard (1939), and twins, Edgar (1942-1990), and Eddie (1942).

Richard Mickey learned farming from his parents. Unlike his parents, Richard Mickey and Carrie saved enough to buy a team of horses and a wagon. This investment allowed them to make more money sharecropping than Nim and Ann had been able to earn.

Life was difficult in Arkansas during the late 1920s and 1930s. My grandparents faced the Depression in 1929, as well as a flood that totally destroyed their crops. Despite these hardships my grandparents kept hoping, praying, farming, and living off the land. Because of these difficulties, a number of Arkansas families migrated North. Richard Mickey did not join the exodus. He thought it safer to stay in the South, where he understood the White power structure and where he knew how to farm.

My grandfather is dark and handsome, with a quiet and calm demeanor. He does not anger easily, but is not pleasant to be around when he does become irritated. My grandparents had to farm actively in order to support themselves and their family, so they only managed to complete the fourth grade. Both, however, are pro education and they strongly encouraged their children to get further education and to complete high school (segregated).

Grandma was temperamentally opposite to my grandfather. Her personality is strong, forceful, and rigid. She managed all activities within her household, but consulted with my grandfather on family matters. An avid believer in God, she expected her entire family to attended church regularly. With both her children and grandchildren, grandmother was a disciplinarian who emphasized hard work, prayer, strict obedience, cleanliness, and perfection in all matters relating to the self. Roles within the family were well defined and grew directly out of the sharecropping system. Thus, family members labored on the farm. Children were expected to attend school and work following school activities.

The Rogers' extended household represented home for children, grandchildren, nieces, nephews, uncles, and grandparents. Everyone who lived in the household contributed economically, even the elderly, who often watched the little ones, cooked, or participated in quilt making activities. Roles were traditionally assigned with females managing children, cooking, cleaning, and laboring in the fields. Field labor for males and females included chopping and picking cotton, harvesting corn, potatoes, okra and other items.

Prior to World War II, the Rogers family appeared to be doing well and were "successful" because they were managing to care for themselves and to save a little. Family members had different clothes for work, school, and Sunday. The land provided food. Richard Mickey and Carrie not only raised crops, they also had many cows, hogs, chickens, and some turkeys. Also, my grandfather would bring home from his outdoor expeditions fish, turtle, frog, rabbit, duck, deer, and raccoon. Both grandparents prepared all these foods. Further, the Rogers would invite nearby families to participate in the "Preparation For Fall Event." Such a collaborative effort represented a festive occasion for family and friends and served to equip all individuals with enough food to get through the winter. My great-cousin Ann described the preparation for winter storage as follows:

"I considered the 40s and early 50s the last of the good ole days as far as being able to live good on the land. I recall the preparation of food for fall and how eventful that was. There was such a strong sense of community, sharing, cooperation, and looking out for one another, especially if one had a lot of children. I can recall the smell of the Sasfas bushes and the spicy smell the smoked leaves carried off the meat, which was placed in a storage house following preparation. This is where the term smoke house came from. I also remember neighbors canning hundreds of fruit, children preparing or grinding sausage, and family members canning vegetables. You know those were the 'good ole' days, that was successful living. I miss those days, the smell of food, good people..."

In the early 1930s and 1940s families would get together frequently. Men talked to each other at church and went on collective hunting expeditions. They assisted widows and large families with game from their hunts or clothing no longer used within their households. People also held a firm belief in family. If anyone cheated on a spouse, one rarely heard about it: such acts were discrete.

With the "boom" resulting from World War II, Richard Mickey and Carrie managed to live well and continued to save a little. Drafted in 1942, Grandpa Mick was dismissed from service because of kidney problems.

World War II sent more and more African American women outside their homes for employment. My grandparents saw families change. Children were not farming the land anymore. Following high school they were joining the military. After the War, African American women elected to removed their aprons and keep their outside jobs. Also, more African American women became heads of households while their husbands were away at war. Moreover, my grandparents put away their kerosene lamps and welcomed the advent of electricity in 1944. Changing technology brought new products stimulating consumption. Cousin Ann describes the impact on our family and on neighbors:

"It seemed to me that families changed a lot. More women were working outside the home and living alone. Families began purchasing more items such as furniture, cars, and clothes. Things were changing. Black families also became more independent and competitive. For some reason folks all of a sudden just got greedy."

My grandparents managed to not only care for their family, but also provided their children with a childhood that was not completely monopolized by work.

The Roger's oldest son Richard, and my mother, Ruby Phillips (1939-1991) met in elementary school. Prior to their wedding in 1961, mom and dad had three children Carrie (1956), Roy (1957), and Ronnie (1959). Following my birth in 1961, mom, dad, and I migrated to Chicago. Eventually, the twins, Edgar (1942-1990) and Eddie (1942) joined their brother Richard and his family in Chicago. All were in search of better economic opportunities.

1960s Life in Chicago

City life was different from rural Arkansas. My parents moved into a third floor, three bedroom apartment on Chicago's West Side. As a small child, I recall my frequent running up and down the many stairs, as I entered and exited home in playful delight.

For my parents, Chicago was quite the opposite of delight. Dad found work with a Construction Company and performed janitorial services for a local church. These two jobs barely paid enough to support the family. Mom continued to care for the home and four additional children, Richard Jr. (1963), Laveller (1964), James (1965), and Elton (1966). The growing family required more money than Dad could supply, so my mother obtained employment. At age twenty-seven my mother was caring for the home, my dad, and was working two to three jobs at any given time.

Our economic situation steadily worsened. I rarely saw my parents; when I did, one parent was coming or going to work, or there was tension, arguments, and fights.

My father was a man who worked hard and appeared to enjoy life in Chicago. My father never came home right away; he would hook up with a couple of his buddies and shoot pool, play cards, or just hang out in the bars. I do not recall my father doing anything inside the home except eating, sleeping, watching T.V., or entertaining guests. I do not remember him playing with me or my brothers and sisters.

My father looked forward to the "Preparation For Fall" held annually on the farm in Arkansas. The "Preparation For Fall" had become an important activity for family members who had migrated from the South. "Preparation For Fall" symbolized the legacy of the Rogers family and acted as a barometer to monitor one's commitment to family. Attracting Rogers from local and far away areas, the even served to reaffirm family ties, exchange information about social and political issues, and to temporarily ease the dominate forces in society such as racism and economic insufficiency.

Economically, things worsened and so did the dynamics within my family. For a time, both my parents were out of work. My father was absent for days at a time. When he did return, he argued with my mother about why they had to have so many children. In reaction to my father's lack of employment, her own low self-esteem, and other outside pressures, my mother turned to alcohol. Due to my mother's drinking, I became an adult at age eight.

There were moments when Miss Ruby would literally be passed out. When father was gone I would have to care for myself and my four brothers and sisters. I remember rare moments of "childish play." My parents marriage was in deep trouble, and they contemplated ways to save their marriage. Dad obtained new employment with a tool and die company; mom found a new job and stopped drinking. Dad said that Chicago was not a place for us kids and that perhaps we should join our three brothers and sisters in Arkansas until things got better economically.

Late 1960s-1970s Farm Labor

My parents' arrival for the "Preparation For Fall" event was timely for us kids, as far as school was concerned. There would be no problem enrolling; my mother had brought all the required documents. Before my parents departed for Chicago, I told my mother that I did not understand why she had to leave me in Arkansas. She responded with a glassy-eyed look, saying that she and Dad would come back for all of us. As my parents drove away, I felt excruciating pain and tears rolled down my face. I knew as I watched their 1967 black and white chevy stir up dust and fade quickly down the old gravel road that Mom and Dad were not coming back to get me or my sisters and brothers.

In Arkansas, I attended Mary Jackson Elementary, an integrated school which happened to be in the same building where my Dad and uncles had attended high school. I recall walking down the halls and reviewing the portraits of high school graduating classes and managed to find pictures of my Dad and an uncle.

Miss Jackson was my fourth grade teacher, and I did not like her very much. It was from Miss Jackson that I discovered physical punishment. This was something new to me, something I had never experienced in the Chicago Public School System. I received a whipping for missing seven words on a spelling test. I received two licks per word. I also remember students teasing me because of my Midwest-ern accent and for being a good student.

I found comfort in school and for the first time a passion for learning. Perhaps my romance with education began as an escape from laboring in the fields. Following school every day my brothers and sisters and I had to help on the farm. In the summer months all the Rogers grand children worked full-time. I recall chopping cotton from five o'clock in the morning to six o'clock at night. The first time I chopped anything, it was okra, and I was given five dollars and a pat on the back by the White landowner. The rows were extremely long. There were moments when I thought that I would faint from exhaustion and discomfort from the sun beaming down on my little body. My hunger and thirst did not seem to impress the adults. There were no breaks. I would have to wait along with my brothers and sisters for lunch which was torturously slow in arriving and, when it did finally come, had to be finished in half an hour.

By age twelve, I was numb to the fields and began to direct my creative energies within school activities. In school I forgot about my strict grandmother, the three brothers and sisters that I did not really know, the cotton fields, and the image of that black and white chevrolet disappearing around the bend, headed to Chicago.

My grandmother told me one day that I had reached the "age of recognition" and that it was time for me to think about heaven, hell, God, and my life. It was revival time, and I was "saved" in the traditional way, being baptized in the Mississippi River. How festive this occasion was for my grandparents as well as the community! My grandmother dili-

gently prepared my white baptismal gown which I wore when I "waded into the water." There were about twelve of us who were dipped that day. Six deacons held me up on each side (due to my small size and the water's depth) and passed me along to the pastor, Reverend Ivory, who immersed me. There were screams of joy and laughter and elaborate singing like I had never before heard as each person was passed along and dipped. A huge church picnic was held following the baptisms. Massive amounts of food included barbecued ribs, banana pudding, sweet potato pie, turkey and dressing, collard greens, cornbread and many other great dishes. The singing continued, and people laughed and talked. I had such a good time that I asked my grandmother, if I could get baptized again? She gazed at me in disbelief.

Grandma Carrie and Grandpa Mick continued to work hard on the farm, even in their old age. Grandpa Mick took me fishing and hunting and taught me, as well as my sisters and brothers, the value of nature, the land, and work. Grandpa Mick often told me that I was bright because I could read and write. He said that if he could read and write, he would stay in school forever doin' noth,' but just readin'.

Economically, the Rogers were barely managing to stay afloat. There was no money for luxury items. A couple times at Christmas we did not receive any gifts. But we had food and clothes, and that mattered more.

Miss Ruby and Richard visited once during the five years I was in Arkansas. By then Miss Ruby had two more children, Sharlene (1970) and Elaine (1971). Miss Ruby and Richard were different, more distant to me. They did not offer to take us back with them, and we did not ask to go. My parent's marital problems escalated, and they separated in 1972. Richard moved from Chicago to Maywood, Illinois. Miss Ruby and her youngest children joined her family in Racine, Wisconsin.

My sisters and brothers were quite fond of farm life. All of us managed to treasure rare moments of fun. My two oldest brothers were master builders and would take remnants of old toys and repair them. My second oldest brother got me my first bicycle by repairing an old bicycle, painting it, and adding tires. Roy, my oldest brother, built us a dirt basketball court.

Life as my grandparents knew it was about to change. The landowner installed bathrooms in the homes of all his tenants except ours. This infuriated my grandfather, and he asked why. Russell replied that, since my grandfather's illness, he was not working the land the way he should. It was time for us to leave his property. Grandpa Mick was tormented. He had lived on the Russell Place for twenty-three years and had raised his family there. His parents had lived there, and so much of himself was tied to the land. But having no choice, he moved his family into the town of Hughes. Although Grandma Carrie was also upset at moving, she was ecstatic to realize that they had saved enough to purchase a home in her old age.

1970s and Movement North

Carrie and Roy were the first of my brothers and sisters to leave Arkansas. Roy moved to Racine, Wisconsin, and lived with my mother and our youngest sisters. Upon my brother's return visit to Arkansas, I asked my grandmother if I could return with him and visit my mother for the summer. My grandmother said yes. As the Greyhound Bus pulled off, I promised myself that I would not go back to Arkansas.

I thought my parents had separated, but apparently they had not. Richard had his apartment in Maywood, Illinois and Miss Ruby had her apartment in Racine, Wisconsin. Miss Ruby welcomed my visit and encouraged me to live with her. Much later, I realized that Miss Ruby was on AFDC (Aid To Families With Dependent Children) and that she received money for each child within her home. Richard and Miss Ruby contemplated living together but did not, partly because she received more money and overall support on welfare than both could earn working.

I found life in Racine interesting. Miss Ruby began to drink more and more. I became more introverted and hid behind my school work. After a while Richard did not visit anymore, and Miss Ruby was hospitalized. I moved in with my aunt and uncle until I graduated from high school in 1979. As I departed for the University of Wisconsin at La Cross, I though that "struggle" would no longer be a constant companion. I was mistaken, but that is a story for another time.

Summary

The Rogers family history, although unique in some ways, is not fundamentally different from the shared experiences of many African-American families. Historically, positive family development has been consistently affected by race, class, and gender in the milieu of capitalism and "progress." As a result of these structural influences, most members of my family have been affected by limited access to educational opportunities and marginal participation in their society's economy.

Nim and Ann Rogers were limited by post emancipation forces which included Nim's inability to read and their general lack of resources. They really did not elevate their status, but passed the "torch" on to Richard Mickey and Carrie.

Richard Mickey and Carrie, both born prior to World War I, were only able to attend primary school although they desperately wanted more education.

Richard and Ruby migrated to Chicago in 1961 but, as was the case for so many other African American families did not find the promised "good-life" of the North. Decreased family ties resulting from migration, and increased work activities outside the home, were instrumental in the separation of my parents.

In an effort to cope with these macro forces, Rogers family members sought protection, comfort, strength, and sharing of common experiences within the context of family. Children were a source of inspiration, particularly for the second and third generations. More importantly, children symbolized hope, hope for a different kind of a success which many I believe many people in my family thought about for themselves but did not discuss. Adults encouraged children to have a strong work ethic, to maintain consistent order with the self and with others, and to be disciplined. These seemed the necessary attributes for success. Thus, discipline of the Rogers' children was an effort to "prepare them to take on not only the appropriate age and sex role, but a racial role as well" (Staples, 1976).

Religious expression also brought strength, comfort, protection, and understanding. "Blacks have been adept at using religion as a mechanism for survival and advancement throughout their history in America" (Hill, 1972).

The gathering of families at the "Preparation For Fall" event also served as a support mechanism. This event originated out of a demand for planning and procuring goods and storing these goods for the year. The "Preparation For Fall" event bridged the gap between the old and the young, as well as those Rogers' who were far away and those who were near. One was expected to attend. This custom of visitation and festivity was typical "among Blacks, especially in Southern and rural areas" (Staples, 1976). Such a ritual increased family cohesiveness, provided economic support, served as a viable agent in the transmission of values to the children, furnished a healthy outlet for the elderly, and more importantly served as an agent for transferring information.

My familial experiences and the nature of my "struggle" have greatly influenced my stance as an educator and as a learner. In reflecting upon my experiences three critical events have emerged and prove useful in understanding the "self" as learner.

My movement South represented a breach in the mother/daughter relationship and fostered the beginning of a new independent way of being for me as a child. Although I was devastated by the

separation, our separation came to symbolize the demands that my particular "slot" required of me in society.

I find that my childhood years spent in Arkansas as a participant of farm labor a second critical event in my life. This life event not only introduced me to the world of work and economics, but also familiarized me with the dynamics of race relations in the South. And it validated my "struggle" within the larger context of the "struggle" of African Americans throughout history. Moreover, this life event was characterized by transitions which included breaking away from life in Chicago as I had known it, a search for meaning, and acquisition of a new experience as a tool for coping with life (Merriam & Cafferella, 1991). In addition, laboring in the fields contributed to the recognition of my own oppression, elevated my level of consciousness, and contributed to my gradual personal transformation (Freire, 1970).

I recognized as a child, within the context of my circumstances, that I was in a box of sorts. If I remained in this box, I would not be a sane, functional being. Hence, I decided to break out in search of what life would be for me. In my attempt to understand the nature of my condition, I exercised silence at home and in the fields. It is through such silence, that I came to understand the nature of my condition, and it is through such silence that I became acquainted with my own voice. I slowly began to recognize and view myself outside of the box as my own "empowered being."

I found my passion for education and the integration of school the

third critical life event. During my years in the South, education became important because it represented escape. School and the desire for an education became a legitimate platform from which to seriously search for my own voice. It also became a battleground on which I was able to recognize and challenge the dimensions of my box..

More importantly, it was at school that I discovered voices similar to my own. I slowly began to interact with and "touch" others in ways that laboring in the fields and my home environment would not permit. I discovered the joy of learning. I am self-directed, and my quest for learning has become a lifelong activity. These characteristics are consistent with the findings of Cross (1981) and Tough (1971).

Due to the influence of my life experiences, my role within the classroom as an educator includes that of change agent. I feel receptive to all students but particularly those who are on the margins. I encourage students to recognize the power of voice, to utilize voice not only as a way to understand themselves in relation to society but as a means of self elevation. I challenge students to critically reflect upon their life experiences as a way to interpret meaning and to validate themselves and their history in the world as they know it to be.

I have found that by investigating my family history, I better understand my "struggle." I see more clearly who I am, what I am, and the importance of my role as an actor among other actors in fostering a better society.

References

Cross, P. (1981). *Adults as learners.* San Francisco: Jossey Bass, pp. 50, 63, 85, 121, 128.

Daniels, R.V. (1966). *Studying history—how and why.* New Jersey: Prentice-Hall, p. 03.

Freire, P. (1970). *Pedagogy of the oppressed.* New York: Seabury, pp. 32, 42.

Gutman, H. (1976). *Black family in slavery and freedom, 1750-1925.* New York: Pantheon Books, p. 433-459.

Hill, R.B. (1972). *The strengths of black families.* New York: Emerson Hall Publishers, Inc., p. 33.

Merriam, S. and R. Caffarella. (1991). *Learning in adulthood.* San Francisco: Jossey Bass, p. 107-110.

Staples, R. (1976). *Introduction to black sociology.* New York: McGraw-Hill Book Company, p. 68, 134.

Tough, A. (1971). *Adult learning projects.* Toronto, Ontario: Institute For Studies In Education, pp. vii, viii, 06, 170.

Zinn, M.B. and D.S. Eitzen (1993) *Diversity and families.* (3rd ed.). New York: Harper Collins College Publishers Press, pp. 24-25, 71.

A somewhat different version of this paper will appear in <u>Thresholds in Education</u> and is preprinted by permission.

Section Two

What's Happened
Along the Way?

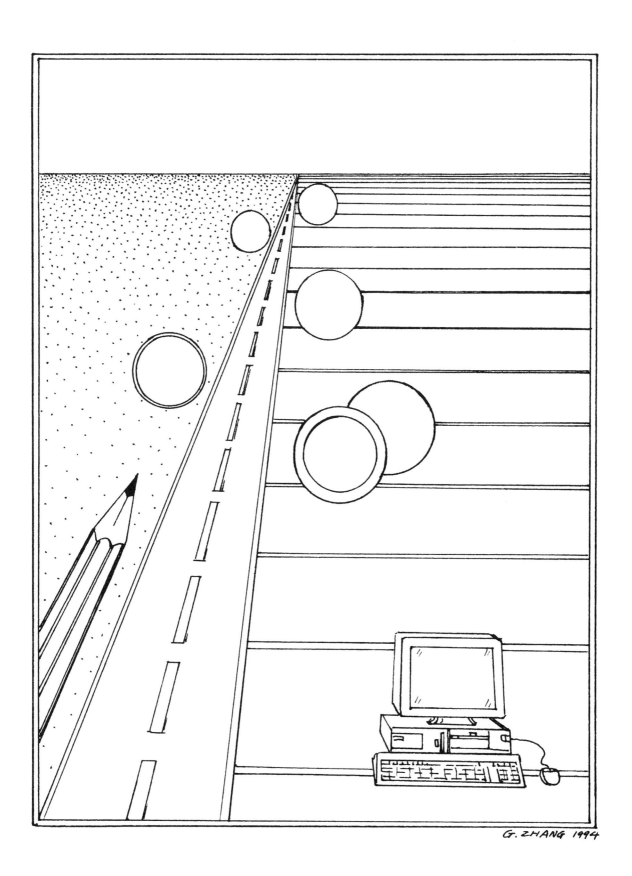

G. ZHANG 1994

Multiculturalism Can Be Taught Only by Multicultural People

Stephen Joel Trachtenberg

Of all the tedious debates that have ever gone nowhere in the academic world, few can equal the one that recently featured western culture in one corner versus a number of alternatives in the other. Ostensibly, the debate was a search for the answer to a difficult question: How shall we go about educating today's young people, and what is most necessary for them to learn? But it quickly turned into a free-for-all that had "traditionalists" slugging it out with representatives of various feminist, ethnic, and political causes vaguely identified as "leftist."

The debate raged almost unchecked for a couple of years, its flames fanned by the nation's drug czar, William Bennett, when he was still secretary of education. Bennett was firmly on the side of western culture as what students really need to know. Arrayed on the other side of the media boxing ring was a sizable group of people, most of them employed as university faculty members, who suggested that Bennett's cause was a cover for various forms of elitism, paternalism, parochialism, and racism—everything the West seems to stand for when viewed through the red glasses of angry people.

The debate helped to fill the pages of a number of academic journals and tabloids. Having gotten entangled with broader laments about the economic and/or cultural and/or political decline of the entire nation, the debate helped to create a number of best sellers that promised to rescue us from barbarism. And now that the controversy is dribbling slowly away, leaving mainly confusion in its wake, it is time to consider what was wrong about the whole debate in the first place.

1. Confusion about the different meanings of culture. The word is commonly used to denote two nearly opposite ideas. In the first use, culture denotes what used to be known as "high culture"—works of literature, art, philosophy, and music so elevated, noble, ambitious, and demanding that they can be described in monumental terms. Examples of this kind of culture include the works of Homer, Sappho, Plato, Virgil, Dante, Michelangelo, Shakespeare, Dickinson, Rembrandt, and Beethoven.

The second meaning of the word can be traced to modern social science and is quite democratic. Culture refers to the ways in which different groups of people organize their daily lives within national or ethnic groups, urban neighborhoods, companies and professions, and other settings. This second meaning doesn't exclude literature and art, but it is less concerned with what people read or what they say they believe than with what they actually do, including the food they eat, their ways of pairing off males and females, and how they go about rearing their children. A high culture approach to the Hispanic world might focus on Cervantes and Goya, while a social scientist is more likely to describe the varieties of Hispanic culture to be found in the neighborhoods of Los Angeles, New York, or Miami.

2. Refusal to acknowledge the extent to which western culture has always been intertwined with other cultures. Scholars in a variety of disciplines are aware of fascinating examples of cultural interconnections. Plato's views on the afterlife, for example, bear interesting resemblances to those of ancient Jews and Hindus, and contact of some kind cannot be ruled out. Ancient Greeks were deeply involved with the civilizations of Egypt and Persia, as their major writers testify. And Roman mirrors have been found in Chinese tombs of the Han dynasty.

In northwestern India, the area conquered by Alexander the Great, sculptors used Greek artistic techniques to depict Buddhist religious themes, including the earliest artistic representations of the Buddha himself. What's more, a statuette of the Buddha was found in a Viking grave in Scandinavia. The famous Benin bronzes of West Africa were influencing westerners as early as the 17th and 18th centuries. In about 1725 one of them found its way into the library of Jesus College, Oxford, where it can still be seen today.

African and Oceanic art, after it had been discovered and imitated by such artists as Gauguin and Picasso in the early 20th century, helped to transform the art of Western Europe. Meanwhile, western art that reached India, China, and Japan had a similarly liberating effect on the artists of those lands—once they had overcome the initial "culture shock." Today there are very few educated people who have not acquired—through museums, universities, public libraries, and major

newspapers—a global cultural awareness, whatever the meaning of the word culture.

White middle-class Americans can empathize with a resident of Barcelona . . . more easily than . . . with a US citizen whose grandparents emigrated from Mexico or Cuba. And there's more pity.

3. Difficulty in understanding that, for the U.S. today, multiculturalism is synonymous with national survival. It is obvious that we have become a multicultural society. Indeed, those who come from what used to be referred to as our "minority subcultures"—including Hispanics and blacks—may soon constitute a numerical majority of Americans.

Like it or not, our ability to reach those Americans and to help them become skilled and productive contributors to the economy will determine our success or failure in the international marketplace. Our rivals in Japan, West Germany, and other industrialized nations are betting that we won't be able to do it, because white middle-class Ameri-

cans can empathize if he or she is a creator or consumer of high culture—more easily than they can empathize with a U.S. citizen whose grandparents emigrated from Mexico of Cuba.

Meanwhile, the primary educational need of Hispanic and black students may be the awareness that their backgrounds are just as "cultural" as those of Americans who trace their origins to Northern Europe, Asia, and the Middle East. Hispanic and black young people need to become conscious of the fact that their roots are as essential to our world as those of Americans with more money who can afford to trace their genealogies and pay for gold rings emblazoned with coats of arms. These young people need to know that the world would be quite a different place if their forebears had never come here. What they—and their white Anglo-Saxon counterparts—need least of all is the feeling that western culture is just one more assignment designed to hold them back.

In short, what we need in our high schools, colleges, and universities are teachers willing to repeat the words of an ancient Roman playwright: "Nothing human can be alien to me." If we are not preparing such teachers right now—if we are turning our specialist who can think only in dichotomies—then we need to ask ourselves why and where our teacher training programs have gone so astray.

Mr. Trachtenberg is President of George Washington University, Washington, DC, and a Professor of Public Administration. Reprinted by permission.

African Americans today are in a position to build upon the gains they have made over the past several decades. While noting recent advances, Howard and Hammond examine factors which continue to hinder the intellectual development of African American students. Analyzing the interrelationship between perception and performance, the authors provide recommendations for promoting intellectual achievement in the African American community.

Rumors of Inferiority: The Hidden Obstacles to Black Success

Jeff Howard and Ray Hammond

Today's black Americans are the beneficiaries of great historical achievements. Our ancestors managed to survive the brutality of slavery and the long history of oppression that followed emancipation. Early in this century they began dismantling the legal structure of segregation that had kept us out of the institutions of American society. In the 1960s they launched the civil rights movement, one of the most effective mass movements for social justice in history. Not all of the battles have been won, but there is no denying the magnitude of our predecessors' achievement.

Nevertheless, black Americans today face deteriorating conditions in sharp contrast to other American groups. The black poverty rate is triple that of whites, and the unemployment rate is double. Black infant mortality not only is double that of whites, but may be rising for the first time in a decade. We have reached the point where more than half of the black children born in this country are born out of wedlock—most to teenage parents. Blacks account for more than 40

percent of the inmates in federal and state prisons, and in 1982 the probability of being murdered was six times greater for blacks than for whites. The officially acknowledged high school dropout rate in many metropolitan areas is more than 30 percent. Some knowledgeable observers say it is over 50 percent in several major cities. These problems not only reflect the current depressed state of black America, but also impose obstacles to future advancement.

The racism, discrimination, and oppression that black people have suffered and continue to suffer are clearly at the root of many of today's problems. Nevertheless, our analysis takes off from a forward-looking, and we believe optimistic, note: we are convinced that black people today, because of the gains in education, economic status, and political leverage that we have won as a result of the civil rights movement, are in a position to substantially improve the conditions of our communities using the resources already at our disposal. Our thesis is simple: the progress of any group is affected not only by public policy and by the racial attitudes of society as a whole, but by that group's capacity to exploit its own strengths. Our concern is about factors that prevent black Americans from using those strengths.

It's important to distinguish between the specific circumstances a group faces and its capacity to marshal its own resources to change those circumstances. Solving the problems of black communities requires a focus on the factors that hinder black people from more effectively managing their own circumstances. What are some of these factors?

Intellectual Development. Intellectual development is the primary focus of this article because it is the key to success in American society. Black people traditionally have understood this. Previous generations decided that segregation had to go because it relegated blacks to the backwater of American society, effectively denying us the opportunities, exposure, and competition that form the basis of intellectual development. Black intellectual development was one of the major benefits expected from newly won access to American institutions. That devel-

opment, in turn, was expected to be a foundation for future advancement.

Yet now, three decades after *Brown v. Board of Education*, there is a pervasive evidence of real problems in the intellectual performance of many black people. From astronomical high school dropout rates among the poor to substandard academic and professional performance among those most privileged, there is a disturbing consistency in reports of lagging development. While some black people perform at the highest levels in every field of endeavor, the percentages who do so are small. Deficiencies in the process of intellectual development are one effect of the long-term suppression of a people; they are also, we believe, one of the chief causes of continued social and economic underdevelopment. Intellectual underdevelopment is one of the most pernicious effects of racism, because it limits the people's ability to solve problems over which they are capable of exercising substantial control.

Black Americans are understandably sensitive about discussions of the data on our performance, since this kind of information has been used too often to justify attacks on affirmative action and other government efforts to improve the position of black and other minorities. Nevertheless, the importance of this issue demands that black people and all others interested in social justice overcome our sensitivities, analyze the problem, and search for solutions.

The Performance Gap. Measuring intellectual performance requires making a comparison. The comparison may be with the performance of others in the same situation, or

with some established standard of excellence, or both. It is typically measured by grades, job performance ratings, and scores on standardized and professional tests. In recent years a flood of articles, scholarly papers, and books have documented an intellectual performance gap between blacks and the population as a whole.

- In 1982 the College Board, for the first time in its history, published data on the performance of various groups on the Scholastic Aptitude Test (SAT). The difference between the combined median scores of blacks and whites on the verbal and math portions of the SAT was slightly more than 200 points. Differences in family income don't explain the gap. Even at incomes over $50,000, there remained a 120-point difference. These differences persisted in the next two years.

- In 1983 the NCAA proposed a requirement that all college athletic recruits have a high school grade-point average of at least 2.0 (out of a maximum of 4.0) and a minimum combined SAT score of 700. This rule, intended to prevent the exploitation of young athletes, was strongly opposed by black college presidents and civil rights leaders. They were painfully aware that in recent years less than half of all black students have achieved a combined score of 700 on the SAT.

- Asian-Americans consistently produce a median SAT score of 140 to 150 points higher than blacks with the same family income.

- The pass rate for black police officers on New York City's sergeant's exam is 1.6 percent. For Hispanics, it's 4.4 percent. For whites, it's 10.6 percent. These are the results *after* $500,000 was spent, by court order, to produce a test that was job-related and non-discriminatory. No one, even those alleging discrimination, could explain how the revised test was biased.

- Florida gives a test to all candidates for teaching positions. The pass rate for whites is more than 80 percent. For blacks, it's 35 percent to 40 percent.

This is just a sampling. All these reports demonstrate a real difference between the performance of blacks and other groups. Many of the results cannot be easily explained by socioeconomic differences or minority status per se.

What is the explanation? Clear thinking about this is inhibited by the tendency to equate performance with ability. Acknowledging the performance gap is, in many minds, tantamount to inferring that blacks are intellectually inferior. But inferior performance and inferior ability are not the same thing. Rather, the performance gap is largely a behavioral problem. It is the result of a remediable tendency to avoid intellectual engagement and competition. Avoidance is rooted in the fears and self-doubt engendered by a major legacy of American racism: the strong negative stereotypes about black intellectual capabilities. Avoidance of intellectual competition is manifested most obviously in the attitudes of many black youths

toward academic work, but it is not limited to children. It affects the intellectual performance of black people of all ages and feeds public doubts about black intellectual ability.

I. Intellectual Development

The performance gap damages the self-confidence of many black people. Black students and professional people cannot help but be bothered by poor showings in competitive academic and professional situations. Black leaders too often have tried to explain away these problems by blaming racism or cultural bias in the tests themselves. These factors haven't disappeared. But for many middle-class black Americans who have had access to educational and economic opportunities for nearly 20 years, the traditional protestations of cultural deprivation and educational disadvantage ring hollow. Given the cultural and educational advantages that many black people now enjoy, the claim that all blacks should be exempt from the performance standards applied to others is interpreted as a tacit admission of inferiority. This admission adds further weight to the questions, in our own minds and in the minds of others, about black intelligence.

The traditional explanations—laziness or inferiority on the one hand; racism, discrimination, and biased tests on the other—are inaccurate and unhelpful. What is required is an explanation that accounts for the subtle influences people exert over the behavior and self-confidence of other people.

Developing an explanation that might serve as a basis for corrective action is important. The record of

the last 20 years suggests that waiting for grand initiatives from the outside to save the black community is futile. Blacks will have to rely on our own ingenuity and resources. We need local and national political leaders. We need skilled administrators and creative business executives. We need a broad base of well-educated volunteers and successful people in all fields as role models for black youths. In short, we need a large number of sophisticated, intellectually developed people who are confident of their ability to operate on an equal level with anyone. Chronic mediocre intellectual performance is deeply troubling because it suggests that we are not developing enough such people.

The Competitive Process. Intellectual development is not a fixed asset that you either have or don't have. Nor is it based on magic. It is a process of expanding mental strength and reach. The development process is demanding. It requires time, discipline, and intense effort. It almost always involves competition as well. Successful groups place high value on intellectual performance. They encourage the drive to excel and use competition to sharpen skills and stimulate development in each succeeding generation. The developed people that result from this competitive process become the pool from which leadership of all kinds is drawn. Competition, in other words, is an essential spur to development.

Competition is clearly not the whole story. Cooperation and solitary study are valuable, too. But of the various keys to intellectual development, competition seems to fare worst in the estimation of many blacks. Black young people, in particular, seem to place a strong negative value on intellectual competition.

Black people have proved to be very competitive at some activities, particularly sports and entertainment. It is our sense, however, that many blacks consider intellectual competition to be inappropriate. It appears to inspire little interest or respect among many youthful peer groups. Often, in fact, it is labeled "grade grubbing," and gives way to sports and social activity as a basis for peer acceptance. The intellectual performance gap is one result of this retreat from competition.

II. The Psychology of Performance

Rumors of Inferiority. The need to avoid intellectual competition is a psychological reaction to an image of black intellectual inferiority that has been projected by the larger society, and to a less than conscious process of internalization of that image by black people over the generations.

The rumor of black intellectual inferiority has been around for a long time. It has been based on grounds as diverse as twisted biblical citations, dubious philosophical arguments, and unscientific measurements of skull capacity. The latest emergence of this old theme has been in the controversy over race and IQ. For 15 years newsmagazines and television talk shows have enthusiastically taken up the topic of black intellectual endowment. We have watched authors and critics debate the proposition that blacks are genetically inferior to whites in intellectual capability.

Genetic explanations have a chilling finality. The ignorant can be educated, the lazy can be motivated, but what can be done for the individual thought to have been born without the basic equipment necessary to compete or develop? Of course the allegation of genetic inferiority has been hotly disputed. But the debate has touched the consciousness of most Americans. We are convinced that this spectacle has negatively affected the way both blacks and whites think about the intellectual capabilities of black people. It also has affected the way blacks behave in intellectually competitive situations. The general expectation of black intellectual inferiority, and the fear this expectation generates, cause many black people to avoid intellectual competition.

Our hypothesis, in short, is this. (1) Black performance problems are caused in large part by a tendency to avoid intellectual competition. (2) This tendency is a psychological phenomenon that arises when the larger society projects an image of black intellectual inferiority and when that image is internalized by black people. (3) Imputing intellectual inferiority to genetic causes, especially in the face of data confirming poorer performance, intensifies the fears and doubts that surround this issue.

Clearly the image of inferiority continues to be projected. The internalization of this image by black people is harder to prove empirically. But there is abundant evidence in the expressed attitudes of many black youths toward intellectual competition; in the inability of most black communities to inspire the same commitment to intellectual excellence that is routinely accorded athletics and entertainment; and in the fact of the performance gap itself—especially when that gap persists among the children of economically and educationally privileged households.

Expectancies and Performance. The problem of black intellectual performance is rooted in human sensitivity to a particular kind of social interaction known as "expectancy communications." These are expressions of belief—verbal or nonverbal—from one person to another about the kind of performance to be expected. "Mary, you're one of the best workers we have, so I know that you won't have any trouble with this assignment." Or, "Joe, since everyone else is busy with other work, do as much as you can on this. When you run into trouble, call Mary." The first is a positive expectancy; the second, a negative expectancy.

Years of research have clearly demonstrated the powerful impact of expectancies on performance. The expectations of teachers for their students have a large effect on academic achievement. Psychological studies under a variety of circumstances demonstrate that communicated expectations induce people to believe that they will do well or poorly at a task, and that such beliefs very often trigger responses that result in performance consistent with the expectation. There is also evidence that "reference group expectancies"—directed at an entire category of people rather than a particular individual—have similar impact on the performance of members of the group.

Expectancies do not always work. If they come from a questionable source or if they predict an outcome that is too inconsistent with previous experience, they won't have much effect. Only credible expectancies—those that come from a source considered reliable and that address a belief or doubt the performer is sensitive to—will have a self-fulfilling impact.

The widespread expectation of black intellectual inferiority—communicated constantly through the projection of stereotyped images, verbal and nonverbal exchanges in daily interaction, and the incessant debate about genetics and intelligence—represents a credible reference-group expectancy. The message of the race/IQ controversy is: "We have scientific evidence that blacks, because of genetic inadequacies, can't be expected to do well at tasks that require great intelligence." As an explanation for past black intellectual performance, the notion of genetic inferiority is absolutely incorrect. As an expectancy communication exerting control over our present intellectual strivings, it has been powerfully effective. These expectancies raise fear and self-doubt in the minds of many blacks, especially when they are young and vulnerable. This has resulted in avoidance of intellectual activity and chronic underperformance by many of our most talented people. Let us explore this process in more detail.

The Expectancy/Performance Model. The powerful effect of expectancies on performance has been proved, but the way the process works is less well understood. Expectancies affect behavior, we think, in two ways. They affect performance behavior: the capacity to marshal the sharpness and intensity required for competitive success. And they influence cognition: the mental process by which people make sense of everyday life.

Behavior. As anyone who has experienced an "off day" knows, effort is variable: it is subject to biological cycles, emotional states, motivation. Most important for our discussion, it depends on levels of confidence going into a task. Credible expectancies influence performance behavior. They affect the intensity of effort, the level of concentration or distractibility, and the willingness to take reasonable risks—a key factor in the development of self-confidence and new skills.

Cognition. Expectations also influence the way people think about or explain their performance outcomes. These explanations are called "attributions." Research in social psychology has demonstrated that the causes to which people attribute their successes and failures have an important impact on subsequent performance.

All of us encounter failure. But a failure we have been led to expect affects us differently from an unexpected failure. When people who are confident of doing well at a task are confronted with unexpected failure, they tend to attribute the failure to inadequate effort. The likely response to another encounter with the same or a similar task is to work harder. People who come into a task expecting to fail, on the other hand, attribute their failure to lack of ability. Once you admit to yourself, in effect, that "I don't have what it takes," you are not likely to approach that task again with great vigor.

Indeed, those who attribute their failures to inadequate effort are likely to conclude that more effort will produce a better outcome. This triggers an adaptive response to failure. In contrast, those who have been led to expect failure will attribute their failures to lack of ability, and will find it difficult to rationalize the investment of greater effort. They will often hesitate to continue "banging my head against the wall." They often, in fact, feel depressed when they attempt to work, since each attempt represents a confrontation with their own feared inadequacy.

This combined effect on behavior and cognition is what makes expectancy so powerful. The negative expectancy first tends to generate failure through its impact on behavior, and then induces the individual to blame the failure on lack of ability, rather than the actual (and correctable) problem of inadequate effort. This misattribution in turn becomes the basis for a new negative expectancy. By this process the individual, in effect, internalizes the low estimation originally held by others. This internalized negative expectancy powerfully affects future competitive behavior and future results.

The process we describe is not limited to black people. It goes on all the time, with individuals from all groups. It helps to explain the superiority of some groups at some areas of endeavor, and the mediocrity of those same groups in other areas. What makes black people unique is that they are singled out for the stigma of genetic intellectual inferiority.

The expectation of intellectual inferiority accompanies a black person into each new intellectual situation. Since each of us enters these tests under the cloud of predicted failure, and since each failure reinforces doubts about our capabilities, all intellectual competition raises the specter of having to admit a lack of intellectual capacity. But hits particular expectancy goes beyond simply predicting and inducing failure.

The expectancy message explicitly ascribes the expected failure to genes, and amounts to an open suggestion to black people to understand any failure in intellectual activity as confirmation of genetic inferiority. Each engagement in intellectual competition carries the weight of a test of one's own genetic endowment and that of black people as a whole. Facing such a terrible prospect, many black people recoil from any situation where the rumor of inferiority might be proved true.

For many black students this avoidance manifests itself in a concentration on athletics and socializing, at the expense of more challenging (and anxiety-provoking) academic work. For black professionals, it may involve a tendency to shy away from competitive situations or projects, or an inability to muster the intensity—or commit the time—necessary to excel. This sort of thinking and behavior certainly does not characterize all black people in competitive settings. But it is characteristic of enough to be a serious problem. When it happens, it should be understood as a less than conscious reaction to the psychological burden of the terrible rumor.

The Intellectual Inferiority Game. There always have been constraints on the intellectual exposure and development of black people in the United States, from laws prohibiting the education of blacks during slavery to the Jim Crow laws and "separate but equal" educational arrangements that persisted until very recently. In dismantling these legal barriers to development, the civil rights movement fundamentally transformed the possibilities for black people. Now, to realize those possibilities, we must address the

mental barriers to competition and performance.

The doctrine of intellectual inferiority acts on many black Americans the way that a "con" or a "hustle" like three-card monte acts on its victim. It is a subtle psychological input that interacts with characteristics of the human cognitive apparatus—in this case, the extreme sensitivity to expectancies—to generate self-defeating behavior and thought processes. It has reduced the intellectual performance of millions of black people.

Intellectual inferiority, like segregation, is a destructive idea whose time has passed. Like segregation, it must be removed as an influence in our lives. Among its other negative effects, fear of the terrible rumor has restricted discussion by all parties, and has limited our capacity to understand and improve our situation. But the intellectual inferiority game withers in the light of discussion and analysis. We must begin now to talk about intellectual performance, work through our expectations and fears of intellectual inferiority, consciously define more adaptive attitudes toward intellectual development, and build our confidence in the capabilities of all people.

The expectancy/performance process works both ways. Credible positive expectancies can generate self-confidence and result in success. An important part of the solution to black performance problems is converting the negative expectancies that work against black development into positive expectancies that nurture it. We must overcome our fears, encourage competition, and support the kind of performance that will dispel the notion of black intellectual inferiority.

III. The Commitment to Development

In our work with black high school and college students and with black professionals, we have shown that education in the psychology of performance can produce strong performance improvement very quickly. Black America needs a nationwide effort, now, to ensure that all black people—but especially black youths—are free to express their intellectual gifts. That effort should be built on three basic elements:

- Deliberate control of expectancy communications. We must begin with the way we talk to one another: the messages we give and the expectations we set. This includes the verbal and nonverbal messages we communicate in day-to-day social intercourse, as well as the expectancies communicated through the educational process and media images.

- Definition of an "intellectual work ethic." Black communities must develop strong positive attitudes toward intellectual competition. We must teach our people, young and mature, the efficacy of intense, committed effort in the arena of intellectual activity and the techniques to develop discipline in study and work habits.

- Influencing thought processes. Teachers, parents, and other authority figures must encourage young blacks to attribute their intellectual successes to ability (thereby boosting confidence) and their failures to lack of effort.

Failures must no longer destroy black children's confidence in their intelligence or in the efficacy of hard work. Failures should be seen instead as feedback indicating the need for more intense effort or for a different approach to the task.

The task that confronts us is no less challenging than the task that faced those Americans who dismantled segregation. To realize the possibilities presented by their achievement, we must silence, once and for all, the rumors of inferiority.

Who's Responsible? Expectations of black inferiority are communicated, consciously or unconsciously, by many whites, including teachers, managers, and those responsible for the often demeaning representations of blacks in the media. These expectations have sad consequences for many blacks, and those whose actions lead to such consequences may be held accountable for them. If the people who shape policy in the United States, from the White House to the local elementary school, do not address the problems of performance and development of blacks and other minorities, all Americans will face the consequences: Instability, disharmony, and a national loss of potential productivity of more than a quarter of the population.

However, when economic necessity and the demands of social justice compel us toward social change, those who have the most to gain from change—or the most to lose from its absence—should be responsible for pointing the way.

It is time that blacks recognize our own responsibility. When we react to the rumor of inferiority by avoiding intellectual engagement, and when we allow our children to do so, black people forfeit the opportunity for intellectual development that could extinguish the debate about our capacities, and set the stage for group progress. Blacks must hold ourselves accountable for the resulting waste of talent—and valuable time. Black people have everything to gain—in stature, self-esteem, and problem-solving capability—from a more aggressive and confident approach to intellectual competition. We must assume responsibility for our own performance and development.

Jeff Howard is a social psychologist; Ray Hammond is a physician and ordained minister.

Racism as a social ill is very much alive and growing in our society. Education can play a vital role in the battle against racism. Pine and Hilliard argue that schools should nurture racial attitudes that lead to a diverse and equitable society.

RX for Racism: Imperatives for America's Schools

Gerald J. Pine and Asa Hilliard, III

Every time we are almost convinced that the nation is rising above the muck of racism, there come reminders of how little headway we have made—even at eliminating the most vulgar and conspicuous manifestations of the disease. Blatant, crude, egregious, and overt racism has come out of the closet again and into our schools. Documented accounts of public slurs, threats, racist slogans, physical assaults, and racial conflicts now ring disturbingly from schools in every region of the country.[1] Schools, which ought to be a civilizing influence in our society, seem instead to be incubators of racial intolerance. Racism, prejudice, and discrimination are shamefully sabotaging our nation's efforts to provide a high-quality education for all children.

The problem of racism demands the attention of all educators. As American society rapidly grows more diverse, we must give top priority to insuring that all students receive their birthright of educational equity. Unfortunately, although America is a multicultural society, "it is not yet a pluralistic society—a place where all racial and cultural groups share equal access to opportunities for quality lives and power over their own lives."[2] To achieve pluralism, racism must be abolished, and the mission of public education must be fully achieved. That mission is to provide all students with a high-quality education that will enable them to function successfully in an interdependent, multiethnic, multicultural, and rapidly changing world. The magnitude of the task is so great that it constitutes the most significant challenge to America's system of education.

Valuing Diversity

Octavio Paz reminds us that "life is plurality, death is uniformity. Every view that becomes extinct, every culture that disappears, diminishes a possibility of life."[3] When education takes place, every individual—teacher, student, or administrator—brings his or her cultural background to that process. Unless we educators learn to prize and value differences and to view them as resources for learning, neither whites nor minority groups will experience the teaching and learning situations best suited to prepare them to live effectively in a world whose population is characterized by diversity.

Many American children are affected by institutional racism. Education is their best hope for breaking racism's chains. Yet, although such issues as equal opportunity, desegregation, and inequities in educational achievement have received considerable attention in recent years, very few schools have developed deliberate and systematic programs to reduce prejudice. The prevailing attitude seems to be that society has done away with the problem of racism through legislative action and special programs.[4] But continuing instances of overt racism belie this notion, and institutionalized manifestations of racism—less blatant and thus more insidious—continue to stunt the aspirations and talents of minority children and to distort the views and psyches of white children.

Educational Inequity

Despite the grave importance of educational equity in our changing society, low-income minority groups have lost ground and are in imminent danger of losing a great deal more. As Asa Hilliard has pointed out elsewhere:

It should not require proof here that the educational outcomes are vastly different for different racial, language, economic, and gender groups in this nation. Look at dropouts, suspensions, and expulsions; look at academic achievement indices of any kind. Look at the patterns of coursework completed by high school graduates. Look at the cultural retardation of all our high school graduates, minority or majority. . . . But most especially look at the ignorance of and alienation from their natal culture experienced by the millions of children who are on the bottom economically, socially, and politically.

It should also require little proof here that the process of education is vastly different for different racial, language, economic, and gender groups in the nation. Look at the scandalously disproportionate place-

ment of students in special education categories, where low-level demands cause them to miss exposure to higher levels of education activity. Look at the meager attempts nationally to pluralize the standard European-centered curriculum so that it conforms to the truth of all human experience, rather than reflecting a glorification of the narrow parochial cultural experience of dominant groups.[5]

These inequities reflect the persistence of racism and bigotry in the general culture. If we have learned anything at all in the last few years, surely it is how difficult and grievous a struggle human beings have in dealing with racial differences. The effort to learn to treat one another as members of the same human family grinds on. Those who discriminate and those who tolerate discrimination are graduates of our schools. We have had our chance to teach lessons about equity and to make them a priority, but it appears that we have failed. Why? Thomas Arciniega's analysis seems to be as relevant today as it was in 1977:

Public education has successfully shifted the blame for the failure of schools to meet the needs of minorities onto the shoulders of the clients they purport to serve. They have pulled off the perfect crime, for they can never be truly held accountable, since the reasons for failure in school are said to be the fault of poor homes, cultural handicaps, linguistic deficiencies, and deprived neighborhoods. The fact that schools are geared primarily to serve monolingual, white, mid-

dle-class, and Anglo clients is never questioned.[6]

How will we meet the challenge of providing a high-quality education for all students in a culturally diverse society? Do we educators know how to deal with institutional racism? Do we know how to develop healthy, prejudice-free attitudes in all our students? Can we be sure that educational practice will reflect a commitment to educational equity so that all Americans can achieve what we now falsely believe only the elite can attain?

Understanding Racism

In order for Americans to embrace diversity, the conscious and unconscious expressions of racism within our society must be identified and done away with. The first step is to develop an understanding of the history and nature of racism and its relationship to prejudice and discrimination. Prejudice consists of unjustifiable negative feelings and beliefs about a racial or ethnic group and its members. It is characterized by preconceived opinions, judgements, or feelings that lack any foundation or substance. *Discrimination* consists of unjustifiable negative behavior toward a racial or ethnic group and its members. It expresses itself in distinctions and decisions made on the basis of prejudice. *Racism* describes the combination of individual prejudice and individual discrimination, on the one hand, and institutional polices and practices, on the other, that result in the unjustified negative treatment and subordination of members of a racial or ethnic group. By convention, the term *racism* has been reserved to describe the mistreatment of members of racial and ethnic groups, that have experienced a history of discrimination.[7] *Prejudice, discrimination, and racism do not require intention.*

Racism can be thought of as a sick belief system.[8] A "healthy" belief system reflects a good match between the real world and the ideal world. A sick belief system reflects a poor match. Colonization, motivated by greed and a lust for power, depended on creating a sick belief system for both the colonizer and the colonized in order to support colonial expansion. Therefore, the concept of race was invented (conceptually separating Europeans from the people to be dominated), and racism emerged.[9]

Racism is a mental illness characterized by perceptual distortion, a denial of reality, delusions of grandeur (belief in white supremacy), the projection of blame (on the victim), and phobic reactions to differences. A colonizer may be racist, but a victim cannot be so. A victim may become pro-racist, however, which means that he or she identifies with the aggressor and initiates many racist behaviors. To make racism work it is necessary to destroy the victim's identity and to claim superiority for the oppressor. Colonizers accomplished this aim by destroying the history and the culture of their victims and rewriting history to assert their own claim to superiority.[10]

The concept of race is an evil ideological and political tool used to exploit and subordinate people of color. It has no scientific validity that would justify its use in categorizing people. Yet bigotry, prejudice, and discrimination based on the concept of race remain powerful parts of our nation's psyche and behavior. For example, a recent national survey of high school biology teachers conducted by researchers from the University of Texas at Arlington revealed that one in four respondents (the majority of whom were white males) agreed with the statement: "Some races of people are more intelligent than others."[11] Unquestionably, racism is one of the most stubborn diseases afflicting this society.

Monocultural Schools

Historically, every academic discipline—psychology, biology, geography, religion, philosophy, anthropology, literature, history—has been used to justify colonialism and racism. Under colonialism, information is rigidly controlled in several ways: it can be destroyed, distorted, fabricated, suppressed, or selectively emphasized. Those in power can also limit the access of others to information or present it in a manner designed to confuse the recipients.[12]

Through the omission of information, America's schools have become mono-cultural environments. They dispense a curriculum centered on western civilization that encapsulates only narrowly the truth, reality, and breadth of human experience. This curriculum reinforces institutional racism by excluding from discourse and from the ethos of the school and the classroom the intellectual thought, scholarship, history, culture, contributions, and experience of minority groups.[13] Schools have become sites for producing and making acceptable myths and ideologies that systematically disorganize and neutralize the cultural identities of minorities.[14] Consequently, schools—where the hearts and minds of children are shaped and controlled—have been dominated for far too long by the attitudes, the beliefs, and the value system of one race and class of people. This is not a politically, socially, morally, or economically justifiable situation in a democratic, multicultural society.

Because the U.S. system of education is built so solidly on a monocultural, Euro-American world view, it tends to benefit white students, whose cultural patterns and styles are more attuned to this world view. As white students progress through the education system and move into the world of work, the development of their cognitive styles and their learning styles is linear and self-reinforcing. Seldom, if ever, are they required to be bicultural, bilingual, or bicognitive.

For children of color, being bicultural is not a free choice but a prerequisite for success in the education system and for eventual success in the society at large. Nonwhite children are generally expected to be bicultural, bilingual, and bicognitive; to measure their performance against a Euro-American yardstick; and to maintain the psychic energy necessary to sustain this orientation. At the same time, they are castigated whenever they attempt to express and validate their indigenous cultural and cognitive styles.[15]

The Consequences of Racism

The consequences of institutional racism and a monocultural education are pervasive and profound. White students tend glibly to accept the idea of equality and multiculturalism or of the superior position of their group in society without speculation or insightful analysis. They become oblivious to all but the most blatant acts of racism or ethnic discrimination and often re-label such acts something else. They seldom give serious thought to cultural, ethnic, or racial differences or to their meaning for and influence on individuals and groups. They are subliminally socialized, enculturated, and oriented to believe that the western experience, culture, and world view are superior and dominant.[16]

Students of color, by contrast, experience conceptual separation from their roots; they are compelled to examine their own experiences and history through the assumptions, paradigms, constructs, and language of other people; they lose their cultural identity; and they find it difficult to develop a sense of affiliation and connection to a school. They become "universal strangers"—disaffected and alienated—and all too many eventually drop out of school.[17]

It is shameful that, more than a quarter of a century after the passage of major civil rights legislation, black children who are handed drawings of a black child and a white child will favor the white child when they are asked which child is beautiful, which child is ugly, which child is smart, and which is dumb.[18] Clearly, racism attacks a black child's very sense of self. Solving the problem of racism is America's unfinished agenda, and it must be regarded by educators as a moral imperative.

The Role of Education in Combating Racism

How can we mobilize the education system to rescue the perishable spirit and the talent of minority children? How can education reduce and eliminate the effects of institutional racism and a monoethnic curriculum? We educators can

address the problems of racism and educational equity by confronting and challenging racism, increasing the pool of minority teachers, developing and implementing a multicultural curriculum, improving pedagogical practices, elevating the self-esteem of all children, and teaching character development.

Confronting and challenging racism. Benign neglect has allowed the momentum of institutional racism to accelerate to the point of overt expressions involving totally unacceptable behaviors and actions. School policies that assert unequivocally that racism is unacceptable, will not be tolerated, and will lead to appropriate sanctions clearly establish the context for active intervention programs to counter racism. For example, in Ferndale, Michigan, the school board has developed a Human Dignity Policy that succinctly states:

> The Board of Education, recognizing that we are a multiracial, multiethnic school district, believes it is part of our mission to provide a positive harmonious environment in which respect for the diverse makeup of the school community is promoted. A major aim of education in the Ferndale School District is the development of a reasoned commitment to the core values of a democratic society.
>
> In accordance with this aim, the school district will not tolerate behavior by students or staff which insults, degrades, or stereotypes any race, gender, handicap, physical condition, ethnic group, or religion.
>
> Appropriate consequences for offending this policy will be specified in the student code of

conduct of each building. Staff members offending this policy will be disciplined in accordance with provisions of the appropriate employee master agreement with the School Board.[19]

Such a policy leaves no doubt about the determination of a school district to address racism.

To augment clearly stated policies, intervention programs must be established to challenge prejudice, discrimination, and racism. The study of the history, purposes, and dynamics of racism must be recognized as a valid endeavor. An examination of stereotyping in the media, in textbooks, and in the popular culture ought to be included in the curriculum. Every controversial issue associated with racism needs to be studied, discussed, debated, and critically confronted.

Racism cuts deep into the psyche. Discussions and debates about racism create anxiety and conflict, which are handled differently by different cultural groups. For example, whites tend to fear open discussion of racial problems because they believe that such discussion will stir up hard feelings and old hatreds. Whites tend to believe that heated arguments about racism lead to divisiveness, loss of control, bitter conflict, and even violence.

Blacks, on the other hand, believe that discussion and debate about racism help to push racial problems to the surface and, perhaps, force society to deal with them. As Thomas Kochman has noted, "Blacks believe that differences can only be worked out by engaging in struggle, even if the arguments resulting from such engagement become heated. . . . Consequently blacks conceive the danger of violence as greater when people are not communicating than when they are."[20]

Such differences in dealing with conflict suggest that, to confront racism in a free and open discussion, students and teachers will have to develop assertiveness, listening skills, group problem-solving skills, and effective strategies for conflict resolution. Dealing with stereotypes, biases, and differing personal values and constructing a climate that fosters intergroup interaction and understanding are complex efforts that demand sensitivity and empathy.

Many American children are affected by institutional racism. Education is their best hope.

Clearly, staff development for administrators, teachers, and support personnel is imperative. Such staff development programs should be designed not to put people on the defensive but to empower them to understand and address the unconscious and overt effects of the institutional racism that pervades all facets of society.

We are engaged in a long-term struggle. Racism and other forms of prejudice and discrimination will not be eliminated in a day or a week or as a result of one workshop. Intervention programs must be sustained efforts. To turn schools into communities of conscience will require a coherent, comprehensive, and strategic plan that interweaves

school policy and active intervention and that is accompanied by a sense of urgency and mission.

Increasing the pool of minority teachers. As America's classrooms are beginning to serve a rapidly expanding proportion of minority students, the pool of candidates for teaching positions is becoming increasingly white. Over the coming decade, the proportion of minority teachers in the public schools will drop from 12% to 5%. At the same time, the minority student population will increase to 33%.[21] Diversity within the public school faculty is a pedagogical necessity, not merely a matter of fair play in the labor market. There are at least two major reasons to insure cultural, racial, and ethnic diversity in America's teaching force. First, the existence of differences among teachers is itself an equity lesson for students, who must be taught respect for understanding of people from groups other than their own. Second, children of all racial and ethnic groups must have access to attractive role models.[22] It is unequivocally clear that the minority teacher as a role model is important both to white students and to students of color, and the importance of such role models will grow as the population of the United States continues to change.

When minority teachers make up a small percentage of a school's teaching staff, they are in triple jeopardy.[23] First, because they lack contact with minority colleagues, those in the majority interpret the behavior of minority teachers through racial and ethnic stereotypes. They more readily attribute the behavior of minority colleagues to ethnic or racial characteristics than to such individual factors as personality or

background. Second, when a teaching staff is strongly skewed toward members of the majority group, the evaluation of performance is consistently (if subtly) biased against minority teachers. Third, members of the majority group often misunderstand affirmative action and assume that those who benefit from it are less competent and less deserving.

It follows, then, that simple representation of minorities does not guarantee a truly diverse teaching staff. Research indicates that numbers matter—that the quality of life in an institution improves for minority group members as their proportion in the overall population increases. The rate of inclusion of minority group members influences the extent to which they can realize equal opportunity and equal treatment and the extent to which members of the majority group can free themselves from stereotypical thinking and prejudice.[24]

Recent research suggests that 20% is the minimum rate of inclusion required to diffuse stereotypes and other negative factors affecting minority members of organizations.[25] If by the year 2000 one-third of all school-age children in America will be members of minority groups, is it too much to ask that we aspire to have a teaching force reflecting a similar distribution?

Developing and implementing a multicultural curriculum. If we are in the "business" of educating people, then we are in the business of communicating truth and reality—of telling the complete story of history and human experience. That means that we must learn how to tap the rich vein of cultural, ethnic, and racial diversity to improve education for all children. A multicultural, gender-fair, nonparochial curriculum is essential if students are to broaden their understanding of their own cultures and of cultural diversity.

We need to incorporate into the curriculum another story, a non-western story of the world. Education has long been used to create distorted perceptions and beliefs about minority groups. By leaving out nonwestern history, culture, and ideas, we have falsified education for everyone. Schools need to integrate into all curricular areas the ideas, the literature, the contributions, and the history of minority groups. A curriculum based on truth and reality can provide students with a sense of continuity, of self-esteem, and of identity. Portland, Oregon, has developed such a curriculum.[26]

As Glenn Pate has pointed out, a genuinely multicultural approach that permeates the K-12 curriculum—horizontally and vertically, in all subject areas—and that is supported by high-quality instructional materials is far more effective than "add-on" programs designed to reduce prejudice, elevate self-esteem, and enhance learning. Programs that are added on to the regular curriculum are viewed as supplementary. They do not effectively attack students' prejudices, may be seen as patronizing, and may be implemented in such a way that they alienate both majority and minority students.[27]

In his review of approaches to a multicultural curriculum, James Banks noted that, while add-on programs can be used as stepping-stones to more intellectually challenging approaches, they do not involve a restructuring of the curriculum. Thus they often trivialize ethnic cultures; they tend to evade significant issues, such as racism, poverty, and oppression; and they view ethnic content from the perspective of mainstream historians, writers, artists, and scientists.[28] An effective multicultural curriculum is achieved when we change the basic assumptions of the curriculum; enable students to view concepts, themes, issues, and problems from several ethnic perspectives; and infuse throughout the curriculum the frames of reference, history, culture, and perspectives of various ethnic groups. Such an approach extends students' understanding of the nature, development, complexity, and dynamics of a multicultural, pluralistic society and leads them to social action and decision making that reduce prejudice and discrimination in their schools.

Genuine multicultural education demands a major commitment of time, energy, and resources. Developing appropriate materials, collecting resources, conducting historical research, and integrating multicultural content into all parts of the curriculum require sustained effort. Such effort can be regarded as a measure of authentic commitment to educational equity. A curriculum that honors and values the rich contributions that culturally diverse groups have made to society and to civilization is the foundation on which to build interactive, multicultural, gender-fair communities of learning.

Improving pedagogical practice. Jeannie Oakes points out that we have made two critical errors in our thinking about equity and excellence in education. First, in looking for solutions to educational problems, we have focused our attention on the individual circumstances of children (e.g., home environment, heredity, culture) rather than on content and processes within the schools. And second, we have failed to acknowledge that the schools cannot be described as excellent as long as large numbers of students pass through or leave them without having their educational needs satisfied.[29]

Excellence in education should be viewed as a combination of intellectual rigor, challenging content, and effective pedagogy.[30] Equity means that every child has access to educational excellence and that every school is a delivery system that enables each of its students to derive the full benefits of intellectual rigor, challenging content, and effective pedagogy.

The widespread academic failure of children from certain ethnic populations, in the face of clear demonstrations that such failure is totally avoidable, is a national disgrace. The traditional pedagogical approaches and educational delivery systems that have been used to deal with at-risk minority students have often proved to be dysfunctional and anachronistic. They have tended to be rigid, uncreative, and characterized by low expectations.[31]

For example, there is little evidence to support the basic assumptions of tracking. Indeed, research findings demonstrate that the net effects of tracking are to exaggerate initial differences among students, to harm poor and minority students disproportionately, to deny students equal access to knowledge and understanding, to place black and Hispanic children in low-ability and non-college bound groups, and to widen the educational gap between the haves and the have-nots.[32] In view of the overwhelming evidence that tracking contributes to educational inequity, its practice should be abandoned.

However, instead of witnessing the demise of tracking, we are now confronted with well-intended but misguided proposals and legislative initiatives calling for school choice. The inevitable outcome of school choice would be the creation of large-scale tracking systems. Equal funding of high-quality education for all children obviates the need for school choice. We do not need school choice as much as we need choice schools that are characterized by challenging curricula and effective pedagogy—characteristics too often found wanting in schools serving large numbers of minority students.

Underachieving minority students are likely to be assigned to less-experienced teachers who have mastered fewer pedagogical strategies. These youngsters are given mind-numbing worksheets that stress isolated skills, but they are not given opportunities to apply these skills to authentic problems. Perhaps the most striking bias in schools is the restricted access of minority students from low-income families to rigourous academic work. At-risk minority students are more likely to be presented with lessons that are shaped by a behavioral or a training perspective and that focus on low-level skills, fragmented knowledge, and easily tested facts.[33]

Improved pedagogical practice springs from the belief that all children—regardless of their cultural, ethnic, and linguistic backgrounds—can learn. Effective pedagogy is characterized by high expectations, sensitivity to cultural patterns, and successful communication to and motivation of stu-

dents. Cooperative learning and interracial learning groups are good examples of pedagogical practice that has not only improved students' academic achievement but also facilitated cross-ethnic and cross-racial friendships.[34]

Schools have been dominated too long by the attitudes, beliefs, and value system of one race and class of people.

Many educators have produced high-quality results with all children, including those identified as at-risk. Reuven Feuerstein's "dynamic assessment and instrumental enrichment" has been used successfully for 30 years with at-risk children—yet it has not attracted the interest of many teacher educators, nor is it found in the repertoire of most classroom teachers. Preservice teachers must be exposed to settings in which children who normally fail are successful. Preservice teachers will never believe that all children can succeed academically unless they themselves have the chance to teach children successfully in settings where they fear failure.[35]

Teaching character development and improving self-esteem. Studies have consistently shown a significant correlation between low self-esteem and prejudice.[36] When we are able to increase students' self-esteem, there is an accompanying decrease in prejudice. Probably one of the most effective actions schools could take to improve intergroup

relations would be to help students develop strong self-concepts.[37] Deliberate psychological education programs can produce positive self-concepts and elevated self-esteem. However, overreliance on such programs is not justified by recent research, which indicates that self-esteem does not cause—but is an effect of—academic success.[38] Increases in self-esteem are preceded by gains in competence; this suggests that high expectations and effective pedagogical practices that foster academic achievement will generate positive self-concepts and enhanced self-esteem.

If we believe that the goals of the schools are to make all children intellectually competent and to foster decency in their interpersonal relations, then our concerns about increasing students' self-esteem need to be viewed in the context of the overall development of character. Schools must institute programs to protect children from the ravages of social and family disorganization. In today's complex world, all students need more support from the schools than they needed in the past. This is especially true of minority students, who "have experienced the most cultural discontinuity and destruction of their organizing and stabilizing institutions and practices, as well as forced exclusion from education and other developmental opportunities."[39] Schools can offer young people meaningful cocurricular and extracurricular activities that will expand and enrich their lives and simultaneously extend the school's socializing influence. A major goal of socialization should be to promote civic virtue and those qualities that enable children to become productive and dependable citizens in a just society.[40]

Schools need to revitalize their approaches to the teaching of civic virtue. The duties of citizenship in a democracy; the rules of interpersonal civility; the nature of equity and justice; and the morality of caring for the weak, the poor, and the disenfranchised are all concepts that can be taught in the classroom.[41] Through cocurricular and extracurricular activities and appropriate coursework, schools can foster the development of psychological and social traits of character: self-esteem (integrity, consistency); self-discipline; vocational aspiration (work as a calling, not a job); idealism; moral judgement; and interpersonal expectations (including altru-

ism, enlightened self-interest, and social justice).

To become moral communities that are supportive and caring, schools need to model empathy, altruism, trust, cooperation, fairness, justice, compassion, democracy, and celebration of diversity. In schools, the quality of communal caring and the sense of community conscience are largely defined by the degree of harmony and mutual respect between white and minority groups. Harmony and mutual respect are measured by how well we live the values we teach and how fully we practice the ideals to which we are committed. Caring and just schools—characterized by intervention programs to counteract racism, by diverse teaching staffs, by truly multicultrual curricula, by appropri-

ate pedagogical practices, by high expectations, and by continuing emphasis on the development of character and self-esteem—are essential to the achievement of genuine educational equity and to the elimination of institutional racism.

The agenda of imperatives that we have prescribed is demanding, challenging, and complex, but it is commensurate with the nature and urgency of the problem confronting American education. The effects of racism that plague the lives of minority children are more than personal problems. They damage not only the health and welfare of children, but the character of our society, the quality of our civilization, and our prospects for the future. Our children are our future—all our children.

Notes

1. Janet Caldwell, "The Need for Anti-Racism Education." *Education Week*, 20 September 1989. p. 32; and Augustine Garcia, "Just When you Though It Was Safe: Racism in the Schools." *Educational Horizons*, Summer 1989, pp. 156-62.

2. Louise Derman-Sparks, "Challenging Diversity with Anti-Bias Curriculum," *Schools Safety*, Winter 1989, pp. 10-13.

3. Octavio Paz, *The Labyrinth of Solitude* (New York: Grove Press, 1985).

4. Glenn S. Pate, "Reducing Prejudice in the Schools," *Multicultural Leader*, Spring 1989, p. 1.

5. Asa G. Hilliard III, "Educational Equity: What Does the Future Hold? Six Equity Steps," paper presented at the annual meeting of the American Association of Colleges for Teacher Education, Crystal City, VA, 1987.

6. Thomas A. Arciniega, "The Challenge of Multicultural Education for Teacher Educators," *Journal of Research and Development in Education*, vol. 11, 1977, p. 123.

7. *The Smith Design for Institutional Diversity* (Northampton, Mass.: Smith College, 1989) p. 8.

8. Asa G. Hilliard III, *Free Your Mind: Return to the Source–African Origins* (Atlanta: Georgia State University, College of Education, 1986), pp. 10-12.

9. Ibid., p. 12. See also Jacques Barzun, *Race: A Study in Superstition* (New York: Harper & Row, 1965); Ruth Benedict, *Race, Science, and Politics* (New York: Viking, 1959); Michael D. Biddis, *Father of Racist Ideology: The Social and Political Thought of Count Govineau* (New York: Weybright and Talley, 1970); Alan Chase, *The Legacy of Malthus: The Social Costs of the*

New Scientific Racism (New York: Knopf, 1977); Ashley Montagu, *Man's Most Dangerous Myth: The Fallacy of Race* (New York: Collier, 1974); and William R. Stanton, *The Leopard's Spots: Scientific Attitudes Towards Race in America* (Chicago: University of Chicago Press, 1960).

10. Hilliard, *Free Your Mind . . .*, p. 12.

11. Derman-Sparks, p. 11.

12. Hilliard, *Free Your Mind . . .*, p. 11.

13. Carl A. Grant and Maureen Gillette, "The Holmes Report and Minorities in Education," *Social Education*, November/December 1987, p. 521.

14. Cameron McCarthy, "Rethinking Liberal and Radical Perspectives on Racial Inequality in School," *Harvard Educational Review*, August 1988, p. 276.

15. James A. Anderson, "Cognitive Styles and Multicultural Populations," *Journal of Teacher Education*, January/February 1988, p. 5.

16. Carole Pigler Christensen, "Cross Cultural Awareness Development: A Conceptual Model," *Counselor Education and Supervision*, June 1989, pp. 270-87.

17. Hilliard, *Free Your Mind . . .*, p. 13.

18. "Black in White America," American Broadcasting Company television news documentary, 29 August 1989.

19. "Human Dignity Policy," City of Ferndale School District, Ferndale, Mich., 1988.

20. Thomas Kochman, *Black and White Styles in Conflict* (Chicago: University of Chicago Press, 1981), p. 20.

21. Jesse T. Zapata, "Early Identification and Recruitment of Hispanic Teacher Candidates," *Journal of Teacher Education*, January/February 1988, p. 19; and Charles Whitaker, "The Disappearing Black Teacher," *Ebony*, January 1989, pp. 124-26.

22. Hilliard, "Educational Equity...."

23. *The Smith Design for Institutional Diversity*, p. 3; and Thomas F. Pettigrew and Joanne Martin, "Shaping the Organizational Context for Black American Inclusion," *Journal of Social Issues*, vol. 43, 1987, pp. 41-78.

24. Pettigrew and Martin, op. cit.: and Walter G. Stephan and Cooke White Stephan, "Intergroup Anxiety," *Journal of Social Issues*, vol. 41, 1985, pp. 157-75.

25. Ibid.

26. Asa G. Hilliard, III, "African and African American Content in School Curriculum: Portland, Oregon, and Beyond," unpublished paper, January 1988, pp. 1-8.

27. Pate, p. 2.

28. James A. Banks, "Approaches to Multicultural Curriculum Reform," *Multicultural Leader*, Spring 1988, pp. 1-2.

29. Jeannie Oakes, *How Schools Structure Inequality* (New Haven CT: Yale University Press, 1985).

30. Frederick John Geis, "A Provocative Analysis of Contemporary School Issues," *Record in Educational Administration and Supervision*, Fall 1986, p. 3.

31. Hilliard, "Educational Equity . . ."; and idem, "Teachers and Cultural Styles: Just What Does Pluralism Mean?," *NEA Today*, January 1989, pp. 65-69.

32. Jeannie Oakes, "Keeping Track, Part I: The Policy and Practice of Curriculum Inequality," *Phi Delta Kappan*, September 1986, pp. 12-17.

33. Oakes, *How Schools Structure Inequality*.

34. David L. DeVries, Keith J. Edwards, and Robert E. Slavin, "Biracial Learning Teams and Race Relations in the Classroom," *Journal of Educational Psychology*, vol. 70, 1978, pp. 356-62; Daniel Goleman, "Psychologists Find Ways to Break Racism's Hold," *New York Times*, 5 September 1989. p. C-1; Brenda Dorn Conrad, "Cooperative Learning and Prejudice Reduction," *Social Education*, April/May 1988, pp. 283-86; Sholomo Sharan, "Cooperative Learning in Small Groups: Recent Methods and Effects on Achievement, Attitudes, and Ethnic Relations," *Review of Educational Research*, vol. 50, 1980, pp. 24-71; and Robert E. Slavin, "Effects of Biracial Learning Teams on Cross Racial Friendships," *Journal of Educational Psychology*, vol. 71, 1979, pp. 381-87.

35. Hilliard, "Educational Equity . . ."; and idem, "Public Support for Successful Instructional Practices for At-Risk Students," in *School Success for Students At Risk: Analysis and Recommendations of the Council of Chief State School Officers* (New York: Harcourt Brace Jovanovich, 1988).

36. Glenn S. Pate, "Research on Reducing Prejudice," *Social Education*, vol. 52, 1988, pp. 287-89.

37. Pate, "Reducing Prejudice . . . ," p. 2.

38. William J. Holly, "Students' Self-Esteem and Academic Achievement," *Research Roundup*, November 1987, pp. 1-4.

39. James P. Comer, "Is Parenting Essential to Good Teaching?," *NEA Today*, January 1988, p. 37.

40. Perry London, "Character Education Clinical Intervention: A Paradigm Shift for, U.S. Schools, *Phi Delta Kappan*, May 1987, pp. 667-73.

41. Ibid.

Gerald J. Pine is a professor of education and dean of the School of Human and Educational Services at Oakland University, Rochester, Michigan.

Asa G. Hilliard, III is Fuller E. Callaway Professor of Education at Georgia State University, Atlanta, Georgia.

Gerald J. Pine and Asa G. Hillard III. "Rx for Racism: Imperatives for America's Schools" Phi Delta Kappan 71, 8, 593-600. Used by permission.

When a conflict arose over what music would be played at the Senior Prom, several African-American students responded by organizing their own event.

Separate Senior Proms Reveal an Unspanned Racial Divide

Isabel Alexis Wilkerson

Chicago, May 4—The rented limousines carrying young men in tuxedos and young women in taffeta began arriving at a Gold Coast hotel shortly after dusk on Friday. It was the official Brother Rice High School prom, and it was virtually all white.

Three miles away at a South Side hotel, about 30 of their classmates—tuxedos young men in kinte cloth cummerbunds—and their dates dressed in satin alighted from Cadillacs and BMW's borrowed from relatives for the school's first all-black prom.

It was a turning point that has torn at the heart of the predominantly white, boys' Catholic school here and, sociologists say, is a telling allegory of race relations in this country 20 years after the civil rights movement brought an end to legalized segregation.

Defining Integration

"For 20 years we have had a kind of token integration," said Dr. Aldon Morris, an associate professor of sociology at Northwestern University. "Now what we're getting is a real debate. What does integration mean and when has it really occurred? It is one of the most fundamental questions facing America right now."

Sociologists say that as society is forced to redefine integration and the forms it may take it has become apparent that putting the races under the same roof does not guarantee integration. Across the country, college campuses that have been desegregated for decades are witnessing growing racial tension and a disenchantment among blacks who have sought out separate cafeterias and dormitories. The situation at Brother Rice appears to be little different.

The college preparatory school is in a virtually all-white, middle-class neighborhood on Chicago's Southwest Side and has 1,330 students, 12 percent of them black, and no black teachers. And while blacks and whites participate in classes and clubs and sports together and many consider each other great friends, they sit at separate tables at lunch time and go their separate ways after school is over.

On a subtler level, black students express a resentment that their culture does not get the attention that white culture does. They say that while they spend the school year learning mostly about the contributions of whites black culture is relegated to a few seconds each morning during black history month when a student reads over a loudspeaker a brief sketch about a black inventor or abolitionist.

Music as Metaphor

"We've been experiencing their culture for four years," said Edward Jones, a black senior. "But they don't seem ready to experience ours."

The prom, with all its ritual and mythic significance, appeared to bring an underlying tension to a head.

The trouble began when the prom committee, virtually all white, hired a rock band and a disc jockey and announced that the play list for the music at the prom would be based on the suggestions of the senior class. The committee devised what it saw as an objective means of gauging what the class wanted to hear: Each student would list three favorite songs, and the songs mentioned most would be the ones played.

Black seniors began to complain that their preferences would be effectively shut out, that Marvin Gaye would be squeezed out by Bon Jovi. "For every vote we had, there were eight votes for what they wanted," said Hosea Hill, a black senior. "If you're paying tuition to the school, you should have some input. But with us being in the minority, we're always outvoted. It's as if we don't count."

Music became a metaphor for culture and race, and black students considered the gap too wide to close. "They want that hard-rocking, bang-your-head-against-the wall kind of stuff," said Sean Young, a black senior.

Negotiations Fall

And others said that even if they could choose half the songs, which they thought was unlikely, they would probably still be unhappy. "We would have sat down during their songs and they would have sat down during ours," Mr. Jones said.

So the black students decided to put together their own prom, with their own site, menu, theme and decorations. When school administrators got wind of the plans, they called a prom committee meeting to discuss grievances, but black students, figuring they would be outvoted, did not show up.

School administrators have refused to discuss the situation. Several of the black prom organizers, including honor students headed for prestigious universities, said they were threatened with suspension and expulsion if they went ahead with an alternative prom. They did it anyway.

And so while about 200 white couples and six black couples danced to rock music in two adjoining ballrooms at the Marriott Hotel, about 30 black couples listened to the Isley Brothers and Roy Ayers, danced the Electric Slide and crowned their own prom king and queen, James Warren and Devona Rogers, in Ballroom 15 at the McCormick Hotel. Several hours into the evening there were bursts of applause as several of the black couples who had gone to the main prom to spend time with their white friends showed up at the McCormick.

The organizers for the black prom, who said they had nothing against their white classmates, said white students were welcome. But by midnight, none had shown up.

White Students' Sorrow and Anger

Many of the white students have taken the situation personally. Some said they were hurt and felt rejected. Others were angry and bitter.

"Now you find out what they really think of you," said Jerry Ficaro a white student. "You're in the same class so you sort of feel like this is against us."

He said the black students should have gone along with the majority. "The majority makes a decision," he said, "That's the way it works."

Mike Kane, another white student, said: "I think the whole thing got out of hand. They should have found some way to comprise. We might as well have separate graduations."

Some said they just missed their friends and felt the class was not whole without the black students. "It's too bad," said Jack Scott, another white senior, "because it's our senior year, and we should be together."

Brother Rice administrators would not allow reporters into the official prom. They have disavowed the black prom, saying the school had nothing to do with it and barring the black students from using the Brother Rice name in their program, napkins and banner.

Integration on Whose Terms?

The principal, Brother Michael Segvich, told the Chicago Tribune earlier this week, "There is only one prom this year at Brother Rice." The black prom "is something we don't want," he said, adding, "I think it has to do with racism. We felt we went out of our way to accommodate. They seemed to have their minds made up to go along with this other party all along."

Dr. Morris, the sociologist, said the situation is symbolic of the misunderstanding that can occur between a majority and minority culture. "What integration has meant for many whites is that blacks had to interact with them on their terms," he said. "It is a kind of cultural arrogance. Not only do many not want to participate in other cultures, but they feel theirs is the culture that is very much American and what America is."

For many of the black students, a black prom became something of a crusade, a chance to show that they could do something on their own, that they did not have to rely on whites.

Isabel Alexis Wilkerson joined The Times in December 1984, after working for a year as a reporter for the Detroit Free Press. She previously worked as a reporting intern for the St. Petersburg (FL) Times, the Atlanta Journal, the Washington Star, the Washington Post, and the Los Angeles Times.

Different historical, social, and political backgrounds offer different arguments for or against employing bilingual education. Betances explains why bilingual education is necessary in our historical, social, and political context.

My People Made it Without Bilingual Education—What's Wrong with Your People?

Samuel Betances

I eagerly embraced the question. There was strong reason to believe that history would be on the side of the proponents of bilingual education.

But it was not meant to be. The critics were correct. A careful search of the historical record clearly indicates that immigrants on the eve of the 20th century and before did not have anything that can remotely be compared to bilingual education in their educational diet. When the critics argue that "my folks made it without bilingual education," they are correct!

As I poured through the dusty records of history and the socio-economic political arena facing the brave newcomers of yesterday, however, I realized that the absence of bilingual education for that generation of future Americans was related to something bigger than just the language issue. The whole history of immigrant education lay before me and I could now put the issues of yesterday's newcomers in its proper perspective.

Yes, it is true that the newcomers of yesterday did not get bilingual education: but that is because they did not get any education. Entry into the economic system was possible without formal education. When the immigrants came from Europe they did not need middle class English language skills and high school diplomas or college degrees to get into the economy. Those brave souls transplanted into what they labeled as the "new world" came with the basics: strong backs and a willingness to work.

When Swedes ran out of farmland on their native soil they came to the land which had belonged to American Indians and which through conquest became available to these Scandinavian Lutherans. They transplanted themselves into a terrain and geography not unlike the one they left behind and on the very day they arrived Swedes began to work. They could speak to those cows in Swedish and the cows would give milk. Germans in Pennsylvania could speak to the corn in German and it would grow. In effect, the newcomers would have success in the economy, build their homes, their centers of worship and later on schools were established. Several generations would pass in the process. The society did not need to build schools to prepare the first generation of non-English speakers and their children for productive lives in the economy. That generation confronted the cow and the corn. Today's newcomers confront not the cow nor the corn; but the computers.

While the generations of yesterday could wait one, perhaps two, and even three generations before their offspring could enter high school and then college the newcomers of today have to leap-frog from the agricultural period well over the industrial period of strong-back and willingness-to-work to the age of information.

Most people who today sit on boards of education, administer school programs and teach in the classrooms are the third or fourth generation descendants of immigrants. Their parents may have earned a high school diploma: but their grandparents did not. The farther back they go, the less formal schooling. In fact, today's education professionals represent, for the most part, the first generation of college graduates in their individual families. It is not accurate to say "we made it without bilingual education" when history says that public education did not exist at all or simply did not figure in any significant way in the progress of immigrants in an economy that required for the most part the strong backs, the farming skills, the entrepreneurial skills of the merchant, the traders, and the fishing skills of newcomers. America was built by non-English speaking people, without formal education.

At the turn of the century the dropout rate for everyone was about 94 percent but there was no dropout problem. Schools were irrelevant to the bulk of newcomers. When schools did not absorb the children of the immigrants to the degree that public schools existed at all, the economy did.

The dropout rate is a problem only if the lack of a diploma is combined with the inability to get into the economy without such certificates. The newcomer of yesterday faced a large dropout rate but a low dropout problem. Today we have a low dropout rate, about 30 percent overall, but a high dropout problem. Why? Because to get into the economy the workforce needs success in high school and post-high school education.

The newcomers of today come to the U.S. with a strong back and willingness to work with the same intelligence of those farmers of old but at the wrong time. They cannot get into the economy and expect a real future for their children, in the age of computers, by growing corn and milking cows. They cannot have success in the economy until they have success in schools. Latinos, along with the Asians, Pacific Islanders and limited English proficient groups, some native to the soil of the Americas, must do what no other group had to do before in the history of American education: attend middle class institutions, compete with mainstream classmates, and achieve success in classes which transfer information in English. That's a tall order. Knowing how to transfer information in English is basic to such expectations. As Moore and Pachon wrote in Hispanics in the United States:

> It is hard for some critics to understand why other immigrant groups managed without bilingual instruction. Actually, arrivals did not manage. Young children left school in such large numbers and at such an early age that failure was scarcely noticed. Furthermore, the dropouts survived by fitting themselves into a much less demanding economy. A high school diploma is now a bare minimum for many jobs. A wider range of children are

now expected to remain in school—not just a chosen few from upper income groups.

However, we must not fall into the trap of teaching Limited English Proficient (LEP) students English at the expense of their education. That happened to me. When I first went to public school in New York City, I didn't know any English and there were no programs to help me understand what the teacher was saying to our class. So I would look around and imitate my classmates.

One day the teacher asked a question. I heard the noise pregnant with meaning fill the classroom and looked on to see the response of my classmates. I was prepared to follow the lead of my peers, but something strange occurred. I panicked as I witnessed only 50 percent of the class raising their hands. What was I to do? With which group should I vote? I always tended to do what the majority of the students did, but I was trapped since the response was not very clear. I listened intensely as the teacher made the same series of noises and I watched for the response. This time about 60 percent of my classmates raised their hands. And then more. When about 80 percent responded with raised hands I did so, mindful of the fact that mine was hidden in the masses of hands. My response to what I could not understand was at least keeping pace with what everyone else was doing.

I ran home. My feet pounded the concrete sidewalk. I ran up the stairs of my apartment building and I pushed the door open. "Mamy, mamy," I asked. "¿Que significa la palabra 'finish?'" ("Mom, mom. what does the word 'finish' mean?") She said. "Terminates la tarea, mi hijito?" (Did you finish your task, my son?) So that's why only 50 percent raised their hands I thought. Only 50 percent were finished! I now understood what the teacher was asking and why the class responded as they did.

That evening at the dinner table, I noticed a long pause between the bites by my older brother Charlie. I asked him, "Charlie, are you finished?" I felt good about how quickly I put my new vocabulary to work. I felt proud that I knew what the word finish meant. I now knew the word "finish," but I had not finished my task. I was learning English at the expense of my education.

Bilingual education is the process whereby LEP students can learn English and finish their task. The issues are separated to create a positive transition of both empowering newcomers to the language with new verbal skills: but learning in the language they know the important curriculum tasks. Bilingual education is an important legitimate education reform for today's youth.

Bilingual education programs respond to the real problem of making instruction understandable. Anyone who argues that one can get along without English in the U.S. is a fool! English has replaced German as the language of science and French as the language of diplomacy. English is the lingua france of the world. The world's commerce largely takes place in international settings in English. When most of the world studies a foreign language, it tends to be English. That's reason enough for us to insist that newcomers who come to the U.S. schools must learn English. But here is even a more powerful reason: English is the common language of American citizens. It must be taught, required, strengthened and perfected in our schooling initiatives.

At their core, all bilingual educational programs worth their salt aim to teach English to LEP students. But while those LEP students are learning English so they can learn in English, they can be learning their math and science in the language they know.

Monolinguals who have never had to learn a second language to compete in a new and different environment, but who have an appreciation for history, know that the conditions facing us on the eve of the 21st Century are very different from conditions faced by those who came on the eve of the 20th century.

We must realize that not only do these newcomers need our enlightened policy; but we may go one step further. Not only must these newcomers learn English, it might be good if we didn't move in too quickly and tell them to forget Spanish or Vietnamese or Chamorro, or Togalo. Maybe we can come of age and realize that we cannot, in the name of turning out good Americans limit the freedom of speech of those new to our shores and or tell people to forget what they know. In the name of education we cannot argue that it is better to know less than more. Bilingual education enriches our best hopes for a democratic society, making it safe for differences as well—powerful, practical reasons why we need it today even though such programs did not exist for yesterday's arrivals.

Samuel Betances is a professor of Sociology at Northeastern Illinois University, Illinois.

Betances, Samuel. "My People Made it Without Bilingual Education— What's Wrong With Your People?" Official Journal of the California School Boards Association, 44, 7 (Winter 1985). Used by permission.

Bilingual education is more than two thousand years old. The phenomenon is also long standing in the United States, as James Crawford notes.

Bilingualism in America: A Forgotten Legacy

James Crawford

Bilingual education figures nowhere in the immigrant myth: the bootstraps rise to success, the fight for social acceptance, the sink-or-swim imperative of learning English. For many Americans today, the idea of teaching children in other languages is an affront to sacred traditions. Yesterday's immigrants allegedly prospered without special programs; glad to blend into the Melting Pot, they struggled to master the language of their adopted homeland. Operating in English only, public schools weaned students from other tongues and opened a new world of opportunities.

Ancestral legends die hard. Undoubtedly, some early newcomers were quick to assimilate and to advance themselves. But more often, "melting" was a process of hardships that lasted several generations. The immigrants' children were typically the first to achieve fluency in English, their grandchildren the first to finish high school, and their great-grandchildren the first to grow up in the middle class. Moreover, language minorities who were also racial minorities never

had the option of joining the main-stream—whether they learned English or not—before the civil rights reforms of the 1960s.

Melting Pot mythology obscures the diversity of cultures that have flourished in North America since the colonial period, and the aggressive efforts to preserve them, among both immigrants and indigenous minorities. In this history, bilingual education has played a central, if overlooked, role.

In 1664, when the settlement of New Netherland was ceded to the British crown, at least eighteen tongues were spoken on Manhattan Island, not counting Indian languages. Although the hegemony of English over the thirteen colonies had been decided by the late 17th century, the sounds of German, Dutch, French, Swedish, and Polish were frequently heard at the time of the American Revolution, and Spanish was dominant in several soon-to-be-acquired territories. Bilingualism, was common among the working classes as well as the educated, especially in the middle colonies of New York, Pennsylvania,

New Jersey, and Delaware. In the mid-18th century, newspaper advertisements for runaway servants, both black and white, made frequent reference to their bilingual or trilingual proficiencies.[1]

Wherever Europeans established schools in the New World, vernacular education was the rule, whether in English or another tongue. New arrivals naturally strived to preserve their heritage, and language loyalties were strong. Indeed, these were among the values that had brought the Pilgrims to America. During a brief exile in Holland, religious freedom had come at a high cost: the refugees' children had begun to lose English. In Plymouth they sought a climate where not only their Puritanism, but their culture could thrive.

German-speaking Americans were operating schools in their mother tongue as early as 1694 in Philadelphia.[2] Sometimes bilingual and sometimes not, German-language schooling prevailed until the early 20th century, notwithstanding external pressures to phase it out in favor of English instruction.

In the 1750s Benjamin Franklin, a politician frustrated by his inability to influence German-speaking voters, promoted one such project under the auspices of the society for the Propagation of Christian Knowledge. All went smoothly until German parents learned that linguistic assimilation, not religious instruction, was the real purpose of these schools, whereupon they refused to enroll their children. Soon after, the Pennsylvania Germans helped to vote Franklin out of the colonial assembly.

Franklin's impatience with German language loyalty was a minority view among the nation's founders.[3] Not only was bilingualism an accepted fact of life, but the Continental Congress accommodated politically significant groups of non-English speakers. For example, it published many official documents in German and French, including the Artikel des Bundes und der immerwahrenden Eintracht zwischen den Staaten, or Articles of Confederation.

No Official Language Policy

Anti-British sentiment aroused by the American Revolution inspired some proposals to discard English in favor of German, French, Greek, or Hebrew as the national language. Notwithstanding the persistent legend that Congress came within one vote of adopting German as our official tongue, no alternative language was seriously considered.[4] As one cynic observed, it would be easier for Americans to keep English and force the British to learn Greek.

Like England, the United States has adopted neither an official language, nor a government-sanc-

tioned body to regulate speech. In 1780 John Adams's proposal to establish an American language academy, "for refining, correcting, improving, and ascertaining" the English tongue, was ignored by the Continental Congress. Evidence suggests that the framers of the U.S. Constitution believed that a democracy should leave language choices up to the individual.[5] They had no interest in promoting diversity, to be sure. But according to Shirley Brice Heath, a Stanford University linguist, our early leaders placed a higher premium on political liberty than on cultural homogeneity.

Benjamin Rush hoped to promote the assimilation of the Pennsylvania Germans without compromising the principles of the new nation. His solution: bilingual higher education. A federally funded German College, Rush argued, would "open the eyes of the Germans to a sense of the importance and utility of the English language and become perhaps the only possible means, consistent with their liberty, of speaking a knowledge of the English language among them" (emphasis in original).

At the same time, the American nationalism unleashed by the Federalist era had ramifications for the American language. With his dictionary and speller, Noah Webster led efforts to develop standards for "Federal English," distinct from those of the stuffy British. During the hiatus in immigration from 1790 to 1815, the domain of English continued to expand at the expense of rival tongues. Increasingly, ethnic schools offered English either as a class or as a medium of instruction. Still, no uniform language policy prevailed. Bilingual education was likely to be accepted

in areas where language-minority groups had influence, and to be rejected where they had none.

By the mid-1800s, public and parochial German-English schools were operating in such cities as Baltimore, Cincinnati, Cleveland, Indianapolis, Milwaukee, and St. Louis. An Ohio law of 1839 authorized instruction in English, German, or both, in areas where parents requested it. In 1847 Louisiana adopted the identical statue, except that it substituted French for German. The Territory of New Mexico, two years after its annexation in 1848, authorized Spanish-English bilingual education. Pennsylvania, Colorado, Illinois, Iowa, Kentucky, Minnesota, Missouri, Nebraska, and Oregon also passed laws sanctioning instruction in languages other than English. By 1900, according to historian Heinz Kloss, more than 600,000 American children (or about 4 percent of the elementary school population at the time, public and parochial) were receiving instruction partly or exclusively in the German language.

Even without legal authorization, local officials often bent the law to permit native-language classes, as a way to ensure immigrant parents' support of the public schools. As Diego Castellanos explains in The Best of Two Worlds, his chronicle of bilingual education in the United States:

> For much of the 19th century, certainly before the 1880s, the [locally controlled] structure of American public education allowed immigrant groups to incorporate linguistic and cultural traditions into the schools. . . . Wherever immigrant groups possessed sufficient political power—be they

Italian, Polish, Czech, French, Dutch, German—foreign languages were introduced into elementary and secondary schools, either as separate subjects or as languages of instruction.

Joel Perlmann, a historian a the Harvard Graduate School of Education, second this assessment. "Ethnic politics," and not discussions of "the psychological advantages or disadvantages of bilingual training," determined the structure of these programs, he says. "The debates did not focus on whether kids would learn math better in German or in English, or whether they were emotionally better off learning German skills first. The central issues, the ones that were always raised, had to do with being a good American and creating a good America."

For the 19th century education establishment, linguistic assimilation was the ultimate goal for immigrant students. And yet, coercive means were seen as counterproductive, especially for groups like the Germans, who felt strongly about maintaining their heritage. William Torrey Harris, superintendent of St. Louis schools in the 1870s and later U.S. Commissioner of Education, believed that the schools must "Americanize" language-minority children. At the same time, he preached cultural tolerance, arguing that "national memories and aspirations, family traditions, customs and habits, moral and religious observances cannot be suddenly removed or changed without disastrously weakening the personality."

Americanization Efforts

A resurgence of nativism in the late 19th century, led by the Ameri-

can Protective Association, marked the beginning of a gradual decline for bilingual education. Earlier opponents of immigration, such as the "Know Nothing" Party of the 1840s and 1850s, had attacked the Germans mainly for their religion or politics; rarely for their foreign speech. By the late 1880s, however, language legislation was discovered to be a convenient weapon against Catholic parochial schools, which in the Midwest were often conducted in German (as were most Lutheran schools, which became unintended victims of anti-catholic fervor). During this period, mandates for English as the basic language of instruction were enacted in Wisconsin, Illinois, and other states. Proponents made little attempt to conceal their real target. Praising these statuses in 1890, the Chicago Tribune criticized "the arrogance and presumption . . . of an Italian priest living in Rome" for opposing them.

Despite the religious bigotry behind the new language laws, the American Catholic hierarchy was ambivalent in its response: disturbed by state meddling with parochial education, yet not entirely averse to the new English requirements. Within the church, language was becoming a focus of contention, as splits developed along nationality lines. Although the English-instruction laws were soon repealed in Wisconsin and Illinois, around this time several cities canceled public bilingual education. St. Louis did so after German voting strength was sapped by gerrymandering and the Irish gained control of the local school board. Louisville and St. Paul banished German to the status of foreign language offered only in the upper grades.

After 1900 new strains of xenophobia multiplied, as Italians, Jews, and Slavs began to outnumber Irish, Germans, and Scandinavians in the immigrant stream. Social workers and educators addressed poverty among the new arrivals with the "Americanization" campaign. Operating through such organizations as the UMCA, these philanthropists provided large-scale adult English instruction for the first time, while indoctrinating immigrants in "free enterprise" values. After the Lawrence textile strike,[6] the campaign was taken up by industrialists hoping to counter the influence of foreign labor agitators. In 1915 the National Americanization Committee launched an "English First" project in Detroit, with the cooperation of the local Board of Commerce. Employers like Henry Ford made attendance at Americanization classes mandatory for their foreign-born workers.

As Americanization took a coercive turn, proficiency in English was increasingly equated with political loyalty; for the first time, an ideological link was forged between language and "Americanism." The U.S. Bureau of Education became active in this propaganda effort, sponsoring conferences on "Americanization work" and publishing an Americanization Bulletin and other literature, financed by private benefactors.

The educational goal was to replace immigrant languages and cultures with those of the United States. As explained by the superintendent of New York City schools in 1918, Americanization would cultivate "an appreciation of the institutions of this country [and] absolute forgetfulness of all obligations or connections with other countries because of descent or birth." Ellwood P. Cubberly, dean of the Stanford University School of Education, added:

> Our task is to break up [immigrant] groups or settlements, to assimilate and amalgamate these people as part of our American race, and to implant in their children, as far as can be done, the Anglo-Saxon conception of righteousness, law and order, and our popular government, and to awaken in them a reverence for our democratic institutions and for those things in our national life which we as a people hold to be of abiding worth.

Following the Spanish-American War, the U.S. government imposed English as the medium of instruction in its new colonies of Puerto Rico and the Philippines. "The need to consolidate the nation's territorial gains and solidify its political processes seems to have played an important role in this drive toward cultural and linguistic homogeneity," writes Josué González, a former director of the federal Office of Bilingual Education and Minority Languages Affairs (OBEMLA). In Puerto Rico, where "the population was entirely Spanish-speaking and 85 percent illiterate," the English-only rule "proved devastating" to educational achievement, according to Castellanos. In 1916 the U.S. Commissioner of Education compromised and allowed Spanish instruction in grades 1 through 4, Spanish and English in the grade 5, and only English thereafter, a policy that lasted until he late 1940s.

The Rise of Language Restrictionism

Back on the mainland, former President Theodore Roosevelt lectured immigrants: "We have room for but one language in this country and that is the English language, for we intend to see that the crucible turns our people out as American, of American nationality, and not as dwellers in a polyglot boarding house." He advocated, on the one hand, expanded opportunities for immigrants to learn English, and on the other, the deportation of those who failed to do so within five years. Roosevelt stressed language difference in his attacks on "hyphenated Americanism," which were aimed increasingly to German speakers as World War I approached.

After the United States entered the war in April 1917, anti-German feeling created in an unprecedented waive of language restrictionism. Several states passed laws and emergency decrees banning German speech in the classroom, on the street, in church, in public meetings, even on the telephone. In the Midwest at least 18,000 persons were charged under these laws by 1921. Six months after Armistice Day, Ohio Governor James M. Cox sought legislation to remove all uses of German from the state's elementary schools, public and private, arguing that the language posed "a distinctive menace to Americanism, and a part of a plot formed by the German government to make the school children loyal to it." Ohio lawmakers readily approved Cox's bill.

Under legal pressure or not, around this time most public school systems in the United States curtailed study of the German lan-

guage. They did so with the blessings of such establishment voices as The New York Times, which editoriazlied in 1919: "Some German-American parents want German to be taught. It pleases their pride, but it does not do their children any good." German language teachers, suddenly thrown out of work, were often reassigned to instruct children in "Americanism" and "citizenship.," Mobs raided schools and burned German textbooks; in Lima, Ohio, they were led by the local school superintendent. In nearby Columbus the school board sold its German books to a waste paper company for fifty cents per hundredweight.

Soon the fervor of Anglo-conformity spilled over into hostility toward all minority tongues. In the year following the war, according to legal historian Arnold Lelbowitz, fifteen states legislated English as the basic language of instruction.[7] Several followed Ohio's example of forbidding any foreign-language study in the elementary grades. The most restrictive of these laws were struck down by the U.S. Supreme Court in the Meyer v. Nebraska case, which involved a parochial school teacher charged with the crime of reading a Bible story in German to a ten-year-old child. In reversing his conviction, the court said:

> The desire of the legislature to foster a homogeneous people with American ideals prepared readily to understand current discussions of civic matters is easy to appreciate. Unfortunate experiences during the late war and aversion toward every characteristic of truculent adversaries were certainly enough to quicken that aspiration. But

the means adopted, we think, exceed the limitations upon the power of the State and conflict with rights assured . . . in time of peace and domestic tranquility . . .

The protection of the Constitution extends to all, to those who speak other languages as well as to those born with English on the tongue. Perhaps it would be highly advantageous if all had a ready understanding of our ordinary speech, but this cannot be coerced by methods which conflict with the Constitution—a desirable end cannot be promoted by prohibited means.

By the time the court handed down this ruling in 1923, the frenzy of Americanization was already starting to subside. Attempts to legislate loyalty to English were on the decline. Big city school systems were beginning to lift bans on German studies.

And yet, public attitudes had changed fundamentally: learning in languages other than English now seemed less than patriotic. European immigrant groups felt strong pressures to assimilate. Enthusiasm waned for preserving old-country ways. Minority tongues were devalued in the eyes of the younger generation. Meanwhile, the stream of non-English-speaking newcomers slowed to trickle after 1924, when Congress enacted the strictest immigration quotas in the nation's history.

Bilingual instruction continued in some parochial schools, mainly in rural areas of the Midwest, but by the late 1930s, it was virtually eradicated throughout the United States. Interest in the study of foreign languages also fell off dramatically. Next to Latin, German had been the most popular foreign language in 1915, with 24 percent of American secondary school students enrolled; by 1922 less than one percent were studying German. Overall, instruction in modern languages declined from 36 percent of secondary students in 1915 to 14 percent in 1948.[8]

Within a generation, Americanization's goal of transforming a polyglot society into a monolingual one was largely achieved. "This linguistic equivalent of 'book burning' worked admirably well" in promoting assimilation, according to Gonzalez. "But it worked best with the Northern European immigrants," who had a "cultural affinity" with American values and shared a "Caucasian racial history."

For other language minorities, especially those with dark complexions, English-only choosing brought difficulties. While their cultures were suppressed, discrimination barred their full acceptance into American life. Also, it was these groups—conquered peoples and racial minorities—who had suffered linguistic repression in the 19th century, a departure from the laissez-faire attitude toward European immigrant tongues.

English as a 'Civilizing' Influence

The U.S. government recognized the language rights of the Cherokee tribe under and 1828 treaty and agreed to subsidize the first newspaper published in an Indian tongue, the Cherokee Phoenix. In the 1830s, however, President Andrew Jackson initiated a policy of forcible Indian removal from the eastern United States, which became known as the Trail of Tears, as more than one-third of the Indians died en route to Oklahoma. When the Cherokees used their printing press to advocate resistance, it was confiscated and destroyed.

After resettlement in Oklahoma, the tribe established an educational system of twenty-one schools, using Sequoyah's Cherokee syllabary to achieve a 90 percent literacy rate in the active language. According to a 1969 Senate report on Indian education, in the 1850s these schools "used bilingual materials to such an extent that Oklahoma Cherokees had a higher English literacy level than the white populations of either Texas or Arkansas."

Soon the federal government moved to dismantle this experiment in Indian bilingual education and to mandate instruction in English only. In 1879 it began separating Indian children from their families and forcing them to attend off-reservation boarding schools. Students were punished when caught speaking their native tongues, or "barbarous dialects," in the words of one federal Indian commissioner. Representative Ben Nighthorse Campbell of Colorado, a member of the Northern Cheyenne tribe, describes the experience: "Both my grandparents were forcibly removed from their homes and placed in boarding schools. One of the first English words Indian students learned was soap, because their mouths were constantly being washed out for using their native language."

This policy coincided with a broader campaign to contain Indians on reservations by repressing their cultures, for example, banning native religious ceremonies and hair braids for Indian men. The rationale was that such "civilizing" measures, including compulsory uses of English, would acclimate nomadic peoples to reservation life. "To teach Indian school children in their native language is practically to exclude English, and to prevent them from acquiring it," declared J. D. C. Atkins, commissioner of Indian affairs, in 1887, "This language, which is good enough for white man and a black man, ought to be good enough for the red man." In defense of the English-only rule, Atkins asked: "Is it cruelty to the Indian to force him to give up his scalping knife and tomahawk? Is it cruelty to force him to abandon the vicious and barbarous sun dance, where he lacerates his flesh, and cancers and tortures himself even unto death!"

The Cherokees' tribal printing press, which had been used to produce native-language teaching materials, again was confiscated. This time it was shipped to Washington, D.C., and put on display at the Smithsonian Institution. Cherokee educational attainment began to decline, by 1969 only 40 percent of the tribe's adults were functionally literate.

In 1934 the Bureau of Indian Affairs rescinded its official policy of repressing Indian vernaculars, although English remained the language of the classroom except in a few mission schools on reservations. Unofficially, punishments for native-language use continued into the 1940s and 1950s, report many Indian educators, testifying from personal experience.

Mexican American students endured similar treatment in the Southwest until even more recently. In the Rio Grande Valley, "Spanish detention," or being kept after school for using Spanish, remained

a formal punishment in the late 1960s, according to an investigation by the U.S. Commission on Civil Rights. One south Texas principal, quoted in the commission's 1972 report, explained the disciplinary policy in this way:

> Our school is predominantly Latin American—97 percent. We try to discourage the use of Spanish on the playground, in the halls, and in the classroom. We feel that the reason so many of our pupils are reading two to three years below grade level is because their English vocabulary is so limited. We are in complete accord that it is excellent to be bilingual or multilingual, but we must . . . stress the fact that practice makes perfect—that English is a very difficult language to master. Our pupils speak Spanish at home, at dances, on the playground, at athletic events. . . . We feel the least they can do is try to speak English at school.

Until 1973 it was a crime in Texas to use a language other than English as the medium of public instruction. The Civil Rights Commission reports that "as recently as October 1970, a Mexican American teacher was indicted in Crystal City, Texas, for conducting a high school history class in Spanish, although the case was subsequently dismissed."

The 'Cultural Deprivation' Era

After World War II, coercion gave way to an emphasis on treating the minority child's "cultural deprivation" and "language disability." Teddy Roosevelt's "military-style assimilation" was replaced by a "missionary style," writes Colman B. Stein, a consultant on immigrant

education now employed by the U.S. Department of Education. "Just as missionaries move in after soldiers have pacified the terrain, educators of the postwar era gradually projected a softer approach to assimilation."

Cultural deprivation theory, which came to dominate educational psychology in the 1950s, rejected genetic explanations for low school achievement by minority children and pointed instead to environmental factors: parents' failure to stress educational attainment, lower-class values that favored "living in the present" rather than planning for the future, and inadequate English language skills. "To make it in American," declared sociologist W. I. Thomas, what these "culturally inferior" children needed most was to master the language and values of the dominant society. The job of the schools, he argued, was to "change their culture," that is, to overcome students' handicaps of ethnic background and enable them to assimilate.

English as a second language (ESL), a methodology developed in the 1930s to meet the needs of foreign diplomats and university students, was now prescribed for language-minority children. "Pull-out classes" were perhaps the most common form of ESL. Students were removed from regular classrooms, typically two to five times a week for a forty-five-minute period of compensatory instruction. Unlike remedial reading, ESL techniques took account of a child's lack of oral English proficiency. Still, its availability was not widespread. In a Civil Rights Commission survey, only 5.5 percent of Mexican American children in California, Arizona, New Mexico, Colorado, and Texas were enrolled in ESL classes in 1968-69 (about half that number were receiving bilingual instruction).

While ESL was an improvement over sink-or-swim language instruction, it was still limited. "By dealing with the student simply as a non-English speaker," the commission observes, "most ESL classes fail to expose children to approaches, attitudes, and materials which take advantage of the rich Mexican American heritage." Educators began to recognize that excluding minority cultures, or providing only "fantasy" stereotypes like "caballeros and senoritas with gardenias behind their ears," was undercutting chidlren's self-image. Instruction that strives to change students "into something else" inevitably discourages academic achievement, notes Josue Gonzalez. "When children are painfully ashamed of who they are, they are not going to do very well in school, whether they be taught monolingually, bilingually, or trilingually."

According to Diego Castellanos, ESL's emphasis on replacing Spanish with English tended to procure "half-lingual children: stutterers in thought, stammerers in spirit." Also, from a strictly academic standpoint, students were learning English too slowly to keep up in other content areas, and so there was little improvement in their long-term outcomes. In the 1960s the dropout rate for Puerto Rican students in New York City was estimated at 60 percent; those who remained were almost automatically assigned to vocational tracks. In 1963 the city's public schools awarded 331 academic diplomas to Puerto Ricans, representing no more than one percent of the total Puerto Rican enrollment; of these graduates, only 28 went on to college.

Meanwhile, based on their performance on IQ tests administered in English, disproportionate numbers of language-minority children ended up in special classes for the educationally handicapped. As late as 1980, Hispanic children in Texas were over-represented by 315 percent in the learning-disabled category.

Bilingual Education Reborn

The renaissance of bilingual education occurred not among Mexican American or Puerto Rican underachievers, but among a relative privileged minority; Cubans who had fled to Miami after the 1959 revolution in their homeland. The early arrivals were Hispanics of European stock, light-skinned, and largely from the professional classes. Proud of their language and culture, they brought with them education and job skills, if little ready cash. Many had taught school in Cuba, and Florida authorities helped them become recertified thorough one of several programs to assist these politically favored refugees.

To serve this group, the Dade County Public Schools provided ESL instruction, and in 1961 it initiated a Spanish-for-Spanish-speakers program. Two years later the district established a full-fledged bilingual program, the first in an American public school in nearly half a century. Launched at the Coral Way Elementary School, the experiment was open to both English and Spanish speakers. It was anything but a compensatory program; the objective was fluent bilingualism for both groups. Pauline Rojas and Ralph Robinett, ESL specialist who had worked in Puerto Rico, directed the effort with the help of well-trained Cuban educators.

Beginning in September 1963, Coral Way's 350 1st, 2nd, and 3rd graders were grouped by language. Cuban children received their morning lessons in Spanish and their afternoon lessons in English; for English-speaking children, the schedule was reversed. During lunch, music, and art, as well as on the playground, the two groups were mixed. Results were immediately promising, as students appeared to progress academically and in both languages. A 1966 report by the district concluded: "The pupils in Coral Way are rapidly becoming 'culturally advantaged:' They are learning to operate effectively in two languages and two cultures."

Indeed, Coral Way was in many respects a success. In English reading, both language groups did as well as or better than their counterparts in monolingual English schools, and the Cuban children achieved equivalent levels in Spanish. The one disappointment was among Anglo students; as a group, they never reached national norms in Spanish reading achievement. "In retrospect," observes psychologist Kenji Hakuta, "the difference between the two groups was not unexpected, since the predominant language of the environment [was] English." The Cuban children had an advantage because, unlike their English-speaking peers, they received high-quality exposure to the second language outside as well as inside the classroom. In any case, Hakuta says, "the feasibility of bilingual education was established." Variants of the Coral Way approach were tried elsewhere in Dade County, and as educators saw its benefits, the "two-way" model spread to other districts (see Chapter 11).

Federal and state bilingual education laws soon followed. Govern-ment intervention changed the focus of the Coral Way experiment, however, from an enrichment model aimed at developing fluency in two languages, to a remedial effort designed to help "disadvantaged" children overcome the "handicap" of not speaking English. From its outset, federal aid to bilin-gual education was regarded as a "poverty program," rather than an innovative approach to language instruction. This decision would shape the development of bilingual programs, and the heated ideological battles surrounding them, over the next two decades.

Notes

1. For example: "Run away . . . from John Orr, Near Skuylkill, Philadelphia, a Servant Man named James Mitchel . . . He has been a Traveller, and can talk Dutch [probably German], Spanish and Irish," and "Run away from Joseph Forman, of New York . . . a Negro Man named JOE. . . . [This] country born, speaks good English and Dutch." Apparently, monolin-gualism was unusual enough to be noteworthy: "Run away from his Master, Theodorus Van Wyck, of Dutches County, in the Province of New York, a Negro Man named JAMES, aged about 22 Years . . . can talk nothing but English, and has a low Voice." These and similar advertisements are cited in Allen Walker Read, "Bilingualism in the Middle Colonies, 1725-1775," American Speech 12 (1973): 93-99.

2. German Americans were the na-tion's largest ethnolinguistic mi-nority in every decennial Census from 1790 to 1960; unfortu-nately, useful figures on lan-guage proficiency are rarely avail-able. In an analysis of the 1790 Census, the American Council of Learned Societies available. In an analysis of the 1790 Census, the American Council of Learned Societies determined that persons of German back-ground represented 8.6 percent of the population of the original thirteen states. See "Report of the Committee on Linguistic and National Stocks in the Population of the United States," in the Annual Report of the American Historical Asso-ciation for the Year 1931, pp. 103-441. By comparison, His-panics made up 7.9 percent of the Association of the Year 1987, according to the Census Bureau.

3. In Observations on the In-crease of Mankind, first publish-ed in 1755 Franklin wrote: "Why should the Palatine Boors be suffered to swarm into our Settlements, and by herding to-gether, establish their Language and Manners, to the Exclusion of ours? Why should Pennsylva-nia, founded by the English, be-come a Colony of Aliens, who will shortly be so numerous as to Germanize us instead of our Anglifying them?" Apparently embarrassed by his outburst of xenophobia, Franklin excised this passage from later editions of his writings. Ironically, in 1738 he had founded one of the earliest German-language news-papers in America. Die Philadel-phische Zeitung, though it soon failed. Toward the end of his life, Franklin became an influential supporter of German-language higher education.

4. The event that generated this confusion was a petition to the U.S. Congress by Virginia Ger-mans who sought the printing of all federal laws in their lan-guage. In 1795 the proposal failed in the House of Repre-sentatives, 42 to 41, with Speaker F. A. Muhlenberg, a Pennsylvania German, casting the deciding vote. Subsequently, numerous federal documents were published in German, but on an ad hoc basis. The tale that German nearly became our offi-cial language apparently origi-nated with 19th century adher-ents of Deutschtum, or German American cultural nationalism, and was given new life by Ri-pley's Believe It or Note in the 1930s. See Heinz Kloss, Ameri-can Bilingual Tradition (Rowley, MA: Newbury House, 1977), 26-33.

5. Seventy years earlier, the British monarchy had rejected a similar scheme by Jonathan Swift, a no-torious language scold who con-demned the "corruptions" of English during the Restoration era. Daniel Defoe, another en-thusiast, favored an English lan-guage academy that would make it "as criminal . . . to coin words as money." Samuel Johnson, however, in the preface to his Dictionary, described the idea of arresting language change by fiat as not only futile but contrary to "the spirit of English liberty." See Albert C. Baugh and Thomas Cable, A History of the English Language, 3rd ed.

(Engelwood Cliffs, NJ: Prentice-Hall, 1978), pp. 254-69.

6. Led by the Industrial Workers of the World, this 1912 strike in Lawrence, Massachusetts, was a watershed event in U.S. labor-management relations. Victorious despite brutal repression, the strikers demonstrated the potential of an unskilled, nonunionized, immigrant workforce composed of many nationalities. Strike meetings were conducted in more than twenty languages.

7. This brought the total to thirty-four states. At the national level, a bill to designate English "the language of instruction in all schools, public and private,"

failed to pass the 66th Congress (1919-20).

8. According to the U.S. Center for Education Statistics, enrollment climbed to 27.7 percent in 1968, but fell to 21.9 percent in 1982 (public schools, grades 9 through 12).

James Crawford is an independent writer in Washington, DC. In addition to Bilingual Education, his books include Hold Your Tongue: Bilingualism and the Politics of "English Only" (Addison-Wesley, 1992) and Language Loyalties: A Source Book on the Official English Controversy (edited volume, University of Chicago Press, 1992). Previously he served as Washington edidtor of Education Week and Congressionall editor of the Federal Times.

Abigail Thernstrom presents a point against bilingual education. She believes that students in bilingual programs have fallen through the cracks. She emphasizes that students need to learn English in order to get jobs, and that schools should transmit the national culture of the United States.

Bilingual Miseducation

Abigail M. Thernstrom

The New York State Board of Regents has recently voted a 74 percent increase in the number of children eligible for the state's bilingual program. Thousands of new students will now be assigned to classes in which instruction is in a language identified as "native" to them-although many of these children will actually be more fluent in English.

In New York, Massachusetts, and elsewhere, students in such "bilingual" classes are often taught by teachers who have been recruited abroad or know little English. If the students are, say, Puerto Rican, they will learn about Puerto Rico; by ninth grade, Abraham Lincoln may mean nothing to them but they will know that the River Culbrinas is a small tributary in the northwest corner of the island. The Bush administration seems committed to these programs. In fact, as part of an evident shift in federal policy, Bush's Secretary of Education, Lauro Cavazos, has appointed a former Hispanic lobbyist to head the department's bilingual-education program.

A heightened commitment to bilingual education on the part of the federal government-sending an important signal to states and local school districts-is hardly what William J. Bennett, as Secretary of Education under Ronald Reagan, had planned. Nor is it what his immediate predecessor had hoped for. One of Terrel Bell's first acts in 1981 was to revise the "unworkable and incredibly costly" bilingual-education regulations put in place in the Carter years.

But perhaps the revived commitment under Bush should come as no surprise. Legislative and administrative action in the realm of civil rights usually has a ratchet effect; backward movement is seldom possible. To return to former ways is read as reneging on a promise. This is the lesson that the Reagan administration was slow to learn but that the Bush administration understands. Since almost all pressure on civil-rights issues comes from the Left, reconsidering any program that touches on "minority rights" is always politically risky. Little is likely to be gained from it—little, that is, in the way of political benefit.

Bilingual education is unusual in that there is actually an organized group opposed to it: U.S. English. But that organization is generally no match for Hispanic and other lobbyists both inside and outside school systems. These advocates know how to mobilize parents and other allies and they stand ready to brand all critics as morally suspect. Thus, in California a measure declaring English to be the official language passed by a margin of three to one in 1986, but the Hispanic leadership blocked state-legislative efforts to enforce the provision. Educational policy was left in local hands, and in both Los Angeles and San Francisco Hispanic activists outside the school system and bilingual teachers and administrators within were able to keep bilingual programs in place.

As a national Commitment, bilingual education is just over twenty years old. But the idea had an earlier life. In the 19th century, Cincinnati, St. Louis, and other communities provided instruction in the public schools in the native tongue of non-English-speaking immigrants. These programs, however,

were strictly local in nature and were never promoted by professional ethnic activists with a moral message to convey.

The Bilingual Education Act of 1968, on the other hand, was the product of its racially conscious time. Witnesses at the congressional hearings on the bill in 1967 were (by and large) ethnic spokesmen and the arguments they made were couched in civil-rights terms. To be sure, the statute did differ from earlier civil-rights acts in one respect: Hispanics, not blacks, were the focus of concern. But Mexican-Americans and other Hispanics were considered "black-like" in the disadvantages they experienced.

The dropout rate for Hispanic students was appallingly high, congressional witnesses argued. The median number of years of schooling completed by Spanish-surnamed adults was half that of Anglos and considerably below that of blacks. In fact, many had no schooling at all. "The fault lies with our educational system," declared Senator Thomas Kuchel of California.

But the fault did not lie entirely with the American educational system: a larger proportion of the Spanish-surnamed adults to whom the Senator referred had been born and raised in Mexico. Nevertheless, bilingual education was said to be the solution. It would, advocates were confident, solve the special educational problems of Hispanic and other children with limited English-speaking ability.

The argument was, first, that bilingual education would allow these children to acquire basic skills and other knowledge at the proper time. In regular classrooms, the Hispanic child with only limited English inevitably fell behind. But if, for ex-

ample, first-grade math were taught in Spanish, it could be learned in first grade.

Second, it was claimed that Spanish, being written as it sounds, was easier to learn than English. Therefore, for the Spanish-speaking child the fastest route to English literacy was actually through Spanish. The child who learned to read and write in the simpler language could transfer those skills to the more difficult one.

The third and most important point of the argument was that bilingual education would make these children feel good about themselves. It would provide an educational environment that honored the culture from which the children came and would thereby foster the self-esteem so crucial to learning.

In this way, the perspective of the radical black-power movement of the mid-1960's was transferred to Hispanics and other linguistic minorities. According to the Supreme Court in Brown v. Board of Education (1954): "To separate [children] from others of similar age and qualifications solely because of their race generates a feeling of inferiority . . . that may affect their hearts and minds in a way unlikely ever to be undone." Black militants turned that contention around: to assimilate children into an alien culture, they said, creates feelings of inferiority. But on this particular issue they made relatively few converts among white liberals. Hispanic activists, by contrast, adopted the same argument and got white liberals to go along.

Indeed, those who spoke at the congressional hearings on bilingual education in 1967 were close to unanimous in rejecting assimilation as an ideal. To "melt" immigrant children had once been central to the mission of public schools. But now the U.S. commissioner of Education urged Americans to abandon the image of the melting pot and substitute that of a mosaic. Congressman James H. Scheuer of New York echoed the sentiment. "I think we have discarded the philosophy of the melting pot," he said. "We have a new concept of the value of enhancing, fortifying, and protecting [people's] differences, the very differences, that make our country [so] vital . . ."

Congressional liberals and witnesses had thus taken a point that was perhaps psychologically sound but culturally and politically problematic—that blacks could and should maintain separate institutions and distinct values—and by applying it to other groups had transformed it into a contention that was psychologically dubious but culturally and politically possible. That is, the psychological damage to blacks had been real, but he proposed remedy—reviving and maintaining a distinct and segregated culture—was impossible: blacks were Americans. But at least for certain sectors of the Hispanic community the problem was the reverse. At the hearings, no one claimed that the psychological damage to Mexican-Americans or Puerto Ricans was equal to that experienced by blacks. But the fact that these groups had close ties to Mexico and to the island made cultural maintenance much more viable.

The Bilingual Education Act, signed into law in January 1968, committed the federal government to supporting some form of bilingual education in school districts that wanted it. Nothing, of course,

had stopped districts from instituting bilingual programs before, and indeed, early in the decade Dade County, Florida, had begun to offer instruction in Spanish to Cuban refugee children. Other jurisdictions in scattered states—New Mexico and California, among them—had followed suit. What is more, some federal assistance was already available. But sponsors of the legislation were worried that, without the spur of additional federal dollars, the number of such programs would remain small. If bilingual education were really to take hold, proponents were convinced, separate and specific funding would be needed, and with the passage of the Act that is what they got.

The provision of funds was clear. But for what sort of instruction was the money to be used? The Act was quite vague. Technically the legislation was an amendment to Title VII of the Elementary and Secondary Education Act (ESEA), although congress did specify that it could be cited as the "Bilingual Education Act." Yet neither in its "Findings" nor in its "Declaration of Policy" did the statute refer specifically to bilingual instruction. Instead, mention was made of "special educational needs" and the necessity for "new and imaginative programs." Given the inattention to educational details in the hearings, the lack of specificity was understandable. The whole enterprise rested on conclusions that could hardly be called considered educational judgements.

In 1974, when the Act was renewed and altered, its purposes were much more clearly stated, and several important changes were made. For instance, bilingual education was no longer depicted as ex-

perimental; its efficacy was now assumed. And while Title VII had initially spoken simply of the need to fund "new and imaginative" programs, the policy in 1974 had become "to encourage the establishment and operation, where appropriate, of educational programs using bilingual practices . . ."

But bilingual instruction now meant instruction using the native language, with perhaps a bit of English thrown in sometime during the day. And it meant education in the native culture as well. "A primary means by which a child learns is through the use of such child's language and cultural heritage," the amendments stated.

The addition of the cultural component was significant. In the 1967 hearings Congress has agreed on the importance of "fortifying"—not simply respecting—cultural differences, but it had stopped short of taking concrete action to realize that unprecedented (and, one would have hoped, controversial) goal. Now, in 1974, the federal government turned its back on the notion that bilingual instruction would be used simply as a means of temporarily sheltering children from the shock of school in an unfamiliar language and became firmly committed to programs that encouraged Hispanic children to see themselves as a group apart—permanently culturally distinct.

The number of children eligible to participate in federally supported bilingual instruction was now also greatly expanded. In 1968 Title VII had funded programs for children from low-income families only—in keeping with the rest of the ESEA. Limited proficiency in English, sponsors of the legislation had assumed, was only a handicap in the context of broader disadvantage. In 1974 that link between linguistic and economic disadvantage was severed. Middle-class children could now participate in federally supported programs. So could certain children whose primary language was English.

For a school system, more children might mean more federal funds. More children also meant more parents and more bilingual teachers and administrators—in short, an expanded lobby. Bilingual education was well on its way to becoming an addition to that confederation of groups of employees, each with its own clientele, that we innocently call an educational system.

This process was pushed along by a number of judicial decisions, the most important of which was Lau v. Nichols, a 1974 Supreme Court ruling. Although, of all groups, Asians have generally been the least eager for bilingual instruction, Lau was a suit brought by the parents of Chinese students with no English in San Francisco. Other Chinese students in the city were getting special help; they wanted it, too. They won their case in a decision that rested not on constitutional but on statutory grounds—specifically on a guideline issued by the Department of Health, Education, and Welfare (HEW) to clarify the meaning of Title VI of the 1964 Civil Rights Act. Title VI had banned discrimination in programs receiving federal funds, and HEW had said that a child who could not understand the instruction in a classroom was experiencing discrimination on the basis of national origin. In the view of the Court, the interpretive guideline, although formulated by an administrative

agency, was part of the legislative Act and the Chinese students were therefore entitled to help.

The court had declined to specify the form that help should take, but HEW was quick to break the silence. In 1975 the agency issued additional guidelines. (According to the Court, HEW in its enforcement capacity spoke for Congress. Did it also speak for the Justices? And could subsequent judicial decisions then be based not on their own ruling but on HEW's version of that ruling?) The new guidelines threatened to deny federal funds to any school that had more than twenty students with limited English and yet failed to provide bilingual-bicultural instruction. Schools that did not want such a program could come up with another, equally effective remedy. But since no one knew how effective the standard "transitional" bilingual education" was, it was exceedingly hard to prove that another approach could be considered its equal.

The plaintiffs in Lau had been Chinese-Americans, but Hispanics had won. The Chinese-American community had run after-school and other privately funded programs but had never had an interest in the preservation of ethnic identity by means of public support. What it had wanted was help with English—access to what was being taught. The Hispanics, for their part, had consistently made quite a different argument: that pride was the key to academic success and that the promotion of pride demanded not help with English but a reinforcement of the Spanish language and Hispanic culture. This was the argument that HEW's new guidelines reflected.

The Lau decision not only defined bilingual education as a right, further empowering ethnic activists, but helped to expand the number of language groups for whom bilingual education was provided. In 1974 only 23 language groups were served and Hispanics got 80 percent of the funding. But Lau suggested that all children with a limited ability to understand English were entitled to help, and by 1978 the number of such language groups had risen to 70. (The figure is now 145.)

What with federal and state statutes, and what with judicial decisions and regulations interpreting those statutes for purposes of enforcement, the bilingual plot is very thick. Are the students for whom all this has been put in place in fact benefiting? Has instruction in a native language given the students a leg up—as promised? Governor Mario Cuomo of New York has declared bilingual education to be "extremely successful in helping students to learn English." He sounds the right liberal notes, but is he right?

Scholars and others who have posed this question have often met with resistance from bilingual-education partisans, who have mounted what Rosalie Pedalino Porter calls in a forthcoming study a "shrill campaign against any alternative programs." In 1978 the director of the U.S. Office of Bilingual Education even maintained that bilingual education could not be evaluated. "It is a philosophy," he said. And so it was and is. A sense of cultural sin, not educational failing, was the driving force behind the original Act. And the conviction that an ethnocentric society must mend its ways still informs much of the discussion of bilingual programs.

Indeed, not everyone agrees even on the importance of learning English. For instance, at a public meeting this past October, Adelaide Sandord, a member of the New York State Board of Regents, reportedly dismissed the importance of learning the nation's language. A lot of people who speak English are not successful, she is said to have noted.

True enough, but is the converse of this proposition—the issue at stake—true as well? Without English, the prospects for success are slim. And on that score, the record of bilingual education —in its usual "transitional form—is not good.

In the first place, there is too often nothing transitional about "transitional" bilingual education. A 1985 Massachusetts Board of Education study reported that substantial numbers of Hispanic children remained in bilingual classrooms for six or more years. In general, children are kept in the programs until they can perform successfully in regular classes. For many children that day is long in coming. Since they are not usually taught much English, they never learn it.

Furthermore, Christine Rossell, one of the country's leading experts on bilingual education, has painstakingly tabulated the findings of studies that have evaluated bilingual and other methods of teaching limited-English-proficient children. Her conclusion: 71 percent of the studies show transitional bilingual education to be no different from or actually worse than doing nothing.

Similarly, in math achievement, 93 percent of the studies show bilingual programs to have either negative effects or no effects at all. As for social studies and other such subjects, too often the children in bilingual classes are not even exposed to the material that others get.

It is no secret to American businesses that the graduates of bilingual programs are inadequately educated. Striking evidence has recently been reported by Con Edison, New York. All applicants for entry-level jobs are required to pass an aptitude test in English. In 1988, 7,000 applicants, primarily from New York city schools, were tested and only 4,000 passed. The personnel manager checked the results and discovered, to her dismay, that not one product of the city's bilingual-education program was among those who had passed. The company also participated in a pilot program in a bilingual school in the Bronx. All the students with limited English from the program failed Con Edison's most basic test.

No wonder, then, that Motorola and other businesses are spending substantial sums to teach their employees to speak, read, and write English. By 1992 Motorola alone expects to have spent some $30 million on a program begun just three years ago. Many professional educators apparently do not realize it, but even low-level jobs require a reasonable command of English.

There are additional reasons for questioning the wisdom of continuing to offer "transitional" bilingual education. According to federal statistics, as many as 60 percent of the children to whom it is offered are not in need of a "transition" to English since English is already their best language. These children have been assigned to bilingual classes perhaps because someone in the household speaks Spanish or because they fall, say, below the 40th percentile on a standardized test. But of course lots of children who know only English do badly on such tests.

In addition, teachers are in short supply. In New York, advocates have charged that local school boards are simply refusing to fill bilingual-teaching positions. The teachers, they claim, are there for the asking. But the evidence suggests otherwise. Yes, teacher-certification requirements can be lowered or waived. Both are being done. And teachers can be recruited from other cities and other countries. That too is regularly tried. Los Angeles, for instance, frequently looks for bilingual teachers in New York. Many systems—including New York's—have sent emissaries to foreign ports to search for staff. And often they find them. But that process raises another question: are children being properly served when their teachers may be unqualified and speak only the most halting English?

If teachers are recruited abroad, the books and workbooks they use in class will often be imported as well. They will rely on the material with which they are comfortable— the material they know how to teach. In a class of Hispanic children, a Puerto Rican teacher will teach about Puerto Rico, using books from the island. The consequence is that the children are likely to learn almost nothing about American culture. And what happens to the two students in the room from the dominican Republic and the three from El Salvador, the supposed reinforcement of whose cultural identity takes the form of lessons in Puerto Rican history and culture?

Beyond all this, the "transitional" bilingual programs are expensive, as the New York State supervisor of bilingual education has admitted. U.S. English estimates that the revised New York plan will add $62 million per year to the state's current annual cost of $21.7 million—at a time of fiscal austerity. Nor is there anything distinctively expensive about providing such education in the Empire State. In Boston, in 1987-88, the per-pupil annual expenditure for students in the regular program was $4,340. The bilingual pupils cost $5,492.

Finally, bilingual classes amount to segregated education. Those who monitor desegregation plans count ethnic and racial heads in a school and pretend that the presence of Hispanic and other language-minority children counts toward integration. Yet there is often little that is integrated about the education of these students. The students may dabble in paints and dribble a ball together but, for most of the day, a bilingual classroom in a school within a school—a world apart.

The cumulative impact of these problems has inspired some second thoughts. Thus, when Congress reauthorized the Bilingual Education Act in 1988, it raised the level of allowable funding for such alternative approaches as ESL (teaching English as a second language) and structured immersion (immersion in English with a teacher who knows the student's native tongue). Prior to that time, 96 percent of the federal grants had gone to the standard "transitional" form of bilingual education—a form that, besides not being transitional, is rarely bilingual either, since English is

often barely in evidence. Today, up to 25 percent of the funds can go to support alternative programs that are judged worthwhile.

Have these congressional second thoughts made a difference? Not much, since local school districts still have enormous discretion with respect to both staffing and student placement. To make matters worse, while William Bennett, in his years as Secretary of Education, did try to change federal bilingual policy, Secretary Cavazos, as already noted, has chosen to hew to the Hispanic line. For the Bush administration, which clearly wishes to cover all political bases, Cavazo's position undoubtedly comes as a relief. For the students in the programs, Republican prudence is their educational loss.

Children in bilingual programs are too often set up to fail. Not all children in all programs, to be sure. There are important exceptions—classrooms in which good teachers ignore the rules, follow their instincts, and provide excellent education. These are school districts that have structured sensible programs to help children really in need—Rochester, New York, being one. But in too many schools, children with limited English start and end their academic life without the basic skills they need if they are ever to thrive.

The Hispanic children fare the worst. Cambodian and Vietnamese, among others, are often luckier: the schools they attend frequently cannot find native-language teachers and are forced to offer English-based instruction. As a result, only Hispanic children "benefit" from the bilingual approach.

Cavazos has recently reassured the National Association of Bilin-

gual Education (to much applause) that "the sink-or-swim days of learning English are over" and must never come back. But no one is advocating their return—not even U.S. English. No one wants to go back to the days in which bewildered and often ridiculed immigrant chidren were left entirely to their own devices. Everyone agrees that children who speak little or no English can benefit from special language instruction. The question is the form that help should take.

This is an educational question. Bilingual education has been a part of a political agenda, and the children whom the programs are supposed to serve have fallen through the cracks. Proponents often seem almost indifferent to the educational needs of these children. The proponents argue that building self-esteem is the first step to learning, and they define enhanced self-esteem as the feeling which comes from knowing one's own ethnic identity. It is a circular argument and it neglects the point that a sense of self-worth is most likely to result from concrete achievements. The child who stare blankly at one of the standard English achievement tests year after year can only feel defeat.

Such a child will learn English only is he is taught it. And there are plenty of hand-holding ways to teach English. Berkeley, California, for instance, last year prevailed in a case in which the relatively heavy use of English in its bilingual program, and the choice it gave to parents to place their children in ESL classes instead, were both challenged. The school system convinced the federal district court that its English-based instruction had yielded good results.

Interviewed recently in the New York Times, a new arrival from the Soviet Union voiced the frustration that all immigrants feel. "Without English," he said, "we cannot work, and without work, we are nowhere." But of course. It is time for educational "experts" to catch on to what most newcomers have always known.

Nor it is enough for children to master only the language of the country in which they live; they also need to learn about its culture. It is exhilarating to work into a school alive with a sense of the wider world. But it is dismaying to visit a classroom in which one feels in a foreign land. In transmitting national values that transcended ethnic lines, schools traditionally served an integrative function. They still can, and they still should.

Abigail M. Thernstrom is the author of the prizewinning Whose Votes Count? Affirmative Action and Minority Voting Rights (Harvard University Press).

Reprinted from COMMENTARY, February 1990, by permission; all rights reserved.

Most discussions about bilingual education have centered on problems that non-English speakers encounter in U.S. schools. Some research, stresses the cognitive advantages of knowing more than one language and culture. Are bilingual people smarter then their monolingual peers? Baker explores this idea.

Bilingualism and Intelligence

Introduction

There is one piece of advice that parents sometimes receive from well-meaning teachers, doctors, speech therapists, school psychologists and other professionals. Don't raise your child bilingually or problems will result. Predicted problems range from bilingualism as a burden on the brain, mental confusion, inhibition of the acquisition of the majority language, even split personality. Parents and teachers are sometimes advised to use only one language with individual children. When children persist in speaking two languages in school, having their mouths washed with soap and water (Isaacs, 1976) and being beaten with a cane for speaking Welsh (the Welsh 'Not') have been offered as a remedy.

A quotation from a Professor at Cambridge University portrays this deficit viewpoint:

If it were possible for a child to live in two languages at once equally well, so much the worse. His intellectual and spiritual growth would not thereby be doubled, but halved. Unity of mind and character would have great difficulty in asserting itself in such circumstances. (Laurie, 1890: p. 15)

. . . Does the ownership of two languages interfere with efficient thinking? Do monolinguals have more effective thinking quarters? Is a bilingual less intelligent than a monolingual due to a dual language system? . . . We start by considering the relationship between intelligence and bilingualism. 'Intelligence' has been a major concept in psychology and often related to bilingualism. It is also a term used by members of the public in phrasing questions about bilingualism.

Bilingualism and 'Intelligence'

The Period of Detrimental Effects

From the early nineteenth century to approximately the 1960s, the dominant belief amongst academics was that bilingualism had a detrimental effect on thinking. For example, the quote from Professor Laurie (1890) suggested that a bilingual's intellectual growth would not be doubled by being bilingual. Rather both intellectual and spiritual growth would be halved. This view of Laurie (1890) tends to parallel a view commonly held amongst the British and US populace right through the twentieth century: that bilingualism has disadvantages rather than advantages in terms of thinking.

The early research on bilingualism and cognition tended to confirm this negative viewpoint, finding that monolinguals were superior to bilinguals on mental tests (Darcy, 1953). Research up to 1960s looked at this issue through one concept—'intelligence'. A typical piece of research gave bilinguals and monolinguals an 'intelligence' test. When bilinguals and monolinguals were compared on their IQ scores, particularly on verbal IQ, the usual result was that bilinguals were behind monolinguals. An example of this early research is by a Welsh researcher, D.J. Saer (1923). He gathered a sample of 1,400 children age seven to fourteen from bilingual and monolingual backgrounds. A 10 point difference in IQ was found between bilinguals and monolingual English speakers from the rural areas of Wales.

Saer (1923, p. 53) concluded that bilinguals were mentally confused and at a disadvantage in thinking compared with monolinguals. Further research by Saer, Smith & Hughes (1924) suggested that University student monolinguals were superior to bilinguals: "the difference in mental ability as revealed by intelligence tests is of a permanent nature since it persists in students throughout their University career."

While it is possible that situations exist where bilinguals will perform on such tests at a lower level than monolinguals, . . . the early research that pointed to detrimental effects has a series of weaknesses. Such weaknesses tend to invalidate the research in terms of individual studies and cumulatively across studies. These limitations may be listed as follows.

Definition

The concept of 'intelligence' and the use of intelligence tests is controversial and hotly debated. One part of the controversy lies in the problems of defining and measuring intelligence. The underlying questions are: what is intelligence and who is intelligent? A thief who cracks a bank vault? A famous football coach? Someone poor who becomes a billionaire? Don Juan? A chairperson who manipulates the members of a board? Is there social intelligence, musical intelligence, military intelligence, marketing intelligence, motoring intelligence, political intelligence? Are all, or indeed any of these forms of intelligence measured by a simple pencil and paper IQ test which requires a single, acceptable, correct solution to each question? What is intelligent behavior or not requires a subjective value judgement as to the kind of behavior and the kind of person regarded as of more worth.

Language of Testing

The second problem is the language of the IQ test given to bilinguals. It is preferable to test the IQ of bilinguals in their stronger language or in both languages. In the early research, many verbal IQ tests were administered in English only. This tended to be to the disadvantage of bilinguals in that they were tested in their weaker language and thus under-performed in the IQ test.

Matched Groups

The final problem is particularly important. To compare a group of bilingual children with monolinguals on IQ, or on any other measure of cognitive ability, requires that the two groups be equal in all other respects. The only difference between the two groups should be in their bilingualism and monolingualism. If such control does not occur, then the results of the research may be due to the other factor or factors on which the groups differ (rather than their monolingualism or bilingualism). Take the example of a monolingual group being mostly of higher socioeconomic status, and the bilingual group being mostly of a lower socioeconomic status. A result (e.g. showing monolinguals to be ahead of bilinguals) may be due to social class rather than, or as well as, bilingualism. The great majority of researches on bilingualism and 'intelligence' failed to match the groups on other factors that might explain the results. It is necessary to match the groups on variables such as sociocultural class, gender, age, type of school attended and urban/rural and subtractive/additive environment.

Conclusion

The period of detrimental effects research lasted from approximately the 1920s to the 1960s. While the dominant result was that bilinguals were inferior to monolinguals, particularly on verbal IQ, these early researchers share many serious methodological weaknesses. Singly and cumulatively, the early research on bilingualism and IQ has so many limitations and methodological flaws that its conclusion of detrimental effects cannot be accepted. While it is possible that, in some contexts, bilinguals may have cognitive advantages, the early research cannot be used to support this claim. Indeed, . . . different conclusions may better reflect the current state of research.

The Period of Neutral Effects

There are a series of researches that reported no difference between bilinguals and monolinguals in IQ. For example, research in the United States by Pintner and Arsenian (1937) found a zero correlation (no relationship) between verbal (and non-verbal) IQ and Yiddish-English bilingualism/monolingualism. While the number of researches with a 'no difference' conclusion is small in number, the period of neutral effects is important because it highlighted the inadequacies of the early detrimental effects research. An example is the research by W.R. Jones (1959) in Wales. Using 2,500 children aged 10 and 11, Jones (1959) initially found that bilinguals were inferior to monolinguals on IQ. A re-analysis showed that this conclusion was invalid. After taking into account the varying socioeconomic class of bilinguals and monolinguals, Jones (1959) concluded that monolinguals and bilinguals did not differ significantly in non-verbal IQ so long as parental occupation was taken into account. He also concluded that socioeconomic class largely accounts for previous research that reported the inferiority of bilinguals on non-verbal IQ. Therefore, his conclusion was that bilingualism is not necessarily a source of intellectual disadvantage.

While the period of neutral effects overlaps chronologically with the detrimental and additive periods, there was a period when (in Wales, for example) such neutral effects were taught and publicized. Such a 'neutral' conclusion was historically important as it gave a boost to parents who wished to support bilingualism in the home and in the school. As a transitional period, it both helped to question a fashionable belief of bilingualism as cerebral confusion, and became a herald for the additive effects period.

The Period of Additive Effects

A major turning point in the history of the relationship between bilingualism and cognition was reached in Canadian research by Peal & Lambert (1962). It is this piece of research that heralded in the modern approach to bilingualism and cognitive functioning. This research broke new territory in three respects, each setting the pattern for future research.

First, the research overcame many of the methodological deficiencies of the period of detrimental effects. Second, the research found evidence that bilingualism need not have detrimental or even neutral consequences. Rather, there is the possibility that bilingualism leads to cognitive advantages over monolingualism. Peal & Lambert's (1962) finding has been widely quoted to support a variety of bilingual policies in various educational contexts. The political implication of the study was that bilingualism within a country was not a source of national intellectual inferiority (Reynolds, 1991). Third, the research by Peal & Lambert (1962), while using IQ tests, moved research to a . . . broader look at cognition. Other areas of mental activity apart from IQ were placed firmly on the agenda for research into bilingualism and cognitive functioning.

Peal & Lambert (1962) commenced with a sample of 364 children age 10 years old drawn form middle-class French schools in Montreal, Canada. The original sample of 364 children reduced to 110 children for two reasons. First, to create a group of balanced bilinguals . . . and a group of monolinguals. Second, to ensure that the bilingual and monolingual groups were matched on socioeconomic class.

Bilinguals performed significantly higher on 15 out of 18 variable measuring IQ. On the other three variables, there was no difference between balanced bilinguals and monolinguals. Peal & Lambert (1962) concluded that bilingualism provides: greater mental flexibility; the ability to think more abstractly, more independently of words, providing superiority in concept formation; that a more enriched bilingual and bicultural environment benefits the development of IQ; and that there is a positive transfer between a bilingual's two languages facilitating the development of verbal IQ.

These conclusions are historically more important than the specific results concerning IQ. That is, it is analysis of the results rather than the details of the results that provided the stimulus for further research and debate.

This completes the examination of Peal & Lambert's (1962) important and pivotal study. Since their research, the dominant approach to bilingualism and cognitive functioning has moved away from IQ testing to a multi-component view of intelligence and cognition. Although there are researches after Peal & Lambert (1962) that examine IQ and bilingualism, most recent studies look at bilingualism in terms of a range of thinking styles, strategies and skills.

Bilingualism and the Brain

A dominant topic in the study of bilingualism and the brain is lateralization. In the majority of right-handed adults, the left hemisphere of the brain is dominant for language processing. The question has naturally arisen as to whether bilinguals are different from monolinguals in this left lateralization? Vaid & Hall (1991) provide a review of this topic in terms of five propositions derived from existing research:

(1) Balanced bilinguals will use the right hemisphere more than monolinguals for first and second language processing.

(2) Second language acquisition will involve the right hemisphere in language processing more than first language acquisition.

(3) As proficiency in a second language grows, right hemisphere involvement will decrease and left hemisphere involvement will increase. This assumes that the right hemisphere is concerned with the more immediate, pragmatic and emotive aspects of language; the left hemisphere with the more analytic

aspects of language (e.g. syntax). That is, the core aspects of language processing are assumed to reside in the left hemisphere.

(4) Those who acquire a second language naturally (e.g. on the street) will use their right hemisphere more for language processing that those who learn a second language formally (e.g. in the language classroom). Learning rules about grammar, spelling and irregular verbs will result in more left hemisphere involvement in second language learning. Picking up a language in a natural manner and using it for straightforward communication will involve more right hemisphere involvement.

(5) Late bilinguals will be more likely to use the right hemisphere than early bilinguals. This proposition states that there might be a "predominance of a left-hemisphere 'semantic-type' strategy in early bilinguals and for a right hemisphere 'acoustic-type' strategy in late bilinguals" (Vaid & Hall, 1991, p. 90).

Using a quantitative procedure called meta-analysis to review previous research in this area, Vaid & Hall (1991) found that the left hemisphere strongly dominated language processing for both monolinguals and bilinguals. However, differences between monolinguals and bilinguals were the exception rather than the rule. Bilinguals did not seem to vary from monolinguals in neuropsychological processes; the lateralization of language of the two groups being relatively similar.

"The largely negative finding form the meta-analysis must be taken seriously as reflecting a general lack of support for the five hypotheses as they have been addressed in the literature to date" (Vaid & Hall, 1991, p. 104).

While the relationship between the brain and bilingualism is an important area, the present state of knowledge makes generalization unsafe, but an area where future research holds some promise.

References

Darcy, N.T. (1953). A review of the literature on the effects of bilingualism upon the measurement of Intelligence. *Journal of Genetic Psychology* 82, 21-57.

Isaacs, E., (1976). *Greed children in Sydney*. Canberra: Australian National University Press.

Jones, W.R. (1959). *Bilingualism and intelligence*. Cardiff: University of Wales.

Laurie, S.S. (1890). *Lectures on language and linguistic method in school*. Cambridge: Cambridge University Press.

Peal, E. & Lambert, W.E. (1962). The relationship of bilingualism

to intelligence. *Psychological Monographs* 76(27), 1-23.

Pintner, R. & Arsenian, S. (1937). The relation of bilingualism to verbal intelligence and school adjustment. *Journal of Educational Research* 31, 255-263.

Reynolds, A.G. (1991). The cognitive consequences of bilingualism. In A.G. Reynolds (ed.) *Bilingualism, multiculturalism and second language learning*. Hillsdale, NJ: Lawrence Erlbaum.

Saer, D.J. (1923). The effects of bilingualism on intelligence. *British Journal of Psychology* 14, 25-38.

Saer, D.J., Smith, F. & Hughes J. (1924). *The bilingual problem*. Wrexham: Hughes & Son.

Vaid, J. & Hall, D.G. (1991). Neuropsychological perspectives on bilingualism: Right, left and center. In A.G. Reynolds (ed.) *Bilingualism, multiculturalism and second language learning*. Hillsdale, NJ: Lawrence Erlbaum.

Extracted and reprinted from Baker, Colin (1993). "Bilingualism and intelligence" Foundations of Bilingual Education, with permission from Multilingual Matters Ltd.

The road to a comprehensive language policy for the United States has been hard, rocky, and not yet complete. Language as an integral part of a person's culture can easily be used to denigrate or validate one's sense of being. U.S. language policies related to Spanish groups in general and to Puerto Rico in particular are explored here.

English Only Jamas

Juan Cartagena

Gobernar es poblar' . . . Will the present majority peaceably hand over its political power to a group that is simply more fertile?

The words noted above were written in 1986 by John Tanton,[1] co-founder of U.S. English, Inc., the largest and wealthiest supporter of the recent wave of legislation declaring English the only language states can use in government operations. They were written in a discussion of the effects that immigrants would have on the quality of life in the U.S. But make no mistake about it, in the context of the language policy debate raging in the 1980s, they were written about Puerto Ricans as well.

The Puerto Rican experience in the U.S. forced a confrontation between the promises of equality and non-discrimination and the boundaries of U.S. language policy. Puerto Ricans positively shaped language policy and transformed it into a discussion of language rights.

The bilingual assistance provisions in the Voting Rights Act, the court decisions mandating bilingual/bicultural education, the constitutional guarantees of bilingual interpreters in criminal proceedings, and a plethora of Spanish language notices, letters and materials regarding government entitlements are unique Puerto Rican contributions to U.S. language policy. Throughout, the community struggles of parents and activists were guided by certain elements: the full preservation of our language and culture and the fulfillment of non-discrimination on the basis of language. And yet as any puertorriqueño knows, that struggle was far from over in the 1980s. Schools refused to appropriately implement what the law mandated; interpreters were rarely trained; the franchise was devalued and access to political power continued to be elusive. For the modern-day language restrictionists, however, the struggle was just beginning in the 1980s.

Invisible in many other aspects of control over their socio-economic status, Puerto Ricans have been largely ignored in the current national language debate. This omission must be rectified. Once the rhetoric of the language restrictionists is shed, the true issue turns on a question of political empowerment: Will Puerto Ricans and others be allowed to shape their own avenues of access to and control over governmental services in languages they can understand? And will the white, majoritarian society "peaceably" continue to accommodate anything other than English? Only a closer look at the historic and idiosyncratic Puerto Rican experience can point us in the right direction.

Language Policy in Puerto Rico

Another important fact that must not be overlooked is that a majority of the people of this island does not speak pure Spanish. Their language is a patois almost unintelligible to the natives of Barcelona and Madrid. It possesses no literature and little value as intellectual medium.–Dr. William W. Clark, President of the Insular Board of Education in Puerto Rico, 1899. [2]

At the time of the U.S. takeover of the island of Puerto Rico in 1898, Spanish had served as the Island's national language for some 390 years. From the start, programs and policies designed to Americanize its war-booty were instituted by the United States. This process has also been described as Anglicization, or the conversion of the language of the Puerto Rican people from Spanish to English. [3] This was the first taste of U.S. language policy for Puerto Ricans within a colonial relationship.

Specific enactments, as in the area of public education, presaged strained relations between the Island and Washington, resulting in confusion for many Puerto Rican youngsters. With the teaching of Spanish and English occupying from one-fifth to one-half of the educational program, language, and not subject-matter content, was the primary emphasis in these schools. [4]

Consistent with Dr. Clark's ignorant perception of Puerto Rican "patois," Spanish was first relegated to a mere subject in Puerto Rican schools and then marked for elimination altogether. This scheme was apparent from Congressional pronouncements that Puerto Rico could not be trusted to operate its own Department of Education (for fear that English would not be taught) to Commissioner of Education Paul Miller's directive to the police, when seeing a Puerto Rican flag at a graduation, to "remove the enemy flag." [5]

The result of this policy on Puerto Rico's schools became clear. In succeeding stages, Puerto Rican students were buffeted between instructional policies which mandated English, Spanish or both to be the medium of instruction. For example, English became the medium of instruction overnight after the U.S. invasion. From 1900 through 1904 both languages were used. Subsequently, differentiations appeared within grade levels. Thus, Spanish became the medium in elementary grades only, followed by English as the medium from 1905-1916. Differentiation among grades continued with Spanish as the medium from 1916-1934 for only the first four grades. Spanish then reassumed its dominant position in all elementary grades through 1937. Its domination did not survive as both languages were used as the mode of instruction until the late 1940s.

By the mid-1940s, the language policies of Puerto Rico's schools became intertwined with the political question of the status of Puerto Rico. [6] Time and again the Puerto Rican community, its teachers, universities and legislature attempted to implement the use of Spanish as the medium of instruction. Each time, the attempt was thwarted. In fact, in 1946 the legislature of Puerto Rico enacted such legislation only to be vetoed by President Truman. This was the only piece of legislation originating in Puerto Rico ever vetoed by an American President. [7] With the 1947 amendments to the Organic Law, Puerto Rico finally gained "control" of its system of education and in 1949 Spanish became the medium of instruction.

The U.S. has thus had an experiment with foisting English Only upon a population in Puerto Rico which soundly rejected it. This episode was not without losses: erosion of some of our culture as students were forced to learn of George Washington and the Star Spangled Banner instead of *La Borinqueña*; an 80 percent dropout rate in the Island's schools at the time; and no full English proficiency.[8]

All other areas were affected as well. In the first year of U.S. occupation, an order was issued by the U.S. Army which authorized the registration of documents drafted in English when accompanied by a Spanish translation.[9] The Spanish translation requirement, however, was modified by the Language Act of 1902 and has survived to this day:

> In all departments of the Commonwealth Government and in all the courts of this island and in all public offices the English language and the Spanish language shall be used indiscriminately; and when necessary translations and oral interpretations shall be made from one language to the other so that all parties interested may understand any proceedings or communications made therein.[10]

This law unequivocally establishes the language policy in Puerto Rico as one that aims toward bilingualism and not monolingualism. In effect, two languages are accommodated. Yet bilingualism is not integrated at all levels in Puerto Rico. Ironically, it is the federal judiciary—the bastion of "American justice"—that has not, and will not be integrated.

In 1968 a federal district court in Puerto Rico was confronted with a constitutional challenge to the conviction of 11 Puerto Rican draft evaders because of the statutory requirement that all proceedings held in that court be conducted in English.[11] The draft evaders argued that both their right to a fair trial and their right to be tried by a jury of their peers were violated by this requirement as well as the federal provision in 28 U.S.C. Sec. 1861 requiring all jurors to be literate in English. The court recognized the unique situation that it confronted by noting that no other federal court was located in a "state or territory in which the primary language of the American citizens residing therein is other than English".[12] Yet it dismissed the arguments of the draft evaders by concluding:

> Just as Spanish is "the language of the Puerto Rican people" . . . the United States has from the time of its independence been an English-speaking nation.[13]

As will be seen below, the Court's description of the United States is not entirely accurate.

Language Policy in the United States

> The protection of the Constitution extends to all to those who speak other languages as well as those born with English on the tongue.—Myer v. Nebraska[14]

The history of U.S. language policy shows a strange quilt of trends and movements that embrace, and at times reject, accommodation of other languages in public life. This history, however, has shown that there has always been resistance to creating an exclusively monolingual society in the United States. Instead a cyclical or spiral pattern best describes U.S. language policy. Twelve of the more significant historical periods and events in the evolution of U.S. language policy can be listed as follows:

Pre-American Revolution: What we now consider the United States has historically functioned in many languages other than English, both before and after the Declaration of Independence. Spanish, Navajo, Cherokee and Eskimo, among others, have all flourished in what is now the United States long before English reached these shores. These same languages are accommodated now by the federal government. This historical period also demonstrated the ugly side of extremist language policies. African slaves were systematically prohibited, under severe punishment, from practicing their culture and languages.

Formation of the U.S. Government—The Constitution: It is of great interest and significance in defining the boundaries of U.S. language policy that the Constitution does not speak at all to English, or any other language, as the official language of the country. The framers, renowned for their eloquence and expressiveness, exhibited a lack of consensus on this issue, and German, Hebrew, French and Spanish had been mentioned as substitutes for English as the official language at that time.[15] Moreover, the Continental Congress had issued a number of proclamations and letters of appeal in German, including a German edition of the Articles of Confederation.[16] Thus Germans, representing a strong language minority eager to join in the armed rebellion, were courted in their native language.

Culmination of the Early Period of Accommodation—The Germans: With close to a quarter million Germans living in the Thirteen colonies, principally in Pennsylvania, Germans became the single most important language minority group to impact upon this country's development of a language policy.[17] Germans created their own private schools to preserve their language and successfully thwarted attempts to establish English schools in the same areas.[18] From 1794 through 1862, Germans repeatedly petitioned Congress to print federal laws and other publications in the German language.[19]

Even today, German ranks behind only Spanish and Italian as the most popular home language of U.S. residents.[20]

Territorial Annexation and Citizenship—The Mexicans: The conclusion of the Mexican-American War in 1848 resulted in the Treaty of Guadalupe Hidalgo. Approximately 75,000 Mexican settlers became U.S. citizens by operation of law.[21] The Treaty, however, preserved the right of these settlers to their land and arguably, to their language and culture.[22] The final treaty made it clear that these residents would enjoy all the rights of U.S. citizenship. English proficiency was not a condition of citizenship for this Spanish-speaking population.

Territorial Annexation and Citizenship—The Puerto Ricans: Citizenship was granted to Puerto Ricans by operation of the Jones Act of 1917. Like Mexicans, Puerto Ricans presented a substantial Spanish-speaking population that was granted citizenship as a result of U.S. armed initiatives. Once again, English proficiency was not imposed as a precondition to citizenship. Neither group, therefore, fits the typical immigrant stereotype.

Bridges remain behind them. Ellis Island and the Statue of Liberty are not their gateways.

Elimination of the First Wave of English Only Legislation—Myer v. Nebraska: As the final arbiter of the federal Constitution, the U.S. Supreme Court also plays a major role in the development of national pol-

icy. Its decision in *Myer v. Nebraska*, culminated an important phase in the development of U.S. language policy. The 1920s was a peak period for anti-immigrant hysteria. The dramatic rise in the membership of the Ku Klux Klan after World War I, which numbered over four million members in 1925, coincided with its proclamation to save the "Nordic race."[23] Restrictionist immigration policy and restrictionist language policy went hand in hand. When *Myer v. Nebraska* was decided, approximately 20 states had English-As-Official-Language legislation and prohibited the teaching of other languages in the schools.[24] In response, the Supreme Court declared these laws unconstitutional inasmuch as they established criminal penalties for teaching foreign languages.

U.S. Language Policy—The International Forum: With the conclusion of World War II, the United States and many other countries founded the United Nations. Prohibitions on discrimination against nationals of all the signatory countries were an essential element in the principles that forged the United Nations. The Charter of the United Nations lists "language as an impermissible basis of discrimination along side the other impermissible bases of race, sex, and religion."[25]

As a signatory to the United Nations Charter, the U.S. also voted in support of the Universal Declaration of Human Rights of 1948.[26] The Declaration also prohibits differentiation on the basis of language. Thus, the U.S. has expressly approved the protection of language rights within the sphere of international law and policy.

Citizenship Through Naturalization—The English Proficiency Requirement: In 1952 knowledge of "ordinary English" was made a requirement for citizenship through naturalization in the United States. Ability to read and write "ordinary English" was the standard for all would-be citizens except those physically unable to satisfy the requirement and those at least 50 years old and residents of the U.S. for over 20 years. Importantly these exemptions demonstrate, as with Puerto Ricans and Mexicans, that not every immigrant had to pass an English hurdle before gaining citizenship. The recent passage of the Immigration Reform and Control Act, established a major exception, however. For the first time, even eligibility for permanent residence under its "amnesty" provisions is contingent on English proficiency.

Realization of America's Linguistic Inferiority—The Cold War: The linguistic inferiority of the U.S. became particularly apparent during World War II. But it was Sputnik and the Cold War that led to action. Sputnik led to the re-evaluation of the work of the schools and to the passage of the National Defense Education Act in 1958. The Act placed emphasis on math, science, and foreign languages—the three areas in which Russian education was seen as superior. It promoted attention to the processes of second language teaching and learning and emphasized the retention and expansion of our foreign language resources.[27] Today the U.S. still has not learned this lesson: it does not promote the acquisition of foreign languages and insists upon being linguistically chauvinistic.

Language Policy and Foreign Policy—The Cubans: As with the Mexicans and Puerto Ricans before them, Cubans made significant contributions to the development of U.S. language policy, especially in education. The surge of Cubans to the U.S. after the Cuban Revolution presented a unique interaction between U.S. foreign and language policies. The country, in its attempt to establish a strong foreign policy against Cuba's new government, opened its arms to the Cubans who were thought to be transient refugees. Special programs for the Spanish-speaking were commonplace in Florida and the pedagogical benefits of native language instruction were proudly highlighted in educational circles.[28] Compared with the treatment of "domestic" language minority groups at the time, Cubans were given preferential treatment.[29]

Language Policy and Civil Rights—Voting: With the passage of the Voting Rights Act of 1965, voting was recognized as an important right, a right that would enhance other rights and privileges because of its obvious effect on public policy. For the nation's linguistic minorities, the Voting Rights Act set the stage for the subsequent enactment in 1970 of its bilingual assistance provisions.

The start of these efforts was section 4(e) of the Act which created an exemption for citizens who attained a 6th grade education in American flag schools conducted in languages other than English. These citizens could not be turned away from registering to vote because they failed an English literacy requirement. In effect, Congress was saying that political participation was too important to await the acquisition of a second language. Rarely discussed, however, is the fact that Congress was specifically addressing the rights of Puerto Ricans. In 1966 the U.S. Supreme Court said:

> More specifically, Sec. 4(e) may be viewed as a measure to secure for the Puerto Rican community residing in New York non-discriminatory treatment by government—both in the imposition of voting qualifications and the provision or administration of governmental services, such as public schools, public housing law enforcement.[30]

Language Policy and Civil Rights—Education: In 1974 the Supreme Court decided *Lau v. Nichols*. Relied upon by bilingual education advocates everywhere, *Lau v. Nichols* was decided more than 100 years after bilingual instruction was introduced in the United States. Throughout the 1850s and thereafter, bilingual instruction was utilized in states such as Illinois, Iowa, Missouri, Michigan, Kentucky, Minnesota, Oregon, Colorado and Nebraska.[31]

The significance of this case lies in its juxtaposition of the concepts of inequality and non-discrimination with the school district's unresponsiveness to language barriers. Thus, it was unlawful for Chinese students in San Francisco's public schools to sit in regular monolingual English classes without any efforts by the school to address their language needs. As the Court noted: ". . . there is no equality of treatment merely by providing students with the same facilities, textbooks, teachers and curriculum; for students who do not understand English are effectively foreclosed from any meaningful education."[32] This case ushered in a new era in civil rights principles and their application to the public schools. In theory, language minority students would no longer be allowed to sink or swim.

Political Empowerment: The Real Target

> As Whites see their power and control over their lives declining, will they simply go quietly into the night? Or will there be an explosion? Why don't non-Hispanic Whites have a group identity, as do Blacks, Jews, Hispanics?

These words are another excerpt from John Tanton's 1986 diatribe. Its distribution in August 1988 led to the resignation of Walter Cronkite from the Board of Advisors of U.S. English, Inc. and Linda Chavez from its Executive Director chair. Tanton would not retract, but resigned as well. Chavez' media-orchestrated resignation bordered on the humorous—as if from the heavens, the combination among the founders and financiers of U.S. English of the programmatic themes of population control, immigration restrictions and language restrictions became evident and unsavory to Chavez.[33] These connections were not hidden to those of us who have opposed English Only; we were merely supplied with more details.

For example, Tanton's affiliation with Zero Population Growth—which advocates sterilization of women—as well as his creation of the Federation of American Immigration Reform (FAIR) was public knowledge. In the early 1980s, FAIR petitioned the courts to halt the arrival of "Marielitos" because they would pollute the environment and in the mid-80s it lobbied frantically against the "amnesty" provisions of the immigration act. But simultaneously with the disclosure of the Tanton memo, financial data revealed that the financiers of both FAIR and U.S. English included heiress Cordelia Scaife May and the Pioneer Fund. The former financed the distribution of a French novel in which Third World immigrants invade and destroy Europe. The latter is dedicated to white racial superiority and eugenics.[34]

The leadership of the English-Only movement fully understands the political and strategic means necessary to stop Latinos from exercising control over local governments. Tanton recognized as much when he said in his 1986 memo that "the issues we're touching must be broached by liberals. The conservatives simply cannot do it without tainting the whole subject." The rhetoric of U.S. English, Inc. and of English First (another organization supporting a federal constitutional amendment declaring English the only official language) lists many superficial reasons for supporting such laws: the need to preserve the English language; the common bond English creates among Americans; the symbolism of English in America; and the need to provide incentives for Latinos because they refuse to learn English. All of these stated reasons have been effectively and empirically countered as false and unnecessary by opponents of English Only. Accordingly, as Puerto Ricans and others pressed forward with their agenda of access and control, the national debate has sought to suspend the quest for full equality and non-discrimination. The best example of this lies in the English Only movement's position on political participation of language minorities.

Bilingual ballots and bilingual registration forms are immediate and practical targets of the English-Only movement. They also represent, not surprisingly, areas that Latinos, Haitians, Asians and others have fought for in order to empower their respective communities. Take away the ballot and you will have dealt a serious blow to these peoples.

This attack on bilingual ballots and registration forms is especially pernicious. Its elements in the public discourse reveal two barely hidden themes: (a) voters who do not know English (as well as voters who are ignorant) are not worthy of participating in the body politic—you have to *earn* the right (read: privilege) to vote; (b) political and community leaders are deliberately keeping linguistic minorities away from learning English for their own political ambitions. Many of us have heard them before. It's a twist of the same pretext to keep people of color away from political power. Its roots are in the literacy tests used to keep Blacks from voting. Its operation in the Latino, Asian and other communities is dangerous at this time in our history when these groups are starting to register and vote in large numbers. For example, a survey in 1984, conducted by the Southwest Voter Participation Project, found in four states that 30 percent of the Mexicans responding would not have registered to vote had it not been for bilingual voting materials. Another survey published in 1988 by the Commonwealth of Puerto Rico found that 29 percent of all Puerto Ricans surveyed in New York City listed language barriers as an impediment to voting.

The second theme noted above follows from the first and stems from the same desire to arrest the "browning of America." John Tanton summarized:

> The way to demean minority citizens is to keep them in language ghettos, where they can be controlled by self-serving ethnic politicians.[35]

The white liberal (and Tanton deems himself one of them) can now be converted blindly into the white liberator, freeing the minorities from the prisons of their own deficiencies. This thinking led San Francisco voters in 1983 to overwhelmingly pass a referendum urging the repeal of bilingual ballots in a city composed of, what some analysts conclude, many liberal voters.[36]

Isn't it convenient that at a time when minority communities begin successfully to challenge structural impediments to political power, successfully register and turn out to vote, and elect representatives of their own people to public office, that these leaders are now attacked as manipulating their constituents? No connections? Do white politicians manipulate voters or is this trait monopolized only by our elected officials? Certain white politicians, such as Assemblyman Walter Kern of New Jersey, sponsor English-Only legislation because without it "there's no common language in the political arena." This politician wants to attract the Latino vote but does not want to go to the trouble of saying "*como está usted*" in Spanish, *al estilo* Frank Purdue!

Puerto Ricans in the U.S. have been responding to this new attack. In 1987 English Only legislation failed to pass in New York, New Jersey, Connecticut and Pennsylvania. Ohio and Massachusetts began organizing communities against these initiatives. In each of these states Puerto Rican organizations have been essential parts of the leadership. Consolidation of these efforts is necessary. We have some unfinished business to complete. It is necessary to get back on course with the plan of fighting for full preservation of our language and culture and against discrimination on the basis of language.[37]

Notes

1. Memorandum on file with author.

2. Garcia Martinez, Alfonso L. "Language Policy in Puerto Rico," *Revista del Colegio de Abogados de Puerto Rico*, Vol. 42, Num. 2, mayo, 1981, p. 92.

3. Ibid., p. 88.

4. Rodriguez Bou, Ismael, "Americanization of Schools in Puerto Rico" adapted from "Significant Factors in the Development of Education in Puerto Rico," in *The Status of Puerto Rico: Selected Background Studies Prepared for the United State–Puerto Rico Commission on the Status of Puerto Rico*, Wash., DC: Gov. Printing Office, 1966.

5. Garcia Martinez, *supra*, p. 97.

6. San Juan Cafferty, Pastora, and Carmen Rivera Martinez, "Bilingual Education In Puerto Rico," in *The Politics of Language: The Dilemma of Bilingual Education for Puerto Ricans*, (Boulder, CO: Westview Press, 1981), p. 46.

7. Ibid.

8. Zentella, Ana Celia, "Language Politics in the USA: The English-Only Movement," paper adapted from presentation at Modern Language Association, Dec. 29, 1987, p. 5.

9. General Orders No. 192, Headquarters of the Army, Adjutant General's Office, Washington, DC, Dec. 30, 1989.

10. Title 1, Sec 51, Laws of Puerto Rico.

11. *United States v. Valentine*, 288 F. Supp. 957 (D.P.R. 1968).

12. Ibid., p. 963.

13. Ibid., (citations omitted).

14. *Myer v. Nebraska*, 262 U.S. 563 (1974).

15. Castellanos, Diego, *The Best of Two Worlds: Bilingual-Bicultural Education in the U.S.*, New Jersey State Department of Education, Trenton, NJ, p. 8.

16. Kloss, Heinz, *The American Bilingual Tradition*, (Rowley, MA: Newbury House Publishers, 1977), p. x.

17. Castellanos, *supra*, p. 5.

18. Ibid., p. 6.

19. Kloss, *supra*, p. x.

20. 1980 Census Data, General & Social Characteristics.

21. Castellanos, *supra*, p. 12.

22. Cartagena, Juan, Gabe Kaimowitz, and Ignacio Pérez, "U.S. Language Policy: Where Do We Go From Here?" Conference Paper, El Español en los Estados Unidos IV, Hunter College, 1983, p. x.

23. Wittke, Carl, *We Who Built America, The Saga of The Immigrant*, (Western Research Univ. Press, 1939).

24. Combs, Mary Carol and John Trasvina, "Legal Implications of the English Language Amendment" in *The "English Plus" Project*, a publication of the League of United Latin American Citizens, June 1986.

25. McDougal, Myres S., and Harold D. Lasswell and Lung-Chu Chen, "Freedom From Discrimination In Choice of Language and International Human Rights," *Southern Illinois Univ. Law Journal*, 1:151 (1976).

26. Macías, Reynaldo F., "Language Choice and Human Rights In the United States," in Georgetown University Round Table on Languages and Linguistics, Proceedings, 1979.

27. Castellanos, *supra*, pp. 60-61.

28. Ibid., p. 63.

29. González, Josué M. "Coming of Age in Bilingual/Bicultural Education: A Historical Perspective," *Inequality in Education*, 1975.

30. *Katzenbach v. Morgan*, 384 U.S. 641, 652 (1966).

31. Castellanos, *supra*, pp. 17-25.

32. *Lau v. Nichols*, 414 U.S. 563, 566 (1974).

33. *The Miami Herald*, "English Only Leader Urged to Quit," Oct. 15, 1988.

34. Crawford, James, "What's Behind English Only II: Strange Bedfellows," *Hispanic Link Weekly Report*, Oct. 31, 1988.

35. *Los Angeles Times*, Oct. 16, 1986.

36. Woolard, Kathryn A., "Sentences in the Language Prison: The Rhetoric of an American Language Policy Debate" (draft), Presented at American Anthropology Assn., Dec. 1986.

37. Reynaldo F. Macías, a noted linguist, has often based his presentations in language policy on the international norms inherent in various international covenants and treaties. These include a right for every individual to have access to his/her home

or community language and a concomitant right to be free from discrimination on the basis of language. My review of the policies, laws and court cases addressing Puerto Rican concerns in the U.S. has led me to conclude that our community has been striving for essentially the same thing. *Y nos falta mucho.*

Juan Cartagena is a civil rights attorney who has litigated a number of cases in the area of language rights. At present he is General Counsel to the Community Service Society of New York.

Reprinted with permission from CENTRO, Bulletin of the Center for Puerto Rican Studies, Hunter College, City University of New York, Spring 2, 5 (1989): 64-76.

In most cultures, girls and boys have received different educational treatment for many centuries. A recent report by the American Association of University Women revealed numerous instances of unequal education and results.

How Schools Shortchange Girls

American Association of University Women (AAUW)

For those who believe that equitable education for all young Americans is the greatest source of our nation's strength, *The AAUW Report: How Schools Shortchange Girls* will not be reassuring. Commissioned by the AAUW Educational Foundation and developed by the Wellesley College Center for Research on Women, the study challenges the common assumption that girls and boys are treated equally in our public schools.

Ironically, AAUW's first national study—undertaken in 1885—was initiated to dispel the commonly accepted myth that higher education was harmful to women's health. This latest report presents the truth behind another myth—that girls and boys receive equal education.

While most of us are painfully aware of the crisis in American education, few understand or acknowledge the inequities that occur daily in classrooms across the country.

Didn't we address that problem in Title IX of the 1972 Education Amendments, which prohibits discrimination in educational institutions receiving federal funds? Many of us worked hard to ensure that this legislation would be passed. Its passage, however, did not solve the problem.

This report is a synthesis of all the available research on the subject of girls in school. It presents compelling evidence that girls are not receiving the same quality, or even quantity, of education as their brothers.

The implications of the report's findings are enormous. Women and children are swelling the ranks of the poor, at great cost to society. Yet our education policymakers are failing to address the relationship between education and the cycle of poverty. The shortchanging of girls is not even mentioned in the current educational restructuring debate.

A well-educated work force is essential to the country's economic development, yet girls are systematically discouraged from courses of study essential to their future employability and economic well-being. Girls are being steered away from the very courses required for their productive participation in the future of America, and we as a nation are losing more than one-half of our human potential. By the turn of the century, two out of three new entrants into the work force will be women and minorities. This work force will have fewer and fewer decently paid openings for the unskilled. It will require strength in science, mathematics, and technology—subjects girls are still being told are not suitable for them.

The AAUW Report presents a base for a new and enlightened education policy—a policy that will ensure that this nation will provide the best possible education for all its children. It provides policymakers with impartial data on the ways in which our school system is failing to meet the needs of girls and with specific strategies that can be used to effect change. The wealth of statistical evidence must convince even the most skeptical that gender bias in our schools is shortchanging girls—and compromising our country.

The AAUW Educational Foundation is proud to present *The AAUW Report: How Schools Shortchange Girls*, made possible through the generosity of the many supporters of the Eleanor Roosevelt Fund. This report is destined to add a new dimension to the education debate. The evidence is in, and the picture is clear: shortchanging girls—the women of tomorrow—shortchanges America. —Alice McKee, President, AAUW Educational Foundation

Why A Report On Girls?

The invisibility of girls in the current education debate suggests that girls and boys have identical educational experiences in school. Nothing could be further from the truth. Whether one looks at achievement scores, curriculum design, or teacher-student interaction, it is clear that sex and gender make a difference in the nation's public elementary and secondary schools.

The educational system is not meeting girls' needs. Girls and boys enter school roughly equal in measured ability. Twelve years later, girls have fallen behind their male classmates in key areas such as higher-level mathematics and measures of self esteem. Yet gender equity is still not a part of the national debate on educational reform.

Neither the *National Education Goals* issued by the National Governors Association in 1990 nor *Amer-*

ica 2000, the 1991 plan of the President and the U.S. Department of Education to "move every community in America toward these goals," makes any mention of providing girls equitable opportunities in the nation's public schools. Girls continue to be left out of the debate—despite the fact that for more than two decades researchers have identified gender bias as a major problem at all levels of schooling.

Schools must prepare both girls and boys for full and active roles in the family, the community, and the work force. Whether we look at the issues from an economic, political, or social perspective, girls are one-half of our future. We must move them from the sidelines to the center of the education-reform debate.

A critical step in correcting educational inequities is identifying them publicly. The *AAUW Report: How Schools Shortchange Girls* provides a comprehensive assessment of the status of girls in public education today. It exposes myths about girls and learning, and it supports the work of the many teachers who have struggled to define and combat gender bias in their schools. The report challenges us all—policymakers, educators, administrators, parents, and citizens—to rethink old assumptions and act now to stop schools from shortchanging girls.

Our public education system is plagued by numerous failings that affect boys as negatively as girls. But in many respects girls are put at a disadvantage simply because they are girls. *The AAUW Report* documents this in hundreds of cited studies.

When our schools become more gender-fair, education will improve for all our students—boys as well as girls—because excellence in educa-

tion cannot be achieved without equity in education. By studying what happens to girls in school, we can gain valuable insights about what has to change in order for each student, every girl and every boy, to do as well as she or he can.

What The Research Reveals

What Happens in the Classroom?

- Girls receive significantly less attention from classroom teachers than do boys.

- African American girls have fewer interactions with teachers than do white girls, despite evidence that they attempt to initiate interactions more frequently.

- Sexual harassment of girls by boys—from innuendo to actual assault—in our nation's schools is increasing.

A large body of research indicates that teachers give more classroom attention and more esteem building encouragement to boys. In a study conducted by Myra and David Sadker, boys in elementary and middle school called out answers eight times more often than girls. When boys called out, teachers listened. But when girls called out, they were told to "raise your hand if you want to speak." Even when boys do not volunteer, teachers are more likely to encourage them to give an answer or an opinion than they are to encourage girls.

Research reveals a tendency, beginning at the preschool level, for educators to choose classroom activities that appeal to boys' interests and to select presentation formats in which boys excel. The teacher-student interaction patterns in science classes are often particularly biased. Even in math classes, where less-biased patterns are found, psychologist Jacquelynne Eccles reports that select boys in each math class she studied received particular attention to the exclusion of all other students, female and male.

Teaching methods that foster competition are still standard, although a considerable body of research has demonstrated that girls—and many boys as well—learn better when they undertake projects and activities cooperatively rather than competitively.

Researchers, including Sandra Damico, Elois Scott, and Linda Grant, report that African American girls have fewer interactions with teachers than do white girls, even though they attempt to initiate interactions more often. Furthermore, when African American girls do as well as white boys in school, teachers often attribute their success to hard work while assuming that the white boys are not working up to their potential.

Girls do not emerge from our schools with the same degree of confidence and self-esteem as boys. The 1990 AAUW poll, *Shortchanging Girls, Shortchanging America*, documents a loss of self-confidence in girls that is twice that for boys as they move from childhood to adolescence. Schools play a crucial role in challenging and changing gender-role expectations that undermine the self-confidence and achievement of girls.

Reports of boys sexually harassing girls in schools are increasing at an alarming rate. When sexual harassment is treated casually, as in "boys will be boys," both girls and boys get a dangerous, damaging message: "girls are not worthy of respect; appropriate behavior for boys includes exerting power over girls."

These issues are discussed in detail and the research fully annotated in Part 4/Chapter 2 of The AAUW Report.

What Do We Teach Our Students?

- The contributions and experiences of girls and women are still marginalized or ignored in many of the textbooks used in our nation's schools.

- Schools, for the most part, provide inadequate education on sexuality and healthy development despite national concern about teen pregnancy, the AIDS crisis, and the increase of sexually transmitted diseases among adolescents.

- Incest, rape, and other physical violence severely compromise the lives of girls and women all across the country. These realities are rarely, if ever, discussed in schools.

Curriculum delivers the central messages of education. It can strengthen or decrease student motivation for engagement, effort, growth, and development through the images it gives to students about themselves and the world. When the curriculum does not reflect the diversity of students' lives and cultures, it delivers an incomplete message.

Studies have shown that multicultural readings produced markedly more favorable attitudes toward non-dominant groups than did the traditional reading lists, that academic achievement for all students was linked to use of nonsexist and multicultural materials, and that sex-role stereotyping was reduced in students whose curriculum portrayed males and females in non-stereotypical roles. Yet during the 1980s, federal support for reform regarding sex and race equity dropped, and a 1989 study showed that of the ten books most frequently assigned in public high school English courses only one was written by a woman and none by members of minority groups.

The "evaded" curriculum is a term coined in this report to refer to matters central to the lives of students that are touched on only briefly, if at all, in most schools. The United States has the highest rate of teenage childbearing in the Western industrialized world. Syphilis rates are now equal for girls and boys, and more teenage girls than boys contract gonorrhea. Although in the adult population AIDS is nine times more prevalent in men than in women, the same is not true for young people. In a District of Columbia study, the rate of HIV infection for girls was almost three times that for boys. Despite all of this, adequate sex and health education is the exception rather than the rule.

Adolescence is a difficult period for all young people, but it is particularly difficult for girls, who are far more likely to develop eating disorders and experience depression. Adolescent girls attempt suicide four to five times as often as boys (although boys, who choose more lethal methods, are more likely to be successful in their attempts).

Perhaps the most evaded of all topics in schools is the issue of gender and power. As girls mature they confront a culture that both idealizes and exploits the sexuality of young women while assigning them roles that are clearly less valued than male roles. If we do not begin to discuss more openly the ways in which ascribed power—whether on the basis of race, sex, class, sexual orientation, or religion—affects individual lives, we cannot truly prepare our students for responsible citizenship.

These issues are discussed in detail and the research fully annotated in Part 4/Chapters 1 and 3 of The AAUW Report.

How Do Race/Ethnicity and Socioeconomic Status Affect Achievement in School?

- Girls from low-income families face particularly severe obstacles. Socioeconomic status, more than any other variable, affects access to school resources and educational outcomes.

- Test scores of low-socioeconomic-status girls are somewhat better than for boys from the same background in the lower grades, but by high school these differences disappear. Among high-socioeconomic status students, boys generally outperform girls regardless of race/ethnicity.

- Too little information is available on differences among various groups of girls. While African Americans are compared to whites, or boys to girls, relatively few studies or published data examine differences by sex and race/ethnicity.

All girls confront barriers to equal participation in school and society. But minority girls, who must confront racism as well as sexism, and girls from low income families face particularly severe obstacles. These obstacles can include poor schools in dangerous neighborhoods, low teacher expectations, and inadequate nutrition and health care.

Few studies focus on issues affecting low-income girls and girls from minority groups—unless they are pregnant or drop out of school. In order to develop effective policies and programs, a wide range of issues—from course-taking patterns to academic self-esteem—require further examination by sex, race/ethnicity, and socioeconomic status.

These issues are discussed in detail and the research fully annotated in Part 2/Chapter 3 of The AAUW Report.

How Are Girls Doing in Math and Science?

- Differences between girls and boys in math achievement are small and declining. Yet in high school, girls are still less likely than boys to take the most advanced courses and be in the top-scoring math groups.

- The gender gap in science, however, is not decreasing and may, in fact, be increasing.

- Even girls who are highly competent in math and science are much less likely to pursue scientific or technological careers than are their male classmates.

Girls who see math as "something men do" do less well in math than girls who do not hold this view. In their classic study, Elizabeth Fennema and Julia Sherman reported a drop in both girls' math confidence and their achievement in the middle school years. The drop in confidence preceded the decline in achievement.

Researcher Jane Kahle found that boys come to science classes with more out-of-school familiarity and experience with the subject matter. This advantage is furthered in the classroom. One study of science classrooms found that 79 percent of all student-assisted science demonstrations were carried out by boys.

We can no longer afford to disregard half our potential scientists and science-literate citizens of the next generation. Even when girls take math and science courses and do well in them, they do not receive the encouragement they need to pursue scientific careers. A study of high school seniors found that 64 percent of the boys who had taken physics and calculus were planning to major in science and engineering in college, compared to only 18.6 percent of the girls who had taken the same subjects. Support from teachers can make a big difference. Studies report that girls rate teacher support as an important factor in decisions to pursue scientific and technological careers.

These issues are discussed in detail and the research fully annotated in Part 2/Chapter 2 of The AAUW Report.

Tests: Stepping Stones or Stop Signs?

- Test scores can provide an inaccurate picture of girls' and boys' abilities. Other factors such as grades, portfolios of student work, and out-of school achievements must be considered in addition to test scores when making judgments about girls' and boys' skills and abilities.

- When scholarships are given based on the Scholastic Aptitude Test (SAT) scores, boys are more apt to receive scholarships than are girls who get equal or slightly better high school grades.

- Girls and boys with the same Math SAT scores do not do equally well in college—girls do better.

In most cases tests reflect rather than cause inequities in American education. The fact that groups score differently on a test does not necessarily mean that the test is biased. If, however, the score differences are related to the validity of the test—for example, if girls and boys know about the same amount of math but boys' test scores are consistently and significantly higher—then the test is biased.

A number of aspects of a test—beyond that which is being tested can affect the score. For example, girls tend to score better than boys on essay tests, boys better than girls on multiple-choice items. Even today many girls and boys come to a testing situation with different interests and experiences. Thus a reading comprehension passage that focuses on baseball scores will tend to favor boys, while a question testing the same skills that focuses on child care will tend to favor girls.

These issues are discussed in detail and the research fully annotated in Part 3 of The AAUW Report.

Why Do Girls Drop Out and What Are The Consequences?

- Pregnancy is not the only reason girls drop out of school. In fact, less than half the girls who leave school give pregnancy as the reason.

- Dropout rates for Hispanic girls vary considerably by national origin: Puerto Rican and Cuban American girls are more likely to drop out than are boys from the same cultures or other Hispanic girls.

- Childhood poverty is almost inescapable in single parent families headed by women without a high school diploma: 77 percent for whites and 87 percent for African Americans.

In a recent study, 37 percent of the female dropouts compared to only 5 percent of the male dropouts cited "family-related problems" as the reason they left high school. Traditional gender roles place greater family responsibilities on adolescent girls than on their brothers. Girls are often expected to "help out" with caretaking responsibilities; boys rarely encounter this expectation.

However, girls as well as boys also drop out of school simply because they do not consider school pleasant or worthwhile. Asked what a worthwhile school experience would be, a group of teenage girls responded, "School would be fun. Our teachers would be excited and lively, not bored. They would act caring and take time to understand how students feel. . . . Boys would treat us with respect. If they run by and grab your tits, they would get into trouble." (As quoted in *In Their Own Voices: Young Women Talk About Dropping Out*, Project on Equal Education Rights (New York, National Organization for Women Legal Defense and Education Fund, 1988), p. 12.)

Women and children are the most impoverished members of our society. Inadequate education not only limits opportunities for women but jeopardizes their children's—and the nation's—future.

These issues are discussed in detail and the research fully annotated in Part 2/Chapters 4 and 6 of The AAUW Report.

Recommendations: Action for Change

The research reviewed in *The AAUW Report: How Schools Shortchange Girls* challenges traditional assumptions about the egalitarian nature of American schools. Girls do not receive equitable amounts of teacher attention, are less apt than boys to see themselves reflected in the materials they study, and often are not expected or encouraged to pursue higher level math and science.

The current education-reform movement cannot succeed if it continues to ignore half of its constituents. We must move girls from the sidelines to the center of education planning. The issues are urgent; our actions must be swift and effective.

The Recommendations

Strengthened reinforcement of Title IX is essential.

1. Require school districts to assess and report on a regular basis to the Office for Civil Rights in the U.S. Department of Education on their own Title IX compliance measures.

2. Fund the Office for Civil Rights at a level that permits increased compliance reviews and full and prompt investigation of Title IX complaints.

3. In assessing the status of Title IX compliance, school districts must include a review of the treatment of pregnant teens and teen

parents. Evidence indicates that these students are still the victims of discriminatory treatment in many schools.

Teachers, administrators, and counselors must be prepared and encouraged to bring gender equity and awareness to every aspect of schooling.

4. State certification standards for teachers and administrators should require course work on gender issues, including new research on women, bias in classroom-interaction patterns, and the ways in which schools can develop and implement gender-fair multicultural curricula.

5. If a national teacher examination is developed, it should include items on methods for achieving gender equity in the classroom and in curricula.

6. Teachers, administrators, and counselors should be evaluated on the degree to which they promote and encourage gender-equitable and multicultural education.

7. Support and released time must be provided by school districts for teacher-initiated research on curricula and classroom variables that affect student learning. Gender equity should be a focus of this research and a criterion for awarding funds.

8. School-improvement efforts must include a focus on the ongoing professional development of teachers and administrators, including those working in specialized areas such as bilingual, compensatory, special, and vocational education.

9. Teacher-training courses must not perpetuate assumptions about the superiority of traits and activities traditionally ascribed to males in our society. Assertive and affiliative skills as well as verbal and mathematical skills must be fostered in both girls and boys.

10. Teachers must help girls develop positive views of themselves and their futures, as well as an understanding of the obstacles women must overcome in a society where their options and opportunities are still limited by gender stereotypes and assumptions.

The formal school curriculum must include the experiences of women and men from all walks of life. Girls and boys must see women and girls reflected and valued in the materials they study.

11. Federal and state funding must be used to support research, development, and follow-up study of gender-fair multicultural curricular models.

12. The Women's Educational Equity Act Program (WEEAP) in the U.S. Department of Education must receive increased funding in order to continue the development of curricular materials and models, and to assist school districts in Title compliance.

13. School curricula should deal directly with issues of power, gender politics, and violence against women. Better-informed girls are better equipped to make decisions about their futures. Girls and young women who have a strong sense of themselves are better able to confront violence and abuse in their lives.

14. Educational organizations must support, via conferences, meetings, budget deliberations, and policy decisions, the development of gender-fair multicultural curricula in all areas of instruction.

15. Curricula for young children must not perpetuate gender stereotypes and should reflect sensitivity to different learning styles.

Girls must be educated and encouraged to understand that mathematics and the sciences are important and relevant to their lives. Girls must be actively supported in pursuing education and employment in these areas.

16. Existing equity guidelines should be effectively implemented in all programs supported by the local, state, and federal governments. Specific attention must be directed toward including women on planning committees and focusing on girls and women in the goals, instructional strategies, teacher training, and research components of these programs.

17. The federal government must fund and encourage research on the effect on girls and boys of new curricula in the sciences and mathematics. Research is needed particularly in science areas where boys appear to be improving their performance while girls are not.

18. Educational institutions, professional organizations, and the business community must work together to dispel myths about math and science as "inappropriate" fields for women.

19. Local schools and communities must encourage and support girls studying science and mathematics by showcasing women role models in scientific and technological fields, disseminating career information, and offering "hands-on" experiences and work groups in science and math classes.

20. Local schools should seek strong links with youth-serving organizations that have developed successful out-of-school programs for girls in mathematics and science and with those girls' schools that have developed effective programs in these areas.

Continued attention to gender equity in vocational education programs must be a high priority at every level of educational governance and administration.

21. Linkages must be developed with the private sector to help ensure that girls with training in nontraditional areas find appropriate employment.

22. The use of a discretionary process for awarding vocational-education funds should be encouraged to prompt innovative efforts.

23. All states should be required to make support services (such as child care and transportation) available to both vocational and prevocational students.

24. There must be continuing research on the effectiveness of vocational education for girls and the extent to which the 1990 Vocational Education Amendments benefit girls.

Testing and assessment must serve as stepping stones not stop signs. New tests and testing techniques must accurately reflect the abilities of both girls and boys.

25. Test scores should not be the only factor considered in admissions or the awarding of scholarships.

26. General aptitude and achievement tests should balance sex differences in item types and contexts. Tests should favor neither females nor males.

27. Tests that relate to "real life situations" should reflect the experiences of both girls and boys.

Girls and women must play a central role in educational reform. The experiences, strengths, and needs of girls from every race and social class must be considered in order to provide excellence and equity for all our nation's students.

28. National, state, and local governing bodies should ensure that women of diverse backgrounds are equitably represented on committees and commissions on educational reform.

29. Receipt of government funding for in-service and professional development programs should be conditioned upon evidence of efforts to increase the number of women in positions in which they are underrepresented. All levels of government have a role to play in increasing the numbers of women, especially women of color, in education-management and policy positions.

30. The U.S. Department of Education's Office of Educational Research and Improvement (OERI) should establish an advisory panel of gender-equity experts to work with OERI to develop a research and dissemination agenda to foster gender-equitable education in the nation's classrooms.

31. Federal and state agencies must collect, analyze, and report data broken down by race/ethnicity, sex, and some measure of socioeconomic status, such as parental income or education. National standards for use by all school districts should be developed so that data is comparable across district and state lines.

32. National standards for computing dropout rates should be developed for use by all school districts.

33. Professional organizations should ensure that women serve on education-focused committees. Organizations should utilize the expertise of their female membership when developing educational initiatives.

34. Local schools must call on the expertise of teachers, a majority of whom are women, in their restructuring efforts.

35. Women teachers must be encouraged and supported to seek administrative positions and elected office, where they can bring the insights gained in the classroom to the formulation of education policies.

A critical goal of education reform must be to enable students to deal effectively with the realities of their lives, particularly in areas such as sexuality and health.

36. Strong policies against sexual harassment must be developed. All school personnel must take responsibility for enforcing these policies.

37. Federal and state funding should be used to promote partnerships between schools and community groups, including social service agencies, youth-serving organizations, medical facilities, and local businesses. The needs of students, particularly as highlighted by pregnant teens and teen mothers, require a multi-institutional response.

38. Comprehensive school-based health- and sex education programs must begin in the early grades and continue sequentially through twelfth grade. These courses must address the topics of reproduction and reproductive health, sexual abuse, drug and alcohol use, and general mental and physical health issues. There must be a special focus on the prevention of AIDS.

39. State and local school board policies should enable and encourage young mothers to complete school, without compromising the quality of education these students receive.

40. Child care for the children of teen mothers must be an integral

part of all programs designed to encourage young women to pursue or complete educational programs.

The AAUW Report: How Schools Shortchange Girls, 1992. Reprinted by permission.

RESOURCES: THE AAUW EQUITY LIBRARY

■

Ground-breaking Works on Gender Bias in Education

Hostile Hallways: The AAUW Survey on Sexual Harassment in America's Schools
The first national study of sexual harassment, based on the experiences of 1,632 students in grades 8 through 11. Gender and ethnic/racial (African American, Hispanic, and white) data breakdowns included. Commissioned by the AAUW Educational Foundation and conducted by Louis Harris and Associates. 28 pages/1993. $8.95 AAUW members/$11.95 nonmembers.

The AAUW Report: How Schools Shortchange Girls
Disturbing report documents girls' second-class treatment in America's schools, grades K-12. The research report, prepared by the Wellesley College Center for Research on Women, includes policy recommendations and strategies for change. 128 pages/1992. $14.95 AAUW members/$16.95 nonmembers.

The AAUW Report Executive Summary
Overview of **The AAUW Report** research, with recommendations for educators and policymakers. 8 pages/1992. $6.95 AAUW members/$8.95 nonmembers.

The AAUW Report Action Guide
Strategies for combating gender bias in school, based on **The AAUW Report** recommendations. 8 pages/1992. $6.95 AAUW members/$8.95 nonmembers.

AAUW Issue Briefs
Package of five briefs, with strategies for change: Equitable Treatment of Girls and Boys in the Classroom; Restructuring Education; Stalled Agenda—Gender Equity and the Training of Educators; College Admission Tests: Opportunities or Roadblocks?; Creating a Gender-Fair Multicultural Curriculum. 1990-92. $7.95 AAUW members/$9.95 nonmembers.

Action Alert
Monthly newsletter published by the AAUW Program and Policy Department monitors congressional action on educational equity as well as reproductive choice, sexual harass-ment, and other vital issues. Gives you the information you need to lobby effectively for change. One-year subscription: $20 AAUW members/$25 nonmembers.

Executive Summary: Shortchanging Girls, Shortchanging America
Highly readable summary of AAUW's 1991 poll, highlighting survey results with charts and graphs. 17 pages/1991. $5.

Full Data Report: Shortchanging Girls, Shortchanging America
Complete data on AAUW's 1991 national poll on girls and self-esteem, with survey questions and responses, and banners displaying cross-tabulations. Includes floppy disk with all data. 500 pages/1991. To order, call 202/785-7761. Nonmembers who purchase the full report can become AAUW members for only $10 more. $60 AAUW members/$85 nonmembers.

Video: Shortchanging Girls, Shortchanging America
A dramatic look at the inequities girls face in school. Features education experts and public policy leaders, AAUW poll results, as well as the compelling voices and faces of American girls. VHS format/15 minutes/1991. $19.95 AAUW members/$24.95 nonmembers.

A Call to Action: Shortchanging Girls, Shortchanging America
Powerful synopsis of AAUW's 1991 poll and national roundtable on gender bias in education and its effects on girls' self-esteem. Contains action ideas for community change. 40 pages/1991. $12.95 AAUW members/$14.95 nonmembers.

"When you shortchange girls, you shortchange America" Mug
Front shows woodblock and slogan with AAUW logo on the back. White with black and teal. $9.50 AAUW members/$10.50 nonmembers.

"When you shortchange girls, you shortchange America" T-shirt
Sports an elegant woodblock of students as well as the slogan. Available in black, white, and teal. Sizes: extra large and oversize. $14.95 AAUW members/$15.95 nonmembers.

Help Make a Difference for Today's Girls and Tomorrow's Leaders.

Hostile Hallways: The AAUW Survey on Sexual Harassment in America's Schools is made possible by charitable contributions to the AAUW Educational Foundation, a not-for-profit 501(c)(3) organization. Help us continue breaking ground toward positive societal changes. Your support can help put an end to sexual harassment and inequity in schools and communities throughout the nation. Your contributions make a difference, supporting research, community action projects, fellowships for women, and teachers. Send your contributions to: AAUW Educational Foundation, Dept. T, 1111 Sixteenth Street N.W., Washington, DC 20036-4873.

Become part of the American Association of University Women, representing 130,000 college graduates, and help promote education and equity for women and girls. You can add your voice as a Member-at-Large or work on critical issues in one of AAUW's 1,750 local branches. For further membership information, write: AAUW Membership, Dept. T, 1111 Sixteenth Street N.W., Washington, DC 20036-4873.

AAUW Sales Office
PO Box 251 ■ Dept. 259 ■ Annapolis Junction, MD 20701-0251
FOR TELEPHONE ORDERS, CALL:
800/225-9998, ext. 259

Conservative commentator Rita Kramer rejects the AAUW report as outdated, trivial, shoddy, and anti-intellectual. Gender bias is not a problem in U.S. schools, she believes.

Are Girls Shortchanged in Schools?

Rita Kramer

In America today, more girls graduate from high school than boys and more of them go on to college, where they make up 55 percent of the total enrollment. Yet according to a report recently released by the American Association of University Women (AAUW), "girls are invisible" in classrooms which "day in, day out, deliver the message that women's lives count for less than men's."

This report, *How Schools Shortchange Girls*, has been enthusiastically greeted by the media. With almost no attempt to evaluate the evidence on which it purports to be based, front-page articles in most of the nation's leading news-papers have simply passed on the report's conclusions: that standardized tests are biased against girls; that curricula and textbooks ignore or stereotype women; that teachers demonstrate bias by paying less attention to girls; and that because of discrimination girls lag behind boys in math and science and tend not to pursue careers in those fields.

All these charges are either false or misleading. And no wonder, since *How Schools Shortchange Girls* is based on a body of research some of which is outdated, much of which is trivial (unpublished doctoral dissertations and obscure publications), and some of which was done under the auspices of the organization issuing the report—a little like quoting yourself as an authority for your own opinions. The report ignores any published evidence—of which there is quite a bit—that does not support its conclusions and overlooks any inconvenient facts that contradict or even tend to modify those occlusions or suggest explanations other than bias for any statistical discrepancy in favor of boys (though not when the numbers favor girls.)

Take, for example, the charge that the Scholastic Aptitude Test (SAT) is biased against girls. True, girls do somewhat less well than boys on the SAT, which is used to help determine admission to college; it is also true that girls get higher grades in college than boys. Since the SAT

thus "underpredicts" the performance of girls in college, it must, says the AAUW report, be biased against them. But this could just as well be turned around and used as evidence that boys are the victims of grading bias. After all, scholars not quoted in the report have pointed out that girls tend to take more courses in which grading is easier (art, music, literature), and which involve the verbal skills in which girls do better, than the tougher math and science courses more boys tend to take.

The charge that textbooks are biased against women is even more bizarre. Thus, a quantitative analysis of the content of three leading high-school texts in American history carried out at the Center for the Study of Social and Political Change at Smith College (and not cited by the AAUW report) found that women are portrayed more favorably than men; that there are proportionately more pictures of women, largely in untraditional roles; that even minor achievements by women are given extensive treatment compared to the achievements of men; that women are never represented unflatteringly, although men may be; that most accounts of historical events such as wars are considered primarily in terms of the terms of the contributions make by women (and minorities).

Students who read nothing but these textbooks (and that means most students in American high schools) wind up knowing more about minor female characters in the American past than about men who have had a significant influence on world and national affairs. The 1987 National Assessment of Educational Progress test of history and literature found that more high-school students should identify Harriet Tubman than Winston Churchill or Joseph Stalin and more knew that the Seneca Falls Declaration concerned women's rights than when Lincoln was President. In *American Voices*, a new Scott, Foresman entry into the lucrative textbook market, the index entries under "Women" and "Women's" are more than twice as long as those under World War I and World War II together.

As for the observation that teachers pay more attention to boys, this is one of those ambiguous findings that the authors of the AAUW report automatically ascribe to bias. It has long been common knowledge that boys are more aggressive and harder to control in the traditional classroom. Calling on them more frequently may be a strategy for keeping them in line, focusing them on the academic task at hand. But even so, there is no evidence to indicate that this kind of attention translates into their learning more, earning better grades, or getting

into college more easily (which, as we have seen, they do not).

Nor is there any evidence that, as the AAUW report charges, girls "are systematically discouraged from" and "are being steered away from" science, mathematics, and technology. The report—ignoring the possibility that biological, developmental, or cultural factors may well have something to do with the relative disinclination of girls to study these subjects—once again simply assumes that bias is at work. Accordingly, it suggests special programs for girls in math and science.

But encouraging girls to go into previously avoided fields, and then to work hard at excelling in them, is not exactly what the authors of the AAUW report have in mind here. We get some notion of what they do have in mind from a talk given by one of them, Dr. Peggy McIntosh, an associate director at the Wellesley College Center for Research on Women, to teachers in Brookline, Massachusetts, in the fall of 1990.

McIntosh begins by describing a little girl who is unable to solve the problems on a worksheet that asks her to add a series of three numbers such as 1+3+5. McIntosh objects to the assignment as an example of the "the right/wrong, win/lose/kill or be killed system" that defines learning as mastery— "vertical thinking," as she calls it.

Vertical thinking involves "competition, exact thinking, decisiveness, being able to make an argument that will persuade others or to turn in the perfect paper." To avoid such evils, McIntosh recommends revising the assignment in terms of "lateral thinking," which instead of asking, "How am I doing?" asks, "What is it to be alive?" One way of

doing this is just to give the child the answers. Another is to let the children solve all problems in a group. (Incidentally, McIntosh's program for curricular innovation involves putting "not just math, but biology and chemistry off the right/wrong axis.")

The AAUW report, then, reflects the increasingly widespread attitude in American life that sees everything in terms of bias and group entitlement and ignores all the subtle and complex aspects of human nature that differentiate individuals—including women —from one another. As usual, the bottom line is a call for remedial legislation—in this case for a reactivation of the Women's Educational Equity Act Program (WEEAP).

It was under WEEAP that federal funding was made available in 1974 for the development of "nonsexist" textbooks and other curricular materials. But since the Department of Education's publication in 1983 of the report of the National Committee on Excellence in Education, *A Nation at Risk*, programs for school reform have concentrated on issues other than gender bias—most notably on why American children of both sexes do so poorly on all measures of academic ability compared to children in other countries, whom they manage to outdo only on measures of self-esteem. Under the present Secretary, Lamar Alexander, the focus of the Department of Education is on raising academic standards throughout the system from kindergarten to college. Along the way, requests for continued funding for WEEAP have been dropped.

It is this process that the AAUW seeks to reverse by persuading us that the problem with our schools is gender bias rather than a bias against academic achievement. But sharing this latter bias to the full, the AAUW report could not be expected to fight it. And indeed, accepting its shoddy analysis and carrying out the predictably anti-intellectual recommendations that follow from it would only make our schools worse—for girls and boys alike.

Rita Kramer's books include Ed School Follies and Maria Montessori: A Biography.

Tracking has been justified by claiming that students possessing different abilities will learn better if they are grouped and separated. However, the results of tracking programs indicate that initial differences in students' cognitive skills are exaggerated, not reduced. Oakes questions the underlying assumptions and highlights the ethical implications inherent in the practice of tracking students in public schools.

Keeping Track, Part 1: The Policy and Practice of Curriculum Inequality

Jeannie Oakes

The idea of educational equality has fallen from favor. In the 1980's policy makers, school practitioners, and the public have turned their attention instead to what many consider a competing goal: excellence. Attempts to "equalize" schooling in the Sixties and Seventies have been judged extravagant and naive. Worse, critics imply that those well-meant efforts to correct inequality may have compromised the central mission of the schools: teaching academics well. And current critics warn that given the precarious position of the United States in the global competition for economic, technological, and military superiority, we can no longer sacrifice the quality of our schools to social goals. This view promotes the judicious spending of limited educational resources in ways that will produce the greatest return on "human capital." Phrased in these economic terms, special provisions for underachieving poor and minority students become a bad investment. In short, equality is out; academic excellence is in.

On the other hand, many people still argue vociferously that the distinction between promoting excellence and providing equality is false, that one cannot be achieved without the other. Unfortunately, whether "tight-fisted", conservatives or "fuzzy-headed" liberals are in the ascendancy, the heat of the rhetoric surrounding the argument largely obscures a more serious problem, the possibility that the unquestioned assumptions that drive school practice and the basic features of schools may themselves lock schools into patterns that make it difficult to achieve either excellence or equality.

The practice of tracking in secondary schools illustrates this possibility and provides evidence of how schools, even as they voice commitment to equality and excellence, organize and deliver curriculum in ways that advance neither. Nearly all schools track students. Because tracking enables schools to provide educational treatments matched in particular groups of students, it is believed to promote higher achievement for all students under conditions of equal educational opportunity. However, rather than promoting higher achievement, tracking contributes to mediocre schooling for most secondary students. And because it places the greatest obstacles to achievement in the path of those children least advantaged in American society—poor and minority children—tracking forces schools to play an active role in perpetuating social and economic inequalities as well. Evidence about the influence of tracking on student outcomes and analyses of how tracking affects the day-to-day school experiences of young people support the argument that such basic elements of schooling can prevent rather than promote educational goals.

What is Tracking?

Tracking is the practice of dividing students into separate classes for high-average, and low-achievers; it lays out different curriculum paths for students headed for college and for those who are bound directly for the workplace. In most senior high schools, students are assigned to one or another curriculum track that lays out sequences of courses for college-preparatory, vocational, or general track students. Junior and senior high schools also make use of ability grouping—that is, they divide academic subjects (typically English, mathematics, science, and social studies) into classes geared to different "levels" for students of different abilities. In many high schools these two systems overlap, as schools provide college-preparatory, general, and vocational sequences of courses and also practice ability grouping in academic subjects. More likely than not, the student in the vocational curriculum track will be in one of the lower ability groups. Because similar overlapping exists for college-bound students, the distinction between the two types of tracking is sometimes difficult to assess.

But tracking does not proceed as neatly as the description above implies. Both curriculum tracking and ability grouping vary from school to school in the number of subjects

that are tracked, in the number of levels provided, and in the ways in which students are placed. Moreover, tracking is confounded by the inflexibilities and idiosyncrasies of "master schedules," which can create unplanned tracking, generate further variations among tracking systems, and affect the courses taken by individual students as well. Elective subjects, such as art and home economics, sometimes become low-track classes because college-preparatory students rarely have time in their schedules to take them; required classes, such as drivers' training, health or physical education, though they are intended to be heterogeneous, become tracked when the requirements of other courses that are tracked keep students together for large portions of the day.

Despite these variations, tracking has common and predictable characteristics:

The intellectual performance of students is judged, and these judgments determine placement with particular groups.

- Classes and tracks are labeled according to the performance levels of the students in them (e.g., advanced, average, remedial) or according to students' postsecondary destinations (e.g., college-preparatory, vocational).

- The curriculum and instruction in various tracks are tailored to the perceived needs and abilities of the students assigned to them.

- The groups that are formed are not merely a collection of different but equally-valued instructional groups. They form a hierarchy, with the

most advanced tracks (and the students in them) seen as being on top.

- Students in various tracks and ability levels experience school in very different ways.

Underlying Assumptions

First, and clearly most important, teachers and administrators generally assume that tracking promotes overall student achievement—that is, that the academic needs of all students will be better met when they learn in groups with similar capabilities or prior levels of achievement. Given the inevitable diversity of student populations, tracking is seen as the best way to address individual need and to cope with individual differences. This assumption stems from a view of human capabilities that includes the belief that students' capacities to master schoolwork are so disparate that they require different and separate schooling experiences. The extreme position contends that some students cannot learn at all.

A second assumption that underlies tracking is that less-capable students will suffer emotional as well as educational damage from daily classroom contact and competition with their brighter peers. Lowered self-concepts and negative attitudes toward learning are widely considered to be consequences of mixed-ability grouping for slower learners. It is also widely assumed that students can be placed in tracks and groups both accurately and fairly. And finally, most teachers and administrators contend that tracking greatly eases the teaching task and is, perhaps, the only way to manage student differences.

The Record of Tracking

Students clearly differ when they enter secondary schools, and these differences just as clearly influence learning. But separating students to better accommodate these differences appears to be neither necessary, effective, nor appropriate.

Does tracking work? At the risk of oversimplifying a complex body of research literature, it is safe to conclude that *there is little evidence to support any of the assumptions about tracking.* The effects of tracking on student outcomes have been widely investigated, and the bulk of this work *does not* support commonly-held beliefs that tracking increases student learning. Nor does the evidence support tracking as a way to improve students' attitudes about themselves or about schooling.[1] Although existing tracking systems *appear* to provide advantages for students who are placed in the top tracks, the literature suggests that students at all ability levels can achieve at least as well in heterogeneous classrooms.

Students who are *not* in top tracks—a group that includes about 60% of senior high school students—suffer clear and consistent disadvantages from tracking. Among students identified as average or slow, tracking often appears to retard academic progress. Indeed, one study documented the fact that the lowered I.Q. scores of senior high school students followed their placement in low tracks.[2] Students who are placed in vocational tracks do not even seem to reap any benefits in the job market. Indeed, graduates of vocational programs may be less employable and, when they do find jobs, may earn lower wages than other high school graduates.[3]

Most tracking research does not support the assumption that slow students suffer emotional strains when enrolled in mixed-ability classes. Often the opposite result has been found. Rather than helping students fell more comfortable about themselves, tracking can reduce self-esteem, lower aspirations, and foster negative attitudes toward school. Some studies have also concluded that tracking leads low-track students to misbehave and eventually to drop out altogether.[4]

> *Even as they voice commitment to equality and excellence, schools organize and deliver curriculum in ways that advance neither.*

The net effect of tracking is to exaggerate the initial differences among students rather than to provide the means to better accommodate them. For example, studies show that senior high school students who are initially similar in background and prior achievement become increasingly different in achievement and future aspirations when they are placed in different tracks.[5] Moreover, this effect is likely to be cumulative over most of the students' school careers, since track placements tend to remain fixed. Students placed in low-ability groups in elementary school are likely to continue in these groups in middle school or junior high school; in senior high school these

students are typically placed in non-college-preparatory tracks. Studies that have documented increased gaps between initially comparable high school students placed in different tracks probably capture only a fraction of this effect.

Is tracking fair? Compounding the lack of empirical evidence to support tracking as a way to enhance student outcomes are compelling arguments that favor exposing all students to a common curriculum, *even if differences among them prevent all students from benefitting equally.* These arguments counter both the assumption that tracking can be carried out "fairly" and the view that tracking is a legitimate means to ease the task of teaching.

Central to the issue of fairness is the well-established link between track placements and student background characteristics. Poor and minority youngsters (principally black and Hispanic) are disproportionately placed in tracks for low-ability or non-college bound students. By the same token, minority students are consistently underrepresented in programs for the gifted and talented. In addition, differentiation by race and class occurs within vocational tracks, with blacks and Hispanics more frequently enrolled in programs that train students for the lowest-level occupations (e.g., building maintenance, commercial sewing, and institutional care). These differences in placement by race and social class appear regardless of whether test scores, counselor and teacher recommendations, or student and parent choices are used as the basis for placement.[6]

Even if these track placements are ostensibly based on merit—that is determined by prior school achievement rather than by race, class, or student choice—they usually come to signify judgments about supposedly fixed abilities. We might find appropriate the disproportionate placements of poor and minority students in low-track classes if these youngsters were, in fact, known to be innately less capable of learning than middle and upper-middle-class whites. but that is not the case. Or we may think of these track placements as appropriate if they served to remediate the obvious educational deficiencies that many poor and minority students exhibit. If being in a low track prepared disadvantaged students for success in higher tracks and opened future educational opportunities to them, we would not question the need for tracking. However, this rarely happens.

The assumption that tracking makes teaching easier pales in importance when held up against the abundant evidence of the general ineffectiveness of tracking and the disproportionate harm it works on poor and minority students. But even if this were not the case, the assumption that tracking makes teaching easier would stand up only if the tracks were made up of only truly homogeneous groups. In fact, they are not. Even within tracks, the variability of students' learning speed, cognitive style, interest, effort, and aptitude for various tasks is often considerable. Tracking simply masks the fact that instruction for any group of 20 to 35 people requires considerable variety in instructional strategies, tasks, materials, feedback, and guidance. It also requires multiple criteria for success and a variety of rewards. Unfortunately, for many schools and teachers, tracking deflects attention from these instructional realities.

When instruction fails, the problem is too often attributed to the child or perhaps to a "wrong placement." The fact that tracking may make teaching easier for some teachers should not cloud our judgment about whether that teaching is best for any group of students—whatever their abilities.

Finally, a profound ethical concern emerges from all the above. In the words of educational philosopher Gary Fenstermacher, "[U]sing individual differences in aptitude, ability, or interest as the basis for curricular variation denies students equal access to the knowledge and understanding available to humankind." he continues, "[I]t is possible that some students may not benefit equally from unrestricted access to knowledge, but this fact does not entitle us to control access in ways that effectively prohibit all students from encountering what Dewey called the funded capital of civilization."[7] Surely educators do not intend any such unfairness when by tracking they seek to accommodate differences among students.

Why Such Disappointing Effects?

As those of us who were working with John Goodlad on A Study of Schooling began to analyze the extensive set of data we had gathered about 38 schools across the U.S., we wanted to find out more about tracking.[8] We wanted to gather specific information about the knowledge and skills that students were taught in tracked classes about the learning activities they experienced, about the ways in which teachers managed instruction, about the classroom relationships, and about how involved students were in their learning. By studying tracked

classes directly and asking over and over whether such classes differed, we hoped to begin to understand why the effects of tracking have been so disappointing for so many students. We wanted to be able to raise some reasonable hypotheses about the ways in which the good intentions of practitioners seem to go wrong.

We selected a representative group of 300 English and mathematics classes. We chose these subjects because they are most often tracked and because nearly all secondary students take them. Our sample included relatively equal numbers of high-, average-, low-, and mixed-ability groups. We had a great deal of information about these classes because teachers and students had completed extensive questionnaires, teachers had been interviewed, and teachers had put together packages of materials about their classes, including lists of the topics and skills they taught, the textbooks they used, and the ways in which they evaluated student learning. Many teachers also gave us sample lesson plans, worksheets, and tests. Trained observers recorded what students and teachers were doing and documented their interactions.

The data gathered on these classes provided some clear and consistent insights. In the three areas we studied—curriculum content, instructional quality, and classroom climate—we found remarkable, and disturbing differences between classes in different tracks. These included important discrepancies in student access to knowledge, in their classroom instructional opportunities, and in their classroom learning environments.

Access to knowledge. In both English and math classes we found that students had access to considerably different types of knowledge and had opportunities to develop quite different intellectual skills. For example, students in high-track English classes were exposed to content that can be called "high-status knowledge." This included topics and skills that are required for college. High-track students studied both classic and modern fiction. They learned the characteristics of literary genres and analyzed the elements of good narrative writing. These students were expected to write thematic essays and reports of library research, and they learned vocabulary that would boost their scores on college entrance exams. It was the high-track students in our sample who had the most opportunities to think critically or to solve interesting problems.

Low-track English classes, on the other hand, rarely, if ever, encountered similar types of knowledge. Nor were they expected to learn the same skills. Instruction in basic reading skills held a prominent place in low-track classes, and these skills were taught mostly through workbooks, kits, and "young adult" fiction. Students wrote simple paragraphs, completed worksheets on English usage, and practiced filling out applications for jobs and other kinds of forms. Their learning tasks were largely restricted to memorization or low-level comprehension.

The differences in mathematics content followed much the same pattern. High-track classes focused primarily on mathematical concepts; low-track classes stressed basic computational skills and math facts.

These differences are not merely curricular adaptations to individual needs, though they are certainly thought of as such. Differences in access to knowledge have important long-term social and educational consequences as well. For example, low-track students are probably prevented from ever encountering at school the knowledge our society values most. Much of the curriculum of low-track classes was likely to lock students into a continuing series of such bottom-level placements because important concepts and skills were neglected. Thus these students were denied the knowledge that would enable them to move successfully into higher-track classes.

Opportunities to learn. We also looked at two classroom conditions known to influence how much students will learn: instructional time and teaching quality. The marked differences we found in our data consistently showed that students in higher tracks had better classroom opportunities. For example, all our data on classroom time pointed to the same conclusion: students in high tracks get more; students in low tracks get less. Teachers of high-track classes set aside more class time for learning, and our observers found that more actual class time was spent on learning activities. High-track students were also expected to spend more time doing homework, fewer high-track students were observed to be off-task during class activities, and more of them told us that learning took up most of their class time, rather than discipline problems, socializing, or class routines.

Instruction in high-track classes more often included a whole ranged of teacher behaviors likely to enhance learning. High-track teachers were more enthusiastic, and their instruction was clearer. They used strong criticism or ridicule less frequently than did teachers of low-track classes. Classroom tasks were more various and more highly organized in high-track classes. Classroom tasks were more various and more highly organized in high-track classes, and grades were more relevant to student learning.

These differences in learning opportunities portray a fundamental irony of schooling: those students who need more time to learn appear to be getting less; those students who have the most difficulty learning are being exposed least to the sort of teaching that best facilitates learning.

> *The net effect of tracking is to exaggerate the initial differences among students rather than to provide the means to better accommodate them.*

Classroom climate. We were interested in studying classroom climates in various tracks because we were convinced that supportive relationships and positive feelings in class are more than just nice accompaniments to learning. When teachers and students trust one another, classroom time and energy are freed for teaching and learning. Without this trust, students spend a great deal of time and energy establishing less productive relationships with others and interfering with the teacher's instructional agenda; teachers spend their time and energy trying to maintain control. In such classes, less learning is likely to occur.

The data from A Study of Schooling permitted us to investigate three important aspects of classroom environments: relationships between teachers and students, relationships among the students themselves, and the intensity of student involvement in learning. Once again, we discovered a distressing pattern of advantages for high-track classes and disadvantages for low-track classes. In high-track classes students thought that their teachers were more concerned about them and less punitive. Teachers in high-track classes spent less time on student behavior, and they more often encouraged their students to become independent, questioning, critical thinkers. In low-track classes teachers were seen as less concerned and more punitive. Teachers in low-track classes emphasized matters of discipline and behavior, and they often listed such things as "following directions," "respecting my position," "punctuality," and "learning to take a direct order" as among the five most important thing they wanted their class to learn during the year.

We found similar differences in the relationships that students established with one another in class. Students in low-track classes agreed far more often that "students in this class are unfriendly to me" or that "I often feel left out of class activities." They said that their classes were interrupted by problems and by arguing in class. Generally, they seemed to like each other less. Not surprisingly, given these differences in relationships, students in high-track classes appeared to be much more involved in their classwork. Students in low-track classes were more apathetic and indicated more often that they didn't care about what went on or that failing didn't bother most of their classmates.

In these data, we found once again a pattern of classroom experience that seems to enhance the possibilities of learning for those students already disposed to do well—that is, those in high-track classes. We saw even more clearly a pattern of classroom experience likely to inhibit the learning of those in the bottom tracks. As with access to knowledge and opportunities to learn, we found that those who most needed support from a positive, nurturing environment got the least.

Although these data do show clear instructional advantages for high-achieving students and clear disadvantages for their low-achieving peers, other data from our work suggest that the quality of the experience of average students falls somewhere between these two extremes. Average students, too, were deprived of the best circumstances schools have to offer, though their classes were typically more like those of high-track students. Taken together, these findings begin to suggest why students who are not in the top tracks are likely to suffer because of their placements: their education is of considerably lower quality.

It would be a serious mistake to interpret these data as the "inevitable" outcome of the differences in the students who populate the various tracks. Many of the mixed-ability classes in our study showed that high-quality experiences are very possible in classes that include all types of students. But neither should we attribute these differences to consciously mean-spirited or blatantly discriminatory actions by schoolpeople.

Obviously, the content teachers decide to teach and the ways in which they teach it are greatly influenced by the students with whom they interact. And it is unlikely that students are passive participants in tracking processes. It seems more likely that students achievements, attitudes, interest, perceptions of themselves, and behaviors (growing increasingly disparate over time) help produce some of the effects of tracking. Thus groups of students who by conventional wisdom, seem less able and less eager to learn are very likely to affect a teacher's ability or even willingness to provide the best possible learning opportunities. The obvious conclusion about the effects of these track specific differences on the ability of the schools to achieve academic excellence is that students who are exposed to less content and lower-quality, teaching are unlikely to get the full benefit out of their schooling. Yet this less-fruitful experience seems to be the norm when average- and low-achieving students are grouped together for instruction.

I believe that these data reveal frightening patterns of curricular inequality. Although these patterns would be disturbing under any circumstances (and though many white, suburban schools consign a good number of their students to mediocre experiences in low-ability and general-track classes), they become particularly distressing in light of the prevailing pattern of placing disproportionate numbers of poor and minority students in the lowest-track classes. A self-fulfilling prophecy can be seen to work at the instructional level to prevent schools from providing equal educational opportunity. Tracking appears to teach and reinforce the notion that those not defined as the best are *expected* to do less well. Few students and teachers can defy those expectations.

Tracking Equality and Excellence

Tracking is assumed to promote educational excellence because it enables schools to provide students with the curriculum and instruction they need to maximize their potential and achieve excellence on their own terms. But the evidence about tracking suggests the contrary. Certainly students bring differences with them to school, but, by tracking, schools help to widen rather than narrow these differences. Students who are judged to be different from one another are separated into different classes and then provided knowledge, opportunities to learn, and classroom envi-

ronments that are vastly different. Many of the students in top tracks (only about 40% of high-schoolers) do benefit from the advantages they receive in their classes. But, in their quest for higher standards and superior academic performance, schools seem to have locked themselves into a structure that may *unnecessarily* buy the achievement of a few at the expense of many. Such a structure provides but a shaky foundation for excellence.

At the same time, the evidence about tracking calls into question the widely held view that schools provide students who have the "right stuff" with a neutral environment in which they can rise to the top (with "special" classes providing an extra boost to those who might need it). Everywhere we turn we find that the differentiate structure of schools throws up barriers to achievement for poor and minority students. Measures of talent clearly seem to work against them, which leads to their disproportionate placement in groups identified as slow. Once there, their achievement seems to be further inhibited by the type of knowledge they are taught and by the quality of the learning opportunities they are af-

forded. Moreover, the social and psychological dimensions of classes at the bottom of the hierarchy of schooling seem to restrict their chances for school success even further.

Good intentions, including those of advocates of "excellence" and of "equity," characterize the rhetoric of schooling. Tracking, because it is usually taken to be a neutral practice and a part of the mechanics of schooling has escaped the attention of those who mean well. But by failing to scrutinize the effects of tracking, schools unwittingly subvert their well-meant efforts to promote academic excellence and to provide conditions that will enable all students to achieve it.

This article is an extension of analyses that appear in Keeping Track: How Schools Structure Inequality, published by Yale University Press in 1985. The work was conducted under the auspices of the Laboratory in School and Community Education, Graduate School of Education, University of California, Los Angeles. "Keeping Track, Part 2: Curriculum Inequality and School Reform," appears in the October *Kappan*.

Notes

1. Some recent reviews of studies on the effects of tracking include: Robert C. Calfee and Roger Brown. "Grouping Students for Instruction" in *Classroom Management* (Chicago 78th Yearbook of the National Society for the Study of Education. University of Chicago Press, 1979). Dominick Esposito, "Homosceous and Heterogeneous Ability Grouping: Principal Findings and Implications for Evaluating and Designing More Effective Educational Environments," *Reviews of Educational Research*, vol. 43, 1973 pp. 163-79; Jeanne Oaks, "Tracking: A Contextual Perspective on How Schools Structure Differences," *Educational Psychologist*, in press; Caroline J. Persoll. *Education and Inequality, The Results and Results of Stratification in America's Schools*, (New York: Free Press, 1977); and James E. Rosenbaum. "The Social Implications of Educational Grouping," in David C Berliner, ed., *Review of Research in Education*, vol. 8 (Washington, DC: American Educational Research Association, 1980) pp. 361-401.

2. James E. Rosenbaum. *Making Inequality: The Hidden Curriculum of High School Tracking*, (New York: Wiley, 1976).

3. See: for example, David Stern et. al. *One Million Hours a Day Vocational Education in California Public Secondary Schools*

(Berkeley: Report to the California Policy Seminar, University of California School of Education, 1985).

4. Rosenbaum, "The Social Implication . . ." and William E. Shafer and Carol Olexa. *Tracking and Opportunity* (Seranton, PA: Chandler, 1971).

5. Karl A. Alexander and Edward L. McDill, "Selection and Allocation Within Schools: Some Causes and Consequences of Curriculum Placement," *American Sociological Review*, vol. 41, 1976 pp. 969-80; Karl A. Alexander, Martha Cook, and Edward L. McDill "Curriculum Tracking and Educational Strati-

fication: Some Further Evidence," *American Sociological Review*, vol. 43, 1978, pp. 47-66, and Donald A. Rock et al., *Study of Excellence in High School Education: Longitudinal Study, 1980-82*, (Princeton, NJ: Educational Testing Service, Final Report, 1985).

6. Persell. *Education and Inequality . . .* and Jeanne Oakes, *Keeping Track How Schools Structure Inequality* (New Haven, CT: Yale University Press, 1985).

7. Gary D. Fensterntacher. "Introduction," in Gary D. Fensterntacher and John I. Goodlad, eds., *Individual Differences and the Common Curriculum* (Chi-

cago: 82nd Yearbook of the National Society for the Study of Education. University of Chicago Press, 1983), p. 3.

8. John I. Goodlad, *A Place Called School* (New York: McGraw Hill, 1984).

Jeannie Oakes is a social scientist with the Rand Corporation, Santa Monica, California.

Oakes, Jeannie, "Keeping Track, Part I: The Policy and Practice of Curriculum Inequality," Phi Delta Kappan (September 1986), pp. 12-17. © by Phi Delta Kappan. Reprinted by permission.

Students' abilities are different. These differences need to be taken into account in order to produce effective learning. Tracking is the response to these differences, argues Nevi.

In Defense of Tracking

Charles Nevi

Students are equal under law, not in ability. Appropriate tracking accommodates individual differences, but makes "high status knowledge available to all."

In his book *A Place Called School*, John Goodlad presents a dire picture of low-level tracked classes. These classes, he says, are characterized by unmotivated teachers teaching uninspired students; the material has little significant content or relevance. The picture he presents is enough to embarrass any educator who ever been associated with tracking in any way other than to rail against it.[1]

In *Keeping Track* Jeanne Oakes takes the same data that were available to Goodlad for *A Place Called School* and adds even more dire information. In addition to considerably more verbiage, Oakes adds a historical perspective and develops the possibility that tracking is a conscious, deliberate conspiracy on the part of the capitalistic bourgeois elements in society. Oakes claims these groups seek to protect their privileges and property by providing low-level educational programs for the less advantaged to keep them content with their menial roles in society.[2]

Goodlad and Oakes muster enough data and emotion so that it is difficult to dispute them. But with a little reflection, something seems amiss in the pictures of tracking that they present. Somehow, one is reminded of a poem by Issa that goes something like this:

The World is a drop of dew,
and yet—and yet. . . .

They are stating the obvious, and one hesitates to dispute them, and yet there still seems to be more to the issue. Despite the criticism of tracking, ability-grouping is a common, even universal characteristic of public education. Others who have studied the issue indicate that it was being practiced at least as early as the turn of the century and that today it is established in "thousands of American schools."[3] Some observers even say that the history of education is the history of tracking. Tracking was born the first time an enterprising young teacher in a one-room schoolhouse in the 1800s divided his or her class into those who knew how to read and those who didn't. Certainly it began when teachers started organizing their students into grade- and age-level groups, a clear indication that some students were going to cover different contents or the same content at a different rate.

Reasons for Tracking

As education has become more complex, content more broad, and students more heterogeneous, tracking has increased. In recent years guide-lines for certain federal funds—special and gifted education. Chapter 7—require that students be grouped for the purpose of different specialized instruction.

Oakes argues that tradition is one of the main reasons for the existence of tracking. And certainly this historical sorting of students into groups was done for one of the reasons that Oakes gives for tracking today: homogeneous groups are easier to teach.

A variety of additional reasons explain why tracking has become a tradition. It is one method of trying to improve the instructional setting for selected students, or what one researcher refers to as a "search for a better match between learner and instructional environment."[4] Tracking becomes a very common way of attempting to provide for individual differences. Unless everyone is going to be taught everything simultaneously, grouping is necessary. It may be as simple and obvious as putting some students in grade three and other students in grade four, or some students into a primer and others into a novel.

Tracking is not an attempt to create differences, but to accommodate them. Not all differences are created by the schools; most differences are inherited. In reading Goodlad, and particularly Oakes, one can get the impression that all students come to school with exactly the same kinds of abilities, aptitudes, and interests. The reality, of course, is that students vary widely. Socioeconomic status does account for differences in students. Learning disabilities may make some students less able to learn than others, and even though educators seldom deal publicly with the fact, some students are more able learners than others. Some students, for whatever reasons, are just plain smarter than others. Other students come to school with a broader and deeper range of experiences, with attitudes that foster learning, and with a positive orientation to school, rather than a neutral or a negative one. The schools

did not create these differences, but the schools must accommodate them, and one way is through grouping students according to their needs and abilities. Even Oakes seems to recognize this.

> Schools must concentrate on equalizing the day-to-day educational experiences for all students. This implies altering the structures and contents of schools that seem to accord greater benefits to some groups of students than to others.[5]

Equalizing Educational Opportunity

But how are educational experiences made equal? It is easy to argue that putting all students in the same classes is not going to equalize their expectations. In fact, an approach that treats all students the same and ignores the real differences among them can guarantee unequal experiences for all. Treating all students the same is not a formula for equity or excellence. Indeed, research supports tracking. A meta-analysis of 52 studies of secondary tracking programs found "only trivial effects on the achievement of average and below average students." The researchers added that "this finding . . . does not support the view of other recent reviewers who claim that grouping has unfavorable effects on the achievement of low-aptitude students. The effect is near zero on the achievement of average and below-average students; it is not negative."[6]

Despite the zero effect on achievement of average and below-average students, these studies did show some benefits for tracking.

The controlled studies that we examined gave a very different

picture of the effects of grouping on student attitudes. Students seemed to enjoy their school subjects more when they studied them with peers of similar ability, and some students in grouped classes even developed more positive attitudes about themselves and about school.[7]

Tracking is more than a tradition. In a balanced view of tracking, the issue becomes not whether tracking is good or bad, but whether any particular example of tracking accomplishes the goal of matching the learner to the instructional environment.

Appropriate Tracking

If there is such a thing as good and bad tracking, how does one tell the difference? Can we establish objective criteria? Obviously no magic formulas exist, but *Keeping Track* provides a basis for distinguishing between good and bad tracking.

Oakes cites the decision in the court case of Hobson v. Hansen, and calls it "the best known and probably still the most important rule on tracking."[8] The court's decision stated that tracking is inappropriate and unlawful when it limits educational opportunities for certain students "on the assumption that they are capable of no more." The court also provided a definition of appropriate tracking.

> Any system of ability grouping which, through a failure to include and implement the concept of compensatory education for the disadvantaged child or otherwise fails in fact to bring the great majority of children into the mainstream of public education denies the

children excluded equal opportunity and thus encounters the constitutional bar.[9]

This decision suggests the characteristics of appropriate tracking. One obvious consideration is content. Oakes uses the term "high-status knowledge," which she defines initially as "a community whose distribution is limited," to enhance its value. But it is also defined as the knowledge that "provides access to the university."[10] For the purpose of this discussion, high-status knowledge can be thought of as the combination of skills, experiences, attitudes, and academic content needed to create an informed and productive member of society. At the risk of using a cliche: It is the idea that knowledge is power, and that the primary function of the schools is to empower students.

Goodlad and Oakes express legitimate concern that students in the lower tracks are denied access to high-status knowledge, increasing the gap between lower- and higher-tracked (or nontracked) students. Tracking is not appropriate when the intent is to provide the lower-track student with an alternative curriculum that does not lead to the high-status knowledge. An appropriate program of tracking has the same expectations for all students and uses low-level tracking only to provide remediation and to upgrade selected students.

Another consideration, not directly addressed by the court but implicit in the decision relates to the quality of instruction. Goodlad and Oakes apparently never observed good instruction in a lower-level tracked class, and they seem to assume that quality instruction in a lower-track is not possible.

It is true that the attitudes, behaviors, and abilities of the students make lower-track classes more difficult to teach. But these conditions do not magically improve when the students are scattered among untracked classes. They only become hidden from view and easier to ignore. Appropriate tracking is an attempt to structure situations in which the students' special needs and abilities can be recognized and considered. It enables students in lower-level tracks to move toward the worthwhile goal of achieving high-status knowledge.

Appropriate tracking then can provide the best possible match between the learner and the instructional environment. Teachers using it can build a good instructional climate and motivate students toward attaining high-status knowledge.

Inappropriate tracking assumes that low-track students are not capable of acquiring high-status knowledge, and they must be given something less.

Oakes points out that the judge in the Hobson v. Hansen decision felt he was making an educational decision that would have been better left to educators. The court's decision concluded. "It is regrettable, of course that in deciding this case, the courts must act in an area so alien to its expertise."[11] But alien or not, the court's decision against limiting educational opportunities for some provides the essential basis for distinguishing between appropriate and inappropriate tracking.

Notes

1. John L. Goodlad. *A Place Called School* (New York: McGraw-Hill, 1983), see esp. pp. 155-57.

2. Jeannie Oakes, *Keeping Track, How School Structure Inequality* (New Haven: Yale University Press, 1985), see esp. pp. 191-213.

3. Chen-Lin C. Kulik and Makes A. Kulik, "Effects of Ability Grouping on Secondary School Students. A Meta-Analysis of Evaluation Findings." *American Educational Research Journal* (Fall 1982): 416.

4. Deborah Burnett Strather, "Adopting Instruction to Individual Needs. An Eclectic Approach." *Phi Delta Kappan* (December 1985): 309.

5. Oakes, p. 205.

6. Kulik, p. 426.

7. Kulik, p. 426.

8. Oakes, p. 184.

9. Oakes, p. 184.

10. Oakes, pp. 199-200.

11. Oakes p. 190.

Charles Nevi is Director of Curriculum and Instruction, Puyallup School District, P.O. Box 370, Puyallup, WA 98371.

Nevi, Charles (1987). "In Defense of Tracking," Educational Leadership 44, 6:24-26. Reprinted by permission of the Association for Supervision and Curriculum Development. Copyright © 1987 by the Association for Supervision and Curriculum Development. All rights reserved.

Standard tracking systems can be detrimental to students, yet the concept of grouping is attractive to most educators. If approached in a creative and innovative fashion, tracking can be modified to work for instead of against our students.

Alternatives to Tracking

Jomills Henry Braddock, II, and James M. McPartland

Studies of schools' attempts to soften the detrimental effects of tracking indicate that reform may come about through modifications to tracking, rather than by its outright elimination.

To call some students "academic" and others "nonacademic" has a devastating impact on how teachers think about students and how students think about themselves. The message to some is: *you are the intellectual leaders, you will go on to further education.* To others it is: *you are not academic, you are not smart enough to do this work.* Students are thus divided between those who think and those who work, when, in fact, life for all of us is a blend of both.—From *An Imperiled Generation.* The Carnegie Foundation for the Advancement of Teaching, 1988.

Education researchers and theorists regularly prescribe doing away with tracking, but it continues to be used almost universally in high schools and is becoming increasingly prominent in middle and elementary schools.[1] Recent reports on restructuring schools list tracking on their agendas for change; many call for "modifications" in tracking rather than its outright elimination.[2] These more circumscribed approaches may have a better chance of success because they take into account forces on each side of the issue.

The Basic Assumption

Schools use tracking to accommodate instruction to the range of student needs, interests, and abilities. The assumption is that students will learn best when the instructional content is matched well to individual knowledge and abilities. Students are divided into homogeneous learning groups so that teachers can offer lessons that no

---

1 See Braddock (1989) and Maryland State Department of Education (1989).
2 See Children's Defense Fund (1988), Carnegie Council on Adolescent Development (1989), Maryland State Department of Education (1989), and Boyer (1983).

student finds too hard or too easy. This, they think, should maximize student motivation and learning.

The term *tracking* is most often used to refer to between-class homogeneous grouping of students. A number of other variations of within-class and between-class grouping practices have been described in the research literature (Slavin 1989, Oakes 1989). Grouping in elementary schools is often accomplished *within* a heterogeneous class by forming smaller subgroups for instruction, such as the three reading groups that exist in most early elementary classes. Middle and high schools typically form homogeneous groups between rather than within classes, by assigning students to classrooms according to their recent performance on tests or their report card grades. High school students are often assigned first to differentiated curriculum programs, such as academic or college prep, general, and vocational, and then to separate classes within these programs based on further assessments of student needs and abilities.

The Detrimental Effects

Arguments against tracking usually emphasize that separate, tracked classes receive unequal shares of the key formal and informal aspects of a good learning environment.

Weaker learning environments. Lower track classrooms are usually assigned the least experienced teachers, even though they enroll the students with the greatest needs who may be the most challenging to

teach. Indeed, some districts and schools, by allowing their most senior teachers to choose the tracks they wish to teach, often create weaker learning environments for students with the greatest need.

Lowered expectations. Students in lower track classes are often stigmatized by a schoolwide attitude that they are not capable learners. When such negative images are shared by lower track teachers and their students, certain instructional consequences follow: fewer curriculum units are covered, the pace of instruction is slower, fewer demands are made for learning higher-order skills, and test and homework requirements are taken less seriously (Oakes 1985, Mitchell 1989).

Cumulative losses. Tracking actually widens the gap in achievement between students in the top and bottom levels over time (Goodlad 1983). A student who is first assigned to a bottom class has an even poorer chance to move up to a higher track at the next grade level. So for those at the bottom, the effects of tracking produce slower and slower rates of learning and smaller and smaller chances of receiving better track assignments. Naturally the cumulative losses are greatest when tracking starts in the early elementary grades.

Resegregation. Tracking can undermine efforts to desegregate schools, because students from poorer socioeconomic background are most likely to wind up in lower tracks (Epstein 1985). Thus, in racially mixed schools, tracking usually produces resegregation of black and white students into different classes within the school, with

fewer chances for minority students to progress to high school completion and college enrollment.

Resistance to change. There are powerful forces in many schools and districts who perceive tracking to be in their own best interests. Often when the elimination of tracking is proposed, parents of the highest achieving students and senior teachers are the most outspoken opponents of doing away with it.[3]

Pragmatic Alternatives

Modifications and alternatives to tracking can address teachers' desires to match instruction to student abilities, without the gross educational inequalities that often accompany lower-tracked classes and without ignoring the legitimate needs of exceptional children. Based on recent research reviews on this topic (Gamoran and Berends 1987, Oakes 1989, Slavin 1989) and information from schools and districts that are struggling with the issue, we offer these recommendations:

1. *Postpone tracking.* Tracking should be deferred as late in the grade span as possible. Elementary grades should feature within-class methods of adapting instruction to student needs (such as within-class ability groups in mathematics or reading and cooperative techniques) or certain cross-age regrouping approaches that emphasize direct instruction in basic subjects.

2. *Limit tracking.* In the later grades tracking should be limited to those basic academic subjects where students' differences in skill levels are clear detriments to whole class

3 See McPartland and Crain (1987), Oakes (1989), and Slavin et al. (1989). For accounts of political battles over tracking reforms, see Frey (1988).

instruction. Research indicates (Slavin 1989) that between-class grouping plans in the later elementary grades are most beneficial when students remain in heterogeneous classes most of the day and are regrouped only in mathematics or reading on the basis of their current skills in each specific subject. It is reasonable to predict that a similarly limited use of tracking would be effective in the middle and high school grades, perhaps restricted even further to subjects that have specific prerequisite requirements at each step of learning.

3. *Create better placement criteria.* The use of a single criterion, such as a student's rank or overall report card average, to determine the general track placement for his or her entire academic program almost always constitutes the misuse of tracking. Tracking makes sense only if it helps students learn better by creating a stronger learning environment more closely matched to their current needs. Criteria for individual students course assignments should be current and differentiated—the placement of a student in an upper level math course and in a lower level English course (or vice versa) should not be unusual. At a minimum, separate recent tests or grades in *each* tracked subject should be used. School and district officials should regularly review distribution placements in tracked subjects by sex and ethnicity to guard against placement biases.

4. *Experiment with new methods of placement.* School and districts should try offering middle and high school students incentives for taking challenging courses. For example, teachers might encourage students to move to upper level courses by offering them interesting grading

options (pass-fail or extra credits for certain offerings).

5. *Minimize separate offerings for special needs students.* Separate offerings for gifted students, limited-English-proficient students, and special education students can be retained at each grade level along with the program of limited tracking described above. But such separate offerings are themselves a version of general curriculum tracking, and they should be clearly restricted to meeting the needs of exceptional children.

Improvements in Untracked Classes

Some methods for improving untracked classes are offered below.

1. *Provide extra help.* Teachers should offer extra help to any student having serious difficulties. For example, additional coaching sessions or peer tutoring services within the regular school schedule could prevent course failures.

2. *Equip teachers with useful teaching methods.* Cooperative learning techniques that actively involve all students from a heterogeneous class in learning activities are effective ways to improve achievement (Slavin 1986, Newmann and Thompson 1987, Cohen 1986). Mastery learning methods can also deliver extra help and provide extra chances for success to selected students within heterogeneous classes (Block and Anderson 1975).

3. *Expand all students' opportunities.* All students should be able to earn good grades. Students should be rewarded for individual effort and progress regardless of their starting point. They should also be able to demonstrate their competence through different avenues, not

merely the traditional linear-sequential modes.

4. *Find alternatives to tracking.* Other innovations in secondary school scheduling and student evaluation policies, such as continuous progress programs where students can complete course units at different rates, can be used to adapt heterogeneous class grouping to individual student differences (Carnegie Council 1989, Boyer 1983).

Making Tracking Reform Happen

There are many innovative and effective alternatives to tracking. San Diego, for example, has implemented (1) an "equity and student placement policy" aimed at ensuring a balanced representation of student subgroups across curricular programs and (2) a "common core curriculum" designed to eliminate the less challenging mathematics courses and have all students take courses such as algebra and geometry (Lytle 1989). Oakland has focused on strengthening the curriculum and instruction in both mathematics and English and is addressing student access to courses and teacher expectations.

In an effort to "eliminate the gross and subtle mechanisms by which schools differentiate the academic careers of [African-American] and white children," the Norfolk school district has undertaken a review of all their programs and services. Along different lines, Pittsburgh has eliminated the general education track in its high schools and greatly strengthened and updated its vocational (applied technology) education program and middle school career counseling services in order to provide better and more marketable training to non-college bound youth.

On a smaller scale, local schools are also implementing innovative alternatives. Recently, in collaboration with the National Education Association, we surveyed a group of such schools (Slavin et al. 1989) and found three major types of changes at the elementary level. The most prevalent changes were experiments with whole-class instruction in reading. Other schools had instituted flexible, usually cross-grade, grouping plans, often with a strong mainstreaming emphasis. Still other schools reported moving from homogeneous to heterogeneous grouping.

Several of the middle and high school in the Hopkins NEA study described efforts to reduce the number of ability groups while still maintaining two or three groups for some or all subjects. For example, one middle school principal described a plan in which the top track remained separate but the other classes (three of the four sections) were heterogeneously mixed and given the same curriculum. And one of the senior high schools also reduced the number of tracks, plac-

ing most students in a large, fairly heterogeneous group.

A few schools used completely heterogeneous grouping in all subjects and grade levels: one is a small K-12 school in which every class is heterogeneous; another is a magnet school for drama in a large urban district. A second magnet school in the same city uses cooperative learning, individualized instruction, and flexible ability grouping. Both of these magnet schools serve predominantly Hispanic and African-American students. A K-9 university lab school also reported using heterogeneous grouping for all subjects.

Some of the middle school respondents also have implemented ambitious mainstreaming plans, combining special education and gifted students in cooperative learning groups to enhance the higher-order thinking skills of both. Surprisingly, the teachers and administrators interviewed in our survey were almost uniformly positive about their efforts to reduce tracking.

The Bottom Line

Modifications that lead to a combination of tracked and untracked

classes may best initiate tracking reform. These include placing sensible limitations and restrictions on tracked offerings, better use of resources to support the learning of students in lower tracks, and implementing changes in untracked classes to help them work better for all students.

Tracking as practiced in many American schools and districts is clearly in need of reform, but turning the suggestions for reform into action will not be easy. In considering their policies concerning this practice, educators would do well to listen to arguments both for and against tracking. Only by listening to both sides can they recognize—and address—the norms and interests that have sustained tracking practices.

Author's note: This research was supported by a grant from the Office of Educational Research and Improvement, Grant R117 R90002. However, the opinions expressed are those of the authors and do not represent OERI positions or policy, and no official endorsement should be inferred.

References

Block, J.H. and R.B. Anderson. (1975). *Mastery Learning in Classroom Instruction.* New York: Macmillan.

Boyer, E.L.(1983). *High School.* New York: Harper and Row.

Braddock, J.H. (1989). "Tracking of Black, Hispanic, Asian, Native American and White Students: National Patterns and Trends." Baltimore, MD: Center for Research on Effective Schooling for Disadvantaged Students, The Johns Hopkins University.

Carnegie Council on Adolescent Development. (1989). *Turning Points.* New York: Carnegie Council on Adolescent Development.

Children's Defense Fund. (1988). *Making the Middle Grades Work.* Washington, DC: Children's Defense Fund.

Cohen, E.G. (1986). *Designing Groupwork Strategies for the Heterogeneous Classroom.* New York: Teachers College Press.

Epstein, J.L. (1985). "After the Bus Arrives: Resegregation in Desegregation Schools." *Journal of Social Issues.* 41, 23-24.

Frey, G.T. (1988). "Equity in Student Placement in the San Diego Unified School District: The Good, the Bad, and the Ugly." Paper presented at the annual meeting of the American Education Research Association.

Gamoran, A. and M. Berends. (1987). "The Effects of Stratification in Secondary Schools: Synthesis of Survey and Ethnographic Research." *Review of Educational Research.* 57, 415-435.

Goodlad, J. (1983). *A Place Called School.* New York: McGraw-Hill.

Lytle, J.H. (1989). "Minority Student Access to and Preparation for Higher Education." Preliminary report presented at the Council of Great City School, fall conference, Miami, FL.

Maryland State Department of Education. (1989). "Task Force on the Middle Learning Years." Baltimore, MD: Maryland State Department of Education.

McPartland, J.M. and R.L. Crain. (1987). "Evaluating the Trade-offs in Student Outcomes from Alternative School Organization Policies." In *The Social Organization of Schools.*

Mitchell, R. (1989). "Off the Tracks." *Perspective.* 1(3): 1-16.

Newmann, F.M. and J.A. Thompson. (1987). *Effects of Cooperative Learning on Achievement in Secondary Schools: A Summary of Research.* Madison, WI: National Center on Effective Secondary Schools, University of Wisconsin.

Oakes, J. (1985). *Keeping Track: How Schools Structure Inequality.* New Haven, CT: Yale University Press.

Oakes, J. (1989). "Tracking in Secondary Schools: A Contextual Perspective." In *School and Classroom Organization.* edited by R.E. Slavin, Hillsdale, NJ: Lawrence Erlbaum Associates.

Slavin, R.E. (1986). *Using Student Team Learning.* Baltimore, MD: Center for Research on Elementary and Middle Schools. The Johns Hopkins University.

Slavin, R.E. (1989). "Grouping for Instruction in the Elementary School." In *School and Classroom Organization.* edited by R.E. Slavin. Hillsdale, NJ: Lawrence Erlbaum Associates.

Slavin, R., Braddock, J., Hall, C., and R. Petza. (1989). "Alternatives to Ability Grouping." Baltimore, MD: Center for Research on Effective Schooling for Disadvantaged Students. The Johns Hopkins University.

Jomills Henry Braddock II is Director and James M. McPartland is Principal Research Scientist at the Center for Research on Effective Schooling for Disadvantaged Students. The Johns Hopkins University, 3505 N. Charles St., Baltimore, MD 21218.

Braddock II, Jomills Henry and James M. McPartland (1990). "Alternatives to Tracking," Educational Leadership. 47, 7:76-79. Reprinted with permission of the Association for Supervision and Curriculum Development. Copyright © 1990 by the Association for Supervision and Curriculum Development. All rights reserved.

If tracking does not lead to maximum learning, why have schools in so many countries used this device? Glenn Smith argues that tracking and standardized testing are interconnected mechanisms for reproducing existing power relationships.

Schools and the Dilemma Over Social Class

Glenn Smith

All industrialized societies have some degree of social differentiation, but the existence of social stratification presents a peculiar dilemma for people in the United States. On the one hand, it is a deeply ingrained and easily recognized phenomenon that seems operationally "right." On the other it contradicts a cherished tradition and self-image of egalitarianism. Does not our Declaration of Independence assert the equality of everyone? Have not oppressed people from many "corrupt" countries flocked here to the bastion of freedom and opportunity? Have we not fought wars to abolish slavery, make the world safe for democracy and stop totalitarian aggression? And have not European observers since Alexis de Tocqueville (1832), told us that people in America "in their social state" exhibit "a greater equality in point of fortune and intellect ... than in any country of the world,

or in any age of which history has preserved the remembrance?"[1]

The reconciliation of these mutually contradictory traditions is accomplished in America by a form of Orwellian "doublethink"—holding simultaneously two opinions that cancel each other out, knowing them to be contradictory, yet believing in both of them. This involves forgetting whatever it is necessary to forget, then drawing it back into memory again at the moment when it is needed, and then promptly forgetting again, all the while achieving the supreme subtlety of applying the same process to the process itself.

The basic premise on which social doublethink rests is that in the U.S., unlike other countries, everyone begins with an equal chance but that differing abilities and effort produce a hierarchy of rewards. The logical inference from this starting point is that those who enjoy envi-

able social positions earned them in a fair contest and are therefore entitled to the accompanying benefits. Conversely, those who do not occupy the stratum they would like in the social structure have only themselves to blame. It is important that most people accept this as fundamental truth, for if most Americans believed their place in the social hierarchy derived primarily from accident of birth, the privileged would be uneasy, and the dispossessed angry. Yet it is equally necessary that it *not* be true, i.e., if birthright did not play an important part, parents in the upper reaches of society would be highly distraught, for many of their children would be displaced by those from below. As Warner and others note: "Most American parents believe that the best measure of their success in this life, and a good indication of their deserts in the future life, are to be found in the rise or fall of their children in the social scale."[2] To leave such an important dimension of life to genetic roulette would be unthinkable. So mechanisms must be found to guarantee the social status quo while appearing to ensure equal opportunity. We are therefore under a deep but largely unconscious compulsion to hold tenaciously to opposite poles of a contradiction.

Where Do Schools Fit?

There are many social institutions that help guarantee social stratification. The single most effective tool of the twentieth century for keeping the social order intact while appearing to offer equal opportunity is the educational system. School "is primarily a skirmishing ground over which our children fight the preliminary rounds of the class battle in which some of them will take more serious part when they grow up," wrote David Frost and Anthony Jay of British schools.[3] In the United States, we regard schools as not merely a skirmishing ground, but the battlefield itself. We acknowledge this in propaganda against dropping out of school. The amount of schooling one has, we constantly tell flagging pupils, is an important determinant of adult social class level. A more accurate statement would be that social class background determines in large measure how much and what kind of schooling one will receive. The context is rigged from the start and most of the winners are predetermined.

How Schools Maintain the Social Status Quo

A complex interweave of factors operates in schools to guarantee

that the academically brilliant will be separated from the academically dull along socially acceptable lines. To isolate one factor from the others does violence to the subtlety of the system, but such separation is necessary for analytical purposes.

Marks, testing, and guidance counselors

Any analysis of schools must include, and probably should begin with, an understanding of the system of rewards and punishments known as marks. These are now so basic to the institutions comprising our educational system that few teachers, administrators, parents, or for that matter pupils can really imagine a school without them. It has not always been this way, and knowledge of the history of when and how the schools changed is helpful in understanding what marks do today.

Until the last quarter of the nineteenth century, elementary schools were not usually graded by level (first, second, third grade, etc.), and few schools of any type, including colleges, used an A, B, C, D, F mark or its equivalent. Neither marks nor graded primary classes were essential. Most children of lower social class parents went to a "common" school just long enough to learn some arithmetic and acquire basic literacy before dropping out to go to work. Children whose parents had the money (i.e., upper class and many middle class parents) went on to academies—tuition charging secondary schools—and often on to college. These latter two groups, however, were quite small (2.0 percent and 1.68 percent, respectively, of the people of high school and college ages in 1870); and any child who could afford to spend the required number of years in school

and who behaved reasonably well could expect to graduate. For the person who could not afford much schooling, there were numerous possibilities for making money in an age of early industrial development and individual enterprise.

As the country industrialized after the Civil War, these conditions changed. Jobs that children had held either disappeared or were taken by adults. Women who had stayed home entered the labor force. The expansive possibilities associated with an open frontier diminished as the free land disappeared. Life became more specialized, complex, interdependent, and anonymous.

During this time, schooling changed in important ways. An ever-growing proportion of the population spent longer periods of time in schools: tax-supported high schools replaced the academies; elementary schools became sequentially structured with one level following another; and all types of schools turned increasingly to a "scientific" marking system, most commonly A, B, C, D, F. In short, the school became the universal church of a secular society in which heaven was replaced by material affluence and the Lamb's Book of Life by permanent record cards, reflecting the level of purgatory to which each sinner was assigned.

The adoption of a marking system per se was probably less important than was the "standardized" testing base on which it rested, for while marks indicated the degree of success or failure, they did not assign responsibility. In a society where merit alone was to be the basis for success and rewards, it was important that people not leave school blaming their failure on the whims of teachers. This was an especially sensitive matter because teachers were themselves overwhelmingly from one social class (lower-middle) in a school system which purported to serve all social classes equally. While it is overly simple to suggest that ability testing grew up as a direct response to the unconscious desire to maintain social inequality, the scientific testing movement would not have been so popular in schools had it not performed this function. Professional schools managers embraced standardized testing because it appeared both objective and scientific—merely describing the unavoidable nature of reality—and at the same time ensured that the "better" classes would remain in control. It met the doublethink test.

The testing movement, on which so much that is important in American schools rests, started in Europe around the turn of the century.

A man named Alfred Binet took up the challenge of devising a practical scheme for measuring "intelligence" in response to a request from the government of France. The French wished to separate out the most severely incapable people from the general population to be institutionalized. The minister of public instruction asked Binet to develop a way of identifying children who were likely to fail in regular schools so they could put them into special asylums. Binet, with the help of one of his students (Theodore Simon) devised a series of tasks that seemed to test childrens' listening, comprehension, recognition, sequencing, and obedience skills. Binet and Simon arranged these tasks from simple to more complicated. They asked each child to perform the tasks in order

of difficulty, beginning with the simplest. Children who could do fewest of the tasks successfully seemed to Binet the most likely candidates for special services. Although Binet cautioned against using the test for any purpose other than the one for which he designed it, people quickly generalized the process. Psychologists in the United States took a leading role in this development.

"If Binet's principles had been followed, and his tests used as he intended," said historian Stephen Jay Gould, "we would have been spared a major misuse of science in this century." Henry Goddard of Vineland, New Jersey, translated Binet's items and a Stanford University professor named Lewis Terman revised the items for American use. This form of the test became known as the Stanford-Binet.

Virtually all children have taken this or a similar test very early in their school careers, and the results have been the basis for assigning marks—"intelligent" children, if they work to capacity, should receive high marks; "dull" children, even if working to capacity, should not receive many top marks. And other things follow from children's marks: the kind of work given in school, teacher expectations for each child and, indirectly, children's expectations for themselves, and the important process of "guidance." The impact of all this on the child's later social class level deserves further treatment, but first a closer look at the nature of the tests themselves is in order.

From the assumptions Terman made, implicit in virtually all intelligence or ability tests since, that it is apparent the very concept "intelligence" is social-class loaded. In

other words, the tests predict future success and failure in terms of present success and failure as measured against the dominant culture's upper and upper-middle class norms.

Terman's test, designed primarily for children, required identifying objects that were common to everyone's experience and performing sequenced tasks involving memory and visual/spacial perceptions. The objects were presented as fairly realistic miniatures or depicted in simple sketches, with each on a separate card so they could be displayed to a child one at a time.

The test was individually administered by an adult to one child at a time. By asking many children of varied ages to perform sequenced tasks and identify objects or sketches, arrived at a "Standard Average Score" for each age. "Norm Tables" reflected these ages, beginning at age two. The test makers assumed that everyone had been exposed to the same basic skills and knowledge. Differences in performance, they thought, must be mainly due to differences in "general ability." Although the Stanford-Binet would eventually consist of fifteen subscales (e.g., vocabulary, verbal relations, copying, paper folding and cutting, memory for digits), the *Technical Manual* emphasized that all the subtests measured g, that is "mental energy" or "primary mental ability." Terman's and Goddard's work led to the concept of an intelligence quotient (I.Q.). The idea was to find the test taker's "mental age" or mental level by seeing which average age mean score was closest to the individual's raw score. This became the person's "mental age" and was expressed in years and months. The person's actual chronological age, also expressed in years and months, could be divided into the mental age to yield a ratio or quotient. Multiplying by 100 to get rid of the decimal resulted in an IQ score.

The "common" objects which the tester asks children to identify are items which all children are supposed to have had an equal chance to know. In one of the editions of the Stanford-Binet, one of the eighteen is a cream pitcher of the sort which is used to pour milk or cream into coffee or tea at the table. The child receives credit for a correct answer if he says either "creamer," "cream pitcher," or "ewer." Any other response, no matter how imaginative, is wrong. Obviously a child who grows up in a home where a cream pitcher is used and referred to by one of these three names (i.e., an upper class or upper-middle class home) stands a much better chance of being rated a good success prospect than a child whose family pours milk into the coffee out of a carton (i.e., a working-class family).

It should be noted that the average raw score difference was often rather small from one age to another. For example, a twelve year old with a quantitative raw score of 23 was average. Five points less would yield a mental age of nine; five points higher would yield a mental age of fifteen years, eight months. Thus, whether a child had an IQ of 120 or 80 might be a rather small difference in actual performance on the test.

In 1917 Harvard professor Robert Yerkes developed two forms of group tests for the Army to help select potential officer candidates. Known as the Army Alpha and Beta tests, these two were the first I.Q. tests to be given on a large scale.

Yerkes and others analyzed the test results and found reinforcement for their beliefs that the most intelligent Americans were those whose family roots were north European, particularly British, Scandinavian, and German. As Terman wrote about two Native American and Mexican children who had taken his test:

Their dullness seems to be racial, or at least inherent in the family stocks from which they come. The fact that one meets this type with such extraordinary frequency among Indians, Mexicans, and negroes suggests quite forcibly that . . . there will be discovered enormously significant racial differences . . . which cannot be wiped out by any scheme of mental culture.

Goddard asked, "How can there be such a thing as social equality with this wide range of mental capacity." Terman worried about preventing "as far as possible the propagation of mental degenerates." Many of the early proponents of testing were active in the eugenics movement, an organized effort which stressed changing social policy to slow down or prevent idiots, imbeciles, criminals, and other "undesirables" from having children.

Although the Stanford-Binet has been replaced by the Wechsler Intelligence Scale for Children (WISC) as the most widely-used sorting device in schools, it is still used extensively for young children. And none of the replacements of the Stanford-Binet is substantially less social-class loaded. Even Joseph L. French's Pictoral Test of Intelligence, published in 1964 and generally conceded to be "reliable," is so biased that children of professionally and technically employed parents score 25 percent higher than children of unskilled working

class parents.[4] Even the most "protest" psychologists now generally concede that there is sufficient culture-loading in even the best of the widely used tests to account for a difference of 15 to 30 IQ points between the average scores of people in the highest social class level society and those in the lowest. While this may mean that no more than one-fifth to one-fourth of a person's "intelligence" is environmentally (as opposed to genetically) determined, it is enough to make all the difference in school and in later life. The difference between an IQ of 95 and one of 125 is the difference in becoming a police officer and a corporation president.

The new "science of mental levels" quickly found two concrete applications of far reaching significance. First, it became the basis for the immigration law of 1924 which set quotas for the first time based upon national origin. In practice, the law was anti-Semitic and racist. It discouraged immigration from Latin and Slavic countries. Second, ability testing became the basis for hiring "guidance counselors" whose jobs included "guiding" high school students (and their parents) into "appropriate" curricular and career choices. Reinforced by "standardized tests," upper middle class students generally chose the college prep track; working or under class students usually populated the vocational track or dropped out.

Educators embraced the testing movement for two main reasons: (1) because it was "scientific" and mathematically precise; and (2) because it solved their problem of organizing and dealing with unprecedented numbers of students who were staying in school longer—the result of changing economic and social conditions. Thus, educators were ready to believe psychometricians who told them that reliable and effective instruments were available for solving their problems. The fact that the tests "objectively" supported the idea that those who had most of the money and control where the ones who *should* have it, may have helped the testing movement gain acceptance.

Although tests are the base upon which much of the social class differentiation takes place in schools, several other factors contribute refinements. Indeed, without these, the test results would be largely meaningless. Among them are tracking (ability grouping), teachers' attitudes and self-fulfilling prophecy.

Ability grouping. One of the most frequent uses to which the results of standardized tests are put is to divide a school population into groups. The theory behind this practice is attractive. It removes the potential embarrassment felt by "dull" children who often do not know the right answers when in the presence of "bright" children who do know. Additionally, the "dulls" do not hold up the "brights" by constantly asking for explanations which the faster children do not need. Such separation is what has almost always been implied in the twentieth century when educators talked about "providing for individual differences."

Taken at face value, ability grouping appears to be a humane practice aimed solely at helping children learn better; however, it performs other tasks far more important and less benign. In other words it possesses the qualities required of any credible mythology, that of combining widely agreed upon values with subtle and deep-seated needs.

The major function of ability grouping is that it separates children according to social class background without appearing to do so. In this way schools that theoretically treat everyone equally serve the children of different social classes in different ways.

A further note of explanation is perhaps in order for those not intimately familiar with the actual operations of schools. If grouping rested on test results alone, social discrimination would be successfully achieved generally, but there would be glaring individual exceptions because tests, like mortuary tables, predict for groups, not individuals. For this reason school people enter a teacher-administrator "judgment" factor for group placement purposes. This permits a quiet adjustment when a child's score seems seriously out of line with her or his background and behavior patterns. Thus, if the daughter of a physician makes a low score that should put her into a lower social class group, her parents will often complain and the principal will usually concur that she would really be happier and do better work if she were "with her friends." Or if the son of one of the local "river rats" should happen to score high on the test, he would stand a good chance of being moved to one of the lower groups because "he is disruptive in class, runs with a rough crowd, and has a bad attitude." But if children of lower class parents score well and show eagerness to assimilate the values, attitudes, and associational patterns for those above him in the social scale—i.e., if they are *upwardly mobile*—they will likely stay in one of the higher "ability" groups. In this way, the school keeps the social stratification intact, but selects a minority for upward mobility. One must keep in mind that social class stratification does not imply the kind of rigidity characteristic of *caste* societies, those in which almost no social movement is possible. The chance for upward mobility acts as a safety valve, attracting the support and talents of the most ambitious and aggressive people in society.

Self-fulfilling prophecy. The practice of ability grouping has been criticized by some educational philosophers and sociologists since its inception in the 1920s. But only recently have researchers discovered that children tend to perform according to teachers' expectations and that these are significantly influenced by the ability group into which children have been placed. Robert Rosenthal and others in several experiments have found that not only is school performance affected by teacher expectation but also that IQ scores change significantly and that the changes appear to be cumulative. If this is true during the short period of six to eight months that the experiments occupied, consider how important twelve years of teacher expectations will be in a child's life.

Neighborhood Schools

Another aspect of the U.S. school system that reinforces inequality is the time-honored concept of the neighborhood school. This is the practice of requiring children to go to a school in their own immediate community, a widely followed practice defended on the basis that it is both productive of community spirit and beneficial to the child. In actual fact, this practice means that children in cities tend to go to school only with other children of their own social class because housing patterns and school subdistrict boundaries tend to follow social class lines. The "blackboard jungles" and ghetto schools which have become commonplace in cities are one result of this practice. When one realizes that working class schools are controlled by upper-middle class boards of education, and are operated by upward-mobile lower-middle class teachers, the incidence of school vandalism, truancy, and dropout in these schools is hardly surprising. Money is unequally distributed among schools in such a system with the general result that middle class schools receive the newest buildings, equipment, and text material, and the most extensively prepared teachers.

The outcome of the U.S. school system, seen in social class terms, is a major reinforcement of the class system. Children of working class parents enter school at a disadvantage, a disadvantage reinforced throughout their school careers. In the 1960s one-fourth of American fourth, fifth, and sixth graders received Ds or Fs, and 50 percent more received Cs. As psychiatrist William Glasser pointed out, a C to most people is less than a satisfactory grade and is cause for internalizing a feeling of failure.[5] A disproportionate share of low marks goes to working class children, while middle class children receive the bulk of the As and Bs. A typical Midwestern city in the mid-1960s reported that 69 percent of the fourth graders in an upper-middle class neighborhood school received As and Bs while only 6 percent in a lower-working class school received those marks. By the time the stu-

dents have reached college age, the school system has done its social class selection effectively. In 1965, approximately 85 percent of children from upper and upper-middle class homes entered higher education, whereas only 6 percent of those from lower-working class families began a collegiate career.

Nor is this the end of selection. The higher a student's social class background, the more likely he or she is to attend an expensive, prestigious Ivy League or liberal arts college or major state university. The lower a student's social class origins, the greater the likelihood of attending a relatively low-prestige state college or municipal university.[6] Furthermore, social scientists have repeatedly found that the higher one's socioeconomic status the more likely he or she is to finish any kind of college once he or she begins. The old process of teacher expectations, self-concept, and parental expectations combines with the high cost of tuition to "cool out" the lower class children in higher education. The entire process is carried out, in the words of Christopher Jencks, "in a low-key way which gives the student at least the illusion of making his own choices."[7] Were this not the case, he goes on, "the rejects would feel that their ambitions had been blocked out by a particular identifiable group, namely the academicians, who judge them inadequate and they might mobilize politically to alter the system."[8]

This, then, is the hidden dimension of the official mythology of the U.S. school system. The belief that it is equally open to all, that every child has a chance to go as high and as far as his or her native talents will permit is as false as it is popular. It

is institutionalized doublethink on a supremely effective scale. The unpalatable truth is that U.S. schools are no more egalitarian than those of the Scandinavian countries, Britain, or Russia. They merely appear to be.[9]

The problem of doublethink in American education cannot be solved simply by damning standardized testing, for the test makers have devised the kinds of instruments which schools have requested. Nor does a blanket condemnation of the school system achieve anything, since we have the kinds of schools that the dominant forces in our social order have wanted. The question is whether we can afford the luxury of a social class system based upon wide disparity in wealth, prestige, power, and influence—whether a social class system based upon scarcity can successfully be maintained in a society characterized by over-abundance. Put differently, does a class system appropriate to an industrializing society, with its emphasis on differentiated status, pay, and styles according to one's job, fit a postindustrial society which is automating jobs into oblivion? And finally, is a school system unconsciously designed to preserve such a social class system desirable? At the very least, teachers and parents must decide whether it makes any sense to try to force all children to stay for twelve years or longer in a school system designed to eliminate most of them at the end of half that time.

The real question is whether this society can or should continue unaltered. The problem is as deep as the roots of Western civilization. Whatever the answer, the time is past when those connected with schools can permit themselves the easy response of unconsciously settling on the side of blind conservatism. Teachers must consciously face up to the doublethink demands made upon them by their society, or be unwitting tools of the vested interests of the past.

Notes

1. Alexis de Tocqueville, *Democracy in America*. Edited and abridged by Richard D. Heffner (New York: Mentor Books, 1956), 54.

2. W. Lloyd Warner, et al., *Who Shall Be Educated? The Challenge of Unequal Opportunities* (New York: Harper & Row, Publishers, 1944), 49.

3. David Frost and Anthony Jay, *The English* (New York: Avon Books, 1968), 33.

4. Joseph L. French, *Pictoral Test of Intelligence Manual* (Boston: Houghton Mifflin Company, 1964), 16.

5. William Glasser, *Schools Without Failure* (New York: Harper & Row, Publishers, 1961).

6. Seventy-five percent of students in Ivy League schools are from upper and upper-middle class backgrounds, and only 5 percent are from working class homes; at typical state colleges, 20 percent of the students are from the top two classes and 30 percent from working class homes. Robert J. Havighurst and Bernice L. Neugarten, *Society and Education*, 3rd ed. (Boston: Allyn & Bacon, Inc., 1967), 107.

7. For every 100 fifth graders in 1959-60, 97 entered the ninth grade, 85 the eleventh, and 72 graduated from high school in 1967. Forty of these entered college, and twenty will receive degrees in 1971. Of the twenty, more than eight will be upper or upper-middle class, about six will be lower-middle class, about five will be upper-working class, and less than one will be from lower-working class parents.

8. Christopher Jencks, "Social Stratification and Higher Education," *Harvard Educational Review*, vol. 38, no. 2 (Spring 1968), 284-85.

9. See, for example, Robert J. Havighurst, "Education, Social Mobility, and Social Change in Four Societies," *International Review of Education*, vol. 4 (1958), 167-83.

Glenn Smith is professor and chair of the department of Leadership and Educational Policy Studies, College of Education, Northern Illinois University, DeKalb, Illinois.

Teachers routinely use "ability" or "achievement" tests as part of their decision base for how to treat children. In a single experiment, teacher's were less than enthusiastic about their own participation in an "ability" testing situation.

Teachers Don't Want to be Labeled

Harry W. Forgan

When teaching a course on tests and measurements at Kent State University recently, I decided to administer an adult group intelligence test to the class. I wanted the students to "feel" what it was like to take such a test and realize what items we use to measure intelligence. I also thought they might be more aware of the short time it takes to obtain a number which is regarded as very important by many educators.

The students were told not to write their names on the test papers, but rather to use a code such as their house number, physical measurements, or any less obvious symbol. I explained that I really didn't have faith in IQ scores; therefore, I didn't want to know their IQs.

The administration of the test required only 50 minutes. The students seemed to enjoy taking it and chuckled at some of the tasks they were expected to perform. I had to

laugh myself when I saw some of them looking at their hands and feet when responding to items concerning right and left.

Upon scoring the test I found that the lowest IQ was 87 and the highest 143. The mean IQ for the 48 students was 117. I was not astonished by the 87, even though all of the students had successfully completed the general education courses and student teaching at Kent State and were ready to graduate by the end of the term. After all, IQ tests have many limitations.

Then I got an idea. I decided to prepare a report for each student, writing his code on the outside and "IQ 87" on the inside of each. I folded and stapled each paper—after all, an IQ is confidential information!

At the next class period I arranged all of the folded papers on a table at the front of the room. I wrote the range and the average IQ

on the chalkboard. Many students snickered at the thought of somebody getting an 87. The students were eager and afraid as I began by explaining the procedures for picking up their papers. I made a point of telling them not to tell others their IQ score, because this would make the other person feel as if he too had to divulge his "total endowment." The students were then directed to come up to the table, row by row, to find their coded paper. I stood sheepishly—ready to laugh out loud as I watched the students carefully open their papers and see "IQ 87." Many opened their mouths with astonishment and then smiled at their friends to indicate they were extremely happy with their scores.

There was dead silence when I began to discuss the implications of the IQ scores. I explained that in some states a person who scores below 90 on an IQ test is classified as a slow learner. The fact that group intelligence tests should not be used to make such a classification was stressed. I also emphasized the fact that *someone* in this class could have been classified as a slow learner and placed in a special class on the basis of this test.

I told how many guidance counselors would discourage a child with an 87 IQ from attending college. Again I emphasized the fact that one person in this room was ready to graduate from college having passed several courses in history, biology, English, and many other areas.

I then went on to explain that the majority of elementary and secondary school teachers believe in ability grouping. This is usually done on the basis of intelligence tests, so I explained that I would like to try ability grouping with this class—again to see "how it feels." Some students objected right away, saying that "I did not want to know their scores." I calmed them by saying it would be a worthwhile learning ex-perience and assured them that I really didn't believe in IQ scores.

I told the students not to move at this time, but I would like all of those with an IQ below 90 to come to the front so they could sit nearer to me for individual help. I told the students who had an average IQ (between 90–109) to go to the back of the room and then take the seats in the middle of the class. The stu-dents with an above average IQ were asked to go to the side of the room and take the seats in the back because they really didn't need much extra help.

"O.K., all those who got an IQ below 90 can come to the front of the room." The students looked around to find those who scored below 90. I said that I knew there was an 87 and maybe a couple of 89's. Again, there was dead silence. "O.K., all those students whose IQ is between 90–109 go to the back of the room." Immediately, to my amazement, 8 or 10 students picked up their books and headed for the back of the room. Before they could get there I said, "Wait a minute! Sit down! I don't want to embarrass you, but you would lie and cheat—the same way we make our students lie and cheat—because you don't want to be classified as 'slow.' I wrote 'IQ 87' on every paper!"

The class erupted. It was in an uproar for about five minutes. Some of the women cried. Some indicated that they needed to use the restroom. All agreed it was a horri-fying and yet valuable experience.

I asked them to do one thing for me: Please don't label kids. Because we are all "gifted," "average," and "slow," depending on the task at hand. They promised.

Harry W. Forgan is currently a Pro-fessor of Education at University of Miami (Florida).

Forgan, Harry W. "Teachers Don't Want to be Labeled" Phi Delta Kap-pan (September 1973) 304-06. Re-printed by permission.

Section Three

Who Are We Now?

In the United States schools have been the main agency for the socialization of young children into the mainstream culture. Mohl traces the historical evolution of this socialization process from assimilation to pluralism; he cites the latter as the more democratic approach.

Cultural Assimilation versus Cultural Pluralism

Raymond A. Mohl

Beginning with the rise of the common school movement in the early nineteenth century, the public school became an increasingly important institution in the United States. Like most social institutions, the public school has had and still retains certain essential functions. One of these functions, of course, is cognitive—the teaching of basic skills such as reading, writing, and mathematics, which are necessary for social and occupational living. But, most importantly, in addition to their cognitive functions, schools have served as central agents for the socialization of children according to acceptable patterns of thought and behavior. The schools serve to transmit prevailing norms and values across the generations. Not surprisingly, the norms and values that are transmitted are not those of minority groups but those of the majority—of mainstream America. Because the schools gener-

ally reflected the interests of those who possessed economic and political power, they sought to assimilate minority groups into the mainstream. They did so by indoctrinating minority children with the cultural values and behavioral norms thought desirable by the majority. The public schools, in short, have been and remain today instruments of socialization and social control.[1]

Historically, the socialization process in the schools was one which cut across ethnic, racial, and economic class lines. All children in public schools were confronted by the same bureaucratic institutional structure, and all were socialized to the same set of values and norms. By the beginning of the twentieth century, for instance, public schools throughout the nation had developed educational programs promoting morality, piety, conformity, industriousness, thrift, temperance, punctuality, cleanliness, self-

discipline, self-reliance, respect for authority, the responsibilities of citizenship, obedience to the law, respect for property, and other values considered important in an orderly, industrial society. The schools served the corporate-industrial state by promoting the importance of work, and by developing industrial and vocational education programs which sent pretrained workers into the factories, mills, shops, and offices. In a variety of daily activities, the schools promoted patriotism and American nationalism. School children, then, were more or less indoctrinated in prevailing American beliefs, in acceptable behavior patterns, and in the values of a competitive economic system. Education meant shaping the lives of children so that they would fit within the standardized and bureaucratic society. For all children, the public schools were agents of social and cultural conformity.

It is only within the framework of the schools' socialization functions that we can fully and properly understand the history of minority education in the United States. Ethnic and racial minorities came to the schools with different languages, cultures, traditions, and values. For the maintenance of social order and cohesion, the socialization and assimilation of these minority groups was thought to be doubly important. As a homogenizing agent, as an institution designed to secure conformity to the American way, the public schools thus took on the special task of breaking down and destroying ethnic and racial cultures. For minority groups—European and other immigrants, American Indians, Chicanos, and blacks—socialization in the public schools meant a vigorous effort to wipe out the old culture and to propagate the new.

The effort to assimilate European immigrants provides an example of the schools' Americanizing function. Between 1820 and 1930, approximately 35 million immigrants came to the United States, primarily from Europe but also from Asia, Mexico, Canada, and other parts of the Western Hemisphere. The especially heavy immigration from southern and eastern Europe after 1890, according to educational historian Callahan, "constituted an educational problem unparalleled in human history." With a diversity of languages, cultures, and traditions, these immigrants came seeking freedom and economic opportunity—the American dream. What they found was often quite different.[2]

The process of immigrant socialization went under the name of Americanization. Cubberley, one of the nation's leading educators, articulated the goals of the Americanizers in 1909 "Our task," he wrote,

. . . is to break these groups or settlements, to assimilate and amalgamate these people as a part of our American race and to implant in their children . . . the Anglo-Saxon conception of righteousness, law and order, and popular government, and to awaken in them a reverence for our democratic institutions and for those things in our national life which we as people hold to be of abiding worth.[3]

The public schools were central to this process of assimilation. The elementary school provided "the earliest opportunity to catch the little Russian, the little Italian, the little German, Pole, Syrian, and the rest and begin to make good American citizens of them." Most Americans simply did not believe that the immigrants brought anything with them worth saving—culture, tradition, or language.

Immigrant and second generation children made their first acquaintance with American life in the public schools. It was not always a pleasant experience. They suffered daily indignities from native-born American students, who made fun of the immigrant children's speech and dress. Their languages and cultures were often denigrated by an overwhelmingly white, Anglo-Saxon, protestant teaching force. Teachers arbitrarily Americanized the names of the immigrant children. They were forced to conform to American patterns of behavior. They were subject to daily doses of

patriotism. They were indoctrinated with capitalist values—often quite different from the spirit of communitarianism and political radicalism which such diverse groups as Finns, Slovenians, Russian Jews, and others brought with them. Immigrant adults in night schools were accorded similar treatment.[4]

The schools' handling of the language problems of immigrant children suggests a rigorous and insensitive approach to Americanization. In most schools, no special provisions were made for non-English speaking children. Immigrant children were simply thrown into the classroom without any preparation and forced to pick up English as they went along. There is little evidence to suggest that school systems made any effort to hire teachers with ethnic backgrounds or with multiple language skills. Despite language difficulties and cultural differences, immigrant children were expected to act like Americans from their first day in school. The public schools often provided an avenue for economic advancement and mobility, but usually at the cost of abandoning the ethnic heritage and the more traditional values the immigrants brought with them. The public schools in the United States have been called great melting pots, but the only melting pot most educators envisioned was one in which the newcomers were quickly melted into Americans.

Interestingly, different ethnic groups responded in different ways to the Americanizing public school. Many immigrants had been drawn into the American dream. It was, after all, the magnet of economic opportunity that drew most of them to the United States. One way up the economic ladder—for their children, if not for themselves—was through education. The rhetoric of opportunity in America said: get as much of it as possible. Moreover, certain immigrant groups—the English, Greeks, Czechs, Romanians, and Jews, for example—had relatively high levels of educational aspiration. Thus, the Americanization and culture destruction that went on in the public schools became acceptable to many immigrants, because education and the accompanying Americanization represented the road to economic success.[5]

Some other ethnic groups, however, rejected public education. A study of immigrants on the Minnesota Iron Range, for instance, demonstrated that Finnish and Slovenian radicals and socialists opposed the public schools because they taught capitalist values and undermined ethnic culture. Southern Italian immigrants, according to another study, rejected public schooling because it indoctrinated their children with "ideas antagonistic to the traditional codes of family life."[6] Other ethnic groups perceived work rather than education as the means to economic success. For these diverse groups of newcomers, several alternatives to public schooling existed. First, they could demonstrate their rejection of education by pulling their children out of school at or even before the legal age—generally age fourteen until well into the twentieth century—and sending them to work. This choice was quite common among Poles, Slovaks, Hungarians, Serbians, Croatians, and Italians.[7] Second, the immigrants could and did establish their own parochial school systems in which the history, languages, and

secular and religious traditions of the old country could be taught and preserved. Finally, many ethnic groups built a network of after-school schools or church schools or folk schools, which children attended daily after the regular public school day.[8] Thus, although the power and the pervasiveness of the American dream led many immigrants to accept public education which destroyed their cultures, many others fought to retain their ethnic heritages.

White ethnic groups were not the only ones subjected to the destructive impact of the American educational system. For other ethnic and minority groups, education was similarly used as an instrument of social control and cultural assimilation. The schooling of the American Indian, for instance, reflected the interest of Christian missionaries and government agencies in eradicating the Indian languages and tribal cultures. In the colonial period, those who rejected a policy of genocide advocated instead the more moderate policy of civilizing the Indians. Essentially, this meant turning them into Protestants and farmers. In the post-Civil War era, the land hunger of Americans stimulated a more intensified policy of culture destruction through education. The Carlisle Indian School in Pennsylvania, founded in 1879, typified the federal government's Indian education program. As a recent U.S. Senate report noted, the goal of the school, and other schools like it, was to speed the assimilation of Indian children into white society. It was "designed to separate a child from his reservation and family, strip him of his tribal lore and mores, force the complete abandonment of his native

language, and prepare him in such a way that he would never return to his people." In the 1930s, the government moved haltingly toward a more humane policy of Indian education—one which rejected harsh assimilation and began to accept bilingualism and the need to respect and preserve Indian tribal culture. Not until the late 1960s, however, did the federal government make a firm commitment to Indian schools controlled by Indians themselves.[9]

The schooling of blacks in the United States reflects a somewhat different pattern, although no less pernicious in its purposes and results. For blacks, segregated and inferior schooling remained a pervasive practice until well past the middle of the twentieth century. Ironically, the public schools which sought to break down ethnic groups into a common and unifying American standard, which sought to integrate Germans and Poles and Italians and even Indians into the American mainstream, purposely excluded the blacks. As historian Tyack has written, blacks "learned that the educational system that was to homogenize other Americans was not meant for them." The second class schooling blacks did receive was designed first, to induce conformity in values and behavior, and second, to fit them for an inferior place in American society. Thus, a widely imitated model for black education in the late nineteenth century was the industrial education plan introduced at Hampton Normal and Agricultural Institute and at Booker T. Washington's Tuskegee Institute. These and other black educational institutions promoted the moral and cultural values of the white majority, while at the same time preparing blacks for menial work roles in American society.[10]

By the twentieth century, sharp divisions among blacks prevented a common struggle against segregated and inferior schooling. One approach, typified by Booker T. Washington, and later the NAACP, sought to demonstrate that blacks were fully as capable as whites, and worked toward full integration in all areas of American life. But because they rejected militant behavior, these advocates were generally unsuccessful in combating segregated schooling. However, a second approach—that of black nationalists such as W.E.B. DuBois and Marcus Garvey—wanted separate black schools, controlled by black administrators, teachers, and parents; schools in which black children could be taught the black heritage and where they could develop racial pride, dignity, and self-respect. This division over aims and methods apparently still prevails today.[11]

Throughout our history, then, schooling has been viewed as a means of socializing children according to the values of the white majority. For immigrants, Indians, blacks, and other minorities, the school was a manipulative and paternalistic institution which sought to destroy ethnic cultures and languages. Cultural assimilation—a sort of cultural imperialism, actually—was the prevailing mode of thought, the ideology which shaped the schools' programs for minority groups. Cultural pluralism simply was not an ideology which meant very much to anyone with decision making authority in American education.

While cultural pluralism has recently become popular among spokespersons for the "new ethnicity," its roots lie in the early twentieth century. The philosopher Kallen is often given credit for first enunciating the ideology of ethnic pluralism in 1915 in a series of articles in The Nation entitled "Democracy versus the Melting Pot." Kallen urged a pluralistic society in which immigrant languages and religions would nourish "the spontaneous and instinctive cultural life of the masses." Language and religion would serve as "the primary inward factors working against assimilation." Kallen envisioned his ideal pluralistic society as a sort of permanent federation of nationalities, although he was never very specific as to how it would function in actual practice. Of this pluralistic society, he simply wrote: "its form would be that of the federal republic; its substance a democracy of nationalities, cooperating voluntarily and autonomously through common institutions in the enterprise of self-realization." The common language would be English, and all citizens would share and participate in the general society's political and economic life. But each nationality and ethnic group would retain its separateness and individuality in the federation through language, religion, and culture. Kallen's idea of ethnic federations represented a vague and naive idealism, and, as Higham has noted, made few converts in the succeeding years.[12]

Kallen's prescription for ethnic pluralism never caught on, but the idea that ethnic cultures and traditions were important was not ignored by other writers. In 1920, for instance, Berkson, a Jewish educator in New York City, published an influential, pluralist tract entitled Theories of Americanization. Like Kallen, Berkson was hostile to the idea of Americanization or assimilation through the melting pot, because this sort of fusion led to "the obliteration of all ethnic distinctions." As an alternative means of ethnic and immigrant adjustment, Berkson proposed a "community theory" which would accommodate "the ethnic will to live." Immigrants and minority groups, he wrote, had a right to preserve their identity, and he insisted on the value of the ethnic group "as a permanent asset in American life." For Berkson, the basic ingredients for the maintenance of ethnic identity could be found in "the history of the ethnic group, its aesthetic, cultural and religious inheritance, its national self-consciousness." As sociologist Gordon has noted, Berkson's theory of cultural pluralism posited that "each ethnic group which desires to do so should be permitted to create its own communal life, preserving and developing its cultural heritage while at the same time participating effectively in the broader life of the nation as a whole."[13]

According to Berkson's ideology of cultural pluralism, ethnic communities would share in the common economic and political life. Ethnic and racial cultures, however, would co-exist alongside mainstream American culture. Berkson admitted that the ethnic group might eventually disintegrate and be assimilated into American life, but this was acceptable as long as no compulsion was involved and the free choice of the individual was maintained. Berkson's ideas were similar to those of Drachsler, whose book Democracy and Assimilation was also published in 1920. Drachsler urged "the recognition of the value for American life of the cultural heritages of the immigrant groups and of the freedom to foster and conserve some of these values through voluntary communal organization"—a position which he called "cultural democracy."[14]

The ideas of Berkson and Drachsler did have an influence in the 1920s among some social reformers and social workers who dealt with ethnic communities. For instance, the International Institutes—a group of immigrant social service agencies in some fifty-five cities—built their programs around the pluralistic philosophy of Berkson and Drachsler. Other institutions such as the public schools, however, were immune to pluralist views and continued their policies of Americanization and culture destruction.[15]

In the 1930s the pluralist vision was elaborated anew. The leading advocate of cultural pluralism during the depression decade and the war years was Louis Adamic, a Slovenian immigrant who became a successful journalist and writer in the United States. In a series of articles and books, Adamic established himself as an articulate and sensitive pluralist. He was especially concerned about the so-called "second generation problem"—the conflict between ethnic newcomers and their American born children. He sought to overcome the sense of inferiority that prevailed among ethnic minorities in the United States through a sort of ethnic renewal which would build pride in ethnic origins and culture. As historian Vecoli has suggested, "the ideological thrust of Adamic's argument was that a new conception of America was necessary, one which recognized that America was no longer an Anglo-Saxon country and that

the children of immigrants should not be expected to become Anglo-Saxons." Adamic sought the eventual integration of ethnic and racial groups into a new "universal" American ideal, and this made him a "short-term pluralist." However, Adamic opposed assimilation which would destroy the cultural qualities of any ethnic groups. The United States, Adamic contended, was "a nation of nations," and only a new vision of America could accommodate cultural diversity. As Vecoli has noted, "Adamic strove tirelessly to move America toward a new definition of itself—one in which Ellis Island would be regarded as historically important as Plymouth Rock."[16]

By the 1940s most social scientists were predicting the end of ethnicity as a force in American life. The ideological demands imposed on the American people by the Great Depression, World War II, and the anti-Communist hysteria of the post-war years created a national mood of consensus in which ethnic and cultural differences were suppressed. Ethnicity seemed to be disappearing as the assimilationist process silently turned immigrants and their children into Americans. Schools, politics, and other institutions of "the dominant American social system," as one classic social science monograph of the 1940s asserted, were successfully working "to destroy the ethnic subsystems and to increase assimilation." Integration and civil rights legislation even promised to make blacks full partners in American society.[17]

These predictions about the end of ethnicity were premature. As we have discovered in the years since the 1960s, ethnicity remains a

strong and vital component of the American social fabric. Group identities, ethnic heritages, and community institutions continue to have an important place, and even a shaping influence, in the lives of millions of Americans. Advocates of pluralism hold that such cultural and ethnic diversity makes for a stronger and healthier democratic society. Greenbaum has written that pluralism must be taken seriously and "ways must be found to honor alternative worth, to revive and reconsider subordinated alternative values, and to create new, self-respecting institutions and communities."[18] A homogenized society poses real dangers to democratic values, while pluralism, writes educator Itzkoff, "constitutes a real bulwark of freedom."[19]

For American educators, cultural pluralism should point the way toward a less destructive, a more humanistic, and a more democratic schooling. A truly democratic society is one which accepts those who are different, which respects and encourages individuality, and which accords dignity to all. "The times are ready for a new kind of pluralism in schooling," Sizer noted in 1976—a schooling which can accept ethnic and racial diversity and work with alternative educational institutions in ethnic communities and neighborhoods.[20] If schools are to be more than simply instruments of majority culture and majority values, they must respect ethnic and racial cultures, values, traditions, and even languages. Cultural pluralism—not cultural assimilation—is an ideology which can make possible the achievement of these humanistic and democratic goals.

Notes

1. This analysis of the functions of schooling owes much to the recent revisionism in educational history. Especially important are the following: Michael B. Katz, *Class, Bureaucracy, and Schools: The Illusion of Educational Change in America*, expanded ed. (New York: Praeger, 1975); Marvin Lazerson, *Origins of the Urban School: Public Education In Massachusetts, 1870-1915* (Cambridge, Ma.: Harvard University Press, 1971); Joel Spring, *Education and the Rise of the Corporate State* (Boston: Beacon Press, 1972); David B. Tyack, *The One Best System: A History of American Urban Education* (Cambridge, Ma.: Harvard University Press, 1974); Samuel Bowles and Herbert Gintis, *Schooling in Capitalist America* (New York: Basic Books, 1976); Paul C. Violas, *The Training of the Urban Working Class A History of Twentieth Century American Education* (Chicago: Rand McNally, 1978); David Nasaw, *Schooled to Order: A Social History of Public Schooling in the United States* (New York: Oxford University Press, 1979).

2. Raymond E. Callahan, *Education and The Cult of Efficiency* (Chicago: University of Chicago Press, 1962), p. 15. See also Frank V. Thompson, *Schooling of the Immigrant* (New York: Harper, 1920); Robert A. Carlson, *The Quest for Conformity: Americanization Through Education* (New York: Wiley, 1975).

3. Ellwood P. Cubberley, *Changing Conceptions of Education* (Boston: Houghton Mifflin, 1909), pp. 15-16; Richard Watson Gilder, "The Kindergarten: An Uplifting Social Influence in the Home and District," National Education Association, *Journal of Proceedings and Addresses of the Forty-Second Annual Meeting* (1903), p. 390.

4. For a case study of immigrant in the schools of one city, see Ronald D. Cohen and Raymond A. Mohl, *The Paradox of Progressive Education: The Gary Plan and Urban Schooling* (Port Washington, N.Y.: Kennikat Press, 1979), pp. 83-109.

5. Timothy L Smith, "Immigrant Social Aspirations and American Education, 1880-1930," *American Quarterly* 21 (Fall 1969):523-43.

6. Hyman Berman, "Education for Work and Labor Solidarity: The Immigrant Miners and Radicalism on the Mesabi Range," Immigration History Research Center, University of Minnesota; Michael R. Olneck and Marvin Lazerson, "The School Achievement of Immigrant Children, 1900-1930," *History of Education Quarterly* 14 (Winter 1974):453-82.

7. John Bodnar, "Materialism and Morality: Slavic-American Immigrants and Education, 1890-1940," *Journal of Ethnic Studies* 3 (Winter 1976):1-19.

8. On ethnic parochial schools and ethnic folk schools, see James W. Sanders, *The Education of an Urban Minority: Catholics In Chicago, l833-1965* (New York: Oxford University Press, 1977); Joshua A. Fishman, *Language Loyalty In the United States* (The Hague: Mouton, 1966), pp. 92-126.

9. *Indian Education: A National Tragedy–A National Challenge*, Report No. 91-501, Committee on Labor and Public Welfare, U.S. Senate, 91st Congress, 1st Session, 1969 (Washington, D.C.: Government Printing Office, 1969), p. 12; Carlson, *Quest for Conformity*, p. 72. See also Meyer Weinberg, *A Chance to Learn: A History of Race and Education In the United States* (Cambridge: Cambridge University Press, 1977), pp. 178-229; Bruce Rubenstein, "To Destroy a Culture: Indian Education in Michigan, 1855-1900," *Michigan History* 60 (September 1976):137-60.

10. Tyack, *The One Best System*, p. 110; James D. Anderson, "Education as a Vehicle for the Manipulation of Black Workers," In Work, *Technology, and Education: Dissenting Essays In the Intellectual Foundations of American Education*, ed. Walter Feinberg and Henry Rosemont, Jr. (Urbana, Il.: University of Illinois Press, 1975), pp. 15-40; Donald Spivey, *Schooling for the New Slavery: Black Industrial Education, 1868-1915* (Westport, Ct.: Greenwood Press, 1978).

11. August Meier, *Negro Thought in America, 1880-1915* (Ann Arbor, MI.: University of Michigan Press, 1963); Neil Betten and Raymond A. Mohl, "The Evolution of Racism In an Industrial City, 1906-1940: A Case Study of Gary, Indiana," *Journal of Negro History* 59 (January 1974):51-64; Vincent P. Franklin, *The Education of Black Philadelphia: The Social and Educational History of a Minority Community, 1900-1950* (Philadelphia: University of Pennsylvania Press, 1979); Judy Jolley Mohraz, *The Separate Problem: Case Studies of Black Education in the North, l900-1930* (Westport, Ct.: Greenwood Press, 1979).

12. Horace M. Kallen, "Democracy Versus the Melting Pot," *The Nation* 100 (February 18 and 25, 1915):190-94, 217-20, reprinted

in Horace M. Kallen, *Culture and Democracy in the United States: Studies in the Group Psychology of the American Peoples* (New York: Boni and Liveright, 1924), pp. 67-125, quotations on pp. 103, 124; John Higham, *Send These to Me: Jews and Other Immigrants In Urban America* (New York: Atheneum, 1975), p. 212.

13. Isaac B. Berkson, *Theories of Americanization: A Critical Study* (New York: Teachers College, Columbia University, 1920), pp. 97-98; Milton M. Gordon, *Assimilation In American Life: The Role of Race, Religion, and National Origins* (New York: Oxford University Press, 1964), p. 154.

14. Julius Drachsler, *Democracy and Assimilation: The Blending of Immigrant Heritages In America* (New York: Macmillan, 1920), p. 215.

15. For information on the International Institutes, see Raymond A. Mohl and Neil Betten, "Ethnic Adjustment In the Industrial City: The International Institute of Gary, 1919-1940," *International Migration Review* 6 (Winter 1972):361-76; Raymond A. Mohl, "The International Institute Movement and Ethnic Pluralism in Twentieth Century America," *Social Science* (forthcoming).

16. Rudolph J. Vecoli, "Louis Adamic and the Contemporary Search for Roots," *Ethnic Studies* 2 (1978):32. Adamic's writings include *My America, 1928-1938* (New York: Harper, 1938); *From Many Lands* (New York: Harper, 1940); *Two-Way Passage* (New York: Harper, 1941); *What's Your Name* (New York: Harper 1942); and *A Nation of Nations* (New York: Harper, 1945). See also Richard Weiss, "Ethnicity and Reform: Minorities and the Ambience of the Depression Years," *Journal of American History* 66 (December 1979):566-85.

17. W. Lloyd Warner and Leo Srole, *The Social Systems of American Ethnic Groups* (New Haven: Yale University Press, 1945), pp. 283-84.

18. William Greenbaum, "America in Search of a New Ideal: An Essay on the Rise of Pluralism," *Harvard Educational Review* 44 (August 1974):440.

19. Seymour W. Itzkoff, "Cultural Diversity and the Democratic Prospect," *Review Journal of Philosophy and Social Science* 1 (1976):35. On the emergence of the new ethnicity, see also Michael Novak, *The Rise of the Unmeltable Ethnics* (New York: Macmillan, 1972).

20. Theodore R. Sizer, "Education and Assimilation: A Fresh Plea for Pluralism," *Phi Delta Kappan* 59 (September 1976):34.

Raymond A. Mohl is Professor, Department of History, Florida Atlantic University, Boca Raton, Florida.

Mohl, Raymond A. "Cultural Assimilation versus Cultural Pluralism," Educational Forum (March 1981), 323-32. Copyright 1981 by Educational Forum, Kappa Delta Pi, an International Honor Society in Education. Reprinted by permission.

Ladson-Billings examines how beliefs about students, content, instructional approaches, educational settings, and teacher training influence the effectiveness of multicultural education.

What We Can Learn from Multicultural Education Research

Gloria Ladson-Billings

Many findings from multicultural education research can be applied in the everyday world of teachers and administrators. This observation holds regardless of whether the educators work with many students of color or with only a few.

The research shows that five areas matter a great deal in the education of a multicultural population: teachers' beliefs about students, curriculum content and materials, instructional approaches, educational settings, and teacher education. One other area—whether the race and ethnicity of teachers affects student learning—remains unclear.

Beliefs About Students Matter

To begin to see how teacher beliefs affect student achievement, imagine two new teachers. Don Wilson and Margie Stewart are starting their first year of teaching.

Don Wilson. After his first weeks of teaching in an urban school, Wilson is exhausted and uncertain about whether he chose the right profession. His class of 28 fourth graders are African Americans and Latinos. Wilson knows that they have not had many advantages, so he doesn't push them too hard. He wants his students to have fun learning. He worries, though, because many of them don't seem to be having fun or learning. Many are one or more achievement levels below national averages, and some attend school sporadically, fail to complete homework assignments, and seem unmotivated in the classroom. Although Wilson has sent several notes home expressing concern, parents have not responded. Wilson doubts that he makes any difference in the lives of his students.

Margie Stewart. The first weeks of teaching in a suburban school have been exhausting for Stewart, too, but she is enjoying herself. Of Stewart's 28 third graders, 23 are white, upper-middle-class children. Three of the remaining five are African American, and two are Mexican American (one speaks limited English). In general, the students test at or above grade level on standardized tests, but the students of color lag behind the others. Stewart is also concerned about José. Because José's English is limited, Stewart must explain everything to him four or five times, and she can seldom work with him one-on-one. She fears that he is a special needs student. Perhaps she will ask the school psychologist to test José.

The research literature suggests that how teachers like Wilson and Stewart think about education and students makes a pronounced difference in student performance and achievement (Apple 1990, Cooper 1979). Winfield (1986) found that teachers expect more from white students than from African-American students, and they expect more from middle-class students than from working- and lower-class students. Teachers often perceive African-American students from working- or lower-class backgrounds as incapable of high-quality academic work. Both Wilson and Stewart are entertaining such thoughts. They are not attributing their problems with students of color to ineffective teaching approaches.

Sometimes, unrecognized or outright racism causes teachers to hold negative beliefs about students of color. A dramatic example from a first-year teacher's journal entry:

> I hate [African-American students'] ethnic attitude and their lingo. I hate to categorize it but ...I am more comfortable with black students who act white (Birrell 1993).

Such negative attitudes toward students of color lower expectations for achievement, which lowers achievement (King and Ladson-Billings 1990, Lipman 1993).

Content and Materials Matter

Teachers who are sincerely committed to multicultural education cannot be satisfied with superficial celebrations of heroes and holidays. This approach to content trivializes multicultural education and conveys the idea that diversity issues come into play only during celebratory moments with foods, fun, and festivals.

In the multicultural festival model, teachers, students, and parents typically spend lots of time and energy preparing for an all-school activity. Students may do background research about a culture, prepare maps, and help create indigenous costumes. Parents may help to prepare various ethnic foods. On the day of the festival, members of the school community go from class to class, visiting the various cultures, sampling the foods, and enjoying dances, songs, and arts and crafts. At the end of the day, everyone agrees that the annual event has been a great success. Then teachers and students go back to their real work.

Educators will be more successful if they understand five variables that matter in working with a diverse student population.

In the transformative model, on the other hand, multicultural education is not a separate, isolated, once-a-year activity. Instead, the regular curriculum includes a range of cultural perspectives, as in the following two classroom scenarios.

In a primary classroom, the teacher reads several versions of the Cinderella story. One is the familiar European tale by the Brothers Grimm, but other versions are Chinese, Egyptian, and Zimbabwean. The teacher helps students compare the different versions. Similarities include story structure, plot development, moral and ethical dilemmas, and the use of magic. Differences include standards of beauty, settings, use of language, and specific characters. The students absorb the importance of understanding cultural differences and similarities.

In an intermediate history class, students study the African slave trade, but not solely from the perspective of the European traders. They also read a range of primary documents, like the slave narrative called *The Interesting Life of Olaudah Equiano* (it compares slavery in Africa with slavery in the Americas). In addition, the teacher introduces information about the European feudal system. The students compare the lives of enslaved people in Africa, the Americas, and medieval Europe. Finally, they generate analytical questions, such as, What is the relationship between slavery and racism? How could a nation striving for equality and justice permit slavery? Why did some people in Africa participate in the slave trade? And how does the textbook's treatment of slavery compare to primary source material?

The teacher in this class plans to do similar in-depth study when the class studies the displacement of Native Americans, the Spanish mission system, European immigration of the 1890s, and Japanese internment. Although the transformative approach requires redesigning the curriculum, searching for additional materials, and limiting the number of topics taught, the teacher thinks the outcome is worth the effort. Students learn more content and develop a real ability to ask and answer critical questions.

The materials used in classrooms have important effects, too. As Banks' comprehensive literature review (1993a) points out, children are aware of their race and ethnicity at an early age. "If realistic images of ethnic and racial groups are included in teaching materials in a consistent, natural, and integrated fashion," Banks (1993b) concludes, all children "can be helped to develop more positive racial attitudes." Similar results are reported on gender issues (Scott and Schau 1985).

If classrooms use materials that do not portray diverse groups realistically, students are likely to develop, maintain, and strengthen the stereotypes and distortions in the traditional curriculum. Text analysis (a common form of multicultural research) indicates that textbook images and representations exclude, distort, and marginalize women, people of color, and people from lower socioeconomic echelons. A growing proportion of textbooks do include diversity, but their images and representations tend to be superficial and incorrect (Swartz 1992).

Instructional Approaches Matter

Changes to make curriculum content more equitable must be accompanied by changes that make pedagogy evenhanded. To ensure "equitable pedagogy," Banks says (see "On Educating for Diversity: A Conversation with James A. Banks," p. 28), teachers must modify instruction to "facilitate academic achievement among students from diverse groups."

To some teachers, simultaneously dealing with the flood of new materials and modifying instructional approaches seems like an overwhelming task. These teachers think that it is all they can do to teach the new material in old ways. In other classrooms, however, teachers have asked themselves,

what one move can I make to ensure that all students have opportunities for success?

For some teachers, providing more equitable pedagogy may be as simple as using more cooperative learning strategies in class. After all, cooperative learning was first developed as a way to create more equitable classroom environments (Cohen and Benton 1988, Slavin 1987).

How teachers think about education and students makes a pronounced difference in student performance and achievement.

For other teachers, equitable pedagogy will demand that they use the language and understandings that children bring to school to bridge the gap between what students know and what they need to learn (Au and Jordan 1981, Erickson and Mohatt 1982, Jordan 1985, Vogt et al. 1987). In addition, the total school context must come to accept whatever students have learned and experienced as legitimate knowledge (Irvine 1990, Ladson-Billings 1992, in press). Teachers can further these ends if they spend time in their students' community and apply in the classroom what they learned in students' homes. Teachers may also profit by learning their students' language. A teacher who

knows how to ask and answer basic questions in a second language can often make the classroom a welcoming and psychologically safe environment for speakers of that language. If a teacher becomes sufficiently fluent to teach academic content in English and a student's home language, the teacher tacitly promotes bilingualism and biliteracy (Hornberger 1988).

Educational Settings Matter

Forty years ago, the Supreme Court handed down a landmark decision, *Brown v. Board of Education*, which declared separate schools inherently unequal. Yet now, after years of hard-fought battles to desegregate the nation's schools, most students of color still attend segregated schools (Orfield 1989). Even when students go to desegregated schools, they are resegregated within the school via tracking and ability grouping (Oakes 1985).

For students of color, perhaps more devastating is the lack of access to high-quality education (Kozol 1991). Clearly, as a society, our care and concern for student learning is differentiated along racial, class, and ethnic lines.

To grasp the impact of these inequities, imagine that our new teachers, Wilson and Stewart, were to participate in a school exchange program. Wilson's students would visit Stewart's class. Then Stewart's class would visit Wilson's. What will each setting informally teach the children?

When Wilson's students arrive at Stewart's school, they are struck by its physical beauty and space. Well-kept grounds have ample playground equipment. Inside the school, the halls gleam, and a lively buzz emanates from the various classrooms. Each brightly lighted classroom has at least one computer. The school library has several computers, CD-ROM, laser disks, and an extensive library of videotapes. The school has many special rooms: a gymnasium, a multipurpose room, vocal and instrumental music rooms, an art room, and a room for enrichment activities. In each of the rooms is a teacher who regularly works with Stewart's students, freeing her for 45 minutes each day. She uses the time to plan, read, hold parent conferences, and do research.

When Stewart's class visits Wilson's school, they enter an old structure built in the 1920s. Its concrete yard is littered with broken glass, graffiti cover the walls, and the only piece of playground equipment is a netless basketball hoop. Inside the building, the dark halls are eerily silent, since room doors are closed and locked from the inside. There is a room where books are stored, but they are not catalogued because there is no librarian. The entire school shares one VCR and monitor. One of the two 16 mm film projectors is broken. A few filmstrips hide in various closets. The one room that does have computers, listening centers, and film loop machines is the Chapter One lab.

Here, students with literacy and mathematics deficits receive small-group instruction and skill practice for 30 to 45 minutes each day. In a corner of the multipurpose room, 12 gifted students in grades 3 to 5 meet one morning a week with a visiting gifted and talented education teacher. Classroom teachers are responsible for all other instruc-

tion, so they rarely have time to plan or confer.

What Stewart's students learn from their encounter is that Wilson's students are underprivileged, and perhaps, undeserving. The students will probably come to see inequities as normal and to equate African Americans and Latinos with poverty.

Meanwhile, Wilson's students learn that material advantages go with being white. Since Stewart's and Wilson's students are all about the same age with similar interests and abilities, the major difference that Wilson's students can see is skin color.

For some teachers, providing more equitable pedagogy may be as simple as using more cooperative learning strategies.

The few students of color in Stewart's class learn that they are very lucky. Under other circumstance, they could be at Wilson's school. Even though they may do poorly in a predominantly white school, they regard being there as a privilege.

Teacher Education Matters

If Wilson's and Stewart's students derive naive conceptions from their exchange visits, the teachers themselves also have trouble making sense of the differences. Neither teacher learned much about cultural variation dur-

ing preservice preparation (Zeichner 1992, Ladson-Billings, in press).

Wilson took an ESL course, but Stewart did not, and she has José. Both Wilson and Stewart took a required human relations course, but although it presented some historical information about Native Americans, African Americans, Asian Americans, and Latinos, it was silent on European-American cultures and the role of culture in learning and achievement. Both Wilson and Stewart believed, further, that the course was designed to make them feel guilty. As a result, they silently resisted the material, and this impact on their eventual practice was sharply reduced.

As inservice teachers, Wilson and Stewart have had some opportunities to learn about multicultural education, but these have taken the form of fleeting, one-time workshops. The experiences had little or no follow-up, and no one attempted to ensure that teachers applied the new information (Sleeter 1992).

Fortunately, one of Wilson's colleagues is a graduate student who has taken several courses dealing with race, class, and gender issues. He has learned from the experiences of two teacher like Vivian Paley (1979) and Jane Elliot (Peters 1987). Wilson's colleague is impressive because he seems to manage his classes easily, and his students achieve well on tasks that go beyond worksheets and drills. Wilson plans to enroll in a multicultural education course next semester. He hopes to learn something that will help him succeed with students of color.

While Wilson is motivated to change, Stewart is not. Because she is successful with most of her students, she thinks her lack of success with students of color stems from their deficiencies. Stewart's colleagues and the parents of her white students reinforce this belief.

Does the Race and Ethnicity of Teachers Matter?

Whether teachers' race and ethnicity affect student achievement remains an open question. We know that most teachers in the United States are white and that the next largest group, African Americans, comprise less than 5 percent of all public school teachers. We also know that the majority of students in the 25 largest public school systems are students of color.

No empirical evidence, however, indicates that students of color learn better when taught by teachers of color. The most recent review of the literature on African-American teachers (King 1993) finds no connection between teacher race/ethnicity and student achievement. The positive aspect of this finding is that it makes all teachers accountable for teaching all students.

If current demographic trends hold, our student population will become more diverse, while the teaching population remains predominantly white. The implication is that if teachers are to be effective, they will need to be prepared to teach children who are not white. If we are lucky, more teachers will follow Wilson's lead. They will know that the multicultural education research literature can help them understand themselves, their culture, and the cultures of colors, and be more successful with all students.

References

Apple, M. (1990). *Ideology and curriculum.* 2nd ed. New York: Routledge.

Au, K., and C. Jordan. (1981). "Teaching reading to Hawaiian children: finding a culturally appropriate solution." In *Culture and the bilingual classroom: Studies in classroom ethnography,* edited by H. Trueba, G. Guthrie, and K. Au. Rowley, MA: Newbury House.

Banks, J. A. (1993a). "Multicultural education for young children: Racial and ethnic attitudes and their modification." In *Handbook of research on the education of young children,* edited by B. Spodek. New York: Macmillan.

Banks, J.A. (1993b). "Multicultural education: Development, dimensions, and challenges." *Phi Delta Kappan* 75: 22-28.

Birrell, J. (February 1993). "A case study of the influence of ethnic encapsulation on a beginning secondary school teacher." Paper presented at the annual meeting of the Association of Teacher Educators, Los Angeles.

Cohen, E., and J. Benton. (Fall 1988). "Making groupwork work." *American Educator:* 10-17, 45-46.

Cooper, H. (1979). "Pygmalion grows up: A model for teacher expectation communication and performance influence." *Review of Educational Research* 49:389-410.

Erickson, F., and G. Mohatt. (1982). "Cultural organization and participation structures in two classrooms of Indian students." In *Doing the ethnography of schooling,* edited by G. Spindler. New York: Holt, Rinehart and Winston.

Hornberger, N. (1988). "Iman Chay?: Quechua children in Peru's schools." In *School and society: Teaching content through culture,* edited by H. Trueba and C. Delgado-Gaitan. New York: Praeger.

Irvine, J. (1990). *Black students and school failure.* Westport, CT: Greenwood Press.

Jordan, C. (1985). "Translating culture: From ethnographic information to educational pro-gram." *Anthropology and Education Quarterly* 16: 105-123.

King, J. and G. Ladson-Billings. (1990). "The teacher education challenge in elite university settings: Developing critical perspectives for teaching in democratic and multicultural societies." *European Journal of Intercultural Education* 1: 15-20.

King, S. H. (1993). "The limited presence of African-American teachers." *Review of Educational Research* 63: 115-149.

Kozol, J. (1991). *Savage inequalities.* New York: Crown Publishers.

Ladson-Billings, G. (1992). "Reading between the lines and pages: A culturally relevant approach to literacy teaching." *Theory into Practice* 31: 312-320.

Ladson-Billings, G. (In press). "Multicultural teacher education: Research, practice, and policy." In *Handbook of research in multicultural education,* edited by J.A. Banks and C.M. Banks. New York: MacMillian.

Lipman, P. (1993). "Teacher ideology toward African-American students in restructured schools." Doctoral diss., University of Wisconsin-Madison.

Oaks, J. (1985). *Keeping track: How schools structure inequality.* New Haven, CT: Yale University Press.

Orfield, G. (1989). *Status of school desegregation 1968-1986.* (Report of Urban Boards of Education and the National School Desegregation Research Project). Washington, DC: National School Boards Association.

Paley, V. (1979). *White teacher.* Cambridge, MA: Harvard University Press.

Peters, W. (1987). *A class divided: Then and now.* New Haven, CT: Yale University Press.

Scott, K. P., and C. G. Schau. (1985). "Sex equity and sex bias instructional materials." In *Handbook for achieving sex equity through education,* edited by S. S.

Klein. Baltimore: Johns Hopkins University Press.

Slavin, R. (November 1987). "Cooperative learning and the cooperative school." *Educational Leadership* 45, 3: 7-13.

Sleeter, C., and C. Grant. (1988). "An analysis of multicultural education in the United States." *Harvard Educational Review* 57: 421-444.

Swartz, E. (1992). "Multicultural education: From a compensatory to a scholarly foundation." In *Research and multicultural education: From the margins to the mainstream,* edited by C. Grant. London: Falmer Press.

Vogt, L., C. Jordan, and R. Tharp. (1987). "Explaining school failure, producing school success: Two cases." *Anthropology and Education Quarterly* 18: 276-286.

Windifeld, L. (1986). "Teacher beliefs toward at-risk students in inner-urban schools." *The Urban Review* 18: 253-267.

Zeichner, K. (1992). *Educating teachers for cultural diversity.* East Lansing, MI: National Center for Research on Teacher Learning.

Gloria Ladson-Billings is an Assistant Professor at the University of Wisconsin-madison, Department of Curriculum and Instruction, 225 N. Mills St., Madison, WI 53706.

Ladson-Billing, Gloria (1994). "What we can learn from multicultural education research." Educational Leadership 5: 22-26. Reprinted with permission of the Association for Supervision and Curriculum Development. Copyright © 1994 by ASCD. All rights reserved.

Schools need to judge the quality of their programs in terms of the input, the output, AND the process. They cannot provide a multiethnic education only by infusing bits and pieces of information. Not only must they evaluate the success or failure of their students but also the process they were engaged in during their schooling.

Multiethnic Education and the Quest for Equality

James A. Banks

We cannot produce multiethnic education simply by infusing bits and pieces of ethnic content into the curriculum, says Mr. Banks. Reform of the total school is required, if educational equality is to become a reality.

Multiethnic education requires that the total school environment be changed so that students from diverse ethnic and racial groups will experience educational equality. Many educators mistakenly assume that they can produce multiethnic education by simply infusing bits and pieces of ethnic content into the curriculum. Not so. Multiethnic education requires reform of the total school.

This reform must encompass staff attitudes and perceptions, the formal curriculum, teaching strategies, tests and testing procedures, and school-sanctioned languages and dialects.[1] Only when the total environment of a school promotes educational equality for all students can multiethnic education be said to exist.

Proponents of multiethnic education assume that schools have the power to substantially increase the academic achievement and life chances of minority students. This assumption contrasts sharply with the arguments set forth by theorists such as Christopher Jencks and by revisionists such as Samuel Bowles and Herbert Gintis, who contend that schools are severely limited in their ability to increase the educational equality that would seem to be a prerequisite of enhanced academic achievement and life chances.[2]

Equality and Equity

From the "separate but equal" Supreme Court ruling in *Plessy v. Ferguson* in 1896 until the mid-Fifties, black schools in the South had been unequal to white schools in terms of such input variables as teachers' salaries, facilities, instructional materials and supplies, and per-pupil expenditures. After the Supreme Court ruling in *Brown v. Board of Education* in 1954, however, southern and border states made major efforts to change all of that. During the Sixties and Seventies, many schools in economically depressed areas used funds authorized by the Elementary and Secondary Education Act of 1965 to make their input variables more equal to those of schools in economically advantaged areas. By the end of 1979 the federal government had granted $23.2 billion under this act to local school districts.[3]

But the massive and controversial Coleman Report, released in 1966, indicated that such input variables as school facilities and curricula are not the most important correlates of academic achievement.[4] James Coleman concluded that such variables as the teachers' verbal ability, the children's sense of control of their environment, and the children's educational background play the most important role in academic achievement.

The gains made in equalizing such school input variables as teachers' salaries and school facilities during the 1960s and 1970s and the findings of the Coleman Report—coupled with the continuing failure of many minority students to attain educational parity with middle-class white youths—made the notion of measuring educational equality by inputs increasingly unpopular during the 1970s.[5] Instead, educators and social scientists began to define educational equality in terms of results or effects of schooling. From this perspective, such groups as blacks, Chicanos, and Native Americans are thought to have equal educational opportunity only when their scores on standardized tests and other leading indicators of educational achievement are roughly equal to those of their white counterparts.

The output conception of educational equality, like other notions of

equality, is both helpful and problematic. This conception does not explicitly recognize the clear relationship between school input variables and pupil achievement. But the school alone cannot bring about educational equality as measured by output; such other institutions as the family, the church, and the mass media also play powerful educational roles. Despite the problems inherent in the output conception of educational equality, this notion can help educators to set specific goals and to measure their progress toward closing the achievement gap between ethnic minorities and middle-class white students.

Clearly, educators must focus on educational equality, but this is not sufficient. They should also focus on the educational process, through which they can help children to experience educational *equity*. According to Patricia Graham, "Equity differentiates itself from equal educational opportunity by attention to the internal process of education, to the circumstances in which teaching and learning are embedded. The focus is not only on the 'input' (such as access) or 'output' (such as result) but on the educational process in between."[6] In other words, input variables, output variables, and the process of education are integrally interrelated; each must receive attention, if education is to help minority youths attain the literacy and other skills essential for survival in our technological society.

I agree with Graham that the process of education should receive the greatest emphasis, since educational outcomes rest to a considerable degree on the quality of this process. Moreover, I believe that multiethnic education offers the

best hope of educational equity for minority students, because it focuses on reforming those variables of the school environment that now prevent minority students from having effective, enriching, and stimulating learning experiences.

During the 1960s and the 1970s educators increasingly realized that children whose family and community cultures differed markedly from the culture of the school were likely to find academic success more elusive than children whose home and community cultures were congruent with that of the school. For example, many Hispanic children are socialized in the barrio. If they are to achieve on the same academic level as middle-class white youths, the school culture—whose norms, goals, and expectations are primarily white and middle class[7]—must be changed substantially. Merely treating such Hispanic children "equally" (i.e., the same as middle-class white children) will not help many of them to attain the knowledge, skills, and attitudes they need to function effectively in this highly technological society. Because of different motivational styles, languages, and values, Hispanic and Anglo students may often have to be taught differently, if we expect them to learn the same skills and knowledge.[8] In other words, children from some ethnic groups may have different educational entitlements and needs. To reflect cultural democracy and to promote educational equality, the school may be required to provide specialized services, programs, and instruction for these students.

It is true that Jewish and Japanese-American students have been very successful academically; yet they have had no federally mandated bilingual programs in the public schools. (Both groups have established private, after-school language classes.) But the academic success of these groups does not necessarily imply that Hispanic children do not need bilingual education in order to attain educational parity with other students. *Some* Hispanic students may need bilingual programs; others may not.

Education and Schooling

The public school must play an important but limited role in bringing about educational equality. The family, the mass media, the community, the church, and the youth culture also play important roles in educating the young.[9] To the extent that these other institutions promote norms, behaviors, and values that contradict those that the school promotes, the school is hindered in achieving its goals. Thus policy makers must recognize both the possibilities and the limitations of the school in bringing about equal educational opportunity.

Within the last decade, the school has been handicapped in helping children to attain basic skills because it has received little help or support from the family, the community, and other important social institutions. The efforts of the school to teach children such values as justice and equality have often been undercut by practices in the larger society that contradict those teachings. Admittedly, the public school has not distinguished itself by its efforts to promote those values we think of as the American Creed. Nevertheless, it rarely gets much community support when it tries to do so. Although I will focus solely on the role of the school in

bringing about educational equality, readers should keep in mind the severe limitations under which the school operates and the extent to which this institution is simply a reflection of the larger society. Our high expectations for the school should be tempered by these realities.

Minority youths are not likely to achieve full educational equality until other institutions within the society implement reforms that support those that I will propose here for the school. Educators should also realize that the notion of equal educational opportunity is an ideal toward which we should work. Working toward this ideal is a continuing process.

To help minority youths attain educational equality during the 1980s, educational programs should reflect the enormous diversity *within* ethnic groups. Too often, social scientists and educators describe ethnic minorities as monolithic groups, rather than as groups that display enormous socioeconomic, regional, cultural, and linguistic diversity. We have all heard or read such oversimplified and misleading statements as: "Blacks made continuous progress during the 1960s and the 1970s," or "Indian children have low self-concepts." Such statements generally conceal more than they reveal and reinforce harmful educational practices.

Like educational programs, educational policy related to ethnic minorities should reflect the tremendous differences *within* ethnic groups. Most Puerto Ricans, blacks, Chicanos, and Native Americans are on the lower rungs of the socioeconomic ladder. But each of these groups also has a sizable middle class—with values, interests, behav-

iors, and educational needs that differ to some extent from those of the rest of the group.

Although these middle-class individuals usually identify to some extent with their ethnic groups, they also have strong social-class interests that bind them in many ways to other middle-class groups in the society. Middle-class members of ethnic groups often find that their class interests conflict with their ethnic allegiances, and their class interests are often more important to them than their ethnic attachments. Thus middle-class blacks and Chicanos often move to suburban communities and send their children to private schools—not to enhance their ethnic identities, but to live in a manner consistent with their social class. Many middle-class black and Chicano parents are more interested in having their children attain the requisite skills for admission to prestigious universities than they are in having their children enrolled in schools sympathetic to black English or barrio Spanish. Many middle-class black and Chicano parents, like their white counterparts, are deserting the public schools.[10] Ethnicity remains a cogent factor in U.S. society, but it is often mediated by class interests.

Shaping and implementing educational policy for minorities in the Eighties will become increasingly complex as more members of lower-status ethnic groups join the middle class.[11] Most middle-class blacks, Chicanos, and Puerto Ricans wish to retain their ethnic identities without sacrificing the full benefits and opportunities afforded other members of their social class. They may encourage their children to apply to prestigious universities, but they also expect them to relate well to their cousins in the inner city and to take active roles in ethnic activities. During the 1960s and 1970s educators focused on helping lower-class minority children to achieve educational parity. Middle-class minority children were often overlooked—or the school assumed that they, too, were poor and "culturally deprived." Educators should be keenly sensitive to the class diversity within minority communities. This diversity is likely to increase throughout the 1980s.

Of course, ethnic minorities include other important subgroups besides the very poor and the middle class. Blue-collar laborers and their families make up one substantial and important segment of ethnic communities, and their educational needs must also be considered when educational policy is shaped for the 1980s. In many working-class ethnic families, both parents work. The children of such parents do not qualify for special programs that benefit children from poorer families. Yet these working-class parents often cannot afford the educational experiences, enrichment activities, and expensive colleges that are within the means of middle-class parents. Consequently, children from working-class ethnic families are often at a disadvantage; their parents simply do not make enough money to provide them with the educational opportunities they need and deserve.

The problems of educating minority and poor youths first attracted serious attention from educators and educational researchers in the 1960s. Yet our understanding of the reasons for the higher rate of academic failure among these youngsters than among other youths remains sparse and uncer-

tain. We can make few conclusive statements about why minority youths often perform poorly in school and about what can be done to increase their academic achievement and emotional growth. Hypotheses abound, but most of the research is inconclusive and contradictory. As is true in other areas of social science, both the research and the hypotheses reflect the ideologies, assumptions, and values of the researchers and theorists.[12]

I do not intend to suggest that we should ignore the hypotheses and research that relate to the education of ethnic groups. Rather, as consumers of these hypotheses and of this research, we should be sensitive to the ideologies, assumptions, and values that underlie them. And we should be aware of our own goals and values as well. Only in this way can we use the hypotheses and the research appropriately, in ways that will enable us to help minority youths reach their full potential.

Hypotheses regarding the education of minority youths are diverse and conflicting. In the 1960s Arthur Jensen and William Shockley revived the genetic explanation for the low academic achievement of minority youths.[13] Richard Herrnstein, by contrast, hypothesized that intelligence is related to social class.[14] The geneticists argue that minority groups do not perform as well academically as nonminorities because of their genetic characteristics; consequently, the capability of the school to bring about educational equality is severely limited. When assessing the genetic hypothesis, educators should remember its history in the U.S. In earlier times, other theorists "explained" the intellectual inferiority of such groups as the Irish and the

Jews as a matter of genes. Moreover, in studies of intelligence in a nation such as the U.S., it is difficult to control for race. Racial purity here is the exception, not the rule.

The cultural-deprivation hypothesis, which also emerged during the 1960s, maintains that poor youths do not achieve well in school because of the poverty-stricken environments in which they have been reared.[15] In these environments, the argument goes, they are unable to experience the kind of cognitive stimulation that develops intellectual skills. Unlike the geneticists, those who believe in cultural deprivation are confirmed environmentalists; they think that the school can and should play a significant role in establishing educational equality for poor youths. The school can do this, they believe, by intervening in the lives of poor youths at the earliest possible age and providing them with a rich and stimulating educational environment. Those who support the cultural-deprivation hypothesis believe that intensive, behaviorally oriented instruction will enable poor youths to greatly increase their academic achievement and emotional growth.

Another group of educators—the integrationists—emerged in the 1950s. The integrationists began to develop their arguments and research during a period of segregated schooling in the U.S. Integrationists contend that the best way to bring about educational equality for minority youths is to place them in racially desegregated, middle-class schools.[16] Like the cultural deprivationists, the integrationists are environmentalists who believe that the school can and should play a significant role in bringing about educational equality. The school, they say, can increase educational equality by creating environments in which students from diverse racial groups and social classes are free to interact and learn in an atmosphere that values and respects each group. School desegregation has become a major target of the neoconservative scholars who emerged during the 1970s.[17] Urban demographic trends have greatly diminished the likelihood of successful school desegregation in the 1980s. Yet the integrationists remain strongly committed to their dream of a racially integrated America.

A fourth group of scholars and researchers, who support the cultural-difference (or multicultural) hypothesis, emerged during the late 1960s and the early 1970s. They reject the views of both the geneticists and the cultural deprivationists. They do not necessarily reject the ideas of the integrationists, but they have different priorities. Led by such researchers as William Labov, Geneva Smitherman, Joan Baratz, Manuel Ramirez, and Alfredo Castaneda,[18] those who support the cultural-difference hypothesis argue that ethnic minorities have rich and diverse, not deprived, cultures. Minority youths do not achieve well in school, these theorists suggest, because the school culture is alien to them and often in conflict with their home cultures. Moreover, the I.Q. tests used to assess the academic aptitude of these youths are invalid because they are grounded in the mainstream culture.[19] To help minority youths increase their academic achievement and emotional growth, they say we must reform the culture of the schools to make it more congruent with the cultures of ethnic minority youths.

Because of the thin, contradictory, and inconclusive nature of the hypotheses and research on the education of poor and ethnic minority youths, our policies and programs must be guided primarily by our own value commitments. In his classic work, *An American Dilemma,* Gunnar Myrdal argued that Americans believe deeply in the American Creed, which includes such core values as equality, justice, and human dignity.[20] But Americans face a dilemma, Myrdal wrote, because their treatment of blacks contradicts this creed. Myrdal believed, however, that the faith of Americans in the American Creed would help them to create a society that would become increasingly more humane and just.

I also believe that the American Creed is deeply embedded in the American conscience. It dictates that we choose hypotheses to guide the education of minority youths that are consistent with equality, justice, and human dignity.

Educational programs that spring from the idea of cultural deprivation show disrespect for students' home cultures. Educational programs that spring from the genetic hypothesis violate human dignity and other values set forth in the American Creed, because they deny the possibility of a dignified existence for many minority youths.[21] Views that foster cultural freedom for minority youths, such as the cultural-difference or multicultural hypothesis, provide the greatest possibility for an education that will engender justice and equity and thus improve the human condition.

Notes

1. For further discussion of these points, see James A. Banks, *Multiethnic Education: Theory and Practice* (Boston: Allyn & Bacon, 1981).

2. Christopher Jencks et al. *Inequality: A Reassessment of the Effect of Family and Schooling in America* (New York: Basic Books, 1972); and Samuel Bowles and Herbert Gintis, *Schooling in Capitalist America* (New York: Basic Books, 1976).

3. Patricia A. Graham, "Whither Equality of Educational Opportunity?" *Daedalus,* Summer 1980, pp. 115-32.

4. James S. Coleman et al., *Equality of Educational Opportunity* (Washington, DC: U.S. Government Printing Office, 1966).

5. James S. Coleman, "The Concept of Equality in Educational Opportunity," in *Equal Educational Opportunity* (Cambridge, MA: Harvard University Press, 1969).

6. Graham, p. 123.

7. William Greenbaum, "America in Search of a New Ideal: An Essay on the Rise of Pluralism," *Harvard Educational Review,* August 1974, pp. 411-40.

8. Geneva Gay, "Interactions in Culturally Pluralistic Classrooms," in James A. Banks, ed., *Education in the '80s: Multiethnic Education* (Washington, DC: National Education Association, 1981).

9. Lawrence Cremin, *Public Education* (New York: Basic Books, 1976).

10. James S. Coleman, Thomas Hoffer, and Sally Kilgore, *Public*

and Private Schools (Chicago: National Opinion Research Center, March 1981).

11. William J. Wilson, *The Declining Significance of Race: Blacks and Changing American Institutions* (Chicago: University of Chicago Press, 1978).

12. Philip Green, *The Pursuit of Inequality* (New York: Pantheon, 1981).

13. Arthur R. Jensen, "How Much Can We Boost I.W. and Scholastic Achievement?" *Harvard Educational Review*, (Winter 1969), pp. 1-123; and William Shockley, "Dysgenics, Geneticity, Raceology: A Challenge to the Intellectual Responsibility of Educators," *Phi Delta Kappan*, January 1972, pp. 297-307.

14. Richard J. Herrnstein, *I.Q. in the Meritocracy* (Boston: Little, Brown, 1971).

15. Carl Bereiter and Siegfried Engelmann, *Teaching Disadvantaged Children in the Preschool* (Englewood Cliffs, NJ: Prentice-Hall, 1966).

16. Thomas Pettigrew and Robert L. Green, "School Desegregation in Large Cities: A Critique of the Coleman 'White Flight' Thesis," *Harvard Educational Review*, (February 1976), pp. 1-53.

17. Peter Steinfels, *The Neoconservatives: The Men Who Are Changing America's Politics* (New York: Simon and Schuster, 1979).

18. William Labov, "The Logic of Nonstandard English," in Frederick Williams, ed., *Language and Poverty: Perspectives on a Theme* (Chicago: Markham Publishing Co., 1970); Geneva Smitherman, *Talkin' and Testifyin': The Language of Black America* (New York: Houghton-Mifflin, 1977); Joan C. Baratz, "Teaching Reading in an Urban Negro School System," in Williams, *Language and Poverty . . .*; and Manuel Ramirez III and Alfredo Castaneda, *Cultural Democracy, Bicognitive Development, and Education* (New York: Academic Press, 1974).

19. Jane R. Mercer, "Testing and Assessment Practices in Multiethnic Education," in Banks, *Education in the '80s . . .*, pp. 93-104.

20. Gunnar Myrdal, *An American Dilemma: The Negro Problem and Modern Democracy*, vols. 1 & 2 (New York: Harper and Row, 1944).

21. Hannah Arendt, *The Human Condition* (Chicago: University of Chicago Press, 1958).

James A. Banks is professor and chairperson, Department of Curriculum and Instruction, College of Education, University of Washington, Seattle.

Banks, James A. "Multiethnic Education And the Quest For Equality," Phi Delta Kappan (April 1983) 582-85. Copyright 1983 by Phi Delta Kappan. Reprinted by permission.

The article summarizes different approaches to multicultural education. He highlights the advantages of the transformation approach, one advantage being that it brings content about currently marginalized groups to the center of the curriculum.

Transforming the Mainstream Curriculum

James A. Banks

Schools today are rich in student diversity. A growing number of American classrooms and schools contain a complex mix of races, cultures, languages, and religious affiliations.

Two other sources of diversity are becoming increasingly prominent as well. The widening gap between rich and poor students is creating more social class diversity, and an increasing number of gay students and teachers are publicly proclaiming their sexual orientations.

Toward an Authentic Unum

The increasing recognitions of diversity within American society poses a significant challenge: how to create a cohesive and democratic society while at the same time allowing citizens to maintain their ethnic, cultural, socioeconomic, and primordial identities.

Our ideal as a nation has been and continues to be *e pluribus unum*—out of many, one. In the past, Americans have tried to reach this goal by eradicating diversity and forcing all citizens into a white Anglo-Saxon Protestant culture (Higham, 1972).

This coerced assimilation does not work very well. An imposed *unum* is not authentic, is not perceived as legitimate by nonmainstream populations, does not have moral authority, and is inconsistent with democratic ideals. To create an authentic, democratic *unum* with moral authority and perceived le-gitimacy, the *pluribus* (diverse peoples) must negotiate and share power.

Even with its shortcomings, the United States has done better in this regard than most nations. Still, citizen expectations for a just *unum* are far outpacing the nation's progress toward its ideal. Many citizens of color, people with low incomes, or speakers of languages other than English feel alienated, left out, abandoned, and forgotten.

Our society has a lot to gain by restructuring institutions in ways that incorporate all citizens. People who now feel disenfranchised will become more effective and productive citizens, and new perspectives will be added to the nation's mainstream institutions. The institutions themselves will then be transformed and enriched.

In the past two decades, multicultural education has emerged as a vehicle for including diverse groups and transforming the nation's educational institutions (Banks, 1994a, Banks and Banks 1992). Multicultural education tries to create equal educational opportunities for all students by ensuring that the total school environment reflects the diversity of groups in classrooms, schools, and the society as a whole.

Considering the Dimensions of Multicultural Education

The following five dimensions of multicultural education can help educators implement and assess programs that respond to student diversity (Banks, 1993, 1994b).

1. The first dimension, *content integration*, deals with the extent to which teachers illuminate key points of instruction with content reflecting diversity. Typically, teachers integrate such content into curriculum in several different ways (Banks, 1991b). One common approach is the recognition of contributions—that is, teachers work into the curriculum various isolated facts about heroes from diverse groups. Otherwise, lesson plans and units are changed. With the additive approach, on the other hand, the curriculum remains unchanged, but teachers add special units on topics like the Women's Right Movement, African Americans in the West, and Famous Americans with Disabilities. While an improvement over the passing mention of contributions, the additive approach still relegates groups like women, Afri-

can Americans, and disabled people to the periphery of the curriculum.

2. A second dimension of multicultural education is *knowledge construction*, or the extent to which teachers help students understand how perspectives of people within a discipline influence the conclusions reached within that discipline. This dimension is also concerned with whether students learn to form knowledge for themselves.

> *Teaching from a range of perspectives will prepare students from diverse groups to work together in a truly unified nation.*

3. The *prejudice reduction* dimension has to do with efforts to help students to develop positive attitudes about different groups. Research has revealed a need for this kind of education and the efficacy of it. For example, researchers have shown that while children enter school with many negative attitudes and misconceptions about different racial and ethnic groups (Phinney & Rotheram, 1987), education can help students develop more positive intergroup attitudes, provided that certain conditions exist. Two such conditions are instructional materials with positive images of diverse groups and the use of such materials in consistent and sustained ways (Banks, 1991a).

4. The *equitable pedagogy* dimension concerns ways to modify teaching as to facilitate academic achievement among students from diverse groups. Research indicates, for example, that the academic achievement of African-American and Mexican-American students improves when teachers use cooperative (rather than competitive) teaching activities and strategies (Aronson & Gonzalez, 1988).

5. The *empowering school culture and social structure* dimension concerns the extent to which a school's culture and organization ensure educational equality and cultural empowerment for students from diverse groups. Some of the variables considered are grouping practices, social climate, assessment practices, participation in extracurricular activities, and staff expectations and responses to diversity.

Knowledge Construction and Transformation

I would like to suggest an alternative to the contributions and additive approaches that are used in the content integration dimension. This alternative, the *transformation approach*, changes the structure, assumptions, and perspectives of the curriculum so that subject matter is viewed from the perspectives and experiences of a range of groups. The transformation approach changes instructional materials, teaching techniques, and student learning.

This approach can be used to teach about our differences as well as our similarities. Teachers can help students understand that, while Americans have a variety of viewpoints, we share many cultural traditions, values, and political ideals that cement us together as a nation.

The transformation approach has several advantages. It brings content about currently marginalized groups to the center of the curriculum. It helps students understand that how people construct knowledge depends on their experiences, values, and perspectives. It helps students learn to construct knowledge themselves. And it helps students grasp the complex group interactions that have produced the American culture and civilization.

Reinterpreting the Montgomery Bus Boycott

The history of the Montgomery (Alabama) bus boycott, which began on December 5, 1955, can be used to illustrate how the transformation approach works. Viewing this event from different perspectives shows how historians construct interpretations, how central figures can be omitted from historical records, how history can be rewritten, and how students can create their own interpretations.

Textbook accounts of the Montgomery bus boycott generally conclude that: (1) when a bus driver asked Rosa Parks to give up her seat to a white person, she refused because she was tired from working hard all day, and (2) the arrest of Rosa Parks triggered the planning and execution of the boycott.

Two important accounts by women who played key roles in the boycott contradict important aspects of the textbook conclusions. The two memoirs are those of Rosa Parks (with Haskins, 1992) and Jo Ann Gibson Robinson (Garrow, 1987). Robinson was an Alabama State College English professor and

president of the Women's Political Council.

Students can compare mainstream accounts of the events (such as those in textbooks) with transformative accounts (such as those by Robinson and Parks). This activity presents an excellent opportunity both to learn content about diverse groups and to gain insights about the construction of knowledge.

According to Robinson, professional African-American women in Montgomery founded the Women's Political Council in 1946 to provide leadership, support, and improvement in the black community and to work for voting rights for African Americans. Many council members were Alabama State College professors. Others were black public school teachers.

> *Multicultural education has emerged as a vehicle for including diverse groups and transforming the nation's educational institutions.*

In 1953, the council received more that 30 complaints concerning bus driver offenses against African Americans. For instance, black people (even seated in the "Negro" section of the bus) were asked to give up their seats to whites. Fur-

ther, blacks often had to pay their fares in the front of the bus, exit, and reenter through the back door—and sometimes when they stepped off the bus, the driver left them.

Robinson and other council members worked with city leaders to improve the treatment of black bus riders, but to no avail. African Americans continued to experience intimidating, demeaning, and hostile encounters with bus drivers. As the negative pattern of incidents persisted, the council concluded that only a boycott against the bus system would end the abuse of black bus riders and bus segregation. A boycott was thought to have good potential for success because about 70 percent of Montgomery's bus riders were African American. The council planned the boycott and then waited for the right time to launch it.

The year 1955 presented three choices for the "right time." On March 2, 1955, Claudette Colvin, a 15-year-old high school student seated in the "Negro" section of a bus, was arrested after refusing to give up her seat to a white rider. Next, Robinson said:

> They dragged her, kicking and screaming hysterically, off the bus. Still half-dragging, half-pushing, they forced her into a patrol car that had been summoned, put handcuffs on her wrists so she would do no physical harm to the arresting police, and drove her to jail. There she was charged with misconduct, resisting arrest, and violating the city segregation laws (Garrow, 1987).

Claudette Colvin was later found guilty and released on probation. The conviction enraged the African-American community. Six months after the Colvin incident, Mary Louise Smith, 18, was arrested on a similar charge. Smith was fined.

Then, on December 1, Rosa Parks was arrested for refusing to give up her seat. She gives quite a different reason for her intransigence than has commonly been reported:

> People always say that I didn't give up my seat because I was tired, but that isn't true. I was not physically tired, or more tired than I usually was at the end of the working day. I was not old, although some people have an image of me being old then. I was 42. No, the only tired I was, was tired of giving in.
>
> The driver of the bus saw me still sitting there, and he asked was I going to stand up. I said, "No." He said, "Well, I'm going to have you arrested." Then I said, "You may do that." These were the only words we said to each other.
>
> . . . People have asked me if it occurred to me that I could be the test case the NAACP had been looking for. I did not think about that at all. In fact if I had let myself think too deeply about what might happen to me, I might have gotten off the bus. But I chose to remain.

Fed up with mistreatment, the African-American women of Montgomery, led by their council, called for a boycott of city buses. Robinson described the preparations for the boycott:

> I sat down and quickly drafted a message and then called a good

friend and colleague, John Cannon, chairman of the business department of the college, who had access to the college's mimeograph equipment. When I told him that the WPC was staging a boycott and needed to run off the notices, he told me that he too had suffered embarrassment on the city buses. Like myself, he had been hurt and angry. He said that he would happily assist me.

The transformation approach brings content about currently marginalized groups to the center of the curriculum.

Along with two of my most trusted students, we quickly agreed to meet almost immediately, in the middle of the night, at the college's duplicating room. We were able to get three messages to a page, greatly reducing the number of pages that had to be mimeographed in order to produce the tens of thousands of leaflets we knew would be needed. By 4 A.M. on Friday, the sheets had been duplicated, cut in thirds, and bundled (Garrow, 1987).

Part of Robinson's leaflets read:

> Another Negro woman has been arrested and thrown in jail because she refused to get up out of her seat on the bus for a white person to sit

down.... This has to be stopped. Negroes have rights, too, for if Negroes did not ride the buses, they could not operate. Three-fourths of the riders are Negroes, yet we are arrested, or have to stand over empty seats. If we do not do something to stop the arrests, they will continue. The next time it may be you, your daughter, or mother. This woman's case will come up on Monday. We are, therefore, asking every Negro to stay off the buses Monday in protest of the arrest and trial. Don't ride the buses to work, to town, to school, or anywhere else on Monday (Garrow, 1987).

Reinterpreting the Past

Robinson's and Parks' accounts of the Montgomery bus boycott reveal that significant players in historical events can be virtually ignored in written history. For instance, most textbook accounts of the Montgomery bus boycott emphasize the work of men (like Martin Luther King Jr. and Ralph D. Abernathy) or organizations headed by men. The work of women like Robinson and her female colleagues in the Women's Political Council simply cannot be found in most textbooks.

Further, Rosa Parks' stated reason for refusing to give up her seat helps students understand that recorded history can be wrong. Students can also see that when people who have been excluded from the construction of historical knowledge begin to play active roles in interpreting history, the resulting accounts can be strikingly different and much more accurate. As Robert Merton (1972) observed, insiders and outsiders often have different perspectives on the same events, and both perspectives are needed to give the total picture of social and historical reality.

Incorporating New Scholarship

Since the 1970s, people of color—who have historically been outsiders and transformative scholars—have produced a prodigious amount of scholarship on multicultural education. Their thoughtful and informative works include Ronald Takaki's *A Different Mirror: A History of Multicultural America* (1993); John Hope Franklin's *The Color Line: Legacy for the Twenty-First Century* (1993); Gloria Anzaldua's *Borderlands: La Frontera* (1987); Patricia Hill Collin's *Black Feminist Thought: Knowledge, Consciousness, and the Politics of Empowerment*

(1991); and Paula Gunn Allen's *The Sacred Hoop* (1986).

Because men of color have often been silent on women's issues as white men have been (hooks [sic] and West 1991), a special effort should be made to include works by women (such as those by Anzaldua, Collins, and Allen). Two important new books edited by women are Carol Dubois and Vicki Ruiz's *Unequal Sisters: A Multicultural Reader in U.S. Women's History* (1990) and Darlene Clark Hine and her colleagues' *Black Women in America: A Historical Encyclopedia* (1993).

Teaching Civic Action

One of the multicultural education's important goals is to help students acquire the knowledge and commitment needed to think, decide, and take personal, social, and civic action. Activism helps students apply what they have learned and develop a sense of personal and

civic efficacy (Banks & Clegg, 1990).

Action activities and projects should be practical, feasible, and attuned to the developmental levels of students. For instance, students in the primary grades can take action by refusing to laugh at ethnic jokes. Students in the early and middle grades can read about and make friends with people from other racial, ethnic, and cultural groups. Upper-grade students can participate in community projects that help people with special needs. Lewis (1991) has written a helpful guide that describes ways to plan and initiate social action activities and projects for students.

When content, concepts, and events are studied from many points of view, all of our students will be ready to play their roles in the life of the nation. They can help to transform the United States from what it is to what it could and should be—many groups working together to build a strong nation that celebrates its diversity.

References

Aronson, E., & A. Gonzalez. (1988). "Desegregation, jigsaw, and the Mexican-American experience." In *Eliminating racism: Profiles in controversy*, edited by P.A. Katz & A. Taylor. New York: Plenum Press.

Banks, J.A. (1991a). "Multicultural education: Its effect on students' racial and gender role attitudes." In *Handbook of research on social teaching and learning*, edited by J.P. Shaver. New York: Macmillan.

Banks, J.A. (1991b). *Teaching strategies for ethnic studies*. 5th ed. Boston: Allyn and Bacon.

Banks, J.A. (1993). "Multicultural education: Historical development, dimensions and practice." In *Review of Research Education*, vol. 19, edited by L. Darling-Hammond, Washington, DC: American Educational Research Association.

Banks, J.A. (1994b). *Multiethnic education: Theory and practice*. 3rd ed. Boston: Allyn and Bacon.

Banks, J.A., & A.A. Clegg Jr. (1990). *Teaching strategies for the social studies: Inquiry, valuing, and decision-making*. 4th ed. New York: Longman.

Banks, J.A., & C.A. McGee Banks, eds. (1992). *Multicultural education: Issues and perspectives*. 2nd ed. Boston: Allyn and Bacon.

Garrow, D.J., ed. (1987). *The Montgomery bus boycott and the women who started it: The memoir of Jo Ann Gibson Robinson*. Knoxville: The University of Tennessee Press.

Higham, J. (1972). *Strangers in the land: Patterns of American nativism 1860-1925*. New York: Atheneum.

Hooks, B., & West C. (1991) *Breaking bread: Insurgent Black intellectual life*. Boston: South End Press.

Lewis, B.A. (1991). *The kid's guide to social action.* Minneapolis: Free Spirit Publishing.

Merton, R.K. (1972). "Insiders and outsiders: A chapter in the sociology of knowledge." *The American Journal of Sociology* 78, 1:9-47.

Parks, R., with J. Haskins (1992). *Rosa Parks: My story.* New York: Dial Books.

Phinney, J.S., & M.J. Rotheram, eds. (1987). *Children's ethnic socialization; Pluralism and development.* Beverly Hills, CA: Sage Publications.

Some critics of
multiculturalism see the
movement as too little and
too late. Others, including
Diane Ravitch, fear that too
much diversity will tear apart
a fragile social fabric.

Multiculturalism: E Pluribus Plures

Diane Ravitch

Questions of race, ethnicity, and religion have been a perennial source of conflict in American education. The schools have often attracted the zealous attention of those who wish to influence the future, as well as those who wish to change the way we view the past. In our history, the schools have been not only an institution in which to teach young people skills and knowledge, but an arena where interest groups fight to preserve their values, or to revise the judgments of history, or to bring about fundamental social change. In the nineteenth century, Protestants and Catholics battled over which version of the Bible should be used in school, or whether the Bible should be used at all. In recent decades, bitter racial disputes—provoked by policies of racial segregation and discrimination—have generated turmoil in the streets and in the schools. The secularization of the schools during the past century has prompted attacks on the curricula and textbooks and library books by fundamentalist Christians, who object to whatever challenges their faith-based views of history, literature, and science.

Given the diversity of American society, it has been impossible to insulate the schools from pressures that result from differences and tensions among groups. When people differ about basic values, sooner or later those disagreements turn up in battles about how schools are organized or what the schools should teach. Sometimes these battles remove a terrible injustice, like racial segregation. Sometimes, however, interest groups politicize the curriculum and attempt to impose their views on teachers, school officials, and textbook publishers. Across the country, even now, interest groups are pressuring local school boards to remove myths and fables and other imaginative literature from children's readers and to inject the teaching of creationism in biology. When groups cross the line into extremism, advancing their own agenda without regard to reason or to others, they threaten public education itself, making it difficult to teach any issues honestly and making the entire curriculum vulnerable to political campaigns.

For many years, the public schools attempted to neutralize controversies over race, religion, and ethnicity by ignoring them. Educators believed, or hoped, that the schools could remain outside politics; this was, of course, a vain hope since the schools were pursuing policies based on race, religion, and ethnicity. Nonetheless, such divisive questions were usually excluded from the curriculum. The textbooks minimized problems among groups and taught a sanitized version of history. Race, religion, and ethnicity were presented as minor elements in the American saga; slavery was treated as an episode, immigrations as a sidebar, and women were largely absent. The textbooks concentrated on presidents, wars, national politics, and issues of state. An occasional "great black" or "great woman" received mention, but the main narrative paid little attention to minority groups and women.

With the ethnic revival of the 1960s, this approach to the teaching of history came under fire, because the history of national leaders—virtually all of whom were white, Anglo-Saxon, and male—ignored the place in American history of those who were none of the above. The traditional history of elites had been complemented by an assimilationist view of American society, which presumed that everyone in the American melting pot would eventually lose or abandon those ethnic characteristics that distinguished them from mainstream Americans. The ethnic revival demonstrated that many groups did not want to be assimilated or melted. Ethnic studies programs popped up on

campuses to teach not only that "black is beautiful," but also that every other variety of ethnicity is "beautiful" as well; everyone who had "roots" began to look for them so that they too could recover that ancestral part of themselves that had not been homogenized.

. . . these painstaking efforts to expand the understanding of American culture into a richer and more varied tapestry have taken a new turn, and not for the better.

As ethnicity became an accepted subject for study in the late 1960s, textbooks were assailed for their failure to portray blacks accurately; within a few years, the textbooks in wide use were carefully screened to eliminate bias against minority groups and women. At the same time, new scholarship about the history for women, blacks and various ethnic minorities found its way into the textbooks. At first, the multicultural content was awkwardly incorporated as little boxes on the side of the main narrative. Then some of the new social historians (like Stephan Thernstrom, Mary Beth Norton, Gary Nash, Winthrop Jordan, and Leon Litwack) themselves

wrote textbooks, and the main narrative itself began to reflect a broadened historical understanding of race, ethnicity, and class in the American past. Consequently, today's history textbooks routinely incorporate the experiences of women, blacks, American Indians, and various immigrant groups.

Although most high school textbooks are deeply unsatisfactory (they still largely neglect religion, they are too long, too encyclopedic, too superficial, and lacking in narrative flow), they are far more sensitive to pluralism than their predecessors. For example, the latest edition of Todd and Curti's *Triumph of the American Nation*, the most popular high school history text, has significantly increased its coverage of blacks in America, including profiles of Phillis Wheatley, the poet; James Karmistead, a revolutionary war spy for Lafayette; Benjamin Banneker, a self-taught scientist and mathematician; Hiram Revels, the first black to serve in the Congress; and Ida B. Wells-Barnett, a tireless crusader against lynching and racism. Even better as a textbook treatment is Jordan and Litwack's *The United States*, which skillfully synthesizes the groups into the mainstream of American social and political history. The latest generation of textbooks bluntly acknowledges the racism of the past, describing the struggle for equality by racial minorities while identifying individuals who achieved success as political leaders, doctors, lawyers, scholars, entrepreneurs, teachers, and scientists.

As a result of the political and social changes of recent decades, cultural pluralism is now generally recognized as an organizing principle of this society. In contrast to the idea of the melting pot, which promised to erase ethnic and group differences, children now learn that variety is the spice of life. They learn that America has provided a haven for many different groups and has allowed them to maintain their cultural heritage or to assimilate, or—as is often the case— to do both; the choice is theirs, not the state's. They learn that cultural pluralism is one of the norms of a free society; that differences among groups is a national resource rather than a problem to be solved. Indeed, the unique feature of the United States is that its common culture has been formed by the interaction of its subsidiary cultures. It is a culture that has been influenced over time by immigrants, American Indians, Africans (slave and free) and by their descendants. American music, art, literature, language, food, clothing, sports, holidays, and customs all show the effects of the commingling of diverse cultures in one nation. Paradoxical though it may seem, the United States has a common culture that is multicultural.

Our schools and our institutions of higher learning have in recent years begun to embrace what Catherine R. Stimpson of Rutgers University has called "cultural democracy," a recognition that we must listen to a "diversity of voices" in order to understand our culture, past and present. This understanding of the pluralistic nature of American culture has taken a long time to forge. It is based on sound scholarship and has led to major revisions in what children are taught and what they read in school. The new history is—indeed, must be—a warts-and-all history; it demands an unflinching examination of racism and discrimination in our

history. Making these changes is difficult, raises tempers, and ignites controversies, but gives a more interesting and accurate account of American history. Accomplishing these changes is valuable, because there is also a useful lesson for the rest of the world in America's relatively successful experience as a pluralistic society. Throughout human history, the clash of different cultures, races, ethnic groups, and religions has often been the cause of bitter hatred, civil conflict, and international war. The ethnic tensions that now are tearing apart Lebanon, Sri Lanka, Kashmir, and various republics of the Soviet Union remind us of the costs of unfettered group rivalry. Thus, it is a matter of more than domestic importance that we closely examine and try to understand that part of our national history in which different groups competed, fought, suffered, but ultimately learned to live together in relative peace and even achieved a sense of common nationhood.

Alas, these painstaking efforts to expand the understanding of American culture into a richer and more varied tapestry have taken a new turn, and not for the better. Almost any idea, carried to its extreme, can be made pernicious, and this is what is happening now to multiculturalism. Today, pluralistic multiculturalism must contend with a new, particularistic multiculturalism. The pluralists seek a richer common culture; the particularists insist that no common culture is possible or desirable. The new particularism is entering the curriculum in a number of school systems across the country. Advocates of particularism propose an ethnocentric curriculum to raise the

self-esteem and academic achievement of children from racial and ethnic minority backgrounds. Without any evidence, they claim that children from minority backgrounds will do well in school only if they are immersed in a positive, prideful version of their ancestral culture. If children are of, for example, Fredonian ancestry, they must hear that Fredonians were important in mathematics, science, history, and literature. If they learn about great Fredonians and if their studies use Fredonian examples and Fredonian concepts, they will do well in school. If they do not, they will have low self-esteem and will do badly.

At first glance, this appears akin to the celebratory activities associated with Black History Month or Women's History Month, when schoolchildren learn about the achievements of blacks and women. But the point of those celebrations is to demonstrate that neither race nor gender is an obstacle to high achievement. They teach all children that everyone, regardless of their race, religion, gender, ethnicity, or family origin, can achieve self-fulfillment, honor, and dignity in society if they aim high and work hard.

By contrast, the particularistic version of multiculturalism is unabashedly filiopietistic and deterministic. It teaches children that their identity is determined by their "cultural genes." That something in their blood or their race memory or their cultural DNA defines who they are and what they may achieve. That the culture in which they live is not their own culture, even though they were born here. That American culture is "Eurocentric," and therefore hostile to anyone whose ancestors are not European. Perhaps the most invidious implication of particularism is that racial and ethnic minorities are not and should not try to be part of American culture; it implies that American culture belongs only to those who are white and European; it implies that those who are neither white nor European are alienated from American culture by virtue of their race or ethnicity; it implies that the only culture they do belong to or can ever belong to is the culture of their ancestors, even if their families have lived in this country for generations.

The war on so-called Eurocentrism is intended to foster self-esteem among those who are not of European descent. But how, in fact, is self-esteem developed? How is the sense of one's own possibilities, one's potential choices, developed? Certainly, the school curriculum plays a relatively small role as compared to the influence of family, community, mass media, and society. But to the extent that curriculum influences what children think of themselves, it should encourage children of all racial and ethnic groups to believe that they are part of this society and that they should develop their talents and minds to the fullest. It is enormously inspiring, for example, to learn about men and women from diverse backgrounds who overcame poverty, discrimination, physical handicaps, and other obstacles to achieve success in a variety of fields. Behind every such biography of accomplishment is a story of heroism, perseverance, and self-discipline. Learning these stories will encourage a healthy spirit of pluralism, of mutual respect, and of self-respect among children of different back-

grounds. The children of American society today will live their lives in a racially and culturally diverse nation, and their education should prepare them to do so.

The pluralist approach to multiculturalism promotes a broader interpretation of the common American culture and seeks due recognition for the ways that the nation's many racial, ethnic, and cultural groups have transformed the national culture. The pluralists say, in effect, "American culture belongs to us, all of us; the U.S. is us, and we remake it in every generation." But particularists have no interest in extending or revising American culture; indeed, they deny that a common culture exists. Particularists reject any accommodation among groups, any interactions that blur the distinct lines between them. The brand of history that they espouse is one in which everyone is either a descendant of victims or oppressors. By doing so, ancient hatreds are fanned and recreated in each new generation. Particularism has its intellectual roots in the ideology of ethnic separatism and in the black nationalist movement. In the particularist analysis, the nation has five cultures: African American, Asian American, European American, Latino/Hispanic, and Native American. The huge cultural, historical, religious, and linguistic differences within these categories are ignored, as is the considerable inter-marriage among these groups, as are the linkages (like gender, class, sexual orientation, and religion) that cut across these five groups. No serious scholar would claim that all Europeans and white Americans are part of the same culture, or that all Asians are part of the same culture, or that

all people of Latin-American descent are of the same culture, or that all people of African descent are of the same culture. Any categorization this broad is essentially meaningless and useless.

> *. . . to the extent that curriculum influences what children think of themselves, it should encourage children of all racial and ethnic groups to believe that they are part of this society and that they should develop their talents and minds to the fullest.*

Several districts—including Detroit, Atlanta, and Washington D.C.—are developing an Afrocentric curriculum. *Afrocentricity* has been described in a book of the same name by Molefi Kete Asante of Temple University. The Afrocentric curriculum puts Africa at the center of the student's universe. African Americans must "move away from an (sic) Eurocentric framework" because "it is difficult to create freely when you use someone else's motifs, styles, images, and perspectives." Because they are not Africans, "white teachers cannot inspire in our children the visions necessary for them to overcome limitations." Asante recommends that African Americans choose an African name (as he did), reject European dress, embrace African religion (not Islam or Christianity) and love "their own" culture. He scorns the idea of universality as a form of Eurocentric arrogance. The Eurocentrist lauds Shakespeare or Twain, while the Afrocentrist prefers Baraka, Shange, or Abiola. Asante is critical of black artists like Arthur Mitchell and Alvin Ailey who ignore Afrocentricity. Likewise, he speaks contemptuously of a group of black university students who spurned the Afrocentrism of the local Black Student Union and formed an organization called Interrace: "Such madness is the direct consequence of self-hatred, obligatory attitudes, false assumptions about society, and stupidity."

The conflict between pluralism and particularism turns on the issue of universalism. Professor Asante warns his readers against the lure of universalism: "Do not be captured by a sense of universality given to you by the Eurocentric viewpoint; such a viewpoint is contradictory to your own ultimate reality." He insists that there is no alternative to Eurocentrism, Afrocentrism, and other ethnocentrisms. In contrast, the pluralist says, with the Roman playwright Terence, "I am a man: nothing human is alien to me." A contemporary Terence would say "I am a person" or might be a woman, but the point remains the same: You don't have to be black to love Zora Neale Hurston's fiction or Langston Hughe's poetry or Duke Ellington's music. In a pluralist cur-

riculum, we expect children to learn a broad and humane culture, to learn about the ideas and art and animating spirit of many cultures. We expect that children, whatever their color, will be inspired by the courage of people like Helen Keller, Vaclav Havel, Harriet Tubman, and Feng Lizhe. We expect that their response to literature will be determined by the ideas and images it evokes, not by the skin color of the writer. But particularists insist that children can learn only from experiences of people from the same race.

Particularism is a bad idea whose time has come. It is also a fashion spreading like wildfire through the education system, actively promoted by organizations and individuals with a political and professional interest in strengthening ethnic power bases in the university, in the education profession, and in society itself. One can scarcely pick up an educational journal without learning about a school district that is converting to an ethnocentric curriculum in an attempt to give "self-esteem" to children from racial minorities. A state-funded project in a Sacramento high school is teaching young black males to think like Africans and to develop the "African Mind Model Technique," in order to free themselves of the racism of American culture. A popular black rap singer, KRS-One, complained in an op-ed in the *New York Times* that the schools should be teaching blacks about their cultural heritage, instead of trying to make everyone Americans. "It's like trying to teach a dog to be a cat," he wrote. KRS-One railed about having to learn about Thomas Jefferson and the

Civil War, which had nothing to do (he said) with black history.

Pluralism can easily be transformed into particularism, as may be seen in the potential uses in the classroom of the Mayan contribution to mathematics. The Mayan example was popularized in a movie called *Stand and Deliver*, about a charismatic Bolivian-born mathematics teacher in Los Angeles who inspired his students (who are Hispanic) to learn calculus. He told them that their ancestors invented the concept of zero; but that wasn't all he did. He used imagination to put across mathematical concepts. He required them to do homework and to go to school on Saturdays and during the Christmas holidays, so that they might pass the Advanced Placement mathematics examination for college entry. The teacher's reference to the Mayans' mathematical genius was a valid instructional device: It was an attention-getter and would have interested even students who were not Hispanic. But the Mayan example would have had little effect without the teacher's insistence that the class study hard for a difficult examination.

Ethnic educators have seized upon the Mayan contribution to mathematics as the key to simultaneously boosting the ethnic pride of Hispanic children and attacking Eurocentrism. One proposal claims that Mexican-American children will be attracted to science and mathematics if they study Mayan mathematics, the Mayan calendar, and Mayan astronomy. Children in primary grades are to be taught that the Mayans were first to discover the zero and that Europeans learned it long afterwards from the Arabs, who had learned it in India. This will help them see that Europeans were latecomers in the discovery of great ideas. Botany is to be learned by study of the agricultural techniques of the Aztecs, a subject of somewhat limited relevance to children in urban areas. Furthermore, "ethnobotanical" classifications of plants are to be substituted for the Eurocentric Linnaean system. At first glance, it may seem curious that Hispanic children are deemed to have no cultural affinity with Spain; but to acknowledge the cultural tie would confuse the ideological assault on Eurocentrism.

> ... particularists have no interest in extending or revising American culture; indeed, they deny that a common culture exists.

This proposal suggests some questions: Is there any evidence that the teaching of "culturally relevant" science and mathematics will draw Mexican-American children to the study of these subjects? Will Mexican-American children lose interest or self-esteem if they discover that their ancestors were Aztecs or Spaniards, rather than Mayans? Are children who learn in this way prepared to study the science and mathematics that are taught in American colleges and universities and that are needed for advanced study in these

fields? Are they even prepared to study the science and mathematics taught in Mexican universities? If the class is half Mexican-American and half something else, will only the Mexican-American children study in a Mayan and Aztec mode or will all the children? But shouldn't all children study what is culturally relevant for them? How will we train teachers who have command of so many different systems of mathematics and science?

The efficacy of particularist proposals seems to be less important to their sponsors than their value as ideological weapons with which to criticize existing disciplines for their alleged Eurocentric bias. In a recent article titled "The Ethnocentric Basis of Social Science Knowledge Production" in the *Review of Research in Education*. John Stanfield of Yale University argues that neither social science nor science are objective studies, that both instead are "Euro-American" knowledge systems which reproduce "hegemonic racial domination." The claim that science and reason are somehow superior to magic and witchcraft, he writes, is the product of Euro-American ethnocentrism. According to Stanfield, current fears about the misuse of science (for instance, "the nuclear arms race, global pollution") and "the power-plays of Third World nations (the Arab oil boycott and the American-Iranian hostage crisis) have made Western people more aware of nonscientific cognitive styles. These last events are beginning to demonstrate politically that which has begun to be understood in intellectual circles: namely, that modes of social knowledge such as theology, science, and magic are different, not inferior or superior. They represent different

ways of perceiving, defining, and organizing knowledge of life experiences." One wonders: If Professor Stanfield broke his leg, would he go to a theologian, a doctor, or a magician?

Every field of study, it seems, has been tainted by Eurocentrism, which was defined by a professor at Manchester University, George Chevarughese Joseph, in *Race and Class* in 1987, as "intellectual racism." Professor Joseph argues that the history of science and technology—and in particular, of mathematics—in non-European societies was distorted by racist Europeans who wanted to establish the dominance of European forms of knowledge. The racists, he writes, traditionally traced mathematics to the Greeks, then claimed that it reached its full development in Europe. These are simply Eurocentric myths to sustain an "imperialist/racist ideology," says Professor Joseph, since mathematics was found in Egypt, Babylonia, Mesopotamia, and India long before the Greeks were supposed to have developed it. Professor Joseph points out too that Arab scientists should be credited with major discoveries traditionally attributed to William Harvey, Isaac Newton, Charles Darwin, and Sir Francis Bacon. But he is not concerned only to argue historical issues; his purpose is to bring all of these different mathematical traditions into the school classroom so that children might study, for example, "traditional African designs, Indian *rangoli* patterns and Islamic art" and "the language and counting systems found across the world."

This interesting proposal to teach ethnomathematics comes at a time when American mathematics educators are trying to overhaul present practices, because of the poor performance of American children on national and international assessments. Mathematics educators are attempting to change the teaching of their subject so that children can see its uses in every day life. There would seem to be an incipient conflict between those who want to introduce real-life applications of mathematics and those who want to teach the mathematical systems used by ancient cultures. I suspect that most mathematics teachers would enjoy doing a bit of both, if there were time or student interest. But any widespread movement to replace modern mathematics with ancient ethnic mathematics runs the risk of disaster in a field that is struggling to update existing curricula. If, as seems likely, ancient mathematics is taught mainly to minority children, the gap between them and middle-class white children is apt to grow. It is worth noting that children in Korea, who score highest in mathematics on international assessments, do not study ancient Korean mathematics.

Particularism is akin to cultural Lysenkoism, for it takes as its premise the spurious notion that cultural traits are inherited. It implies a dubious, dangerous form of cultural predestination. Children are taught that if their ancestors could do it, so could they. But what happens if a child is from a cultural group that made no significant contribution to science or mathematics? Does this mean that children from that background must find a culturally appropriate field in which to strive? How does a teacher find the right cultural buttons for children of mixed heritage? And how in the world will teachers use this technique when the children in their classes are drawn from many different cultures, as is usually the case? By the time that every culture gets its due, there may be no time left to teach the subject itself. This explosion of filiopietism (which, we should remember, comes from adults, not from students) is reminiscent of the period some years ago when the Russians claimed that they had invented everything first; as we now know, this nationalistic braggadocio did little for their self-esteem and nothing for their economic development. We might reflect, too, on how little social prestige has been accorded in this country to immigrants from Greece and Italy, even though the achievements of their ancestors were at the heart of the classical curriculum.

Particularists reject any accommodation among groups, any interactions that blur the distinct lines between them.

Filiopietism and ethnic boosterism lead to all sorts of odd practices. In New York State, for example, the curriculum guide for eleventh grade American history lists three "foundations" for the United States Constitution, as follows:

A. Foundations

1. 17th and 18th century Enlightenment thought

2. Haudenosaunee political system

   a. Influence upon colonial leadership and European intellectuals (Locke, Montesquieu, Voltaire, Rousseau

   b. Impact on Albany Plan of Union, Articles of Confederation, and U.S. Constitution

3. Colonial experience

Those who are unfamiliar with the Haudenosaunee political system might wonder what it is, particularly since educational authorities in New York State rank it as equal in importance to the European Enlightenment and suggest that it strongly influenced not only colonial leaders but the leading intellectuals of Europe. The Haudenosaunee political system was the Iroquois confederation of five (later six) Indian tribes in upper New York State, which conducted war and civil affairs through a council of chiefs, each with one vote. In 1754, Benjamin Franklin proposed a colonial union at a conference in Albany; his plan, said to be inspired by the Iroquois Confederation, was rejected by the other colonies. Today, Indian activists believe that the Iroquois Confederation was the model for the American Constitution, and the New York State Department of Education has decided that they are right. That no other state see fit to give the American Indians equal billing with the European Enlightenment may be owing to the fact that the Indians in New York State (numbering less than forty thousand) have been more politically effective than elsewhere or that other states have not yet learned about this method of reducing "Eurocentrism" in their American history classes.

Particularism can easily be carried to extremes. Students of Fredonian descent must hear that their ancestors were seminal in the development of all human civilization and that without the Fredonian contribution, we would all be living in caves or trees, bereft of art, technology, and culture. To explain why Fredonians today are in modest circumstances, given their historic imminence, children are taught that somewhere, long ago, another culture stole the Fredonians' achievements, palmed them off as their own, and oppressed the Fredonians.

A debate currently raging among some classicists is whether the Greeks "stole" the philosophy, art, and religion of the ancient Egyptians and whether the ancient Egyptians were black Africans.

I first encountered this argument almost twenty years ago, when I was a graduate student. I shared a small office with a young professor, and I listened as she patiently explained to a student why she had given him a D on a term paper. In his paper, he argued that the Arabs had stolen mathematics from the Nubians in the desert long ago (I forget in which century this theft allegedly occurred). She tried to explain to him about the necessity of historical evidence. He was unconvinced, since he believed that he had uncovered a great truth that was beyond proof. The part I couldn't understand was how anyone could lose knowledge by sharing it. After all, cultures are constantly influencing one another, exchanging ideas and art and technology, and the exchange usually is enriching, not depleting.

Today, there are a number of books and articles advancing controversial theories about the origins of civilization. An important work, *The African Origin of Civilization: Myth or Reality*, by Senegalese scholar Cheikh Anta Diop, argues that ancient Egypt was a black civilization, that all races are descended from the black race, and that the achievements of "western" civilization originated in Egypt. The views of Diop and other Africanists have been condensed into an everyman's paperback titled *What they Never Told You in History Class* by Indus Khamit Kush. This latter book claims that Moses, Jesus, Buddha, Mohammed, and Wishnu were Africans; that the first Indians, Chinese, Hebrews, Greeks, Romans, Britains, and Americans were Africans; and that the first mathematicians, scientists, astronomers, and physicians were Africans. A debate currently raging among some classicists is whether the Greeks "stole" the philosophy, art, and religion of the ancient Egyptians and whether the ancient Egyptians were black

Africans. George G. M. James's *Stolen Legacy* insists that the Greeks "stole the Legacy of the African Continent and called it their own." James argues that the civilization of Greece, the vaunted foundation of European culture, owed everything it knew and did to its African predecessors. Thus, the roots of western civilization lie not in Greece and Rome, but in Egypt and, ultimately, in black Africa.Similar speculation was fueled by the publication in 1987 of Martin Bernal's *Black Athena: The Afroasiatic Roots of Classical Civilization*, Volume 1, *The Fabrication of Ancient Greece, 1785-1985*, although the controversy predates Bernal's book. In a fascinating foray into the politics of knowledge, Bernal attributes the preference of Western European scholars for Greece over Egypt as the fount of knowledge to nearly two centuries of racism and "Europocentrism," but he is uncertain about the color of the ancient Egyptians. However, a review of Bernal's book last year in the *Village Voice* began, "What color were the ancient Egyptians? Blacker than Mubarak, baby." The same article claimed that white racist archaeologists chiseled the noses off ancient Egyptian statues so that future generations would not see the typically African facial characteristics. The debate reached the pages of the *Biblical Archeology Review* last year in an article titled "Were the Ancient Egyptians Black or White?" The author, classicist Frank J. Yurco, "is a chimera, cultural baggage from our own society that can only be imposed artificially on ancient Egyptian society."

Most educationists are not even aware of the debate about whether the ancient Egyptians were black or white, but they are very sensitive to charges that the schools' curricula are Eurocentric, and they are eager to rid the schools of the taint of Eurocentrism. It is hardly surprising that America's schools would recognize strong cultural ties with Europe since our nation's political, religious, educational, and economic institutions were created chiefly by people of European descent, our government was shaped by European ideas, and nearly 80 percent of the people who live here are of European descent. The particularists treat all of this history as a racist bias toward Europe, rather than as the matter-of-fact consequences of European immigration. Even so, American education is not centered on Europe. American education, if it is centered on anything, is centered on itself. It is "Americentric." Most American students today have never studied any world history; they know very little about Europe, and even less about the rest of the world. Their minds are rooted solidly in the here and now. When the Berlin Wall was opened in the fall of 1989, journalists discovered that most American teenagers had no idea what it was, nor why its opening was such a big deal. Nonetheless, Eurocentrism provides a better target than Americentrism.

In school districts where most children are black and Hispanic, there has been a growing tendency to embrace particularism rather than pluralism. Many of the children in these districts performs poorly in academic classes and leave school without graduating. They would fare better in school if they had well-educated and well-paid teachers, small classes, good materials, encouragement at home and

school, summer academic programs, protection from the drugs and crime that ravage their neighborhoods, and higher expectations of satisfying careers upon graduation. These are expensive and time-consuming remedies that must also engage the larger society beyond the school. The lure of particularism is that it offers a less complicated anodyne, one in which the children's academic deficiencies may be addressed—or set aside—by inflating their racial pride. The danger of this remedy is that it will detract attention from the real needs of schools and the real interests of children, while simultaneously arousing distorted race pride in children of all races, increasing racial antagonism and producing fresh recruits for white and black racist groups.

The brand of history that they espouse is one in which everyone is either a descendant of victims or oppressors.

The particularist critique gained a major forum in New York in 1989, with the release of a report called " A Curriculum of Inclusion," produced by a task force created by the State Commissioner of Education, Thomas Sobol. In 1987, soon after his appointment, Sobol appointed a Task Force on Minorities to review

the state's curriculum for instances of bias. He did this not because there had been complaints about bias in the curriculum, but because—as a newly appointed state commissioner whose previous job had been to superintend the public schools of a wealthy suburb, Scarsdale—he wanted to demonstrate his sensitivity to minority concerns. The Sobol task force was composed of representatives of African American, Hispanic, Asian American, and American Indian groups. The task force engaged four consultants, one from each of the aforementioned racial or ethnic minorities, to review nearly one hundred teachers' guides prepared by the state. These guides define the state's curriculum, usually as a list of facts and concepts to be taught, along with model activities. The primary focus of the consultants, not surprisingly, was the history and social studies curriculum. As it happened, the history curriculum had been extensively revised in 1987 to make it multicultural, in both American and world history. In the 1987 revision the time given to Western Europe was reduced to one-quarter of one year, as part of a two-year global studies sequence in which equal time was allotted to seven major world regions, including Africa and Latin America.

As a result of the 1987 revisions in American and world history, New York State had one of the most advanced multicultural history-social studies curricula in the country. Dozens of social studies teachers and consultants had participated, and the final draft was reviewed by such historians as Eric Foner of Columbia University, and Christopher Lasch of the University of Rochester. The curriculum was overloaded with facts, almost to the point of numbing students with details and trivia, but it was not insensitive to ethnicity in American history or unduly devoted to European history.

But the Sobol task force decided that this curriculum was biased and Eurocentric. The first sentence of the task force report summarizes its major thesis: "African Americans, Asian Americans, Puerto Ricans/Latinos, and Native Americans have all been the victims of an intellectual and educational oppression that has characterized the culture and institutions of the United States and the European American world for centuries."

The task force report was remarkable in that it vigorously denounced bias without identifying a single instance of bias in the curricular guides under review. Instead, the consultants employed harsh, sometimes inflammatory, rhetoric to treat every difference of opinion or interpretation as an example of racial bias. The African-American consultant, for example, excoriates the curriculum for its "White Anglo-Saxon (WASP) value system and norms," its "deep-seated pathologies of racial hatred" and its "white nationalism"; he decries as bias the fact that children study Egypt as part of the Middle East instead of as part of Africa. Perhaps Egypt should be studied as part of the African unit (geographically, it is located on the African continent); but placing it in one region rather than the other is not what most people think of as racism or bias. The "Latino" consultant criticizes the use of the term "Spanish-American War" instead of "Spanish-Cuban-American War." The Native American consultant complains that tribal lan-

guages are classified as "foreign languages."

When people differ about basic values, sooner or later those disagreements turn up in battles about how schools are organized or what the schools should teach.

The report is consistently Europhobic. It repeatedly expresses negative judgments on "European Americans" and on everything Western and European. All people with a white skin are referred to as "Anglo-Saxons" and "WASPs." Europe, says the report, is uniquely responsible for producing aggressive individuals who "were ready to discover, invade and conquer foreign land because of greed, racism and national egoism." All white people are held collectively guilty for the historical crimes of slavery and racism. There is no mention of the "Anglo-Saxons" who opposed slavery and racism. Nor does the report acknowledge that some whites have been victims of discrimination and oppression. The African-American consultant writes of the Constitution. "There is something vulgar and revolting in glorifying a process that heaped undeserved rewards on a segment of

the population while oppressing the majority."

The New York task force proposal is not merely about the reconstruction of what is taught. It goes a step further to suggest that the history curriculum may be used to ensure that "children from Native American, Puerto Rican/Latino, Asian American, and African American cultures will have higher self-esteem and self-respect, while children from European cultures will have a less arrogant perspective of being part of the group that had 'done it all.'"

In February 1990, Commissioner Sobol asked the New York Board of Regents to endorse a sweeping revision of the history curriculum to make it more multicultural. His recommendations were couched in measured tones, not in the angry rhetoric of his task force. The board supported his request unanimously. It remains to be seen whether New York pursues the particularist path marked out by the Commissioner's advisory group or finds its way to the concept of pluralism within a democratic tradition.

The rising tide of particularism encourages the politicization of all curricula in the schools. If education bureaucrats bend to the political and ideological winds, as is their wont, we can anticipate a generation of struggle over the content of the curriculum in mathematics, science, literature, and history. Demands for "culturally relevant" studies, for ethnostudies of all kinds, will open the classroom to unending battles over whose version is taught, who gets credit for what, and which ethno-interpretation is appropriate. Only recently have districts begun to resist the demands of fundamentalist groups to censor textbooks and library books (and some have not yet begun to do so).

The spread of particularism throws into question the very idea of American public education. Public schools exist to teach children the general skills and knowledge that they need to succeed in American society, and the specific skills and knowledge that they need in order to function as American citizens. They receive public support because they have a public function. Historically, the public schools were known as "common schools" because they were schools for all, even if the children of all the people did not attend them. Over the years, the courts have found that it was unconstitutional to teach religion in the common schools, or to separate children on the basis of their race in the common schools. In their curriculum, their hiring practices, and their general philosophy, the public schools must not discriminate against or give preference to any racial or ethnic group. Yet they are permitted to accommodate cultural diversity by, for example, serving food that is culturally appropriate or providing library collections that emphasize the interests of the local community. However, they should not be expected to teach children to view the world through an ethnocentric perspective that rejects or ignores the common culture. For generations, those groups that wanted to inculcate their religion or their ethnic heritage have instituted private schools—after school, on weekends, or on a full-time basis. There, children learn with others of the same group—Greeks, Poles, Germans, Japanese, Chinese, Jews, Lutherans, Catho-

lics, and so on—and are taught by people from the same group. Valuable as this exclusive experience has been for those who choose it, this has not been the role of public education. One of the primary purposes of public education has been to create a national community, a definition of citizenship and culture that is both expansive and inclusive.

The curriculum in public schools must be based on whatever knowledge and practices have been determined to be best by professionals—experienced teachers and scholars—who are competent to make these judgments. Professional societies must be prepared to defend the integrity of their disciplines. When called upon, they should establish review committees to examine disputes over curriculum and to render judgment, in order to help school officials fend off improper political pressure. Where genuine controversies exist, they should be taught and debated in the classroom. Was Egypt a black civilization? Why not raise the question, read the arguments of the different sides in the debate, show slides of Egyptian collections? If scholars disagree, students should know it. One great advantage of this approach is that students will see that history is a lively study, that textbooks are fallible, that historian's politics and ideology, that history is written by people who make choices among alternative facts and interpretations, and that history changes as new facts are uncovered and new interpretations win adherents. They will also learn that cultures and civilizations constantly interact, exchange ideas, and influence one another, and that the idea of racial or ethnic purity is a myth. Another advantage is that

students might once again study ancient history, which has all but disappeared from the curricula of American schools. (California recently introduced a required sixth grade course in ancient civilizations, but ancient history is otherwise *terra incognita* in American education.)

Demands for "culturally relevant" studies, for ethnostudies of all kinds, will open the classroom to unending battles over whose version is taught, who gets credit for what, and which ethno-interpretation is appropriate.

The multicultural controversy may do wonders for the study of history, which has been neglected for years in American schools. At this time, only half of our high school graduates ever study any world history. Any serious attempt to broaden student's knowledge of Africa, Europe, Asia, and Latin America will require at least two, and possibly three years of world history (a requirement thus far only in California). American history, too, will need more time than the one-year high-school survey course. Those of us who have insisted for years on the importance of history in the curriculum may not be ready to assent to its redemptive power, but hope that our new allies will ultimately join a constructive dialogue that strengthens the place of history in the schools.

As cultural controversies arise, educators must adhere to the principle of "E Pluribus Unum." That is, they must maintain a balance between the demands of the one—the nation of which we are common citizens—and the many—the varied histories of the American people. It is not necessary to denigrate either the one or the many. Pluralism is a positive value, but it is also important that we preserve a sense of an American community—a society and a culture to which we all belong. If there is no overall community with an agreed-upon vision of liberty and justice, if all we have is a collection of racial and ethnic cultures, lacking any common bonds, then we have no means to mobilize public opinion on behalf of people who are not members of our particular group. We have, for example, no reason to support public education. If there is no larger community, then each group will want to teach its own children in its own way, and public education ceases to exist.

History should not be confused with filiopietism. History gives no grounds for race pride. No race has a monopoly on virtue. If anything, a study of history should inspire humility, rather than pride. People of every racial group have committed terrible crimes, often against others of the same group. Whether one looks at the history of Europe or Africa or Latin America or Asia,

every continent offers examples of inhumanity. Slavery has existed in civilizations around the world for centuries. Examples of genocide can be found around the world, throughout history, from ancient times right through to our own day. Governments and cultures, sometimes by edict, sometimes simply following tradition, have practiced not only slavery, but human sacrifice, infanticide, clitoridectomy, and mass murder. If we teach children this, they might recognize how absurd both racial hatred and racial chauvinism are.

What must be preserved in the study of history is the spirit of inquiry, the readiness to open new questions and to pursue new understandings. History, at its best, is a search for truth. The best way to portray this search is through debate and controversy, rather than through imposition of fixed beliefs and immutable facts. Perhaps the most dangerous aspect of school history is its tendency to become Official History, a sanctified version of the Truth taught by the state to captive audiences and embedded in beautiful mass-market textbooks as holy writ. When Official History is written by committees responding to political pressures, rather than by scholars synthesizing the best available research, then the errors of the past are replaced by the politically fashionable errors of the present. It may be difficult to teach children that history is both important and uncertain, and that even the best historians never have all the pieces of the jigsaw puzzle, but it is necessary to do so. If state education departments permit the revision of their history courses and textbooks to become an exercise in power politics, then the entire process of state-

level curriculum-making becomes suspect, as does public education itself.

The curriculum in public schools must be based on whatever knowledge and practices have been determined to be best by professionals—experi enced teachers and scholars—who are competent to make these judgments.

The question of self-esteem is extraordinarily complex, and it goes well beyond the content of the curriculum. Most of what we call self-esteem is formed in the home and in a variety of life experiences, not only in school. Nonetheless, it has been important for blacks—and for other racial groups—to learn about the history of slavery and of the civil rights movement; it has been important for blacks to know that their ancestors actively resisted enslavement and actively pursued equality; and it has been important for blacks and others to learn about black men and women who fought courageously against racism and who provide models of courage, persistence, and intellect. These are instances where the content of the curriculum reflects sound scholarship, and at the same time probably lessens racial prejudice and provides inspiration for those who are descendants of slaves. But knowing about the travails and triumphs of one's forebears does not necessarily translate into either self-esteem or personal accomplishment. For most children, self-esteem—the self-confidence that grows out of having reached a goal—comes not from hearing about the monuments of their ancestors but as a consequence of what they are able to do and accomplish through their own efforts.

As I reflected on these issues, I recalled reading an interview a few years ago with a talented black runner. She said that her model is Mikhail Baryshnikov. She admires him because his is a magnificent athlete. He is not black; he is not female; he is not American-born; he is not even a runner. But he inspires her because of the way he trained and used his body. When I read this, I thought how narrow-minded it is to believe that people can be inspired only by those who are exactly like them in race and ethnicity.

Diane Ravitch is adjunct professor of history and education at Teachers College, Columbia University, and the author of several books including The Troubled Crusade: American Education, 1945-1980.

From The American Scholar, Volume 60, Number 3, Summer 1991. Copyright © 1991 by the author. Reprinted with permission.

Many critics of traditional historical accounts find either distortions or see nothing about any cultural contributions by members of the racial, ethnic, or national groups with which they identify. Floyd Hayes counters arguments by Diane Ravitch, E.D. Hirsch, Allan Bloom, and others who want a unitary, Eurocentric account.

Politics and Education in America's Mutlicultural Society: An African-American Studies' Response to Allan Bloom

Floyd W. Hayes, III

With the 1987 publication of *The Closing of the American Mind*, Allan Bloom has emerged from being an obscure professor of political philosophy to become a prominent, if not popular, would-be philosopher of education. His ideas—or perhaps his book's catchy subtitle, *How Higher Education Has Failed Democracy and Impoverished the Souls of Today's Students*—have captured the attention of academicians, journalists, and knowledgeable sectors of the lay public. Bloom's supporters point to the book's widely-heralded publishing success and praise his cold-blooded assessment of America's current educational crisis. Bloom's critics, bewildered by the book's public ac-claim, charge that his text is poorly written and that his neo-conservative diagnosis of the nation's educational dilemma is faulty and mean-spirited.

The central problem in American education, however, is not exclusively academic. Rather, as both Bloom's text and responses to it indicate, that problem is a result of a clash of cultures, a conflict of interests and a struggle for power. There is a contest between proponents of tradition and proponents of change, between those who look to the past and those who look to the future, between old ideas and new ideas, between hegemonic forces and counter-hegemonic forces and between historically in-cluded groups and historically excluded groups. These developments are taking place in the midst of a dramatic transformation of American society.

In America's emerging postindustrial-managerial society, in which knowledge is expanding and innovation has become a central feature, learning is the indispensable investment required for social development. Therefore, formal education has become increasingly a focal point of public attention and the struggle for power. While the present issue of educational crisis and the call for reform in America are not new—educational crises seem to emerge about every twenty years in the United States—the national concern about the decline in the quality of education exemplifies the critical role education plays in the new social order.

Seductive in some ways and dangerous in others, Bloom's text reflects the American public's anxiety about the nation's educational disarray. His text is seductive because some of his lamentations about the decline of American education seem to ring true, even to many who labor in the higher education vineyard; yet, his explanations for this state of affairs are largely flawed. Hence Bloom sometimes says the right thing, but for the wrong reason. His book is dangerous because he generally blames the social changes of the 1960s and, ultimately, African-Americans for the present crisis in higher education. Clearly, the challenges to tradition and the demand for inclusion and partnership by historically excluded groups and individuals must be traumatizing to Bloom's elitist sensibilities.

The intent here is to examine critically and respond to Bloom's assault on African-American university students in the 1960s and his observations about the role and significance of the "new studies," particularly African-American Studies, within the academy. I am attentive not only to what Bloom says but also to what he does not say about the "new studies" and what they represent.

Bloom's Lament

Allan Bloom makes disturbing, yet revealing, remarks about the historical and current nature of racial interaction in American society and its universities. He notes the increased numbers of African-American students in major universities

since the 1960s, but laments the absence of real friendship between them and their White counterparts. Although universities are integrated, Bloom laments that African-American and White students walk separate paths. He exonerates White students of any racist tendencies. In Bloom's portrait, White students are uncomfortable with, but have come to accept, special entry policies for African-American students. Moreover, since the legal exclusion of African-Americans from the university is no longer in practice, Bloom declares that White students have done all they can possibly do to improve racial interaction on the campus.

According to Bloom, the real blame for this racial impasse rests with African-American students. He complains: "Thus, just at the moment when everyone else has become a 'person,' blacks have become black" (p. 92). He laments that they associate mainly with each other. Bloom considers this strange, particularly since he says that the early 1960s witnessed the pursuit of racial integration. Additionally, Bloom contends that African-Americans strangely are the only group to embrace its own cultural identity and he claims that this effort goes against the American grain. In a vicious attack Bloom declares:

> . . . the movement of the blacks goes counter not only to that of the rest of society, and tends to put them at odds with it, but also to their own noblest claims and traditions in this country. And it is connected with a dangerous severing of the races in the intellectual world, where there can be no justification for separatism and where the ideal of common

humanity must prevail. The confrontations and indignation of the political realm have become firmly fixed in the university (p. 93).

For Bloom, racism in the academy no longer exists; therefore, he assails African-Americans for perpetuating racial separatism.

Bloom also blames the university for abandoning its "universalizing mission," which apparently should have or would have overcome racially separatist tendencies. Although major universities began to educate more African-Americans following World War II, Bloom contends that as a result of the civil rights movement, when "everyone was still integrationist," universities sought a dramatic increase in African-American student enrollment to discount the appearance of racism. However, in this period of exuberance, many universities lent priority to quantity over quality, resulting in substantial numbers of African-American students with less academic preparation. To accommodate this situation, Bloom observes, many institutions lowered academic standards, creating a class of less-educated African-Americans.

If Bloom is critical of the academy's fall from grace, he is hostile to the post-civil rights Black Power movement and its intellectual representation at the university—the ascendancy of African-American Studies. Bloom is angered by the movement's rejection of integrationism and threatened by the challenge of African-American to the academy's received "truth." For him, this emerging field of study is a "cop-out" that has set in motion a "new segregationism." As Bloom laments: "The way was opened for black students to live and study the black experience, to be comfortable, rather than be constrained by the learning accessible to man as man" (p. 95). However according to Bloom, even with all of its political and ideological energy, African-American Studies is a failure and is largely ignored by the academy.

Western Cultural Domination and Educational Politics

What are we to make of Bloom's interpretation? In view of the current resurgence of White student's verbal and physical attacks on African-American students on university campuses across the nation, Bloom displays a racist distemper when he blames the historically assaulted people for these conflicts. Lacking historical depth, his argument is seriously flawed.

Incredibly, Bloom asserts that there are in principle no outsiders in America (p.53) and that the enslavement of Africans was an aberration in "American history" (p. 248). On the contrary, it is well-documented that the trade in African flesh and the institution of chattel slavery laid the foundation for the development of colonial America's political economy. Moreover, this sordid history's legacy is deeply rooted in American culture and thought (Baron, 1971; Blackburn, 1988; David's, 1966; Bois, 1965; Genovese, 1967; Williams, 1966). African-Americans' forebears were enslaved for 250 years, not because they were "savages" and "uncivilized" as claimed, but rather because there was born in those days in the Western world a new form of government founded largely on the Calvinist concept of "the elect and the unelect"—theological

doctrine based on the premise that some persons are born outside salvation. Actually this form of government arose in response to a desire on the part of a select minority to dominate the majority. Later, that minority of Whites could strengthen its position with the profits, power, and pleasure derived from enslaved Africans (Bercovitch, 1975; Greene, 1968; Harkness, 1931; Tawney, 1952; Weber, 1968; Woodard, 1982).

Sixteenth-century Calvinist social ethics and theological absolutism together with the progressive rise of capitalism and the seventeenth/eighteenth-century enlightenment rationalist absolutism, set in motion the accepted belief in the superiority of Western civilization. Defined by Calvinist Puritans as beings without souls and declared by Enlightenment thinkers as persons unable to reason, Africans were relegated to a class of sub-humanity (Davis, 1984; Fitch, 1987; Gates, 1986; Hodge, Struckmann, and Trost, 1975; Mazique, 1959; Richards, 1980; Tannenbaum, 1946). Hence, the theory and practice of Eurocentrism and Western imperialism defined Western culture and thought as superior to other cultures and peoples and rationalized both the dehumanizing institution of chattel slavery and the exploitation of African labor.

Since no person, Black nor White, voluntarily submits to slavery, it became necessary, in order to institutionalize the system, to break up their family and social structure as quickly as Africans departed from the slave ship. Another essential for guaranteed control over chattel slaves was to deny them literacy, while educating them for service on the plantation and in the

slave master's house. Thus, in a larger sense, it cannot be asserted that Africans were totally denied education, for they were engaged in weaving and sewing, cooking and housekeeping, and carpentry and numerous skills. However, American slave owners immediately frowned upon teaching slaves reading and mathematics, then implemented this sentiment absolutely. Slave owners feared that literate slaves would be able to acquire knowledge of their heritage, preserve their history, and obtain information about the outside world. They dreaded the possibility that literate slaves would communicate in writing, plot insurrections, and plan escape through the underground railroad. The tradition of dehumanizing, exploiting, and robbing the minds of African slaves and their American descendants became embedded in all aspects of American culture, thought and institutions.

Following chattel slavery, African-Americans waged a relentless battle against this culturally hegemonic tradition, but its legacy survived. The great majority of African-Americans have participated in a continuing struggle for human rights-human dignity and personal worth, family stability and parental control over their children's destiny, literacy and quality education, economic well being and self-sufficiency, and political rights and self-determination. Clearly, the contours and content of this historic project are broader than the limited agenda of citizenship rights and racial integration which civil rights leaders have articulated since the 1940s. Therefore, Bloom is incorrect to suggest that "everyone was integrationist" in the early 1960s.

Particularly in the area of education, the vast multitude of African-Americans desired neither the segregationist regime of the Old South nor the integrationist strategies and tactics put forward by the liberal educational managerial elite. Rather, African-Americans sought quality education and self-determination: good schools and the right to enter the school of their choice.

In the late 1950s and early 1960s, after the Supreme Court's historic Brown desegregation ruling, African-American residents in many big cities across the nation battled urban public school regimes that sought to evade or distort the court's decision. For example, community groups in Washington, D.C., struggled against the school system's pupil assignment policy of tracking which channeled the majority of African-American students into the lowest track early in their educational career. Community participants labeled the policy "programmed retardation," declaring that tracking was more harmful than segregation in the Old South. Significantly, they did not call for racial integration; rather, community leaders demanded quality education. They defined this educational goal unambiguously: (1) the distribution and mastery of the fundamental tools of knowledge: reading, writing, and computational skills; (2) academic motivation; and (3) positive character-building.

Like so many residents in other urban areas, Washington's African-American community lost the political contest for quality education. Although the tracking policy strategy eventually was terminated in the late 1960s, liberal educational managerial elites—big city school administrators, educational special-

ists, university professors (on the rise of educational managerialism, see Tyack and Hansot, 1982)—and civil rights advocates won the day with the implementation of various integration policies: racial-balance busing, magnet school programs, and other educational experiments. Because integration is at best only a *means* to achieve an end, the contradictions quickly became apparent. Thus, as educational managers and civil rights leaders put forward integration as the *goal* of education and forced it on public schools at all costs, good classroom teaching declined, the fundamental tools of knowledge were abandoned, academic motivation was subverted, and positive character-building was perverted. The consequences of this course of events are evident in the continued decline in the quality of education in the public schools in the District of Columbia and in many other urban areas. Ironically, school budgets have continued to rise along with the growing bureaucratization of urban school systems (Hayes, 1987).

Additionally, to rationalize the denial of quality education to African-Americans, liberal members of the educational managerial elite applied various theories of cultural deprivation to African-American youth (see Clark, 1965). Categorizing African-descended Americans as "culturally deprived" or "culturally disadvantaged" merely continues into the contemporary era the legacy of cultural domination and denial of African-American human dignity originally established during the Atlantic slave trade and chattel slavery in colonial America. To refer to African-Americans as "educationally handicapped" when there has been a historic conspiracy

to deny them quality education is comparable to breaking a person's leg and then criticizing that person when he or she limps. In spite of it all, America's Judeo-Calvinist tradition of an "elect-unelect" pervades educational theory and practice, providing a means for keeping the oppressed in an oppressed situation.

These unfortunate educational trends and developments characterized urban less affluent public school systems in the 1960s and 1970s. Today, many suburban and more affluent public school systems also are experiencing an educational crisis. Public schools confront a growing rate of complex problems: functional illiteracy, drop/push-outs, discipline, drug use, teenage pregnancy, gang activity, and teacher burn-out (NAEP, 1987; NCEE, 1983). What is to be expected of youngsters—African-American, Latino, White, or any other nationality—who were never taught to read, who never developed the responsibility to carry out an assignment and to follow directions, who never learned to respect knowledge or its purveyors, and who never became masters of their own souls with self-discipline? Hence Bloom's diagnosis is largely correct; there is an educational crisis in America. However, he misreads the dilemma's cause. The source is not cultural relativism or intellectual openness or the ascendancy of assertive African-American students in the university as Bloom urges us to believe; rather, America's educational tragedy is related to the betrayal in public schools from which the vast majority of university students come (Washington, 1969). This is not an attack on public school systems;

however, it is a critique of the educational managerial elite who dominate them and retard the development of quality education.

In the current stage of American postindustrial-managerial development, there is less emphasis on quality education and learning and more stress on *managing* schools, students, and teachers. The result is a techno-bureaucratic educational process that tends to produce students who posses less of an independent and critical sensibility and more of a pragmatic and instrumentally rationalist consciousness (McNeil, 1986, Misgeld, 1985; Wise, 1979; Zeigler, Kehoe, and Reisman, 1985). This is why today's students are reading less, are less intellectually curious, and are more socially indifferent than their counterparts of a few generations ago. Hence, the theory and practice of denying quality education to African-Americans, as well as to others, and implementing various managerial educational policy experiments have placed the nation increasingly at risk.

Hegemony/Counter-Hegemony: The Critical Practice of African-American Studies

Since Bloom misunderstands the origin and nature of America's current educational dilemma and ultimately incriminates African-Americans, it is not surprising that the more assertive African-American university students, and their demand for African-American Studies in the late 1960s threaten his elitist sensibilities. Bloom champions the Eurocentric perspective and Western cultural supremacy of the American academy. In contrast, the emerging field of African-American Studies, as well as the other "new studies" (Latino, Asian-American, Native American, and Women's Studies) it spawned in the late 1960s and early 1970s, seeks to expose and dismantle the ideological and political foundation of Eurocentrism and Western cultural hegemony.

In general terms, African-American Studies, as an organized academic enterprise, emerged at historically White universities and colleges during the late 1960s in the context of complex social change affecting virtually every sector of American society. The African-American Studies movement converged with mass protest movements against the brutalizing effects of social injustice, socioeconomic inequality, racial antagonism, and the Vietnam War. Assertive students contested the hegemony of traditional modes of thinking and social practice and set in motion an assault on the hypocrisy and immorality of many of the nation's social institutions. Institutions of higher learning became primary targets of criticism as students challenged them to deal with the burning questions and urgent social problems of the day. Students attacked the university's conventional aloofness from a concern about their everyday life experiences. And students increasingly demanded that the content and contours of their university education be "relevant" and point toward the solution of complex social difficulties.

More specifically, the eruption of African-American Studies can best be understood as a radical intellectual turn and institutional representation of the contemporary stage of the African-American struggle for collective survival, social development, and human rights. Following the beatings, arrests, bombings and assignations that characterized the White South's response to nonviolent, direction action protests by hundreds of thousands of liberal civil rights activitists from the late 1950s to the mid-1960s, not even the most naive utopian could believe unequivocally that the American social order would soon terminate the cultural domination, racial oppression, and economic subordination of African-Americans.

In the face of southern White terrorism, the strategic limitations of the civil rights movement became apparent to the large mass of urban African-Americans in the north. A more assertive group of leaders, including Malcolm X, Congressman Adam Clayton Powell, and Stokely Carmichael, urged African-Americans across the nation to unite on the basis of Black nationalism, take responsibility for their own advancement, and expand their struggle beyond the confines of civil rights to the broader global contest for human rights: human dignity, social development, economic self-sufficiency, and political self-determination (Breitman, 1965; Stone, 1968).

Reacting to historic frustration with subordination and disenfranchisement, masses of African-Americans punctuated their quest for social and political self-determination through violent insurrections in Harlem, Watts, Detroit, Cleveland, Newark and other northern cities throughout America. Their powerful and defiant protests shook the nation and, in the summer of 1966, ushered in a new era, signaled by the discourse of "Black Power" (see Forman, 1972; Stone, 1968).

As with any political slogan, interpretations of Black Power differed. Although traditional civil rights leaders criticized the term, other African-American spokespersons put forward a variety of meanings: group solidarity, cultural pride, political power, economic power, defensive violence, anti-integrationism, community control, and human rights. In 1967, then Student Non-Violent Coordinating Committee leader Stokely Carmichael and Roosevelt University political scientist Charles V. Hamilton sought to define and clarify this new social vision:

> [Black Power] is a call for black people in this country to unite, to recognize their heritage, to build a sense of community. It is a call for black people to begin to define their own goals to lead their own organizations and to support those organizations. It is a call to reject the racist institutions and values of this society. (1967, p. 44)

This definition of Black Power sets forth the vivid necessity for African-Americans to center political outlook and social practice on their own particular interests. The concentrated focus on Black Power—its pointed emphasis on the immediate and collective concerns of African-Americans—characterized the ideological milieu within which African-American Studies emerged.

The establishment of African-American Studies was insurrectionary and emanicpatory in at least two ways. First, as case studies of the events at San Francisco State University (Chrisman, 1969; McEvoy and Miller, 1969), Merritt College (Walton, 1969), and Cornell University (Edwards, 1970 and 1980) disclose, disruption. African-

American Studies erupted in the context of university protests and disruption. African-American students and their supporters sought to challenge and transform the policies and practices of institutional racism. Students clearly were aware of how the conventional politics of education largely denied higher learning to African-Americans in the past. Thus, African-American Studies and its necessarily disquieting beginning represented the enactment of the dialectics of domination and emancipation, tradition and change.

Second, African-American Studies represented a bold insurrectionary and emancipatory movement that undertook to unmask and contest the power/knowledge configuration of Eurocentrism and Western cultural authority characteristic of the American academy. In addition to challenging the ideological assumptions of the Eurocentric paradigm, the new field of intellectual inquiry attempted to resist the rigid barriers between traditional academic disciplines by emphasizing an interdisciplinary and multidisciplinary approach to teaching and learning.

The traditional Eurocentric view within the American academy, which Bloom guards, assumes that the Western structure of knowledge is true, objective, and politically-neutral, applicable equally to all people and circumstances. Yet, this organization of knowledge resulted in a representation of civilization which privileges Western culture and thought, but marginalizes all Others. From the standpoint of the Eurocentric paradigm, European views and values are and should be the human norm.

Because they are different from the West, other peoples and their cultural expressions are defined negatively as evil, irrational, valueless, ugly, savage, aberrant, amoral, undeveloped, primitive and inferior. Furthermore, the difference takes on an enormous importance in the context of Western cultural domination: by stressing the difference, the West seeks to intensify or affect the disenfranchisement, the isolation by which the Other is situated outside society or even outside humanity. Within the modalities of domination and exploitation established and rationalized by the Western structure of knowledge—for example, lower classes, women, undesirable nationalities, the aged, the young, the insane, the physically handicapped, and criminals—the African and African-descended Others are marked as the absolutely different and negative. The negative marking of Africans and American-descended Americans as a class of sub-humanity is deeply rooted in Western, and particularly North American, culture and thought (Fanon, 1964; Gerald, 1972; Jordan, 1968; Said, 1983; West, 1988).

If Western cultural hegemony has been institutionalized as the dominant discourse within the American academy, permeating the human sciences, African-American Studies theorists and practitioners have produced an oppositional knowledge, seeking to contest and transform the received ideas, entrenched institutions, questionable values of that tradition. African-American Studies critics charge that the prevailing Eurocentric perspective is narrow, ethnocentric, and culture-bound. They have exposed its particularistic, fragmented, and ideological character by revealing how the dominant discourse of the West wittingly or otherwise played down, distorted or omitted the contributions of African and African-descended peoples to world development. In the process, African-American Studies laid the foundation for the growing awareness that the Western structure of knowledge excludes far more than it includes. Thus, the emerging field of study unmasked the power/knowledge nexus of Western cultural despotism and its assertion of universality and truth. Focusing on the global African experience, which the White academy had largely omitted or distorted, represented a bold stroke designed by African-American Studies critics to break the cultural tyranny of the Eurocentric paradigm and nullify the interpretive authority of conventional White scholars (Alkalimat & Associates, 1986; Asante, 1987, 1988; Butler, 1981; Cruse, 1968; Jackson, 1970; Karenga, 1982).

For African-American Studies, dislodging and dismantling the power/knowledge configuration of Eurocentrism requires the critical analysis of the complex structures of exclusion and repression that dominate the life and culture of African-descended people. Western education developed alongside Western civilization and, understandably, to serve the interests of the West. The global problem emerged, however, when the peoples of Western Europe, a minority of the world's population groups, sought to enthrone and enshrine themselves and their culture by subverting and neutralizing Others (Robinson and Gallagher, 1961; Van Laue, 1987). Although forced into cultural chaos, invisibility, and

silence as a result of Western cultural imperialism, the formerly enslaved, colonized, and conquered Others rapidly are emerging to take their rightful place on the global stage. They too desire to leave their footprints on the sands of time. African-American Studies, as an intellectual expression of African descended people's struggle for cultural ascendancy, endeavors to play its role in the developing cultural renaissance among the world's historically dispossessed populations. One can almost hear the echo of the late Frantz Fanon's distant and defiant summons:

> come, then, comrades; it would be as well to decide at once to change our ways. We must shake off the heavy darkness in which we were plunged, and leave it behind. The new day which is already at hand must find us firm, prudent and resolute . . . Let us waste no time in sterile litanies and nauseating mimicry. Leave this Europe where they are never done talking of Man, yet murder men everywhere they find them, at the corner of every one of their own streets, in all the corners of the globe. For centuries they have stifled almost the whole of humanity in the name of a so-called spiritual experience. Look at them today swaying between atomic and spiritual disintegration. . . . Let us decide not to imitate Europe; let us combine our muscles and our brains in a new direction. Let us try to create the whole man, whom Europe has been incapable of bringing to triumphant birth. (1966, pp. 252-253)

Within the relatively new field of African-American Studies, the Afrocentric critical perspective is an important intellectual strategy. It seeks the radical critique of the dominant Eurocentric ideology and the undoing of Western cultural hegemony, a challenge Bloom seeks to subvert. While maintaining that the Eurocentric tradition is valid within its own context, Afrocentric criticism soundly rejects that tradition's universalist and absolutist self-representation. Nor does this new critical perspective arrogantly suggest that it is the only interpretation of the world. Afrocentric critical practice is an interpretation of the world from a particular philosophical and ideological standpoint. The Afrocentric perspective finds its essential grounding in the history, culture, and thought of African and African-descended people. Hence, there is an assumption that there exist a distinct and valid African-centered world view. For example, Temple University professor and chairman of the Department of African-American Studies, Molefi K. Asante, the foremost theorist of the Afrocentric interpretive critique, states that one of its crucial elements is the notion of harmony or complementarily. Here the idea is that entities can be different and yet complement each other. As Asante remarks:

> In the Afrocentric conception of literature and orature, the critical method would be employed to determine to what degree the writer or speaker contributed to the unity of the symbols, the elimination of chaos, the making of peace among disparate views, and the creation of an opportunity for harmony and hence balance. . . Harmony, in the sense that I am

speaklng of it, is an equilibrium among the various factors impinging upon communication (1987, pp. 177-178).

Asante points out that the Afrocentric concept of harmony is quite distinct from the conception of oppositional dichotomies so fundamental to the Eurocentric consciousness. He notes that dichotomization pervades the Eurocentric structure of knowledge in which people and things are generally grouped on the basis of their opposition to each other—for example, European/African, male/female, mind/body, reason/emotion, science/nature. Generally, the opposing categories, are hierarchically related within the Eurocentric dualist conception of the world. That is, one of the dichotomous elements is superior to and therefore should dominate, silence, or negate the other: European over African, male over female, mind over body, reason over emotion. This central dimension of the Eurocentric outlook is the driving force behind Western cultural aggression, resulting in the complex structures of domination and exploitation based on class, race, and sex.

The displacement of Western cultural hegemony also demands the development of an emancipatory theory and practice that cultivates and empowers a conception of public life that respects the multicultural and multiracial character of America's emerging postindustrial-managerial society. Critical intellectuals from within historically dispossessed and disenfranchised cultural and racial groups must emerge so that they can be looked to directly for new knowledge and its application to this increasingly complex and technologically advanced age. This is a necessity so that with the passing of the industrial-capitalist era, there will not come an even more destructive society of intellectual and managerial imperialism, a society which is already in process.

This forward-looking project will require, among other things, the stimulation of strategic solidarity among the progressive forces within the heterogeneous "new studies." However, the idea of developing a field of compatibility among these and other heterogeneous groups is not necessarily a call for a multicultural and multiracial united front in which differences are suppressed for the sake of a totalized sameness. Neither does it advocate some larger multicultural institutional arrangement within the academy which merges the "new studies." These are Eurocentric ideals. Thus, unanimity and collective responsibility among these culturally diverse groups may not always be the objective, but the recognition and appreciation of differences, in the context of contesting the power/knowledge configuration of Western cultural domination.

Conclusion

Significantly, the United States, and indeed other Western nations, is presently undergoing a phase of neo-conservatism in regard to such matters as the role of government and social, economic, and educational policy. Allan Bloom and his neo-conservative ideas have achieved recent popularity because they are ideologically compatible with perspectives characterizing the ascendancy of Reaganism—anxiety about the decline of American power, the breakdown of the family, the decay of moral development, and nostalgia about a past golden age of Western cultural authority. This has been clearly indicated, for example, by former Secretary of Education William Bennett's embrace of Bloom's text in public discourse about American higher education. Thus, the convergence of power, knowledge, and ideology contributes enormously to Bloom's widespread influence. Moreover, in America's increasingly complex and knowledge-dependent society, political decision-makers, journalists, and the knowledgeable sectors of the lay public are more and more attentive to intellectuals who produce novel ideas.

Correctly noting America's current educational crisis, Bloom disingenuously argues that African-Americans are substantially responsible for it and for the current racial antagonism in institutions of higher learning. However, the source of the educational crisis is located in America's historic conspiracy to deny quality education to African-Americans and the educational managerial elite's current policy experiments.

A champion of the Eurocentric perspective and of Western cultural supremacy, Bloom is clearly threatened by the "new studies," particularly African-American Studies, that emerged in the late 1960s. Going beyond Bloom's lament means addressing the significant role of African-American Studies in unmasking and dislodging the power/knowledge nexus of Eurocentrism and Western cultural domination in the American academy. Achieving this goal demands that African-American Studies and other "new studies" forge an emancipatory theory and practice that encourages and empowers a view of civic life that privileges the multicultural and multiracial nature of America's evolving postindustrial-managerial society.

References

Alkalimat, Abdul and Associates. *Introduction to Afro-American Studies: A Peoples College Primer.* Twenty-First Century Books & Publications. (1986).

Asante, Molefi Kete. *The Afrocentric Idea.* Temple University Press. (1987).

Asante, Molefi Kete. *Afrocentricity.* Africa World Press, Inc. (1988).

Baron, Harold M. *The Demand for Black Labor: Historical Notes on the Political Economy of Racism.* New England Free Press. (1972).

Bercovitch, Sacvan. *The Puritan Origins of the American Self.* Yale University Press. (1975).

Blackburn, Robin. *The Overthrow of Colonial Slavery 1776-1848.* Verso. (1988).

Bloom, Allan. *The Closing of the American Mind: How Higher Education Has Failed Democracy and Impoverished the Souls of Today's Students.* Simon and Schuster. (1987).

Breitman, George, ed. *Malcolm X Speaks: Selected Speeches and Statements.* Grove Press. (1965).

Butler, Johnnella E. *Black Studies: Pedagogy and Revolution–A Study of Afro-American Studies and the Liberal Arts Tradition Through the Discipline of Afro-American Literature.* University Press of America, Inc. (1981).

Carmichael, Stokely and Charles V. Hamilton. *Black Power: The Politics of Liberation in America.* Random House. (1967).

Chrisman, Robert. "Observations on Race and Class at San Francisco State," in James McEvoy and Abraham Miller, eds., *Black Power and Student Rebellion: Conflict on the American Campus.* Wadsworth Publishing Company, Inc., (1969).

Clark, Kenneth B. *Dark Ghetto: Dilemmas of Social Power.* Harper & Row, Publishers. (1965).

Cruse, Harold. "The Integrationist Ethic as a Basis for Scholarly Endeavors," Armstead L. Robinson, Craig C. Foster, and Donald H. Ogilvie, eds., *Black Studies in the University: A Symposium.* Yale University Press. (1969).

Davis, David Brion. *The Problem of Slavery in Western Culture.* Cornell University Press. (1966).

Davis, David Brion. *Slavery and Human Progress.* Oxford University Press. (1964).

DuBois, W.E. Burghardt. *The Suppression of the African Slave-Trade to the United States of America 1638-1870,* Russell & Russell, Inc. (1965).

Edwards, Harry. *Black Students.* Free Press. (1970).

Edwards, Harry. *The Struggle That Must Be: An Autobiography.* Macmillan Publishing Company, Inc. (1980).

Fanon, Frantz. *The Wretched of the Earth.* Grove Press. (1964).

Fitch, Nancy E. "The Reconstruction of the Black Mind: African American Improvisations Upon Historical Texts and the Historical Process in the United States," paper presented at the International Convention of American Studies Association and the Canadian Association for American Studies. (1987).

Forman, James. *The Making of Black Revolutionaries.* The Macmillan Company. (1972).

Floyd W. Hayes, III is in the Department of Afro-American Studies at San Diego State University.

The Journal of Ethnic Studies, Western Washington University. Reprinted by permission.

Unlike Eurocentric advocates, Jack Weatherford acknowledges the positive influence of Native Americans on the European Enlightenment and on U.S. political thought. Native Americans, he says, living without social class, private property, or a system of government separate from kinship systems, exhibited an individualism, equality and freedom which was novel to Europeans who explored and settled North American.

Liberty, Anarchism, and The Noble Savage

Jack Weatherford

On a hot Friday afternoon in the last week of August, cars, pickup trucks, camping vans, and school buses slowly pull into a park on the edge of Fargo, North Dakota. Young people greet their friends excitedly, and old Ojibwa women solemnly shake hands with one another with greetings of "Bozhoo, Bozhoo" and look over one another's grandchildren. Dakota men greet one another with the friendly "Hau, Kota" before exchanging stories and jokes. Lakota families carve out small pieces of territory around their vehicles, making the park into a series of encampments, each with its own blanket on the ground, aluminum folding chairs, and grill.

As for an unknown number of generations in the past, the Indians of the Great Plains gather once again for an annual powwow. For much of the afternoon, everyone seems to be helping everyone else get dressed. A father straps a bustle of brightly colored feathers on his adolescent son, and then he holds up a mirror for the boy to adjust the roach of hair cascading down his scalp. Young girls fasten each other's deerskin dresses and help untangle the fringes of their shawls from the hundreds of jingle bells on their dresses. A group of men gather near the cars out of sight of spectators to paint one another's faces with irregular and markedly asymmetrical designs of black and

red, and they braid one another's hair. Women sew their torn moccasins, and girls string pendants of embroidered beads into their hair. A young girl helps her father fluff up the feathers in his headdress, and mothers and grandmothers put headbands and small bracelets on babies they carry in their arms.

In the central arena, a young man sets up a microphone system and checks the lighting. An announcer takes up the microphone and asks if a drum group has arrived. When no one answers, he calls out the names of various drum groups from White Earth, Pine Ridge, Red Wing, Lake Nipigon, and The Cities, but he gets no response. Twenty minutes later he repeats the same request, emphasizing that some of the people are now dressed and ready to dance, but there is no drum group ready to drum.

About dusk, an older man and his adolescent grandson appear from the edge of the arena with a large drum. They set it up and wait for several more men of various ages to join them in a circle around it. The oldest man puts his left hand over his ear, cocks his head to the side, and seemingly shuts his eyes before he cries out a long high wail that sounds almost like a woman's shriek, and immediately all of the men start pounding on the drum and singing in the same high voices.

Young children dance energetically on the sidelines, but no one moves into the arena. The announcer's voice booms over the microphone for some warriors to please come forward to carry the flag so that they can begin. He repeats the call seven times before the first two men emerge, dressed in feathers and beads. These men are in their sixties, veterans of World War II, and they march out carrying the flags of the United States and Canada. They must wait for the younger veterans of the Korean and Vietnam wars, who straggle forward singly, some dressed in denim pants and cowboy hats while others wear traditional feathers and boast large beer bellies protruding over the ample loincloths that cover their bathing trunks. These middle-aged men carry the North Dakota flag and several flags from neighboring states and Canadian provinces as well as a series of colorful Indian reservation flags. Among the cloth flags some men carry staffs lined with eagle feathers. All seated people rise, and the already quiet crowd becomes absolutely si-

lent for a few moments before the singing of the national anthems of Canada and the United States. The men dance slowly around the arena with the brightly colored flags and then sing a special song honoring the flags themselves.

Following the flag ceremony, the same warriors lead off the first dance of the powwow, with the eldest veterans dancing first, and slowly other people join them in the Intertribal Dance. Grandmothers shuffle with their grandchildren in their arms while teenage boys dance widely around them. Beaming young women dance while flourishing long and very colorful shawls in front of them, and studiously ignore the boys. Some people in street clothes join in the ceremony, and finally nearly a hundred people slowly move clockwise around the arena, all moving at the same speed but dancing the particular steps appropriate to their gender and dress. Most subsequent dances that night permit only one of the five categories of dancers into the arena: Men's Traditional Dance, Shawl Dance, Men's Fancy Dance, Women's Traditional Dance, and Jingle-Dress Dance. Each category wears the correct clothing and follows an exact choreography. The announcer and a panel of judges award occasional prizes as high as $100 to different dancers. Between rounds of competition, someone will make the call for another Intertribal Dance in which participants of all categories as well as the audience dance together.

English predominates among the people representing a dozen different tribes, but among the smaller groups and families, people speak one or more of the Indian languages and some words of a French creole

used in many of the languages of the area. All singing and praying is done in Dakota, the language of the powwow hosts.

Between one set of dances, a family comes to the fore to distribute presents in honor of their teenage daughter, who has taken her grandmother's Indian name. The young girl presents gifts of blankets, embroidered pieces of Indian bead jewelry, cartons of cigarettes, and money to people who have helped her mature to this stage in life. She then leads off a dance in their honor.

Between dances, someone occasionally rises to honor another person, commemorate an event, announce an upcoming powwow, or welcome a group that has traveled particularly far to participate in that night's festivities. Various announcers remind the assembled people that part of the money collected for admission to the powwow will be donated to a program combating alcohol and drug addiction among Indian people, and they denounce the evils that these two substances have brought to them.

On the side, a food concessionaire sells fry bread, Indian tacos, hamburgers, and bratwurst, as well as a selection of cold soft drinks and hot coffee. Vendors hawk Indian ornaments and items of dance wear made from diverse synthetic and natural materials. A man offers a selection of buttons and bumper stickers with slogans such as "Red Power," "Proud to be an Indian," "I powwowed in Fargo," "Squaw on Board," and "I'd rather be dancing."

The dancing and eating continue late into the night, when some people leave to go home or to a motel and others drift off to their vans and campers. The activities resume the next day and continue until the afternoon, when some people pack up and start the long drive home. Others settle in for another night's rest before starting their own trek.

Today the powwow blends traits of a dozen different Indian groups together with items borrowed from white culture, just as some of the Indians have blond hair and green eyes. Some have "typical" Indian names while others have Norwegian, Irish, or French names. Despite all of the blending, however, some very basic Indian values dominate.

To an outsider, such powwows often appear chaotic. Even though posted signs promise that the dances will begin at four o'clock, there is still no dancing at five-thirty. Drummers scheduled to play never arrive, and some groups drum without being on the program. Impromptu family ceremonies intertwine with the official scheduled events, and the microphone passes among a score of announcers during the evening. No one is in control.

This seems to be typical of Indian community events: no one is in control. No master of ceremonies tell everyone what to do, and no one orders the dancers to appear. The announcer acts as herald or possibly as facilitator of ceremonies, but no chief rises to demand anything of anyone. The event flows in an orderly fashion like hundreds of powwows before it, but leaders can only lead by example, by pleas, or by exhortations. Everyone shows great respect for the elders and for warriors, who are repeatedly singled out for recognition, but at the same time children receive great respect for dancing and even the audience re-

ceives praise for watching. The powwow grows in an organic fashion as dancers slowly become activated by the drums and the singing. The event unfolds as a collective activity of all participant, not as one mandated and controlled from the top. Each participant responds to the collective mentality and mood of the whole group but not to a single, directing voice.

This Indian penchant for respectful individualism and equality seems as strong today in Fargo, North Dakota, as when the first explorers wrote about it five centuries ago. Much to the dismay of contemporary bureaucrats and to the shock of the Old World observers, Indian societies operated without strong positions of leadership and coercive political institutions.

Freedom does not have a long pedigree in the Old World. When it appears in the ancient literature of the Mediterranean, freedom usually refers to the freedom of a tribe, a nation, or a city from the domination of another such group, as in the freedom of the Jews from Egyptian bondage or the freedom of the Greek cities from Persian rule. In this sense the word echoes our contemporary notion of national sovereignty, but it resembles only slightly our concept of freedom as personal liberty. Occasionally, this sense of the word appeared in connection with a Roman or Greek slave who was freed, but this was a very specialized use that meant a person became human and was no longer merely the property of someone else.

After the people of the Old World learned to accept the strange animals reported from America and had at least a slight acquain-

tance with the new plants, they began to examine more closely the people and their culture. By this time the Spanish had virtually decapitated the native societies that they had encountered, and they had then grafted the Spanish monarchy, the Spanish language, and Spanish Catholicism to the native roots of American culture. In contrast, the more marginal areas of America that fell into the hands of the French and British still had flourishing native societies.

The most consistent theme in the descriptions penned about the New World was amazement at the Indians' personal liberty, in particular their freedom from rulers and from social classes based on ownership of property. For the first time the French and the British became aware of the possibility of living in social harmony and prosperity without the rule of a king.

As the first reports of this new place filtered into Europe, they provoked much philosophical and political writing. Sir Thomas More incorporated into his 1516 book *Utopia* those characteristics then being reported by the first travelers to America, especially in the much-discussed letters of Amerigo Vespucci. More made his utopia one of equality without money. The following year, More's brother-in-law John Ratsell set out in search of some such paradise in America. Although his trip failed, he continued to advocate the colonization of America in his writings, and his son did make the trip in 1536 (Brandon, p. 10).

More's work was translated into all the major European languages and has stayed in print until the present day. His thought carried influence throughout the European continent, and in the following century, other writers strengthened and developed the idea of freedom that he described and the ways that the Indians in America maintained it.

Writing a little later in the sixteenth century, the French essayist Michel de Montaigne presented a similar description of American Indian life based primarily on the early reports from Brazil. In his essay "On Cannibals," Montaigne wrote that they are "still governed by natural laws and very little corrupted by our own." He specifically cited their lack of magistrates, forced services, riches, poverty, and inheritance. As in More's utopia, Brazil emerged as the ideal place and Indians as having created the ideal society (Montaigne, pp. 109-10). Most of these early writings contained strongly satirical veins—the writers indicated that even so-called savages lived better than civilized Europeans—but the satire grew out of the unavoidable truth that the technologically simple Indians usually lived in more just, equitable, and egalitarian social conditions.

Not until a century after Montaigne did the first French ethnography on the North American Indians appear. Louis Armand de Lom d'Arce, Baron de Lahontan, wrote several short books on the Huron Indians of Canada based on his stay with them from 1683 to 1694. An adventurer far more than an anthropologist, Lahontan nevertheless managed to rise above the genre of adventure stories to give the French reader the worldview of the Hurons from inside the Indian mind. By the time of Lahontan's sojourn among the Hurons, they had already survived several dec-

ades of sporadic interactions with European explorers and traders, and they had been the subject of numerous commentaries by Jesuit missionaries. From these interaction the Hurons were able to compare their own way of life and the Europeans'. The Indians particularly decried the European obsession with money that compelled European women to sell their bodies to lusty men and compelled men to sell their lives to the armies of greedy men who used them to enslave yet more people. By contrast, the Hurons lived a life of liberty and equality. According to the Hurons, the Europeans lost their freedom in their incessant use of "thine" and "mine."

One of the Hurons explained to Lahontan, "We are born free and united brothers, each as much a great lord as the other, while you are all the slaves of one sole man. I am the master of my body, I dispose of myself, I do what I wish, I am the first and the last of my Nation . . . subject only to the great Spirit" (Brandon, p. 90). It is difficult to tell where the Huron philosopher speaks and where Lahontan may be promoting his own political philosophy, but still the book rested on a base of solid ethnographic fact: the Hurons lived without social classes, without a government separate from their kinship system, and without private property. To describe this political situation, Lahontan revived the Greek-derived work "anarchy," using it in the literal sense meaning "no ruler." Lahontan found an orderly society, but one lacking a formal government that compelled such order.

After the appearance of Lahontan's New Voyages to North America in 1703 in The Hague and his

Curious Dialogues soon there-after, Lahontan became an international celebrity feted in all the liberal circles. The playwright Delisle de la Drevetière adapted these ideas to the stage in a play about an American Indian's visit to Paris. Performed in Paris in 1721 as Arlequin Sauvage, the play ends with a young Parisian woman named Violette falling in love with the Indian and fleeing with him to live in the liberty of America beyond law and money.

As usually happens in the theatrical world, this success initiated dozens of imitations, and there soon followed a spate of plays, farces, burlesques, and operas on the wonderful life of liberty among the Indians of America. Impresarios brought over Indians in droves to tour the European capitals and entertain at parties with their tales of liberty and freedom in the American paradise. Plays such as Indes Galantes and Le Nouveau Monde followed in the 1730s. The original play Arlequin Sauvage had a major impact on a young man named Jean Jacques Rousseau, who set about in 1742 to write an operetta on the discovery of the New World featuring Christopher Columbus's arrival with a sword while singing to the Indians the refrain "Lose your liberty!" (Brandon, p. 104). This contrast between the liberty of the Indians and the virtual enslavement of the Europeans became a lifelong concern for Rousseau and eventually led to publication of his best-known work, Discourse on the Origins of Inequality, in 1754.

Despite the excessive literary commercialization of the notion of American liberty, a number of good ethnographic studies of the Indians also appeared during this period. The social descriptions of Lahontan found subsequent corroboration in the more ethnographic but less dramatic writings of the Jesuit Father Joseph Francois Lafitau, who published in 1724 *Customs of the American Savages Compared with Those of Earliest Times*, describing the Mohawks. The virtues of Indian society so impressed Lafitau that he saw in it a reflection of ancient Greek society. He intimated that the Indians actually might be descendants of refugees from the Trojan wars who managed to transfer their Greek ideals to America.

During this era the thinkers of Europe forged the ideas that became known as the European Enlightenment, and much of its light came from the torch of Indian liberty that still burned brightly in the brief interregnum between their first contact with the Europeans and their decimation by the Europeans. The Indian, particularly the Huron, became the "noble savage," the man of liberty living in the "natural state." While a few Europeans chose the path of Violette and left the corrupt world of Europe for America, others began working on ideas and plans to change Europe by incorporating some of the ideas of liberty into their own world. Almost all of the plans involved revolutionary changes to overthrow the monarchy, the aristocracy, or the church, and in some cases even to abolish money and private property.

The greatest political radical to follow the example of the Indians was probably Thomas Paine (1737-1809), the English Quaker and former craftsman who arrived in Philadelphia to visit Benjamin Franklin just in time for Christmas of 1774.

Because the Quakerism of his family restricted his study of Latin, the language of learning, Paine was not an intellectual trained in philosophy. He left school at age thirteen to become an apprentice staymaker. He earned his education in life, something that many people have attempted and few have accomplished. His experiences made him a radical proponent of democracy.

After arriving in America he developed a sharp interest in the Indians, who seemed to be living in the natural state so alien to the urban and supposedly civilized life he encountered around himself. When the American Revolution started, Paine served as secretary to the commissioners sent to negotiate with the Iroquois at the town of Easton near Philadelphia on the Delaware River in January 1777 (Johansen, p. 116). Through this and subsequent encounters with the Indians, Paine sought to learn their language, and throughout the remainder of his political and writing career he used the Indians as models of how society might be organized.

In his writings, Paine castigated Britain for her abusive treatment of the Indians, and he became the first American to call for the abolition of slavery. He refined his knowledge and opinions in order to disseminate them to the world in eloquent works bearing such simple titles as Common Sense, which he issued in January 1776 as the first call for American independence. Subsequently he became the first to propose the name "United States of America" for the emerging nation. After the revolutionary victory in America, he returned to Europe in 1787 to carry the Indian spark of liberty. The French made him an honorary French citizen, and they

offered him a seat in the National Assembly in order to help draft a just constitution for their nation. He fought hard for the French Revolution, but despite his belief in revolutionary democracy, he abhorred terrorism, including the French reign of terror. Despite these excesses of the French, Paine laid out his logical defense of revolution in The Rights of Man in 1792, and then turned his attention to the role of religion by writing the book that gave its name to the whole Enlightenment, *The Age of Reason* (1794-95).

After this life of activism and writing, Paine wrote *Agrarian Justice* (1797), in which he asked a question that still haunts our own time: can civilized society ever cure the poverty it has created? He was not entirely optimistic that it could. He returned once again to the Iroquois, among whom he had learned democracy, when he wrote, "The fact is, that the condition of millions, in every country in Europe, is far worse than if they had been born before civilization began, or had been born among the Indians of North-America at the present day" (Paine, p. 338). Unfortunately, however, Paine concluded that "it is always possible to go from the natural to the civilized state, but it is never possible to go from the civilized to the natural state" (Paine, p. 337).

When the French so ardently embraced Napoleon as emperor, Paine felt that they had betrayed everything he had been preaching, and he left France in disgust in 1802 to return to America, which still struggled with the implementation of liberty. He found the citizens of America now more complacent. Following their revolution they seemed intent on settling down, making money, and enjoying the pursuit of happiness. They showed no tolerant mood for an aging radical who held up savage Indians to them as paragons of the proper human values.

By the time Paine died, the Indians had been permanently enshrined in European thought as exemplars of liberty. In the next generation, Alexis de Tocqueville, writing in the first volume of Democracy in America, repeatedly used phrases such as "equal and free." He said that the ancient European republics never showed more love of independence than did the Indians of North America. He compared the social system and the values of the Indians to those of the ancient European tribes prior to becoming "civilized" and domesticated (Tocqueville, Vol. I, p. 357).

Even in the twentieth century, French anthropologists continued the analysis of liberty and equality among surviving American Indian groups, particularly those in the jungles of South America. Describing it as "society against the state," Pierre Clastres analyzed political institutions in Indian America to determine anew whether society could function without political oppression and coercion. He found that even in societies with chiefs, "the chief's word carries no force of law." He quoted the great cacique, or chief, Alaykin of the Argentine Chaco as saying that "if I were to use orders or force with my comrades, they could turn their backs on me at once." He continued, "I prefer to be loved and not feared by them." Clastres summed up the office of chief by observing that "the chief who tries to act the chief is abandoned" (Clastres, pp. 176, 131).

From the moment the notion of democracy and the noble savage appeared in Europe, some skeptical thinkers rejected it entirely. Thomas Hobbes launched one of the first attacks against this primitivism. Although he had never been to America, he claimed in his Leviathan (1651) that the savage people in many places of America led a life that was "solitary, poor, nasty, brutish, and short." He than went on to attack the ideas of liberty. For Hobbes the natural state of man was the horror of "war of all against all," and only through total subjugation of everyone to a ruler could the individual be protected from the perfidy and savagery of others.

In the next century a philosopher as eminent as Voltaire joined Hobbes in belittling the American Indians, but he used Indian characters in several of his works. Even the German philosopher Immanuel Kant attacked the idea of the noble American savage. In his 1772 lectures on philosophical anthropology at the University of Konigsberg, Kant proclaimed that the American Indians "are incapable of civilization." He described them as having "no motive force, for they are without affection and passion. They are not drawn to one another by love, and are thus unfruitful. They hardly speak at all, never caress one another, care about nothing, and are lazy." In a note in his lecture he foreshadowed two long centuries of racist thought in Germany when he wrote that the Indians "are incapable of governing themselves" and are "destined for extermination" (Commager, p. 89).

As the eighteenth century closed in the bloodshed of the French Revolution, Europeans momentarily tired of constant political debate

and the question of the natural social or political state of man. They turned away from the American Indian and let their fantasies flow to the south Pacific, where they envisioned a paradise of sensuality. Unlike the Indians who had suffered no rulers, many of the island people of Polynesia had rulers, and yet they seemed to be happy and to have found sexual, if not political, liberation. The notion of the noble savage took a new turn away from politics and into a frivolous image that still persists in some writings today.

Egalitarian democracy and liberty as we know them today owe little to Europe. They are not Greco-Roman derivatives somehow revived by the French in the eighteenth century. They entered modern western though as American Indian notions translated into European language and culture.

In language, custom, religion, and written law, the Spaniards descended directly from ancient Rome, yet they brought nothing resembling a democratic tradition with them to America. The French and Dutch who settled parts of North America also settled many other parts of the world that did not become democratic. Democracy did not spring up on French-speaking Haiti any more than in South Africa, where the British and Dutch settled about the same time that they settled in North America.

Even the Netherlands and Britain, the two showcases for European democracy, had difficulty grafting democracy onto monarchical and aristocratic systems soaked in the strong traditions of class privilege. During the reign of George III of Great Britain, while the United States was fighting for its independence, only one person in twenty could vote in England. In all of Scotland three thousand men could vote, and in Ireland no Catholic could hold office or vote (Commager, pp. 146-48). In their centuries of struggle to suppress the Irish, the British possibly encumbered their own democratic development.

American anglophiles occasionally point to the signing of the Magna Carta by King John on the battlefield of Runnymede in 1215 as the start of civil liberties and democracy in the English-speaking world. This document, however, merely moved slightly away from monarchy and toward oligarchy by increasing the power of the aristocracy. It continued the traditional European vacillation between government by a single strong ruler and by an oligarchic class. An oligarchy is not an incipient democracy, and a step away from monarchy does not necessarily mean a step toward democracy. In the same tradition, the election of the pope by a college of cardinals did not make the Vatican into a democratic institution, nor did the Holy Roman Empire become a democracy merely because a congress of aristocrats elected the emperor.

When the Dutch built colonies in America, power in their homeland rested securely in the hands of the aristocracy and the burghers, who composed only a quarter of the population. A city such as Amsterdam fell under the rule of a council of thirty-six men, none of whom was elected; instead each council member inherited his office and held it until death (Commager, p. 153).

Henry Steele Commager wrote that during the Enlightenment "Europe was ruled by the wellborn, the rich, the privileged, by those who held their places by divine favor, inheritance, prescription, or purchase" (Commager, p. 154). The philosophers and thinkers of the Enlightenment became quite complacent and self-congratulatory because the "enlightened despots" such as Catherine of Russia and Frederick of Prussia read widely and showed literary inclinations. Too many philosophers became court pets and because of that believed that Europe was moving toward enlightened democracy. As Commager explained it, Europe only imagined the Enlightenment, but America enacted it. This Enlightenment grew as much from its roots in Indian culture as from any other source.

When Americans try to trace their democratic heritage back through the writings of French and English political thinkers of the Enlightenment, they often forget that these people's thoughts were heavily shaped by the democratic traditions and the state of nature of the American Indians. The concept of the "noble savage" derived largely from writings about the American Indians, and even though the picture grew romanticized and distorted, the writers were only romanticizing and distorting something that really did exist. The Indians did live in a fairly democratic condition, they were egalitarian, and they did live in greater harmony with nature.

The modern notions of democracy based on egalitarian principles and federated government of overlapping powers arose from the unique blend of European and Indian political ideas and institutions along the Atlantic coast between 1607 and 1776. Modern democracy as we know it today is as much the legacy of the American Indians, particularly the Iroquois and the Algonquians, as it is of the British settlers, of French political theory, or of all the failed efforts of the Greeks and Romans.

The American Revolution did not stop with the thirteen Atlantic colonies; it soon spread around the world. As Thomas Paine wrote in The Rights of Man, "from a small spark, kindled in America, a flame has arisen, not to be extinguished." He went on to say that the flame "winds its progress from nation to nation, and conquers by silent operation" (Paine, p. 223).

Although today the notion of the noble savage usually reaps only scorn and historical footnotes as a quaint idea of a less-informed era, the idea had ramifications of great width and magnitude. The noble savage represented a new ideal of human political relations that mutated into the hundreds of political theories that have swept the world in the past five hundred years. The discovery of new forms of political life in America freed the imaginations of Old World thinkers to envision utopias, socialism, communism, anarchism, and dozens of other social forms. Scarcely any political theory or movement of the last three centuries has not shown the impact of this great political awakening that the Indians provoked among the Europeans.

The descriptions of the Baron de Lahontan and other New World travelers of the so-called anarchy among the American Indians contributed to several different brands of anarchistic theory in the nineteenth century. Today, anarchism is often equated with terrorism and nihilism, which denies any values, but early anarchism lacked both of these qualities. Peirrre Joseph Proudhon (1809-1865), the father of modern anarchistic theory, stressed the notion of "mutualism" in a society based on cooperation without the use of coercion from any quarter. This was to be brought about peacefully through workers helping one another in labor associations.

From these simple ideas about the noble savage, there followed a wild array of theories as varied and exotic as the different types of birds in the Amazon. Michael Bakunin developed anarchist collectivism. Peter Kropotkin became associated with the ideas of anarchist communism that achieved popularity in Spain, while in France anarcho-syndicalism helped inspire the work of Georges Sorel. Pacifist anarchism developed around the ideas of the Russian writer Leo Tolstoy and the Dutch political philosopher Domela Nieuwenhuis.

In one of its mildest expressions, these ideas of pacific anarchism showed up in America in the writings of Henry David Thoreau (1817-1862). Worshiping the New England countryside by then denuded of its aboriginal Indian inhabitants, Thoreau withdrew from society in order to practice his individualistic anarchism. In 1849 these ideas of the individual's right to refuse cooperation with the state received its highest expression in his essay "Civil Disobedience." In the twentieth century the ideas of Thoreau came to play almost as important a role in world politics as did the many revolutionary theories that developed from more activist brands of anarchism. In 1907 Thoreau's essay helped Gandhi to select the appropriate means of struggle for Indian independence from Britain. Rather than launch a war of liberation, he launched a peaceful movement of civil disobedience. This movement eventually liberated Pakistan and India, and in so doing, sealed the fate of colonialism everywhere in the world. The peaceful movements of Gandhi did more to bring independence than did all the twentieth-century wars of independence.

Thoreau and Gandhi together inspired many different versions of their struggle, one of the most notable being that of the civil rights movement in the United States. Opting for the same peaceful struggle and for civil disobedience, the movement under Martin Luther King, Jr., ended virtually all legal forms of racism in the United States.

Like the American plants that spread all over the world and changed forever the economic, social and demographic patterns of the world, the Indian love of liberty, freedom, and individuality have also spread. Even though the Indians never had a monopoly on these values, they did achieve the highest cultural development of them. Thus, today in the ordered anarchy of a powwow in North Dakota these same values are articulated even better and more eloquently than in the writings of Paine, Rousseau, Thoreau, and Gandhi.

Those first Americans had developed and constructed their own civilization including temples, customs, and technical life necessities, such as daily baths. The constructive Native American lifestyles were destroyed, distorted, and ignored by European immigrants.

Those First Americans

Lewis Lord with Sarah Burke

Most vacationers driving along Interstate 55-70 in Illinois speed right by ancient Cahokia and its 15-acre ceremonial mound. Only the curious pull off to learn how a 12th-century feather-crowned ruler known as the Great Sun kneeled atop the earthen temple in the morning and howled when the real sun came up.

At its peak this city across the Mississippi from present-day St. Louis boasted probably as many residents as London at that time, and a trading network that stretched from the Gulf of Mexico to the Great Lakes. But basic history textbooks in classrooms today barely take notice. Cahokia's problem is that American history, in the minds of many, started just 500 years ago, with Columbus's arrival in the New World in 1492. By then, Cahokia had already thrived and vanished.

Like many modern metropolises, Cahokia could not handle growth. Cornfields that fed 20,000 to 30,000 urbanites gradually lost their fertility, and forests were stripped. Warfare, disease and social unrest may have added to the decline. When French settlers arrived at Cahokia in the mid-1700s, they found only grown-over mounds.

Yet the New World was anything but empty in Columbus's day. The first Americans were Asians, who came over 12,000 years ago, probably crossing a glacial land bridge between Siberia and Alaska. By 1492, the Western Hemisphere may have contained 90 million people. Most lived south of the Rio Grande, but about ten million inhabited what is now the United States and Canada. Ancient societies had been rising and falling here for centuries.

Daily Bath

Newcomers from Europe, though accustomed to people being burned at the stake or beheaded, were shocked at what went on in America. Columbus claimed he had to take hundreds of Carib Indians to Spain for their own good and that of their Arawak neighbors, whom they were eating. (He had a harder time explaining why he also enslaved the gentle Arawaks.) While cannibalism and human sacrifice were rare among Indians north of Mexico, people in some tribes killed unwanted infants and took multiple wives.

Other customs seemed alien as well: most Indians took a daily bath, a practice the Europeans abhorred. America was not new, but it was different.

As whites moved across the country, the tribesmen they encountered asked a recurring question: "Why do you call us Indians?" The answer, of course, was that Columbus was mistaken. He called all the natives *los indios* thinking he was in the distant Indies, somewhere between Japan and India. The natives had no word for their race. They called themselves "people" or "real people," and gave other tribes names like "friend," "enemy" or "snake."

The diversity that Americans relish today existed long before Columbus arrived. Most of the hundreds of languages the Indians spoke were as different from one another as Farsi is from French. Some Indians loved war; others hated it. After every reluctant fight, Arizona's Pimas subjected their warriors to a 16-day cure for insanity.

Ancient caste systems endured. The Great Sun used his feet to push leftovers to his Natchez tribe subordinates. But three centuries before the U.S. Constitution was adopted, the Iroquois League had a Congress-like council, exercised the veto, protected freedom of speech—and ran a classless society.

Some tribes banned women from their councils. Others were ruled by female chiefs, like the "Lady of Coftachequi," who in 1540 greeted Hernando de Soto with pearls from the Savannah River. (He ungraciously kidnapped her.) Premarital sex was unthinkable among the Apache, but the Natchez tribe of Mississippi encouraged teenagers to have flings while they could. Once a Creek Indian of Alabama wed, an extramarital affair could cost a nose or an ear. Still, some tribes allowed a woman to end her marriage by putting her husband's belongings outside their door—a sign for him to live with his mother.

America's Stonehenge

Pioneers who found thousands of abandoned mounds in the Ohio and Mississippi valleys refused to believe they had been built by "naturally indolent" Indians. The Mound Builders, they speculated, were stray Vikings, Phoenicians or a lost tribe of Israel. Not until the 1890s did educated people agree that the mounds in fact had been built by the Indians' ancestors.

The genius of the Mound Builders has become even more evident in recent years. In northeastern Louisiana, for example, lies Poverty Point, a 3000-year-old collection of concentric semicircles of earth, the biggest extending for nearly three-quarters of a mile. Visitors can stand atop a mound just west of Poverty Point's rings. "At the time of the spring and fall equinoxes," writes Roger G. Kennedy in *Rediscovering America*, "one can still have a clear view of the sun rising over the central 37-acre plaza, a view like that found at similar conjunctions of earth and sun at Stonehenge." In Newark, Ohio, the 20-centuries-old Hopewell Indian earthworks contain circles, squares and octagons that once covered four square miles. "Such nice equivalences of shape and size are not the work of savages," says Kennedy, who is director of the Smithsonian's National Museum of American History. "I doubt that the Harvard freshman class would be capable of similar intellectual achievements."

Every explorer and early settler seemed to notice the aromas of America that the Indians had long enjoyed. Robert Beverley was awed by "the pleasantest smell" of Virginia's magnolias. Henry Hudson paused in New York's harbor to enjoy the "very sweet smells" of

grass and flowers on the New Jersey shore. But the visitors also smelled smoke. Every autumn, Indians burned chunks of woodland to clear the way for cornfields fertilized by the ashes and to create meadows for grazing deer and elk. The animals flourished, and so did the trees that survived. Sycamores in Ohio grew seven feet in diameter, and the white pines of New England towered 200 to 250 feet.

Animals were bigger then. New England trout, nearly two feet long, were easy targets for Algonquian arrows. Virginia sturgeon stretched six to nine feet, and Mississippi catfish topped 100 pounds. Off Cape Cod, Indians caught 20-pound lobsters, and many oysters had to be sliced into thirds to be swallowed.

Heavy Toll

The Bible taught that it is better to give than to receive, and the Indians couldn't have agreed more. Their desire to share perplexed the newcomers. Long after the Arawaks showered Columbus with birds, cloth and "trifles too tedious to describe," natives were offering Europeans anything from fish and turkeys to persimmon bread and the companionship of a chief's daughter.

Colonists interpreted the Indian's generosity as evidence they were childlike. That they had no desire to accumulate wealth was seen as laziness. But many Indian tribes were traders. Colorado's Pueblos kept parrots that came from Mexico. The Ottawas, whose name meant "to trade," traveled the Great Lakes exchanging goods. "Hootchenoo," the Northwest Chinooks' word for homemade liquor, became the slang expression "hootch."

Twenty years after Columbus colonized Hispaniola—the island shared by Haiti and the Dominican Republic—diseases and taskmasters reduced its Arawaks from a quarter-million to under 20,000. In a short time Old World diseases killed millions of the New World's natives. Death rates of up to 90 percent were common among some tribes. Two years before De Soto visited Coftachequi's female chief, pestilence swept her province, decimating her town and emptying others nearby. And four years before the *Mayflower* landed, a disease—probably smallpox or chicken pox— killed thousands of Indians on the New England coast.

Fifteen years after the Powhatan Indians' gifts of corn saved England's toehold settlement at Jamestown, the tribe was systematically wiped out, its crops and villages torched by settlers who wanted more land to grow tobacco. Indians shuddered every time they found honeybees in a hollow tree. These "English flies" moved a hundred miles ahead of the frontier—a sign that the white man was on his way. Some tribes moved west; others perished.

Yet, at least one ancient American community that didn't move endures today. In Acoma, atop a mesa in the New Mexico desert, Pueblo Indians have continuously occupied the dwellings for 1000 years, through droughts, Apache raids and a brutal Spanish occupation. Acoma is twice as old as St. Augustine, Fla., the Spanish-settled city that is generally considered the nation's oldest community.

Reprinted with permission from the January 1992 Reader's Digest. Copyright, 1991, U.S. News & World Report.

Racial and ethnic prejudices have deep roots in European languages, including English. Many contemporary accounts of Native Americans, unconsciously transmit negative interpretations.

Forked Tongues: Moral Judgments in Indian History

James Axtell

After the previous essay appeared in print, I received an opportunity to practice what I preached. Mildred Alpern, co-editor of an historical column devoted to classroom applications, invited me to write about teaching moral judgments in undergraduate classes in Indian history. So I sat down to analyze how I dealt with value judgments—those of the historical sources, the students', and mine—in my own classes in ethnohistory. The following essay, minus one paragraph, was published in *Perspectives: AHA Newsletter* in February 1987.

As might be expected, ordinary words—nouns, adverbs, and adjectives—provide the most numerous and most fruitful sources of exercise. The normative resonance of *savage* is quite different from that of *sauvage*; *invaders* packs more wallop than *strangers* or even *intruders*. *Shot* and *slain* convey moral messages different from those emanating from *murdered* or *massacred*. From analyzing individual words it is a natural step to distinguishing *obser-*

vations (more or less objective) from *interpretations* of the objects or events observed. To note that the Montagnais did not practice regular field agriculture is correct; to conclude from that fact that they did not have a concept of private or communal property is erroneous. Finally, students need to grapple with the normative implications of different narrative "emplotments," the larger structures of meaning that all viable histories must have. A history of Indian-white relations played as romance or tragedy is clearly different from one cast in a comic or satirical mode. Complications arise when sub-plots play different themes for the sake of ironic contrast or simply because the writer did not complete his literary tasks, and students should be enabled to cope with them.

Most of the words we use in history and everyday speech are like mental depth-charges. When heard or read they quickly sink into our consciousness and explode, sending off cognitive shrapnel in all direc-

tions. On the surface they may look harmless enough, or resemble something equally benign. But as they descend and detonate, their resonant power is unleashed, showering our understanding with fragments of accumulated meaning and association.

In our search for professional disinterestedness, fairness, and objectivity it is easy to give our students and readers the impression that words are strictly denotative (rather than detonative) instruments of scientific precision and emotional neutrality. Nothing could be farther from the truth. There is no neutral vocabulary for historians that is not either aesthetically void or technically esoteric. Any historian who employs nouns, verbs, adjectives, and adverbs to tell his story and puts them together in calculated patterns of meaning will unavoidably express moral or value judgments about his subjects.[1]

Teaching the history of Indian-white relations, whether independently or as part of an American survey course, quickly brings us face to face with some of the classic problems posed by our loaded vocabularies. The first problem is shared by all students of history: the tendency to apply our own limited range of modern meanings to words we share with the past but which may have meant different things to the historical educators who used them. Here the *Oxford English Dictionary* or the American equivalents are needed to clarify the usage of each age and to prevent anachronism.

Francis Jennings is particularly adept at this kind of semantic sleuthing. In *The Invasion of America* he used the *OED* to probe such elements of the English "cant of conquest" as *king, pagan, heathen, peasant, savage, and filthy.* Neal Salisbury, on the other hand, was caught by a generally complimentary reviewer in the act of giving a seventeenth-century word a twentieth-century meaning. In the space of twenty pages, Salisbury referred three times to the Massachusetts Bay Company's plans in 1629 to purchase land from any Indians who *"pretend* right of inheritance" so as to "avoyde the least scruple in intrusion." He concluded (not wholly without reason) that the English colonizers were utterly contemptuous of Indian land rights. But, as Alden Vaughan pointed out, "the standard seventeenth-century meaning of *pretend* was *claim,* without modern implications of deception."

Another problem faced by many historians, particularly those who study the history of native peoples largely through the documents produced by European invaders, is the tendency to adopt uncritically the intruders' descriptions and value

judgments of the natives as their own. Despite our best efforts, we are all, to some extent, the unwitting dupes and victims of our sources. It is all to easy to accept as objective description the colonists' unflattering characterizations of the natives, particularly when we happen to share the writers' race, religion, or nationality. While we teach our students to be critical of every source they use, we tend to drop our own guard when a source seems relatively familiar and intellectually congenial.

A third problem, related to the first two, is our tendency to make moral judgments without admitting that we do or without sufficient attention to the normative content of the words we use in making them. Some historians have no trouble with either issue. Jennings, for one, writes unabashedly moral history because he fears that "what we approve in past conduct will be repeated in the future." Assuming that "human persons do have some power of choice over their own conduct and that their adherence to moral standards, whatever those standards may be, is a matter of historical concern," he does not hesitate to use highly charged language to describe and interpret the past.[4] The Puritan clergy "thundered their wrath and called it God's." Colonial leaders resorted to "mendacity extraordinary even among adepts" to "put a fair face on fraud," and shamefully played "deed games," the "missionary racket," and "brutal charades." The colonists' "heedless grasping and bellicosity" were spearheaded by "mercenary buccaneers" and "backcountry Euramerican thugs," who resembled nothing so much as "great [feudal] hulks on horseback."

No reader has any difficulty interpreting Jennings's moral stance or recognizing that he has one.

But most historians are, by nature or nurture, more judicious in their use of overtly moral language. Yet they do not fail to make normative judgments all the time; often they are blissfully unaware that they are doing so, or they try to wrap them in the cloak of professional objectivity or the mantle of esoteric dullness. Even seemingly mild unpointed words are capable of carrying a great deal of moral freight. Take, for instance, the following two passages:

> One [of the two competing societies in colonial New England] was unified, visionary, disciplined, and dynamic. The other was divided, self-satisfied, undisciplined, and static. It would be unreasonable to expect that such societies could live side by side indefinitely with no penetration of the more fragmented and passive by the more consolidated and active.[5]

The second moral issue raised by the scalp bounties is not that Europeans taught the Indians how to scalp—they already knew how—but that Europeans adopted the Indian practice of scalping even though their cultures offered no moral or religious warrant for it and the traditional standards of Christian behavior condemned it.[6]

When asked to choose the least "moral," most "objective" passage, students invariably pick the first because the adjectives seem temperate and disinterested; it helps that they are also polysyllabic and abstract (the warp and woof of scientific "objectivity"). The second passage, by contrast, is sprinkled with normative-*sounding* words, such as *moral, religious, standards, Christian,* and *condemned.* But in fact, as students realize after a brief session of Socratic questioning, the first passage is much more "personal" and value-laden than the second, which simply describes, without judgment, the historical status of a moral issue raised by contemporaries themselves. The first passage is objectionable, not only because we cannot define or describe a person or society by negation (divided vs. unified, etc.), but because the unconscious sexual metaphor that concludes it betrays the male Eurocentric bias of its author.

In attempting to teach students to be fair to both Indian and white cultures and sensitive to the normative challenge of our historical vocabularies, I spend considerable time making them watch their words in speech and in writing. As we read the materials of the course together, I draw their attention to words commonly used to describe native peoples. Some of them, notably in the newer ethnohistories, are unobjectionable to Indians and historians alike. But most of the descriptive nouns and adjectives used by historical contemporaries and even modern historians to portray native life are biased, pejorative, demeaning, or simply inaccurate.

So pervasive is our literary bias against Indian people and culture that perhaps the best way to spend the few class hours we devote to the Indians in our American survey courses is to attack head-on our student's stereotypes. Asking for a list of words to describe "Indians" (tribe and time unspecified) will usually provide more than enough to work with. Another source is the

collection of colonial documents in my *The Indian Peoples of Eastern American: A Documentary History of the Sexes* (New York, 1981). Then the list can be attacked, item by item, with reliable ammunition from books such as Jennings's *The Invasion of America* (particularly the first ten chapter), Gary Nash's *Red, White, and Black: The Peoples of Early America* (Englewood Cliffs, N.J., 1974; 2d ed., 1982), Robert Berkhofer's *The White Man's Indian: Images of the American Indian from Columbus to the Present* (New York, 1978), Wilcomb Washburn's *The Indian in America* (New York, 1975) or my *The European and the Indian: Essays in the Ethnohistory of Colonial North America* (New York, 1981).

Many of the words we use to describe native people and culture are relative, having no concrete reality in themselves; their meaning depends on other words that are equally slippery. Take, for instance, the following:

Savage: In European writings this is the most common synonym for 'Indian.' it is based, of course, on an ethnocentric ranking of societies, with those of Western Europe at the top. Derived from the Latin word for 'forest' *(silva)* through the French word for 'wild' or 'untamed' *(sauvage), savage* by the late sixteenth century had come to mean 'and uncivilized, wild person' in the 'lowest stage of culture.' The key term of reference is *civilize,* which by circular definition means 'to bring out of a state of barbarism.' *Barbarism,* as one might guess, means a 'barbarous social or intellectual condition.' And *barbarous* is defined no more helpfully as 'rude, savage,' the opposite of 'civilized.' In other words, the meanings

of all these terms depend on an imaginary construct, a social-evolutionary hierarchy in the speaker's mind which has no objective or historical reality.

Understandably, the criteria for this ranking of societies are never stated explicitly because they are the familiar products of cultural habit rather than the earned results of philosophical analysis. From early documents it is relatively easy and very useful for students to discover some of the unarticulated standards by which European observers judged a "savage" American society. Consonant with the definiton of *savage* as 'uncivilized,' these benchmarks are usually stated as deficiencies: *lack* of clothing; large towns and cities; statutory law; centralized and compulsory forms of government; literacy and printing; draft animals and fences; iron, cloth, and glass; scriptural and ecclesiastical religion.

Primitive: In the discussion surrounding thee social judgments, this word usually appears. Derived from the Latin *primus* ('first'), *primitive* in the late seventeenth century meant 'having the quality or style of that which is early or ancient; simple, rude, or rough.' But since then it has acquired more pejorative connotations from social evolutionists. Sensitive anthropologists recently have urged their colleagues to expunge the word from their vocabularies, because the concept is as value-laden and descriptively useless as *savage.*[7] When so-called "primitive" or tribal societies are examined carefully, usually the only thing remotely "simple" or "rude" about them is their technology. While the North American Indians had no wheels, ships, paper, guns, compasses, or cathedrals, some of the shrewdest students of society have struggled mightily to plumb the complexity and sophistication of the polytheist religions, kinship systems, "barter" economies, suasive governments, arts of war and peace, and languages.

Once the last vestige of crude evolutionism has been disposed of, students should be urged to consider more worthy criteria for comparing human societies, namely those things that contribute to the *quality* of life. Without succumbing to "noble savagism," our classes are likely to give the Indians higher marks than did their colonial predecessors by measuring native and colonial societies—all members of them—against standards of health, life expectancy, physical security, individual freedom, personal fulfillment, leisure, emotional support, and aesthetic and religious expression.

Pagan: With the exception of kinship, religion was the least understood aspect of Indian life. Seeing no familiar churches, crosses, clergymen, or Scripture, Europeans concluded that the natives were "without faith," godless, "pagan." But of course *pagan* (and its synonym *heathen*) is simply a Christian definition of—or rather epithet for—a *non-*Christian, one who 'does not worship the *true* God.' To the natives who worshipped them, Indian deities were no less 'true.'

Superstition: Instead of "true religion," Indian religion was thought to be devil-worship and rank "superstition." From the early sixteenth century, Englishmen used *superstition* to denote 'religious belief or practice founded upon fear or ignorance.' In the next century, however, Thomas Hobbes reminded his countrymen that "fear

of things invisible, is the natural seed of that which every one in himself calleth religion; and in them that worship, or fear that power otherwise than they do, superstition."[8] Students of history can use the same reminder.

Even well-meaning modern historians occasionally use terms that are inappropriate or vaguely insulting.

Red Man and *Redskin* are inappropriate for two reasons. First because they refer to a physical characteristic, they lend themselves to racial stereotyping and discrimination, as does (upper case) "Whites" to denot Europeans or Anglo-Americans. Historians should be discriminating only in their respect for cultural and human diversity. Second, the color is objectively wrong. As Alden Vaughan has shown, the colonists described the Indians' pigmentation as brown, copper, olive, black, tawny, and even white, but not red. When *Red* slowly came into use in the second half of the eighteenth century, the color referred to the Indians' warpaint and, by extension, their allegedly ethnic or racial antipathy to the "White Man."[9]

Brave is a nineteenth-century word for an Indian warrior of the Plains, so it is inappropriately used to describe a warrior of an Eastern Woodland tribe or an Indian male who did not join war parties.

Squaw, a neutral Algonquian word for 'woman,' quickly acquired pejorative coloration from European descriptions of native women as "drudges" and "slaves" who did most of the farming, transported lodge material and household items in their travels, collected firewood and water, and hauled game home from the spot where it was killed by

their menfolk. Indian people today eschew it for that reason.

Half-breed: Miscegenation (there should be a better word) between Europeans and Indians produced numerous descendants who were often referred to, pejoratively, as *mixed bloods, half-breeds, or simply breeds.* Objectively, of course, the blood of members of two different ethnic or racial groups does not "mix" except in a genetic sense, at the chromosomal level. In order to unload "the freight of a phony and damning folk biology," therefore, we should use the neutral French term *metis* for 'mixed.'[10] The original *Metis* were the nineteenth-century descendants of French and Indian parents from the Red River settlement in Manitoba. But today the term applies more generally to any person of mixed Indian-white ancestry, particularly in Canada and in the northern border states of the United States. (In areas settled by the Spanish the equivalent term is *mestizo*.) Jennings has coined the uneuphonious term *synethnic* for such people, but historians should avoid such cumbrous jargon like the plague.[11]

Almost invariably our textbooks commit three other verbal *faux pas*, to which students should be alerted.

Prehistory is used to describe the Indian past before the arrival of Europeans and written records, as if the natives had no real history until the white man gave it to them. Such a condescending attitude does an injustice to the historical value of archaeology, glottochronology, and oral tradition. *Precontact* is a better word.

Masacre is typically what Indians (i.e., "savages") did to (innocent) white folks, as in the Virginia "Massacres" of 1622 and 1644 when the Powhatans surprised the encroaching colonists and in brilliant coordinated attacks claimed nearly 850 victims. The English attack on the Pequot Fort in 1637, on the other hand, is rarely described as a massacre, although between three and eight hundred men, women, and children lost their lives in the fiery onslaught. If there is to be an historical standard of judgment, it should not be double.

French and Indian War appears in nearly every American history textbook—and should give way to "Seven Years' War" (even though in America the war lasted nine years, thanks to George Washington). Indians fought on both sides in that and every other *intercolonial war*. From the French perspective, the encounter could have been seen as the "English and Indian War." To the Indians it was simply another "French and English" or (by that time) "White Man's" War. contemporaries, of course, called it none of these. To them it was just "the war" or "the last war." The "French and Indian" tag apparently was hung by Anglo-American historians in the nineteenth century.

As they move through texts and documents, students will discover that other words bear watching. Buffalo, not Indians, "roam." The "nomadic" Indians of the Eastern Woodlands did not wander; they commuted on an annual cycle between familiar residences. By the same token, the American environment was a "wilderness" only to the European newcomers, not to the native who called it home. And only the rare certifiable homicidal maniac sought to commit "genocide" upon the Indians. The vast majority of settlers had no interest in killing Indians and those who did took careful aim at temporary political or military enemies. *Genocide* was coined in 1944 to denote the systematic "annihilation of a *race*," and the settlers' animus was directed at *cultural or social* foes.

Virtually any course will provide abundant materials for the teacher and student interested in exploring the moral dimensions of history. But the history of Indian-white relations offers a particularly rich field because it features five centuries of sustained, sometimes deadly, combat over the most basic cultural values. The moral complexion and complexity of the contest for the continent provides students with an historical experience which raises the full range of normative issues in the relative safety and quite of the past, but also reminds them that few of those issues are dead. And to prepare them to deal sensitively and intelligently with the moral dilemmas of their own time is, after all, the main purpose of moral history.

Notes

1. James Axtell, "A Moral History of Indian-White Relations Revisited," *The History Teacher*, 16 (1983), 169-90.

2. Francis Jennings, *The Invasion of America: Indians, Colonialism, and the Cant of Conquest* (Chapel Hill, 1975), 43, 49n, 73-74, 114.

3. Neal Salisbury, *manitou and Providence: Indians, Europeans, and the Making of New England, 1500-1643* (New York, 1982), 181, 195, 200; review of Salisbury by Alden Vaughan, *new England Quarterly*, 56(1983), 129-32 at 131.

4. Jennings, *Invasion of America*, ix-x.

5. Alden T. Vaughan, *New England Frontier: Puritans and Indians, 1620-1675* (Boston, 1965), 323. In fairness, Vaughan has considerably modified this statement in his revised edition (New York, 1979).

6. James Axtell and William C. Sturtevant, "The Unkindest Cut, or Who invented scalping?" *William and Mary Quarterly*, 3d ser. 37 (1980), 451-72 at 470.

7. Francis L. K. Hsu, "Rethinking the Concept 'Primitive,'" *Current Anthropology*, 5 (1964), 169-78.

8. Thomas Hobbes, *Leviathan*, ed. Michael Oakshott (Oxford, 1946), 69.

9. Alden T. Vaughan, "From White Man to Redskin: Changing Anglo-American Perceptions of the American Indian," *American Historical Review*, 87 (1982), 917-53.

10. Jacqueline Peterson and Jennifer S. H. Brown, eds., *The New Peoples: Being and Becoming Métis in North America* (Winnipeg, 1985), 4-6.

11. Francis Jennings, *The Ambiguous Iroquois Empire* (New York, 1984), 58-60.

Axtell, James. "Forked Tongues." After Columbus (New York: Oxford University Press, 1988). Reprinted by permission.

Native American education after European conquest has almost always meant assimilation. Native Americans were forced to give up their values and culture and were to replace them with a European way of life.

The Demise of Native American Education: Part I

Eileen M. O'Brien

A history of "mis-education" is all the white man has given the American Indian until very recently. Though American Indians sought education from the U.S. government almost from their first interactions, formalized education has almost always meant relinquishing their culture and becoming "white."

In the past few decades, American Indian advocates and educators have won major victories in their struggle to gain more control over their children's education and influence the public schools they attend. But these successes have not been widespread, and they cannot overcome centuries of forced assimilation, Indian leaders admit.

The Indians requested education in their earliest dealings with the federal government. In more than one-quarter of the approximately 400 treaties entered into by the U.S. government between 1778 and 1871, education was one of the specific services Indian tribes asked for in exchange for their lands.

Yet for the most part, American Indian students in formalized education in the U.S. were "forced to embrace European life and renounce their own culture," a 1989 report from the Carnegie Foundation for the Advancement of Teaching noted. "Many students were forced into a cultural no-man's land, where they remained torn between two worlds, suffering deeply from the schism," the report continued.

"The respect of knowledge held by Native Americans makes the failure of effective education policies for the Indian nations these past two centuries all the more tragic," Education Secretary Lauro Cavazos said last October. Recognizing "the history of failure in Indian education," Cavazos announced the Education Department would launch a major study of the Indian experience in education, to be called Indian Nation at Risk.

During a recent meeting of minority researchers in San Francisco, "we agreed that we had a paucity of data on American Indians that there is no national database," said Dr. Robert Wells, professor of government at St. Lawrence University. Wells said he decided after the meeting to conduct a survey of all tribal chiefs to determine their satisfaction level with the education provided.

The data shortage on information was also a motivating factor for Cavazos' project. "One of the biggest problems facing us today in Indian education is that there is much we do not know . . . [We] do not know . . . what types of education practices work best among these groups," he said.

Statistically, Indians have either been ignored or placed in the "other" category for most national education data. So even though their history in American education is longer than that of any other minority group, very little is known about their participation rates and achievement levels, and what is known is not good.

The available data paints a very bleak picture:

- *American Indians have the highest dropout rate of all minorities.* According to the National Center for Education Statistics' *Dropout Rates in the United States: 1988*, American Indians' dropout rate is 35.5 percent, compared to 22.2 percent for Blacks, and 27.9 percent for Hispanics. The report also shows they represent 3.1 percent of all dropouts, despite the fact that they account for only 0.9 percent of all elementary and secondary students.

- *American Indians are disproportionately placed in special education and learning disabled programs.* A 1988 Bureau of Indian Affairs (BIA) report note that 11 percent of Indian sophomores in public and private schools were enrolled in special education programs; 36 percent were classified as having some form of handicap; and only 53 percent were termed "not handicapped." But comparison, only 9 percent of Blacks and 7 percent of Hispanics were in special education programs.

- *Poverty and unemployment are constant afflictions to the American Indian population.* Male unemployment on reservations is 58 percent, according to a 1986 Department of Interior study, and on some reservations it reaches as high as 80 percent. The average income for Indian families was $13,680, compared to the overall median of $19,920.

Indian advocates argue that the plight of their population is often ignored because of its small numbers. Indeed, they are a minority among minorities: In the 1980 Census, their numbers totalled 1.4 million—less than 1 percent of the nation's population.

While the population is growing significantly, Indian researchers worry that their people will continue to be neglected or overlooked. "We are constantly urging people not to forget us," said Dr. Karen Swisher, director of the Center for American Indian Education at Arizona State University.

Swisher, a member of the Standing Rock Sioux tribe of North Dakota, recounted, "As the demographer Harold Hodgkinson says, 'When you're too small, you tend to get left off the list and you get forgotten,' But we have a special relationship with the people of this country and we shouldn't be forgotten."

Jojo Hunt, executive director of the National Advisory Council on Indian Education (NACIE), predicted the Indian population will reach 2 million in the 1990 Census, due to better counting methods and the community's large growth over the past decade. Yet Hunt, a Lumbee Indian of North Carolina, is "not sure that the increase will have an effect on getting national attention focused on our issues, because regardless of whether we're 2 million, 4 million or 6 million, we're still such a small minority."

Even if the figure does reach 2 million, "it's still a drop in the bucket," agreed Clara Sue Kidwell, professor of Native American studies at the University of California-Berkeley. "I doubt that [such an increase] would focus that much more attention on Indians. The change between the 1970 Census and the 1980 Census was quite dramatic and no one paid attention then."

American Indians also suffer from a misperception common to many minority groups: They are viewed as "one people with one need," when in fact there is wide diversity among Indian peoples. According to Bill Mahojeh, chief of the elementary and secondary educa-

---

Distribution of 1.4 Million American Indians

- The 1980 Census supplementary questionnaire showed that one-third of all American Indians lived on reservations and in the historic areas of Oklahoma (excluding Urbanized areas).

- One-fourth or 340,000 of all American Indians lived on reservations in 1980. Reservations are areas with boundaries established by treaty, stature and/or executive or court order.

- The American Indian population in the historic areas of Oklahoma (excluding urbanized areas) numbered 116,000, comprising 9 percent of the total American Indian population. The historic areas consist of the former reservations, which had legally established boundaries during the 1900-1907 period.

tion branch of the Bureau of Indian Affairs, there are more than 30 tribes in the continental U.S., and in Alaska, where every village is considered a tribe, there are 200 villages. Also, even though some of the tribal languages have vanished, some 200 still exist.

In addition, Hunt noted, the population is no longer concentrated on reservations. Only 25 percent of Indian people are on reservations, she said, and a significant number are located in Oklahoma on trust land areas, in urban areas, and especially in California, many tribes that are not federally recognized live in rural nonreservation areas.

However, this multiplicity has its downside, as well. "At times, this diversity prevents national unity among American Indians." according to a recent paper by Dr. John Tipperconnic, editor of the Journal of American Indian Education and associate professor of education at Arizona State University. Because Indians do not speak in one voice, they are unable to exert the necessary political pressure that leads to action, he argued.

It is also difficult to attack educational problems because Indian students are served by several types of schools. Even the data on how many elementary and secondary students are Indian are fuzzy, but NACIE estimates that there are 400,000. Most of these students—82 percent—are enrolled in state-run public schools. About 7 percent are in private schools, many of them missionary schools that sprang up near reservations. The remaining 11 percent, are in BIA-funded schools, about 70 of which are operated by tribes under contract with BIA.

Ten States with the Largest Number of American Indians

- According to the 1980 Census, most American Indians lived west of the Mississippi River.

- Two in three Indians lived in the 10 states with the largest Indian populations. Of these states, only North Carolina, Michigan and New York are east of the Mississippi River.

- In 1980, more than half of the Indian Population lived in fives states: California (198,275), Oklahoma (169,292), Arizona (152,498), New Mexico (105,976), and North Carolina (64,536).

- California had the largest Indian population in 1980, climbing from third position in 1970. Between 1970 and 1980, Oklahoma dropped from first to second place. Arizona fell from second to third, and New Mexico stayed fourth.

Indian advocates say the schools funded by the Bureau are doing better now since they are run with more input from Indians, yet the nation's public school system is not meeting the needs of Indian students, nor are these schools offering many programs to help Indian students retain their cultural heritage.

"If we rank at the bottom or near the bottom in achievement levels and have such a high dropout rate, we can't say they're doing a good job," said NACIE's Hunt. "Some [public schools] are, and those typically have a lot of involvement from Indian parents. But for a variety of factors, I don't believe the public school systems or the supplemental programs some schools offer are providing what's needed for Indian students."

Swisher said a particular problem with some public schools is the lack of English as a second language programs for those Indian students who come to school not knowing English.

"There is a great concern for the restoration and maintenance of the native languages" among Indian communities and students, she said, adding that BIA schools typically do a better job of helping students maintain their languages. But in both BIA schools and public schools, many of the students "speak Indian English, a combination of English and their tribe's language."

Indians and mainstream society have usually had different agendas in receiving an education. Wells said, "Education has been one way in which Indians have tried to preserve their cultural identity. Yet white society has tried to do the opposite with education."

The pressure of assimilation—or becoming "white"—is still a problem with formalized education, Swisher argued. At a recent meeting held by BIA in Sante Fe, NM, Swisher was inspired by "some Indian students who wanted to speak out. They gave some really impassioned speeches about wanting to be Indian, to remain an Indian but still to excel and go on to college."

Percent Distribution of American Indians by Age

- The American Indian population is young. The age distribution of the American Indian population differed substantially from that of the total population in 1980.

- Forty-four percent of the Indian population was under 20 years of age, compared with 32 percent of the nation's total population.

- About 6 percent of all Indians were 60 years old or over in 1980, about half of the proportion (16 percent) for the total population.

- The median age of the Indian population was 22.9 years, considerably younger than the U.S. median age of 30.0 years. (The median age is the age where half the population is older and half the population is younger.) The younger Indian population is partially the result of higher fertility rates.

Historically, public education often alienated students from their tribes and even their parents, she explained. "But from my experience, that is changing. There are some very traditional areas where parents do fear that their children will forget the traditional ways . . . but students are gaining what I call 'cultural confidence,' knowing when to do what and when to act in certain ways."

Speaking at the National Indian Education Association meeting last year, Cavazos agreed that public education has typically failed Indians because of the lack of consideration for Indian culture. "From the Anglo perspective, the primary purpose of education was assimilation. Well into the 20th century . . . the federal government adopted a uniform curriculum for all Indian schools that ignored Indian cultural heritage, language, mores and traditions," he said.

Unfortunately, Indians don't have many alternatives to public education, noted Ruth Myers, assis-

tant director of the Center for American Indian and Minority health in Duluth, MN. "With compulsory attendance laws, you don't have much choice," she said. She knows of many Indian parents in Minnesota who send their children to Indian schools in South Dakota, rather than have them go to Minnesota public schools.

The school system has failed Indians, much like other minority groups, she added. "Indian students, particularly males, are over represented in special education programs, and there is a disproportionate number in juvenile detention centers. Indian student bring in X number of dollars [to the school system], but they don't get the services they should for that money," she said.

In her position, Myers recruits Indian students and other minority students into health, biomedical and aquatic science fields. "From where I sit [recruiting students into competitive fields], it's not an easy

job after the system's beat them down for 12 years," Myers said.

"Indian learners have the same problem learners everywhere have: schools too rarely base their strategies on the best research that's available," stated Bob Arnold, an aide for the Senate Select Committee on Indian Affairs. "But also some of their problems arise simply from their 'Indianness,' the difference in their language and their culture; and some of their problems arise from their minorityness'—discrimination is a fact of life in America."

There are bright spots, both in specific schools and programs and on the horizon, Indian leaders note. Change is coming, Swisher said, "People are realizing that cultural diversity is here to stay and what we have been doing isn't working. There used to be this attitude [of majority educators], 'If they'd [Indian students] just change—the system worked for these little white kids, why shouldn't it work for these little brown kids?'"

Swisher also pointed to the Sante Fe Indian School as an exceptional example of a BIA-funded tribally controlled schools that offers "a strong balance of the affective and the cognitive. They offer an academically rigorous program, but they couple it with caring." The boarding school has a dropout rate of only 2 percent to 3 percent and sends a high percentage of students on to college.

"Not surprisingly, the key is teachers who want to teach Indian kids and who are willing to be a part of the community," she said.

Another success story is also BIA-funded; the Rocky Boy Tribal High School in Montana. Part of the Rocky Boy district, which is encompassed by the Rocky Boy Indian Reservation and includes a public elementary school controlled by Indians, the high school was established because reservation leaders were concerned over the high dropout rate (54 percent) of their students, explained Dr. Robert Swan, acting superintendent for the two schools.

Swan, a Chippawa-Cree said that the school receives funding not only from BIA, but from an Education Department discretionary grant as well. "If we only had BIA funding, we would have to get rid of a lot of our programs—home ec, foreign languages, computers, business, industrial arts, et cetera." Because of "drastic" underfunding from BIA, the high school has petitioned to become a state public school, was

approved and will start next year as one.

"We're a step above a lot of other schools," Swan said. "We set high standards and goals for the schools. We're graduating our seniors at grade level, and we've lowered the dropout rate to less than 15 percent."

Admittedly, there are few shining examples in the public school system Indian educators could point to, with one exception: the Buffalo, NY magnet school for Native Americans. Cavazos praised the school last October, saying. "During the past five years, the number of third-graders at this school needing remedial language instruction has dropped from 58 percent to 11 percent." The school is changing

negative self-images American Indian students have and showing Indian children they can succeed in school, according to Principal Lloyd Elms.

Despite history, Indian advocates still think education is the key in the economic survival of their people and are optimistic that improvements will be made. "Change comes slow," said Tippeconnic, "[but] education remains the ray of hope to economic self-sufficiency."

From O'Brien, Eileen M. "The Demise of Native American Education: Part I" Black Issues in Higher Education, 15 March 1990. Reprinted with permission.

One-fourth of African-American males currently encounter the criminal justice system. Urban underemployment and long-standing patterns of racial discrimination continue unabated according to the following Chicago Tribune account.

Odds Against Growing up Black and Male

Jean Latz Griffin, Karen M. Thomas, and George Curry

It is 4 A.M. in the Cook County Hospital Trauma Unit. Two black teenagers, Anthony Buchanan and Chris Wilson, are lying on gurneys within a foot of each other while doctors and nurses await the results of their X-rays.

At 2 A.M., Buchanan, 19, was standing in an alley in the Austin neighborhood on Chicago's West Side when he was shot in the right shoulder. At 3 A.M., Wilson, 17 was shot in the thigh and buttocks as he stood near 57th and Laflin Streets on the South Side.

"I'm lucky I didn't get killed. I thought he was going to pop me in the belly. I lay there for 10, 15 minutes, then one of my friends called an ambulance," Wilson said.

Buchanan says all he heard was the soft whiz of passing bullets. He was on the ground by the time he realized he had been shot.

The boys will be patched up, nursed to health and returned to the streets, two young soldiers, wounds bandaged, heading back to the front.

There was a time when the shooting of a teenager would have drawn angry parents and preachers into the streets for protest marches. But now these incidents are so common that the public's sense of outrage seems dulled.

Like an old boxer who has taken too many punches to the head, society covers its eyes and ears and waits for the latest pummeling to pass.

Within a month, Wilson and Buchanan will become part of a set of lifeless, but revealing, statistics. Among them, black boys between the ages of 15 and 19 are 11 times more likely than whites to die by gunfire. Through September, the latest month for which statistics are available, 87 had been fatally shot this year in Chicago.

Gang fights, vendettas, drug battles, accidents, drive-by shootings, the violence is overwhelming, but it is only one force threatening the lives of black men and boys in America.

They are also more likely than whites to face a number of other problems—malnutrition, poor education, drug or alcohol addiction, the collapse of families, a series of medical problems linked to poverty, lifestyle and heredity—as they mature.

Chicago, New York, Los Angeles, Miami, Detroit, Washington, Boston, no big city in America has found a way to break the cycle.

In the black community, a boy's unsolved problems are carried through life, and continually compounded, creating layer upon layer of other troubles as he grows to manhood.

Even if a black man can avoid or escape the violence and other environmental hazards, more obstacles lie ahead.

Charles Williams, 36, a financial planner with Massachusetts Mutual Life and Insurance Co., says he is not quite sure how to react when people point to him as a remarkable success.

"If I were white, would you be talking to me as an example of success?" he asks. "No, I'd be just like everybody else. By whose standards am I judged to be a success?"

Williams cites his son and daughter "as my highest achievements" and says he feels acutely the need for black men to "reinforce family values."

To gauge the scope and severity of problems facing black males, the Tribune analyzed data on birth, death, health, illness, violence, educational achievement, employment, home ownership, net worth, crime and imprisonment.

Information was gathered from a variety of sources, including the Illinois Department of Health, the National Center for Health Statistics, the Illinois State Board of Education, the Chicago Board of Education, the U.S. Census Bureau, the Illinois Department of Employment Security, the Chicago Fire Department, and the Illinois Department of Criminal Justice.

The Tribune also interviewed dozens of black men and boys across the area, visited schools and hospitals, attended funerals and church services.

To be sure, there are powerful stories of personal and financial success. Nearly 67 percent of African-Americans have escaped poverty, according to 1989 census figures, and 59 percent own their own homes.

However, the net worth of a middle-class black family is still only one-third that of a white family, and a black family is more likely than a white family to need two incomes to reach middle-class status. College-educated black men earn only 74 cents for every dollar earned by college educated white men.

Moreover, behind every successful black family like the Williams family, this other nation persists, a distant backdrop where the Anthony Buchanans and Chris Wilson live, where the problems seem insoluble, the despair grinding and perpetual.

In a wealthy nation that readily sends its dollars and sympathies to whales trapped under the ice, disappearing rain forests, threatened owls and abandoned pets, to visit these troubled lives is to witness the perils faced by one of America's most threatened, and yet potentially most valuable, resources.

A Hard Start

DuJuan Boston, 4, was the first black boy to die in a Chicago fire in 1991. His brothers, Nathan, 8, and Jonathan, 6, were severely burned.

Scars criss-cross Jonathan's chest, arms and back. For at least a year, says Norma Jean Boston, his mother, he will have to wear a clear plastic mask to keep the scar tissue from disfiguring his face.

Nathan breathes through a tube in his throat because of injuries from smoke inhalation. He seldom speaks above a whisper. Nurses at Schwab Rehabilitation Center, 1401 S. California Ave., have tried to wean him from the tube, but he panics when they try to get him to breathe without it.

Despite the easy availability of smoke alarms and decades of fire-

prevention education, fire remains the most frequent cause of death for black boys between the ages of 1 and 5, most often those trapped by poverty in dilapidated rental housing. They are three times as likely to die from fire as white boys in Illinois.

This is where the sad measure of youth begins for many black males in America, but it is not where they end. The longer-term statistics on black males are equally disturbing, revealing everything from low birth weights to dropping out of school to prison terms.

They will face a nightmarish series of threats and challenges. And many will face it without their most important male role model—their fathers.

Nearly 80 percent of American black children had a father living in their home in 1960. But by 1988, only 57 percent did. The comparable figure for white children in 1988 was 87 percent.

Of every 1,000 black baby boys who will be born in the next year in Illinois, fewer than half—only 423—will survive childhood, graduate from high school, stay out of jail, and obtain the skills necessary to become functioning members of society by age 35, based on mortality, high school dropout and incarceration rates. For white boys, the number is 764.

The seeds of these problems may take root when a baby's mother is growing up, the troubles in her own life setting an equally difficult course for her children. Nagging anxiety, long-term stress, drug abuse, malnutrition, psychological problems, they can all play a role.

A Tribune examination of 156,902 Illinois Department of Public Health birth and death certificates issued from 1985 to 1987 shows black babies in Chicago are twice as likely as white babies to have a low birth weight, even when their mothers have the same education and income level as white mothers.

Within that group of babies, nearly 72 percent of the black males who died before they were a year old were simply too small to survive. There is evidence that the stress on the mothers, the tension of poverty central among them, was instrumental in the premature births.

But waiting until pregnancy to identify and try to repair the damages of stress may be too late.

Children who are exposed to severe, repeated stress may lose the ability to cope as adults, according to the National Health/Education consortium, part of the National Commission to Prevent Infant Mortality.

Poor nutrition in their childhoods also may predispose women to early labor, according to Dr. Naomi Morris, professor at the University of Illinois at Chicago School of Public Health. Women who were low birth weight babies also are more likely to have low birth weight babies.

In all races, poor women fare worse than more affluent women, but black middle-class women have not yet caught up with white women in reducing the numbers of low birth weight babies they have or infants they lose before their first birthday.

"We really don't know what is happening with black middle-class women," said Dr. Kuang Sund Lee, head of the neonatology department at the University of Chicago.

"We spend millions of dollars on infant mortality, but we do it piece-meal, and until we understand what is really going on with black premature birth, we are just spinning our wheels."

Rejection at School

By the time an inner-city black boy steps into his first classroom, he is more likely than his white counterpart to have suffered untreated infections, witnessed violence and experienced hunger or homelessness.

The schoolhouse door can lead to a world where he is taught, encouraged, challenged and molded into a productive man. Or it can begin a slide to ever-lessening expectations and stunted achievements. Public school can offer salvation, but it can also damage a student almost beyond repair.

"Black boys go into the school system, and they have more problems," said Dr. Alvin Poussaint, a Harvard University psychiatrist who specializes in black family life. "Some are rejected by teachers. Some are in schools that aren't structured to deal with their behavior. . . The black male child feels very early that he doesn't belong."

There are pressures from many directions. Outside the school walls, there are gangs, drugs and the money they can produce, splintered families and a mainstream society that has very low expectations for the urban black male.

Inside there are lowered expectations from teachers, inadequate facilities and peer pressure against academic success. Because of these problems, the door to success as an adult can slam shut for black boys even before they are 10 years old.

Standardized test results may present the first red flag.

By 3rd grade, black boys trail all other groups in mathematics, testing lower than Asians, whites and Hispanics on a statewide math exam. In every other ethnic group, boys significantly outscored girls, but black boys and girls showed the same results in math test.

Statewide, black boys are also three times as likely as white boys to be labeled mildly mentally retarded and to never attend a regular class. The high rate of special education placements has drawn changes that as many as a third of the boys are mislabeled, placed in slower classes that focus on only the most simple skills.

But for many black males, classroom problems pale in comparison to their problems at home or on the street. Within this age group, it is clear, there are other priorities and bigger dangers.

Sylvester "Rocky" Jones, the oldest son of Norma Jean Boston, was born when his mother was 13. She could not read or write.

Rocky, 14, has been raised by his mother, both grandmothers, his father and an aunt. His father and one uncle are in prison.

Two of his school chums have been shot. A friend's mother has been killed by gunfire.

"I read good and spell good. I'm good in math, but not as good as I am in reading and spelling."

Rocky's eyes light up when he talks about a swimming program offered by the University of Illinois at Chicago last summer. But they also light up when he talks about gangs. He thinks he knows a lot about gangs and a lot about their big business: drugs.

"It's like this. The government give the drugs to the syndicate, the syndicate give it to the gang leader, he give it to his general, the general give it to the right hand man and he give it to the workers," he said.

"And the money go back up the same way."

Rocky was arrested the first time when he was 10 years old, when he was with friends who were stealing annual stickers from license plates. He can't remember all the arrests that followed that one.

"Once I got arrested when a kid's head got busted. He was trying to stab me with a butcher knife and I hit him with a log and his head got busted," he said.

He has his own dreams, perhaps crafted from his experiences.

He wants to go to Disneyland, finish high school, become an undertaker and "marry a Puerto Rican lady and have twin boys. I'd name them Don Antonio Jones and Sean Antonio Jones, and I'd teach them to be good and be like their selves, not like anybody else."

Handling dead bodies wouldn't bother him in the undertaking business, he says.

"I've seen my brother dead and my uncle. And a man. The man, I didn't see his shot, but I saw his brains on the sidewalk. It looked nasty. All kinds of gray stuff with hunks of blood."

In May, Rocky's father sent the family a picture from prison. He is standing in front of a chain link fence at Vandalia.

"I love all of you," says the inscription.

A Time to Choose

When Jeremy Borders speaks, his body moves in rhythm with his words, his frame, over 6 feet, gliding gracefully around the living room of his mother's apartment on Chicago's West Side.

His hands roam from a family photo album to a basketball trophy, his fingers finally pointing to a large portrait hanging on the wall of his friend, 15-year-old Jumaani Jackson.

The portrait is Borders' reminder of what to avoid on the streets outside of his mother's fourth-floor apartment on Central Avenue. Jackson was fatally shot last year during a robbery in which his drug money was taken.

"He got caught up in the fast lane," said Borders, 16. "I guess he thought it was cool. I just didn't think anything like that would happen to him. He was just 15. It was real shocking."

"It could happen to me."

Borders is growing up quickly, and he faces a collection of major decisions in his life. One involves the lure of the street, another a dream about basketball, a third the dream of becoming a doctor.

Borders, a Collins High School student, has had academic problems. His school record includes flunking a year and spending time at Montefiore School for Boys after his behavior had spun out of control.

Montefiore, a Chicago public school at 1300 S. Ashland Ave., takes boys after other school officials say they no longer fit in their classrooms.

Some students have prison records. Some are gang members. Some have been abused—sexually, emotionally or physically. Some, like Borders, watched their families unravel and then unleashed their rage in classrooms.

All share one thing. They are below grade level, left educationally adrift because of their conduct. About 10 percent are white, 19 percent are Hispanic and 71 percent are black.

At Montefiore, Borders was placed in a small class. There were school rules, discipline, routines that had to followed.

Students are recognized for good attendance, good behavior, improving reading and math scores—even their birthdays—anything school officials can think of to boost sagging esteem.

None of this was lost on Borders. His teachers pushed him, threatened him and nurtured him. One teacher signed his 8th-grade yearbook: "Good luck in high school, you better make it or else." They made him want to succeed academically for the first time in his life.

Although he graduated from Montefiore two years ago, Borders keeps a well-worn copy of a short essay he wrote in 1989.

"Graduation will make my mother and my family very happy," he read from the two-page essay, written at the urging of Charles Cashaw, assistant principal of Montefiore.

"I must step up and do something for myself before it is too late. Positive attitude and control, that's what I need."

This fall at Collins High School, Jeremy Borders made the honor roll.

Behind Bars

The statistics are staggering. Black men make up only 14.8 percent of the Illinois population but 62.4 percent of the adult prison population. The state sends more black men to prison per capita than does South Africa. Black men are more likely to be in jail, on probation or on parole than in college.

Joseph Reed is typical of those incarcerated adults, a black man who got in trouble because of drugs and guns.

As a Chicago teenager selling "happy sticks" (marijuana laced with the animal tranquilizer PCP) in 1984, a customer accused him of delivering poor quality drugs. An argument erupted. A friend of Reed's joined in.

"We whipped him," said Reed, 24, during an interview at Cook County Jail, where he was being held on an unrelated charge. "He said, 'You better not be out here when I come back.' So he got into his car and left."

"He came back. At this time, I had went home and got a gun, a .25 automatic. He had his hand behind his back and he was talking to some of my partners. He's saying, 'I'm going to do this and I'm going to do that.'"

"I thought he had a pistol. I snuck up behind him, he didn't see me. When he turned around, I was up in his face and pow—shot him. Right here, right here in the cheekbone."

The man didn't die. Reed pleaded guilty to assault charges and received a 2-year sentence.

"For too many inner-city kids, activities like drug dealing appear to be one of the better employment opportunities, if not the only one, around," said Marc Mauer of the Sentencing Project, a Washington-based group that promotes sentencing reform.

"There's quick money to be made, you don't have to pass a civil service test and you don't need any particular training to enter the field."

Pouissant says that temptation is compounded because male violence

---

Black Males—Infancy to Young Adults

- Infant mortality: Black newborn males are twice as likely to die before they are a year old than white newborn males.

- Poverty rate: 43% of all black males under age 6 live at or below the federal poverty level.

- Chances of survival: Between birth and age 5, twice as many black children die as white children.

- Asthma: Black males ages 5 to 34 are nearly five times more likely to die from asthma than are whites, and 1.5 times more likely than black females.

- High school dropouts: More than half of the black boys, 55%, fail to complete high school; black girls, 44%; white boys, 22%; white girls, 16%.

- Attending college: One-fifth of all black men ages 18-34 are currently in college, compared with one-third the college-age white men.

- Bachelor's degrees: Although blacks comprise 16% of the Illinois population, they earned only 7.4% of all bachelor's degrees awarded in 1989.

- Chances of jail: 28 black males per 1,000 are incarcerated for some period of time, compared with two white males and less than one black or white female.

- U.S. criminal system: Almost one in four black men is either is prison, in jail, on probation or on parole.

---

has become acceptable in American culture. That, and the fact that a segment of the population has lost its self-esteem, can produce deadly results.

"The self-esteem and control issues is so powerful that they put aside the fact that they are self-destructing," Poussaint said, citing a recent rise in shooting deaths among young black males. "They will shoot someone and go to jail for life for that moment of control. There is no understanding or concern."

At 24, Bernard Taylor has spent every summer since 1982 locked in a prison cell. He has robbed at gunpoint, sold drugs, snatched purses and jewelry.

He has separated himself from his family because he fears that he will influence his younger brothers, who once looked up to him as a role model.

"Up in here . . . your meal is prepared for you. The whole day is prepared for you," Taylor said during an interview last summer at Cook County Jail, where he was awaiting trial for armed robbery.

"The challenge is out there in the real world. I think I was afraid of that challenge out there."

Once a man has served prison time, he is marked for life.

Education and training programs to prepare for employment are scarce within prison walls. Outside, the job market is virtually closed to those with prison records.

"Prison is a repository for all of life's [problems]," said Mike Mahoney, executive director of the John Howard Association, an inmate advocacy group. "It is the last stop on a train to nowhere."

Seeking to Help

Whenever, over a few beers or even a cup of tea, the discussion among white people turns to the problems encountered by blacks, someone is bound to say, "Why can't they help themselves like we did when we first came over here?"

The issue is complex. The experiences of blacks in America are significantly different than those of others. Blacks were the only "immigrants" who were brought to America as slaves, kept enslaved for 239 years and then prevented from voting in any numbers for another 100 years.

Unlike whites, they could never just blend in, virtually unnoticed, with earlier waves of immigrants. Unlike Cubans or many Asians, they did not have accumulated wealth and professional degrees or

banks back home to lend them money.

Blacks are the only group for whom it was once a crime to learn to read.

Despite these obstacles, blacks over the generations have worked together to improve their lot.

And today, as hurdles once thought nearly leveled start to rise again for black men and their families, the men themselves are coming together in cities across the nation to try to help their brothers.

Concerned Black Men Inc. pairs successful black men as role models with students. Project Image works with schools and churches to strengthen the black family and build the self-esteem of young black boys. The 500 African-American Men for Justice rid rough neighborhoods of drugs and gangs. 100 Black Men motivates and nurtures young black men in local schools. All are national groups with local chapters in Chicago.

"I know the argument, I am not here to be the father, uncle, or grandparent," said Spurgeon

Smith, a 7th grade Chicago public school teacher. "But as a black male, I accept that role. If the problem is there, how can you say no? You would be a coward and fool if you did that."

However, because blacks are an economically depressed minority; the argument that they should just pull themselves up is unrealistic.

"The notion that the black middle class can turn this around is unreasonable," Poussaint said. "They can't create jobs. They have minimum control over the economy."

Jean Latz Griffin is a public health writer for the Chicago Tribune. Prior to joining the Tribune she reported for the Joliet Herald News and the Raleigh Times. She was one of the lead reporters on a team which produced the series, "Chicago Schools: The Worst in the Nation," which received three awards and honors.

© Copyrighted 1991, Chicago Tribune Company, all rights reserved, used by permission.

African-American students whose cultural history includes dislocation, racism, discrimination, and harrassment have been encouraged to abandon their traditions and to conform to white middle class norms. The Afrocentric curriculum, in contrast, encourages respect for each student's heritage.

Afrocentric Curriculum

Molefi Kete Asante

Recently I spoke about Afrocentric teaching at a gathering of thousands of teachers in a large urban district. After my speech, I was pleased that two teachers wanted to share their classroom experiences with the audience.

After a trip to Africa, one teacher said, he returned to his classroom of mostly African-American students and began identifying them with various ethnic groups, "You look like a Fulani boy I saw in Northern Nigeria," he commented to a young man. "You're definitely Ibo," he said to a female student. "Yes. I have seen that face in the Ibo region." Turning to another student, he said, "I see Mandinka features in your face." Soon, all the children were clamoring for identification: "Me, who do I look like?" "Tell me my ethnic group," each one asked the teacher.

The other teacher remarked that she asks her students to write about their family's genealogy. The best way to approach the subject of identity and connectiveness, she suggested, is to begin with the family, because students have both personal and collective identities.

I applauded both teachers for doing precisely what all teachers should do: place children, or center them, within the context of familiar cultural and social references from their own historical settings.

The Breakthrough

The discovery of the centric idea was a major breakthrough in my educational conceptualization. It allowed me to explain what happens to white children who attend American schools, what happens to Asian children who are rooted in

Asian culture and attend schools in their countries, what happens to children of the African continent who are grounded in their own culture and attend their own schools.

In my 17 journeys to Africa during the past 20 years, I have visited schools and colleges in all parts of the continent and been impressed with the eagerness of the children to learn. Back home in Philadelphia, I wanted to explore why children in Africa seemed more motivated than African-American children here. Why did Africans on the continent learn four and five languages, when in some schools African-American children were often not encouraged to take even one foreign language? To say the least, I have been disturbed by the lack of direction and confidence that plague many African-American children. I believe it is because they are not culturally centered and empowered in their classrooms.

Empowering Children Through Their Culture

One of the principal aspects of empowerment is respect. Students are empowered when information is presented in such a way that they can walk out of the classroom feeling that they are a part of the information.

The times I am able to relate a class topic to the background of a Native American, Chinese, Hispanic, or African child in a multicultural classroom make me very pleased, because I see the centering immediately register in the child's countenance. Self-perception and self-acceptance are the principle tools for communicating and receiving communication. And teaching is preeminently a communicating profession.

Most teachers do not have to think about using the white child's culture to empower the white child. The white child's language is the language of the classroom. Information that is being conveyed is "white" cultural information in most cases; indeed, the curriculum in most schools is a "white self-esteem curriculum."

Teachers are empowered if they walk into class and there is an air of credibility. How do teachers empower themselves in a classroom with children of African-American or other heritages? They must use the same tools used to empower white children.

When I enter a classroom of white college students and demonstrate in the course of my lecture that I know not only the words of Ogotommeli, Seti, and Ptahhotep

but also Shakespeare, Homer, and Stephen J. Gould, I am usually empowered as a teacher with my white students. They understand that I have no problem centering them within their cultural framework. The reason they understand it is simple: this is the language of the dominant culture.

The fact that an African-American or an Hispanic person—in order to master the white cultural information—has had to experience the death of his or her own culture does not register with most teachers. The true "centric" curriculum seeks for the African, Asian, and Hispanic child the same kind of experience that is provided for the white child.

Centering the African-American Child

The centric idea gave me some idea of what happened to African-American children whose culture has been ravaged by racism, discrimination, harassment, and the Great Enslavement. These children, with cultural handicaps, are forced to complete with students whose ancestors have not suffered such devastation.

What centers the African-American child? I began working with this question many years ago when I observed what happened to the African-American child in the large school systems of northern urban communities. Being brought up in Valdosta, Georgia, during the era of segregation, I have been nourished and nurtured by teachers who had mastered the nuances and idiosyncrasies of my culture. This is something that teachers often seem unable to do in many urban schools.

Of course, segregation was legally and morally wrong, but something was given to black children in those

schools that was just as important in some senses as the new books, better educated teachers, and improved buildings of this era. The children were centered in cultural ways that made learning interesting and intimate.

African-American children who have never heard the Spirituals; never heard the names of African ethnic groups; never read Paul Laurence Dunbar, Langston Hughes, and Phillis Wheatley nor the stories of High John de Conqueror, Anansi, and the Signifying Monkey are severely injured in the most fragile parts of their psyches. Lacking reinforcement in their own historical experiences, they become psychologically crippled, hobbling along in the margins of the European experiences of most of the curriculum.

While I am not nostalgic for the era of segregated schools, we should remember what was best in those schools and use that knowledge to assist in centering African-American children. Through observations, inquiry, and discussions, I've found that children who are centered in their own cultural information are better students, more disciplined, and have greater motivation for schoolwork.

A neighbor of mine often speaks to elementary classes in one of the most economically devastated communities in Philadelphia. He tells the young children, "You're going to be somebody." Later, the children are often heard saying to their peers, "I am going to be somebody."

It sounds so ridiculously corny to say this, but many of these children have never been touched at their psychological centers, never been reached in their cultural homes. They see school as a foreign place because schools do foreign things. Of course, many students master the "alien" cultural information, but others have great difficulty getting beyond the margin in which they have been placed.

A Dislocated Culture

When it comes to facing the reality of social and cultural dislocation, teachers are on the front lines. They are among the first in the society to see the devastation that has occurred to the African-American child's spirit. If they've been teaching for more than 20 years, they have seen more and more students who seem to have been dislocated culturally, socially, and psychologically.

I contend that the movement of Africans from the continent of Africa was the first massive dislocation. The African person was physically separated from place, from culture, and from traditions. In the Americas, the African person was punished for remembering Africa. Drums were outlawed in most of the colonies soon after the arrival of large numbers of Africans. And since the drum was an instrument intimate to the cultural transmission of values and traditions, its disappearance was one of the great losses in the African-American psyche. Physical movement became in reality a precursor to a more damaging dislocation and decentering.

Numerous educational, social, religious, and political structures and institutions have tried to minimize the dislocation. But the despair has intensified since the '60s, because of questions of equity and lack of economic opportunities. Schools are affected inasmuch as their students are filled with the emptiness of their own self-dislocation.

Indeed, schools have often contributed to the dilemma by encouraging African-American children to concentrate on mastering only information about the majority culture. These children may learn, but, without cultural grounding, the learning will have destroyed their sense of place. Increasing numbers of children abandon, in their minds, their own cultures in order to become like others culturally, hoping this will bring them closer to the white norms.

Schools also reinforce feelings of limited self-worth and cultural dislocation by ignoring the historical contributions of African Americans or devaluing their culture. The teacher who teaches American literature and does not refer to one African-American writer is doing a disservice to students of all cultural backgrounds. Equally so, the teacher who teaches music and does not mention one composition by an African American is de-centering the African-American child and miseducating the rest of the children.

Certainly some schools and teachers do better than others. And, in some cases, the child will get a sense of the importance of African and African-American contributions to human knowledge. But, for the most part, the African-American child fails to find a sense of identification with the information being presented.

The rise of cultural manifestations in the clothing, concepts, and motifs of African Americans is a direct result of the Afrocentric movement. Growing from a sense of the necessity for relocation, the reawakening within the African-American community portends positive developments on the educational level.

> By "centering" their students of color, teachers can reduce feelings of dislocation engendered by our society's predominantly "white self-esteem curriculums."

Achieving Success Through Congruence

The role of the teacher is to make the student's world and the classroom congruent. Language, examples, and concepts must be relevant. As all teachers know, this is a risky maneuver because relating classroom experience to outside experience depends to a large degree on the teacher's ability to know the student's cultural location as well as the subject. One does not have to constantly maintain congruence to be successful, however, one needs only to have an openness to the possibility that the student who is not of European ancestry may need to be centered in a particular way. Such centering techniques as examples from history, from books, from real life situations may also be helpful to other students.

Of course, the choice of examples is as important as knowing that you should have some centering devices. I once knew a white teacher in California who thought that he was being aware of his Mexican-American students by referring to an incident with "wetbacks" along the Texas-Mexico border. He thought the students would understand that he was trying to bring them into his discussion on the politics of the third world. When the students complained to him and the principal, the teacher was shocked and still could not see his mistake.

Therefore, teachers must read information from the cultures of their students. Should teachers have Cambodian students, then they must know something about Cambodians. Should teachers teach African-American students, then they must read information from African-American studies. This means that teachers must examine their lessons to see that they do not contain pejoratives about African Americans or other ethnic groups. Otherwise, they will not be empowered with the class.

Ideally, an Afrocentric program should be infused throughout the class period, not merely tagged on or added as a once-a-month feature. Resources for teaching with an Afrocentric approach are available from two major sources: Africa World Press of Trenton, New Jersey, and the GRIO publishing company of Philadelphia. Materials include books for all grades, informational packets, Afrocentric Kits, bibliographies, and sample lessons plans.

Toward Multicultural Classrooms

What do the principles of an Afrocentric approach look like in the classroom? In the Hatch Middle School in Camden, New Jersey, Principal Jan Gillespie and her teachers have organized the Molefi Asante Multicultural Academy. Utilizing the resources of the students' families, the academy's emphasis is on centering the children, treating each person's heritage with respect, and studying to learn about each other as a way to knowledge about self and the world.

Beyond raising the level of self-confidence among its students, the academy has become a training ground for teachers interested in building respect for cultural diversity as a way to empower teachers.

Students often do what they see their teachers doing and, consequently, as the best teachers soar like eagles, their students soar with them.

Our society is a composite of many ethnic and racial groups, and all students should be able to converse about the cultural diversity of the nation. Thus, both content and process are important in an Afrocentric approach to teaching. By combining the best elements of the centering process reminiscent of the segregation era with the best of today's more sophisticated techniques and equipment, we might find a new synthesis in our ability to teach children.

Molefi Kete Asante is Professor and Chair, Department of African-American Studies, Temple University, Philadelphia, PA 19122. His books include The Afrocentric Idea *and* Kemet, Afrocentricity, and Knowledge.

Asante, Molefi Kete. (Dec 92/Jan 93). "Afrocentric Curriculum." Educational Leadership, 49, 4:28-31. Reprinted with permission of the Association for Supervision and Curriculum Development. Copyright © 1992 by the Association for Supervision and Curriculum Development. All rights reserved.

The media has played a strong role in mystifying and stereotyping Asian Americans as a "model minority". The following article explores some of the recurring myths.

Asian Americans: Model Minority or Double Minority?

Arthur Hu

If the 1980's herald the start of the "New Age," then Asian Americans are America's "New" minority. Although Asians have been a part of America for over a century, it has only been in the past decade that they are slowly making an impact on mainstream society. Their population has tripled since 1970 when they were only two-thirds of one percent of Americans.[1]

Even today, Asians compose barely more than 2 percent of the population. However, they have become the largest, not smallest, minority in many career fields and also at many elite colleges. In 1980, when Asian Americans were just 1.5 percent of the population, they were 5 percent of the engineers and 8 percent of all doctors in the country.[2] In either field, Asians outnumbered Blacks and Hispanics combined. Asian businesses generated more revenues nationally than any other minority group.[3] As history

has often shown, the overall population proportion of a group can have little bearing on its actual impact on a society.

The striking presence of Asians in America's elite colleges is probably the most important portent of how they will affect the future. In 1987, Asian Americans were 13 percent of admitted freshmen at Harvard[4] and 25 percent at UC Berkeley.[5] But that was not all. Asians were some 30 percent of the entering women students at MIT[6] and over half of newly admitted engineering students at UC Berkeley.[7]

The ultimate impact of Asians is likely to be even greater as their numbers continue to increase. By the end of this century, the population of Asian Americans will grow again by one-half at current rates of birth and immigration.[8]

Even in the year 2000, Asians will be but a deceptively small 3

percent of all Americans. But judging by their success now, it is likely that by then, Asian Americans may comprise more than one-third of students at MIT and a clear majority of engineering students at UC Berkeley. Nationally, it is likely that they will be 10 percent of engineers and 16 percent of doctors.[9]

Since the 1970 Census, the average household income and education level of Asian Americans have been reported to be the highest of any racial group, and Asians have been promoted as the "Model Minority." There is also resentment from those who may have judged Asians as too successful. But perhaps the biggest controversy is whether this image of success is appropriate at all.

Many Asians live in urban areas where living costs are high, and their families have more workers than other American families, so median income data do not really provide a valid measure of their economic status.[10] Ronald Takaki of UC Berkeley has pointed out that Asian males in the San Francisco Bay area earned less than white males with comparable education. Though the Asian presence at Harvard and MIT may be strong, the much greater numbers of typical urban Asian youth stand very little chance of ever making it into such a school.

But closer examination of the 1980 Census reveals more details. The data show that Asians have the highest income of any racial group per household. But median per capita, or per person, income of $7,307 was 10 percent lower than for white households. This is mostly due to the large size of Asian families, which, at 3.8 persons, nearly matches that of the Hispanics. This is not the result of a high fertility rate, because Asians actually bear the fewest number of children per woman. Rather, the lower per capita findings are based on extended families and an immigrant population with many young adults who have small children. Though white families actually have more children, they are more likely to have grown up and left the household.[11]

"Model Minority" Thesis: Reality or Media Myth?

There seems to be a raging battle as to whether the "Model Minority" thesis is real or only a media myth. In my analysis of U.S. Census data and College Board statistics, I believe that both viewpoints are wrong and perhaps also a bit right. Asians, in my view, are the only major racial group that can be best characterized as a "double" minority. Depending on which Asians you

choose, they fit both the pattern of a privileged "overminority" and a disadvantaged "underminority."

But how can this be? Traditional "Civil Rights" thinking classifies all persons into only two categories. The white majority predominates among the rich and upper levels, while it discriminates against a weaker, nonwhite minority. Depending on one's political philosophy, Asians are either considered to be White because they do better than average, or they are seen as a minority because of the persistence of discrimination and poverty in urban neighborhoods. There have been few, if any, studies that take into account the possibility that Asians equally fit both patterns at the same time.

The problem lies with the use of a single average to characterize an entire population. Only a small number of people in any given group are exactly average. Populations are better described by a hill-shaped, normal distribution curve where the greatest number is close to the average. Usually, the bulk in any given group lies either clearly above or below the average. A high, white median income is indicative of consistently higher incomes for Whites and lower incomes for Blacks.

But Asians have what has been called a "square," or "bipolar," distribution. In fact, the normal curve is much wider for Asians than for other groups, with proportionally far more people both above and below the average, and relatively fewer persons in the middle. This is the result of the history of Asian immigration, which includes substantial numbers of both professional and unskilled immigrants. Moreover, groups such as the Japa-

nese and Chinese have assimilated over four or more generations, while other Asians are recent immigrants, many of them impoverished refugees.

When persons at the extremes balance each other out, the result is an average that would lead one to believe that Asians are either just a bit better than average if judging by household income, or a bit worse on a per capita basis. But this hides the fact that Asians have unusual amounts of both wealth and poverty. In 1980, the proportion of Asians earning above $50,000 a year was 50 percent greater than for whites. But the poverty rate for Asians was also 38 percent greater. In contrast, the proportion of Asians in the middle, earning $15,000 per year, was 13 percent smaller than for whites.[12]

A study by the National Committee on Pay Equity found Asian American men to most likely to be both in high-paying fields, such as medicine and engineering, and in low status jobs, such as restaurant workers, porters, and groundskeepers.[13] In my own analysis of U.S. Census data, Asians were three to five times as likely as Whites to be engineers and doctors, but they were also two to four times as likely to be working long hours for low pay in sweatshops or restaurants.[14]

Low-paying jobs held by Asians often are at or below minimum wage and may not include health insurance. A study by the city of Boston found that 27 percent of Asians were uninsured, a rate two-and-a-half times greater than for Whites in the city.[15] Female garment workers were often the sole source of health insurance for their families.[16] Nationally, 90 percent of adult Chinese spoke their ancestral language, and nearly a third had difficulty with English, meaning that many were disqualified from jobs in mainstream American because of language handicaps.[17]

Do Asian American Women Face "Double Oppression?"

Even if we factor in the greater education of Asian males, the U.S. Census data show that median wages of all Asian males are still lower than for Whites. But what of Asian women? Many have stated that Asian women, as women of color, bear a double burden of being both female and minority.[18] But surprisingly, this is not borne out by the facts. The truth is that Asian American women working fulltime actually earned $11,502, 10 percent more than $10,512 for white women.[19] (Another little noted fact is that black women earned only 10 percent less than white women.) Another study showed that immigrant women reach earning parity with non-immigrant women sooner than do immigrant men, a finding that may be due in large part to the impact of Asian immigrant groups.[20]

Asian women are three and twelve times more likely than white women to be engineers and doctors.[21] Although women generally do not score as well as men on the math section of the SAT, Asian women in particular score nearly the same as white males.[22] Still, they are only half as likely as white males to tend to study engineering. In contrast, Asian women are 30 percent less likely than Whites to be in women's traditional occupations, such as school teachers, librarians, and secretaries.[23]

Compared to Whites, a higher percentage of Asian women work full-time, perhaps because of the underemployment of their husbands. In fact, if we combine the median wages for Asian men and women, it would be $28,905, slightly higher than $28,498 for a corresponding white couple.[24]

Although much has been made of the poverty in female-headed minority households, Asians have the smallest proportion of such households in Massachusetts. Nationally, only 11 percent of Asian households are headed by women, the same as for Whites, and considerably less than 20 percent for Hispanics and 38 percent for Blacks. The median income for female-headed Asian families was the highest at $12,126, compared with $11,384 for Whites, $7,271 for Blacks, and $6,937 for Hispanics.

The surprisingly high socioeconomic status of Asian women flies in the face of both traditional stereotypes and the activist view that all women of color are disadvantaged. Indeed, it seems that it is precisely because of such views that this phenomenon has been such well-kept secret. But why do Asian women do so well?

Although there is obviously need for further study, I would like to venture two contributing factors. Jayjia Hsia, a researcher for the Educational Testing Service, has observed that Asian women in this society are somewhat better accepted than men. Typically Asian traits such as reserve in manner and deference to authority may be interpreted as being "wimpy" in men. But they may be more favorably accepted in women, and many college admissions offices seem to be acting on this assumption.

Many immigrant women left Asia precisely to get away from gender restrictions. Many professional women came here in the fifties and sixties believing that American was truly the land of equal opportunity. But when they arrived, they found that most American women were housewives. Francis L.K. Hsu in *Americans and Chinese* observes that although Asian tradition holds back many women from advancement, they are often far less inhibited than Western women once barriers are removed, and they are far more likely to be taken seriously in society.

Although in the United States, we have been taught that women are, or, at least, should be equal to men, in reality the American concepts of "masculinity" and "femininity" enforce a host of cultural barriers to the advancement of women. It seems that Asian women do well not only because they have discarded their traditional barriers but also have not been assimilated enough to be affected by the cultural checks of American norms.

The relative success of Asian women is clearly an important factor in pushing household incomes above the average since Asian males continue to be paid less than white males despite their higher education. Thus, the view that Asians are better off than other Americans is at best misleading and at worse quite false.

The "Dual Minority" Effect in Education

The dual minority effect is also reflected in education. Fully one-third of Asian American adults have completed college, double the rate of Whites. Yet 6 percent have not even completed elementary school, triple the rate of Whites.[25] Asians received 19 percent of the highest SAT scores in 1988, if we count the number who received top scores in either math or verbal tests, so their presence in elite schools should not be surprising. But 14 percent of the worst SAT scores also went to Asian students, primarily because of poor verbal performance.[26]

Just how many of Asian students are super-students and under-students? In 1985, the top fifth of Asian students scored better than their white counterparts. But an even larger group, the bottom one-quarter, scored worse. Although Asian students in high income brackets and native speakers score even higher on their combined SATs than white students, the average verbal score of the one-quarter of Asian students who speak English as a second language was worse than for black students at any income level. Their combined math and verbal scores were not much better than for Blacks, even though their math scores were very strong, even better than the native, English-speaking Asians. This indicates that although the two groups of Asians are probably equally smart, one might not know this from their combined SAT scores. Over half of college-age Asians take the SATs, compared to 30 percent for Whites and 18 percent for Blacks.[27] It is difficult to use SAT averages to compare groups because we are comparing many of the weaker Asian candidates with the strongest candidates from other groups. But clearly, not all Asian students are star performers. *Newsweek* and *Time* may proclaim Asian Americans to be academic whizzes because of their slightly higher math scores.

But since Asians actually score lower than Whites on the combined sum of both math and verbal tests—and this is what colleges usually count—the SATs actually put Asians at a disadvantage.

The Split between Rich and Poor Asian Americans

The 1980 U.S. Census for the state of Massachusetts provides the most graphic example of the split between rich and poor Asians.[28] This state has a higher than average concentration of immigrant Asians, 69 percent compared to 58 percent nationally. Asians are about evenly split between urban and suburban areas. Though the state average household income for Asians is nearly the same as the overall average for all in the state, there is a substantial difference between suburban and urban Asians.

Suburban Asians had an average income some 20 percent greater than that of Whites. Over one-half have completed four years of college. One-fifth are scientists, engineers or doctors, compared to only 4 percent for Whites. There is little doubt that this group is at least relatively well-off, though even in the suburbs Asians have a slightly higher poverty rate than Whites.

But urban Asians in Massachusetts are quite another story. The median household income of $15,958 and the poverty rate of 28 percent were virtually the same for Blacks in the state, and the median family size of 3.9 is the largest of any group. Consequently, per capita income is even less than for Blacks. Even so, only 12 percent of urban Asian families received public assis-

tance, compared with 25 percent of Blacks.

Median full-time wages for either urban Asian men or women in Massachusetts were as low or lower than for either Blacks or Hispanics. One in eight of urban Asian adults did not complete elementary school, a higher rate than any other racial group in the state and a reflection of the large number of Asian immigrants from rural areas. Nearly 40 percent of Asian men worked in restaurants, and one-quarter of women worked in garment factories in 1980.

Ethnic origins also divide the Asians economically. Nationally, only two Asian American groups, the Japanese and Asian Indians, have national, full-time employment median household incomes that are appreciably greater than that of white households. All other Asian groups do no better, or even worse, than Whites. Vietnamese median incomes are among the lowest, falling between the incomes of Blacks and Hispanics.[29]

There are many components to this ethnic disparity. Measured by household income in the 1980 Census, the Japanese Americans at $22,157 have the highest, and the Vietnamese at $12,549 the lowest socioeconomic status of any Asian ethnic group. The poverty rate of Japanese is only 6.5 percent but for the Vietnamese, it is 35.5 percent. While the Affluence of the Japanese Americans exceeds even that of Whites, the poverty of the Vietnamese is comparable to that of Blacks.

Separate census figures are not available for other Southeast Asian refugee groups, many of whom have immigrated since the 1980 Census. It is also important to note that a large percentage of the pre-1980 Southeast Asians were from the educated Vietnamese middle classes. But many of the newest arrivals are not well educated or accustomed to western culture. We can only assume that Laotians, Cambodians, and the latest wave of Vietnamese will fare even worse than the 1980 Census sample.

All but 10 percent of Vietnamese Americans are foreign born. In comparison, 72 percent of Japanese Americans are well-established, American-born natives, with the third generation already having children of their own. The recently released 1980 Census subject reports of Asian and Pacific Islanders show that among all Asians nationally, the mean income of foreign-born households was $23,190, or $1,437 less than the American-born households. Of Chinese households, 74 percent were foreign born in 1980. While the mean household income of $22,470 was nearly the same as the $21,173 of Whites, American-born Chinese earned $26,900. This is very significant disparity of some 20 percent and $4,434 due solely to immigrant status.

The median age of Vietnamese is 21.5, so nearly half of Vietnamese Americans are children. In contrast, the Japanese are the eldest of Asian Americans. With a median age of 33.5 years, a clear majority are well-established adults. At 3.24 and 4.68 persons respectively, Japanese have the smallest and Vietnamese the largest Asian families. The Vietnamese have birth rates and fertility rates which are double that of the Japanese. The California Health Department reported that in 1980, Vietnamese infant mortality rates were double that for most other Asians. Of Vietnamese families, 25 percent were not headed by both parents, compared to only 13 percent for the Japanese.

Interestingly enough, unlike the poverty statistics for other minorities, the figures for Asians do not have a proportional effect on education. Nearly half of all Vietnamese aged twenty to twenty-one are in school, presumably in college, not far behind the 61 percent for Japanese. Vietnamese consistently do well in math classes and on tests, and they are the recipients of numerous awards in the nation's high schools. Among adults, the median education for Vietnamese is 12.4 years, only a half year less than for Japanese. (A table summarizing 1980 Census data for Asian American groups is provided as an appendix to this article.)

In Boston and Seattle, Asian high school students have a dropout rate which is barely half that of other students.[30] But there is a great disparity between Chinese and Japanese American students, some of whom are the American-born fifth generation, and recent Southeast Asian refugees. Much has been made of the achievement level of many Vietnamese and Cambodian students. Yet relatively little has been said about the considerable toll taken on Southeast Asian youngsters by social adjustment and economic problems which have caused a disturbing increase in the Asian dropout rate in Boston since the start of the decade.

Asian Americans and Affirmative Action

Should Asians be a minority in terms of affirmative action? Although many federal laws and affirmative action programs specifically mention Asian Americans as a minority, this practice is increasingly being questioned as it is no longer obvious that Asians are disadvantaged. When Asian incomes and representation in many key fields surpass that of Whites, how can one argue that Asians deserve special consideration?

We now hear the terms "under-represented" and "non-Asian" minorities. Even "under-represented" is not necessarily appropriate because Puerto Rican students are actually over proportion at MIT due to the proximity to their ethnic concentration in the Northeast. It is becoming obvious that "nonwhite" is not the same as "disadvantaged."

At Tufts University, Asian students continue to receive admissions consideration as minority students, even though Asians are already over four times their national proportion.[31] At MIT, women are admitted at twice the rate of men, and Asian women are no exception. But while women in general may be under-represented at MIT, Asian women were already ten times over their proportion in 1986. In some years, MIT has admitted Asians at a higher rate than other groups. But upon analysis of statistics, I found that this was only because Asians had the largest proportion of women, not because of any preference for Asians as a group.[32]

When the stated goal of many affirmative action advocates is for representation which "reflects the diversity of that of the population," how can this be reconciled with the fact that Asian Americans are seven times over their proportion at Harvard, and Chinese are twenty times over their proportion at MIT? At either Stanford, Harvard, or MIT,

Asians and Jews combined comprise over one-third of all new undergraduates, even though together they account for less than 5 percent of Americans.[33]

Some fear that Asians are crowding out other minorities. Indeed, since the early 1980s, Asians have become the largest minority on many campuses. But, if anything, Blacks and Hispanics have actually gained at MIT, even though Asians quadrupled from 5 percent to 20 percent over the past decade. Rather, it is the proportion of white students that has fallen from 90 percent in 1974 to 68 percent at MIT in 1985. While the national proportion of white students was 73 percent, Whites have become an under-represented majority at MIT. This is also the case at Stanford and Harvard. At UCLA and UC Berkeley, non-Hispanic Whites are not even a 50 percent majority of entering students, and every group is now a minority.[34]

In the early part of the century, the Jews presented a similar "problem," which was simply addressed by the use of quotas. Today, such practices would be banned by the Civil Rights Act of 1964. Yet certain trends have led many to ask if the same sort of thing is now secretly happening to Asians. Judging by admission rates, Brown University evidently dropped affirmative action for Asians in 1979. By 1983 there were charges that the lower admission rates for Asians were indicative of admissions bias against Asians who had to score higher on their SATs than white applicants. Many other Ivy League schools, including Yale and Harvard, admit Asians at a lower rate than other students, even though their academic credentials, and often their

non-academic credentials, are as good as or better than other students.[35]

In 1986, Stanford nearly doubled the number of admitted Asian American students after a special committee concluded that Asian applicants were probably the victims of "subjective" bias.[36] Both UC Berkeley and UCLA have been under scrutiny since 1984 when the number of Asians admitted decreased despite increasing applications. That year, admission rates for Asians were 20 percent lower than rates for Whites at either campus. Minorities increased by 5 percentage points at Berkeley in response to a legislative mandate, but Asians decreased by nearly the same amount without explanation. Evidently in response to the controversy, parity with white admission rates was quietly restored by both campuses by 1986. It has also been noted that the number of Chinese students at UC Berkeley is now fewer than at any time before 1975.[37]

Though evidently no school has a Bakke-style, fixed quota that could be immediately struck down, there do seem to be a number of adverse factors. Asians who have learned English as a second language score on the average 160 points lower on the combined SATs than native speakers even though their math scores and grade points are comparable. This can make an otherwise excellent student appear unqualified solely on the basis of test scores. There were rumors that verbal score test cutoffs had much to do with the decrease in Asians at UC Berkeley. While the admissions office at MIT greatly discounts the significance of verbal scores of non-native speak-

ers, not all schools are so sophisticated.

At some liberal arts colleges, including Brown and Princeton, Asian students have been judged to be "narrower" in background than Whites. However, other schools, such as MIT have not found this to be the case, and the Stanford admissions committee concluded that such judgments may be largely subjective.

Harvard and Brown claim that Asians are admitted at a lower rate solely because of preferences for athletes and children of alumni. Alumni children are admitted at 2.5 times the average rate, and one of four white students falls under this category. With a bit of algebra, one can compute that if Asian American students are even one-half as likely as Whites to be alumni children, this preference alone can account for the 10 percent gap between white and Asian admission rates before 1982. But it does not explain why Asian admission rates were 20 percent lower than Whites after 1982, and why they changed back to 10 percent after 1986 following campus controversies. Harvard dismissed as irrelevant in 1985 the fact that enrollments of Asians and Hispanics, the two groups most threatening to maintaining white and black enrollments, did not increase at all between 1982 and 1985. Both Harvard and UCLA are now under investigation by the Department of Education to determine if they have discriminated against Asian Americans.[38]

Parents could encourage their children to be more active in sports. But how fair is an alumni preference when the vast majority of parents of Asian students are immigrants who never had a chance to attend Harvard? Black and Hispanic students have affirmative action to compensate for this imbalance, but Asian students do not. Though alumni preferences are not strictly racial in intent, they do seem to have the same effect, and this may have interesting legal ramifications.

Another problem is the reluctance of admissions offices to release information on test score distributions and admission and enrollment rates by race and gender. Some data is made public to the campus newspaper year by year, but it is often extremely difficult to get concise summary data for several years. Despite making requests for such data from Harvard officials for three years, I could not get this information. Such protection from public scrutiny may enable schools to preach equality while actually practicing a complex system of preferences.

What does all this mean for affirmative action? For one thing, admissions committees really cannot apply blanket preferences to a group strictly on the basis of over- and under-representation. Though Asians are an extreme case, all ethnic groups have both privileged and disadvantaged members who should be treated individually. The bilingual student in an inner city school whose parents work overtime to earn poverty level wages in Chinatown is clearly not the same

as the suburban Asian who goes to an upper middle class high school that sends everyone to college.

Using strict population proportions cause problems simply because they bear no resemblance to the actual distribution of academic skills in America. How could one justify setting a goal of 2 percent for Asians at MIT when 14 percent of those who scored high enough on the SATs to qualify were Asian?

UC Berkeley has taken proportional minority representation to such an extent that black students are over their state proportion, while it is Whites who are actually 15 percent below their state proportion. It is already widely acknowledged that many more minorities are admitted to the UC system than actually meet the normal minimal qualifications in order to meet affirmative action goals.[39]

"Over-minorities," such as Asians, may take more than their share, but this is because of higher academic qualifications. This may reduce the number of spots for other students, but to do otherwise would require the use of illegal restrictive quotas. The remaining spots should be divided fairly among other groups, and current population estimates should be used. However, admissions committees should realize that the figures for Asians and Hispanics in the eighteen-year-old category may have

grown by as much as 50 percent since the 1980 Census. So goals based on old census data could be unfair to these immigrant groups.

"Diversity" should not be used as a justification to exclude those who have the diligence and will to perform better than others. It is one thing to help those who have fallen behind, but it is quite another thing to penalize excellence in order to preserve mediocrity.

With there recent rise in racial violence against Asians, it would appear that Asian success rates may be causing resentment. But Asian academic performance should not be seen as a problem. Rather, it should serve as an example of how the American system still provides opportunities through education and how even low income families can send their children to the best schools.

America was built by immigrants. If every immigrant took away one job, America would have gone out of business long ago. Instead, America has grown into an economic powerhouse. Asians are a new and dynamic, if unusual, addition to America's great mosaic of cultural heritage. Rather than fearing the newcomers, we should welcome their arrival as an opportunity to learn from each other as we live and work together in this diverse land.

Notes

1. Department of Commerce, Bureau of the Census, 1980 *Census of Population PC801C1, Vol. 1, Chapter C, General Social and Economic Characteristics.* See also 1970 Census.

2. Computed from data in *Census 1980 PC801C1*, tables 125 and 126 (Occupation and Industry by Race).

3. "Asians, Native Americans Top Minority Entrepreneurs," *USA Today* (5 December 1986), 11A.

4. "Harvard to Offer 2166 Spots in Class of 1991," *Harvard Crimson* (10 April 1987), 1.

5. Office of Student Research, University of California, Berkeley.

6. MIT admissions office.

7. "Admissiongate: U.C. Berkeley Discriminates Against Qualified Asians," *East/West* (11 December 1986), 1.

8. Computed estimates based on 1970 Census and 1980 Census and current immigration and birth rates.

9. 1980 proportions are scaled by projected growth in population.

10. "Success of Asian Americans: Fact or Fiction?" U.S. Commission on Civil Rights, September 1980.

11. 1980 Census, table 111 (Income), table 121 (Fertility and Family Composition), and table 120 (General Characteristics).

12. 1980 Census, tables 111 and 113 (Income and Poverty by Race).

13. "Study: Race, Sex Bias in Work Force," *Boston Globe* (30 June 1987), 1.

14. 1980 Census, tables 125 and 126 (Industry and Occupation by Race).

15. Larry Tye, "Hub Study: 15% Have No Health Plan," *Boston Globe* (30 June 1987), 1. Based on *Boston Committee on Access to Health Care Report*, June 1987.

16. Shirley Mark Yuen and Teresa Feng, "Coping with Unemployment, the Struggle of the PSC Garment Workers," *Asian American Resource Workshop Newsletter*, Boston, Massachusetts, June 1986.

17. Department of Commerce, Bureau of the Census, *Statistical Abstract of the United States 1985*, table 43 (Current Languages Spoken at Home).

18. "Asian Women Are Still Paid Far Less Than Their White Counterparts," AARW Newsletter, April 1987. Excerpts taken from a speech by Rahan Jalan at Smith College, "Issues Concerning Asian Women in America."

19. 1980 Census table 128 (Income by Race). Data for all working women, age fifteen and above, indicate that Whites earned $5336 and Asians $6685, or 24 percent higher than for Whites. For full-time workers, median wages for white women were $10,512, compared to the 9.4 percent higher wage of $11,502 for Asian women. I have talked to a number of Asian American Studies experts who disbelieve this statistic. But it has been cited in studies since 1965 and in the 1970 Census as well.

20. Susan Edmiston, "1986: Year of the Woman Immigrant," *Working Woman* (July 1986), 53.

21. 1980 Census, tables 125 and 126 (Occupation and Industry by Race).

22. SAT Math scores for 1986 admissions applicants indicate that white males scored 721 females 694; Asian males 729 and females 714. See also Leonard Ramist and Solomon Arbeiter, "Profiles, College-bound Seniors, 1985," available from the College Board.

23. 1980 Census, table 128.

24. 1980 Census, table 123 (Education by Race).

25. Ibid.

26. Ramist and Arbeiter, "Profiles," unpublished data, 1988.

27. Actually, the College Board in "Profiles" says that 70 percent of Asian American eighteen-year-olds took the SAT. However, this figure is based on the 1980 population and does not take new immigration into account. The 50 percent figure is based on my own, more accurate population estimate of Asian Eighteen-year-olds and 1980 SAT registration forms.

28. U.S. Department of Commerce, Bureau of the Census, *1980 Census of the Population PC801C23, General Social and Economic Characteristics, State of Massachusetts*.

29. "A Super Minority Tops Out," *Newsweek* (11 May 1987).

30. "New Test Figures Clarify Minority Gap," *Seattle Post Intelligencer* (16 January 1987), E1. See also "Crisis in Immigrants Dropout Rate," *Boston Globe* (1 November 1986), 19.

31. Tufts Admissions Office, 1984.

32. Arthur Hu, "College Enrollments Suggest Asian Quotas," *The Tech* (MIT) (20 February 1987), 4. See also Arthur Hu, "Women Are Favored at MIT," *The Tech* (27 February 1988), 4.

33. See "Top Scholars Spearhead Jewish Studies Program," *Stanford Observer* (November 1986); "Book Details Discrimination Against Jewish Students," *Boston Globe* (9 March 1986), A23; and "Yale's Limit on Jewish Enrollment Lasted until Early 1960s, Book Says," *New York Times* (4 March 1986), B1.

34. "Over Half of UCLA's Freshman Are Now Minorities," *East/West* (25 September 1988), 4. See also "Asian Students, Numerous and Successful, Change Berkeley Campus," *Boston Globe* (5 January 1986), B1.

35. "Asian Americans Question Ivy League's Policies," *New York Times* (30 May 1985), B1.

36. "Asian Freshmen at Stanford Officially Double in One Year," *East/West* (19 September 1988), 4. Reprinted from *San Francisco Examiner* (29 August 1986).

37. "Admissionsgate"; see also, Office of Student Research, UCB, *Report by the Auditor General Review of the First-Year Admissions of Asians and Caucasians at UC Berkeley*, UCLA Planning Office.

38. Suzie Chao and Dean William Fitzsimmons, "Statement on

Asian American Admissions," *Harvard Gazette* (22 January 1988). Alumni childrens' admit rate is from Harvard Admissions Office. Applications and admit data from *Harvard Crimson* articles, 1980-1988. See also, "Limit on Minorities Denied," *Harvard Crimson* (6 December 1985); and "Federal Probers Check Harvard for Asian Quota," *Boston Globe* (18 November 1988), 21.

39. James S. Gibney, "The Berkeley Squeeze," *The New Republic* (11 April 1988), 15.

Arthur Hu is an independent researcher and writer who lives in Stoneham, Massachusetts. He works as the R&D group leader at Mosaic Software in Cambridge, Massachusetts. He received a B.S. and M.S. in Electrical Engineering and Computer Science from MIT in 1981.

Hu, Arthur. "Asian Americans: Model Minority or Double Minority?" Amerasia Journal 15:1 (1989): 243-57. Reprinted by permission.

Positive stereotypes can be just as distressing as negative ones. The pressure to conform to expectations based on racial or ethnic group membership is particularly difficult for high school students to withstand.

Fighting Stereotypes: 'Yellow' Among the White

Amy Wu and Elys A. McLean

I often wish that I could live in a place where yellow, red, white and black could become one. This dream has not come true.

In the land of white men, white crust and white suburban neighborhoods, I grew up as one of the few "yellow" kids in the neighborhood. Being spatters of yellow on a canvas of white male made us proud.

My father always taught me to stick my chin up high and hold my head straight. Ever since early childhood, I lived by the premise: "You are Chinese. Do not disappoint your race. Always accept defeat."

Defeat in a white world came often. Almost every "white" I encountered in school, neighborhood and even church had an image of a "yellow" person.

In junior high I was coaxed into the math club and practically forced to join the science club. When I failed miserably in the first math tournament, I endured weeks of laughter and mockery. "What kind of Chinese person doesn't do well in math?" I heard one fellow "yellow" math genius say to her friend. I had disappointed my race, quickly becoming the center of curiosity and then dislike. The few other "yellows" in the school seemed to satisfy everyone's expectation of what an Oriental should be-a genius, high IQ, math whiz, science star, honor roll every quarter, Harvard material. They fit the mold.

I was the only yellow person who didn't seem to excel in math or science-and my father's being a biochemist made it even worse. During a dissection of worms, I almost cut off the worm's head accidentally. Once, when I decided to pursue acting, I was met with frowns of disapproval.

"I didn't know a Chinese could act," one white slice said.

What many whites didn't know was that I grew up in cruelty and confusion. When I was 9, I came home to find "chink" sprayed across our newly paved driveway. I wanted to kill whoever wrote that.

From elementary school on, my very Chinese last name became the center of jokes. I learned to cope with the ignorance by pretending not to hear or see it. There were times when I would fall into a world of depression, once wishing that I had been born white, another time wishing that the "yellows" outnumbered the "whites." Some white people who decided I was "OK" would ask me questions that made me laugh inside.

"Are you Buddhist?" "Are you a communist?"

Once, in global studies, we discussed the history of Japan.

"Ask Amy, she'll know!" voices began to cry.

"I'm not Japanese!" I said, seething with anger.

Another time, a scroll filled with Chinese characters was placed before me.

"What does it mean?" they asked.

It was very difficult explaining to 26 blank faces that I could not read Chinese, and the only thing that I could write was my name. I learned that being one of the few "yellows" in the land of white makes everything into a world of proving and explaining.

My mom once told me that I was a representative of the Chinese race and that I would have to prove to those Mei *gua yuan* (Americans) that I was more capable of doing things than they. I have not reached that goal. I often wish that I could live in a place where yellow, red, white and black could become one. This dream has not come true. For now, I am still-the yellow.

Amy Wu is a student at Thornwood, New York.

Elys A. McLean is a writer for USA Today.

USA Today, July 7, 1992, 11A. Copyright 1992, USA TODAY. Reprinted by permission.

Hispanics, one of the largest minority groups in the United States today, are becoming a growing presence in our urban as well as rural schools. To better serve this group of students, educators must be trained in the cultural and linguistic differences found within this group.

Understanding the Hispanic Student

John M. Dodd, J. Ron Nelson, and Esther Peralez

Hispanics are becoming the largest minority group in the United States (Valero-Figueroa, 1988, Yates, 1988). Many Hispanics drop out of high school without graduating and very few continue on to graduate from college (Fields, 1988). There is also concern and vigilance regarding the over-representation of minority groups in special education (e.g., Chinn and Hughes, 1987). Experts have pointed out the importance of differentiating between behaviors which indicate the presence of learning disabilities and those which are characteristic of student' cultural or linguistic backgrounds (e.g. Collier & Hoover, 1987). As the number of Hispanic students increases in rural schools, personnel must consider students' cultural and linguistic characteristics when they are evaluating these students for special education services.

Many Spanish language editions of tests have been developed and are available to assess the potential and achievement in the Spanish-speaking students' primary language (McLaughlin & Lewis, 1986). Educational testers can use the language which elicits maximal performance from the student. Nuttal (1987) reported there is a scarcity of qualified bilingual testers available to use these instruments. Additionally, Kelker (1981) said expectations of resource room teachers are particularly high in rural areas. However, Dodd (1981) pointed out that P1-94-142 provides a free and appropriate education for all children, without regard to whether they live in rural or urban areas.

In addition to identifying and classifying Hispanic students with learning disabilities, teachers must consider cultural and linguistic characteristics and increase opportunities for positive school experiences for Hispanic students and their families. There is a growing conviction that Hispanic students should become thoroughly grounded in the language in which their parents feel most comfortable (e.g., Cummins, 1983). Supporting this notion, there is evidence to suggest that learning a second language (i.e. English) is easier after a thorough grounding in a first language (Cummins, 1979).

Although some Hispanic students are fully assimilated, serving the needs of those less assimilated as well as those with learning disabilities requires a variety of special services and technologies. Teachers who are aware of Hispanic cultural and linguistic characteristics can use such services to maximize the students' learning experience.

It is easier to implement adaptations in urban areas, where one finds a large neighborhood ("el barrio") of Hispanic persons and even a majority of Hispanic students than in rural areas. Students in "el barrio," which abound with bilingual persons, are able to experience a feeling of belonging within the Hispanic culture where a great many customs are maintained.

Dodd (1981) pointed out that rural schools must often form partnerships with other schools in order to provide appropriate services. However, the number of at-risk students is increasing in rural areas (Helge, 1988). They may be permanent residents of the community or they may be children of migrant workers, the highest percentage of whom come from Spanish-speaking homes (Baca and Harris, 1988). There are hundreds of small communities with schools in which there are only a few Hispanic students who are in the minority and can not experience the same feeling of belonging as their urban counterparts.

Chavex, Burton, and Lopez (1986; 1987) reported both rural and urban teachers indicate they lack skills required for teaching bilingual children. The requirement for appropriate services, however, does not respect the shortage of resources in rural areas. Solutions may require more creativity and effort in rural areas, but the problem must be addressed. While it is important to recognize that there are distinct cultures and values among the various Hispanic groups and regions, the purpose of this paper is to present information on cultural and linguistic characteristics of His-

panic students in non-urban environments which school personnel must recognize. In addition, suggested techniques for dealing with cultural and linguistic differences are presented.

Mexican-American Families

Family and community are central to Hispanic and/or Mexican-American society. It is essential for teachers who work with these children to have an understanding of and sensitivity to both the Hispanic family and their community. The family is the most valued institution in the Hispanic and Mexican-American society (Riding, 1984). One remains loyal to the family at all costs (Gomez, 1972). Within the family, respect is based on both age and gender. The oldest male is the head of the household (Gomez, 1972). However, although the father is the authority figure, it is the mother who is the source of strength for the family. In addition, the older members of the family command the younger members, and the males command the females.

The extended family is important. For example, one becomes an aunt to second cousins and the respect offered is similar to that given any aunt. Even moving to a distant location does not break down the family. In place of those who have left the family, there are godparents, elders, and neighbors. They are treated with the same respect as would be any member of the family. For instance, children who do not have a grandfather or grandmother living in their community will be nurtured and cared for by another family's grandparents. They will ex-

change invitations with the child and his family for special functions and holiday celebrations. In addition, their religious training and values are provided by the adoptive grandparents.

Language

Students whose primary language is Spanish or who have learned English from parents or guardians whose primary language is Spanish may exhibit language differences. For example, the possessive is formed differently and a student may say "the family of Roy" rather than "Roy's family." In Spanish the sound of every letter is pronounced. Therefore, the bilingual student may pronounce more syllables than the English-speaking person would. For example, in the name Laura the u may also be pronounced, adding an extra syllable. Also, because the word order is different, the Hispanic may say "the house blue is mine."

In addition, there are a great many cognates between English and Spanish. For instance, "el carro" is car in Spanish and Hispanics may have a tendency to add an o sound to the word car. The Hispanic may pronounce the word as though it were in Spanish although it is embedded in an English sentence. Inflections or accents follow different rules in Spanish. The Hispanic may talk about a "cowboy" with the "boy" rather than "cow" being accented. Many students growing up in Hispanic homes may have learned "Spanglish." For example, "truck" may be "trocka" and "sandwich," "sangewiche." They also may engage in "code switching," meaning that sentences will contain both Spanish and English.

If teachers have a Spanish speaker in their classrooms, every attempt must be made to meet that student's needs. It is important to teach the student the conventions used in the English language, to point out the rationale for them and to indicate the differences between Spanish and English. Initially directions, reprimands, and endearments can be given in Spanish which may have more meaning for the child. If children are told "escuchen," it may have more of an impact than "listen." Talking to "la familia" may help in finding out what those key terms are. Using a Spanish/English dictionary is often necessary. The teacher must not confuse accent with inability to communicate as some of the most eloquent English speakers of Hispanic origin are those who are articulate first in their own language.

Motivation

Hispanic children are encouraged at a very early age to become educated. For example, many Hispanics have grown up hearing "Estudio para que no seas burros como nosotros," which means "Study and learn everything you can so you are not ignorant like us (parents)." If children have the "ganas" (want), they will achieve that goal.

Typically, teachers use instructional practices in their classrooms that emphasize competition and individualism (Buffington, 1988). In contrast, Hispanic children are taught to be cooperative and to have a sense of community (Connoly and Tucker, 1982). As a result of this conflict, many times Hispanic children do not see the relevance of the instruction in their school. Therefore, they may not achieve academi-

cally or appear to have high academic aspirations. For some Hispanic students their "ganas" fades.

Schools must help these children keep their "ganas." This can be accomplished by activities in which the children can work together since Hispanic children feel more comfortable when attempting new tasks or being placed in new situations if they are allowed to work together. In addition, including Mexican role models in school presentations, and materials that address Mexican culture, as well as celebrating Mexican holidays along with American holidays can be useful.

Mysticism

Mysticism, the doctrine of attaining knowledge of spiritual truths, plays a significant role in Mexican American society. When inexplicable things happen, Mexicans might explain it by saying that the person was bewitched or "embrujado" (Elsasser, MacKenzie, Tixier y Vigil, 1980). An example of this phenomenon would be "el ojo" (the evil eye). Sometimes it may be given innocently, such as in a case when a person admires a child so much and leaves without hugging or kissing the child. Or, it may be given to cause "bad luck" or illness to someone who may have caused problems or pain to the family. In either case, sickness may be the result. If this happens, las "curanderas" or "curanderos," people who have healed others for centuries, are called upon for an explanation of what happened or to bring healing. The "curandero" has an important role because it is he who makes house calls when something goes wrong.

Machismo

Machismo is part of the Hispanic and/or Mexican American culture. Men are taught to act proud, self-reliant, and virile. Next to devotion to the family, a man's manliness outweighs all other aspects of prestige. He represents his family and must do so with honor and devotion. This honor and respect are associated with lack of indebtedness (Gomez, 1972). For example, a Mexican-American man will be reluctant to seek help from institutions because acceptance of charity is humiliating. Additionally, he must not be wrong and will not state his opinion unless he is willing to defend it. Therefore, when asked his opinion he may only smile and look knowingly and perhaps say "maybe so" until he is willing to state and defend his opinion.

However, there is a contradiction. While he is trying to be strong and manly, he is also taught to respect his elders, and to love his family. Furthermore, he is taught that he can show his emotions. He can hug another man or cry. However, it must be done without embarrassment to the family. It is not unusual to see a man become putty in the hands of his mother, aunts, or children.

Touching

Touching is an important part of interpersonal communication in the Mexican-American and/or Hispanic culture. A required distance between people is almost non-existent. Handshakes are frequent among acquaintances and hugs are expected among family and close friends. In addition, touching is used in everyday conversation to make a statement or to emphasize a particular point. More importantly, it is used spontaneously, without threat of rejection, to show excitement, love, and affection between people.

Time

To the Hispanic "ahora" (now) means sometime around the present. It is understood that other events may intervene and "now" may be extended considerably. The use of time is leisurely and considerate and waits for everyone. It does not preclude things being accomplished or completed, but it includes interruptions and delays.

Learning Disabled Hispanic Students

Understanding and accepting Hispanics and their culture, as well as the differences the children exhibit, may help prevent their overclassification for special education. However, there are Hispanic children who are learning disabled and need appropriate special education services. Those children need to be identified and provided the needed services. If their parents speak primarily Spanish, they should be communicated with in Spanish in order to obtain the necessary signed parental permission. It may be necessary to seek help from the high school Spanish teacher, but the parents have the right to be addressed in their language.

Learning disabled Hispanic children who are bilingual would exhibit the deficit regardless of the language employed to identify the learning disability. It is crucial that testers go that extra mile to deter-

mine if the problem is exhibited only when English is spoken. To determine this, it may be necessary to turn to one of the greatest strengths of the culture, the family, for linguistic support. Many of the child's family members are likely to be bilingual and the family will be interested in the welfare and progress of the child. Bilingual family members can be asked to elicit various responses from the child in Spanish. If the appropriate response is elicited in Spanish it would indicate the learning problem was due to cultural or language differences and the child should not be identified as a candidate for classification for special education.

When a Hispanic child is being considered of for special education placement the parents should be notified and invited in Spanish to participate in inter-disciplinary team meetings if Spanish is their primary language. However, school personnel should understand that for Hispanics, caring for children is the women's role. It will probably be the mother who attends the meeting. She will need to talk with her husband before she will feel comfortable about signing the individualized education plan (IEP). Therefore, she should be allowed time to discuss it with her husband. However, because she will regard time more flexibly than the school personnel do, it may be necessary to indicate to her the specific day and time she should return to the school to sign the IEP.

Implications-Summary

Ironically, the values instilled in Hispanic children who grow up with a strong cultural identity may also contribute to the difficulties

they experience as minority group members. Such children may find it difficult to adjust to an educational system that is designed to meet the needs of the majority population.

Hispanic students may feel incompetent or worthless because there may be little at school to which they can relate. Additionally, they may feel that they lack identity because school personnel give them names other than their own. For example, "Ricardo" may become "Richard" or "Ricky," "Raquael" may become "Rachel" and "Jesue," "Jesse." The implication is that the Anglicized name is somehow better or more proper which is disrespectful to the child and may have a negative effect. Although it may be difficult to pronounce the Spanish name, it is important to do so since a child's name is part of his or her identity.

The male Hispanic is responsible for maintaining the family's honor. However, because of this responsibility he may be made to believe he has less self-worth than the female child. Being reprimanded or told he is wrong may appear to him and other family members as diminishing family honor. The male Hispanic may "act up" to show that he is still "macho." Additionally, he may respond inappropriately to punishment because he must demonstrate he is manly and "can take it." Consequently, if a child needs to be reprimanded it should be done on an individual basis and the child should not be singled out if others have done the same thing.

It is important not to make sexist remarks when disciplining a Mexican child who already has well-defined sex roles as males or females. It may help to key Spanish terms-respecto (respect), ganas (want), estudia (study)—when pointing out misbehavior to the student. Also, whether disciplining a child or not, one must take the time to touch. For Hispanic children, communication is enhanced when there is no reluctance to show warmth or affection or just friendliness by touching.

The child may confront racist stereotypes for the first time in school. School personnel must be aware of ethnic stereotypes that may seem insignificant or funny, but which can be devastating to a child. Some examples of persisting stereotypes are:

1. The picture of the Mexican leaning against the cactus, wearing a huge sombrero and sleeping, which implies that Mexicans are lazy.

2. The song that has the sentence "Manana is good enough for me," which says that Mexicans put things off and do not take tasks seriously.

3. "Chicano time" implies that Mexicans cannot and will not be on time.

4. The term "wet back" or asking someone if they have a "green card" tells someone that they are not Americans.

There is a clear distinction in Hispanic cultures between male and female jobs. For example, if there is a project requiring food preparation the Hispanic male would be unlikely to participate. Therefore, teachers should avoid asking Hispanic male students to complete tasks which would be considered inappropriate within the Hispanic community, or to include other males so he does not feel he has been signaled out or that the task is anything he should feel bad about doing. If such assignments are not handled appropriately, the student will feel that his values have been attacked and he will have to make a decision about remaining in the classroom.

While the teacher may not understand the concept of "el ojo" the teacher should recognize that it is real for Mexican children and their parents. The reality and the reason

for being ill should be accepted without questioning.

Teachers need to realize that North American society is time-oriented; everything has to happen now and in the right sequence. In contrast, the Hispanic child may have grown up in a home where time is imprecise. They plan to go to class or to complete their assignment "some-time." Although this may seem to be evidence of lack of interest, in reality, the child wants to do what is required. However, the child has no sense of urgency to get it completed right now. If something needs to be done right now it may be best to point out when it is to be completed. For example, it would be appropriate to show where the hands on the clock should be when the task is completed. Since now has greater latitude in meaning it may be necessary to say "ahora mismo" (right now) when referring to things that must be done immediately. Similarly, in dealing with Hispanic parents, it is necessary to realize that they may view time flexibly and without a sense of urgency.

References

Baca, L. and Harris, K.C. "Teaching Migrant Exceptional Children," *Teaching Exceptional Children*, 20: 32-35.

Buffington, P.W. "Competition vs. Cooperation," *Sky*, 22-25, December, 1988.

Chavez, J. A., Burton, L. F. "The Needs of Rural and Urban Teachers in Bilingual Special Education," *The Rural Educator*, 8:8-12; Winter, 1986-87.

Chinn, P.C. and Hughes, S. "Representation of Minority Students in Special Education

Classes," *Remedial and Special Education*, 20:41-46; 1987.

Collier, C. & Hoover, J.J. "Sociocultural Consideration When Referring Minority Children," *Learning Disabilities Focus*, 3:39-45; 1987.

Connoly, L. H. and Tucker, S. M. "Motivating the Mexican American Student," Fact Sheet. ERIC Clearinghouse on Rural Education and Small Schools, Las Cruces: NM; 1982. (EIRC Document Reproduction Service No. ED 287-0657.

Cummins, J. "Linguistic Interdependence and the Educational Development of Bilingual Children," *Review of Education Research*, 49:222-251; 1979.

Cummins, J. "Bilingualism and Special Education: Program and Pedagogical Issues," *Learning Disabilities Quarterly*, 6:373-386; 1983.

Dodd, J.M. "Toward Special Services-Minue Prejudice," *Educational Considerations*, 8:13; 1981.

Elsasser, N., MacKenzie, K. and Tixier y Vigil, Y. *Las Mujeres*

Conversations from a Hispanic Community, The Feminist Press and the McGraw Book Co. New York, 1980.

Fields, C. "The Hispanic Pipeline: Narrow, Leaking and Needing Repair," *Change*, 20, 18-33; 1987.

Gomez, R. *The Changing Mexican American: A Reader*, The University of Texas Press, Austin, 1972.

Helge, D. "Serving At-Rick Populations in Rural America" *Teaching Exceptional Children*, 20:17-18; 1988.

Kelker, K.A. "Role Confusion in Rural Schools," *Educational Considerations*, 8:20-22; 1981.

McLoughlin, J. A. and Lewis, R. B. *Assessing Special Students*, Merrill Publishing Co., 1986.

Nuttal, E. V. "Survey of Current Practices on the Psychological Assessment of Limited-English Proficient Handicapped Children," *Journal of School Psychology*, 25:53-61; 1987.

Riding, A. *Distant Neighbors*, Random House, New York, 1984.

Valer-Figueroa, E. "Hispanic Children," *Teaching Exceptional Children*, 20:47-49; 1988.

John M. Dodd is Professor of Special Education, Institute for Habilitative Services at Eastern Montana College and Research Associate, American Indian Rehabilitation Research and Training Center at Northern Arizona University.

J. Ron Nelson is a doctoral candidate at Purdue University.

Esther Peralez is Director of the Student Opportunity Services at Eastern Montana College.

Reprinted by permission: The Rural Educator—Published by the National Rural Education Association.

To Juan Andrade,
assimilation was inevitable,
but, as he states, for him the
dominant institutional
influence was "several
formative years too late." As
you read this piece you will
come to understand how the
dominant culture attempted
to deny him any sense of
himself. With a strength born
long before his schooling,
Juan not only survived the
system but spends his life
seeing that others are
empowered and not destroyed.

Reflections on My Public Education

Juan Andrade, Jr.

Introduction: The Seeds of Endurance

A little over forty years ago I took the first of many steps toward that elusive high school diploma. As we who have successfully completed the process have realized in retrospect, it was really no big deal. But if it was no big deal, then why has it been so elusive to such a high percentage of White Americans, African Americans, and most Hispanics?

I don't know why everyone else drops out of school, but my Hispanidad is not wasted when it comes to knowing why Hispanics quit school.

We don't drop out, we are pushed out.

Well, if we're pushed, then how did some of us manage to finish high school? The answer does not lie in our ability to achieve, but in our ability to endure. Let me explain.

In northern occupied Mexico, a.k.a. Texas since 1848, Spanish-speaking children were expected to know English before they started school. In other words, we had to master a foreign language before entering the first grade! That wasn't such a bad idea, but it was not, unfortunately, required of all first graders. Welcome to Injustice 101.

Besides, with no television in the house and essentially monolingual (Spanish-speaking) parents and relatives around, English on our side of the tracks just wasn't going to happen. Language schools were out of the question. What's more, we weren't about to have our Hispanidad questioned by publicly harboring the silly notion of wanting to learn the language of those who conquered our ancestors, occupied our land, and exercised every means possible to relegate us to second-class citizenship (No soy pendejo!/I'm not stupid!).

It wasn't cool to pretend you were better than anybody else, and speaking English would trigger the whispers "se cree mucho" (he thinks he's too good) or "quiere ser bolillo" (he's a white wannabe). No thanks.

Unbelievable as it may sound, neo-nativists and others who have not learned from history are again proposing a return to the double standard of requiring Hispanic children to learn a foreign language before they enter the first grade. The reason is said to be financial, but it also provides cover for those that are simply anti-Hispanic, or anti language and cultural minority students. Still, I wouldn't disagree, if they would require all students to do the same.

For the record, I believe Hispanic children should learn English. Anybody who believes they don't need to learn English is a fool. But anybody who believes that English is the only language they need to learn is a bigger fool.

It would probably help to mention that the right to our Hispanidad (the right to maintain our language, customs, traditions, etc.) was guaranteed in the Treaty of Guadalupe Hidalgo between Mexico and the United States. But I'll defer to my Native American brothers and sisters to enlighten us on the sanctity of such guarantees.

At best we could be, or choose to remain, what we were (are), Spanish-speaking people, but society, in this case public education, was under no obligation to accept us or respect us for it. In other words, a double-edged sword.

But hey, what normal seven year old is not capable of making a responsible decision when having to choose between what he is and what he ought to be (according to those who believe they have the divine right to hold our future in their hands and can't understand why we want to be who we are, especially if that makes us different from them)?

But that wasn't all that was wrong. The teachers were, shall we say, "Spanish challenged." Bilingualism was not, and still is not, an accepted standard of excellence. Teachers were not required to know Spanish, and those who did were not allowed to speak it. I know, I was arrested on the third day of my teaching career for explaining democracy (of all things) in Spanish to a class that was predominantly Hispanic.

Monolingualism is the single most backward standard of education ever adopted by this country. Incredibly, we are the only nation in the world that believes a person can be educated and speak only one language. It's almost a contradiction in terms. Even in Haiti, the poorest nation in the western hemisphere with an illiteracy rate of 85 percent, most people speak French and Creole and many speak English too.

Ironically, the poorest and least educated people in America (Hispanics and Native Americans) speak two languages. It's like Mark Twain said, he never let his schooling get in the way of his education.

Humor, Church And Family: The Tools of Endurance

I should have seen it coming. "Looney" is no name for a school. Yet for two years, it would be the elementary school for my first and second grades. I'll never forget those first two years, the beginning of the great transformation from what I was, to what I ought to be, or, at the very least, to what I would become.

In retrospect, it was more like a sanctioned melt-down of my cultural constitution. Fortunately, school was not the dominant insti-

tutional force in my life. Had it been dominant, there is no telling who I would be today, or where I would be, doing what, let alone knowing why.

To be the most dominant force in my life, school would have had to take the place of my church and my family, and that wasn't going to happen. Frankly, had I not known who I was and been totally secure in who I was before I entered the first grade, I would have lost total control of the assimilation process that was about to begin.

Assimilation was inevitable. The question was to what degree and whether I would determine the degree. My greatest single achievement is probably that I never relinquished control over the process and that assimilation was contained. I am what I ought to be, a considerable enlargement of who I was, with all the rights and privileges pertaining thereto, and I like being who and what I am.

School never stood a chance in terms of being the dominant institutional influence in my life. In fact, it was several formative years too late for the dance. My very first recollection of childhood is being held in my mother's arms as a toddler while she stood in church singing "He lives, He lives, Christ Jesus lives today . . . you ask me how I know He lives, He lives within my heart." That's the English version of course. She actually sang it en Español, commonly known among the more enlightened sorts in the barrio as God's language.

I literally memorized hymns like "Holy, Holy, Holy," "When the Roll Is Called Up Yonder," and "How Great Thou Art" long before I learned to sing or read music, or just plain read! But "He Lives" was my favorite and the one my mother sang best.

I remember those services in that little Baptist mission in Brownwood, Texas very well. I almost never slept during the worship services. I couldn't. The preaching and the music was usually loud. But what was really loud was my mother's singing! The Bible says to make a joyful noise unto the Lord. My mother believed the Bible was the inspired word of God, and if He said to make a joyful noise, that's exactly what she was going to do! And man, what a joyful noise! I didn't yet know Christ as Lord of my life but my mother did. She explained to me what it meant to have Him living in your heart. She said I'd never be alone, that my sins would be forgiven, that He would sustain me during difficult times, help me make the right choices and decisions in life, and that I would have eternal life. I obviously had no idea what life had in store for me, but hey, God's gift was just too good to reject.

While I didn't receive Him as Lord and Savior until the ripe young age of 11, by the time I reached the first grade I had been told for years that I was special, that God loved me, that He had a purpose for me in life, and that it was my responsibility to prepare myself for whatever His will for me would be. What's more, it was made very clear to me that I was ultimately accountable for whatever use I made of the talent(s) God had given me.

These teachings did wonders for my self-esteem, and instilled in me a sense of invincibility and a dogged determination to persevere regardless of the obstacles that I would have to confront. Early in life I began to feel secure in who I was,

and was anxious to begin discovering whatever it was that I was to become.

To put it simply, the protective shield that would enable me to endure the twelve years of public education that awaited me began to manifest itself long before the first grade. In fact, by the time I reached the first grade I could speak Spanish, read Spanish, write Spanish, and sing, pray, think, and worship in Spanish. I became everything that was Spanish, and everything that was Spanish became me.

Thanks to my Christian parents, especially my mother's obediently joyful noise, the church quickly became the most powerful institutional force in my young life, a force that would sustain me through school.

My second recollection of childhood is picking cotton at roughly four years of age. We were migrant farmworkers. It was a rough life. The work was hard. The pay was bad. The dangers were endless. The working conditions were hazardous. Health care was nonexistent. There was no job security. An early death was commonplace, usually accidental or merely the results of a life expectancy of only 49 years.

Cesar Chavez was stuck in the same rut. The union that could give us hope and perhaps even a little justice was still years away. But there was a silver lining to our circumstances. What a way to learn and experience family unity.

For those who don't know, migrant housing is not just usually dilapidated, it's also extremely crowded. An entire family can live in one room, and if they're lucky, two rooms. If there's a house, it's normally shared by more than one family. We shared a small house

with our relatives on a cotton farm in McGregor, Texas. My father got a job with the railroad so he stayed in our hometown. Mother would take us five kids to work at the only place we could work, and that was in the cotton, onion, cabbage, cantaloupe, watermelon, and peanut fields in Texas. I was the baby of the family.

Before I was born my parents and older siblings would travel out of state to work in the fields. But my parents made a fundamental decision at that point. They decided that under no circumstances would their children be forced to miss school. That decision changed our lives and meant staying in Texas.

That was the good news. The bad news was the crowded housing. Our family developed a great sense of humor however. We used to laugh and say that we were so crowded in that little house that we had to go outside to change our minds! And our poor dog had to learn to wag its tail up and down because there was no room to do it from side to side without hitting someone. Still, it taught me the value of laughter and the importance of a good sense of humor. It helped us survive some difficult years. Laughter is good for the soul. It helps you keep a positive perspective.

In retrospect, maybe that's where the Spanish saying came from, "me rio por no llorár" (I laugh to keep from crying). My mother had the best sense of humor. And no one could match her laugh. Whenever she laughed everybody knew it. Perhaps she was trying to teach us that not only was laughter good for you, it was occasionally necessary.

I didn't find out until many years later that my mother and father had no house at all in which to live when they first met and began their life together as farmworkers. I saw the weeds and tall Johnson grass on which they used to sleep under the moon and stars of the Texas sky. I guess our crowded housing was actually a major improvement to her!

She never complained, but she always reminded us of her wish that we would make a better life for ourselves and our children. And she constantly told us that school was the only way to succeed. It wasn't true, of course, but we got the point.

The choice was clear. And the 100+ degree heat day after day made the choice easy. When school started every year, we were going to be the first ones in line to enroll. It would be a family act.

Toys are not readily found in farmworker families so we created our own ways to have fun. The best was a large stack of hay that sat below a window in the barn. Whenever we had a chance to play that's where we would go. We loved that stack of hay and the thrill of jumping out the old barn's window to bounce off of it and roll on the ground. It scared my mother half to death but she knew how much fun it was for us. It was good clean family fun.

Some years later we went back to search for the old cotton farm. We found it, or what was left of it. It was abandoned and there was no more cotton to be picked. The house in which we used to live was gone. The barn in which we used to play was gone too. About the only thing still standing was that old stack of hay. It's color had long since faded and it had lost all of its bounce as well. But it wasn't the color or bounce that mattered. What mattered was

that we still remembered it the way it used to be. We could still see ourselves jumping on and rolling off the old stack. And we could still hear the laughter. It's amazing to think about how our family was held together by the laughter from playing on that old stack of hay, the joy we shared, and all the hard work we had to do on that cotton farm.

You just can't imagine how much cotton can be grown on a farm until you've had to pick it all. I was too small to have my own cotton sack, so I had to help my mother. She would always pick two rows at a time. She wasn't trying to finish fast, just trying to pick 100 pounds for two bucks as quickly and as often as possible each day.

I would run ahead of her and try to pick as much cotton as I could and stack it up in as big a mound as possible. When my mother would catch up with me, I would help her put the cotton into her sack. It was always a pleasure to help her. She worked so hard. But no matter how tired she was, she always had a little smile for me, and I loved to hear her say "gracias mi hijo" (thank you my son). She would stand for a second, take a deep breath and walk the relatively short distance I'd cleared for her, and then she would start picking more cotton. And, I would run ahead and repeat the process again.

By summer's end, I had earned my own sack, even if it was just a potato sack. It was mine. I had earned it. I would even take it in to be weighed whenever I filled it. I would proudly climb to the top of the truck with my sack perfectly balanced on my shoulder, just like the grown-ups and empty it. It never took long, so I would go to extremes to savor the moment. I would jump

into the truck as if to claim all the space I could. Then I would holler to get my mother's attention and wave. I wanted her to see how much work I was doing on my own. I never got paid. I would just tell the boss to add it to my mother's total. He would just smile and say "sure kid." Hey, we're talking two cents a pound here!

Before I ever reached the first grade I had developed a deep respect for hard working people. And I still don't know who works harder or does more for less than farmworkers.

Before my first day of school I knew what hard work was. I had done it and I knew hard work never hurt anybody. I also knew that you had to work hard for whatever you got. Picking cotton is about as hard work as anybody can do. But perhaps the best lesson that picking cotton taught me was that hard work was the only way to make it in the fields, and hard work was the only way to make it out of the fields.

The dominant forces in my life, my church and my family, were clearly intact and secure. The school culture that would comprise the bulk of the next twelve years would also take these two dominant forces to task many times in many ways. But for now I was ready to see how the rest of the world lived. I was ready for the first grade.

Have You Seen This Niño?

Well, here I am in the first grade. Except for my cousin and a couple of friends, I don't know any of these kids. But hey, once we get past the first day and start learning, I'm sure everyone will get along fine. There's no sense being defensive. Hell, we don't even know these kids. Well, the teacher is about to begin. It's time to start learning. I'm ready and don't want to miss a thing. This is the first hour of the first day of the next twelve years of my public education.

Now what's wrong? I can't understand the teacher. She's speaking, but it's not Spanish. That much I can tell. She's going on and on. How long is this going to last? It seems like forever. Be patient I tell myself. Soon she will begin speaking Spanish, God's language. Everybody speaks Spanish, don't they? Hey, especially the teacher. What intelligent (and educated) teacher is not going to know Spanish? Surely she's heard of heaven. If Spanish is God's language, then surely everyone who wants to go there is going to know Spanish. Hell is no place for teachers. She's going to get into Spanish any minute now.

My God, it's time for recess and the teacher is still going on and on. Everybody seems to understand her except my cousin, my friends, and me. I look at my cousin. He looks at me. We're both lost and it shows on our faces. We shrug our shoulders and try to hide our fear. Not that we are afraid of fear, we just didn't know that fear would be our first educational experience. Thank God for recess period.

It's time to caucus. Does anybody know what's wrong with the teacher? Surely she knows Spanish. So why isn't she using it? When is she going to say something we can understand? Finally, somebody gets it! Remember the teachings of the apostle Paul? In his letter to the First Baptist Church of Corinth, he talked about the gifts of the spirit. Some of the gifts of the spirit were the ability to preach, teach, heal, handle snakes, and speak in tongues. That had to be it. She was having a major religious experience! She was speaking in tongues! She'll get over it and get back into Spanish soon.

Well, it's almost 3:00 P.M. and she's on a roll. This is one massive religious experience. It's lasted all day. It's almost time to go home and I haven't understood a damn thing she has said all day. It's been exhausting for me. I can imagine how she must feel. It's been like a marathon. My God, how could she go all day without saying a single word in Spanish? It had to be some kind of record.

There goes the bell. It's time to go home. I feel like running all the way. Well, at least to the railroad tracks. It'll be safer on that side of the tracks. But hey, no running in school. Nobody had to tell us. Just look at all the other kids. They must have understood something we missed. Ha! What an understatement. We missed everything! Could they possibly know something we don't? They sure do and it's called English.

My cousin and I are walking down the hall. It's a long walk to that door. I can't wait to get out of here. But the faster we walk the further the door seems to get. I think I feel an anxiety attack coming on. My God, I'm too young for this. I'm only in the first grade and it's the first day of school. It wasn't supposed to be like this. What's wrong? I don't know. But my cousin and I are looking at each other, both of us thinking, "va estar pelón!" (it's going to be tough).

One thing is for sure. We're going to have to learn this teacher's language. She's obviously not going to learn our language. I don't know what she's going to do if and when she gets to heaven. But I'm going to have to learn English if I'm going to get to the second grade.

My first two years of school, at Looney Elementary, were a clash between my home culture and a strange school culture. Perhaps the clash was inevitable. But I was not at all prepared for one particular thing that happened in the first grade that, in retrospect, may have been an omen.

The long and short of these two years was a classic struggle over my identity. I had a very strong sense of who and what I was, but the school clearly had a very different idea about that and was going to make it as difficult as possible for me to remember who and what I was, let alone continue being who I was. You see, one of the ways kids have of remembering each school year, especially what we looked like, is through our school pictures. Everybody usually tried to look their very best, especially kids like me because there was every likelihood that posing for school pictures would be the only time we would ever be photographed during the entire year. Why? Because absolutely no one owned a camera in the entire barrio, that we knew of!

Being the last of five kids, I was use to this annual occasion when all school-aged kids would bring home their pictures to show their parents, usually proudly, and letting them choose the one they wanted before exchanging the rest with relatives and friends.

Well, as my luck would have it, my first grade pictures never arrived at good ol' Looney. So there I was with no visible proof that I was even in school! And I had nothing to show my parents who always seemed to look forward to seeing the school pictures of my brothers and sister. That had never happened to anyone I knew, so I didn't know if that was just one of those bureaucratic foul-ups. But somehow it just seemed to follow right along with everything else that was happening to me. There was something that I was supposed to lose, and from the looks of this, it must have been my self-identity. And if my picture was going to help me remember what I looked like and who and what I was, well, I was just going to have to be the only kid in that particular first grade class without a school picture.

I can't say my pictures were lost intentionally, but if they were, the school had failed to realize that I had not had a picture taken of myself since I was born. But I didn't need a damn picture to know who I was.

My self-image was already deeply engraved in my own heart, soul, and mind. Besides, what I was, was what I was from within, and not just what I looked like. There was a whole lot more to me than my outward appearance. Oh, I knew what I looked like. I had a mirror at home, thank you very much! Furthermore, my mother always told me that I was "chulo" (cute), and not to believe whatever anybody else said! I think it's called having a face only a mother could love. Who needs pictures anyway? So there! But to this day there is only a blank space above my name in my first grade yearbook.

Looney Tunes: Adventures Beyond The Classroom

Well, believe it or not, I made it. I successfully completed two years at Looney Elementary School. I

have some fond memories, despite that God-forsaken first day. In a nutshell, I learned that I had to learn English. With more than a little bit of speech therapy, I learned to say chicken instead of "sshicken," and church instead of "sshursh," and show instead of "cho." I also befriended a few non-Hispanics. Man, that was a first! And oddly enough, we remained friends for all twelve years.

I had two profound experiences at Looney. I was in a school play. It wasn't much, just a small part. In fact, it was such a small part that I was an elf. Talk about small! I remember that my mother asked a woman in the barrio, I can't remember her name, to make my costume. She took one look at me and agreed. That was the last time I saw her until the night before the play. My God! Elves are small, but those little britches were entirely too small. The pants fit tight around my ankles like they were supposed to, but I could barely get my two legs through the small waist. And my feet couldn't get past the calves!

What to do, what to do but improvise. A little rip here and a little rip there, and bingo, there's your feet! And what were those little green things? Left over fabric? I should be so lucky. Those were my shoes! Oh no, and what do you do with the back half of your foot? What else? Sew a patch around the heel, like a sandal! It's okay, he's young. I know, I just won't tell anyone at school and no one will ever know. Fat chance.

I'll never forget the look on my poor teacher's face when she saw me dressed as an elf. I looked like a little stuffed green pepper bursting at the seams!

One day, at lunch time, we were playing softball. I was a fairly good player. In fact, I had already played on a real team. Some guy, I think he was one of my older brother's teacher, organized a team of Mexican kids to play on Saturdays against white kids. That was the first time I saw the park where whites played, Coggin Park. It was a big park. Lots of trees. Huge trees. They had tennis courts, picnic tables, basketball courts, playground equipment, a water fountain, and a pond.

Where we played there were none of those things. Why? I didn't know. Or I didn't want to let myself know that I knew. I knew, but I didn't want to know.

More importantly, white kids played baseball with gloves. I couldn't believe it! Gloves? My brother was a good ballplayer, so he was the pitcher. But like the rest of us, he wasn't allowed to play sports in school beyond grade school. Junior high and high school sports was for white kids. Occasionally a Mexican was allowed to play. But even if we were better athletes, almost none of us were allowed to play. My brother eventually became a football and basketball coach at the same school that wouldn't let him play. Call it poetic justice.

It was amazing. I couldn't believe all the equipment these guys had. I played catcher. My brothers and I often played catch. But for the game, I was issued a catcher's mitt, shin guards, a mask, and a chest protector. There was no time to get use to all the equipment, it was time to play ball.

I didn't know the signals for a fastball, curve, or drop. So for a curve I would move my hand in a snake-like motion. For a drop I would simply move my hand toward my brother and then quickly drive my hand toward the ground. When I wanted a fastball I would simply pound my fist into the mitt repeatedly. My brother had no trouble reading my signals. But then, neither did anyone else! Talk about telegraphing signals.

I don't remember who won the game. I guess it didn't really matter. What I learned about life, people, unequal treatment, and double standards was more important. What I do remember is that on the first pop fly, I took off my mask and threw it. When I spotted the ball I took off my mitt and threw it away too. Then I ran and caught the ball bare-handed, the only way I knew how. You don't always need what everybody else has to make the play, in baseball or in life.

When it came to playing baseball at school, well, you might say that my cousins, friends, and I had a little more experience than the other kids. I'll never forget when the difference in experience showed, and probably saved my life. I stepped up to the plate and proceeded to hit a home run. As I rounded third base, running fast to beat the throw, I looked up to see my friend Craig standing in the batter's box totally oblivious to my impending score. He was wildly swinging his bat, getting ready for his turn. The batter's box is no place to take practice swings, especially when your teammate is fixing to score. Well, he never saw me coming. I couldn't stop. The only thing to do was slide, hoping to come in low enough to avoid the bat he was swinging. It was close, but he managed to catch just enough of my head to scare me and everybody else half to death. Craig and I became

good friends, but from then on he batted first!

I'll never forget those experiences. Who could? Being embarrassed beyond belief in my acting debut and nearly killed playing ball, what could be worse than that? Answer, the third grade.

Dissed-advantaged: Was It Something I said?

I guess it's only human to expect fairness but, presumably, not when it comes to respecting the ability to speak a second language. I mean, since the first day of school I made the conscious decision to learn English because my teachers either couldn't or wouldn't learn Spanish. I never considered my ability to learn a second language would make me superior to anyone, and certainly not inferior. If anything, it certainly made me wiser than my teachers, but not superior. So why would my teachers and school administrators, none of whom were Hispanic, try to make me feel inferior? Was it discrimination, or just their ego-defense mechanisms at work? Quién sébe. (Who knows.)

English was not an easy language to learn. What's worse, there were certain stigmas attached to the process of learning English. Poor pronunciation often would bring ridicule upon the learner. And our limited English ability would often preclude us from performing at the same level as our white counterparts. Incredibly, teachers seemed to always find the best ways to make a bad situation worse.

To avoid having the less English-proficient children hinder the progress of the more proficient English-speakers, "slower" students were separated from the "faster" students based on our ability to read

English. This was the first real aspersion cast upon our intelligence. Our intelligence was not based on our ability to read. After all, the same exercise in Spanish would have reversed the results. Would white kids, let alone their parents, have allowed their intelligence to be measured in a foreign language? Would they have excelled as well or graduated from high school in the same high percentages? I doubt it.

I have often wondered what would have happened to my white counterparts had they had to learn Spanish like we had to learn English. But nosotros, well, we were told not to question authority, respect your elders, and for God's sake "pórtate bién" (behave)! So we accepted "slowness," our new found lower self-esteem, with all the grace becoming of conquered peoples whose rights were protected only by a worthless treaty.

The poisonous seeds of academic humiliation were successfully planted, the results of which would be in full bloom in approximately six to nine years, depending on the tolerance level of the victims (us). Those who were unable or unwilling to tolerate the cultural humiliation and indignities imposed by our school system would drop out, or be pushed out, first. Others would endure perhaps another year or two. But most would be gone by the ninth grade.

It never made any sense to me that the schools would deprive us from speaking Spanish. On the one hand they would acknowledge, albeit reluctantly, that there was certainly an advantage to speaking a language other than English. But then they would warn us that if we had to speak Spanish to a classmate, to please do so only in the restroom!

Carámba, don't hold back. What do you mean? Spanish belongs in the restroom? What are you trying to say? Hey, I'm in the third grade now. I can handle it! Confused? Chale ese. (No way.) I read you loud and clear, and I don't like what you're saying.

Spanish was not allowed to be spoken in the classroom. That of course was understandable. Teachers had enough problems without being paranoid about us obviously talking about them. I mean, what else could we possibly be saying in that "restroom lingo"? And if we dared giggle, it was off to the principal's office with specific instructions to stay there until we told him the truth about what we said about her that made us giggle. In other words, until we vindicated her paranoia!

It was a lose-lose situation. How are you going to convince an equally paranoid and insecure principal that you weren't really laughing at her. After all, he's thinking he's next! So even if there was nothing to confess, the longer it took for us to do so the madder she was going to get. What was worse, we knew we were going to "get it" when we got home. There was just no way to keep it from our parents.

If only the teacher had learned Spanish, life would have been so much better. No trouble for me, and no mental illness for her. But curse her? Never. No, it wasn't her fault. It was mine! Teachers and school administrators are never wrong. If only I had not listened to my parents, I would never have learned Spanish. And if I had not gone to that Baptist Church I would never have learned to read, pray, sing, or worship in Spanish.

Worship! A lot of good that was doing me now. Look at all the trouble I was in. All because of Spanish! Maybe it would have been better after all to have learned just English. I should have stopped being who I am long ago. Just be whatever they want me to be. Who needs cultural pride? Who needs self-esteem? Who needs a positive self-identity? Who needs Spanish?

Hey, I'm practically white. If I just stayed out of the sun and didn't have to work in those stupid fields, I bet I could pass for white. That's it! Of course, that's the answer. I should just go through life pretending to be white and everything will work out just fine. No one will ever know I'm really a Mexican. What am I crazy? Somebody slap me, please! You know, life shouldn't be this complicated in the third grade.

Patrol Boys: Life In The Fast Lane

Well, after that peak into my rear view mirror, it's plain to see how most of us got "pushed" out of school. Our first so-called "professional" role models who had "made it," we found, had nothing in common with us. They couldn't speak Spanish (el idioma de Dios/God's language), they'd never heard of "El Piporro," they couldn't dance rancheras, they'd all probably had their own bedroom, never gone to bed hungry, never gone to a public health clinic because their parents could afford a private dentist, and probably had never picked cotton or lived in farmhouses. It wasn't long before their inability to teach would be conveniently re-defined as our inability to learn.

But hey, I survived the fourth and now I'm in the mighty fifth

grade! Practically a man! Heck, my dad was hiking across Mexico and jumping on boxcars at my age. I can handle it. Give me your best shot.

What now? We can't speak Spanish on the school grounds either? What's wrong with these people? What did we ever do to them? Damn, they won the war! What else do they want? I'm beginning to feel like an onion, having a layer of my Hispanidad peeled off one at a time. But why aren't they crying? Isn't peeling an onion supposed to make you cry? It's making me cry, so why are they laughing?

I feel like I'm being raped. If I stay around much longer, there's going to be less of me than when I started. I'm no longer who I was. That's okay. But I'm not sure that what I am becoming is any better. That's not okay. I thought school was going to add to what I was and make me what I ought to be. Instead it's taking me away from myself. It's getting close to being time to quit. These people aren't going to be satisfied until I am illiterate in two languages!

If I'm going to survive much longer, I'm going to have to get involved in something. There has to be more to school than classrooms, books I can hardly read, teachers that can't teach, and policies that punish me for being who I am. I can handle the humiliation, injustice, discrimination, and ridicule. After all, soy hombre! (I'm a man!)

Thank God for Patrol Boys. This was better than school. All I had to do was stand in the middle of the busiest four-lane road in town (by legal definition a highway), with no street light, and stop the traffic with only a yellow flag hanging off a pole . . . so the white kids could safely cross the street!! Que pendejo! (How stupid!)

Maybe the teachers were right. I was a few trees short of a forest! But there were three fringe benefits that made it all worthwhile.

First, I got to wear a badge on a white strap and a blue hat that was similar to the one the police wore, which made me feel like I was braver than the other kids. (My self-esteem needed a real boost.)

Second, I got out of class five minutes early to get my gear on and to get ready to stop the cars that were speeding by. The danger was worth the break from class. (Interestingly enough, not a single Patrol Boy that I can remember dropped out of school.)

Third, we had a "hamburger party" at the end of school every year. The hamburgers were from Bill's Drive-In. Talk about Texas-size hamburgers! My mother could have made three or four hamburgers out of just one of those patties. But these were for us, as many as we could eat, compliments of the Brownwood Police Department. Oddly enough, the party was at Coggin Park, where I played my first baseball game as a six year old.

The other activity that helped me survive was sports, despite nearly being killed with a bat!

No Meskins Allowed

What is it now? No speaking Spanish on the way to or from school either! Man, these people are serious. Am I dangerous or what? I'm only in the seventh grade, almost out of here. They gotta be losing sleep to come up with all this crap. God, how many years is elementary school anyway?

We just beat the socks off the "linguistically correct" schools in basketball. We won the championship! My cousins and I had a blast. Running up and down the court, setting up plays in Spanish! From the opening tip-off, who would get the ball, who would pass it to whom, who would shoot . . . every word in Spanish. There is a God! But what about the rules? Hey, the coach didn't mind. He just wanted to win. He wasn't an English teacher anyway. His nickname was "Choc," short for chocolate, which may have had something to do with coaching brown kids. He never said, and we didn't ask.

We had a pretty good football team too. We won quite a few games. We used to run circles around the guys from the other elementary schools—East, North, South, Coggin, and Woodland Heights. The other schools had no Hispanics on their teams. But what we noticed the most about them was that they all wore shoes! I don't know if our ability to run circles around them was because they had no Hispanics on their teams, or because we played barefoot. I think we just ran faster, and running barefoot didn't hurt.

A strange thing happened to me in the seventh grade. My cousin (Amado) and I were invited to a birthday party. I'd never had a birthday party, so this was all new to me. But perhaps what was even more different was that the birthday party was for Glenda. Glenda was obviously white, and lived down the street. Her best friend was Hazel. All of us were in the same grade, the same classes, and had had the same teachers since the first grade—the grade from hell.

We never thought about why they lived in the barrio. Probably just didn't have enough money to live anywhere else. There were just a few white families who lived among us. In fact, Hazel lived next door to me with her grandparents.

Her grandfather worked for the city sanitation department and would often bring us toys that other people had thrown away. He also had a television set, the only one in the barrio.

In the evenings he would always let a few of us come inside and sit on the floor and watch television. The rest of us would watch through the screen doors or through the windows. It was always crowded when the favorites were on—*Rin Tin Tin, The Thin Man, Tarzan, Jim Bowie, The Life of Riley, Groucho Marx, I Love Lucy, Dragnet,* etc. Hazel's grandfather liked us a lot. His own kids had dropped out of school early on, and I think he approved of the fact that my mother and father made sure we always went to school. He probably thought, or hoped, that we would have a positive influence on his grandchildren.

Well, whatever positive reasons I may have had for feeling good about myself were promptly shattered by Glenda's grandmother. Immediately after Amado and I walked in the front door, after having knocked of course and been allowed in by both Glenda and Hazel, Glenda's grandmother called both girls into the next room and told us to wait at the door. Amado and I had no idea what was going on, and no clue as to what was about to happen. All we knew was that the only time we ever got this clean before was to go to church. We never got this clean to go anywhere else. It was party time!

Forget the games and forget the party. Glenda's grandmother came back into the living room and asked us to leave. She said that no "meskin" boys were allowed in her house, that she didn't want her granddaughter playing with us, and that she wanted us to leave that very minute.

My cousin and I were momentarily stunned. We had just experienced something for the first time. Sure I had had trouble in school because of who and what I was. But this was different. Indeed it was bad for her to make us leave, but perhaps what made it worse was that it happened to us in our own barrio. All the other humiliation, injustice, discrimination, and ridicule had occurred in or around school. It happened on their turf where they controlled "la movida" (the agenda). But this was on my side of the tracks!

There was something particularly mean, cruel, and offensive to being discriminated against by whites in my own barrio. Was nothing sacred anymore?

Incredibly, our pain and anger was erased by the obvious embarrassment that Glenda and Hazel were suffering. They were at the point of tears. My cousin and I were deeply moved as they apologized over and over. Hey, it wasn't their fault. They weren't responsible for the grandmother's ignorance. (Thank God it obviously had not occurred to the old bird that we were together all day at school. Hell, she might've died!) As we left, my cousin and I said, "see y'all Monday."

My cousin and I didn't know what to make of what had happened. We had just been insulted by whites in our own barrio. We felt so bad we did the only thing that had ever helped before. We laughed. We laughed at ourselves, at Glenda's

grandmother, and at Glenda and Hazel, the only kids in the whole damn barrio who were more poor than we.

My mother and sister didn't know why we were home so early, or what we were laughing about. When we told them, my sister took care of business quickly. She got Glenda's grandmother on the telephone and proceeded to cut that grandmother a new one. It was quite a sight. My sister, who was on the National Honor Society and had just been chosen Most Beautiful in high school, was extremely impressive in conveying our family's outrage and defending our culture. No one had ever stood up for us before. My sister never went on to champion our cause for civil rights, but she made it clear that, in her own mind, no one was culturally superior to her or to any of us.

I'll never forget that incident, or my sister's gallant defense. In retrospect, maybe that's what I needed because, after that night, I began rediscovering my pride. And with that, my years in elementary school came to a close.

Now my friends are talking about quitting. They've had enough. I can't say I blame them. Hell, we're just kids for God's sake. Yes, we were all raped. We are no longer quite as Hispanic as we were when we started. And, if we stay we will probably end up being even less Hispanic.

Our Spanish is not so hot anymore. My parents and relatives say we should be ashamed. We are, but we couldn't help it. It was all part of our education. Part of becoming what we ought to be. There is less to my Hispanidad now.

I never realized how important language was to my Hispanidad. It's

not the same to say I'm proud to be Hispanic, if I can't even say it in Spanish, the language of God and of my ancestors. Some of the pride is definitely gone. And so is my Dad. He died two days after Christmas. I'm only thirteen. What the hell am I going to do now? I really needed my Dad. At least I could look at him and remember who and what I was.

Discrimination In Living Color

Check it out, there are blacks in my eighth grade class! Now there's a first. How did that happen? Do they just get to start in the eighth grade? What about grades one through seven? I mean, I just went through hell to get this far. How is it that these guys get to start in the eighth grade?

Hardin. What's Hardin? A school? Where? At Cordell Park? You mean that itty-bitty house made of rock at Cordell? That's a school? All these folks went to school in that tiny little house? There's more? What? Get out of here. All the rest of the black kids in town are still there in that tiny school? How can that be? Why didn't they just come to school where I did—Looney and then Central? They would not have had to walk any further than we did to get there. They weren't allowed? Why? Segregation! What in the hell is segregation? Naaww. They weren't allowed to attend school with us because they're black? Hell, they still look black to me! What's the difference?

This is crazy. I'm all confused now. Sure, I knew blacks lived at "the flat." My older brother had a paper route over there. Yep, sometimes we'd stop collecting money on Saturdays long enough to play a little baseball or football in the street with them. But, shoot, we never discussed school! I guess I just figured they didn't have to go! They didn't go to any of the elementary schools we played against. Damn I was stupid! Of course they had to go to school. Why shouldn't they? They were kids too! This system wasn't just screwing me, it was screwing a whole race of people!

I don't know why it never occurred to me to ask them where they went to school. I must have been preoccupied with my own problems. If somebody didn't have to go to school and endure the same crap I was having to deal with, more power to them. But I can't believe we weren't allowed to attend the same schools because they were black and I wasn't. Man, these people are seriously paranoid about us "colored" folks. Paranoid or racist.

I know my being brown must have cost them a lot of sleep, considering the clues and all they'd been giving me for seven years. But man, they didn't want to go to school with blacks at all! That was wrong. That was evil. That was segregation. And they say it was the law? Some law. God help us all.

James is the best athlete on our football team; the best on our track team; and the best on our basketball team. James is fast. He can run, jump, catch, shoot, dribble, anything, better than anyone. And, James is black. James would eventually make All-State in football, All-State in basketball, and set the state record for the hundred yard dash. A disbelieving out-of-town reporter once asked him if it was true he ran the hundred in 9.6. James replied, "no no no," as if denying the claim. Then he paused, and said, in 9.4! That was mighty fast 30 years ago.

James won a college scholarship and eventually played professional football. But in the eighth grade, all the talent in the world didn't change the fact that James was black. And to some people that was all that mattered. It wasn't enough that he was a superior athlete. His personal safety could not be guaranteed in those little red-neck towns around Brownwood.

This was a long way from the sanctuary of my barrio, but I was quickly starting to realize that the color of my skin would have everything to do with whatever happened to me, good as well as bad, just like James.

There never was much to do in Brownwood, especially if you were just in junior high. But during school, on Friday nights, we had what was called "Teen Timers." Only junior high kids were allowed to attend, so most of us would usually gather there at the Adams Street Community Center. At Teen Timers we could dance, play ping pong, watch television, or just sit around and have a Coke or Pepsi. We mostly just sat around. Hispanic girls didn't much care for it, and rarely attended.

The white kids did everything there was to do. We sat around and watched them dance. We sat around and watched whatever they wanted to watch on television, something called The Twilight Zone. We sat around and watched them drink their soft drinks and tried to listen to whatever they talked about. One night I walked with a white kid to the refreshment stand just to watch him buy a soda pop. He declined several choices which made me think he was crazy. I would've taken any of them if I'd had a dime. He objected to the "carbonated water,"

whatever that was. I couldn't help thinking that there was something different about us and these white kids, and it was more than just the color of our skin. For one thing, they sure were picky about their soda pops.

Such were our Friday nights. Certainly not more fun than we could stand! Afterwards the parents would park outside in a long row of cars to drive their kids home, and we would start the long walk back to the barrio. But once again it was just us and the white kids. Blacks never attended, either because they were not allowed, or because they weren't sure they'd be welcomed.

One Friday night something most unusual happened. Several black students in junior high decided to go to Teen Timers. Nobody tried to stop them, fortunately, and they headed straight for the dance floor. All of a sudden the most popular white girls excitedly jumped up from their seats around the dance floor and started screaming and hugging the black girls! This all seemed very strange because at school they hardly ever talked to each other. And then for some strange reason the white girls, who seemed to always wear black or white shoes, sat down and started exchanging shoes with the black girls!

The black girls were wearing shoes of many different colors, like pink, green, orange, purple, red, etc. I think the white girls were subconsciously thinking, or hoping, that they would be able to dance as well as the black girls by merely wearing the same shoes. Wrong. It was going to take more than just different color shoes to make good dancers out of these girls.

The black girls were obviously excellent dancers, but it wasn't because of the color of their shoes. Shoot, they were just good! Even when they had to wear the black or white shoes worn by their white schoolmates, their dancing was not hindered in the least that night, while the white girls were trying to see if the colored shoes could help them dance as good as colored folks. Once again, in a totally different vein, a highly disproportionate value had been placed on color, only this time it was the color of shoes and not skin. Maybe there was hope for this crowd.

For a brief moment they may have unconsciously accepted a basic equality between the races, and assumed that the difference in dancing ability was artificially attributed to the color of one's shoes and not to the color of one's feet. But perhaps most importantly, we all had the opportunity to socialize together, without oppressive policies or administrators, and, not surprisingly, we got along great.

I have to believe that all the white kids that experienced that most unusual evening at Teen Timers went home and told their parents, and, in the process, planted a little mustard seed that would then begin the slow, but long overdue process of changing their views and attitudes toward us and blacks.

Spanish II: The White Way

These people are totally insane. Spanish is required as a foreign language, and now I have to take it. Can you believe it? They just spent seven years denying me the right to speak it practically anywhere outside my home. And now I have to learn it all over again! The "right"

way this time, I'm sure, and from a Non-Hispanic no less.

I knew I was in trouble on that very first day of Spanish class when I heard the teacher say, '"Buenos días cláse, me llámo señorita Cole." I couldn't believe it. It was as though I was back in the first grade. To quote that great American linguist, Yogi Berra, "it was deja vu all over again." Another language problem! Only this time, the teacher could speak Spanish! Or could she? What is this "proper" Spanish? Mine's different? According to whom? God these people are stupid. Now I'll probably have to speak Spanish with an accent!

I know it's typical of teenagers to question everything. But that wasn't why I was questioning this nonsense about Spanish in junior high. If they knew this was going to happen, why didn't they just teach Spanish in the first grade so my little culturally deprived white friends could learn it? It certainly would have leveled the playing field a little better. It certainly would have made me feel a lot better about myself. It certainly would have put some of us native-speakers in the "fast" group occasionally, for a change. I think I just answered my own question. That just wasn't the way things were meant to be, or so they thought. It just wouldn't be right to have a bunch of little Mexicans running around thinking they were just as good as little white kids. Heaven forbid! Ha! But they didn't know what I had learned from my sister the year before!!

It was bad enough that none of this made sense. I mean, requiring us to re-learn our first language was nothing short of ludicrous. I must admit that I was not the concerned taxpayer in junior high that I am

now. But even then I had to ask myself, how much does it cost to teach Spanish to hundreds of thousands of Hispanic kids who had already known the language, before the schools made them "un-learn" it? I mean, after paying for all those teachers and all the books, it had to cost a small fortune. It would have made much more sense, not to mention saving a lot of money, to just let us continue using our native language. Instead they punished us for using it, humiliated us for not functioning as well in English as our white counterparts, and tried to destroy our positive self-esteem.

Junior high has definitely taken its toll. With only high school left, how many more of us won't make it?

Achievement: The Triumph Of Endurance

I chose to stay in the ring for round three, "high school," and that elusive diploma. Oh well, it wasn't the end of the world. But, unfortunately, for three-fourths of my friends, it was already the end of the line. As for me, it was no longer about how much I could achieve, but about how much more I could endure.

For me there was no turning back. Quitting school, whether by dropping out or being pushed out, was never a real alternative to me or my siblings. Our parents had focused us properly since childhood and there was no way we were going to disappoint them. It is also fair to say, that by the time we got to this point, there was no way we were going to deny ourselves the pleasure of surviving the "endurance test from hell," our public school education. Our eyes were on the prize!

I had an interesting encounter with my English teacher. She got upset with me over something, I can't remember what. But it must have been serious for her to so promptly condemn me to fail. She told me, in front of the entire class, that I was never going to "make it." That I was never going to "amount to anything." And that I was never going "anywhere in life." I didn't know why she was holding back. She should have just let me have it, or, as they say, lowered the boom!

My dad told me there would be days like this. He also told me to always defend myself. (He must have told my sister the same thing! She was the oldest and I was the baby.) He would have been disappointed if I hadn't. So I stood up to my teacher and said, "I demand a second opinion." She marched me straight to the counselor's office. I felt better already. If I hadn't ask for a second opinion, I may never have met my counselor!

Unfortunately, after telling her what she (the teacher) said and I said, my counselor said she agreed with my teacher! So much for encouragement. And small wonder that I never asked the counselor for any advice or guidance concerning college!

Those who were unable or unwilling to tolerate the cultural humiliation and indignities imposed on us by our school system dropped out early. Most were gone soon after the ninth grade. Others endured a year or two later. The rest of us, the few of us, who were willing to become less in order to eventually become more, endured to the end and earned a high school diploma, an invitation to higher education.

Conclusion: Let The Record Speak For Itself

Is it any wonder that barely half of all Hispanics have graduated from high school? Or that the overwhelming majority of Hispanic high school graduates have chosen not to pursue a college education? Is it any wonder that most of those who did choose to pursue a college education didn't finish? Is it any wonder that, as recently as twenty-five years ago, only 2 percent of all Hispanics in the United States had a college education? Or that today, only 6 percent of all Hispanics have a college education. It is any wonder that there are so few Hispanics with advanced degrees? Or that there are so few Hispanic teachers and public school administrators? Is it any wonder that there are so few Hispanic professors or university administrators? Or that the percent of Hispanics attending college is the lowest among all ethnic or racial groups in the United States?

Why? I'm sure there are at least a million reasons. But I would submit that those million reasons probably have a common thread. And that common thread is simply that the reflections of millions of Hispanics would probably sound very similar to mine, but, unfortunately, with a different ending.

Public education has clearly taken its toll on our people and our community. Some scholars have described that toll as a "national tragedy." It's true, but unfortunately, it's actually worse than that. In fact, I believe it's worse than anyone would ever have imagined. As for me, I too could have been a casualty of the public schools like 80 percent of my childhood friends. But the strength of my family unity and the providence of God enabled me to achieve, or should I say, endure my public education.

Juan Andrade, Jr., is President and Executive Director of the Midwest Northeast Voter Registration and Education Project. Headquartered in Chicago, he travels throughout Latin America and annually hosts the U.S. Hispanic Leadership Conference.

Section Four

Where Are We?

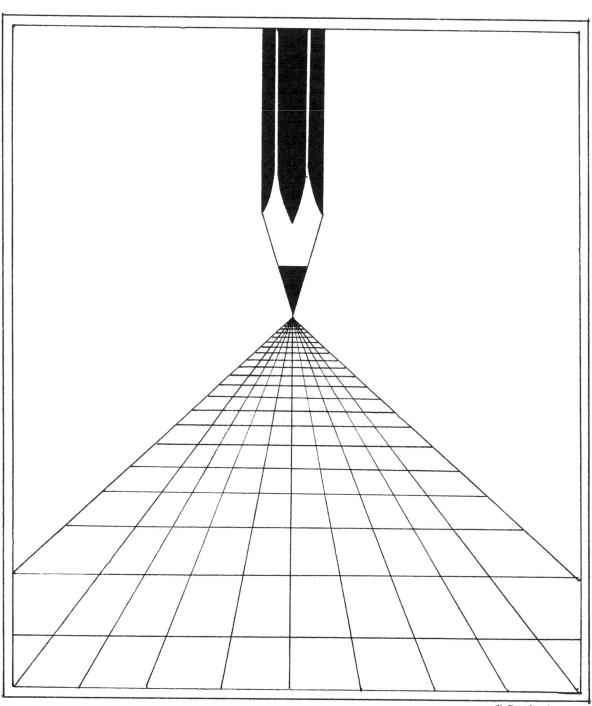

G.ZHANG 1994

The good intentions of
affirmative action are often
offset by the harsh realities of
conscious or unconscious
racial preferences of
employment. What are the
advantages and
disadvantages of affirmative
action? Who benefits from
this policy?

Affirmative Action: The Price of Preference

Shelby Steele

In a few short years, when my two children will be applying to college, the affirmative action policies by which most universities offer black students some form of preferential treatment will present me with a dilemma. I am a middle-class black, a college professor, far from wealthy, but also well-removed from the kind of deprivation that would qualify my children for the label "disadvantaged." Both of them have endured racial insensitivity from whites. They have been called names, have suffered slights, and have experienced firsthand the peculiar malevolence that racism brings out in people. Yet, they have never experienced racial discrimination, have never been stopped by their race on any path they have chosen to follow. Still, their society now tells them that if they will only designate themselves as black on their college applications, they will likely do better in the college lottery than if they

conceal this fact. I think there is something of a Faustian bargain in this.

Of course, many blacks and a considerable number of whites would say that I was sanctimoniously making affirmative action into a test of character. They would say that this small preference is the meagerest recompense for centuries of unrelieved oppression. And to these arguments other very obvious facts must be added. In America, many marginally competent or flatly incompetent whites are hired everyday—some because their white skin suits the conscious or unconscious racial preference of their employer. The white children of alumni are often grandfathered into elite universities in what can only be seen as a residual benefit of historic white privilege. Worse, white incompetence is always an individual matter, while for blacks it is often confirmation of ugly stereotypes.

The Peter Principle was not conceived with only blacks in mind. Given that unfairness cuts both ways, doesn't it only balance the scales of history that my children now receive a slight preference over whites? Doesn't this repay, in a small way, the systematic denial under which their grandfather lived out his days?

So, in theory, affirmative action certainly has all the moral symmetry that fairness requires—the injustice of historical and even contemporary white advantage is offset with black advantage; preference replaces prejudice, inclusion answers exclusion. It is reformist and corrective, even repentant and redemptive. And I would never sneer at these good intentions. Born in the late forties in Chicago, I started my education (a charitable term in this case) in a segregated school and suffered all the indignities that come to blacks in a segregated society. My father, born in the South, only made it to the third grade before the white man's fields took permanent priority over his formal education. And though he educated himself into an advanced reader with an almost professional authority, he could only drive a truck for a living and never earned more than ninety dollars a week in his entire life. So yes, it is crucial to my sense of citizenship, to my ability to identify with the spirit and the interests of America, to know that this country, however imperfectly, recognizes its past sins and wishes to correct them.

Yet good intentions, because of the opportunity for innocence they offer us, are very seductive and can blind us to the effects they generate when implemented. In our society, affirmative action is, among other things, a testament to white goodwill and to black power, and in the midst of these heavy investments, its effects can be hard to see. But after twenty years of implementation, I think affirmative action has shown itself to be more bad than good and that blacks—whom I will focus on in this essay—now stand to lose more from it than they gain.

In talking with affirmative action administrators and with blacks and whites in general, it is clear that supporters of affirmative action focus on its good intentions while detractors emphasize its negative effects. Proponents talk about "diversity" and "pluralism"; opponents speak of "reverse discrimination," the unfairness of quotas and set-asides. It was virtually impossible to find people outside either camp. The closet I came was a white male manager at a large computer company who said, "I think it amounts to reverse discrimination, but I'll

put up with a little of that for a little more diversity." I'll live with a little of the effect to gain a little of the intention, he seemed to be saying. But this only makes him a half-hearted supporter of affirmative action. I think many people who don't really like affirmative action support it to one degree or another anyway.

I believe they do this because of what happened to white and black Americans in the crucible of the sixties when whites were confronted with their racial guilt and blacks tasted their first real power. In this stormy time white absolution and black power coalesced into virtual mandates for society. Affirmative action became a meeting ground for these mandates in the law, and in the late sixties and early seventies it underwent a remarkable escalation of its mission from simple anti-discrimination enforcement to social engineering by means of quotas, goals, timetables, set-asides and other forms of preferential treatment.

Legally, this was achieved through a series of executive orders and EEOC guidelines that allowed racial imbalances in the workplace to stand as proof of racial discrimination. Once it could be assumed that discrimination explained racial imbalances, it became easy to justify group remedies to presumed discrimination, rather than the normal case-by-case redress for proven discrimination. Preferential treatment through quotas, goals, and so on is designed to correct imbalances based on the assumption that they always indicate discrimination. This expansion of what constitutes discrimination allowed affirmative action to escalate into the business of social engineering in the name of

anti-discrimination, to push society toward statistically proportionate racial representation, without any obligation of proving actual discrimination.

What accounted for this shift, I believe, was the white mandate to achieve a new racial innocence and the black mandate to gain power. Even though blacks had made great advances during the sixties without quotas, these mandates, which came to a head in the very late sixties, could no longer be satisfied by anything less than racial preferences. I don't think these mandates in themselves were wrong, since whites clearly needed to do better by blacks and blacks needed more real power in society. But, as they came together in affirmative action, their effect was to distort our understanding of racial discrimination in a way that allowed us to offer the remediation of preference on the basis of mere color rather than actual injury. By making black the color of preference, these mandates have reburdened society with the very marriage of color and preference (in reverse) that we set out to eradicate. The old sin is reaffirmed in a new guise.

But the essential problem with this form of affirmative action is the way it leaps over the hard business of developing a formerly oppressed people to the point where they can achieve proportionate representation on their own (given equal opportunity) and goes straight for the proportionate representation. This may satisfy some whites of their innocence and some blacks of their power, but it does very little to truly uplift blacks.

A white female affirmative action officer at an Ivy League university told me what many supporters of affirmative action now say: "We're after diversity. We ideally want a student body where racial and ethnic groups are represented according to their proportion in society." When affirmative action escalated into social engineering, diversity became a golden word. It grants whites an egalitarian fairness (innocence) and blacks an entitlement to proportionate representation (power). *Diversity* is a term that applies democratic principles to races and cultures rather than to citizens, despite the fact that there is nothing to indicate that real diversity is the same thing as proportionate representation. Too often the result of this on campuses (for example) has been a democracy of colors rather than of people, an artificial diversity that gives the appearance of an educational parity between black and white students that has not yet been achieved in reality. Here again, racial preferences allow society to leapfrog over the difficult problem of developing blacks to parity with whites and into a cosmetic diversity that covers the blemish of disparity—a full six years after admission, only about 26 percent of black students graduate from college.

Racial representation is not the same thing as racial development, yet affirmative action fosters a confusion of these very different needs. Representation can be manufactured; development is always hard-earned. However, it is the music of innocence and power that we hear in affirmative action that causes us to cling to it and to its distracting emphasis on representation. The fact is that after twenty years of racial preferences, the gap between white and black median income is greater than it was in the seventies. None of this is to say that blacks don't need policies that ensure our right to equal opportunity, but what we need more is the development that will let us take advantage of society's efforts to include us.

I think that one of the most troubling effects of racial preferences for blacks is a kind of demoralization, or put another way, an enlargement of self-doubt. Under affirmative action the quality that earns us preferential treatment is an implied inferiority. However this inferiority is explained—and it is easily enough explained by the myriad deprivations that grew out of our oppression—it is still inferiority. There are explanations, and then there is the fact. And the fact must be borne by the individual as a condition apart from the explanation, apart even from the fact that others like himself also bear this condition. In integrated situations where blacks must compete with whites who may be better prepared, these explanations may quickly wear thin and expose the individual to racial as well as personal self-doubt.

All of this is compounded by the cultural myth of black inferiority that blacks have always lived with. What this means in practical terms is that when blacks deliver themselves into integrated situations, they encounter nasty little reflex in whites, a mindless, atavistic reflex that responds to the color black with alarm. Attributions may follow this alarm if the white cares to indulge them, and if they do, they will most likely be negative—one such attribution is intellectual ineptness. I think this reflex and the attributions that may follow it embarrass most whites today, therefore, it is usually quickly repressed. Nevertheless, on an equally atavistic level, the black will be aware of the reflex his color triggers and will feel a stab of horror at seeing himself reflected in this way. He, too, will do a quick repression, but a lifetime of such stabbings is what constitutes his inner realm of racial doubt.

The effects of this may be a subject for another essay. The point here is that the implication of inferiority that racial preferences engender in both the white and black mind expands rather than contracts this doubt. Even when the black sees no implication of inferiority in racial preferences, he knows that whites do, so that—consciously or unconsciously—the result is virtually the same. The effect of preferential treatment—the lowering of normal standards to increase black representation—puts blacks at war with an expanded realm of debilitating doubt, so that the doubt itself becomes an unrecognized preoccupation that undermines their ability to perform, especially in integrated situations. On largely white campuses, blacks are five times more likely to drop out than whites. Preferential treatment, no matter how it is justified in the light of day, subjects blacks to a midnight of self-doubt, and so often transforms their advantage into a revolving door.

Another liability of affirmative action comes from the fact that it indirectly encourages blacks to exploit their own past victimization as a source of power and privilege. Victimization, like implied inferiority, is what justifies preference, so that to receive the benefits of preferential treatment one must, to some extent, become invested in the view of one's self as a victim. In this way, affirmative action nurtures a victim-focused identity in blacks. The obvious irony here is that we become inadvertently invested in the very condition we are trying to overcome. Racial preferences send us the message that there is more power in our past suffering than our present achievements— none of which could bring us a *preference* over others.

When power itself grows out of suffering, then blacks are encouraged to expand the boundaries of what qualifies as racial oppression, a situation that can lead us to paint our victimization in vivid colors, even as we receive the benefits of preference. The same corporations and institutions that give us preference are also seen as our oppressors. At Stanford University minority students—some of whom enjoy as much as $15,000 a year in financial aid—recently took over the president's office demanding, among other things, more financial aid. The power to be found in victimization, like any power, is intoxicating and can lend itself to the creation of a new class of super-victims who can feel the pea of victimization under twenty mattresses. Preferential treatment rewards us for being underdogs rather than for moving beyond that status—a misplacement of incentives that, along with its deepening of our doubt, is more a yoke than a spur.

But, I think, one of the worst prices that blacks pay for preference has to do with an illusion. I saw this illusion at work recently in the mother of a middle-class black student who was going off to his first semester of college. "They owe us this, so don't think for a minute that you don't belong there." This is the logic by which many blacks, and some whites, justify affirmative action—it is something "owed," a form of reparation. But this logic over-

looks a much harder and less digestible reality, that it is impossible to repay blacks living today for the historic suffering of the race. If all blacks were given a million dollars tomorrow morning it would not amount to a dime on the dollar of three centuries of oppression, nor would it obviate the residues of that oppression that we still carry today. The concept of historic reparation grows out of man's need to impose a degree of justice on the world that simply does not exist. Suffering can be endured and overcome, it cannot be repaid. Blacks cannot be repaid for the injustice done to the race, but we can be corrupted by society's guilty gestures of repayment.

Affirmative action is such a gesture. It tells us that racial preferences can do for us what we cannot do for ourselves. The corruption here is in the hidden incentive *not* to do what we believe preferences will do. This is an incentive to be reliant on others just as we are struggling for self-reliance. And it keeps alive the illusion that we can find some deliverance in repayment. The hardest thing for any sufferer to accept is that his suffering excuses him from very little and never has enough currency to restore him. To think otherwise is to prolong the suffering.

Several blacks I spoke with said they were still in favor of affirmative action because of the "subtle" discrimination blacks were subject to once on the job. One photojournalist said, "They have ways of ignoring you." A black female television producer said, "You can't file a lawsuit when your boss doesn't invite you to the insider meetings without ruining your career. So we still need affirmative action." Others mentioned the infamous "glass ceiling"

through which blacks can see the top positions of authority but never reach them. But I don't think racial preferences are a protection against this subtle discrimination; I think they contribute to it.

In any workplace, racial preferences will always create two-tiered populations composed of preferreds and unpreferreds. This division makes automatic a perception of enhanced competence for the unpreferreds and of questionable competence for the preferreds—the former earned his way, even though others were given preference, while the latter made it by color as much as by competence. Racial preferences implicitly mark whites with an exaggerated superiority just as they mark blacks with an exaggerated inferiority. They not only reinforce America's oldest racial myth but, for blacks, they have the effect of stigmatizing the already stigmatized.

I think that much of the "subtle" discrimination that blacks talk about is often (not always) discrimination against the stigma of questionable competence that affirmative action delivers to blacks. In this sense, preferences scapegoat the very people they seek to help. And it may be that at a certain level employers impose a glass ceiling, but this may not be against the race so much as against the race's reputation for having advanced by color as much as by competence. Affirmative action makes a glass ceiling virtually necessary as a protection against the corruptions of preferential treatment. This ceiling is the point at which corporations shift the emphasis from color to competency and stop playing the affirmative action game. Here preference backfires for blacks and becomes a taint that holds them back. Of course, one could argue that this taint, which is, after all, in the minds of whites, becomes nothing more than an excuse to discriminate against blacks. And certainly the result is the same in either case—blacks don't get past the glass ceiling. But this argument does not get around the fact that racial preferences now taint this color with a new theme of suspicion that makes it even more vulnerable to the impulse in others to discriminate. In this crucial yet gray area of perceived competence, preferences make whites look better than they are and blacks worse, while doing nothing whatever to stop the very real discrimination that blacks may encounter. I don't wish to justify the glass ceiling here, but only to suggest the very subtle ways that affirmative action revives rather than extinguishes the old rationalizations for racial discrimination.

In education, a revolving door; in employment, a glass ceiling.

I believe affirmative action is problematic in our society because it tries to function like a social program. Rather than ask it to ensure equal opportunity we have demanded that it create parity between the races. But preferential treatment does not teach skills, or educate, or instill motivation. It only passes out entitlement by color, a situation that in my profession has created an unrealistically high demand for black professors. The social engineer's assumption is that this high demand will inspire more blacks to earn Ph.D.'s and join the profession. In fact, the number of blacks earning Ph.D.'s has declined in recent years. A Ph.D. must be developed from preschool on. He requires family and community sup-port. He must acquire an entire system of values that enables him to work hard while delaying gratification. There are social programs, I believe, that can (and should) help blacks *develop* in all these areas, but entitlement by color is not a social program; it is a dubious reward for being black.

It now seems clear that the Supreme Court, in a series of recent decisions, is moving away from racial preferences. It has disallowed preferences except in instances of "identified discrimination," eroded the precedent that statistical racial imbalances are *prima facie* evidence of discrimination, and in effect granted white males the right to challenge consent degrees that use preference to achieve racial balances in the workplace. One civil rights leader said, "Night has fallen on civil rights." But I am not so sure. The effect of these decisions is to protect the constitutional rights of everyone rather than take rights away from blacks. What they do take away from blacks is the special entitlement to more rights than others that preferences always grant. Night has fallen on racial preferences, not on the fundamental rights of black Americans. The reason for this shift, I believe, is that the white mandate for absolution from past racial sins has weakened considerably during the eighties. Whites are now less willing to endure unfairness to themselves in order to grant special entitlement to blacks, even when these entitlement are justified in the name of past suffering. Yet the black mandate for more power in society has remained unchanged. And I think part of the anxiety that many blacks feel over these decisions has to do with the loss of black power they may signal.

We had won a certain specialness and now we are losing it.

But the power we've lost by these decisions is really only the power that grows out of our victimization—the power to claim special entitlments under the law because of past oppression. This is not a very substantial or reliable power, and it is important that we know this so we can focus more exclusively on the kind of development that will bring enduring power. There is talk now that Congress will pass new legislation to compensate for these new limits on affirmative action. If this happens, I hope that their focus will be on development and anti-discrimination rather than entitlement, on achieving racial party rather than jerry-building racial diversity.

I would also like to see affirmative action go back to its original purpose of enforcing equal opportunity—a purpose that in itself disallows racial preferences. We cannot be sure that the discriminatory impulse in America has yet been shamed into extinction, and I believe affirmative action can make its greatest contribution by providing a rigorous vigilance in this area. It can guard constitutional rather than racial rights, and help institutions evolve standards of merit and selection that are appropriate to the institution's needs yet as free of racial bias as possible (again, with the understanding that racial imbalances are not always an indication of racial bias). One of the most important things affirmative action can do is to define exactly what racial discrimination is and how it might manifest itself within a specific institution. The impulse to discriminate is subtle and cannot be ferreted out unless its many guises are made clear to people. Along with this there should be monitoring of institutions and heavy sanctions brought to bear when actual discrimination is found. This the sort of affirmative action that America owes to blacks and to itself. It goes after the evil of discrimination itself, while preferences only side-step the evil and grant entitlement to its *presumed* victims.

But if not preferences, than what? I think we need social policies that are committed to two goals: the educational and economic development of disadvantaged people, regardless of race, and the eradication from our society—through close monitoring and severe sanctions—of racial, ethnic, or gender discrimination. Preferences will not deliver us to either of these goals, since they tend to benefit those who are not disadvantaged—middle-class white women and middle-class blacks—and attack one form of discrimination with another. Preferences are inexpensive and carry the glamour

of good intentions—change the numbers and the good deed is done. To be against them is to be unkind. But I think the unkindest cut is to bestow on children like my own an undeserved advantage while neglecting the development of those disadvantaged children on the East Side of my city who will likely never be in a position to benefit from a preference. Give my children fairness; give disadvantaged children a better shot at development—better elementary and secondary schools, job training, safer neighborhoods, better financial assistance for college, and so on. Fewer blacks go to college today than ten years ago; more black males of college age are in prison or under the control of the criminal justice system than in college. This despite racial preferences.

The mandates of black power and white absolution out of which preferences emerged were not wrong in themselves. What was wrong was that both races focused more on the goals of these man-

dates than on the means to the goals. Blacks can have no real power without taking responsibility for their own educational and economic development. Whites can have no racial innocence without earning it by eradicating discrimination and helping the disadvantaged to develop. Because we ignored the means, the goals have not been reached, and the real work remains to be done.

Instead of assuming that absence means noncaring, educators must understand the barriers that hinder some parents from participating in their child's education, such as fear or diverse linguistic and cultural experience. The article includes some suggestions from parents for teachers and administrators about ways to promote active involvement.

Why Some Parents Don't Come to School

Margaret Finders and Cynthia Lewis

In our roles as teachers and as parents, we have been privy to the conversations of both teachers and parents. Until recently, however, we did not acknowledge that our view of parental involvement conflicts with the views of many parents. It was not until we began talking with parents in different communities that we were forced to examine our own deeply seated assumptions about parental involvement.

From talking with Latino parents and parents in two low-income Anglo neighborhoods, we have gained insights about why they feel disenfranchised from school settings. In order to include such parents in educational conversations, we need to understand the barriers to their involvement from the vantage point, as that of outsiders. When asked, these parents had many sug-

gestions that may help educators re-envision family involvement in the schools.

The Institutional Perspective

The institutional perspective holds that children who do not succeed in school have parents who do not get involved in school activities or support school goals at home. Recent research emphasizes the importance of parent involvement in promoting school success (Comer, 1984; Lareau, 1987). At the same time, lack of participation among parents of socially and culturally diverse students is also well documented (Clark, 1983; Delgado-Gaitan, 1991).

The model for family involvement, despite enormous changes in

the reality of family structures, is that of a two-parent, economically self-sufficient nuclear family, with a working father and homemaker mother (David, 1989). As educators, we talk about "the changing family," but the language we use has changed little. The institutional view of nonparticipating parents remains based on a deficit model. "Those who need to come, don't come," a teacher explains, revealing an assumption that one of the main reasons for involving parents is to remediate them. It is assumed that involved parents bring a body of knowledge about the purposes of schooling to match institutional knowledge. Unless they bring such knowledge to the school, they themselves are thought to need education in becoming legitimate participants.

Administrators, too, frustrated by lack of parental involvement, express their concern in terms of a deficit model. An administrator expresses his bewilderment:

> Our parent-teacher group is the foundation of our school programs. . . . This group (gestures to the all-Anglo, all-women group seated in the library) is the most important organization in the school. You know, I just don't understand why those other parents won't even show up.

Discussions about family involvement often center on what families lack and how educators can best teach parents to support instructional agendas at home (Mansbach, 1993). To revise this limited model for interaction between home and school, we must look outside of the institutional perspective.

The Voices of "Those Other Parents"

We asked some of "those other parents" what they think about building positive home/school relations. In what follows, parents whose voices are rarely heard at school explain how the diverse contexts of their lives creates tensions that interfere with positive home/school relations. For them, school experiences, economic and time constraints, and linguistic and cultural practices have produced a body of knowledge about school settings that frequently goes unacknowledged.

Diverse school experiences among parents. Educators often don't take into account how a parent's own school experiences may influence school relationships. Listen in as one father describes his son's school progress:

> They expect me to go to school so they can tell me my kid is stupid or crazy. They've been telling me that for three years, so why should I go and hear it again? They don't do anything. They just tell me my kid is bad.
>
> See, I've been there. I know. And it scares me. They called me a boy in trouble but I was a troubled boy. Nobody helped me because they like it when I didn't show up. If I was gone for the semester, fine with them. I dropped out nine times. They wanted me gone.

Instead of assuming that absence means noncaring, educators must understand the barriers that hinder some parents from participating in their child's education.

This father's experiences created mistrust and prevent him from participating more fully in his son's education. Yet, we cannot say that he doesn't care about his son. On the contrary, his message is urgent.

For many parents, their own personal school experiences create obstacles to involvement. Parents who have dropped out of school do not feel confident in school settings. Needed to help support their families or care for siblings at home, these individuals' limited schooling makes it difficult for them to help their children with homework beyond the early primary level. For some, this situation is compounded by language barriers and lack of written literacy skills. One mother who attended school through 6th grade in Mexico, and whose first language is Spanish, comments about homework that "sometimes we can't help because it's too hard." Yet the norm in most schools is to send home schoolwork with little information for parents about how it should be completed.

Diverse economic and time constraints. Time constraints are a primary obstacle for parents whose work doesn't allow them the autonomy and flexibility characteristic of professional positions. Here, a mother expresses her frustrations:

> Teachers just don't understand that I can't come to school at just any old time. I think Judy told you that we don't have a car right now. . . . Andrew catches a different bus than Dawn. He gets here a half an hour before her, and then I have to make sure Judy is home because I got three kids in three different schools. And I feel like the teachers are under pressure, and they're turning it around and putting the pressure on me cause they want me to check up on Judy and I really can't.

Often, parents work at physically demanding jobs, with mothers expected to take care of child-care responsibilities as well as school-related issues. In one mother's words:

> What most people don't understand about the Hispanic community is that you come home and you take care of your husband and your family first. Then if there's time you can go out to your meetings.

Other parents work nights, making it impossible to attend evening programs and difficult to appear at daytime meetings that interfere with family obligations and sleep.

At times, parents' financial concerns present a major obstacle to participation in their child's school activities. One mother expresses frustration that she cannot send eight dollars to school so her daughter can have a yearbook to sign like the other girls.

> I do not understand why they assume that everybody has tons of money, and every time I turn around it's more money for this and more money for that. Where do they get the idea that we've go all this money?

This mother is torn between the pressures of stretching a tight budget and wanting her daughter to belong. As is the case for others, economic constraints prevent her child from full participation in the culture of the school. This lack of a sense of belonging creates many barriers for parents.

Diverse linguistic and cultural practices. Parents who don't speak fluent English often feel inadequate in school contexts. One parent explains that "an extreme language barrier" prevented her own mother from ever going to anything at the school. Cultural mismatches can occur as often as linguistic conflicts. One Latino educator explained that asking young children to translate for their parents during conferences grates against a cultural norm. Placing children in a position of equal status with adults creates dysfunction within the family hierarchy.

One mother poignantly expresses the cultural discomfort she feels when communicating with Anglo teachers and parents:

> [In] the Hispanic culture and the Anglo culture things are done different and you really don't know—am I doing the right thing? When they call me and say 'You bring the plates' [for class parties], do they think I can't do the cookies, too? You really don't know.

Voicing a set of values that conflicts with institutional constructions of the parent's role, a mother gives this culturally-based explanation for not attending her 12-year old's school functions:

> It's her education, not mine. I've had to teach her to take care of herself. I work nights, so she's had to get up and get herself ready for school. I'm not going to be there all the time. She's gotta do it. She's a tough cookie. . . . She's almost an adult, and I get the impression that they want me to walk her through her work. And it's not that I don't care either. I really do. I think it's important, but I don't think it's my place.

This mother does not lack concern for her child. In her view, independence is essential for her daughter's cultural, linguistic, or economic reasons, these parents' voices are rarely heard at school. Perhaps, as educators, we too readily categorize them as "those other parents" and fail to hear the concern that permeates such conversations. Because the experiences of these families vary greatly from our own, we operate on assumptions that interfere with our best intentions. What can be done to address the widening gap between parents who participate and those who don't?

For many parents, their own personal school experiences create obstacles to involvement. Those who have dropped out of school do not feel confident in school settings.

Getting Involved: Suggestions from Parents

Parents have many suggestions for teachers and administrators about ways to promote active involvement. Their views, however, do not always match the role envisioned by educators. Possessing fewer economic resources and educational skills to participate in traditional ways (Lareau, 1987), these parents operate at a disadvantage until they understand how schools are organized and how they can promote systemic change (Delgado-Gaitan, 1991).

If we're truly interested in establishing a dialogue with the parents of all our nation's students, however, we need to understand what parents think can be done. Here are some of their suggestions.

Clarify how parents can help. Parents need to know exactly how they can help. Some are active in church and other community groups, but lack information about how to become more involved in their children's schooling. One Latina mother explains that most of the parents she knows think that school involvement means attending school parties.

As Concha Delgado-Gaitan (1991) points out ". . . the difference between parents who participate and those who do not is that those who do have recognized that they are a critical part in their children's education." Many of the parents we spoke to don't see themselves in this capacity.

Encourage parents to be assertive. Parents who do see themselves as needed participants feel strongly that they must provide their children with a positive view of their history and culture not usually presented at school.

Some emphasize the importance of speaking up for their children. Several, for instance, have argued for or against special education placement or retention for their children; others have discussed with teachers what they saw as inappropriate disciplinary procedures. In one parent's words:

> Sometimes kids are taken advantage of because their parents don't fight for them. I say to parents, if you don't fight for your child, no one's going to fight for them.

Although it may sound as if these parents are advocating adversarial positions, they are simply pleading for inclusion. Having spent much time on the teacher side of these conversations, we realize that teachers might see such talk as challenging their positions as professional decision makers. Yet, it is crucial that we expand the dialogue to include parent knowledge about school settings, even when that knowledge conflicts with our own.

Develop trust. Parents affirm the importance of establishing trust. One mother attributes a particular teacher's good turnout for parent/teacher conferences to her ability to establish a "personal relationship" with parents. Another comments on her need to be reassured that the school is open, that it's OK to drop by "anytime you can."

In many cases, severe economic constraints prevent children from full participation in the culture of the school.

In the opportunities we provide for involvement, we must regularly ask ourselves what messages we convey through our dress, gestures, and talk. In one study, for example, a teacher described her school's open house in a middle-class neighborhood as "a cocktail party without the cocktails" (Lareau, 1987). This is the sort of "party" that many parents wouldn't feel comfortable attending.

Fear was a recurrent theme among the parents we interviewed: fear of appearing foolish or being misunderstood, fear about their children's academic standing. One mother explained:

> Parents feel the teachers are looking at you, and I know how they feel, because I feel like that here. There are certain things and places where I still feel uncomfortable, so I won't go, and I feel bad, and I think maybe it's just me.

This mother is relaying how it feels to be culturally, linguistically, and ethnically different. Her body of knowledge does not match the institutional knowledge of the school and she is therefore excluded from home/school conversations.

Build on home experiences. Our assumptions about the home environments of our students can either build or sever links between home and school. An assumption that "these kids don't live in good environments" can destroy the very network we are trying to create. Too often we tell parents what we want them to do at home with no understanding of the rich social interaction that already occurs there (Keenan, et al. 1993). One mother expresses her frustrations:

> Whenever I go to school, they want to tell me what to do at home. They want to tell me how to raise my kid. They never ask me what I think. They never ask me anything.

When we asked parents general questions about their home activities and how these activities might build on what happens at school, most thought there was no connection. They claimed not to engage in much reading and writing at home, although their specific answers to questions contradicted this belief. One mother talks about her time at home with her teenage daughter:

> My husband works nights and sometimes she sleeps with me. . . . We would lay down in bed and discuss the books she reads.

Many of the parents we spoke to mentioned Bible readings as a regular family event, yet they did not see this reading in relation to schoolwork. In one mother's words:

> I read the Bible to the children in Spanish, but when I see they're not understanding me, I stop (laughing). Then they go and look in the English Bible to find out what I said.

Although the Bible is not a text read at public schools, we can build on the literacy practices and social interactions that surround it. For instance, we can draw upon a student's ability to compare multiple versions of a text. We also can include among the texts we read legends, folktales, and mythology—literature that, like the Bible, is meant to teach us about our strengths and weaknesses as we strive to make our lives meaningful.

As teachers, of course, we marvel at the way in which such home interactions do, indeed, support our goals for learning at school; but we won't know about these practices unless we begin to form relationships with parents that allow them to share such knowledge.

Use parent expertise. Moll (1992) underscores the importance of empowering parents to contribute "*intellectually* to the development of lessons." He recommends assessing the "funds of knowledge" in the community, citing a teacher who discovered that many parents in the Latino community where she taught had expertise in the field of construction. Consequently, the class developed a unit on construction, which included reading, writing, speaking and building, all with the help of responsive community experts—the children's parents.

Parents made similar suggestions—for example, cooking ethnic foods with students, sharing information about multicultural heritage, and bringing in role models from the community. Latino parents repeatedly emphasized that the presence of more teachers from their culture would benefit their children as role models and would help them in home/school interactions.

Parents also suggested extending literacy by writing pen pal letters with students or involving their older children in tutoring and letter writing with younger students. To help break down the barriers that language differences create, one parent suggested that bilingual and monolingual parents form partnerships to participate in school functions together.

An Invitation for Involvement

Too often, the social, economic, linguistic, and cultural practices of parents are represented as serious problems rather than valued knowledge. When we reexamine our assumptions about parental absence, we may find that our interpretations of parents who care may simply be parents who are like us, parents who feel comfortable in the teacher's domain.

Instead of operating on the assumption that absence translates into non-caring, we need to focus on ways to draw parents into the schools. If we make explicit the multiple ways we value the language, culture, and knowledge of the parents in our communities, parents may more readily accept our invitations.

References

Clark, R.M. (1983). *Family life and school achievement: Why poor black children succeed or fail.* Chicago: University of Chicago Press.

Comer, J.P. (1984). "Homeschool relationships as they affect the academic success of children." *Education and Urban Society* 16: 323-337.

David, M.E. (1989). "Schooling and the family." In *Critical pedagogy, the state, and cultural struggle,* edited by H. Giroux and P. McLaren. Albany, NY: State University of New York Press.

Delgado-Gaitan, C. (1991). "Involving parents in the schools: A process of empowerment." *American Journal of Education* 100: 20-46.

Keenan J.W., J. Willett, & J. Solsken. (1993). "Constructing an urban village: School/home collaboration in a multicultural classroom." *Language Arts* 70: 204-214.

Lareau, A. (1987). "Social class differences in family-school relationships: The importance of cultural capital." *Sociology of Education* 60: 73-85.

Mansbach, S.C. (February/March 1993). "We Must Put Family Literacy on the National Agenda." *Reading Today*: 37.

Moll, L. (1992). "Bilingual classroom studies and community analysis: Some recent trends." *Educational Researcher* 21; 20-24.

Margaret Finders is completing a doctoral program in English Education at The University of Iowa and will be an Assistant Professor at Purdue University as of August 1994.

Cynthia Lewis is completing a doctoral program in Reading at The University of Iowa and will be on the faculty at Grinnell College as of August 1994.

What can administrators, teachers, and support do to provide the necessary educational opportunities for homeless children and youth? This article discusses the number of homeless children attending our school institutions. It points out the physical and psychological effects of homelessness. It also lists practical suggestions from current research.

Homeless Students at the School Door

George E. Pawlas

Every night anywhere from 225,000 to 500,000 children go to sleep homeless in America.[1] Of the total number of homeless people in the nation, almost one-third are families,[2] the fastest growing segment of the homeless population.[3]

Estimates of the number of homeless students vary. According to one source, the figure is equal to the number of students in the Montgomery County, Maryland, Schools (the 15th largest system in the country).[4] Another source estimates that the figure parallels the number of children living in Atlanta, Boston, Miami, or Newark.[5]

No matter the exact number, the fact that there are so many homeless children in America is alarming.

What is being done to provide for these children and youth?

Support for Homeless Students

In 1987, Congress passed the first comprehensive law to provide emergency and long-term assistance for homeless persons, in particular, children and youth. Under the Stewart B. McKinney Act, the 50 states, Puerto Rico, and the District of Columbia receive funding to investigate the number and the needs of homeless children, to identify obstacles that prevent them from receiving an education, and to develop a plan to overcome these problems (Stronge and Helm 1990).

The $7.2 million that Congress appropriated in 1991 to serve the needs of homeless children was increased to $24.8 million in 1992 (American Political Network 1992). While the increase appears dramatic, those who are actively involved with the students claim that it is not nearly sufficient. The McKinney Act also provides emergency food assistance, adult literacy instruction, job training, health services, and other programs. Under the act, Homeless children are ensured access to the same free, appropriate, public education that other children in the state receive.

In 1990, the Center for Law and Education commissioned Kathleen McCall to identify programs that served the needs of the homeless. Her study located 29 alternative programs that provided remedial education, appropriate time and conditions for study, and continuity of instruction. In addition, the programs attempted to remedy many school officials' lack of knowledge and understanding of the problems homeless students face. With a focus on involving homeless and indigent parents in their children's education, the projects coordinate educational services with social service programs and other community efforts, while also implementing flexible enrollment policies that emphasize individualized instruction (McCall 1990). Although successful, these programs hang by a slender thread. Uncertain funding and the difficulties of serving a transient population are two of the major obstacles they face.

Some of the educational problems confronting homeless children center on whether they will receive better opportunities at the school they formerly attended or at a school near their temporary shelter. Some benefits of remaining at their former school include greater stability, more continuity of instruction and friendships, and possibly more satisfaction with the school and the teacher. For many homeless students, however, this option is not a viable alternative, either because transportation is not readily available or it presents more problems than it is worth.

Each time a child transfers to a new school, time irrevocably lost. The effects of those losses, even if a quality education program is available, contribute to academic underachievement, holdover rates, and a break in continuity of learning. The transfer of school records takes time and prevents new school personnel from preparing an appropriate

learning program for the student. Each time a student moves to a new shelter, he or she typically misses four to five days of school.

With the number of homeless students on the rise, schools encounter new educational challenges, including how to make transferring from school to school least destructive to a child's education.

Rather than create schools specifically for homeless students, which isolates them from their peers who live in homes, a better solution is for public schools to develop programs that incorporate many of the positive qualities of the school projects mentioned earlier. Many public schools have done just that. For example, the collaborative efforts of agencies in Orange County, Florida, provide an excellent model (see "A Safety Net for Homeless Students," p.82).

Physical and Psychological Effects of Homelessness

The sensitivity that teachers exhibit to their special needs students can make a big difference in how children feel when they enter the

school. Homeless children may have experienced a number of problems including:

- physical abuse,
- health problems,
- eating and sleeping problems,
- lags in language skills,
- low self-esteem,
- learning disabilities, and
- attention deficit disorder.

Observations of behaviors of homeless children in 14 early childhood programs in New York City found the following developmental delays:

- short attention span,
- withdrawal,
- aggression,
- speech delays,
- sleep disorders,
- regressive behaviors,
- inappropriate social interaction with adults,
- immature peer interaction, and
- immature motor behavior (Coe et al. 1991).

The same can be said for homeless elementary students. In addition, the psychological impact of homelessness is manifested by a greater prevalence and intensity of anxiety, depression, and behavioral disturbances. Homeless children scored significantly higher than housed children on sleep problems, extreme shyness, speech difficulties, withdrawal, and aggression (Reinherz and Gracey 1982).

Frequently, the majority of homeless students read below grade level. Also, a very high percentage of them scored below grade level on mathematics ability. These poor showings in two critical areas usually result in homeless children being two or more years over age for their grade.

A Baker's Dozen of Ideas

What can administrators, teachers, and support staff do to provide the necessary educational opportunities for homeless children and youth? Here are some practical suggestions culled from the research.

1. Find out if there are any shelters or hotels/motels housing homeless families in the school district. Arrange a meeting to share information about district programs and policies and to learn about the shelter's program.

2. Identify a volunteer advocate at each school for any homeless children who may come to that school. This person can be trained to help overcome the needless delays most homeless people encounter when they try to register their children.

3. Share copies of all school newsletters, school calendars, and bulletins with the shelters. Having access to this information keeps shelter personnel informed about school activities.

4. If possible, develop opportunities for teachers to meet with parents at the shelters. This could be an effective way to share ideas about how the parents can be involved in their child's education and ways the school can be of help.

5. Enlist the support of parent groups and civic organizations to collect school supplies and clothing. Crayons, paper, pencils, and items of clothing are examples of supplies to have on hand at the school to share with needy students.

> *The poor showings of homeless children in reading and mathematics ability usually result in their being two or more years over age for their grade.*

6. Have a buddy system. When a homeless child moves into the school, assign a buddy to show him or her around the school and make introductions to people.

7. Provide homeless children with conveyable resources for completing homework, and incorporate play time into their school day. Children in shelters may not have any physical space in which to do their homework. Try to provide a "transportable desk" such as a notebook or clipboard. Homeless children need play time, too. This may need to be incorporated into the school's program, since space might not be available in a shelter.

8. Provide homeless students with structure in the classroom. A consistent daily schedule should be maintained.

9. Incorporate life skills into the curriculum. These skills include listening, following instructions, social skills, and self-esteem enhancers.

10. When you know a homeless child is leaving the school, try to bring some degree of ending for the child. Ways to provide completion to the school experience include allowing time to gather up personal items and to say good-bye to friends and teachers.

11. Try to reduce the time it will take a student to begin working in a new school setting. Ways to accomplish this include having students take transfer cards, records, and IEPs when they leave.

12. Enlist volunteer students or adults as tutors. These helpers should plan to tutor homeless students at the shelter.

13. Finally, remember that homeless children and youth didn't create the unfortunate situation they are in, nor can they participate in the political process to alleviate it. They need all the support, love, and consideration they can get.

Notes

1. According to James Stronge, researcher at the College of William and Mary, as reported by D. Kelly, (March 9, 1993), "A Haven for Homeless Students," USA Today, p.10.

2. See Mihaly (1991).

3. House of Representatives, Select Committee on Children, Youth, and Families, (1987), Crisis in Homelessness: Effects on Children and Families, (Washington, DC: U.S. Government Printing Office).

4. According to figures released by the U.S. Department of Education, National Center for Education Statistics, (1992), Digest of Educational Statistics 1991, (Washington, DC: U.S. Government Printing Office).

5. See Mihaly (1991).

References

American Political Network. (December 10, 1992). Daily Report Card: Children in Crisis. Washington, DC: American Political Network.

Coe, J., L. Salamon, and J. Molnar (1991). Homeless Children and Youth. New Brunswick, NJ: Transaction Publishers.

McCall, K. (1990). "Educating Homeless Children and Youth: A Sample of Programs, policies, and Procedures." Cambridge, MA: Harvard University Center for Law and Education.

Mihaly, L. (1991). Homeless Families: Failed Policies and Young Victims. Washington, DC: Children's Defense Fund.

Reinherz, H., and C.A. Gracey. (1982). The Summons Checklist: Technical Information. Boston: Simmons School for Social Work.

Stronge, J., and V. Helm. (April 1990). "Residency and Guardianship Requirements as Barriers to the Education of Homeless Children and Youth." Paper presented at the annual meeting of the American Educational Research Association.

Reprinted by permission of Educational Leadership, May 1994. George E. Pawlas earned a Ph.D. in Educational Administration from the University of South Carolina. He coordinates the College of Education programs at the Brevard Campus of the University of Central Florida.

Pawlas, George E. (1994). "Homeless Students at the School Door." Educational Leadership 5: 79-82.

With violence erupting all around, educators need to foster peaceful relations in their classrooms. Molnar suggests that the consequences of not providing this atmosphere are catastrophic.

Too Many Kids Are Getting Killed

Alex Molnar

On my ride into New Orleans for the 1992 ASCD conference, I struck up a conversation with the driver of the airport shuttle. He was a young man in his mid-twenties, a college graduate. From his conversation about national politics and local affairs, I could tell he was well informed and looking for ways to contribute to his community.

For example, he told me that the neighborhood swimming pools had been threatened with closing because there was no money to pay lifeguards. He and a group of friends, all of whom had learned how to swim at community-supported pools, offered to life-guard for nothing so that the pools could be opened. The city turned them down. Ultimately, a wealthy benefactor stepped in at the last moment and contributed the funds necessary to open the pools. Despite his story's happy ending, the driver said he felt sorry for children today because they have fewer opportunities than he did when he was growing up.

As we continued talking, our conversation turned to the topic violence. I listened in numb silence as the young man told me that he was going to a wake the next day for a fellow driver who had been murdered by her boyfriend; that a few days before my arrival a police-woman had been found bludgeoned to death in her apartment; that the day before I arrived a 15-year-old student had been shot to death in a school hallway. Finally, he told me that he had been shot in the chest at point-blank range and almost killed in an armed robbery that had netted his assailants $40.

In my room, as I unpacked my clothes, I thought about my conversation with the van driver. My mind was filled with a jumble of recollections. I remembered news reports. Reports of two students shot dead in a New York high school the month before; reports of a teenager murdered for his jacket in Milwau-kee a few months earlier; reports of a high school athlete killed in his school cafeteria in a small Texas town at the start of the school year. Then I remembered that in my relatively affluent urban-suburb, the deli where I regularly eat breakfast had been robbed twice in the last year, the bank where I do business had been robbed recently, and that shortly before departing for New Orleans the hardware store where I buy the odds and ends that keep our home from coming apart was robbed. Every incident involved a gun. Each could have resulted in a death.

Our world is awash in violence. And no one is suffering more than our children. Some psychologists talk of the children suffering post-traumatic stress disorder, a psychological condition first associated with combat veterans returning from Vietnam. Sociologists speak of a lost generation, and tell us they are unable to predict the individual and social consequences of children forced to grow up in fearful and dehumanizing circumstances. Poor children are growing up in fear for their lives, and affluent kids, to use Paul Goodman's term, are growing up absurd. For too many children, our society is a fearful wasteland that mocks adult pieties and nurtures nihilism.

When educators cannot escape violence, they often focus their energy on immediate needs such as metal detectors, weapons checks, secured hallways, and so on. This is the educational equivalent of our government's focus on incarceration. The United States imprisons 10 times more people per capita than Japan or any nation in Western Europe. The threat of violence can, at best, be held at bay by such tactics, tactics that are no substitute for a long-term social strategy to build a more peaceful world for our children and ourselves.

If we are to construct a more peaceful world, we have work to do both inside and outside of schools.

As educators, it is logical for us to begin with questions of classroom method and curriculum content. We should ask ourselves the extent to which our classroom practices promote and strengthen peaceful relations among our students. We should ask ourselves the extent to which students study that part of our history and culture that affirms the pursuit of peace and provides role models. These are important questions, but they are only the beginning.

Unless we are content to limit our role to bandaging the wounded literally and figuratively, we will have to become much more effective advocates for our students and their families. As a profession, we have been too willing to allow the terrible anti-child bias of our culture to express itself unchallenged. It is essential that we begin to speak out against political values that treat children and their families as if they are spare parts whose principal value is as units of consumption.

Speak out against values that begin and end at the bottom line. If we do not participate in trying to reshape our society into something more humane, decent, and fair, then we shouldn't be surprised when violent offspring turn up at the schoolhouse door.

Alex Molnar is a Professor of Education at the University of Wisconsin–Milwaukee, School of Education, Department of Curriculum and Instruction, Enderis Hall, P.O. Box 413, Milwaukee, WI 53201. He is consultant to Educational Leadership for Contemporary Issues.

Molnar, Alex. (1992). "Too Many Kids Are Getting Killed," Educational Leadership 50, 1:4-5. Reprinted with permission of the Association for Supervision and Curriculum Development. Copyright © 1992 by the Association for Supervision and Curriculum Development. All rights reserved.

Steve Blancarte joins with Barbara Azeke, in describing how Long Beach used networking to provide alternatives to gangs. The success of this program rests in the recognition that it is everyone's problem and everyone's challenge.

A Pluralistic Approach to Gang Prevention: The Long Beach Model

Steve Blancarte and Barbara J. Azeka

In the past few decades, the population of Long Beach, California, currently 429,433 (1990 Census), has evolved from a primarily white, homogeneous community to a multicultural mix of people. Demographic statistics indicate that the current racial composition is 50 percent white, 24 percent Hispanic, 13 percent black, and 13 percent Asian-pacific islander or other. Benefits of the city's cultural diversity include the positive sharing of art, food, celebrations, and customs. Yet, with diversity comes the challenge of new approaches and problems that arise from cultural differences. For instance, cultural diversity and recent immigration has led to communication and language difficulties and cultural clashes among groups, and requires a reassessment of traditional recreational and social programming. The experience in Long Beach called for the development of innovative leisure. A growing, cul-turally diverse youth population was especially affected by the changing needs of this community. Unfortunately, conflict among some of the young people in Long Beach resulted in gang involvement and criminal activity.

Through intensive study and evaluation of both gang and substance abuse problems, city leaders hoped to identify the scope of the problem and develop solutions.

In November 1986, the mayor and the city council appointed a Task Force on Gangs. Reflecting the diversity of the city's population, task force members represented areas most affected by substance abuse and gangs. The final report, completed in 1987, provided 116 recommendations affecting nine different organizations in the Long Beach area. While several of the recommendations required new funding for implementation, many called for service collaboration among the identified agencies and organizations (City of Long Beach, 1987).

In response to this report, the mayor and city council appropriated $200,000 from the general fund in fiscal year 1989-90. City staff were directed to structure and implement a one-year pilot program that best addressed the recommendations of the Task Force on Gangs. In general, task force recommendations called for year-round activities for at-risk youth; a resource network for positive diversion programs; incorporation of existing resources; and training and awareness for individuals working with youth who live in at-risk environments. The overriding thrust of the recommendations was to channel at-risk youth into positive activities before they became involved with gangs, placing higher priority upon prevention rather than rehabilitation of those already involved in gangs (City of

Long Beach, 1987). Funding levels for the program have grown from $200,000 in 1989-90 to $328,000 for fiscal year 1991-92, $100,000 of which comes from community development block grant (CDBG) funds for specifically targeted neighborhoods.

In 1991-92, the program's third year, ten components were implemented to provide a comprehensive, pluralistic approach to gang prevention. The city's parks and recreation department currently coordinates the program. Services are targeted at youth aged 8 to 18 who meet the following criteria: 1) lives in a low income or ethnically diverse neighborhood; 2) has a family member, neighbor or friend who belongs to a gang; 3) comes in contact with gang members at school, work, or in a social setting; or 4) has shown signs of delinquency, including poor performance or behavior problems at school. The city has identified gangs from several ethnic groups, including white, Hispanic, black, Cambodian, Laotian, Filipino, Samoan, and Vietnamese.

The program structure involves the following separate, but interdependent, components:

- school classroom anti-gang instruction;
- consultant and staff to coordinate the program;
- recreational programming;
- employment training and development;
- collaboration of a peer counseling program between the school district and parks and recreation department;
- training for service providers to at-risk youth;
- extensive case management services for "high-risk" youth;

- independent program evaluation; and
- a parent education component.

1. Anti-Gang Instruction

The 1991-92 Gang Prevention Program has a $28,000 contract with the Long Beach Unified School District to provide anti-gang classroom lessons. Started in September 1989 with a $56,000 contract for a certified school teacher, this component was modified to involve the services of an instructional aide in the following years. The anti-gang education component consists of a pullout program for one period a week for ten weeks, which is offered to sixth and seventh grade students (12-to 13-year-olds) in all of the district's middle schools. In the pullout program, students from different classrooms come together for instruction in a specific subject.

Lessons are taught by an instructional aide with specific training and experience in anti-gang classroom instruction. Curriculum effectiveness is measured by a pre- and post-program survey of the participants which measures their attitudes about gangs and gang-related activities. The survey results indicated that the anti-gang lessons contribute to a significant attitudinal change in youth not yet fully involved in the gang lifestyle. Approximately 3,000 students will go through this instruction course each year in the program. In addition to receiving instruction, 125 at-risk youth who need additional support services and activities as a deterrent to potential gang involvement are identified yearly, and through this component, are then

referred to the program coordinator, who serves as the "hub," or central component of the program.

2. Program Consultant/Coordinator

In 1991-92, the amount of this contract is $54,000 for the equivalent of a full-time position. The coordinator must intake, refer, and track 350 youth through the program referral process, 125 referred by the school district, and the remainder from a variety of sources. Although the program components have been designed to receive the majority of the referrals, the coordinator may refer youth to any existing program in the area. The coordinator also must compile a service resource directory, develop a training video, make training presentations, and assist with new programs and fun development. In addition, as funding for coordinating the program has increased—$186,000 for 1991-92—program counselors have been added to assist the coordinator.

3. Recreation Programming

New and existing recreational activities are tailored to the specific interests of the program participants. Two hundred forty-five youth participate yearly. Although a majority of youth recreational activities offered by the parks and recreation department are free, some specialty classes have fees for enrollment. Fee waivers ensure that at-risk youth have no economic barriers to recreational opportunities. In addition, free bus transportation allows program participants to attend recreational activities of specific interest.

This component is facilitated by a parks and recreation department Gang Prevention Committee, comprised of 12 selected department staff members with experience in working with at-risk youth or who can facilitate the process of fee waivers and new program development. Through this committee, the continuing involvement of the department as a whole is strengthened and ensured. The 1991-92 budget for this component is $31,000.

The first new recreational activity to be developed for the Gang Prevention Program was a three-day overnight camping excursion to the local southern California mountains. In an interest survey distributed through the educational component of the program, students selected overnight camping as their number one choice of recreational activity. In 1990, a collaborative effort which drew resources from the parks and recreation department's Gang Prevention Committee, the school district, and the South East Partnership on Youth Violence (a coalition of youth servicing organizations who work with at-risk youth in the area) reduced the direct costs of the camping program to only $5,000, and provided an activity for approximately 60 youth, supervised by 30 professional staff. Total in-kind costs were estimated at $15,000. This camp was repeated successfully in 1991.

4. Employment Training and Development

Special employment development projects designed for up to 23 program participants annually received a $30,000 budget in 1991-92, and are supervised by the parks and recreation department's arts section. The purpose of these projects

is not only to create fun, artistic activity, but to provide youth with some marketable work experience. For example, one project was designed to focus on landscaping. A city park site was identified, and a professional consultant was hired to work with 15 youth to design and plan the project, which included blueprint drafting. This project targeted older program participants— 14 and 15 years of age—who were paid minimum wage. For many of these youth, earning a steady wage and working hard for their money helped to develop a sense of pride and self-esteem which they had not experienced. Most of the participants used their earnings to help supplement the family income.

5. Collaboration Between the School District and the Parks and Recreation Department

A formal collaboration between the school district and the parks and recreation department exists. The district offers a peer counseling training program at all of its high schools. Additionally, Long Beach City College's Human Resources Department offers advanced peer counseling as an extension course to high school students who have successfully passed the high school program. Subjects covered in the training courses include substance abuse, crisis intervention, communication skills, teen pregnancy, and gang awareness. As a result of their advanced training, these high school students, mostly 16- to 18-year-olds, are excellent prospects for employment in the parks and recreation departments's summer day camps. Ten peer counselors are hired for each of ten summer recreation day camp programs each year.

The positions are part-time, 25 hours per week, and have a salary of approximately $5 per hour. There are no direct costs to the Gang Prevention Program since all funding for staff salaries and course instruction is absorbed by the two agencies.

6. Training for Service Providers

Training is provided for individuals who work with and around at-risk youth. To supplement the training, the program coordinator developed a training video, "Giving Our Kids a Chance." Because of the diversity of the individuals it will serve, content for the video was gathered from a wide range of technically mixed youth and adults. The final product assists the program coordinator and staff with inservice presentations to the various service providers, parents, and teachers. Total cost to develop the video was $16,000. This component has targeted the training of 200 individuals each year.

7. Case Management Services

Case management for 50 of the highest risk youth referred into the program each year addresses youth who have "one foot in and one foot out the door" and may already be involved in gangs or on the verge of gang involvement. A $50,000-a-year contract has been awarded to the Long Beach Community Services Development Corporation. Referral youth are channeled through the City Gang Prevention Program Coordinator to receive extensive outreach and support services, including counseling, job training, court assistance, and remedial education.

8. A Resource Directory of Services

A resource directory of area services available to at-risk youth was designed in workbook form to assist service providers with a viable network they can use to help the at-risk youth they serve. More than 200 directories are distributed annually.

9. Independent Program Evaluation

Although no longer considered a pilot program since it has been operating for three years, the model program is innovative and was developed because of the absence of other programs. The program focus on prevention makes it difficult to identify and measure specific results. An annual evaluation by an independent consultant provides a cursory evaluation of the program. Funding of $3,000 per year in 1991-92 is minimal, but prospective grant funding for this component is being researched.

10. Parent Education

Many of the problems with "at-risk" youth lie not only with them, but also with their parents. Parent and family alienation exacerbates the situation, which seems to be linked to a variety of serious social and economic problems, some of which may be multigenerational.

Family outreach—support groups, education, and linkage with other necessary services—are used to strengthen the family unit and make gang affiliation less desirable. Parenting classes are being planned using existing staff and volunteers. While no formal funding is earmarked for this component, program staff hope to find a source in the near future.

A collaborative model which recognizes the complexity of gang membership and involvement in criminal activity can be difficult to implement and monitor. Coordination that relies upon the cooperation and sharing of resources among several large agencies and organizations requires regular communication and involvement from the various contracting and referral agencies. While the program and its structure resulted from Task Force on Gangs' recommendations, continued community involvement has been critical to the program's success. To facilitate this involvement, the city manager formed an advisory committee of community representatives and city staff to provide program direction.

To date, the program has been received very well throughout the city. Since the pilot program was first developed in 1989, the City Gang Prevention Program has provided over 25,000 hours of services for over 7,000 youth and 300 adults. Although limited by funding constraints, the program represents an important step toward investing in the future by preventing gang membership and criminal activity. The future of this project will be based not only on it's effectiveness, but also on funding availability. Although continued funding seems assured, the city's general fund, from which this program receives the majority of its support, is subject to economic fluctuations and other city spending priorities. Consistent with the need for long-term funding strategies, staff is pursuing fund development through grants, corporate sponsorships, and private foundations.

Prevention is said to be less expensive than rehabilitation. The value of this message is seen in the complexity of programs and services designed to mold and restructure the values of today's youth. It is a message that has become part of the language of recreation professionals who have accepted the challenge of diversity. Recognizing the evolution of demographic changes and impact upon service delivery is our responsibility. Educators must commit to this concept and be willing to support and work towards new and innovative approaches which stress collaboration and the sharing of resources.

References

United States Census. (1990).

City of Long Beach. (1987). Mayor and city council's task force on substance abuse and gangs final report.

Steve Blancarte is the director of Parks and Recreation in Montebello, California 90640.

Barbara Azeka is special assistant to the city manager in Long Beach, California 90802.

This article is reprinted with permission from the Journal of Physical Education, Recreation and Dance, April 1992, 31-34, 51. JOPERD is a publication of the American Alliance for Health, Physical Education, Recreation and Dance, 1900 Association Drive, Reston, VA 22091.

Nancy Gibbs discusses the myths and realities of rape. She defines terms we have read about in newspaper accounts of rape cases.

When Is It Rape?

Nancy Gibbs

Be careful of strangers and hurry home, says a mother to her daughter, knowing that the world is a frightful place but not wishing to swaddle a child in fear. Girls grow up scarred by caution and enter adulthood eager to shake free of their parents' worst nightmares. They still know to be wary of strangers. What they don't know is whether they have more to fear from their friends.

Most women who get raped are raped by people they already know—like the boy in biology class, or the guy in the office down the hall, or their friend's brother. The familiarity is enough to make them let down their guard, sometimes even enough to make them wonder afterward whether they were "really raped." What people think of as "real rape"—the assault by a monstrous stranger lurking in the shadows—accounts for only 1 out of 5 attacks.

So the phrase "acquaintance rape" was coined to describe the rest, all the cases of forced sex between people who already knew each other, however casually. But

that was too clinical for headline writers, and so the popular term is the narrower "date rape," which suggests an ugly ending to a ravenous night on the town.

These are not idle distinctions. Behind the search for labels is the central mythology about rape: that rapists are always strangers, and victims are women who ask for it. The mythology is hard to dispel because the crime is so rarely exposed. The experts guess—that's all they can do under the circumstances—that while 1 in 4 women will be raped in her lifetime, less than 10 percent will report the assault, and less than 5 percent of the rapists will go to jail.

When a story of the crime lodges in the headlines, the myths have a way of cluttering the search for the truth. The tale of Good Friday in Palm Beach landed in the news because it involved a Kennedy, but it may end up as a watershed case, because all the mysteries and passions surrounding date rape are here to be dissected. William Kennedy Smith met a woman at a bar, invited her back home late at night and apparently had sex with her on

the lawn. She says it was rape, and the police believed her story enough to charge him with the crime. Perhaps it was the bruises on her leg; or the instincts of the investigators who found her, panicked and shaking, curled up in the fetal position on a couch; or the lie-detector tests she passed.

On the other side, Smith has adamantly protested that he is a man falsely accused. His friends and family testify to his gentle nature and moral fiber and insist that he could not possibly have committed such a crime. Maybe the truth will come out in court—but regardless of its finale, the case has shoved the debate over date rape into the minds of average men and women. Plant the topic in a conversation, and chances are it will ripen into a bitter argument or a jittery sequence of pale jokes.

Women charge that date rape is the hidden crime; men complain it is hard to prevent a crime they can't define. Women say it isn't taken seriously; men say it is a concept invented by women who like to tease but not take the consequences.

Women say the date-rape debate is the first time the nation has talked frankly about sex; men say it is women's unconscious reaction to the excesses of the sexual revolution. Meanwhile, men and women argue among themselves about the "gray area" that surrounds the whole murky arena of sexual relations, and there is no consensus in sight.

In court, on campus, in conversation, the issue turns on the elasticity of the word *rape*, one of the few words in the language with the power to summon a shared image of a horrible crime.

At one extreme are those who argue that for the word to retain its impact, it must be strictly defined as forced sexual intercourse: a gang of thugs jumping a jogger in Central Park, a psychopath preying on old women in a housing complex, a man with an ice pick in a side street. To stretch the definition of the word risks stripping away its power. In this view, if it happened on a date, it wasn't rape. A romantic encounter is a context in which sex *could* occur, so what omniscient judge will decide whether there was genuine mutual consent?

Others are willing to concede that date rape sometimes occurs, that sometimes a man goes too far on a date without a woman's consent. But this infraction, they say, is not as ghastly a crime as street rape, and it should not be taken as seriously. The New York *Post* alarmed by the Willy Smith case, wrote in a recent editorial, "If the sexual encounter, *forced or not*, has been preceded by a series of consensual activities—drinking, a trip to the man's home, a walk on a deserted beach at 3 in the morning—the charge that's leveled against the al-

Do you believe a woman who is raped is partly to blame if:			
	Age	Yes	No
She is under the influence of drugs or alcohol	18-34	31%	68%
	35-49	35%	58%
	50+	57%	36%
She initially says yes to having sex and then changes her mind	18-34	34%	60%
	35-49	43%	53%
	50+	43%	46%
She dresses provocatively	18-34	28%	70%
	35-49	31%	67%
	50+	53%	42%
She agrees to go to the man's room or home	18-34	20%	76%
	35-49	29%	70%
	50+	53%	41%
Have you ever been in a situation with a man in which you said no but ended up having sex anyway?	Asked of females	Yes 18%	No 80%

leged offender should, it seems to us, be different than the one filed against, say, the youths who raped and beat the jogger."

This attitude sparks rage among women who carry scars received at the hands of men they knew. It makes no difference if the victim shared a drink or a moonlit walk or even a passionate kiss, they protest, if the encounter ended with her being thrown to the ground and forcibly violated. Date rape is not about a misunderstanding, they say. It is not a communications problem. It is not about a woman's having regrets in the morning for a decision she made the night before. It is not about a "decision" at all. Rape is rape, and any form of forced sex—even between neighbors, co-workers, classmates and casual friends—is a crime.

A more extreme form of that view comes from activists who see rape as a metaphor, its definition swelling to cover any kind of oppression of women. Rape, seen in this light, can occur not only on a date but also in a marriage, not only by violent assault but also by psychological pressure. A Swarthmore College training pamphlet once explained that acquaintance rape "spans a spectrum of incidents and behaviors, ranging from crimes legally defined as rape to verbal harassment and inappropriate innuendo."

No wonder, then, that the battles become so heated. When innuendo qualifies as rape, the definitions have become so slippery that the entire subject sinks into a political swamp. The only way to capture the hard reality is to tell the story.

A 32-year old woman was on business in Tampa last year for the Florida supreme court. Stranded at the courthouse, she accepted a lift from a lawyer involved in her project. As they chatted on the ride home, she recalls, "he was saying all the right things, so I started to trust him." She agreed to have dinner, and afterward, at her hotel door, he convinced her to let him come in to talk. "I went through the whole thing about being old-fashioned," she says. "I was a virgin until I was 21. So I told him talk was all we were going to do."

But as they sat on the couch, she found herself falling asleep. "By now, I'm comfortable with him, and I put my head on his shoulder. He's not tried anything all evening, after all." Which is when the rape came. "I woke up to find him on top of me, forcing himself on me. I didn't scream or run. All I could think about was my business contacts and what if they saw me run out of my room screaming rape.

"I thought it was my fault. I felt so filthy. I washed myself over and over in hot water. Did he rape me? I kept asking myself. I didn't consent. But who's gonna believe me? I had a man in my hotel room after midnight." More than a year later, she still can't tell the story without a visible struggle to maintain her composure. Police referred the case to the state attorney's office in Tampa, but without more evidence it decided not to prosecute. Although her attacker has admitted that he heard her say no, maintains the woman, "he says he didn't know what I meant by no. He didn't feel he'd raped me, and he even wanted to see me again."

Her story is typical in many ways. The victim herself may not be sure

right away that she has been raped, that she had said no and been physically forced into having sex anyway. And the rapist commonly hears but does not heed the protest. "A date rapist will follow through no matter what the woman wants because his agenda is to get laid," says Claire Walsh, a Florida-based consultant on sexual assaults. "First comes the dinner, then a dance, then a drink, then the coercion begins." Gentle persuasion gives way to physical intimidation, with alcohol as the ubiquitous lubricant. "When that fails, force is used," she says. "Real men don't take no for an answer."

The Palm Beach case serves to remind women that if they go ahead and press charges, they can expect to go on trial along with their attacker, if not in a courtroom then in the court of public opinion. The New York *Times* caused an uproar on its own staff not only for publishing the victim's name but also for laying out in detail her background, her high school grades, her driving record, along with an unattributed quote from a school official about her "little wild streak." A freshman at Carleton College in Minnesota, who says she was repeatedly raped for four hours by a fellow student, claims that she was asked at an administrative hearing if she performed oral sex on dates. In 1989 a man charged with raping at knife point a woman he knew was acquitted in Florida because his victim had been wearing lace shorts and no underwear.

From a purely legal point of view, if she wants to put her attacker in jail, the survivor had better be beaten as well as raped, since bruises become a badge of credibility. She had better have reported the crime right away, before taking

the hours-long shower that she craves, before burning her clothes, before curling up with the blinds down. And she would do well to be a woman of shining character. Otherwise the strict constructionist definitions of rape will prevail in court. "Juries don't have a great deal of sympathy for the victim if she's a willing participant up to the non-consensual sexual intercourse," says Norman Kinne, a prosecutor in Dallas. "They feel that many times the victim has placed herself in the situation." Absent eyewitnesses or broken bones, a case comes down to her word against his, and the mythology of rape rarely lends her the benefit of the doubt.

She should also hope for an all-male jury, preferably composed of fathers with daughters. Prosecutors have found that women tend to be harsh judges of one another—perhaps because to find a defendant guilty is to entertain two grim realities: that anyone might be a rapist, and that every woman could find herself a victim. It may be easier to believe, the experts muse, that at some level the victim asked for it. "But just because a woman makes a bad judgment, does that give the guy a moral right to rape her?" asks Dean Kilpatrick, director of the Crime Victim Research and Treatment Center at the Medical University of South Carolina. "The bottom line is, Why does a woman's having a drink give a man the right to rape her?"

Last week the Supreme Court waded into the debate with a 7-to-2 ruling that protects victims from being harassed on the witness stand with questions about their sexual history. The Justices, in their first decision on "rape shield laws," said an accused rapist could not present evidence about a previous sexual relationship with the victim unless he notified the court ahead of time. In her decision, Justice Sandra Day O'Connor wrote that "rape victims deserve heightened protection against surprise, harassment and unnecessary invasions of privacy."

That was welcome news to prosecutors who understand the reluctance of victims to come forward. But there are other impediments to justice as well. An internal investigation of the Oakland police department found that officers ignored a quarter of all reports of sexual assaults or attempts, though 90 percent actually warranted investigation. Departments are getting better at educating officers in handling rape cases, but the courts remain behind. A New York City task force on women in the courts charged that judges and lawyers were routinely less inclined to believe a woman's testimony than a man's.

The present debate over degrees of rape is nothing new: all through history, rapes have been divided between those that mattered and those that did not. For the first few thousand years, the only rape that was punished was the defiling of a virgin, and that was viewed as a property crime. A girl's virtue was a marketable asset, and so a rapist was often ordered to pay the victim's father the equivalent of her price on the marriage market. In early Babylonian and Hebrew societies, a married woman who was raped suffered the same fate as an adulteress—death by stoning or drowning. Under William the Conqueror, the penalty for raping a virgin was castration and loss of both eyes—unless the violated woman agreed to marry her attacker, as she

was often pressured to do. "Stealing an heiress" became a perfectly conventional means of taking—literally—a wife.

It may be easier to prove a rape case now, but not much. Until the 1960s it was virtually impossible without an eyewitness; judges were often required to instruct jurors that "rape is a charge easily made and hard to defend against, so examine the testimony of this witness with caution." But sometimes a rape was taken very seriously, particularly if it involved a black man attacking a white woman—a crime for which black men were often executed or lynched.

Susan Estrich, author of *Real Rape*, considers herself a lucky victim. This is not just because she survived an attack 17 years ago by a stranger with an ice pick, one day before her graduation from Wellesley. It's because police, and her friends, believed her. "The first thing the Boston police asked was whether it was a black guy," recalls Estrich, now a University of Southern California law professor. When she said yes and gave the details of the attack, their reaction was, "So, you were really raped." It was an instructive lesson, she says, in understanding how racism and sexism are factored into perceptions of the crime.

A new twist in society's perception came in 1975, when Susan Brownmiller published her book *Against Our Will: Men, Women and Rape*. In it she attacked the concept that rape was a sex crime, arguing instead that it was a crime of violence and power over women. Throughout history, she wrote, rape has played a critical function. "It is nothing more or less than a conscious process of intimidation,

by which *all men* keep *all women* in a state of fear."

Out of this contention was born a set of arguments that have become politically correct wisdom on campus and in academic circles. This view holds that rape is a symbol of women's vulnerability to male institutions and attitudes. "It's sociopolitical," insists Gina Rayfield, a New Jersey psychologist. "In our culture men hold the power, politically, economically. They're socialized not to see women as equals."

This line of reasoning has led some women, especially radicalized victims, to justify flinging around the term rape as a political weapon, referring to everything from violent sexual assaults to inappropriate innuendos. Ginny, a college senior who was really raped when she was 16, suggests that false accusations of rape can serve a useful purpose. "Penetration is not the only form of violation," she explains. In her view, rape is a subjective term, one that women must use to draw attention to other, nonviolent, even nonsexual forms of oppression. "If a woman did falsely accuse a man of rape, she may have had reasons to," Ginny says. "Maybe she wasn't raped, but he clearly violated her in some way."

Catherine Comins, assistant dean of student life at Vassar, also sees some value in this loose use of "rape." She says angry victims of various forms of sexual intimidation cry rape to regain their sense of power. "To use the word carefully would be to be careful for the sake of the violator, and the survivors don't care a hoot about him." Comins argues that men who are unjustly accused can sometimes gain from the experience." They have a lot of pain, but it is not a pain that I would necessarily have spared them. I think it ideally initiates a process of self-exploration. 'How do I see women?' 'If I didn't violate her, could I have?' 'Do I have the potential to do to her what they say I did?' Those are good questions."

Taken to extremes, there is an ugly element of vengeance at work here. Rape is an abuse of power. But so are false accusations of rape, and to suggest that men whose reputations are destroyed might benefit because it will make them more sensitive is an attitude that is sure to backfire on women who are seeking justice for all victims. On campuses where the issue is most in-flamed, male students are outraged that their names can be scrawled on a bathroom-wall list of rapists and they have no chance to tell their side of the story.

"Rape is what you read about in the New York *Post* about 17 little boys raping a jogger in Central Park," says a male freshman at a liberal-arts college, who learned that he had been branded a rapist after a one-night stand with a friend. He acknowledges that they were both very drunk when she started kissing him at a party and ended up back in his room. Even through his haze, he had some qualms about sleeping with her:

"I'm fighting against my hormonal instincts, and my moral instincts are saying, 'This is my friend and if I were sober, I wouldn't be doing this.'" But he went ahead anyway. "When you're drunk, and there are all sorts of ambiguity, and the woman says, 'Please, please' and then she says no sometime later, even in the middle of the act, there still may very well be some kind of violation, but it's not the same thing. It's not rape. If you don't hear her say no, if she doesn't say it, if she's playing around with you—oh, I could get squashed for saying it—there is an element of say no, mean yes."

The morning after their encounter, he recalls, both students woke up hung over and eager to put the memory behind them. Only months later did he learn that she had told a friend that he had torn her clothing and raped her. At this point in the story, the accused man starts using the language of rape. "I felt violated," he says. "I felt like she was taking advantage of me when she was very drunk. I never heard her say 'No!,' 'Stop!,' anything." He is angry and hurt at the charges, worried that they will get around, shatter his reputation and force him to leave the small campus.

So here, of course, is the heart of the debate. If rape is sex without consent, how exactly should consent be defined and communicated, when and by whom? Those who view rape through a political lens tend to place all responsibility on men to make sure that their partners are consenting at every point of a sexual encounter. At the extreme, sexual relations come to resemble major surgery, requiring a signed consent form. Clinical psychologist Mary P. Koss of the Uni-

Would you classify the following as rape or not?		Rape	Not Rape
A man has sex with a woman who has passed out after drinking too much	Female	88%	9%
	Male	77%	17%
A married man has sex with his wife even though she does not want him to	Female	61%	30%
	Male	56%	38%
A man argues with a woman who does not want to have sex until she agrees to have sex	Female	42%	53%
	Male	33%	59%
A man uses emotional pressure, but no physical force, to get a woman to have sex	Female	39%	55%
	Male	33%	59%
		Yes	No
Do you believe that some women like to be talked into haveing sex?	Male	54%	33%
	Female	69%	20%

From a telephone poll of 500 American adults taken for TIME/CNN on May 8 ...
Sampling error is plus or minus 4.5% ...

versity of Arizona in Tucson, who is a leading scholar on the issue, puts it rather bluntly, "It's the man's penis that is doing the raping, and ultimately he's responsible for where he puts it."

Historically, of course, this has never been the case, and there are some who argue that it shouldn't be that women too must take responsibility for their behavior, and that the whole realm of intimate encounters defies regulation from on high. Anthropologist Lionel Tiger has little patience for trendy sexual politics that make no reference to biology. Since the dawn of time, he argues, men and women have always gone to bed with different goals. In the effort to keep one's genes in the gene pool, "it is to the male advantage to fertilize as many females as possible, as quickly as possible and as efficiently as possible." For the female, however, who looks at the large investment she will have to make in the offspring, the opposite is true. Her concern is to "select who will provide the best set-up for their offspring." So, in general, "the pressure is on the male to be aggressive and on the female to be coy."

No one defends the use of physical force, but when the coercion involved is purely psychological, it becomes hard to assign blame after the fact. Journalist Stephanie Gutmann is an ardent foe of what she calls the date-rape dogmatists. "How can you make sex completely safe?" she asks. "What a horribly bland, unerotic thing that would be! Sex is, by nature, a risky endeavor, emotionally. And desire is a violent emotion. These people in the date-rape movement have erected so many rules and regulations that I

don't know how people can have erotic or desire-driven sex."

Nonsense, retorts Cornell professor Andrea Pattot, co-author of *Acquaintance Rape: The Hidden Crime*. Seduction should not be about lies, manipulation, game playing or coercion of any kind, she says. "Too bad that people think that the only way you can have passion and excitement and sex is if there are miscommunications, and one person is forced to do something he or she doesn't want to do." The very pleasures of sexual encounters should lie in the fact of mutual comfort and consent: "You can hang from the ceiling, you can use fruit, you can go crazy and have really wonderful sensual erotic sex, if both parties are consenting."

It would be easy to accuse feminists of being too quick to classify sex as rape, but feminists are to be found on all sides of the debate, and many protest the idea that all the onus is on the man. It demeans women to suggest that they are so vulnerable to coercion or emotional manipulation that they must always be escorted by the strong arm of the Law. "You can't solve society's ills by making everything a crime," says Albuquerque attorney Nancy Hollander. "That comes out of the sense of overprotection of women, and in the long run that is going to be harmful to us."

What is lost in the ideological debate over date rape is the fact that men and women, especially when they are young, and drunk, and aroused, are not very good at communicating. "In many cases," says Estrich, "the man thought it was sex, and the woman thought it was rape, and they are both telling the truth." The man may envision a celluloid seduction, in which he is

being commanding, she is being coy. A woman may experience the same event as a degrading violation of her will. That some men do not believe a woman's protests is scarcely surprising in a society so drenched with messages that women have rape fantasies and a desire to be overpowered.

By the time they reach college, men and women are loaded with cultural baggage, drawn from movies, television, music videos, and "bodice ripper" romance novels. Over the years they have watched Rhett sweep Scarlett up the stairs in *Gone With the Wind*; or Errol Flynn, who was charged twice with statutory rape, overpower a protesting heroine who then melts in his arms; or Stanley rape his sister-in-law Blanche du Bois while his wife is in the hospital giving birth to a child in *A Streetcar Named Desire*. Higher up the cultural food chain, young people can read of date rape in Homer or Jane Austen, watch it in *Don Giovanni* or *Rigoletto*.

The messages come early and often, and nothing in the feminist revolution has been able to counter them. A recent survey of sixth- to ninth graders in Rhode Island found that a fourth of the boys and a sixth of the girls said it was acceptable for a man to force a woman to kiss him or have sex if he has spent money on her. A third of the children said it would not be wrong for a man to rape a woman who had had previous sexual experiences.

Certainly cases like Palm Beach, movies like *The Accused*, and novels like Avery Corman's *Prized Possessions* may force young people to reexamine assumptions they have inherited. The use of new terms, like acquaintance rape and date rape, while controversial, has given men and women the vocabulary they need to express their experiences with both force and precision. This dialogue would be useful if it helps strip away some of the dogmas, old and new, surrounding the issue. Those who hope to raise society's sensitivity to the problem of date rape would do well to concede that it is not precisely the same sort of crime as street rape, that there may be very murky issues of intent and degree involved.

On the other hand, those who downplay the problem should come to realize that date rape is a crime of uniquely intimate cruelty. While the body is violated, the spirit is maimed. How long will it take, once the wounds have healed, before it is possible to share a walk on a beach, a drive home from work or an evening's conversation without always listening for a quiet alarm to start ringing deep in the back of the memory of a terrible crime?

Reported by Sylvester Monroe/Los Angeles, Priscilla Painton and Anastasia Toufexis/New York.

What if a Wife Says No?

"But if you can't rape your wife, who can you rape?" A crude joke, but a fair reflection of a common attitude for most of history. Until 1979, most states had rape laws that explicitly protected husbands from prosecution for even the most violent rapes of their wives. For a woman to refuse to sleep with her husband was grounds for divorce. But over the past decade, the attitudes and the laws have slowly shifted. A generation that saw an epidemic of wife beating and wife murder could hardly pretend that sexual violence within marriage was

not also a crime. In a 1990 study, a House committee estimated that 1 in 7 married women will be raped by their spouses. Very few crimes will be reported, however, since women assume that no one will believe them. "People think marital rape is she has a headache and doesn't want to have sex and she gives in," says Ann Marie Tucker, executive director of the Citizens Committee on Rape, Sexual Assault and Sexual Abuse in Buffalo. "That isn't it at all. The sexual abuse is often part of an ongoing pattern of physical intimidation and violence."

Women who do press charges face a heavy burden of proof. The National Clearinghouse on Marital and Date Rape in Berkeley reports that though 20 states have completely eliminated preferential treatment for husbands, 26 other states hover in a gray zone: without gross brutality, the husband has the benefit of the doubt. If prosecutors decide they have enough for a case, however, they usually win; between 1978 and 1985, only 118 cases of spousal rape went to trial, but 104 wound up with a conviction.

Can a Man Be Raped?

One answer, of course, is yes—by another man. In fact, by some estimates, 10 percent of rape victims are men, though they rarely report the crime. But the interesting question, in light of the current debate, is how a man could be raped by a woman.

Most men would say, with physiological confidence, that if a man doesn't want to have sex, he can't be tied down and forced. Human anatomy provides him a special protec-

tion. But there are sex therapists who dispute this notion, some point to "masochistic titillation," while others speculate that panic, along with fear of bodily harm, does not necessarily rule out sexual arousal and may even increase it in some cases.

In any event, the most expansive definitions of rape include psychological coercion, which raises the question, Couldn't a woman emotionally pressure a man to have sex, by, for instance, impugning his manhood if he refused, and thus be guilty of rape?

If the word is given to mean unwanted sex, then men are vulnerable, too. A 1988 study of sexually active college students found that 46.3 percent of the women and 62.7 percent of the men reported having had unwanted intercourse. Peer pressure, coercion, intimidation all led students into situations they later regretted.

Some researchers fear that even raising the question trivializes the whole issue of rape. But there are paradoxes here that might shed light on the issue. How is it that when an adolescent boy is coerced into sleeping with an older woman, it is viewed with a wink as an accepted rite of passage, while the reverse—the coercion of a girl by an older man—is clearly not?

Nancy Gibbs is Senior Editor for Time Magazine. She is a frequent guest on radio and television talk shows. Her most recent book is entitled Children of Light.

Copyright 1991 Time Inc. Reprinted by permission.

Sautter chronicles the growing crisis of babies born with drug addictions. He presents several case studies of these children and advocates early intervention programs that seem to be successful.

Crack: Healing the Children

R. Craig Sautter

Antoine was on the run again. The emotionally distraught 10-year-old had just appeared in court on a parole violation for a burglary charge. A juvenile judge took extra time to review Antoine's case history, and he offered the timid-looking youngster reprieve from the hardships of a juvenile home on one condition: that Antoine enroll in a residential treatment program for children fighting the effects of crack, the drug that had damaged their young biological systems even before they were born.

Antoine was, the judge knew, what the three-inch headlines of the weekly news magazines call a "crack kid," a label some experts charge does more harm than good. Yet to the judge, Antoine wasn't a label. He was just another youngster in need of help, and a special kind of help at that.

Antoine agreed to the judge's placement. However, he'd already been in other—though unsuccessful—treatment programs during his young life, and he'd been in and out of a variety of public schools that quickly gave up on him. So as soon as he saw his chance, Antoine bolted from the guard escorting him from the courthouse to the treatment center.

The judge had no alternative except to issue an arrest warrant for the child. The authorities haven't found Antoine yet, but they assume he's spent the last several months living on the streets—sleeping in alleys, in abandoned cars, and on back porches.

Antoine is a real child, and his story is a recent one. "Unfortunately, Antoine is just the tip of the iceberg," declares Cook County Circuit Court Judge Stuart Lubin. "In the next decade, the courts will be swamped with cases like Antoine's. He hasn't run away from us. We've run away from him. The schools and the public welfare system have failed to help him and thousands of kids like him. These institutions seem to seek the least expensive solutions to difficult problems instead of what needs to be done to help the child. This is a tragedy that every social agency must confront, or the consequences could be disastrous for us all. It won't do any good to ignore the Antoines of the world. He ran back to the streets. But many others are likely to appear quickly in his place."

A Social Epidemic

The United States is experiencing an explosion in the number of drug-exposed children, according to U.S. Rep. Charles Rangel (D-N.Y.), who chairs the House Select Committee on Narcotics Abuse and Control and has sponsored hearings on the subject. "Some hospitals report that over 20% of their deliveries are infants who were prenatally exposed to drugs," he said at one such hearing.

The noted pediatrician T. Berry Brazelton agrees that "intrauterine exposure to drugs is the epidemic of the 1990's. Drug abuse is not new. . . . But the threat today is like a tidal wave."[1]

In fact, according to the National Institute on Drug Abuse, the number of drug-exposed children born each year ranges from 375,000 to 739,000—possibly 18% of all newborns in the United States. Of these nearly 5% have been exposed to cocaine, from which crack is derived. By contrast, 17% have been exposed to marijuana and 73% to alcohol.

But despite the relatively small number of children affected, the annual cost to the nation of intrauterine exposure to cocaine is enormous, now running between $33 million and $1 billion for newborns and between $351 million and $1.4 billion for first-year care. At the same time, the nation spends $375 million for alcohol-exposed newborns, $652 million for tobacco-exposed newborns, and as much as $852 million for the care of tobacco-exposed children. Moreover, all of these costs are likely to increase, according to experts, because the fastest-growing group of drug abusers in this country is adolescent girls, many of whom will soon be mothers.

The bottom line for educators, though, comes from the March of Dimes, which predicts that by the year 2000 as many as four million drug-exposed children will be attending school.

Already, teachers are seeing an unusually high proportion of kindergartners functioning at low levels and exhibiting behavioral problems. Rep. Rangel said at a congressional hearing on the topic that he has heard from anxious teachers around the nation who are struggling with the consequences of

children's exposure to drugs.[2] "Many veteran teachers say such children's characteristics are different from those of other problem pupils," he noted. "Unable to concentrate, overwhelmed by the slightest stimulation, suffering from delayed speech development, drug-exposed children are overwhelming America's teachers, many of whom have no formal preparation for dealing with this kind of disabled student."

"Teachers feel alone," Rangel added. "Although they feel a problem exists, they often do not know how to identify, let alone counsel, drug-exposed children. And they rarely receive guidance or assistance."

In addition to anecdotal evidence, hard data show that the numbers of 3-to 5-year-old children enrolled in special education in Los Angeles and Miami, for example, have doubled since 1986. A substantial portion of these children have been exposed in utero to drugs.

"Unable to cope with drug-exposed children while paying enough attention to their other students, teachers often send these difficult-to-handle children to special education," Rep. Rangel noted. "In New York City, special education referrals increased in the 1989-90 school year from 1,071 to 1,600 due largely to the drug-exposed. The rest of the nation experienced a similar trend. Special education services, however, are unable to absorb all drug-exposed children. Such services can cost three to five times as much as regular education."

No Social Boundaries

Inner cities seem particularly hard hit. Some researchers predict

that, by the end of the decade, up to 60% of all inner-city children will be prenatally drug-exposed. New York City alone could have 72,000 children who were exposed to crack in the womb. But the phenomenon is not restricted to the nation's cities.

Drug use cuts across all socioeconomic and racial boundaries. A recent study in Pinellas County, Florida, conducted by the National Association for Perinatal Addiction, found that low-income minority women were 10 times more likely to be reported as drug users. But urine tests of 3,000 pregnant women in both private and public health facilities showed that middle-class women used illicit drugs at virtually the same rate. Thus public and private schools in every community can expect to be confronted with drug-exposed children during the next decade. The middle-class children just may not be as readily identifiable.

William Schipper, executive director of the National Association of State Directors of Special Education, which has its headquarters in Alexandria, Virginia, told Congress, "There is no typical profile. We are beginning to learn that drug abuse among middle-class women is substantial and increasing. Yet we know less about the children born to these women because they have better access to health care, are able to afford private medical services, do not need to interact with the public health system, and are not as readily reported as drug users."

Damage to the children

Evelyn Davis, M.D., assistant clinical professor of pediatrics at Harlem Hospital Center in New York City, believes that cocaine remains the illicit drug choice among the pregnant women she sees.[3] About 13% of all babies delivered at her hospital are affected by cocaine.

Many of these babies are delivered prematurely and must be placed in intensive care. Many exhibit uncontrollable shaking and endless shrieking. Some are intensively colicky and have a variety of neurological impairments; others display underdeveloped craniums, autism, blindness, attention deficit disorder, hyperactivity, severe learning disabilities, emotional disorders, and other abnormalities. Later, some exhibit tremors, language delays, poor task organizational ability, and attachment and separation problems.

Dr. Davis notes that the head circumferences of children affected by drugs are below the fifth percentile in about one-third of the children. "A small head, a small cranium, means a small brain," she said. "Children who are severely microcephalic cannot process information, cannot think logically. And growth retardation continues well beyond infancy. This certainly has implications for the school system."

According to Dr. Davis, roughly 90% of these children are language delayed. "These are youngsters who do not coo on time, do not babble on time," she said. "They very often reach age 2 without having said the first two words that most children say, namely, 'mommy' and 'daddy.' Many of these youngsters, at ages 4 and 5, cannot speak in phrases. They are speaking in single words. And many of these youngsters, when they speak, are not really quite sure of what they are saying; some of them don't quite understand what they are hearing. Many are

hyperactive, and the group as a whole has an alarming rate of autistic disorder."

At Harlem Hospital, the typical cocaine-using mother is not a teenager. The mean age of these drug-using mothers is 27. The typical case is an older woman who, according to Dr. Davis, "has pretty much given up on society, a woman who has been deserted by society and in many instances by her partner—and very often it is a mother who plays Russian roulette. She really does not think about the outcome of her pregnancy."

A Question of Definitions

The situation is even more complicated because the majority of drug-using mothers seen at Harlem Hospital are polysubstance abusers. Well over 50% used alcohol along with some other drugs during their pregnancy. In reality, then, the term crack children is as inaccurate as it was sensational when the label first hit the newsstands. Most studies of "crack children" are really studies of children whose mothers abused more than one drug, including cigarettes and alcohol. Thus not everyone is convinced that the rash of cocaine-exposed children presents a kind of medical problem that is qualitatively different from that presented by children exposed to other drugs.

One recent study conducted at Emory University even suggested that, by itself, cocaine has no observable impact on children and that the worrisome condition of so-called crack babies results from a combination of factors, such as inadequate prenatal health care and general neglect and abuse.

But Dr. Davis disagrees and stressed the need for early interven-

tion. "Cocaine and alcohol are neurological in nature," she says. "Roughly 15% of the drug-exposed children I see at Harlem Hospital have handicapping conditions that will require a lifetime of care. The needs must be recognized early, and intervention must be provided. With early intervention, many of these children will not require special education after 5 years of age."

Educators and politicians, such as Rep. Rangel, don't want to wait for more studies to resolve the issue. "We must accept the reality of this trend and prepare for it," Rangel warns. "Our schools are the primary line of defense in this war against suffering. As these children grow up, they enroll in school systems that are largely unprepared to accommodate them."

Special Education Mandate

Schipper, executive director of the National Association of State Directors of Special Education, concludes that "there is no question that many of these children will require special education and related services in order for them to succeed in school. State and federal laws require schools to provide free and appropriate public education to children with disabilities. This takes the form of special education, or specially designed instruction, to meet the unique needs of a child with an identified disability, along, with related services that help a child with disabilities to benefit from [his or her] educational program."

Schipper notes that, over the last six years, the federal government has worked with the states to develop a system of support for infants and toddlers with disabilities through Part H of the Individuals with Disabilities Education Act, administered by the U.S. Department of Education. In 1986 Congress enacted P.L. 99-457, a grant program that provides early intervention services for infants and toddlers with disabilities and for their families.

"Under Part H, states have developed an interagency coordinating council to oversee the development of the services delivery system," Schipper said, "and within about two years all states hope to be providing early intervention services to all eligible children on a statewide basis."

"I stress the term hope," he continued, "because the financing for this early intervention system in many states is proving difficult. The limited federal funding for Part H is intended for planning and coordinating activities. State and local revenues are supposed to pay for the actual delivery of early intervention services to children and families. At present, resources within many of the states are not adequate to finance service delivery."[4]

When Congress enacted the Part H program, "it was envisioned that 100,000 to 160,000 eligible infants and toddlers would be served," said Schipper. "But, given the numbers of infants exposed to cocaine and other illicit drugs, as many as 300,000 to 375,00 infants and toddlers may be eligible to receive these services. At this time, resources are inadequate to provide such services to all children who might benefit from them."

Schipper argues that one important component of this legislation pertains to infants and toddlers who do not have disabilities but are at risk of having substantial developmental delays. Many infants and toddlers who have been exposed to illicit drugs in utero do have substantial impairments that qualify them for Part H services. Many others, however, are only at risk of experiencing developmental delays and therefore may not necessarily receive appropriate intervention.

Indeed, according to the Florida Department of Health and Rehabilitative Services, the annual cost of getting crack babies ready for school by age 5 is $40,000 per child. In Pennsylvania in 1990-91, the cost of special education for children who had a learning disability was $7,000 per year. In that state, a year of residential treatment and special education for an emotionally disturbed child could range in cost from $25,000 to $47,000. A child sent to juvenile detention for 15 days cost the state $2,500; a child sent to a residential drug treatment program cost $15,000 per year. According to the U.S. General Accounting Office, as many as 50% of drug-exposed children will be placed in foster care in years to come. It is clear that the sad aftermath of epidemic crack use has cost U.S. taxpayers and non-profit agencies plenty.

But the federal government must take the lead, Dr. Davis of Harlem Hospital insists. "The monies are not available at the city and state levels. The very well-being of our nation is at stake," she warns. "We have never seen any thing like crack before."

Early Intervention Offers Hope

Of course, the answer lies in stopping the drug epidemic, in drug education and prevention, and in providing drug treatment programs for men and women before they have children. But the question today is, What do we do about those children who have already been affected by drugs?

As grim as the statistics and testimonies seem, there is some reason for hope. Judith Burmison, executive director of the Chicago-based National Association for Perinatal Addiction Research and Education (NAPARE), testified at a congressional hearing that educators are finding success with intervention strategies for children now entering the school system who were exposed to drugs prenatally.[5]

"Helping these children is uppermost in the minds of educators all across the country," she explained. "Some administrators and teachers are fearful. They have read about or seen TV stories that depict drug or alcohol-exposed children as little monsters, uncontrollable, and uneducable."

"That picture is distorted, unfair to children, and certainly unproductive," she added. "Writing off hundreds of thousands of children as lost will only create a self-fulfilling prophecy and will burden various social service, education, and medical agencies to their limits, when, in fact, with intervention for mothers, children, and families, most of these children have the potential to become productive adults."

NAPARE is conducting the nation's lengthiest longitudinal study of the developmental progress of 300 children who were prenatally exposed to illicit drugs. Funded by the National Institute on Drug Abuse, the study provides some encouraging data of importance to every school that works with drug-exposed children. For example, according to Burnison, the NAPARE study has yielded the following findings:

- Almost 100% of these drug-exposed children test within normal range cognitively. They can be taught, and they can learn.

- While all drug-exposed children exhibit signs of neurobehavioral deficiencies as infants, the majority of them at ages 3 and 4 have achieved levels of social, emotional, and intellectual development that place them within the normal range.

- Between 30% and 40% of the cocaine-exposed children continue to display problems of varying degrees of severity in langauge development and/or attention. Attention difficulties range from mild distractibility to attention deficit disorder with hyperactivity. However, less than 5% of these children exhibit true attention deficit disorder with hyperactivity.

Burnison notes that "the attentional problems seem to be related to the types of self-regulatory problems we see in cocaine-exposed infants. These children have low thresholds for overstimulation and frustration. They react by losing control or withdrawing. Obviously, either reaction would be a problem when a child is in a classroom with 20 or more other children."

"The easily overstimulated child requires consistent, predictable care," she advises. "Some require physical therapists, speech therapists, Head Start." But Burnison warns, "if the mother has no treatment, the fragile, drug-exposed infant goes to an environment that exacerbates his or her behavioral problems. The infant may be exposed to the risks of poor nutrition, inadequate medical care, a chaotic lifestyle, possible abuse and neglect, and passive exposure to illicit drugs."

Yet, while many teachers remain justifiably anxious about how best to respond to the educational problems of children exposed prenatally to drugs or worry about the impact that these youngsters will have on other students, a few school systems have taken the lead in developing models that can and should be studied by schools around the nation.

Harlem Hospital Program

In February 1991 the New York City Board of Education collaborated with Harlem Hospital to set up a preschool therapeutic nursery for 2-to 4-year-old children exposed to drugs in utero. The program places seven children in each class, along with two special education teachers, a speech therapist, and a play therapist.

Psychiatrists from Harlem Hospital provide treatment for those children who require such help. A major component of the program is outreach to local District 5. Teachers from the district have already begun to rotate through the nursery school for eight-week introductions to the spectrum of disabilities that in utero exposure to drugs produces and the range of intervention strategies that ameliorate these conditions.

Dr. Davis of Harlem Hospital notes that early intervention works. "It makes no sense," he warns, "to throw 5-year-old youngsters prenatally exposed to drugs into the public school system without having worked with them from infancy and without having worked with their families. But this is not a hopeless generation of youngsters."

Allan Sheldin, Jr., executive director of the Elementary School Center in East Harlem, New York, sponsored a summer institute in 1991 on crack-exposed children. Practitioners concluded then that, in Sheldin's words, "it is not especially important to identify why and how a child became disabled. What is important is a thorough assessment and a plan of action . . . Schools must form active working partnerships across the spectrum of child-serving professions. This is good practice for all children. Schools should look carefully for these children's strengths and skills," Shedlin insists, "so we can build upon them and develop individual learning and teaching strategies, which is again what we ought to be doing for all children."

Shedlin also wants legislators to resist the temptation to divert money from regular education to special services for drug-exposed children. Instead, he believes more funding must be made available for all students. That includes expanding the Head Start model down to birth and up through grade 6.

Project Daisy in Washington, D.C.

In 1989 the superintendent of schools in the District of Columbia convened a Superintendent's Roundtable of private and public agencies to develop strategies for young children who were prenatally exposed to drugs. One of the strategies was to design an educational intervention program under the school district's Office of Early Childhood Programs. The program became known as Project DAISY

(Developing Appropriate Intervention Strategies for Young Children).

Project DAISY was designed as a three-year longitudinal study that will then follow children for five additional years to determine the impact of the early intervention. It completed its second full year of operation in June 1992.

The project serves a total of 60 children: one classroom of 15 students in each of four D.C. schools. Of the 15 children in each classroom, five have documented prenatal exposure to drugs, and 10 are children who come from the neighborhood and have no documented prenatal exposure. The program is housed in schools located in areas where the incidence of drug use is known to be high.

Children are identified as prenatally exposed through a tracking system operated by the District of Columbia General Hospital. The hospital database includes information on prenatal exposure to PCP (phencyclidine), crack/cocaine, alcohol, heroin, methadone, and tobacco.

Between January 1991 and May 1992, the hospital tracked 2,600 newborns who were prenatally exposed to these drugs. The tracking system is not mandatory, so not all births in the District are reported. However, hospitals are strongly encouraged to be part of the linkage system so that children who need it can receive early intervention. And the majority of District hospitals now participate.

Using this tracking system, 20 children were placed in the Project DAISY experimental group because their birth records showed that they had been exposed to drugs. The program has several key features:

Developmentally appropriate. The Project DAISY classrooms contain multi-age groupings of children between the ages of 3 and 5. "We believe in using developmentally appropriate practices and strategies with young children," says Diane Powell, director of Project DAISY. "We recognize that children may have problems in attachment and bonding, and we want to provide them with opportunities to develop long-lasting relationships with a consistent significant adult or team of adults."

None of the children in Project DAISY have been identified for special education. "DAISY is a fully inclusionary program, held in a regular early childhood classroom, with an early childhood educator and classroom assistant, and supported by a multidisciplinary consultation team," emphasizes Powell.

Support team. The support team, whose responsibilities are multifaceted, includes a clinical psychologist, a clinical social worker, a speech/language pathologist, and a nutritionist. The entire team participates in the initial screening of all children in the program. The children are evaluated using the Developmental Individualized Assessment of Learning Revised, a screening test, and the Vineland, which looks at cognitive adaptive behavior skills so that the parent and teacher can report on what they have observed in terms of behavior.

The team also meets with the regular early childhood classroom teacher for 2-1/2 hours each month. The team discusses the needs of each child and suggests intervention strategies. It also develops a plan for each child that anyone on the team may be responsible for carrying out.

The team provides home support and tracks the intervention strategies from the previous month to see how they worked. If team members know that a child is leaving the program, they plan the transition. Though Project DAISY is a multi-age grouping of children between the ages of 3 and 5, it is considered a regular kindergarten, and its graduates go on to a regular first-grade classroom.

Plug-in services. "Ours is a plug-in model," explains Powell. "Instead of pulling children out to deliver services in isolation, we incorporate the work of our specialists into the normal routine of the classroom. Because the classroom is developmentally appropriate, it is centered on choices for children. If the child were to choose to work in the socio-dramatic play area, the clinical social worker might work with the child in that area. Or if a child is involved in prewriting activities or in emergent literacy activities, such as using a big book, that's where you might find the speech/languages pathologist working with the child. But they also work with any other child who might be working in that area. We support the children in the context of their real experience."

In addition to providing direct support, the specialists give teachers prescriptive follow-up activities, so that the interventions they are using as an interdisciplinary team can be continuously integrated throughout a child's time in the classroom. If a child is receiving direct service from a speech pathologist twice a week, the teacher can follow up with activities on the other three days.

Family partnerships. Because home-based intervention is a very strong component of Project DAISY, the team also contributes support to families. The family may be a foster mother, a grandmother, a biological mother, a father or grandfather, or the staff in a residential program. Two members of the team visit the home. For example, the classroom teacher and the speech pathologist—or the classroom assistant and the social worker, or the director and the social worker, or the nutritionist and the social worker—could visit to share strategies with the family in the home.

If the speech pathologist is working on language development, the team doesn't ask the family to do anything very different from its normal routine. But the team might suggest that, as family members fix dinner, they talk with the child about what they are doing and ask questions to see whether he or she understands. Project DAISY tries to make strategies realistic for each family situation.

In addition, Project DAISY teachers coordinate a parent group at each school. When the parents come in, they learn actual support techniques from the staff by participating in activities centered on their children, such as a school picnic. Parent involvement is further stimulated by a new Suzuki music program and by a tumbling program that focuses on motor development.

"When the kids are playing on their Suzuki violins, parents watch the children perform, and then they may be invited to participate in a beginning lesson themselves," Powell notes. "As a result, many parents have asked that the violins be sent home and have followed up with individual lessons for their children. It is very enjoyable for them, and the self-esteem the kids gain

from the experience is just unbelievable."

Student choices. What teaching strategies does Project DAISY use to reach children who have been prenatally exposed to drugs when they are integrated with unexposed children? "We recognize that good early childhood practices are very important with these groups of children," Powell observes. "We felt the classrooms should be environmentally appropriate and user-friendly. We have opportunities for children to initiate and choose activities."

Project DAISY's strategies include whole-language, emergent-literacy, and hands-on experiences. Instead of being directive, teachers act as guides in the classroom. The project tries to make the environment reflect the children's experiences and accommodate their individual differences.

More than play. Project DAISY classrooms maintain a balance between individual activities and those that nurture collaboration and group discussion. The guiding premise of the project's child-centered instructional curriculum is that the primary work of young children is play. Play is taken as an indicator of mental growth and social development.

Project DAISY classrooms have successfully employed strategies from the "social curriculum" to foster interactions among children. Each morning, at the "Morning Meeting," children greet one another and talk about their experiences. Each child asks the group for questions and comments. The exercise promotes the development of language and social skills.

"One of the children we had was extremely resistant to touch," recalls Powell. "And now he greets his

peers with a hug." (See "The Story of Kahlil.") Powell continues, "It is so exciting to see. People who come in can't even identify who was and who wasn't drug-exposed. Using sound early childhood practices with these children is clearly making a difference, and having the support of a team for continued problem solving and assessment of the learning experience is important for these children."

Districtwide staff training. Project DAISY is just one of 36 early childhood initiatives in the District of Columbia, all of them interrelated. The D.C. schools are using the findings of Project DAISY to shape the training of people throughout the school system.

Maurice Sykes, director of early childhood programs for the school district, said that, in order to get the primary grades ready for all the children who have been victimized by desperate biological and social environments, he launched intensive training for all teachers in the city's early childhood unit, which spans Head Start through grade 3. More than 400 teachers were trained this past summer. In addition, all Head Start, prekindergarten, kindergarten, and first-grade classrooms have been restocked with developmentally appropriate materials and equipment.

Consequently, when Project DAISY children and those from the other early childhood initiatives go into a first-grade classroom, it is not unlike their previous experience and should not cause trauma. The teachers have been trained to use center-based instruction and experiential hands-on curriculum materials.

Next, the District of Columbia schools will extend the same training to teachers in the fourth, fifth, and sixth grades. "The change is having a mammoth impact," observes Powell. "We are transforming the expectations so that teachers support the needs of children in the early years."

Project DAISY staff members have been in demand as local and national speakers. "We have an intensive training plan designed for next year in 60 schools, Head Start to third grade, as well as for day-care providers," Powell said. "We are attractive to districts because this whole project is funded in the regular budget with no federal subsidies. The per-pupil expenditure for regular students in the District is $6,236. To fund children for special education is extremely expensive. Project DAISY is very cost-effective. And the children don't have to be labeled to get services."

Prognosis good. Project DAISY has shared its preliminary findings with us. Those findings are encouraging because they seem to further support the proposition that early intervention makes a big difference and that, if school systems can aggressively gear up a "developmentally appropriate" response, they can significantly reduce the problems schools will face in serving these children in the years ahead. As the end of the second year, the Project DAISY staff felt that none of the drug-exposed children needed special education and that all could be fully integrated into regular education if a model similar to Project DAISY were provided.

Those feelings were supported by the data collected by Project DAISY on control groups in two schools. The researcher found greater cognitive weaknesses in the control groups of children who were presumed to have been exposed to drugs than in the Project DAISY group of children who were known to have been exposed. The cognitive strengths of Project DAISY children known to have been exposed were also greater than the cognitive strengths of those in the control groups.

Moreover, the drug-exposed students in Project DAISY had significantly greater social and emotional strengths than children in the control groups, and exposed students in Project DAISY had significantly fewer social and emotional weaknesses than the children in the control groups.

"The prognosis for all the Project DAISY children is extremely good," reports Powell. "The drug-exposed children were totally integrated with youngsters who were not prenatally exposed, which gave them language modeling and literacy exposure in a classroom—just like any other child between the ages of 3 and 5."

In 1992-93 Project DAISY will begin to use its classrooms as model visitation sites for teachers throughout the District of Columbia, so that other teachers can learn from the Project DAISY experience and can take successful practices back to their classrooms.

The Los Angeles Experience

The Los Angeles Unified School District established its pilot program for prenatally drug-exposed children between the ages of 3 and 6 at the Salvin Special Education Center. Salvin's program is individualized and family-focused. It includes interdisciplinary assessments and emphasizes consistency in teaching. The program aims to help children make successful transitions to a regular classroom or to the least-restrictive special education program.

Based on the Salvin experience and other research, the district developed a book of teaching strategies that is now being adapted and used throughout the district and the nation. That book, *Today's Challenge: Teaching Strategies for Working with Young Children at Risk Due to Prenatal Substance Exposure*, presents parents and preschool and primary teachers with strategies to foster children's learning, social and emotional development, communication, and motor development—and with strategies to establish home/school partnerships.

The book's first recommendation is that "these children should not be grouped together solely on the basis of the prenatal substance exposure." The fear is that such segregation can create a self-fulfilling cycle of behavior. Experts who work with cocaine-exposed children want these youngsters to have a chance to succeed, and they believe that early intervention can help the vast majority of them to make the transition to responsible social and community life.

But school officials in Los Angeles also warn that prenatally exposed preschoolers are known to exhibit extreme behaviors, ranging from passivity to hyperactivity, from apathy to aggression, from indiscriminate trust to extreme fear and suspicion. The good news is that Los Angeles educators agree that children who were prenatally exposed can adjust to a school environment if they receive high-quality intervention that helps them gain self-esteem, self-control, and an ability to solve problems.

One way to promote this adjustment, the school district suggests, is by providing these children with a predictable, secure, and stable environment. This means a defined structure with clearly stated expectations and boundaries, as well as the provision of ongoing nurturance and support. This also means that teachers need to find ways for young children to cope appropriately with stress.

However, Marci Schoenbaum, special education and early childhood teacher at Salvin, reports, "After working with children for six years, we have found that 55% are still showing learning disabilities, regardless of whether they have intervention or a stable environment. At first we didn't want to say this. But now we know that some children will have learning problems. These are problems that can be addressed in a regular class or a special day class, but they are problems that have to be addressed."

The Salvin project is based on the premise that "early positive responsive care is crucial for the child's emotional and cognitive well-being. Establishing a strong attachment with each child through understanding and acceptance is a teacher's major priority." From the Salvin experience, school officials in Los Angeles recommend in their book that programs for prenatally drug-exposed children include eight elements.

Curriculum. "The curriculum should promote active learning through interaction, exploration, and play"—as well as concrete experiences, decision makind, and problem solving— "to encourage competency and self-esteem" and to provide "motivation for new learning."

Play. "Children at risk need a setting which allows extended periods of play," the Los Angeles plan suggests. Through play children "learn to learn; to explore and to manipulate the environment; to cope with the perplexities of life experience; to express feelings, and to become symbolic thinkers."

Adults. Children need contact with enough adults to promote "attachment, predictability, nurturing, and ongoing assistance in learning appropriate coping styles."

Flexible rooms. These students need classrooms that are flexible enough that materials and equipment can be removed to "reduce stimuli" or added to provide enrichment.

Transition time. "At-risk children need a setting in which transition time is seen as an activity in and of itself," with a "beginning, middle, and end." Transition time is one of the "best times of day to teach the child how to prepare for and cope with change and ambivalence."

Routines and rituals. The environment should give children "continuity and reliability through routines and rituals. Scheduling activities in a predictable order over time strengthens a child's self-control and sense of mastery over the environment."

Such professionals as speech and language therapists, psychologists, and social workers also need a routine for reintroducing themselves to the children and for future scheduling.

Classroom rules. The book recommends limiting the number of explicit rules so that children "can explore and actively engage in their social and physical environment."

Too many classroom rules can hinder this development, the book cautions.

Observation and assessment. Children at risk need more than a simple assessment of their skills in such areas as language, social and emotional development, and cognitive and motor development. They also need to have these skills judged in practice during transitional times to see how they manage, how they relieve tension, how they cope with other children and adults, and how they solve problems. Such authentic assessment will help the teacher determine which skills need further work.

Today's Challenge insists that children exposed to drugs prenatally need classrooms that give them respect. They need positive experiences and personal attachment to an adult. They need a setting in which adults acknowledge and deal with their feelings. Teachers also need to discuss the decisions that the children make. "Talking about behavior and feelings (done with empathy rather than judgment) validates the child's experiences and sets up an accepting atmosphere. Permission to have these feelings leads to the increased ability to distinguish between wishes and fantasies on the one hand and reality on the other."

The book also notes that "verbal expression allows the child to integrate past and present events into a total experience. This integrating process leads to the child's increased ability to modulate behavior, gain self-control, and express feelings."

Beyond an appropriately designed classroom environment, the Los Angeles model makes home/school partnership an essential part of the curriculum. Teachers and service providers plan and evaluate the support needed by each child and family.

Dignity and a Fair Chance

Rep. Rangel argues that "drug-exposed children should not be considered doomed to failure. We should not designate them a 'bio-underclass' or a 'lost generation.' Our society does not condemn epileptics to asylums or exclude the blind from the work force. Instead, we endeavor to incorporate handicapped people into the mainstream."

"By the same token, we should not give up on drug-exposed children before we have even tried to help them . . . Our challenge is to find the best way to integrate drug-exposed children into schools so that they may be productive members of society. A failure to do so will [be] detrimental [not only] to the children in question but to all their classmates who will not receive teachers' full attention."

Thus it is possible that a large percentage of children exposed to drugs in utero can survive and even prosper in public schools. But our schools must immediately learn how to accommodate these children and offer them an environment and a series of learning experiences that build on their strengths and avoid exacerbating their weaknesses. These informed responses must be found in both the regular and the special education programs. And they must be carried out in ways that show respect, rather than disdain, toward the children whom the headlines so mislabel "Crack Kids."

Notes

1. Identifying the Needs of Drug-Affected Children: 1990 Issue Forum (Washington, DC: Office for Substance Abuse Prevention, U.S. Department of Health and Human Services, 1990), p.1.

2. "Drug-Exposed Children in the Schools: Problems and Policy," hearing before the U.S. House of Representatives Select Committee on Narcotics Abuse and Control, 30 July 1991, p. 4.

3. Ibid., p. 41.

4. Ibid., p. 51.

5. Ibid., p. 17.

A Resource Guide

A number of educational, medical, and legal organizations and various publications have focused on the problems of children born to drug-using mothers and their impact on the schools. A sample of such resources follows.

Organizations

■ Birth to Three Linkage and Tracking Project is located at the District of Columbia General Hospital. For more information, contact Dr. Elaine Vowels, Director, 1900 Massachusetts Ave. S.E., Washington, DC 20003

■ Center for Applied Research and Urban Policy at the University of the District of Columbia has sponsored a series of forums on substance abuse and exposure and their effects and has set up a resource library for national use. For more information, contact Dr. Vijaya L. Melnick, Director, Center for Applied Research and Urban Policy, University of the District of Columbia, 4200 Connecticut Ave. N.W., Washington, DC 20008

■ Elementary School Center is a national child advocacy and policy center with an interdisciplinary staff of child-serving professionals. Education Children from the World of Drugs and Alcohol is a package of publications and videos available from the ESC, which includes: Neither Damned Nor Doomed: Educating Children Prenatally Exposed to Drugs and Alcohol ($25); and Educating Children from the World of Crack: Realities and Myths Concerning Children Prenatally Exposed to Drugs and Alcohol, 200 pages of reprinted articles and research findings ($25). The two videos in the package are: "Neither Damned nor Doomed: Teachers' Perspectives" ($95) and "Neither Damned nor Doomed: Mothers' Perspectives" ($95). ESC also has a two-week previewing rate of $30 for both videos, which is deducted from the purchase price if previewers choose to buy the package. To obtain any of the above materials, write to ESC, Two East 103rd St., New York, NY 10029

■ Project DAISY is a special programs for early intervention with children at risk from prenatal drug exposure. For more information, contact Diane Powell, Director, Project DAISY, Rudolph Elementary Annex, Second and Hamilton Sts. N.W., Washington, DC 20011.

■ Office of Educational Research and Improvement in the U.S. Department of Education recently conducted a survey of all domestic programs and made recommendations regarding best practices. For more information, write Shirley Jackson, Comprehensive School Health Education Program, Office of Educational Research and Improvement, U.S. Department of Education, 555 New Jersey Ave, N.W., Room 400K, Washington, DC 20208.

Books

■ Sergio Fabro and Anthony R. Scialli, eds., *Drug and Chemical Action in Pregnancy: Pharmacologic and Toxicologic Principles* (Marcel Dekker, Cimarron Rd., P.O. Box 3005, Monticello, NY 12701, 1986).

■ Avital Ronell, *Crack Wars* (University of Nebraska Press, 901 N. 17th St., Lincoln, NE 68588-0520, 1991).

Articles

■ Leslie Baldacci, "Crack Mom's Baby 'Gonna Do Fine,'" Chicago Sun-Times, 2 December 1991, Sect. 1 pp. 1, 41; and idem, "Study Bashes Stereotypes of Drug Abuse in Pregnancy," Chicago Sun-Times, 18 December 1991, pp. 1, 32.

■ Yolanda Bellisimo, "Crack Babies The Schools' New High-Risk Students," *Thrust*, January 1990, pp. 23-26.

■ Sandra Blakeslee, "Crack's Toll on Infants Found to Be Emotional Devastation," *New York Times*, 17 September 1989, p. A-1.

■ Adele M. Brodkin and Barry Zuckerman, M.D., "Are Crack Babies doomed to School Failure?," *Instructor*, March 1992, p. 16.

■ Ira Chasnoff, M.D., "Perinatal Effects of Cocaine," *Contemporary Ob/Gyn*, May 1987, pp. 163-79; and Ira Chasnoff, M.D., et al,. "Prenatal cocaine Exposure is Associated with Respiratory Pattern Abnormalities," *American Journal of Disabled Children*, May 1989, pp. 583-87.

■ Susan Chira, "Crack Babies Turn Five, and Schools Brace," *New York Times*, 25 May 1990, p. A-1.

■ Suzanne Daley, "Born on Crack and Coping with Kindergarten," *New York Times*, 7 February 1991, p. A-1.

■ Howard French, "Rise in Babies Hurt by Drugs Is Predicted: Five Percent in New York City Could Need Care by '95," *New York Times*, 18 October 1989, pp. B-1—B-2.

■ Josephine Gittler and Dr. Merle McPherson, "Prenatal Substance Abuse," *Children Today*, July/August 1990, pp. 3-7.

■ Lameece Atallah Gregorchik, "The Cocaine-Exposed Children Are Here," *Phi Delta Kappan*, May 1992, pp. 709-11.

■ Jean Latz Griffin and Teresa Wiltz, "Schools OFfer Hope for Cocaine Babies," *Chicago Tribune*, 1 December 1991, Sect 1, p. 1.

■ Dan R. Griffith, "Prenatal Exposure to Cocaine and Other Drugs: Developmental and Educational Prognoses," *Phi Delta Kappan*, September 1992, pp. 30-34.

■ Clara Hemphill, "A Tormented Cry: As Crack Babies Grow, So Do Their Problems," *Newsday*, 28 September 1990, pp. 6, 28-29.

■ J. Howard, "Annotation: Cocaine and Its Effects on the Newborn," Developmental Medicine and Child Neurology, vol. 31, 1989, pp. 255-57.

■ J. Howard et al., "The Development of Young Children of

Substance-Abusing Parents: Insights from Seven Years of Intervention and Research," Zero to Three: Bulletin of the National Center for Clinical Infant Programs, June 1989, pp. 8-12.

- Janice Hutchinson, "What Crack Does to Babies," American Educator, Spring 1991, pp. 31-32.

- Barbara Kantrowitz et al., "The Crack Children," Newsweek, 12 February 1990, pp. 62-63.

- Katharin A. Keller, "Acquiring School Services for Drug-Addicted Children," Education Digest, March 1991, pp. 46-48.

- Peter Kerr, "Crack Addiction: The Tragic Toll on Women and Their Children," New York Times, 9 February 1987, p. B-1.

- Diane Alken Laderman, "Crack Babies: Ready or Not, Here They Come," American Teacher, November 1990, pp. 10-11.

- S. MacGregor et al., "Cocaine Use During Pregnancy: Adverse Prenatal Outcome," American Journal of Obstetrics and Gynecology, September 1987, pp. 686-90.

- G. Miller, "Addicted Infants and Their Mothers,: Zero to Three: Bulletin of the National Center for Clinical Infant Programs, June 1989, pp. 20-23.

- "Newborns and Addiction," Newsweek, 20 April 1992, p. 75.

- Michele L. Norris, "The Class of Crack's Innocent Victims," Washington Post, National Weekly Edition, 8 July 1991, pp. 11-12.

- Andrew C. Revkin, "Crack in the Cradle," Discover, September 1989, pp. 63-69.

- Marilee C. Rist, "'Crack Babies' in School," Education Digest, May 1990, pp. 30-33; and idem, "The Shadow Children Preparing for the Arrival of Crack Babies in School," Phi Delta Kappa Research Bulletin, July 1990, pp. 1-6.

- J. Schneider and Ira Chasnoff, M.D., "Cocaine abuse During Pregnancy: Its Effects on Infant Motor Development: A Clinical Perspective," Topics in Acute Care and Trauma Rehabilitation, July 1987, pp. 59-69.

- "Smoking Out Cocaine's 'In Utero' Impact," Science News, 9 November 1991, p. 302.

- T.B. Sonderegger, "Overview" (a symposium of papers presented at the meeting of the Committee on Problems of Drug Dependence, Tahoe City, Calif., 1986), Neurotoxicology and Teratology, vol. 9, 1987, pp. 289-90.

- B. Tittle and N. St. Claire, "Promoting the Health and Development of Drug-Exposed Infants Through a Comprehensive Clinical Model," Zero to Three: Bulletin of the National Center for Clinical Infant Programs, June 1989, pp. 18-20.

- Anastasia Toufexis, "Innocent Victims," Time, 13 May 1991, pp. 56-60.

- Rachelle Tyler, M.D., "Prenatal Drug Exposure: An Overview of Associated Problems and Intervention Strategies," Phi Delta Kappan, May 1992, pp. 705-8.

- Priscilla Van Tassel, "Schools Trying to Cope with 'Crack Babies,'" New York Times, 5 January 1992, Sect. 12, p. 1.

- Debra Viadero, "New Research Finds Little Lasting Harm for 'Crack' Children," Education Week, 29 January 1992, p. 1.

- Donna Weston et al., "Drug Exposed Babies: Research and Clinical Issues," Zero to Three: Bulletin of the National Center for Clinical Infant Programs, June 1989, pp. 1-7.

- Robert C. Yeager, "Kids Who Can't Say No," Reader's Digest, February 1991, pp. 66-71.

- B. Zuckerman et al., "Effects of Maternal Marijuana and Cocaine Use on Fetal Growth," New England Journal of Medicine, vol. 320, 1989, pp. 762-68.

Reports/Transcripts

- "Born Hooked: Confronting the Impact of Perinatal Substance Abuse," summary of a hearing before the Select Committee on Children, Youth and Families, U.S. House of Representatives, 27 April 1989.

- Cocaine Babies: Florida's Substance-Exposed Youth, developed by the Prevention Center of the Florida Department of Education's Office of Policy Research and Improvement, distributed by the North Central Regional Educational Laboratory, 1900 Spring Rd., Oakbrook, IL 60521. For information, contact Dan Thomas, 414 Florida Education Center, Tallahassee, FL 32399-0400.

- Cocaine/Crack, The Big Lie, National Clearinghouse for Drug

Information, P.O. Box 2345, Rockville, MD 20052; pamphlet, single copies are free.

- "Drug-Exposed Infants," The Future of Children, Spring 1991. This special issued of the quarterly journal is available from the Center for the Future of Children, David and Lucile Packard Foundation, 300 Second St., Suite 102, Lost Altos, CA 94022; it is free.

- Robert L. DuPont, M.D., ed., Crack Cocaine: A Challenge for Prevention, a project of the Office for Substance Abuse Prevention, 5600 Fishers Lane, Rockwall II, Rockville, MD 20857, 1991; it is free

- "The Enemy Within: Crack Cocaine and America's Families," report prepared by the Committe on Ways and Means, U.S. House of Representatives, 12 June 1990.

- Fetal Alcohol Syndrome and Other Drugs Update, a newsletter of information about fetal alcohol syndrome and the impact of drug addiction, published by the Prevention Resource Center, 822 S. College St., Springfield, IL 62704; vol. 10, no. 4; it is free. A 1991 special issue, Not One Life to Lose, includes features on the Drug-Free Families with a Future initiatives and information on programs throughout Illinois and in other states.

- Identifying the Needs of Drug-Affected Children: 1990 Issue Forum, presented by the Office for Substance Abuse Prevention; the report is distributed by the Midwest Center for Drug-Free Schools and Communities, 1900 Spring Rd., Oakbrook, IL 60321.

- "Impact of Crack Cocaine on the Child Welfare System," hearing before the Sub-committee on Human Resources of the Committee on Ways and Means, U.S. House of Representatives, 101st Congress, 2nd Session, 3 April 1990.

- "Prenatal Cocaine Exposure: The South Looks for Answers," a SACUS Special Report, available from the Southern Association on Children Under Six, P.O. Box 5403; the price is $6.

- "Principal Findings on Addicted Infants and Their Mothers," Select Committee on Children, Youth, and Families Staff Survey, U.S. House of Representatives, 27 April 1989.

Teaching Resources

- Danni Odom-Winn and Dianne Dunagan, "Crack Kids" in School—What to Do, How to Do It (Educational Activities Inc., P.O. Box 392, Freeport, NY 11520); ph. 800/645-3739; the price is $14.95 plus $2 for shipping; bulk discounts are available.

- Project Healthy Choices is a teacher-training program for working with children exposed to drugs. For information, write to Robin Ruhf, Safe Spaces, Project Healthy Choices, Bank Street College of Education, 610 W. 112th St., New York, NY 10025; ph. 212/875-4510.

- Strategies for Teaching Young Children Prenatally Exposed to Drugs is a publication that is part of a training program for educators, school district officials, and department of education staff. For information, contact Teaching Strategies, Hillsborough County Public Schools, 1202 E. Palm Ave., Tampa, FL 33605.

- Today's Challenge: Teaching Strategies for Working with Young Children at Risk Due to Prenatal Substance Exposure, developed by the Los Angeles Unified School District, Division of Special Education, Prenatally Exposed to Drugs Program; it is distributed free of charge by the Midwest Regional Center for Drug-Free Schools and Communities, 1900 Spring Rd., Suite 300, Oakbrook, IL 60521.

The Story of Kahlil

How could a public school make a dramatic impact on a crack-exposed child who seemed destined to wind up in the same kind of trouble as Antoine, the boy who escaped from custody in Cook County?

Kahlil (not his real name) is the 6-year-old who could not bear human touch when he first entered Project DAISY at age 4 during the first year of the program. His behavior indicated depression, and he had problems bonding with adults. He was extremely angry and anxious and had poor socialization skills. He was easily intimidated by other children's play behaviors and would often become aggressive. The Project DAISY specialists suspected that Kahlil had vision problems as well.

His grandmother reported that Kahlil was hyperactive and extremely difficult to discipline. He had formed no attachment with his mother, who was a polysubstance abuser with a history of numerous incarcerations. There were a number of family members living at home.

Kahlil's grandmother was Project DAISY's contact during the first year of the project, when he received psychological counseling in the classroom. Social service support was also given to his family. He received speech and language screening, home-based consultation, and a developmentally appro-priate learning experience within the Project DAISY classroom.

At the end of two years, Project DAISY expanded social services to his mother, who was then out of jail. The project social worker addressed the family's housing and clothing needs and helped to get Kahlil's mother enrolled in a drug treatment program. The project also dealt with Kahlil's medical needs.

The child and family received support from the multidisciplinary team and were given counseling regarding nutrition. The home-based intervention then included six weeks of consultation during the summer.

Kahlil's preschool teacher implemented a social curriculum that included the use of Montessori techniques and a child-centered, choice-driven curriculum. His classroom experience was with a heterogeneous group of students and included many options, the use of a computer center, and the integration of literacy techniques with Kahlil's work in different learning centers throughout the school day.

The staff began to see differences in Kahlil's self-perception and in his use of positive social risk-taking. The Project DAISY staff concluded that the "Morning Meeting," in particular, fostered positive social interaction and provided multiple opportunities for modeling and rehearsing langauge, which was one way Kahlil could learn to get his needs met.

"We no longer witnessed his physical aggression when he had a problem," confirms project director Diane Powell. "He was using language. By the end of the second year, we noted a remarkable reduction of anger. He exhibited appropriate social interaction, heightened interest in the classroom activities, and strong bonding with classroom staff and project staff. And he no longer exhibited any aggression. Kahlil had developed a very strong sense of self and purpose."

While his home situation still remains chaotic because of multiple changes in the family, Kahlil is able to state his wants and needs. During an interview with the social worker at the end of the year, Kahlil poignantly stated, "I don't want to be on drugs like my Mommy."

"This fall," Powell says with satisfaction, "Kahlil was moved to first grade. He has no need for special education or multidisciplinary team intervention. He is functioning above grade level and is a very confident little boy."

Kahlil will continue to receive monitoring by the psychologist. Project DAISY research staff will follow his progress to keep track of his educational outcomes over the next three to five years. And the project's support team will follow him at three key points during the transitional year to see how he is doing in first grade.—RCS

Ten Recommendations for Educators

At the Federal level, the U.S. Department of Education (ED) does not take any particular position on how schools ought to educate children exposed to drugs prenatally. But Shirley Jackson, director of ED's Comprehensive School Health Education Program, has just completed her own two-year nationwide study of school programs for prenatally drug-exposed children.

Jackson makes 10 recommendations to help guide schools and teachers.

1. Cease using the labels *crack babies and crack children*. "We don't know whether crack children exist," insists Jackson, "We know from research on other self-fulfilling prophecies on grouping children that when you identify children with derogatory terms, you set low expectations for them that are likely in and of themselves to be fulfilled," she explains.

And I've seen many cases of schools that worried hysterically about "crack kids" and how different these children are. But they did not actually know that the children were born prenatally exposed. Lots of people don't know what they are talking about.

As important the literature and researchers say that most drug-abusing mothers are polysubstance abusers. So it is not clear which drug may or may not have done damage to the child. For example, alcohol and tobacco are in many cases far more detrimental in terms of effect on the child. Additionally, many children are misdiagnosed by teachers or

schools that have no medical evidence for their fears. So that's why it makes little sense to label these children.

2. Do not identify, label, and segregate children because it is believed that they have been prenatally exposed to drugs. "There appears to be no educational reason to set up an early identification system," Jackson says. "If the child has been prenatally exposed to crack cocaine, how will the teacher treat that differently from a case of prenatal exposure to alcohol or just coming from a dysfunctional environment? The manifesting behaviors are the same.

"Children affected by psychosocial trauma and children who may be affected by prenatal exposure to drugs have the same kind of behaviors. The researchers cannot tell the difference between children exposed to drugs in utero and those with postnatal psychosocial traumatic conditions."

"So there is no need for [teachers] to do anything differently. All they could do is label and segregate the children and start a cycle of self-fulfilling prophecies. These students for the most part will be in regular classrooms. About 40% have developmental lags, but they are the same kind of things you find among children traumatized by poverty—attention disorders, the restlessness that these children show, and some of the antisocial behaviors are similar."

"If a child is living in an environment with the using parents, then that child is being exposed to a lot

of neglect and trauma," Jackson explains, "Whether it is prenatal or postnatal you have to deal with the behavior of that particular child."

"Identification systems by schools could also lead to legal entanglements. If they get mothers to tell of their prenatal drug use, many states have laws that punish those whom the schools may get involved in something that they do not really need."

3. Provide all teachers with staff development to prepare and encourage them to use practices that have been learned from research about the ways to successfully teach children who are experiencing psychosocial trauma. "All regular classroom teachers need to know how to teach children who are experiencing some kind of difficulty because of psychosocial trauma," Jackson says. "More and more of our schools, even in the richest school districts, are finding a lot more of their children with a lot of behaviors that in the past were associated with poor children."

"There is a lot of destabilization going on in the society," she notes, "economic destabilization, lots of latchkey children. The schools—whether the richest or the poorest—are seeing a different kind of child. So teachers are going to have to learn, from some of the excellent techniques that have been developed through special education and through Head Start, ways to deal with children who have less readiness or eagerness to learn."

4. Schools should provide developmentally appropriate early childhood education programs for all children—but especially poor children. "If these kids, don't receive the sound early intervention, then it is unlikely that they are going to experience success in school," Jackson asserts.

5. Plan the guidance of social and emotion development as an integral part of the curriculum. Positive social behaviors should be modeled and taught directly, not incidentally, especially for children experiencing behavioral difficulties. Such behaviors "include perseverance, industry, independence, cooperation, negotiating, solving interpersonal problems nonviolently, self-control, dealing with fears, and intrinsic motivation," explains Jackson. "Some children just don't come from environments where they have learned these things. If they come to school not knowing these things, especially in the primary grades, our job has to be the guidance of social/emotional development as an integral part of the curriculum.

6. Schools should remember that classroom limits of two adults for every 20 children are recommended for the preschool and primary years. Early childhood educators concur on this standard for developmentally appropriate programs. "In all of the programs I contacted," says Jackson, "the directors spoke emphatically to the question of class size."

7. Schools should organize multidisciplinary trans-agency teams of providers of health and social services to assist children and families in solving problems that transcend the reach of schools and teachers. "Teachers can only do so much, and we have to support them" so that they have time enough "to actually teach children as their number one priority," Jackson argues. This requires an easy system of teacher referral to medical or counseling aid. Schools have to reach out to public health-care providers to create these networks.

"The schools see a lot of things that need attention, but the teacher should not be responsible for solving all the problems. But so many of these problems are presenting barriers to learning that we can't ignore them anymore."

8. Establish effective home/school partnerships that help care givers become actively involved in the education of their children. "The important thing to emphasize is the real care giver," says Jackson, "whether grandmother or foster parent or other family member. We must deal with the reality of the new family."

9. Schools should plan active and intensive drug-prevention programs for all children, especially those living in communities with a widespread drug culture.

10. Schools should cooperate with others in the community to provide drug prevention treatment or seminars for women of child-bearing age, including middle and high school students.

Jackson insists that the entire area is a "rapidly emerging field that schools need to keep track of as new developments occur. We want to give these children the best chance."—RCS

R. Craig Sautter is a writer and editor based in Chicago.

Sautter, R. Craig. "Crack: Healing the Children." Phi Delta Kappan (November 1992): pp. K1-K10. Used with permission.

Although education and religion have been historically interwined, conflicting beliefs and traditions in the U. S. have led to official neutrality in state supported schools. Kathan traces some of the history of this controversy.

Prayer and the Public Schools: The Issue in Historical Perspective and Implications for Religious Education Today

Boardman W. Kathan

The controversy over the role of religion and public education has continued throughout the history of the United States and shows no signs of abating. Arrayed on various sides of the conflict are fundamentally different philosophies of education and sharply divided understandings of the relationship between Church and State in a modern democratic republic. Battles have been fought over prayer and Bible reading, textbooks and curriculum, religious holidays and religious symbols, evolution and creationism, released time inside and outside the school building. The landscape is littered with countless tracts, sermons, addresses, articles,

books, laws, and court decisions. In every generation the contending forces have found new resolve, fresh recruits, and replenished ammunition.

This paper is an attempt to explain the persistence of the issue of school prayer and to provide a historical framework for understanding the changes in the issue over time. Why has the issue demonstrated such staying power? Whereas Bible reading has been the predominant subject through the years, why have the proposals to override the 1962-63 Supreme Court decisions been primarily prayer amendments? How has the issue of school prayer changed dur-

ing the course of American history? Is the practice of prayer in the classroom as long-standing a custom or as widespread and universal as commonly assumed?

There is a large body of literature on the subject. In the nineteenth century much of it was polemical, revolving around Protestant-Catholic battles over the King James Version of the Bible and the division of school funds. In the last two decades the discussion has centered around the legal issues and the interpretation of the U.S. Constitution. For example, in *Religion in the Public Schools: An Introduction*, Richard C. McMillan has intentionally chosen the legal frame of reference because "in a pluralistic society, given the idea of religious liberty to which the country is constitutionally dedicated, solutions that will protect the rights of all persons can be found only in a legal context."[1] One of the best historical studies is *Piety in the Public School* by Robert Michaelsen, but the author's main interest is the attempt in different generations to find common religion for the public schools, whether the "common Christianity" of Horace Mann or the "common faith" of John Dewey.[2] A bibliography was prepared by Albert J. Menendez, *School Prayer and Other Religious Issues in American Public Education*, but of 1,566 entries only 12 are listed under "School Prayer: History," while there are 165 listed under "School Prayer in the Courts."[3] What is lacking, even in these 12 entries, is a systematic treatment of the subject in American educational history.

Persistence of the Issue

The issue of prayer in the public schools is one that will not go away. Since the rulings of the Supreme Court in 1962 and 1963, there have been many attempts by the Congress to amend the Constitution. The two most active leaders of this period of time were Representative Frank Becker of New York and Senator Everett Dirksen of Illinois. In 1966 the Senate lacked a two-thirds majority by nine votes, and in 1971 the House missed the two-thirds majority for an amendment by 23 votes. Undoubtedly, the best

organized and most carefully orchestrated campaign was in March 1984, when 50 proamendment speakers kept the House of Representatives in a rare all-night session; when demonstrations, rallies, and prayer vigils were held at the Capitol and the Supreme Court building; when Pat Boone and other celebrities organized letter, postcard, and telephone drives; and when the Senate finally voted on a prayer amendment, after two weeks of debate, which fell 11 votes short of the two-thirds majority required. Over 20 years after the Supreme Court decisions, the issue of school prayer is more controversial and politicized than ever before. Advocacy for an amendment was added to the platform of the Republican Party in 1980 and became part of the "social issues" agenda in the 97th and 98th Congress along with anti-abortion and anti-busing for school desegregation.

Conservative religious groups such as the National Association of Evangelicals, the re-named Moral Majority, and others have lobbied extensively for school prayer and have threatened retribution at the polls. Many Protestant and Jewish organizations are just as strongly opposed to it, along with the American Civil Liberties Union, People for the American Way, and Americans United for the Separation of Church and State. Fierce battles are being fought in the largest Protestant denomination, the Southern Baptist Convention, over the school prayer issue.

There are at least six factors that help to explain this persistence. The first is ideological. In its simplest terms the movement to "restore" prayer to the classroom is a struggle for control of the public schools of the country. This struggle is nothing new. In every generation a host of special interest groups has seen universal free education as a way of capturing the hearts and minds of the American people for a particular cause or ideology. The history of American education is full of efforts to influence classroom instruction, textbook publishing, and teacher education. Those eager to bring God and religion "back to the classroom" are seeking to rid the schools of what they perceive as a religion of secularism or secular humanism. These same individuals have a fervent, nostalgic longing for a "Christian America," God-fearing and law-abiding, and they feel that mandated or organized prayer is one way to reclaim it.

Closely related is the moral factor. People sense a loss of traditional values, a decline in discipline, a rise in crime and violence, equating these trends with the ejection of prayer and God from the schools. Moral education and character-building have always been tasks assigned to the schools; and at least since Horace Mann and the common school reform movement, there has been a healthy debate about the sources of morality and the relationship of religion to ethics, as far as American schools are concerned. Mann himself saw the schools as solving all the problems

1   Richard C. McMillan, *Religion in the Public Schools: An Introduction* (Macon, Georgia: Mercer University Press, 1984).

2   Robert Michaelsen, *Piety in the Public School* (New York: The Macmillan Co., 1970).

3   Albert J. Menendez, *School Prayer and Other Religious Issues in American Public Education: A Bibliography* (New York: Garland Publishing, Inc., 1985).

of society through moral instruction, but he was opposed to sectarian religious teaching: that was the job of the church and Sunday school. Modern attempts to make prayer a formal part of the daily classroom routine have the danger of foreclosing the debate about moral education and of offering a simplistic solution to the problems of drug abuse, alcoholism, vandalism, and teenage pregnancy.

The third factor is civil-religious. The sociologist, Robert Bellah, propounded the view that "there actually exists alongside of and rather clearly differentiated from the churches an elaborate and well-institutionalized civil religion in America."[4] This religion has its creeds and dogmas, rituals, symbols, saints, holy days, and scriptures. G. K. Chesterton could observe that "America is the only nation in the world that is founded on a creed," and he called the United States "a nation with the soul of a church."[5] The public schools have been perceived as the primary institution for the practice and inculcation of this civil religion; therefore, a major reason for the outcry against the 1962 and 1963 decisions was that it seemed to be banished from the schools. Overlooked was the fact that in these same decisions the justices recommended the use of documents, addresses, anthems, and other literature in American history where faith in God is expressed.

A fourth factor is nationalism. Since World War II the United States has been locked in a struggle with the Soviet Union for economic, political, and military supremacy. In this battle with godless, atheistic Communism, it was essential to enlist God on the side of America. This helps to explain why, at the height of the cold war in the 1950s, "under God" was added to the pledge to the flag, and "In God we trust" was adopted as the official motto of the country. Not only is prayer essential to elevate morality and to maintain our civil religion, but it is a strategic weapon to use in our conflict with the USSR. This use or mis-use of God for reasons of statecraft and international competition is frightening at the very least.

The fifth factor is political. In the two decades since the Supreme Court decisions the American people have been regularly polled on their attitude toward school prayer. The Gallup Poll has shown consistently that about 80 percent of the people support school prayer and would favor an amendment to the Constitution. Not only are these figures quoted extensively in the halls of Congress, but those running for office use them for political gain. One incumbent Republican senator, challenged by a more conservative opponent, announced the day before the primary that he would vote in favor of the prayer amendment: He won the primary. We live in a day of single-issue candidates and pressure groups, and school prayer persists as an attractive platform because there is so much political mileage to be gained from it.

A sixth and final factor is that of states' rights and local control. The Constitution left matters of education to the people and the states, and the states in turn have delegated much power to school districts and their boards of education. The First Amendment prohibited only the Congress from making laws relative to the establishment of religion, and it was not until 1940 that the Supreme Court used the 14th Amendment to interpret the religion clauses in a state case. Is it any wonder that people were stunned when a simple prayer written by the New York Board of Regents was declared unconstitutional or when in 1963 Bible readings and the Lord's Prayer were declared an establishment of religion. One of the most passionate arguments for a prayer amendment is that it will return policy and decision-making to the states and school districts. One hotly debated amendment on the floor of the Senate would have removed federal court jurisdiction over school prayer cases and, if passed, could have led to 50 different interpretations of the First Amendment.

In answer to the question of why there have been persistent attempts to pass a prayer amendment rather than a Bible reading amendment, it is clear that the devotional use of the Bible is too specific, too concrete, and that a movement in this direction would break down over which translation, which testament, which passages. Prayer has more symbolic power. It is like motherhood, the flag, and apple pie: Who could be against it? It becomes a convenient rallying point for all those who are critical of humanistic and secular trends in public education. And if anyone questions the power of symbols and their manipulation, a glance at the book *Symbolic Crusade*

---

4   Robert N. Bellah, "Civil Religion in America," *Daedalus 96* (Winter 1967): 1.
5   Sidney E. Mead, *The Nation with the Soul of a Church* (New York: Harper & Row, 1975): 20, 48.

by Joseph Gusfield would be enlightening.[6]

For a historical analysis of the school prayer issue, I suggest that we look at six periods of American history: 1) the colonial era; 2) the revolution era or early national period and decline of common schools; 3) the mid-nineteenth century and common school reform; 4) the late nineteenth century and the development of modern secular education; 5) the first half of the twentieth century and the era of state prayer and Bible laws; 6) the second half of the twentieth century and the era of the U.S. Supreme Court decisions regarding prayer and Bible reading.

1. *Colonial Era.* School prayer was not an issue in the colonial period, since the public school, as we know it today, simply did not exist. Earlier historians like Ellwood Cubberly were fond of reciting the story of how the seeds of public schooling were planted in the seventeenth century and finally brought to glorious fruition in the nineteenth century.[7] Educational historiography has been flawed by a preoccupation with formal pedagogy and educational institutions and an attempt to find precursors of present forms in the past. Bernard Bailyn corrected these assumptions with an understanding of education "as the entire process by which a culture transmits itself across the generations." According to Bailyn, the most important agency in this process was the family, extended and formalized in apprenticeship and the local community. The church carried on a more explicit or formal educational function, but at the local level the church was coterminous with the community. In other words, the line between "private" and "public" was blurred. "The modern conception of public education," wrote Bailyn, "was unknown before the end of the eighteenth century."[8]

Churches were expected to start schools in order that everyone would be trained in literacy and therefore be able to read the Bible and not be "deluded by Satan." For example, the Congregational Church of Wilton, Connecticut, was organized in 1726 with five purposes: 1) to hold worship; 2) to recruit; 3) to train the militia; 4) to raise taxes; 5) to educate all the children of the community. Schools in this early period were predominantly Protestant in ethos and content, and it was common for the school day to include prayers, hymns, and Bible reading. Lawrence Cremin, in his *American Education: The Colonial Experience 1607-1783*, indicated that the rules and regulations of the Hopkins Grammar School in New Haven in 1684 were typical: "The master is instructed to begin each day with a short prayer and then to set his pupils in the schoolroom according to their degrees of learning."[9] In the more Anglican colony of Virginia the teachers of the Society for the Propagation of the Gospel were enjoined, among other things, to teach the Holy Scriptures, to catechize, and to lead pupils in morning and evening prayers.[10]

By the end of the colonial period schools had assumed a new importance, and education became more "deliberate, self-conscious and explicit."[11] Cremin distinguishes three general types of institution: "the English (or petty, or common) school; the Latin grammar school; and the academy."[12] However, there was another important development by the end of this period, namely, the growth of a diversity of religious groups. Among other things, this meant that sectarian religious teachings and practices in the common schools would not go unchallenged.

2. *Revolutionary Era or Early National Period.* School prayer continued in this period as a custom or tradition in the common schools, but with less frequency, support, and favor. It is generally recognized that at the end of the eighteenth century and the beginning of the nineteenth, there was a decline in religion. According to Syndey Ahlstrom, "The revolutionary era was a period of decline for American Christianity as a whole. The churches reached a lower ebb of vitality during the two decades after the end of hostilities than at any other time in the country's religious history."[13] The Great Awakening

6   Joseph Gusfield, *Symbolic Crusade: Status, Politics and the American Temperance Movement* (Urbana: University of Illinois Press, 1966).
7   Ellwood P. Cubberly, *Public Education in the United States* (Boston: Houghton Mifflin Co., 1919). See also Lawrence A. Cremin, *The Wonderful World of Ellwood Patterson Cubberly* (New York: Teachers College, Columbia University, 1965).
8   Bernard Bailyn, *Education in the Forming of American Society* (New York: W.W. Norton Co., 1960): 14, 11.
9   Lawrence A. Cremin, *American Education: The Colonial Experience, 1607-1783* (New York: Harper & Row, 1970): 186.
10   *Ibid.*, 343.
11   Bernard Bailyn, *op cit.*, 41.
12   Lawrence Cremin, *op cit.*, 500.

had run its course, and the war for independence had taken its toll on churches, ministers, and church membership. In addition, there was a growth of religious rationalism (Thomas Paine had his followers in the new nation), Enlightenment ideas, and deism. Another factor was the disestablishment of the churches and the First Amendment guarantees of free exercise of religion. To those who claim that this was only to prevent a national church, the story is told of the Declaration of Religious Liberty in Virginia, supported by Madison and Jefferson, in opposition to Patrick Henry's bill to pay for Christian teachers in the schools.

There was also a decline in the common schools during this period. It is ironic that in this critical time of nation-building, with the need for an educated citizenry with republican virtues, education deteriorated. Horace Mann pointed out some reasons in the first issue of *The Common School Journal*, which he edited. Other causes and preoccupations had deflected interest in the schools, such as the revolutionary struggle, the fiscal condition of the new government, other philanthropic enterprises, and the attention given to material prosperity.[14] I believe that a major factor in this decline was the system of local control without any checks or balances. The new Constitution had left education to the people and the states. Proposals by Jefferson, Benjamin Rush, and others to organize state systems were not passed. Laws

passed by state legislatures were not enforced. Local communities resisted the additional taxes and kept the decentralized district schools, resulting in a lack of supervision, accountability, financial support, and a great deal of public apathy and indifference. It is clear that, before the common school reform movement, the schoolhouses were deplorable and lacked equipment; classes were ungraded and crowded; teachers were untrained, ill-paid, and transient; libraries were unknown; and textbooks were lacking. Those who could afford it sent their children to an increasing number of private schools and academies.

Given these conditions, it is no wonder that religious instruction and religious exercises were haphazard, perfunctory, or neglected altogether. In his first annual report as Secretary of the Board in Connecticut in 1839, Henry Barnard wrote: "The whole field of moral education is almost abandoned," despite the fact that the Bible or New Testament was found in almost every school.[15] Barnard and other school reformers discovered that the Bible was used as a reading and spelling book and sometimes as a religious exercise at the opening of school. School visitors reported that in some districts there was the reciting of the Lord's Prayer and the Ten Commandments once a week, while others reported that there was prayer only when the visitors, especially clergy, were present to lead them. The purpose of education

had shifted to training for morality, but the common schools were inadequate for the task.

3. *Mid-Nineteenth Century or Era of Common School Reform.* Carl Kaestle has pointed out in his writings and addresses that the traditional view of this period has emphasized the work of individuals like Mann and Barnard and has perpetuated the "great man" approach to history. In a presentation before the Connecticut Historical Society, Kaestle said:

> Where the conditions were right—in much of the Midwest and even in the upcountry non-plantation South—advocates of common school systems emerged. Though they often cited Yankee authorities and even invited Barnard and Mann to their communities to give advice, one can imagine that they would have invented a public school tradition on their own even if the New England model had not been available.[16]

Conditions were ripe for the reform of the common schools beginning in the 1830s. State systems of education were created; teachers institutes and normal schools were started; textbooks were written; and a vast network of publications, speakers' bureaus, and other resources was developed.

Parallel to the reforms in education and contributing to them was the revival of religion, often called the Second Great Awakening. In their book, *Managers of Virtue: Pub-*

13 Sydney E. Ahlstrom, *A Religious History of the American People* (New Haven: Yale University Press, 1972), 365.

14 Horace Mann, "Editorial," *The Common School Journal* 1, 1 (November 1838): 2-3.

15 Henry Barnard, *First Annual Report of the Secretary of the Board* (Hartford: Case, Tiffany and Burnham, 1839), 42.

16 Carl Kaestle, "Yankee Educators to the Nation: A Reassessment," *To Enlighten, Correct and Form: Yankee Educators to the Nation* (West Hartford, CT: Noah Webster Foundation and Historical Society, 1986), 17.

lic School Leadership in America, 1820-1980, David Tyack and Elisabeth Hansot have demonstrated that the religious revival in the 1800s and the millennial vision of the Protestant-republican ideology laid the foundation for public schools.[17] In two "Monographs in Christian Education," Robert Lynn and Will Kennedy showed that these schools were an important part of a dual Protestant strategy in education. The purpose of the public school was to teach morality and a common Protestant Christianity, while the Sunday school was developed to provide the more specific teaching of the different denominations.[18]

When Horace Mann became secretary of the newly created Board of Education in Massachusetts in 1837, sectarian religious doctrine was still being taught by teachers and visiting clergy, even though the state legislature had passed a law in 1827 prohibiting sectarian textbooks. In order to develop a school system that would be open to all students and supported by the taxes of all people, he had to work out a compromise, so that the schools would be neither sectarian on the one hand or "godless" on the other. His solution was to encourage the teaching of a common morality or natural religion and to promote the reading of the Bible "without comment." Mann could not recognize

the sectarian nature of the King James Version of the Bible, which was objectionable to Catholics.

In his 12th and final report as secretary in 1848, he was proud of the fact that the Bible had been restored to the schools of the state. He was relatively quiet on the matter of prayer. On a trip to Europe in 1843, he visited some Catholic schools and wrote in his journal an unfavorable comment about "the number of prayers which the children are obliged to make."[19] In his book, *Public Schools and Moral Education,* Neil McCluskey wrote that for Mann, genuine religion consisted of love for humanity, the golden rule, and the social betterment of the race: "This meant *doing* for one's fellow rather than preoccupying one's self with private prayer and worship."[20]

Henry Barnard considered Mann his mentor, colleague, and confidant, and turned to him for advice on many problems, including religion in the schools. In a letter to Barnard on June 23, 1844, the older educator included this recommendation: "The other suggestions relates to a matter which has been of late exciting considerable interest in this State. It is that of the *neutrality* of schools between the different religious parties among us."[21]

I have underlined the word, *neutrality,* because it is a key concept in

later discussion and court decisions. Just as nonsectarian striving did not deter Mann from the Protestant Bible, so the search for neutrality did not preclude the use of prayers and Protestant worship for Barnard. Paul Mattingly has shown that the early teachers institutes of Barnard were revival meetings: "Prayers and hymns not only were incorporated into the actual proceedings but usually began and concluded the main exercises and lectures of an institute."[22] In the *American Journal of Education,* which he edited for many years, Barnard published articles that included the answer to the question as to what the public school can do regarding Christianity: "It can, in many instances, with the universal consent of the community, affix a more decidedly religious character to the school duties of each day, by the observance of daily prayers."[23]

Barnard's successor as school commissioner in Rhode Island, E.R. Potter, dealt extensively with the problem of the Bible and prayer in the public schools in his 1853 and 1854 reports. Potter decided cases of objection to prayer on a voluntary bases; there would be no coercion; students who object could be excused; the right of conscience would be upheld. Yet, it was claimed, "Religious exercises, if conducted in a really Christian spirit, would seldom be objected to. The

---

17 David Tyack and Elisabeth Hansot, *Managers of Virtue: Public School Leadership in America, 1820-1980* (New York: Basic Books, Inc., 1982), 15-28.

18 Robert W. Lynn, *Protestant Strategies in Education* (New York: Association Press, 1964), and William B. Kennedy, *The Shaping of Protestant Education: An Interpretation of the Sunday School and the Development of Protestant Educational Strategy in the United States, 1789-1860* (New York: Association Press, 1966).

19 Neil G. McGluskey, *Public Schools and Moral Education* (New York: Columbia University Press, 1958), 49.

20 *Ibid,* 2.

21 Vincent P. Lannie, Editor, *Henry Barnard: American Educator* (New York: Teachers College Press, 1974), 86-87.

22 Paul H. Mattingly, *The Classless Profession* (New York: New York University Press, 1975), 67.

23 Henry Barnard, Editor, *Papers for the Teacher* (New York: F.C. Brownell and Hartford: F.B. Perkins, 1860), 8 (Reprinted from *American Journal of Education*).

Lord's Prayer, or one similar in substance, would probably never be objected to."[24]

By the 1840s, prayer and Bible reading had become the rule but also a bone of contention. As long as communities were predominantly or entirely Protestant, no objection was raised. However, the immigration of Irish and German Catholics, especially to urban centers, challenged Protestant hegemony in education. Meeting in Baltimore in 1840, the Fourth Provincial Council of Roman Catholics requested that parish priests resist Protestant prayers and readings from the Protestant Bible in public schools. Conflict erupted in New York City in the following years, and when prayers and the KJV of the Bible continued in use, Bishop John Hughes urged Catholics to attend parochial schools. Finally, in 1853 there was a ruling by the New York State Superintendent of Schools that prayer could not be mandated as a part of daily classroom activities, and that Catholic pupils could not be required to attend schools were the KJV Bible was used. The controversy between Protestants and Catholics became violent in Philadelphia, and people lost their lives. Homes and churches were burned. The stage had been set for a bitter "Bible war" and a change in policy by boards and courts.

4. *Late Nineteenth Century and Development of Modern Secular Education.* Whereas the "Bible Wars" in New York and Philadelphia pitted Protestants against Catholics, in Cincinnati, Ohio, a coalition was formed of Catholics, Jews, and Protestants to protest religious practices in the public schools. In 1869 the Board of Education voted to eliminate prayers, Bible reading, hymns, and other sectarian religion from classrooms, but the decision split the board and the city. It was appealed to the Superior Court where it was overturned and then to the Supreme Court of Ohio where it was upheld. It is worth noting that the dissenting vote in the Superior Court was cast by Judge Alphonso Taft (father of William Howard Taft, later President of the United States), who argues that in its attitude toward religion "the government is neutral."[25] The Ohio Supreme Court ruled that the Constitution of the State does not enjoin or require religious instruction, or the reading of religious books, in the public schools of the state.[26] Anson Phelps Stokes in his comprehensive work, *Church and State in the United States,* called this "one of the most important decisions in the relation between church and state in this country."[27]

A common practice in the nineteenth century in schools was to allow students to be excused if there was objection to prayer and Bible reading. It was felt that this practice protected the free expression of religion and the sensibilities of minority religious groups. However, in an important decision in 1910 the Illinois Supreme Court declared:

The exclusion of a pupil from this part of the school exercise in which the rest of the school joins, separates him from his fellows, puts him in a class by himself, deprives him of his equality with the other pupils, subjects him to a religious stigma and places him at a disadvantage in the school, which was never contemplated. All this is because of his religious belief. If the instruction or exercises is such that certain of the pupils must be excused from it because it is hostile to their or their parents' religious beliefs, the said instruction or exercise is sectarian, and forbidden by the Constitution.[28]

The lawsuit was instituted by a group of taxpayers in District 24, who felt as Roman Catholics that they could not allow their children to be taught from a different version of the Bible or be led in a different version of the Lord's Prayer than that approved by the church. Since school attendance was compulsory and there existed no alternative school in the country, their children were virtually coerced into attending a place of worship contrary to their beliefs and conscience. The majority opinion sided with the parents and added that the state and school were civil or secular institutions, not religious, and it was not the duty of the state to teach religion. Practices that were struck down in the Illinois case were the reading of the Bible, recitation of the Lord's Prayer, and the singing of sacred

24 E.R. Potter, *Report Upon Public Schools and Education in Rhode Island* (Providence: Knowles, Anthony & Co., 1855), 12-13.
25 *The Bible in Public Schools: Arguments in the Case of John D. Minor et al. v. Board of Education* (Cincinnati: Robert Clarke & Co., 1870), 415.
26 *Ibid.,* reprinted with appendix, Supreme Court decision of 1872, (New York: Da Capo Press, 1967), 238-54.
27 Anson Phelps Stokes, *Church and State in the United States,* 2 (New York: Harper & Brothers, 1950), 562.
28 Samuel W. Brown, *Secularization of American Education* (New York: Teachers College, Columbia, 1912), 139-40.

hymns, for all of which students were required to assume a devotional attitude.

In 1903 in Nebraska the court ruled that Bible reading, prayers, and hymns were devotional exercises and, therefore, constituted sectarian instruction. Likewise, in 1890 the Wisconsin Supreme Court had ruled that such religious practices were illegal. The high courts in Louisiana, South Dakota, and Washington also decided against religious exercises. Courts in other states let the practices stand. In an Iowa case in 1884, the court refused to interfere with the custom of teachers to use the first few minutes of each school day to read from the Bible and lead in the Lord's Prayer and religious songs, as long as students were not required to be present during those exercises. The court declared in a 1904 Kansas case that nothing in the state constitution served to exclude the Bible or prohibit a teacher, for the purpose of quieting the pupils and preparing them for their regular lessons, from repeating the Lord's Prayer and the Twenty-Third Psalm, again under the condition that none of the pupils be required to participate. Similar decisions were made in Kentucky, Massachusetts, and Texas. All in all, eight courts declared Bible reading, prayer, and other religious exercises unconstitutional, while 14 courts declared them legal. In many states no action was taken either way.

In 1912 Samuel W. Brown wrote a book entitled *The Secularization of American Education*, in which he analyzed legislation, state constitu-

tions, and court decisions in the nineteenth century, which removed church control and sectarian religion from the public schools. According to this author, the aims of education in the seventeenth and eighteenth centuries were largely religious and ecclesiastical, but by the twentieth century they had become civic. Laws were enacted in many states to prohibit sectarian religious instruction and sectarian textbooks in the schools. In many cases this took the form of a constitutional provision. Brown felt that this secularization of public education represented but one phase of the differentiation and separation of the ecclesiastical and the civil powers that had been going on in the country from the earliest years of its history.[29]

This process of secularization reached a peak during the career of William Torrey Harris (1835-1909). Long before he went to St. Louis as a teacher in 1858, the school system had decided not to hold religious exercises in the schools. Contrary to Horace Mann, Harris did not feel that the reading of the Bible without comment had a place in the classroom, and he rejected the idea of non-sectarian religious instruction. For Harris, "the reading of the Bible, the offering of prayers, the teaching of some simple catechism" were all particular forms of Protestantism and were therefore sectarian. It was not that Harris did not have a high regard for religion and the Bible; it was just that he felt that they belonged in the home and church where they could be taught with full respect for truth and integ-

rity.[30] Besides serving as Superintendent of Schools in St. Louis for 12 years, he also was U.S. Commissioner of Education from 1889 to 1906, and in this capacity he did much to influence American schooling through his writing and lecturing.

Samuel Brown had argued that the secularization of the public schools had occurred by the time his study was published in 1912. In his book, *Piety in the Public School*, Robert Michaelsen takes issue with Brown on the basis that church religion was not eliminated from the schools, nor had "secularism" triumphed. Michaelsen admits, however, that it depends upon one's definition of "secular," and that in a formal or legal sense American education did become increasingly secularized in the nineteenth century. Even where the courts did allow Bible reading and other devotional practices, it was because they considered them nonsectarian and a traditional part of a secular program of education.[31] Prayer in the public schools as a policy was turned down by boards of education and courts in different parts of the country, but in other places it continued into the twentieth century.

5. *First Half of the Twentieth Century and State Legislation.* By the beginning of the twentieth century, many religious and educational leaders perceived that religion had been eliminated from the public schools. Ministers preached about the lack of prayer and Bible. Church assemblies, like the Presbyterians in 1890, voted to deplore the absence

---

29 *Ibid.*, see esp. 155f.
30 Neil G. McGluskey, *op. cit.*, 166-171.
31 Robert Michaelsen, *op. cit.*, 109-110.

of the Bible. Many articles were written. Religious and educational associations took action including the Religious Education Association, which was founded in 1903 explicitly for the purpose of promoting religious and moral education in elementary and secondary schools as well as other institutions. One of the most influential organizations in this period was the National Reform Association with its headquarters in Pittsburgh. In his doctoral dissertation, "The Holy Experiment and Education: The 1913 Public School Bible Reading Legislation in Pennsylvania," Jack Low has shown how this relatively small group was instrumental in passing a state law mandating prayer and Bible reading in the schools.[32] With the help of other organizations, this movement spread to other states.

Whereas only one state, Massachusetts, had a statute on the books before 1900, 11 states and the District of Columbia passed laws between 1910 and 1930 that made either morning prayer or Bible reading (or both) mandatory. In addition, six states approved laws that permitted Bible selections, and one state, Mississippi, added a provision to its State Constitution, which provided that the Bible could not be excluded from the public schools. According to Don Conway, who did a comprehensive study of the situation for the University of Chicago in 1956, there were also 19 states where Bible reading was permitted under general terms of silence (no

statute) or by interpretation of the Attorney General. Bible reading was not permitted in 11 states by statute or under interpretation of the State Constitution. All the states requiring Bible (and prayer) were in the East and South, except for Idaho. All the states not permitting it were in the West or Mid-West except for New York and Louisiana.[33] These regional differences also showed up in the research of Richard Dierenfield in 1962.[34] With a crazy quilt of local district policies, state laws, contradictory court decisions, and legal opinions, the stage was set for the momentous and historic rulings by the U.S. Supreme Court in 1962 and 1963.

6. *Second Half of the Twentieth Century and U.S. Supreme Court Decisions.* In spite of the diversity of state court rulings, the U.S. Supreme Court consistently refused to accept jurisdiction in cases because of a lack of a substantial federal question. For example, a case was brought to the high court in 1931 from the State of Washington on the grounds that the Bible and religious teachings in public schools were contrary to the First and Fourteenth Amendments to the Constitution, but the justices refused to hear the case. The Supreme Court's decision in the 1940 case, Cantwell v. Connecticut, opened the way for future appeals on First Amendment grounds, since it ruled that free exercise of religion was one of the liberties falling within the due process clause of the 14th Amendment. In 1952 a New Jersey law providing

for Bible reading in the school was appealed to the Supreme Court on the basis that it violated the First Amendment clause prohibiting an establishment of religion. The majority of the justices decided that the opinion of the New Jersey court should stand, since no claims of injury were made and the appellant's child has graduated from high school before the case was appealed (Doremus v. Board of Education).

In the 1961-62 term the Court agreed to hear the Engle v. Vitale case from New York, and in the 1962-63 term they combined two cases, Abington v. Schempp from Pennsylvania and Murray v. Curlett from Maryland. In the former case the Court ruled "it is no part of the business of government to compose official prayers for any group of the American people to recite as a part of a religious program carried on by government." In the latter two cases the Court decided that Bible reading, even without comment, and prayers, including the Lord's Prayer, were sectarian religious exercises and were unconstitutional. A provision for excusing or dismissing students did not mitigate the situation. The justices went out of their way to indicate that the rulings did not mean they were hostile toward religion or that they were rendering the schools "godless." The issue of prayer in public schools had changed considerably through the years from an inherited custom or tradition, often neglected, to a district rule, then to a board policy, sometimes upheld and sometimes

---

32 John W. Lowe, "The Holy Experiment and Education: The 1913 Public School Bible Reading Legislation in Pennsylvania," Ph.D. dissertation submitted to the faculty of Union Theological Seminary and Teachers College, Columbia University, 1986.

33 Don Conway, *Summary: State Regulations Concerning Religion and Public Education*, unpublished report printed by the Committee on Religion and Public Education, National Council of Churches of Christ in the U.S.A., Chicago, Illinois, 1955.

34 Richard B. Dierenfield, *Religion in American Public Schools* (Washington, DC: Public Affairs Press, 1962).

overturned by the courts, then a state law, and finally a practice declared unconstitutional by the U.S. Supreme Court.

In summary, this historical review has shown that school prayer is neither as long-standing a custom or as widespread and universal as commonly assumed.

Conclusion

There are at least three implications for religious education. The first is a challenge to churches and other religious institutions not to turn to the public schools for the teaching and practice of religion, but to strengthen and improve their methods and models of education.

The second is the recognition that religion has not been excluded from public schools: The courts have encouraged or permitted the academic study of religion; the use of historic documents, addresses, and anthems that express religious faith; the practice of voluntary prayer or even an organized period of silence as long as prayer is not promoted; the use of songs and stories of religious holidays within an educational program; and the existence of extracurricular religious groups in non-instructional periods. The third is an acceptance of the invitation posed by Jack Seymour, Bob O'Gorman, and Chuck Foster to join in "the continuing venture to shape the church's education for this pub-

lic role and responsibility," namely to reclaim its role in the education of the public.[35]

The Rev. Mr. Kathan is associate professor of the Cheshire United Church of Christ in Cheshire, CT; archivist of the Religious Education Association; and was Executive Secretary of the Religious Education Association from 1970 to 1981.

Reprinted from the journal, RELIGIOUS EDUCATION, volume 84, number 2, by permission from the publisher, The Religious Education Association, 409 Prospect Street, New Haven, CT 06511-2177. Membership information available upon request.

---

35 Jack L. Seymour, Robert T. O'Gorman and Charles R. Foster, *The Church in the Education of the Public* (Nashville: Abingdon Press, 1984), 153.

This excerpt from a 1992 U.S. Supreme Court decision shows the continuing reluctance of a majority of even a conservative court to condone the appearance of officially approved religious expression.

Lee v. Weisman

Supreme Court Reporter

Deborah Weisman graduated from Nathan Bishop Middle School, a public school in Providence, at a formal ceremony in June 1989. She was about 14 years old. For many years it has been the policy of the Providence School Committee and the Superintendent of Schools to permit principals to invite members of the clergy to give invocations and benedictions at middle school and high school graduations. Many, but not all, of the principals elected to include prayers as part of the graduation ceremonies. Acting for himself and his daughter, Deborah's father, Daniel Weisman, objected to any prayers at Deborah's middle school graduation, but to no avail. The school principal, petitioner Robert E. Lee, invited a rabbi to deliver prayers at the graduation exercises for Deborah's class. Rabbi Leslie

Gutterman, of the Temple Beth El in Providence, accepted.

It has been the custom of Providence school officials to provide invited clergy with a pamphlet entitled "Guidelines for Civic Occasions," prepared by the National Conference of Christians and Jews. The Guidelines recommend that public prayers at nonsectarian civic ceremonies be composed with "inclusiveness and sensitivity," though they acknowledge that "[p]rayer of any kind may be inappropriate on some civic occasions." App. 20-21. The principal gave Rabbi Gutterman the pamphlet before the graduation and advised him the invocation and benediction should be nonsectarian. Agreed Statement of Facts 17, id., at 13.

Rabbi Gutterman's prayers were as follows:

"Invocation

"God of the Free, Hope of the Brave:

For the legacy of America where diversity is celebrated and the rights of minorities are protected, we thank You. May these young men and women grow up to enrich it.

For the liberty of America, we thank You. May these new graduates grow up to guard it.

For the political process of America in which all its citizens may participate, for its court system where all may seek justice we thank You. May those we honor this morning always turn to it in trust.

For the destiny of America we thank You. May the graduate of Nathan Bishop Middle

School so live that they might help to share it.

May our aspirations for our country and for these young people, who are our hope for the future, be richly fulfilled. Amen.

Benediction

O God, we are grateful to You for having endowed us with the capacity for learning which we have celebrated on this joyous commencement.

Happy families give thanks for seeing their children achieve an important milestone. Send Your blessings upon the teachers and administrators who helped prepare them.

The graduates now need strength and guidance for the future, help them to understand that we are not complete with academic knowledge alone. We must each strive to fulfill what You require of us all: To do justly, to love mercy, to walk humbly.

We give thanks to You, Lord, for keeping us alive, sustaining us and allowing us to reach this special, happy occasion. Amen

High school graduations are such an integral part of American cultural life that we can with confidence describe their customary features, confirmed by aspects of the record and by the parties' representations at oral argument. . . . The parties stipulate that attendance at graduation ceremonies is voluntary. . . . The graduating students enter as a group in a processional, subject to the direction of teachers and school officials, and sit together, apart from their families. We assume the clergy's participation in any high school gradu-

ation exercise would be about what it was at Deborah's middle school ceremony. There the students stood for the Pledge of Allegiance and remained standing during the Rabbi's prayers. . . . Even on the assumption that there was a respectful moment of silence both before and after the prayers, the Rabbi's two presentations must not have extended much beyond a minute each, if that. We do not know whether he remained on stage during the whole ceremony, or whether the students received individual diplomas on stage, or if he helped to congratulate them.

The school board . . . argued that these short prayers and others like them at graduation exercises are of profound meaning to many students and parents throughout this country who consider that due respect and acknowledgement for divine guidance and for the deepest spiritual aspirations of our people ought to be expressed at an event as important in life as a graduation. We assume this to be so in addressing the difficult case now before us, for the significance of the prayers lies also at the heart of Daniel and Deborah Wesiman's case.

Deborah's graduation was held on the premises of Nathan Bishop Middle School on June 29, 1989. Four days before the ceremony, Daniel Weisman, in his individual capacity as a Providence taxpayer and as next friend of Deborah, sought a temporary restraining order in the United States District Court for the District of Rhode Island to prohibit school officials from including an invocation or benediction in the graduation ceremony. The court denied the motion for lack of adequate time to consider it. Deborah and her family attended

the graduation, where the prayers were recited. In July 1989, Daniel Weisman filed an amended complaint seeking a permanent injunction barring petitioners, various officials of the Providence public schools, from inviting the clergy to deliver invocations and benedictions at future graduations. . . .

The case was submitted on stipulated facts. The District Court held that petitioners' practice of including invocations and benedictions in public school graduations violated the Establishment Clause of the First Amendment, and it enjoined petitioners from continuing the practice. 728 F.Supp. 68 (RI 1990). The court applied the three-part Establishment clause test set forth in *Lemon v. Kurtzman*, 403 U.S. 602, 91 S.Ct. 2105, 29 L.Ed.2d 745 (1971). Under that test as described in our past cases, to satisfy the Establishment Clause a governmental practice must (1) reflect a clearly secular purpose; (2) have a primary effect that neither advances nor inhibits religion; and (3) avoid excessive government entanglement with religion. . . . The court decided, based on its reading of our precedents, that the effects test of *Lemon* is violated whenever government action "creates an identification of the state with a religion, or with religion in general," . . . or when "the effect of the governmental action is to endorse one religion over another or to endorse religion in general." . . . The court determined that the practice of including invocations and benedictions, even so-called nonsectarian ones, in public school graduations creates an identification of governmental power with religious practice, endorses religion, and violates the Establishment Clause. . . .

These dominant facts mark and control the confines of our decision: State officials direct the performance of a formal religious exercise at promotional and graduation ceremonies for secondary schools. Even for those students who object to the religious exercise, their attendance and participation in the state-sponsored religious activity are in a fair and real sense obligatory, though the school district does not require attendance as a condition for receipt of the diploma. . . .

The principle that government may accommodate the free exercise of religion does not supersede the fundamental limitations imposed by the Establishment Clause. It is beyond dispute that, at a minimum, the Constitution guarantees that government may not coerce anyone to support or participate in religion or its exercise, or otherwise act in a way which "establishes a [state] religion or religious faith, or tends to do so." *Lynch, supra,* at 678, 104 SCt., at 1361; see also *Allegheny County, supra,* 492 U.S., at 591 109 S. Ct., at 3100 quoting *Everson v. Board of Education of Ewing,* 330 U.S. 1, 15-16, 67 S.CT. 504, 511-512, 91 L.Ed. 711 (1947). The State's involvement in the school prayers challenged today violates these central principles. . . .

Petitioners argue, and we find nothing in the case to refute it, that the directions for the content of the prayers were a goodfaith attempt by the school to ensure that the sectarianism which is so often the flashpoint for religious animosity be removed from the graduation ceremony. The concern is understandable, as a prayer which uses ideas or images identified with a particular religion may foster a different sort of sectarian rivalry than

an invocation or benediction in terms more neutral. The school's explanation, however, does not resolve the dilemma caused by its participation. The question is not the good faith of the school in attempting to make the prayer acceptable to most persons, but the legitimacy of its undertaking that enterprise at all when the object is to produce a prayer to be used in a formal religious exercise which students, for all practical purposes, are obliged to attend. . . .

The First Amendment's Religion Clauses mean that religious beliefs and religious expression are too precious to be either proscribed or prescribed by the State. The design of the Constitution is that preservation and transmission of religious beliefs and worship is a responsibility and a choice committed to the private sphere, which itself is promised freedom to pursue that mission. It must not be forgotten then, that while concern must be given to define the protection granted to an objector or a dissenting nonbeliever, these same Clauses exist to protect religion from government interference. James Madison, the principal author of the Bill of Rights, did not rest his opposition to a religious establishment on the sole ground of its effect on the minority. A principal ground for his view was: "[E]xperience witnesseth that ecclesiastical establishments, instead of maintaining the purity and efficacy of Religion, have had a contrary operation."

. . . These concerns have particular application in the case of school officials, whose effort to monitor prayer will be perceived by the students as inducing a participation they might otherwise reject. Though the efforts of the school

officials in this case to find common ground appear to have been a good-faith attempt to recognize the common aspects of religions and not the divisive ones, our precedents do no permit school officials to assist in composing prayers as an incident to a formal exercise for their students. *Engel v. Vitale, supra,* 370 U.S., at 425, 82 S.Ct., at 1264. And these same precedents caution us to measure the idea of a civic religion against the central meaning of the Religion Clauses of the First Amendment, which is that all creeds must be tolerated and non favored. The suggestion that government may establish an official or civic religion as a means of avoiding the establishment of a religion with more specific creeds strikes us as a contradiction that cannot be accepted.

The degree of school involvement here made it clear that the graduation prayers before the imprint of the State and thus put school-age children who objected in an untenable position. We turn our attention now to consider the position of the students, both those who desired the prayer and she who did not.

To endure the speech of false ideas or offensive content and then to counter it is part of learning how to live in a pluralistic society, a society which insists upon open discourse towards the end of a tolerant citizenry. And tolerance presupposes some mutuality of obligation. It is argued that our constitutional vision of a free society requires confidence in our own ability to accept or reject ideas of which we do not approve, and that prayer at a high school graduation does nothing more than offer a choice. By the time they are seniors, high school students no doubt have been required to attend classes and assemblies and to complete assignments exposing them to ideas they find distasteful or immoral or absurd or all of these. Against this background, students may consider it an odd measure of justice to be subjected during the course of their education to ideas deemed offensive and irreligious, but to be denied a brief, formal prayer ceremony that the school offers in return. This argument cannot prevail, however. . . .

The lessons of the First Amendment are as urgent in the modern world as in the 18th Century when it was written. One timeless lesson is that if citizens are subjected to state-sponsored religious exercises, the State disavows its own duty to guard and respect that sphere of inviolable conscience and belief which is the mark of a free people. To compromise that principle today would be to deny our own tradition and forfeit our standing to urge others to secure the protections of that tradition for themselves.

As we have observed before, there are heightened concerns with protecting freedom of conscience from subtle coercive pressure in the elementary and secondary public schools. Our decisions in *Engel v. Vitale*, 370 U.S. 421, 82 S.Ct. 1261, 8 L.Ed.2d 601 (1962), and *Abington School District, supra*, recognize, among other things, that prayer exercises in public schools carry a particular risk of indirect coercion. The concern may not be limited to the context of schools, but it is most pronounced there. . . What to most believers may seem nothing more than a reasonable request that the nonbeliever respect their religious practices, in a school context may

appear to the nonbeliever or dissenter to be an attempt to employ the machinery of the State to enforce a religious orthodoxy.

We need not look beyond the circumstances of this case to see the phenomenon at work. The undeniable fact is that the school district's supervision and control of a high school graduation ceremony places public pressure, as well as peer pressure, on attending students to stand as a group or, at least, maintain respectful silence during the Invocation and Benediction. This pressure, though subtle and indirect, can be as real as any overt compulsion. Of course, in our culture standing or remaining silent can signify adherence to a view or simple respect for the views of others. And no doubt some persons who have no desire to join a prayer have little objection to standing as a sign of respect for those who do. But for the dissenter of high school age, who has a reasonable perception that she is being forced by the State to pray in a manner her conscience will not allow, the injury is no less real. There can be no doubt that for many, if not most, of the students at the graduation, the act of standing or remaining silent was an expression of participation in the Rabbi's prayer. That was the very point of the religious exercise. It is of little comfort to a dissenter, then, to be told that for her the act of standing or remaining in silence signifies mere respect, rather than participation. What matters is that, given our social conventions, a reasonable dissenter in this milieu could believe that the group exercise signified her own participation or approval of it. . . .

The injury caused by the government's action, and the reason why

Daniel and Deborah Weisman object to it, is that the State, in a school setting, in effect required participation in a religious exercise. It is, we concede, a brief exercise during which the individual can concentrate on joining its message, meditate on her own religion, or let her mind wander. But the embarrassment and the intrusion of the religious exercise cannot be refuted by arguing that these prayers, and similar ones to be said in the future, are of a *de minimis* character. To do so would be an affront to the Rabbi who offered them and to all those for whom the prayers were an essential and profound recognition of divine authority. And for the same reason, we think that the intrusion is greater than the two minutes or so of time consumed for prayers like these. Assuming, as we must, that the prayers were offensive to the student and the parent who now object, the intrusion was both real and, in the context of a secondary school, a violation of the objectors' rights. That the intrusion was in the course of promulgating religion that sought to be civic or nonsectarian rather than pertaining to one sect does not lessen the offense or isolation to the objectors. At best it narrows their number, at worst increases their sense of isolation and affront. . . .

We do not hold that every state action implicating religion is invalid if one or a few citizens find it offensive. People may take offense at all manner of religious as well as nonreligious messages, but offense alone does not in every case show a violation. We know too that sometimes to endure social isolation or even anger may be the price of conscience or nonconformity. But, by any reading of our cases, the conformity required of the student in this case was too high an exaction to withstand the test of the Establishment Clause. The prayer exercises in this case are especially improper because the State has in every practical sense compelled attendance and participation in an explicit religious exercise at an event of singular importance to every student, one the objecting student had no real alternative to avoid. . . .

Our society would be less than true to its heritage if it lacked abiding concern for the values of its young people, and we acknowledge the profound belief of adherents to many faiths that there must be a place in the student's life for precepts of a morality higher even than the law we today enforce. We express no hostility to those aspirations, nor would our oath permit us to do so. A relentless and all-pervasive attempt to exclude religion from every aspect of public life could itself become inconsistent with the Constitution. . . . We recognize that, at graduation time and throughout the course of the educational process, there will be instances when religious values, religious practices, and religious persons will have some interaction with the public schools and their students. See *Westside Community Bd. of Ed. v. Mergens*, 496 U.S. 226, 110 S.Ct. 2356, 110 L.Ed.2d 191 (1990). But these matters, often questions of accommodation of religion, are not before us. The sole question presented is whether a religious exercise may be conducted at a graduation ceremony in circumstances where, as we have found, young graduates who object are induced to conform. No holding by this Court suggests that a school can persuade or compel a student to participate in a religious exercise. . . .

Section Five

Where Do We Go From Here?

Jesus Garcia compares textbooks past and present. He provides examples of how power shifts are reflected in the curriculum. Mr. Garcia suggests that perhaps the issue of "multiculturalizing" the curriculum is best stated as a political questions: Who is going to control the curriculum?

The Changing Image of Ethnic Groups in Textbooks

Jesus Garcia

In preparing to write this article, I pulled from my bookshelf a dusty U.S. history text for secondary schools published in 1952 and one published in 1992 and skimmed each for its portrayal of minority groups (African Americans, Asian Americans, Native Americans, and Hispanics) and white ethnic groups (e.g., Jewish, Irish, and Italian Americans). Real changes in the depiction of these groups have occurred during this 40-year period. The portrayal of minorities has improved, and coverage of Irish, Jewish, and other white ethnic groups is evident. A look at other textbooks used in both elementary and secondary schools suggests that multicultural content has increased in the prose, illustrations, and highlighted material.

Is such progress sufficient? Or should greater attention be directed at what some critics—pressure groups inside and outside the education community—allege publishers have failed to accomplish? Textbook publishers would want educators to focus on the "positive," while critics would want us to focus on the "continued distorted and stereotypic depictions of minorities in textbooks." But is following the pronouncements of either of these camps an effective approach for examining this issue? Perhaps a broader look would prove more valuable in helping readers assess the depiction of societal groups in textbooks.

One approach might be to discuss societal groups and textbooks within a historical context—that is, to begin by examining why textbooks and minorities have become an issue and what progress, if any, has occurred in the portrayal of minorities and other societal groups in textbooks. The related issue of the influence of interest groups on the textbook industry would also be worthy of scrutiny. Finally, the discussion should focus on a concluding question, Do multicultural textbooks make a difference? That is, Do textbooks that attempt to chronicle accurately the experiences of minorities with advantages that nonminority students experience (e.g., self-esteem, school success, cultural pride)? And do they afford all students a greater understanding of and sensitivity to the pluralistic nature of American society than do Eurocentric textbooks?

Historical Perspective

It may prove useful to take a look at the historical purpose of U.S. public schools and at the role of textbooks in them before discussing the treatment of societal groups in textbooks since the 1970s. According to William Reese, in the 19th century "public schools taught children and adolescents that America was Christian, republican, and the greatest nation on earth."[1] Given this perspective, textbook authors manufactured a world that Ruth Elson described as:

a fantasy made up by adults as a guide for their children. It is an ideal world, peopled by ideal villains as well as real heroes. . . . Individuals are to be understood in terms of easily discernible, inherent characteristics of their race and nationality as much as in terms of their individual character. Virtue is always rewarded, vice punished.[2]

The textbook authors of the time were "mostly New England born, Protestant, white men who often attended college or other higher schools"—an "atypical slice of the American populace."[3] Individuals who were not white were omitted from the textbooks or received a treatment that reinforced widespread beliefs about their "proper" station in life. In the 19th century, while some authors spoke of American Indians as brave and alert, many more descriptions referred to them as cruel, vengeful, and barbarous. Textbook descriptions of Latin Americans from the same period were equally disdainful:

The creoles have all the bad qualities of the Spaniards from whom they descended, without the courage, firmness and patience which makes the praiseworthy part of the Spanish character. Naturally weak and effeminate, they dedicate the greatest part of their lives to

loitering and inactive pleasures.[4]

Elson summed up the treatment African Americans received in 19th-century textbooks:

It should be noted that the image of the Negro is of the same gay, foolish, childlike creature who appeared in the writings of George Fitzhugh and Thomas Nelsen Page, as well as in the consciousness of the old Southern aristocracy, and finally in the minstrel show. It is not the bestial Negro in the writings of Thomas Dixon at the end of the century, nor in the thinking of the Ku Klux Klan and the Southerners who fixed a rigid and all-pervasive segregation of the race. The Negro of the schoolbooks must be cared for by the whites as one would care for a child; he is not vicious, nor is it necessary to quarantine him. His place in America's future is quite clear; he will assist the whites from his menial but useful position.[5]

By the 1840s most textbooks writers had drawn clear distinctions between Americans whose roots were in Northern and Western Europe and those whose roots were in Southern and Eastern Europe. Sister Marie Lenore Fell, surveying textbooks written between 1783 and 1860, cites Jesse Olney's *Geography*, written in 1844, as being representative of the treatment afforded certain religious and immigrant groups:

The Dutch are honest, patient, and persevering; and remarkable for their industry, frugality and neatness. . . . The Irish in general are quick of apprehen-

sion, active, brave, and hospitable; but passionate, ignorant, vain and superstitious. . . . The Italians are affable and polite; and excel in music, painting, sculpture; but they are effeminate, superstitious, slavish and revengeful. . . . The English are intelligent, brave, industrious and enterprising; but possess great national pride.[6]

At the turn of the 19th century, the treatment of European immigrants in textbooks was dictated not by objectivity, but by how closely the immigrant group in question mirrored the values and peculiarities of specific Northern European groups. It seems to be accurate to generalize that early textbooks favored an American prototype that reflected Northern European characteristics.

Up to the first half of the 20th century, few researchers showed an interest in the depiction of minorities in textbooks. One can only speculate about why this was the case. Perhaps it was because most of the educators writing at the time were white, and their interests lay in other areas. Perhaps it was because, at the beginning of the 20th century, desegregation was so firmly embedded in public education that the prevailing questions were: given the present education system, what inherent qualities do minorities possess that stymie their growth and development in schools? What can schools do to help minorities attain their station in life? Certainly descriptions of minorities in textbooks and in other writings only seemed to confirm the supposedly inherent weaknesses of these groups.

With the publication of *Land of the Free* in the late 1960s,[7] a change occurred in the portrayal of minorities in textbooks. *Land of the Free*, a U.S. history textbook for secondary students, includes a significant amount of content describing the African American experience. Why is this book more multicultural? Perhaps the publishing company decided to commit itself to multiculturalism and, as a result, selected as one of the three authors of the text the distinguished African American historian John Hope Franklin. Whether it was Franklin's influence, the commitment of all three authors, or the publisher's commitment, *Land of the Free* acknowledges the experiences of minorities in U.S. history and is the first serious attempt to integrate these experiences into a textbook marketed for public schools. In the ensuing years other publishing companies would attempt to "multiculturalize" their textbooks.

The Civil Rights Movement

One of the goals of the civil rights movement of the 1960s was to improve the school performance of minorities at all levels of education. This effort received its first real impetus at the university level with the creation of ethnic studies departments and quickly spread to the public schools. On the West Coast the "Los Angeles Blowouts" of 1968 are representative of attempts by minorities to define their grievances for the officials of public education.[8] Chicano students in Los Angeles walked out of their classrooms and schools and joined parents and community activists to protest the lack of Mexican American teachers and administrators, the absence of a curriculum that included the experiences of Mexicans and Mexican Americans, and

a school staff—made up primarily of Anglo teachers and administrators—that, according to the protesters, exhibited little concern for the educational needs of minority students, particularly Mexican Americans. As more and more minorities across the country launched their own "blowouts," the rationale for a more relevant curriculum crystallized.

To the many who were doing battle with the public schools, there was sufficient evidence to suggest that schools took little interest in the welfare of minority students. In this volatile decade critics could point to a basal reader, an elementary science text, or a secondary health textbook and cite the lack of content and illustrations depicting minorities of their experiences. When such material was included, it was usually minimal and, according to critics, distorted or stereotypical. In social studies textbooks, where historical accuracy would seem to be of utmost importance, the quality of the content was generally no better. If the sin was not one of omission, it was certainly one of distortion and stereotyping. Interestingly, no one bothered to ask whether, in depicting various groups in society, there was a difference between the purpose of, say, a science textbook and that of a U.S. history textbook.

Perhaps as a result of these distortions, stereotypes, and omissions, textbook critics began defining "broad and comprehensive" textbooks as those that included depictions of African, Mexican, and Native Americans that were similar to the treatment accorded to white Americans. At both the elementary and the secondary levels, critics lobbied for textbooks that described

and illustrated the targeted groups performing scientific and mathematical experiments, executing reading and writing tasks, and taking part in occupations that required more than a high school diploma. In the social studies, critics called for textbooks that depicted the groups fighting, dying, inventing, writing, and legislating—just as white Americans had always been depicted.

At a very basic level, critics argued that giving minorities more prominence in textbooks would provide students with a more accurate description of society. In the social studies it would ensure that all students would be provided with a more comprehensive view of American history. However, some critics took the argument further by suggesting that multicultural textbooks would enhance intergroup relations. They reasoned that, as students gained a more accurate understanding of one another, ignorance, misunderstanding, and racial conflict would begin to disappear from classrooms and society. Some also claimed that a more positive account of the role of minority groups in American society would help minority students raise their self-esteem, improve their school performance, and reduce their dropout rate.

Early Textbook Reviews

How did 20th-century authors of textbooks published prior to the civil rights movement depict minorities and white ethnic groups? Did the authors, as critics charge, ignore the experiences of the minority groups? Did they portray minority groups stereotypically? A number of textbook reviews that have been conducted since 1949 should reveal the answers.

What is obvious in the following survey of textbook reviews is that most of the studies were conducted not by social science organizations or by social scientists but by education organizations and educators. The first major review of textbooks published in the 20th century was sponsored by the American Council on Education in 1949.[9] The Committee on the Study of Teaching Materials in Intergroup Relations examined more that 300 elementary, secondary, and postsecondary textbooks used in the 1940s to determine the treatment of the topic "intergroup relations." The committee "found textbooks in use throughout the United States to be distressingly inadequate, inappropriate and even damaging to intergroup relations."[10] Five years later Morton Sobel examined 15 social studies texts used in the seventh grade for their treatment of social class, racial groups, religious groups, and nationality.[11] He concluded that some stereotypes persisted in the descriptions of minorities but that text material was not necessarily derogatory.

In the 1960s more studies appeared. Lloyd Marcus examined 48 textbooks used in the 1950s and early 1960s for treatment of Jews, African Americans, and other minorities.[12] Marcus concluded that, while gains had occurred since 1949, they were uneven.

Roger Zimmerman examined the treatment of famous individuals in fourth-, fifth-, and sixth-grade U.S. history textbooks used in Minnesota school districts during the 1960-64 academic years.[13] According to Zimmerman, with few exceptions, Caucasian men identified

with the development of Western civilization received the most coverage. In 1975 Zimmerman replicated his study with revised editions of the textbooks used in his previous study. His conclusions varied only slightly from the 1965 study.[14]

In 1969 James Banks reviewed elementary history textbooks used in grade 4 through 9 for their treatment of African Americans and of race relations. He used a thematic analysis to tabulate the frequency of 11 categories (discrimination, achievement, and so on). For a subsample of six textbooks, he also compared the frequency of themes in textbooks from 1964 and 1968. He found that many authors rarely depicted violence and in some instance failed to explain prejudice and deliberate discrimination. However, he also found that textbook writers relied less on stereotypes in 1968 and that the treatment accorded African Americans had improved significantly since 1964.[15]

In 1970 Michael Kane examined 45 social studies textbooks published in the 1960s, using the criteria from the 1961 Marcus study. Kane's conclusions were that, although textbooks had improved, the treatment of groups was uneven, especially for Asian groups, Chicanos, Puerto Ricans, and Native Americans.[16]

Richard Simms reported on a study conducted by the Dallas chapter of the American Jewish Committee. The group examined those history textbooks on Texas' 1975 official adoption list for the treatment of African Americans, Chicanos, and Native Americans. The American Jewish Committee used guidelines that took account of errors of omission and commission—

including stereotyping, ethnocentrism, Eurocentrism, and the use of prejudicial statements or caricatures that demean minorities—to sort and measure the statements made about the three groups. The conclusion of the group's yearlong study was that textbooks continued to be less than equitable in treating these three minority groups.[17]

With these and other studies in hand, critics began pressuring teachers and local school boards for changes. But they quickly learned that it was far more effective to pressure teacher organizations, state school boards, and publishing houses. They also sought assistance from pressure groups and politicians to force a change in the status quo. Some state school boards and publishing houses reacted to the initial pressure by issuing guidelines on what is an "acceptable presentation of minorities" and on "how to evaluate a textbook for ethnic bias." While many critics did not view this as a valuable step, additional changes did occur in the portrayal of societal groups in textbooks. Whether these changes have satisfied particular pressure groups remains an open question. Before examining what changes have occurred in the presentation of minorities in textbooks in the past 20 years, it may be germane to examine the role of pressure groups in the production of textbooks.

Pressure Groups And Publishing

Today, most publishing companies that plan to develop a textbook or series engage in a process of information gathering in which they solicit information from a variety of organizations. The purpose is to identify the positions these groups hold with respect to particular topics (e.g., cultural lifestyles, evolution, abortion). Some of the groups that publishers listen to are discipline-oriented organizations (e.g., the National Council for Social Studies, the International Reading Association, the National Council of Teachers of Mathematics), state education agencies, and national organizations (e.g., the National Education Association, the National School Boards Association). These are organizations with large constituencies that represent a wide variety of views on education. Publishers also listen to groups that hold particular views of society and that target schools and textbooks to promote their goals. These are groups that may have large constituencies but are narrowly focused. In this article I will concentrate on the influence of these lesser-known groups.

In the past the major pressure groups were manufacturing organizations and business and community groups. In the late 1960s and early 1970s the Council on Interracial Books for Children (CIBC) altered students, parents, and educators to the treatment of minorities and women were accorded in U.S. history textbooks and other texts marketed by the publishing industry. In *Stereotypes, Distortions, and Omissions in U.S. History Textbooks*, for example, the CIBC pointed out inadequate portrayals of minorities and women in 13 textbooks published in the 1970s and outlined what would be an accurate presentation of the groups.[18] At another level, the CIBC suggests to its readers strategies that are intended to influence the textbook industry. These strategies call on students, teachers, and parents to become activists and to work for the removal of texts that do not present what CIBC views as a balanced picture of U.S. history. This was the typical approach of most pressure groups that flourished during the 1970s.

Today the more influential of the narrowly focused groups seem to be the National Association of Christian Educators, Educational Research Analysts (Mel and Norma Gabler), and Citizens for Excellence in Education. Many of these groups are conservative and oriented toward religious fundamentalism. They differ from the pressure groups that flourished in the 1970s in that they are more aggressive and desire to control the textbook industry.

Why are these groups so influential? The keys to their success are organization and action. Most have a prescribed agenda and plan of action. Many of the Christian organizations, for example, send out newsletters on a regular basis and encourage their members and individuals sympathetic to their goals to run for local school board positions, to volunteer to serve on textbook adoption committees, and to seek appointments to other school and community groups that may have some influence on the curriculum. Their messages are heard daily on Christian radio and television stations and in local newspapers. Some even hire state and national lobbyists.

What makes these groups so effective is that they possess the political expertise to influence local and state boards of education, state legislatures, and other agencies responsible for what should be included in a textbook. People involved in the adoption process listen to these groups because of their political savvy. What makes these groups dangerous is that they are no longer interested in airing the views in the marketplace of ideas; they are interested in controlling the textbook industry. It appears that the voices of the CIBC and other organizations and individuals interested in textbooks that are multicultural may be drowned out by these new conservative pressure groups.

Textbook Reviews, 1970-1990

In the last 20 years a small number of studies of textbook content have appeared. And they make it clear that a major problem textbook authors face is selecting which groups to cover and at what depth. Frances FitzGerald reviewed a number of textbooks for their treatment of U.S. history. Among the topics she discussed was the treatment of minorities. According to FitzGerald, the treatment of minorities represents a compromise, "an America sculpted and sanded down by the pressures of diverse constituents and interest groups."[19] The inclusion of particular African American individuals, for example, represents ideological victories rather than historical scholarship. I examined eight U.S. history textbooks for secondary students published in 1978 and 1979 and found that "textbook writers provide readers with limited descriptions of Hispanics."[20] I also examined 20 secondary U.S. history textbooks published in the 1970s and found that authors used a variety of themes to chronicle the role of Native Americans in U.S. history.[21] However, the treatment of Native Americans remains uneven. Such issues as U.S. land policy and treaty rights are superficially covered, while other content (e.g., pre-Columbian experiences) tends to reinforce the stereotype of the "noble savage." William Rupley, Bonnie Longnion, and I examined basal readers published between 1976 and 1978 and found that, when compared with previously published basal readers, the newer ones had a greater number of stories with females as major characters.[22]

Nathan Glazer and Reed Ueda examined six U.S. history textbooks for secondary students published in the 1970s for their treatment of racial and ethnic groups. In these texts African Americans, Native Americans, and Americans whose roots are in Southern and Eastern Europe receive more thorough treatment than do Hispanics, Asian Americans, and Americans with roots in Northern and Western Europe. And in this content Glazer and Ueda see a new myth being proclaimed, "a Manichaean inversion in which whites are malevolent and blacks, Indians, Asians, and Hispanics are tragic victims."[23]

To identify changes in the treatment of African Americans, Julie Goeble and I examined a group of five texts written between 1956 and 1975 and compared them with a group of 10 texts written in the 1980s.[24] Not surprisingly, coverage of the group had increased, but the descriptions remained focused on such issues as slavery, Reconstruction, and the civil rights movement. While a number of other topics were included (e.g., black organizations, free blacks in Colonial America, the development of black churches), the treatment remained superficial. The breadth of coverage had increased, but the depth of coverage had not.

I also conducted a comparative study to determine the breadth and depth of coverage provided to white ethnic groups—Irish, Italian, Jewish, and Polish Americans.[25] Three sets of textbooks, representing three different time periods—1956-1974, 1977-1978, and 1984-1986—were examined. The early set of texts provide general information about the groups but do not identify when and why they immigrated, do not discuss their major interactions with established Americans, and do not draw distinctions among the groups. Textbooks published in 1977-1978 devote more space to the groups, but the additional sentences describing when and why groups came to the U.S. However, as with textbooks in the two earlier periods, there is little or no content describing interactions between the newly arrived white ethnic groups and established Americans and little or no content highlighting the distinctions among the groups. In other words, the textbooks published in the 1980s do not provide greater insights into the experiences of white ethnic groups than did textbooks published in the 1970s.

Richard Powell and I studied the quantitative and qualitative portrayal of females and minorities in the illustrations of seven contemporary elementary science textbook series.[26] The textbooks evaluated in this study present females and minorities actively involved in science. More recently, Nancy Harrison, Jose Luis Torres, and I replicated the study using elementary mathematics series published in 1985.[27] We found that elementary mathematics series are also multicultural.

In sum, the literature seems to suggest that textbooks have improved since the *Land of the Free*.

Textbooks are more multicultural; descriptions and illustrations of minorities now appear in U.S. history textbooks and in elementary science and math texts. While content that deals with minorities has increased in quantity, it is not clear that it has improved in quality. For example, the few studies cited here suggest that the treatment of minorities has not improved dramatically in the social sciences. In other subject areas (e.g., science, reading, health science) minorities are better represented, but the purpose of the representation is not clear.

This short review of the literature also suggests that most publishing houses have interpreted cultural diversity to mean "the experiences of minority groups and women in the United States." In most contemporary social studies textbooks the quality of content describing white ethnic groups is no more informative than the content found in texts published before the 1960s. In textbooks in other disciplines, descriptions of various white ethnic groups are nonexistent. Moreover, there is little or no content suggesting a global connection to cultural diversity. Except in such obvious cases as immigration patterns or the Bering Strait theory, textbook authors do not attempt to suggest the interconnectedness of the world's societies. Thus readers are provided with a limited view of multiculturalism.

Do Multicultural Texts Make A Difference?

Over the last two decades activists who have argued for greater coverage of societal groups in textbooks have failed to address a number of questions. Perhaps the two most important are: What is the purpose of a textbook? And what is the purpose of a text in a classroom?

One answer to the first question is that the purpose of a textbook is to familiarize the reader with the subject being described. The purpose of a social studies text, for example, is to describe U.S. history, economics, government, and the like. But some would argue that the purpose of a textbook in U.S. history is not just to familiarize readers with the subject, but to provide content that introduces the reader to key documents (e.g., the Constitution or the Bill of Rights), that highlights citizenship skills, and that nurtures patriotism. Does a U.S. history textbook have other purposes? Perhaps. A few critics would argue that a U.S. history textbook should provide relevant content and make learning interesting and fun; some would focus on self-esteem; still others would suggest that it is to show the reader the evils of communism, fascism, and other nondemocratic forms of government.

The discussion with regard to purpose is not limited to social studies textbooks, however. There is a general agreement that the major purpose of a math book, for example is to teach children mathematics. "Multiculturalizing" math books, it is claimed, encourages children to want to learn mathematics by offering a relevant curriculum, by fostering improved student self-esteem, and by enhancing intergroup relations in the classroom. Similar arguments can be employed to promote the inclusion of minority content in elementary and secondary science textbooks.

While the literature illustrates that publishing houses have inserted their brand of multicultural content into textbooks, we must ask, Can more be done? Certainly. Will there ever be a time when everyone will be satisfied with the content provided to children and young adults in textbooks? Certainly not. From an educational perspective, there will always be questions to be asked about what content to include in a textbook. For example, what are the reading interests of young children? Do boys have the same interests as girls? What are the connections between reading, reading interests, and learning how to read? When given a choice what kind of texts do Hispanic children choose? Do children enjoy reading Martin Luther King, Jr., about Jane Addams, about Henry Cisneros, and about Sacajawea?

However, perhaps the issue of "multiculturalizing" the curriculum is best stated as a political question: Who is going to control the curriculum? As Michael Apple states:

> Curricula aren't imposed in countries like the United States. Rather, they are the products of often intense conflicts, negotiations, and attempts at rebuilding hegemonic control, of actually incorporating the knowledge and perspectives of the less powerful under the umbrella of the discourse of the dominant groups.[28]

What if we could assume for a moment that oppressed groups have removed themselves from the "umbrella of discourse," have

gained control of the curriculum in the inner city, and have rewritten their history? What would that history look like? Would Hispanics, for example, be able to agree on a "legitimate" view of Hispanic history? Or would conflicts and negotiations be part of a neverending struggle among Mexican American, Puerto Ricans, Cuban Americans, and others to present Hispanic history?

Little information is available in the literature to answer the second question I raised above: What is the purpose of a textbook in a classroom? Studies to date have concentrated on the content rather than on the use of the textbook. Research that explores how teachers use textbooks in the classroom is much needed.

Why are so many people concerned about what is included in a textbook? Is it because the textbook establishes the boundaries of what students are expected to learn? Are texts able to do all that advocates for a variety of positions say they can? Perhaps we give the textbook too much credit. The literature indicates that students find textbooks less than appealing; in fact, they describe them as "boring." Could it be that students simply are not interested in what is in a textbook because it is a textbook? And, when forced to learn textbook content, many students retain the information long enough to regurgitate it on a test but then quickly forget it. Certainly textbooks should be multicultural, but they will never be a panacea for what ails education.

Notes

1. William J. Reese, *An Aristocracy of Intellect* (New Haven, CT: Yale University Press, forthcoming).

2. Ruth Elson, *Guardians of Tradition* (Lincoln: University of Nebraska Press, 1964), p.98.

3. Reese, op. cit.

4. Quoted in Elson, p. 156.

5. Ibid., p.98.

6. Quoted in Sister Marie Lenore Fell, "The Foundations of Nativism in American Textbooks" (Doctoral Dissertation, Catholic University, 1941), p. 157.

7. John W. Caughey, John Hope Franklin, and Ernest R. May, *Land of the Free: A History of the United States* (New York: Benziger Brothers, 1967).

8. Kaye Briegel, "Chicano Student Militancy: The Los Angeles High School Strike of 1968," in Manuel P. Servin, ed., *An Awakened Minority: The Mexican Americans*, 2nd ed. (Beverly Hills, CA: Glencoe Press, 1974), pp. 215-25.

9. Committee on the Study of Teaching Materials in Intergroup Relations, *Intergroup Relations in Teaching Materials* (Washington, DC: American Council on Education, 1949).

10. Michael B. Kane, *Minorities in Textbooks* (Chicago: Quandrangle Books, 1970), p. 1.

11. Morton J. Sobel, "An Analysis of Social Studies Texts in Relation to Their Treatment of Four Areas in Human Relations" (Doctoral Dissertation, Wayne State University, 1954.)

12. Lloyd Marcus, *The Treatment of Minorities in Secondary School Textbooks* (New York: Anti-Defamation League of B'nai B'rith, 1961.)

13. Roger M. Zimmermann, "An Analysis of the Treatment of Famous Individuals in Six Elementary School Social Studies Textbook Series" (Doctoral Dissertation, University of Minnesota, 1968).

14. Roger M. Zimmermann, "Social Studies Textbooks Still Neglect Racial Minorities and Women, and Shortchange Children," *Negro Educational Review*, April/July 1975, pp. 116-23.

15. James A. Banks, "A Content Analysis of the Black American in Textbooks," *Social Education*, December 1969, pp. 954-57, pp. 963ff.

16. Kane, op. cit.

17. Richard L. Simms, "Bias in Textbooks: Not Yet Corrected," *Phi Delta Kappan*, November 1975, pp. 201-2.

18. Council on Interracial Books for Children, *Stereotypes, Distortions, and Omissions in U.S. History Textbooks* (New York: Racism and Sexism Resource Center for Education, 1977).

19. Frances FitzGerald, *America Revised* (New York: Vintage Books, 1980), p. 46.

20. Jesus Garcia, "Hispanic Perspective: Textbooks and Other Curricular Materials," *History Teacher*, November 1980, p. 110.

21. Jesus Garcia, "The American Indian: No Longer a Forgotten American in U.S. History Textbooks Published in the 1970s," *Social Education*, February 1980, pp. 148-52.

22. William H. Rupley, Jesus Garcia, and Bonnie Longnion, "Sex Role Portrayal in Reading Materials," *Reading Teacher*, April 1981, pp. 786-91.

23. Nathan Glazer and Reed Ueda, *Ethnic Groups in History Textbooks* (Washington, DC: Ethics and Public Policy Center, 1983), p. 60.

24. Jesus Garcia and Julie Goebel, "A Comparative Study of the Portrayal of Black Americans in Selected U.S. History Textbooks," *Negro Educational Review*, July/October 1985, pp. 118-27.

25. Jesus Garcia, "The White Ethnic Experience in Selected Secondary U.S. History Textbooks," *Social Studies*, July/August 1986, pp. 169-75.

26. Richard R. Powell and Jesus Garcia, "The Portrayal of Females and Minorities in Selected Elementary Science Series," *Journal of Research in Science Teaching*, September 1985, pp. 519-33.

27. Jesus Garcia, Nancy Harrison, and Jose Luis Torres, "The Portrayal of Females and Minorities in Selected Elementary Mathematics Series," *School Science and Mathematics*, January 1990, pp. 2-11.

28. Michael Apple, "The Text and Cultural Politics," *Educational Researcher*, October 1992, p. 8.

Reprinted from Phi Delta Kappan "The Changing Image of Ethnic Groups in Textbooks," September 1993: 29-35, with permission from author.

The power issues within the walls of the classroom have always been an expression of control especially for the teacher. Providing an environment of empowerment for students is also an issue that has been explored in recent years. This article provides an insight into power sharing between student and teacher.

But . . . the Curriculum

Carolyn Mamchur

June Sikler was tired. She had been marking papers half the night. So her patience wore a little thin when her eleventh-grade English class responded to her request to "go over the errors and rework your papers" with groans, quick sidelong glances, and a general lack of interest. "Okay, fail then," she felt like saying. "You'll have to stay after class and write out each story five times," she thought of threatening. "Don't come to my class if you don't want to work. Take a little visit to the principal's office. Just get lost," she wanted to say. But she didn't. She made her voice even and low, she smiled a thin smile, and she walked between the rows and commanded obedience with her small, tight body.

Like everyone else, secondary teachers get tired and frustrated—even fed up—from time to time. They see their best-laid plans and hardest work wasted on students who seem not to care. Their frustration is to be expected. It's like mind depression or occasional migraine—it comes, it goes. Usually it comes when a teacher is tense, overworked, and in a stressful situation.

Although it may seem so at the time, it is not always the students who put the teacher in such a situation. If teachers tend to blame students—to bemoan their lack of interest, their laziness, their resistance—then perhaps the teachers had better ask themselves a few tough questions.

When things were going wrong for me as a secondary teacher, I asked myself 10 tough questions. I now ask them of my preservice students when they are having difficulty in their teaching practicum. The same 10 questions keep popping into my mind when teachers or school districts request inservice workshop on motivation or discipline or classroom management. For 25 years now—as a high school teacher, as a teacher educator, as a troubleshooter—I have been asking the same set of questions. Either they are awfully important questions, or my mind is stuck on them—imprinted, like the images on a computer screen left on bright when the owner goes to the south of France for a three-month vacation.

These are the questions imprinted on my mental screen:

1. How often do students have choices in the classroom?

2. How often do students feel in control, in charge of themselves?

3. How many decisions that really count are students allowed to make?

4. How are students responsible for their own learning?

5. How do your students know when they have pleased you?

6. How do you know when you have pleased them?

7. How often is there a right answer to the questions you ask of your students?

8. How often do students feel important in your classroom?

9. How often do you and your students share laughter and pleasure?

10. How do the students react when they walk into your classroom? Happy? Calm? Safe? Excited? Assured? Afraid? Bored? Sorry?

In all my 25 years of teaching secondary students and training teachers, I have *never* known teachers who are having trouble with discipline or motivation to say that their students have choices, control, or true responsibility for their schooling. Yet when I ask why students don't have control, I hear a standard set of responses. "We have no time to allow for choices—the curriculum has to be covered!" argues one teacher. "Students aren't able to make decisions regarding curriculum," asserts another. "It's on the exam, and that's that!" a third states flatly. "This is secondary school!"

An analysis of the questions themselves reveals that they deal with power, not with curriculum. Could it be that secondary teachers hide behind the safe excuse, the cop-out excuse, the excuse that blames curricular requirements when what we really want is power? "I believe that the need for power is the core—the absolute core—of almost all school problems," William Glasser told *Kappan* readers.[1] Could it be that, if we gave power to our students, they would cease to appear lazy, uncaring, and undisciplined?

> *Does giving students "power" mean choosing "students" over "curriculum"? Not at all. Curriculum is the tool.*

Teachers who have not tried to run their classrooms in ways that allow students to satisfy their need for power often mistakenly worry that in giving power to students they will lose their own. Teachers who encourage their students to make choices, to take responsibility for their learning, to be independent and fulfilled in classrooms in which autonomy, decisiveness, risk-taking, and caring are recognized and appreciated know that power shared is not lost—but increased. In a power struggle, on the other hand, someone always loses.

Does this mean that the teacher must stop being concerned about the curriculum? Does giving students "power" mean choosing "students" over "curriculum"? Not at all. Curriculum is the tool, the "stuff" of education. Through curriculum students learn the skills, the attitudes, and the knowledge they need. Curriculum is a vehicle, a device.

As an English teacher working with "tough" students, I was asked by the school board to leave classroom teaching and become a counselor. "Why?" I asked.

"Because students don't have discipline problems or truancy problems or 'failing exam' problems with you. You're good with them."

"*I'm* not good. The way we work together is good."

"Well, work with more students, as a counselor."

Work with what? I asked myself. The "stuff" we worked with in my English classes was the curriculum. Literature, drama, writing. How could I teach without these? *I* didn't keep my students quiet, interested, working. They did that themselves, using curriculum they cared about in ways that were interesting and meaningful to them. They gained power over language, thought, and ideas. And they had so many choices to make: What stories will we study? How should we choose? How can we express our ideas about the stories? How can we help one another? What use can we make of our new knowledge? They read, wrote, put on plays, made films, bought an old school bus, went on the road, entertained in nursing homes, and tutored other young people having academic problems. How could you keep these students out of school? Have you ever visited the home of a really "troubled" youngster? Did you see much peace and quiet? Much time or energy devoted to caring? Much excitement over what the child had to say or was doing? Troubled young people come to school starved.

Curriculum can become a delicious feast, tempting students to taste, to satisfy their appetites. Having once eaten, though, they are not forever full. Indeed, tomorrow's hunger will be even keener, and the palate will be even more sophisticated. Curriculum must never be the "stuff" we rub our students' noses in as if they had just dirtied the carpet; that doesn't do much for the appetite.

The happy truth is that students learn the curriculum best when we give them power over how they learn it. But what about students who don't seem to want to cooperate? We can be sure that such students won't learn the curriculum by force. What have they—or we—got to lose by trying an alternative method? Forced smiles, thin voices, tight bodies? Which method is easier on us, their teachers? Which one makes us feel good about ourselves at the end of the day, the week, the year?

Giving students choices may seem to be a complex issue. But actually, it is dead simple. The rule is this: whenever you can give a student a choice of any kind, do it.

Some of these choices will be big ones. Early in September a young teacher working in a remarkably student-centered school phoned me for some advice. She and two other teachers were dividing fifth- and sixth-grade students into three groups to work on a science project. She knew that I had done work on learning styles, and she wanted to

know if it would be wise to put these students into groups matched for learning style.

"How are you organizing the project?" I wanted to know.

"We are having three themes: the human factor, research, and the world around us."

"Why not let each student choose the area of study that he or she wants to start with? Try to help the students make informed choices. Describe what's going to happen in each area, and suggest that they base their choices on their own interests and abilities."

"Won't they have to take part in all three? We planned for them to do all three," she said. She sounded worried.

Curriculum must never be the "stuff" we rub our students' noses in—as if they had just dirtied the carpet.

I assured her that the students would eventually work in all three areas. But why not let them choose the order? It makes sense, and research bears out the fact that "matching" students' learning styles, interests, and abilities to a task at the introductory stage is effective.[2] "Mismatching"—or moving to the more difficult or unfamiliar tasks—should take place once students have built up confidence and

a more sophisticated level of interest and knowledge.

"What about learning styles?" the teacher wanted to know. "Shouldn't we group that way at all?"

The power of understanding differences in students' learning styles is that it allows the teacher to offer better-informed choices. A teacher can design learning centers, assignments, or tests in a variety of ways. By designing them with the different learning styles of the students in mind, the teacher can feel confident that all students will have the opportunity to learn in a way that suits them best.

Matching assignments to learning styles works even better if the students are also informed. The teacher could help students to understand their own learning-style preferences; then, when they make choices—in projects, in ways to learn new concepts, or in ways to demonstrate mastery—or when they find themselves performing better in one mode than another, the students will understand why. The students might even develop their own alternatives. The one thing better than having students choose from a variety of modes of learning is having them generate their own options.

Choice can come in many shapes. For example, there is the large choice of which programs to begin studying. Last spring a friend of mine was challenged by a school district to conduct a workshop on "the writing process" for resistant learners. She accepted the challenge on the condition that she could offer the students choices throughout the three-day workshop. The first choice she offered her group of 78 students from grades 7 through

11 was this: "If you would, for any reason, rather not be in this workshop, please don't stay. You are free to go to the library, to your regular class, or to the sunny side of the building. The one choice you don't have is to stay in this workshop if you don't feel that this is a good time to learn to improve your writing skills."

That was the big choice. At the beginning of each session she repeated the offer. By the end of the three days, she had lost 22 students. Of the 56 who remained, everyone completed a polished composition—many, for the first time that school year.

Every chance she got, my friend offered these students choices. They were allowed to choose the topics they were going to write about. She suggested the general topic of "an awkward moment." She suggested subtopics related to being happy or surprised or embarrassed or shy or frightened. She used an overhead projector to share several of her own pieces of writing. She let students choose the ones they liked best and asked them to tell her why. She invited the class to ask her any questions they wished about her awkward moments or about the ways she chose to write about them. She offered students the opportunity to write about their own awkward moments, to write on any other topic, or to act as observers/reporters for the next hour—recording what was happening in the class in order to explain it to their teachers when they went back to their regular classrooms.

The students were free to determine the genre, the length, and whether they wanted to talk over their intended topics with partners before writing or to read more sam-ples of awkward moments written by the teacher or by other writers. They chose whether to speak into a tape recorder or to write their papers—and, if they chose the latter, whether to use a pencil or a pen or a crayon or a computer. They could work in pairs, in threes, or alone. They could sit on the floor, at a desk, or at a table. They could listen to music with headphones while they wrote. They could *not* choose to interfere with the work of others or to have no task.

Teachers marveled at the success my friend was having. One who had taken a previous workshop with her asked permission to sit in on this workshop during the second day. She had tried my friend's methods of teaching the writing process with limited success.

If you give choices, you must mean it. Our job is not to judge students' choices but to work with them.

During the second day's session a young man who was considered severely learning disabled had difficulty understanding the idea of "showing, not telling." He simply couldn't grasp the concept. My friend, who is very open and fun-loving by nature, asked the young man whether he liked her. The boy grinned and shyly dropped his head. "I'll take that for a yes," she said and gave the boy's hair a gentle tousle. "How would you let me know you liked me if you were too shy to tell me?" The boy looked up at her and smiled. At recess he went to the schoolyard and picked my friend a bouquet of daisies and put them on her desk. She went to the board and wrote the sentence, "He liked her." Then she wrote beneath it, "He brought her a bouquet of daisies the color of sunshine." She announced to the class that Ronald had just provided a perfect example of "showing, not telling." The first sentence told, the second showed.

Ronald was so proud and so confident that he even decided to try to write about his own awkward moment. His teacher, who wished to be more successful in teaching the writing process, peered over his shoulder to see what he was writing. Ronald had written, "I passed a fart in class." His teacher said, "Be serious, Ronald. It isn't nice to make fun when Miss Simpson is working with us. Don't write something stupid."

Ronald decided not to come to the third workshop session. And Miss Simpson knew why her method of teaching the writing process didn't work for this teacher. If you give choices, you must mean it. Our job is not to judge students' choices but to work with them. If we choose not to, we have made an important choice.

June Sikler is having a conference with a student. They are analyzing ways to improve the student's ability to clarify ideas. "What is your main thought here?" the teacher asks. "What did you really want to say?"

"I really believe that responsibility is a loaded word. I want to show how my ideas about it have changed," the student replies. The teacher is relaxed. She is listening carefully. The student is deeply engaged, concentrating her energy.

Miss Sikler can focus so much attention on one student because the rest of the students are also engaged. Working alone, in pairs, or in larger groups, they are busy with writing topics that they have chosen themselves. They are writing about things they know and care about. They help one another with their work, sharing ideas and skills. Their knowledge and judgment count. What they say to one another is important.

"Does my story make sense to you?"

"Can you visualize this part?"

"What does this remind you of?"

"What's another word for lazy?"

I wasn't there to hear the response to this last question. But when the word is applied to students, I might suggest "controlled, bored, unsatisfied, powerless."

Notes

1. Pauline B. Gough, "The Key to Improving Schools: An Interview with William Glasser," *Phi Delta Kappan*, May 1987, pp. 656-63.

2. Daniel Solomon and Arthur J. Kendall, *Final Report: Individual Characteristics and Children's Performance in Varied Educational Settings* (Rockville, MD: Spencer Foundation Project, 1976).

Carolyn Mamchur is an Associate Professor in the Faculty of Education at Simon Fraser University, Burnaby, British Columbia.

Reprinted with permission. Carolyn Mamchur, "But . . . the Curriculum," Phi Delta Kappan (April 1990) pp. 634-37.

Illich proposes that the inevitable disestablishment of the school should fill us with hope. He welcomes the reevaluation that shifts responsibility for teaching and learning, and proposes that educational institutions—if they are needed at all—take the form of centers where one can get a roof of the right size over his/her head and access to a piano or a kiln, and to records, books, slides, etc.

In Lieu of Education

Ivan Illich

During the late sixties I conducted a series of seminars at the Centro Intercultural de Documentacion (CIDOC) in Cuernavaca, Mexico, that dealt with the monopoly of the industrial mode of production and with conceptual alternatives that would fit a postindustrial age. The first industrial sector that I analyzed was the school system and its presumed output, education. Seven papers written during this period were published in 1971 under the title Deschooling Society. From the reactions to that book I saw that my description of the undesirable latent functions of compulsory schools (the "hidden curriculum" of schooling) was being abused not only by the promoters of so-called free schools but even more by schoolmasters who were anxious to transmogrify themselves into adult educators. The following essay was written in mid-1971. I here insist that the alternative to the dependence of a society on its schools is not the creation of new devices to make people learn what experts have decided they need to know; rather, it is the creation of a radically new relationship between human beings and their environment. A society committed to high levels of shared learning and personal intercourse, free yet critical, cannot exist unless it sets pedagogically motivated constraints on its institutional and industrial growth.

For generations we have tried to make the world a better place by providing more and more schooling, but so far the endeavor has failed. What we have learned instead is that forcing all children to climb an open-ended education ladder cannot enhance equality but must favor the individual who starts out earlier, healthier, or better prepared; that enforced instruction deadens for most people the will for independent learning; and that knowledge treated as a commodity, delivered in packages, and accepted as private property once it is acquired must always be scarce.

People have suddenly become aware that public education by means of compulsory schooling has lost its social, it pedagogical, and its economic legitimacy. In response, critics of the educational system are now proposing strong and unorthodox remedies that range from the voucher plan, which would enable each person to buy the education of his choice on an open market, to shifting the responsibility for education from the school to the media and to apprenticeship on the job. Some individuals foresee that the school will have to be disestablished just as the Church was disestablished all over the world during the last two centuries. Other reformers propose to replace the universal school with various new systems that would, they claim, better prepare everybody for life in modern society. These proposals for new educational institutions fall into three broad categories: the reformation of the classroom within the school system; the dispersal of free classrooms throughout society; and the transformation of all society into one huge classroom. But these three approaches—the reformed classroom, the free classroom, and the world-wide classroom—represent three stages in a proposed escalation of education in which each step threatens more subtle and more pervasive social control than the one it replaces.

I believe that the disestablishment of the school has become inevitable and that this end of an illusion should fill us with hope. But I also believe that the end of the "age of schooling" cold usher in the epoch of a global schoolhouse that would be distinguishable only in name from a global madhouse or a global prison in which education, correction, and adjustment became synonymous. I therefore believe that the breakdown of the school forces us to look beyond its imminent demise and to face fundamental alternatives in education. Either we can work for new and fearsome educational devices that teach about a world which progressively becomes more opaque and forbidding for man, or we can set the conditions for a new era in which technology would be used to make society more simple and transparent, so that all men could once again know the facts and use the tools that shape their lives. In short, we can disestablish schools or we can deschool culture.

The Hidden Curriculum

In order to see clearly the alternatives we face, we must first distinguish learning from schooling, which means separating the humanistic goal of the teacher from the impact of the invariant structure of the school. This hidden structure constitutes a course of instruction that remains forever beyond the control of the teacher or of the school board. It necessarily conveys the message that only through schooling can an individual prepare for adulthood in society, that what is not taught in school is of little value, and that what is learned outside school is not worth knowing. I call it the hidden curriculum because it constitutes the unalterable framework of the schooling system, within which all changes in the visible curriculum are made.

The hidden curriculum is always the same regardless of school or place. It requires all children of a certain age to assemble in groups of about thirty, under the authority of a certified teacher, for some 500 or 1,000 or more hours per year. It does not matter whether the curriculum is designed to teach the principles of fascism, liberalism, Catholicism, socialism, or liberation, so long as the institution claims the authority to define which activities are legitimate "education." It does not matter whether the purpose of the school is to produce Soviet or United States citizens, mechanics, or doctors, so long as you cannot be a legitimate citizen or doctor unless you are a graduate. It makes no difference where the meetings occur—in the auto repair shop, the legislature, or the hospital—so long as they are understood as attendance.

What is important in the hidden curriculum is that students learn that education is valuable when it is acquired in the school through a graded process of consumption; that the degree of success the individual will enjoy in society depends on the amount of learning he consumes; and that learning *about* the world is more valuable than learning *from* the world. The imposition of this hidden curriculum within an educational program distinguishes schooling from other forms of planned education. All the world's school systems have common characteristics as distinguished from their institutional output, and these are the result of the common hidden curriculum of all schools.

It must be clearly understood that the hidden curriculum translates learning from an activity into a commodity for which the school monopolizes the market. The name we now give to this commodity is "education," a quantifiable and cumulative output of a professionally designed institution called school, whose value can be measured by the duration and the costliness of the application of a process (the hidden curriculum) to the student. The grammar school teacher with an M.A. commands a greater salary than one with fewer hours of academic credit, regardless of the relevance of the degree to the task of teaching.

In all "schooled" countries knowledge is regarded as the first necessity for survival, but also as a form of currency more liquid than rubles or dollars. We have become accustomed, through Karl Marx's writings, to speak of the alienation of the worker from his work in a class society. We must now recognize the estrangement of man from his learning when it becomes the product of a service profession and he becomes the consumer.

The more education an individual consumes, the more "knowledge stock" he acquires and the higher he rises in the hierarchy of knowledge capitalists. Education thus defines a new class structure for society within which the large consumers of knowledge—those who have acquired greater quantities of knowledge stock—can claim to be of superior value to society. They represent gilt-edged securities in a society's portfolio of human capital, and access to the more powerful or scarcer tools of production is reserved to them.

The hidden curriculum thus both defines and measures what education is, and to what level of productivity it entitles the consumer. It serves as a rationale for the growing correlation between jobs and corresponding privilege—which translates into personal income in some societies and into direct claims to time-saving services, further education, and prestige in others. (This point is especially important in the light of the lack of correspondence between schooling and occupational competence established in studies such as Ivar Berg's *Education and Jobs: The Great Training Robbery* [New York, 1970].)

The endeavor to put all men through successive stages of enlightenment is rooted deeply in alchemy, the Great Art of the waning Middle Ages. John Amos Comenius (1592-1670), a Moravian bishop, self-styled pansophist, and pedagogue, is rightly considered one of the founders of modern schools. He was among the first to propose seven to twelve grades of compulsory learning. In his *Didactica ntagna*, he described schools as devices to "teach everybody everything" and outlined a blueprint for an assembly-line production of knowledge, which according to his ideas would make education cheaper and better and make growth into full humanity possible for all. But Comenius was not only an early efficiency expert; he was an alchemist who adopted the technical language of his craft to describe the art of rearing children. The alchemist sought to refine base elements by conducting their distilled spirits through seven successive stages of sublimation, so that for their own and all the world's benefit they might be transmuted into gold. Of course, the alchemists failed no matter how often they tried, but each time their "science" yielded new reasons for their failure, and they tried again.

Pedagogy opened a new chapter in the history of the Ars Magna. Education became the search for an alchemic process that would bring forth a new type of man, who would fit into an environment created by scientific magic. But no matter how much each generation spent on its schools, it always turned out that the majority of people were unfit for enlightenment by this process and had to be discarded as unprepared for life in a man-made world.

Educational reformers who accept the idea that schools have failed fall into three groups. The most respectable are certainly the great masters of alchemy who promise better schools. The most seductive are the popular magicians who promise to make every kitchen into an alchemical laboratory. The most sinister are the new masons of the universe who want to transform the entire world into one huge temple of learning.

Notable among today's masters of alchemy are certain research directors employed or sponsored by the large foundations who believe that schools, if they could somehow be improved, could also become economically more feasible than those that are now in trouble, and simultaneously could sell a larger package of services. Those who are concerned mainly with the curriculum claim that it is outdated or irrelevant. So, the curriculum is filled with new packaged courses on African Culture, North American Imperialism, Women's Lib, Pollution, or the Consumer Society. Passive learning is wrong—it is, indeed—so students are graciously allowed to decide what and how they want to be taught. Schools are prison houses; therefore principals are authorized to approve teachouts, moving the school desks to a roped-off Harlem street. Sensitivity training becomes fashionable, so we import group therapy into the classroom. School, which was supposed to teach everybody everything, now becomes all things to all children.

Other critics insist that schools make inefficient use of modern science. Some would administer drugs to make it easier for the instructor to change the child's behavior. Others would transform school into a stadium for educational gaming. Still others would electrify the classroom. If they are simplistic disciples of McLuhan, they replace blackboards and textbooks with multimedia happenings; if they follow Skinner, they claim to be able to modify behavior more efficiently than old-fashioned classroom practitioners.

Most of these changes have, of course, some good effects. The experimental schools have fewer truants. Parents do have a greater feeling of participation in a decentralized district. Pupils assigned by their teacher to an apprenticeship often do turn out more competent than those who stay in the classroom. Some children do improve their knowledge of Spanish in the language lab because they prefer playing with the knobs of a tape recorder to conversing with their Puerto Rican peers. Yet all these improvements operate within predictably narrow limits, since they leave the hidden curriculum intact.

Some reformers would like to shake loose from the hidden curriculum of public schools, but they rarely succeed. Free schools that lead to further free schools produce a mirage of freedom, even though the chain of attendance is often interrupted by long stretches of loafing. Attendance through seduction inculcates the need for educational treatment more persuasively than reluctant attendance enforced by a truant officer. Permissive teachers in a padded classroom can easily render their pupils impotent to survive once they leave.

Learning in these schools often remains nothing more than the acquisition of socially valued skills defined, in this instance, by the consensus of a commune rather than by the decree of a school board. New presbyter is but old priest writ large.

Free schools, to be truly free, must meet two conditions: first, they must be run in such a way as to prevent the reintroduction of the hidden curriculum of graded attendance and certified students study-

ing at the feet of certified teachers. And more important, they must provide a framework in which all participants, staff and pupils, can free themselves from the hidden assumptions of a schooled society. The first condition is frequently stated in the aims of a free school. The second condition is only rarely recognized and is difficult to state as the goal of a free school.

The Hidden Assumptions of Education

It is useful to distinguish between the hidden curriculum, which I have described, and the occult foundations of schooling. The hidden curriculum is a ritual that can be considered the official initiation into modern society, institutionally established through the school. It is the purpose of this ritual to hide from its participants the contradictions between the myth of an egalitarian society and the class-conscious reality it certifies. Once they are recognized as such, rituals lose their power, and this is what is now beginning to happen to schooling. But there are certain fundamental assumptions about growing up—the occult foundations—which now find their expression in the ceremonial of schooling, and which could easily be reinforced by what free schools do.

On first sight, any generalization about free schools seems rash. Especially in the United States, in Canada, and in Germany of 1971, they are the thousand flowers of a new spring. About those experimental enterprises which claim to be *educational institutions*, generalizations can be made. But first we must gain some deeper insight into

the relationship between schooling and education.

We often forget that the word "education" is of recent coinage. It was unknown before the Reformation. The education of children is first mentioned in French in a document of 1498. This was the year when Erasmus settled in Oxford, when Savonarola was burned at the stake in Florence, and when Durer etched his *Apocalypse*, which speaks to us powerfully about the sense of doom hanging over the end of the Middle Ages. In the English language the word "education" first appeared in 1530-the year when Henry VIII divorced Catherine of Aragon and when the Lutheran Church separated from Rome at the Diet of Augsburg. In Spanish lands another century passed before the word and idea of education became known. In 1632 Lope de Vega still refers to "education" as a novelty. That year, the University of San Marcos in Lima celebrated its sixtieth anniversary. Learning centers did exist before the term "education" entered common parlance. You "read" the classics or the law; you were not educated for life.

During the sixteenth century the universal need for "justification" was at the core of theological disputes. It rationalized politics and served as a pretext for large-scale slaughter. The Church split, and it became possible to hold widely divergent opinions of the degree to which all men were born sinful and corrupt and predestined. But by the early seventeenth century a new consensus began to arise: the idea that man was born incompetent for society and remained so unless he was provided with "education." Education came to mean the inverse of vital competence. It came to mean a process rather than the plain knowledge of the facts and the ability to use tools which shape a man's concrete life. Education came to mean an intangible commodity that had to be produced for the benefit of all, and imparted to them in the manner in which the visible Church formerly imparted invisible grace. Justification in the sight of society became the first necessity for a man born in original stupidity, analogous to original sin.

Schooling and education are related to each other like Church and religion, or in more general terms, like ritual and myth. The ritual created and sustains the myth; it is mythopoeic, and the myth generates the curriculum through which it is perpetuated. "Education" as the designation for an all-embracing category of social justification is an idea for which we cannot find (outside Christian theology) a specific analogue in other cultures. And the production of education through the process of schooling sets schools apart from other institutions for learning that existed in other epochs. This point must be understood if we want to clarify the shortcomings of most free, unstructured, or independent schools.

To go beyond the simple reform of the classroom, a free school must avoid incorporating the hidden curriculum of schooling which I have described above. An ideal free school tries to provide education and at the same time tries to prevent that education from being used to establish or justify a class structure, from becoming a rationale for measuring the pupil against some abstract scale, and from repressing, controlling, and cutting him down to size. But as long as the free school tries to provide "general educa-

tion," it cannot move beyond the hidden assumptions of education.

Among these assumptions is what Peter Schrag calls the "immigration syndrome," which impels us to treat all people as if they were newcomers who must go through a naturalization process. Only certified consumers of knowledge are admitted to citizenship. Men are not born equal but are made equal through gestation by Alma Mater. They must be guided away from their natural environment and pass through a social womb in which they are formed sufficiently to fit into everyday life. Free schools often perform this function better than schools of a less seductive kind.

Free educational establishments share with less free establishments another characteristic: they depersonalize the responsibility for education. They place an institution in loco parentis. They perpetuate the idea that teaching, if done outside the family, ought to be done by an agency, for which the individual teacher is but an agent. In a schooled society even the family is reduced to an "agency of acculturation." Educational agencies that employ teachers to perform the corporate intent of their boards are instruments for the depersonalization of intimate relations.

Of course, many free schools do function without accredited teachers. By doing so, they represent a serious threat to the established teachers' unions. But they do not represent a threat to the professional structure of society. A school in which the board appoints people of its own choice to carry out its educational endeavor even though they hold no professional certificate, license, or union card is not

thereby challenging the legitimacy of the teaching profession any more than a madam, operating in a country which for legal operation demands a police license, challenges the social legitimacy of the oldest profession by running a private house.

Most teachers who teach in free schools have no opportunity to teach in their own name. They carry out the corporate task of teaching in the name of a board, the less transparent function of teaching in the name of their pupils, or the more mystical function of teaching in the name of "society" at large. The best proof of this is that most teachers in free schools spend even more time than their professional colleagues planning with a committee how the school should educate. When they are faced with the evidence of their illusion, the length of committee meetings drives many generous teachers from public into free school and after one year beyond it.

The rhetoric of all educational establishments states that they form men for something, for the future. But they do not release them for this task before they have developed a high level of tolerance to the ways of their elders: education for life rather than in everyday life. Few free schools can avoid doing precisely this. Nevertheless, they are among the most important centers from which a new life-style will radiate, not because of the effect their graduates will have, but rather because elders who choose to bring up their children without the benefit of properly ordained teachers frequently belong to a radical minority and because their preoccupation with the rearing of their children sustains them in their new style.

The Hidden Hand in an Educational Market

The most dangerous category of educational reformers are those who maintain that knowledge can be produced and sold much more effectively on an open market than on one controlled by the school. These people argue that skills can be easily acquired from skill models if the learner is truly interested in their acquisition, that individual entitlement can provide a more equal purchasing power for education. They demand a careful separation of the process by which knowledge is measured and certified. These seem to me obvious statements. But it would be a fallacy to believe that the establishment of a free market for knowledge would constitute a radical alternative in education.

The establishment of a free market would indeed abolish what I have previously called the hidden curriculum of present schooling—its age-specific attendance in a graded curriculum. Equally, a free market would at first give the appearance of counteracting what I have called the occult foundations of a schooled society: the "immigration syndrome," the institutional monopoly of teaching, and the ritual of linear initiation. But at the same time a free market in education would provide the alchemist with innumerable hidden hands to fit each man into the multiple tight little niches a more complex technocracy can provide.

Many decades of reliance on schooling have turned knowledge into a commodity, a marketable staple of a special kind. Knowledge is now regarded simultaneously as a first necessity and as society's most precious currency. (The transformation of knowledge into a commod-

ity is reflected in a corresponding transformation of language. Words that formerly functioned as verbs are becoming nouns that designate possessions. Until recently "dwelling" and "learning" and "healing" designated activities. They are now usually conceived as commodities or services to be delivered. We talk about the manufacture of housing or the delivery of medical care; people are no longer regarded as fit to heal or house themselves. In such a society people come to believe that professional services are more valuable than personal care. Instead of learning how to nurse grandmother, the teenager learns to picket the hospital that does not admit her.) This attitude could easily survive the disestablishment of school, just as affiliation with a church remained a condition for office long after the adoption of the First Amendment. It is even more evident that batteries of tests measuring complex knowledge packages could easily survive the disestablishment of school—and along with them the compulsion to oblige everybody to acquire a minimum package of knowledge stock. The scientific measurement of each person's worth and the alchemistic dream of each person's "educability to his full humanity" would finally coincide. Under the appearance of a free market, the global village would turn into an environmental womb where pedagogic therapists controlled the complex placenta by which each human being was nourished.

At present schools limit the teacher's competence to the classroom. They prevent him from claiming man's whole life as his domain. The demise of school would remove this restriction and give a semblance of legitimacy to the

lifelong pedagogical invasion of everybody's privacy. It would open the way for a scramble for "knowledge" on a free market, which would lead us toward the paradox of a vulgar, albeit seemingly egalitarian, meritocracy.

Schools are by no means the only or the most efficient institutions that pretend to translate information, understanding, and wisdom into behavioral traits the measurement of which is the key to prestige and power. Nor are schools the first institutions used to convert education into an entitlement. The Chinese mandarin system, for example, was for centuries a stable and effective incentive for education in the service of a relatively open class whose privilege depended on the acquisition of measurable knowledge. Promotion to a scholarly rank did not provide entitlement to any of the coveted jobs, but it did provide a ticket for a public lottery at which offices were distributed by lot among the certified mandarins. No schools, much less universities, developed in China until that country began to wage war with European powers. The testing of independently acquired measurable knowledge enabled the Chinese Empire for three thousand years, alone among nation states in having neither a true church nor a school system, to select its governing elite without establishing a large hereditary aristocracy. Access to this elite was open to the emperor's family and to those who passed tests.

Voltaire and his contemporaries praised the Chinese system of promotion through proven learning. Civil service testing was introduced in France in 1791, only to be abolished by Napoleon. It would be fascinating to speculate what would have happened had the mandarin system been chosen to propagate the ideals of the French Revolution, instead of the school system, which inevitably supported nationalism and military discipline. As it happened, Napoleon strengthened the polytechnic, residential school. The Jesuit model of ritual, sequential promotion in a cloistered establishment prevailed over the mandarin system as the preferred method by which Western societies gave legitimacy to their elites.

Principals became the abbots in a world-wide chain of monasteries in which everybody was busy accumulating the knowledge necessary to enter the constantly obsolescent heaven on earth. Just as the Calvinists disestablished monasteries only to turn all of Geneva into one, so we must fear that the disestablishment of school may bring forth a world-wide factory for knowledge. Unless the concept of learning or knowledge is transformed, the disestablishment of school will lead to a wedding between the mandarin system—which separates learning from certification—and a society committed to provide therapy for each man until he be ripe for the gilded age.

The Contradiction of Schools as Tools of Technocratic Progress

Education for a consumer society is equivalent to consumer training. The reform of the classroom, the dispersal of the classroom, and the diffusion of the classroom are different ways of shaping consumers of obsolescent commodities. The survival of a society in which technocracies can constantly redefine human happiness as the consumption of their latest product depends on

educational institutions (from schools to ads) that translate education into social control.

In rich countries such as the United States, Canada, or the Soviet Union, huge investments in schooling make the institutional contradictions of technocratic progress very evident. In these countries the ideological defense of unlimited progress rests on the claim that the equalizing effects of open-ended schooling can counteract the disequalizing force of constant obsolescence. The legitimacy of industrial society itself comes to depend on the credibility of schools, and it does not matter if the GOP or the Communist Party is in power. Under these circumstances the public is avid for books like Charles Silberman's report to the Carnegie Commission, published as *Crisis in the Classroom* (New York, 1970). Such research inspires confidence because of its well-documented indictment of the present school, in the light of which the insignificant attempts to save the system by manicuring its most obvious faults can create a new wave of futile expectations.

Neither alchemy nor magic nor masonry can solve the problem of the present crisis "in education." The deschooling of our world-view demands that we recognize the illegitimate and religious nature of the educational enterprise itself. Its hubris lies in its attempt to make man a social being as the result of his treatment in an engineered process.

For those who subscribe to the technocratic ethos, whatever is technically possible must be made available at least to a few whether they want it or not. Neither the privation nor the frustration of the majority counts. If cobalt treatment is possi-

ble, then the city of Tegucigalpa must have one apparatus in each of its two major hospitals, at a cost that would free an important part of the population of Honduras from parasites. If supersonic speeds are possible, then some must travel at such speeds. If the flight to Mars can be conceived, then a rationale must be found to make it appear a necessity. In the technocratic ethos poverty is modernized: not only are old alternatives closed off by new monopolies, but the lack of necessities is also compounded by a growing distance between those services that are technologically feasible and those that are in fact available to the majority.

A teacher turns "educator" when he adopts this technocratic ethos. He then acts as if education were a technological enterprise designed to make man fit into whatever environment the "progress" of science creates. He seems blind to the evidence that constant obsolescence of all commodities comes at a high price: the mounting cost of training people to know about them. He seems to forget that the rising cost of tools is purchased at a high price in education: they decrease the labor-intensiveness of the economy and make learning on the job impossible, or at best the privilege of a few. All over the world the cost of educating men for society rises faster than the productivity of the entire economy, and fewer people have a sense of intelligent participation in the commonwealth.

Further investments in school everywhere render the futility of schooling monumental. Paradoxically, the poor are the first victims of more school. The Wright Commission in Ontario had to report to its government sponsors that postsecondary education is inevitably and without remedy the disproportionate taxing of the poor for an education that will always be enjoyed mainly by the rich.

Experience confirms these warnings. For several decades a quota system in the Soviet Union favored the admission to the university of sons of working parents over sons of university graduates. Nevertheless, the latter are overrepresented in Russian graduating classes much more than they are in those of the United States.

In poor countries, schools rationalize the economic lag of an entire nation. The majority of citizens are excluded from the scarce modern means of production and consumption, but long to enter the economy by way of the school door. The legitimization of hierarchical distribution of privilege and power has shifted from lineage, inheritance, the favor of king or pope, and ruthlessness on the market or on the battlefield to a more subtle form of capitalism: the hierarchical but liberal institution of compulsory schooling, which permits the well-schooled to impute guilt to the lagging consumer of knowledge for holding a certificate of lower denomination. Yet this rationalization of inequality can never square with the facts, and populist regimes find it increasingly difficult to hide the conflict between rhetoric and reality.

For ten years Castro's Cuba has devoted great energies to rapid-growth popular education, relying on available manpower, without the usual respect for professional credentials. The initial spectacular successes of this campaign, especially in diminishing illiteracy, have been cited as evidence for the claim that

the slow growth rate of other Latin American school systems is due to corruption, militarism, and a capitalist market economy. Yet now the logic of hierarchical schooling is catching up with Fidel and his attempt to school-produce the New Man. Even when students spend half the year in the cane fields and fully subscribe to the egalitarian ideals of *companero* Fidel, the school trains every year a crop of self-conscious knowledge consumers ready to move on to new levels of consumption. Also Dr. Castro faces evidence that the school system will never turn out enough certified technical manpower. Those licensed graduates who do get the new jobs destroy by their conservatism the results obtained by noncertified cadres who muddled into their positions through on-the-job training. Teachers simply cannot be blamed for the failures of a revolutionary government that insists on the institutional capitalization of manpower through a hidden curriculum guaranteed to produce a universal bourgeoisie.

On March 8, 1971, an act of the United States Supreme Court made it possible to begin the legal challenge of the hidden curriculum's legitimacy in that country. Expressing the unanimous opinion of the Court in the case of *Griggs et al.* vs. *Duke Power Company*, Chief Justice Warren E. Burger stated that "diplomas and tests are useful servants, but Congress has mandated the commonsense proposition that they are not to become masters of reality." The Chief Justice was interpreting the intent of Congress in the equal-opportunities section of the 1964 Civil Rights Act, and the Court was ruling that any school degree or any test given prospective

employees must "measure the man for the job" and not the "man in the abstract." The burden of proving that educational requirements are a "reasonable measure of job performance" rests with the employer. In this decision, the Court ruled only on tests and diplomas as means of racial discrimination, but the logic of the Chief Justice's argument applies to any use of an educational pedigree as a prerequisite for employment. Employers will find it difficult to show that schooling is a necessary prerequisite for any job. It is easy to show that it is necessarily antidemocratic because it inevitably discriminates. The Great Training Robbery so effectively exposed by Ivar Berg should now face repeated challenges from students, employers, and taxpayers.

The Recovery of Responsibility for Teaching and Learning

A revolution against those forms of privilege and power that are based on claims to professional knowledge must start with a transformation of consciousness about the nature of learning. This means, above all, a shift of responsibility for teaching and learning. Knowledge can be defined as a commodity only so long as it is viewed as the result of institutional enterprise or as the fulfillment of institutional objectives. When a man recovers the sense of personal responsibility for what he learns and teaches, this spell can be broken and the alienation of learning from living be overcome.

The recovery of the power to learn or to teach means that the teacher who takes the risk of interfering in somebody else's private affairs also assumes responsibility for the results. Similarly, the student who exposes himself to the influence of a teacher must take responsibility for his own education. For such purposes educational institutions—if they are needed at all —ideally take the form of facility centers where one can get a roof of the right size over his head and access to a piano or a kiln and to records, books, or slides. Schools, television stations, theaters, and the like are designed primarily for use by professionals. Deschooling society means above all the denial of professional status to the second oldest profession, namely, teaching. The certification of teachers now constitutes an undue restriction on the right to free speech; the corporate structure and professional pretensions of journalism an undue restriction on the right to a free press. Compulsory-attendance rules interfere with free assembly. The deschooling of society is nothing less than a cultural mutation by which a people recovers the effective use of its constitutional freedoms: learning and teaching by men who know they are born free rather than treated to freedom. Most people learn most of the time when they do whatever they enjoy; most people are curious and want to give meaning to whatever they come in contact with; and most people are capable of personal, intimate intercourse with others unless they are stupefied by inhuman work or turned off by schooling.

The fact that people in rich countries do not learn much on their own constitutes no proof to the contrary. Rather it is a consequence of life in an environment from which, paradoxically, they cannot learn much precisely because it is so highly programmed. They are constantly frustrated by the structure of contemporary society in which the facts that are the basis for making decisions have become more elusive. They live in an environment where tools that can be used for creative purposes have become luxuries, an environment where the channels of communication allow a few to talk to the many.

A New Technology Rather Than a New Education

During the Kennedy years, a peculiar image appeared: knowledge stock. It then gained wide currency in economic thought through Kenneth Boulding. This valuable social good is viewed as the cumulative accretion of the mental excrement of our brightest and best. We here succeed in imagining an anal "capital" that replaces the heaps of earth or gold of previous capitalisms. Instead of bankers and brinksmen, scientists and information storage and retrieval specialists guard it. Meanwhile, thanks to its accruement in a critical mass, it produces interest. A special kind of marketing specialist called an "educator" distributes the stock by channeling it toward those privileged enough to have access to the higher reaches of the international knowledge exchange called "school." Here, these acquire knowledge-holding certificates, which increase the possessor's social value. In some societies, this value translates principally into increased personal income, while in those where knowledge capital is considered too valuable to end up as private property, the value translates into power, rank, and privilege. Such singular treatment is rationalized by the pomp due the guardians of such stock when they put it to further use.

Such a view also affects the manner in which we think of modern technology's development. A contemporary myth would make us believe that the sense of impotence with which most men live today is the consequence of a technology that cannot but create huge systems. But it is not technology that makes systems huge, tools immensely powerful, channels of communication one-directional. Quite the contrary. Properly controlled, technology could provide each man with the ability to understand his environment better and to shape it powerfully with his own hands, and would permit him full intercommunication to a degree never before possible. Such an alternative use of technology constitutes the central alternative in education.

If a person is to grow up he needs, first of all, access to things, to places, and to processes, to events and to records. He needs to see, to touch, to tinker with, to grasp whatever there is in a meaningful setting. This access is now largely denied. When knowledge became a commodity, it acquired the protections of private property, and thus a principle designed to guard personal intimacy became a rationale for declaring facts off limits for people without proper credentials. In schools teachers keep knowledge to themselves unless it fits into the day's program. The media inform, but exclude those things they regard as unfit to print. Information is locked into special languages, and specialized teachers live off its retranslation. Patents are protected by corporations, secrets are guarded by bureaucracies, and the power to keep others out of private preserves—be they cockpits, law offices, junkyards, or clinics—is jealously guarded by professions, institutions, and nations. Neither the political nor the professional structure of our societies, East and West, could withstand the elimination of the power to keep entire classes of people from facts that could serve them. The access to facts that I advocate goes far beyond truth in labeling. Access must be built into reality, while all we ask of advertising is a guarantee that it does not mislead. Access to reality constitutes a fundamental alternative in education to a system that only purports to teach about it.

Abolishing the right to corporate secrecy—even when professional opinion holds that this secrecy serves the common good—is, as shall presently appear, a much more radical political goal than the traditional demand for public ownership or control of the tools of production. The socialization of tools without the effective socialization of know-how in their use tends to put the knowledge capitalist into the position formerly held by the financier. The technocrat's only claim to power is the stock he holds in some class of scarce and secret knowledge, and the best means to protect its value is a large and capital intensive organization that renders access to know-how formidable and forbidding.

It does not take much time for the interested learner to acquire almost any skill that he wants to use. We tend to forget this in a society where professional teachers monopolize entrance into all fields and thereby stamp teaching by uncertified individuals as quackery. There are few mechanical skills used in industry or research that are as demanding, complex, and dangerous as driving a car, a skill that most people

quickly acquire from a peer. Not all people are suited for advanced logic, yet those who are make rapid progress if they are challenged to play mathematical games at an early age. One out of twenty kids in Cuernavaca can beat me at Whiff 'n' Proof after a couple of weeks training. In four months all but a small percentage of motivated adults at our CIDOC center were able to learn Spanish well enough to conduct academic business in the new language.

A first step toward opening up access to skills would be to provide various incentives for skilled individuals to share their knowledge. Inevitably, this would run counter to the interest of guilds and professions and unions. Yet multiple apprenticeship is attractive; it provides everybody with an opportunity to learn something about almost anything. There is no reason why a person should not combine the abilities to drive a car, repair telephones and toilets, act as a midwife, and function as an architectural draftsman. Special-interest groups and their disciplined consumers would, of course, claim that the public needs the protection of a professional guarantee. But this argument is now steadily being challenged by consumer-protection associations. We have to take much more seriously the objection that economists raise to the radical socialization of skills: that "progress" will be impeded if knowledge—patents, skills, and all the rest—is democratized. Their arguments can be faced only if we demonstrate to them the growth rate of futile diseconomies generated by any existing educational system.

Access to people willing to share their skills is no guarantee of learn-

ing. Such access is restricted not only by the monopoly of educational programs over learning and of unions over licensing but also by a technology of scarcity. The skills that count today are know-how in the use of tools that were designed to be scarce. These tools produce goods or render services that everybody wants but only a few can enjoy, and which only a limited number of people know how to use. Only a few privileged individuals out of the total number of people who have a given disease ever benefit from the results of sophisticated medical technology, and even fewer doctors develop the skill to use them.

The same results of medical research have, however, also been employed to create a basic tool kit that permits army and navy medics, with only a few months of training, to obtain results under battlefield conditions that would have been beyond the expectations of full-fledged doctors during World War II. On an even simpler level, any peasant girl could learn how to diagnose and treat most infections if medical scientists prepared dosages and instructions specifically for a given geographic area.

All these examples illustrate the fact that educational considerations alone suffice to demand a radical reduction of the professional structure that now impedes the relationship between the scientist and the majority of people who want access to science. If this demand' were heeded, all men could learn to use yesterday's tools, rendered more effective and durable by modern science, to create tomorrow's world.

Unfortunately, precisely the contrary trend prevails at present. I know a coastal area in South America where most people support themselves by fishing from small boats. The outboard motor is certainly the tool that has changed the lives of these coastal fishermen most dramatically. But in the area I have surveyed, half of all outboard motors that were purchased between 1945 and 1950 are still kept running by constant tinkering, while half the motors purchased in 1965 no longer run because they were not built to be repaired. Technological progress provides the majority of people with gadgets they cannot afford and deprives them of the simpler tools they need.

Metals, plastics, and ferroconcrete used in building have greatly improved since the 1940s and ought to provide more people the opportunity to create their own homes. But' while in 1948 more than 30 per cent of all one-family homes in the United States were owner-built, by the end of the 1960s the percentage of those who acted as their own contractors had dropped to less than 20 per cent.

The lowering of the skill level through so-called economic development has become even more visible in Latin America. Here most people still build their own homes from floor to roof. Often they use mud in the form of adobe and thatchwork of unsurpassed utility in the moist, hot, and windy climate. In other places they make their dwellings out of cardboard, oil drums, and other industrial refuse. Instead of providing people with simple tools and highly standardized, durable, and easily repaired components, all governments have gone in for the mass production of low-cost buildings. It is clear that not one single country can afford to provide satisfactory modern dwelling units for the majority of its

people. Yet everywhere this policy makes it progressively more difficult for the majority to acquire the knowledge and skills they need to build better houses for themselves.

Self-Chosen "Poverty"

Educational considerations permit us to formulate a second fundamental characteristic that any post industrial society must possess: a basic tool kit that by its very nature counteracts technocratic control. For educational reasons we must work toward a society in which scientific knowledge is incorporated in tools and components that can be used meaningfully in units small enough to be within the reach of all. Only such tools can socialize access to skills. Only such tools favor temporary associations among those who want to use them on specific occasions. Only such tools allow specific goals to emerge in the process of their use, as any tinkerer knows. Only the combination of guaranteed access to facts and of limited power in most tools renders it possible to envisage a subsistence economy capable of incorporating the fruits of modern science.

The development of such a scientific subsistence economy is unquestionably to the advantage of the overwhelming majority of the people in poor countries. It is also the only alternative to progressive pollution, exploitation, and opaqueness in rich countries. But as we have seen, the dethroning of GNP cannot be achieved without simultaneously subverting GNE—Gross National Education, usually conceived as manpower capitalization. An egalitarian economy cannot exist in a society in which the right to produce is conferred by schools.

The feasibility of a modern subsistence economy does not depend on new scientific inventions. It depends primarily on the ability of a society to agree on fundamental, self-chosen antibureaucratic and antitechnocratic restraints.

These restraints can take many forms, but they will not work unless they touch the basic dimensions of life. (The decision of the United States Congress against development of the supersonic transport plane is one of the most encouraging steps in the right direction.) The substance of these voluntary social restraints would be very simple matters that could be fully understood and judged by any prudent man. (The issues at stake in the SST controversy provide a good example.) All such restraints would be chosen to promote stable and equal enjoyment of scientific know-how. The French say that it takes a thousand years to educate a peasant to deal with a cow. It would not take two generations to help all people in Latin America or Africa to use and repair outboard motors, simple cars, pumps, medicine kits, and ferroconcrete machines if their design did not change every few years. And since a joyful life is one of constant meaningful intercourse with others in a meaningful environment, equal enjoyment does translate into equal education.

At present a consensus on austerity is difficult to imagine. The reason usually given for the impotence of the majority is stated in terms of political or economic class. What is not usually understood is that the new class structure of a schooled society is even more powerfully controlled by vested interests. No doubt an imperialist and capitalist organization of society provides the social structure within which a minority can have disproportionate influence over the effective opinion of the majority. But in a technocratic society the power of a minority of knowledge capitalists can prevent the formation of true public opinion through control of scientific know-how and the media of communication. Constitutional guarantees of free speech, free press, and free assembly were meant to ensure government by the people. Modern electronics, photo-offset presses, timesharing computers, and telephones have in principle provided the hardware that could give an entirely new meaning to these freedoms. Unfortunately these things are used in modern media to increase the power of knowledge bankers to funnel their program-packages through international chains to more people, instead of being used to increase true networks that would provide equal opportunity for encounter among the members of the majority.

Deschooling the culture and social structure requires the use of technology to make participatory politics possible. Only on the basis of a majority coalition can limits to secrecy and growing power be determined without dictatorship: We need a new environment in which growing up can be classless, or we will get a brave new world in which Big Brother educates us all.

Ivan Illich was born in Austria and educated in Europe. His first assignment after being ordained a Roman Catholic priest was in New York. There he learned Spanish and accepted a post as Vice Rector of the Catholic University of Ponce in Puerto Rico. He and a few colleagues founded the Centro Intercultural de Documentacion (CIDOC) in Cuernavaca, Mexico.

From Toward a History of Needs, *Heyday Books, 1987. Copyright © Valentina Borremans. Reprinted by permission.*

For Sherry Turkle, computers are not simply a new form of technology but a screen on which we project our innermost fears and distress. Computer terminology has entered everyday language as a reflection of what we think about ourselves.

The Evocative Object

Sherry Turkle

On a cold January dawn in 1800, a boy of about thirteen came out of the woods near the village of Saint-Sernin in the Aveyron region of southern France. No one knew where he had come from. To all appearances he had survived alone, finding food and shelter in an inhospitable mountain climate since early childhood. He could not speak, and he made only weird meaningless cries.

The Wild Child was human, yet he had lived apart from culture and language. He walked out of the woods to enter history and, what is perhaps more to the point, to enter modern mythology as someone with a secret to tell. As a human being who had lapsed back to the animal condition, he was thought to embody the "natural." His way of thinking, if he could be taught to

communicate, would testify to the condition of "man in nature." The life of the Wild Child became the occasion for what has been called "the forbidden experiment," the experiment that would reveal what human beings really are beneath the overlay of society and culture.[1] Are people "blank slates," malleable, infinitely perfectible, or is there a human nature that constrains human possibility? And if there is a human nature, what is it? Are we gentle creatures ill-equipped for the strains of life in society? Or are we brutish and aggressive animals barely tamed by the demands of social life?

A young French doctor, Jean-Marc-Gaspard Itard, tried to teach the Wild Child, rechristened as Victor. He undertook the forbidden experiment. But even after seven

years of the most painstaking, systematic, and often inspired pedagogy, the boy never learned to speak, to read, or to write. He never told what he knew. He never told if he knew.

Although the experiment resolved nothing, the story of the Wild Child did not lose its power. The forbidden experiment did not settle opposing views about nature and nurture, about the innate and the social, but it provided a concrete image with which to think about them. People could imagine themselves in the story. They could say, "I am Itard. I have the job of teaching the Wild Child. What am I going to try? What do I think will happen? And why?" And when they went through the thought experiment, their ideas about what people are and how they develop came to the surface.

The Wild Child appeared soon after the French Revolution. It was a time when theories about human nature seemed up for grabs. It mattered desperately whether our nature was forever fixed or could be reformed. Fascination with the forbidden experiment and fascination with playing through its possibilities in one's mind were fed by widespread uncertainties. Now, as during that time, we are plagued with questions about who we are. Now, as then, we are drawn to whatever permits us, or forces us, to think the problem through. Not surprisingly, we have of late "rediscovered" Victor's story. There has been a flood of new studies of the Wild Child: historical, literary, psychological. The story is still evocative, "good to think with." But there is something new. There is a new focus for a forbidden experiment. A new mind that is not yet a mind. A new object, betwixt and between, equally shrouded in superstition as well as science. This is the computer.

We asked of the Wild Child to speak to us about our relationship to nature. But of the computer we ask more. We ask not just about where we stand in nature, but about where we stand in the world of artifact. We search for a link between who we are and what we have made, between who we are and what we might create, between who we are and what, through our intimacy with our own creations, we might become.

The schoolbook history of new technologies concentrates on the practical. In these accounts, the telescope led to the discovery of new stars, the railroad to the opening of new territories. But there is another

history whose consequences are deep and far-reaching. A new sense of the earth's place in the solar system made it necessary to rethink our relation to God; the ability to cross a continent within days meant a new notion of distance and communication. Clocks brought more than the ability to measure time precisely; they made time into something "divisible" and abstract.[2] Time was no longer what it took to get a job done. Time was no longer tied to the movement of the sun or the moon or to the changing of a season. Time was what it took for hands to move on a mechanism. With digital timekeeping devices, our notion of time is once more being touched by technical changes. Time is made more abstract still. Time is no longer a process; time is information.

Technology catalyzes changes not only in what we do but in how we think. It changes people's awareness of themselves, of one another, of their relationship with the world. The new machine that stands behind the flashing digital signal, unlike the clock, the telescope, or the train, is a machine that "thinks." It challenges our notions not only of time and distance, but of mind.

Most considerations of the computer concentrate on the "instrumental computer," on what work the computer will do. But my focus here is on something different, on the "subjective computer." This is the machine as it enters into social life and psychological development, the computer as it effects the way that we think, especially the way we think about ourselves. I believe that what fascinates me is the unstated question that lies behind much of our preoccupation with the computer's capabilities. That question is

not what will the computer be like in the future, but instead, what will we be like? What kind of people are we becoming?

Most considerations of the computer describe it as rational, uniform, constrained by logic. I look at the computer in a different light, not in terms of its nature as an "analytical engine," but in terms of its "second nature" as an evocative object, an object that fascinates, disturbs equanimity, and precipitates thought.

Computers call up strong feelings, even for those who are not in direct contact with them. People sense the presence of something new and exciting. But they fear the machine as powerful and threatening. They read newspapers that speak of "computer widows" and warn of "computer addiction." Parents are torn about their children's involvement not only with computers but with the machines' little brothers and sisters, the new generation of electronic toys. The toys hold the attention of children who never before sat quietly, even in front of a television screen. Parents see how the toys may be educational, but fear the quality of children's engagement with them. "It's eerie when their playmates are machines." "I wish my son wouldn't take his 'Little Professor' to bed. I don't mind a book, would welcome a stuffed animal—but taking the machine to bed gives me a funny feeling." I sit on a park bench with the mother of a six-year-old girl who is playing a question-and-answer game with a computer-controlled robot. The child talks back to the machine when it chides her for a wrong answer or congratulates her for a right one. "My God," says the mother, "she treats that thing like a person.

Do you suppose she thinks that people are machines?"

This mother shows us the shock of a first encounter. But the computer is evocative in an even more profound way for those who know it well, who interact with it directly, who are in a position to experience its second nature.

From them, there is testimony about the computer's "holding power." They say the machine is fascinating. They say it is hard to put away. For some, the "hold" is a source of puzzled amusement: a lawyer whose Wall Street firm has installed a computer system in the office and who finds himself "making work" to use it comments, "It's a cross between the Sunday *Times* crossword and Rubik's Cube." For others, the feelings are more intense, even threatening. They speak of being grabbed in a more compelling, even more intimate way than by almost anything else they have ever know. A variety of people, ranging form virtuoso programmers to those whose contact with computers goes no further than playing video games, compare their experiences with computers to sex, to drugs, or to transcendental meditation. The computer's reactivity and complexity stimulate a certain extravagance of description. "When I play pinball," says a thirty-five-year-old account executive who plays several hours of video games a day, "I am playing with a material. When I play Asteroids, it's like playing with a mind."

The computer is evocative not only because of its holding power, but because holding power creates the condition for other things to happen. An analogy captures the first of these: the computer, like a Rorschach inkblot test, is a power-ful projective medium. Unlike stereotypes of a machine with which there is only one way of relating—stereotypes built from images of workers following the rhythm of a computer-controlled machine tool or children sitting at computers that administer math problems for drill—we shall see the computer as partner in a great diversity of relationships.

. . . I choose to look at settings where the computer can be taken up as an expressive medium. Not all encounters between people and computers are as open. But as computers become commonplace objects in daily life—in leisure and learning as well as in work—everyone will have the opportunity to interact with them in ways where the machine can act as a projection of part of the self, a mirror of the mind.

The Rorschach provides ambiguous images onto which different forms can be projected. The computer too takes on many shapes and meanings. In what follows, we shall see that, as with the Rorschach, what people make of the computer speaks of their larger concerns, speaks of who they are as individual personalities.

When different people sit down at computers, even when they sit down at the same computer to do the "same" job, their styles of interacting with the machine are very different. Nowhere is this more true than when they program. For many, computer programming is experienced as creating a world apart. Some create worlds that are highly predictable and use their experiences in them to develop a sense of themselves as capable of exerting firm control. Others have different needs, different desires, and create worlds whose complexity is always on the verge of getting out of hand, worlds where they can feel themselves to be wizards of brinkmanship.

But of course there is a difference between the computer and the Rorschach. The blots stay on the page. The computer becomes part of everyday life. It is a constructive as well as a projective medium. When you create a programmed world, you work in it, you experiment in it, you live in it. The computer's chameleonlike quality, the fact that when you program it, it becomes your creature, make it an ideal medium for the construction of a wide variety of private worlds and, through them, for self-exploration.[3] Computers are more than screens onto which personality is projected. They have already become a part of how a new generation is growing up. For adults and for children who play computer games, who use the computer for manipulating words, information, visual images, and especially for those who learn to program, computers enter into the development of personality, of identity, and even of sexuality.

As this happens, experiences with computers become reference points for thinking and talking about other things. Computers provoke debate about education, society, politics, and, . . . about human nature. In this, the computer, is a "metaphysical machine." Children too are provoked. The computer creates new occasions for thinking through the fundamental questions to which childhood must give a response, among them the question "What is life?"[4]

In the adult world, experts argue about whether or not computers will ever become true "artificial intelligences," themselves capable of autonomous, humanlike thought. But irrespective of the future of machine intelligence, computers are affecting how today's children think, influencing how they construct such concepts as animate and inanimate, conscious and not conscious.

Some objects, and in our time the computer is preeminent among them, provoke reflection on fundamentals. Children playing with toys that they imagine to be alive and adults playing with the idea of mind as program are both drawn by the computer's ability to provoke and to color self-reflection. The computer is a "metaphysical machine," a "psychological machine," not just because it might be said to have a psychology, but because it influences how we think about our own.

I came to this study of computers and people six years ago after joining the faculty at MIT. I was struck by the psychological discourse that surrounded computers, and by the extent to which it was used by my students and my faculty colleagues to describe the machine's processes. A chess program wasn't working. Its programmers spoke of its problems as follows: "When it feels threatened, under attack, it wants to advance its king. It confuses value and power, and this leads to self-destructive behavior." Even the most technical discussions about computers use terms borrowed from human mental functioning. In the language of their creators, programs have intentions, try their best, are more or less intelligent or stupid, communicate with one another, and become confused. This psychological vocabulary should not be surprising. Many people think of computers as mathematical objects,

but when you get closer to them you realize that they are information objects, manipulators of symbols, of language. You inevitably find yourself interacting with a computer as you would with a mind, even if a limited one. This is why the language that grows up around computers has a special flavor. Computer jargon is specifically "mind jargon."

And not only is the computer thought of in human mental terms. There is movement in the other direction as well. People are thinking of themselves in computational terms. A computer scientist says, "my next lecture is hardwired," meaning that he can deliver it without thinking, and he refuses to be interrupted during an excited dinner conversation, insisting that he needs "to clear his buffer." Another refers to psychotherapy as debugging," the technique used to clean out the final errors from almost-working programs and to her "default solutions" for dealing with men.

These people are not just using computer jargon as a manner of speaking. Their language carries an implicit psychology that equates the processes that takes place in people to those that take place in machines. It suggests that we are information systems whose thought is carried in "hardware," that we have a buffer, a mental terrain that must be cleared and crossed before we can interact with other people, that for every problem there is a preprogrammed solution on which we can fall back "by default," and that emotional problems are errors that we can extirpate.

"Hardwired," "buffer," "default," "debug"—these were among the computer metaphors I met within

the MIT computer culture. Others, that came before them, have already moved out into the common language, for example the very notion of programming. When I was in the earliest stages of writing this book I had lunch with a friend to whom I tried to explain this process of computational ideas moving out. My problem was solved when two young women sat down at the table next to us. "The hard part," said one to the other, "is reprogramming yourself to live alone." The language of computers is moved out so effectively that we forget its origins. But although we may forget, we do not so easily escape the new assumptions that our language carries about what we are and how we can change.

Amid this discussion of minds as machines and of machines having minds I felt some of the dislocation and change of perspective that can make being a stranger in a foreign place both difficult and exciting. For the anthropologist this experience brings more than the shock of the new. There is a privilege and a responsibility to see the new world through a prism not available to its members, and (and this the part that is often the most difficult) to use the new lenses to see one's own world differently as well. . . . I try to meet both of these responsibilities. And in the end, the second became even more central to my concerns than the first. Because as I worked, it became clear that what I was studying was not confined to computer experts and computer professionals. The computer was moving out into the culture as a whole.

When I began my work, studying the computer culture meant working with easily identifiable groups of people, among these virtuoso programmers known as "hackers," members of the artificial intelligence community, and the first generation of people who owned home computers. But my subject had a special quality. Unlike most ethnographies, which explore a well-defined and delimited community, whether it be a primitive society or a rural commune, I was studying a moving target. When I began my work, personal computers had just come on the market. The first computer toys and games had not yet appeared. Most people had never heard the phrase "artificial intelligence." [Now] . . . computer toys are commonplace in toddler playrooms, college freshmen arrive on campus with computers rather than electric typewriters, and the importance of a "fifth-generation" supercomputer has become a theme of public debate.

Thus, this . . . became a study of a culture in the making. A computer culture that in one way or another touches us all. And because it affects our lives in so many ways, [it] . . . takes its questions about this nascent culture from many perspectives.

From the perspective of psychological development I ask how computers enter into the process of growing up. Computers affect children very differently at different ages.

I found three stages in children's relationships with computers. First there is a "metaphysical" stage: when very young children meet computers they are concerned with whether the machines think, feel, are alive. Older children, from age seven or eight on, are less concerned with speculating about the nature of the world than with mastering it. For many of them, the first time they stand in front of a computer they can master is when they play their first video game. I discuss games—the computational medium that first made it into the general culture—and then I follow elementary-school-age children out of the games arcade and into the classroom, where they are learning to master computers by programming them. These children are all involved with the question of their own competence and effectiveness. When they work with computers they don't want to philosophize, they want to win. The second stage is one of mastery.[5]

In adolescence, experience is polarized around the question of identity, and the child's relation to the computer takes on a third character.[6] Some adolescents adopt the computer as their major activity, throwing themselves into programming the way others devote themselves to fixing cars. But there is a more subtle and widespread way that computers enter the adolescent's world of self-definition and self-creation. A computer program is a reflection of its programmer's mind. If you are the one who wrote it, then working with it can mean getting to know yourself differently. We shall see that in adolescence computers become part of a return to reflection, this time not about the machine but about oneself.

A psychological perspective also led me to study what computers come to mean for different kinds of people. I look at differences of gender, of personality, and I look most carefully at what seems to place some people "at risk." In particular, there is the risk of forming a relationship with the computer that will close rather than open opportunities for personal development.

While for some children the computer enhances personal growth, for others it becomes a place to "get stuck." For adults as well as children, computers, reactive and interactive, offer companionship without the mutuality and complexity of a human relationship. They seduce because they provide a chance to be in complete control, but they can trap people into an infatuation with control, with building one's own private world.

I describe metaphysics, mastery, and identity as organizing issues for children as they grow up. I return to them from another perspective, an anthropological one, when I write about cultures within the computer world where one or another of these issues emerges as a central theme. I look at the culture of artificial intelligence, the culture of virtuoso programmers, and the culture of personal computer owners.

The connection between artificial intelligence and the "metaphysical computer" is apparent. As soon as you take seriously the idea of creating an artificial intelligence, you face questions such as whether we have any more than sentimental reasons to believe that there is something about people that makes it impossible to capture our intelligence in machines. Can an intelligence without a living body, without sexuality, ever really understand human beings? Artificial intelligence researchers study minds in order to build programs, and they use programs to think about mind. In the course of exercising their profession, they have made questions about human intelligence and human essence their stock in trade. For the "hacker," the virtuoso programmer, what is most important about the computer is what you can make it do. Hackers use their mastery over the machine to build a culture of prowess that defines itself in terms of winning over ever more complex systems. And in talking to personal computer owners I heard echoes of the search for identity. I found that for them the computer is important not just for what it does but for how it makes you feel. It is described as a machine that lets you see yourself differently, as in control, as "smart enough to do science," as more fully participant in the future. . . .

But what we see today "larger than life" within computer cultures will not remain within their confines. As the computer presence becomes more widespread, relationships between people and computers that now take place within them prefigure changes for our culture as a whole—new forms of intimacy with machines, and a new model of mind as machine.

Because the computer is no longer confined to expert subcultures, . . . yet another kind of question [arises]: How do ideas born within the technical communities around computation find their way out to the culture beyond? This is the province of the sociology of knowledge. Ideas that begin their life in the world of science can move out; they are popularized and simplified, often only half understood, but they can have a profound effect on how people think. This diffusion has special importance in the case of the computer. The computer is a "thinking" machine. Ideas about computation come to influence our ideas about mind. So, above all, what "moves out" is the notion of mind as program, carried beyond the academy not only by the

spoken and written word, but because it is embedded in an actual physical object: the computer.

My approach to theories about mind as program is not that of a philosopher. My concern is not with the truth of such theories, but with the way in which they capture the popular imagination. What happens when people consider the computer as a model of human mind? What happens when people begin to think that they are machines? . . .

These efforts to capture the impact of the computer on people involve me in a long-standing debate about the relationship between technology and culture. At one pole there is "technological determinism," the assertion that technology itself has a determinative impact, that understanding a technology allows us to predict its effects. "What does television do to children?" The question assumes that television, independent of its content, or its social context, has an effect, for example that it creates a passive viewer, or that it breaks down the linear way of thinking produced by the printed word. At the opposite pole is the idea that the influence of a technology can be understood only in terms of the meanings people give it. What does it come to represent? How is it woven into a web of other representations, other symbols?[7]

. . . In my interviews I heard discourse about computers being used to think about free will and determinism, about consciousness and intelligence. . . . That this is not surprising from a philosophical point of view. But I was not talking to philosophers. I was talking to sophomores in high-school computer clubs, five-year-olds playing with computer games and toys, college freshmen taking their first pro-

gramming course, engineers in industrial settings, and electronics hobbyists who had recently switched from building model trains to building computers from kits. . . . I report on interviews with over four hundred people, about half of them children and half of them adults. The computer brought many of them to talk about things they might otherwise not have discussed. It provided a descriptive language that gave them the means to do so. The computer has become an "object-to-think-with."[8] It brings philosophy into everyday life.

For children a computer toy that steadily wins at tic-tac-toe can spark questions about consciousness and intention. For adults such primitive machines do not have this power. Since almost everyone knows a mechanical strategy for playing tic-tac-toe, the game can easily be brought under the reassuring dictum that "machines do only what they are programmed to do." Tic-tac-toe computers are not metaphysically "evocative objects" for adults. But other computers are. Conversations about computers that play chess, about robotics, about computers that might display judgment, creativity, or wit lead to heated discussions of the limits of machines and the uniqueness of the human mind. In the past, this debate has been carried on in academic circles, among philosophers, cognitive psychologists, and researchers working on the development of intelligent machines. The growing computer presence has significantly widened the circle of debate. It is coming to include us all.

Steve is a college sophomore, an engineering student who had never thought much about psychology. In the first month of an introductory computer-science course he saw how seemingly intelligent and autonomous systems could be programmed. This led him to the idea that there might be something illusory in his own subjective sense of autonomy and self-determination.

Steve's classmate Paul had a very different reaction. He too came to ask whether free will was illusory. The programming course was his first brush with an idea that many other people encounter through philosophy, theology, or psychoanalysis: the idea that the conscious ego might not be a free agent. Having seen this possibility, he rejected it, with arguments about free will and the irreducibility of people's conscious sense of themselves. In his reaction to the computer, Paul made explicit a commitment to a concept of his own nature to which he had never before felt the need to pay any deliberate attention. For Paul, the programmed computer became the very antithesis of what it is to be human. The programmed computer became part of Paul's identity as not-computer.

Paul and Steve disagree. But their disagreement is really not about computers. It is about determinism and free will. At different points in history this same debate has played on different stages. Traditionally a theological issue, in the first quarter of this century it was played out in debate about psychoanalysis. In the last quarter of this century it looks as though it is going to be played out in debate about machines.

The analogy with psychoanalysis goes further. For several generations, popular language has been rich in terms borrowed from psychoanalysis, terms like "repression," "the unconscious," "the Oedipus complex" and, of course, "the Freudian slip." These ideas make a difference in how people think about their pasts, their presents, and their possibilities for change. They influence people who have never seen a psychoanalyst, who scarcely understand Freudian theory, and who are thoroughly skeptical about its "truth." So, when we reflect on the social impact it makes more sense to speak of the development of psychoanalytic culture than to talk about the truth of particular psychoanalytic ideas.[9] What fueled the development of a psychoanalytic culture is not the validity of psychoanalysis as a science, but the power of its psychology of everyday life. Freud's theory of dreams, jokes puns, and slips allows people to take it up as a fascinating plaything. The theory is evocative. It gives people new ways to think about themselves. Interpreting dreams and slips allows us all to have contact with taboo preoccupations, with our sexuality, our aggression, our unconscious wishes.

My interpretation of the computer's cultural impact rests on its ability to do something of the same sort. For me, one of the most important cultural effects of the computer presence is that the machines are entering into our thinking about ourselves. If behind popular fascination with Freudian theory there was a nervous, often guilty preoccupation with the self as sexual, behind increasingly interest in computational interpretations of mind is an equally nervous preoccupation with the idea of self as machine.

The debate about artificial intelligence has centered on the question "Will machines think like people?" For our nascent computer culture another question is more relevant: not whether machines will ever think like people, but whether people have always thought like machines. And if the latter is true, is this the most important thing about us? Is this what is most essential about being human?

The computer stands betwixt and between.[10] In some ways on the edge of mind, it raises questions about mind itself. Other marginal objects carry their own questions: the figure of the clown and the madman, both within and outside the normal social order, the myths of Dracula and Frankenstein, both within and outside our normal categories of what is alive. And then, on the border between nature and culture, there is the image of the Wild Child of Aveyron, the child who grew up in nature, never, it was believed, having had the influence of society, language, and civilization.

The Wild Child of Aveyron was an evocative object, inciting self-reflection, not because of anything that he did, but because of who he was, because of his position on the border between nature and culture. The computer too stands on a border. Its evocative nature does not depend on assumptions about the eventual success of artificial intelligence researches in actually making machines that duplicate people. It depends on the fact that people tend to perceive a "machine that thinks" as a "machine who thinks." They begin to consider the workings of that machine in psychological terms. . . .

Notes

1. Roger Shattuck, *The Forbidden Experiment* (New York: Farrar, Straus, and Giroux, 1980).

2. See, for example, Lewis Mumford *Technics and Civilization* (New York: Harcourt, Brace and World, 1934), particularly the classic discussion of time in "The Monastery and the Clock," pp. 12-18.

3. My discussion of personalized computer worlds builds on the notion of "microworlds" for learning developed by Seymour Papert in *Mindstorms: Children, Computers, and Powerful Ideas* (New York: Basic Books, 1980).

4. The classic discussion of how children develop the concept of life is found in Jean Piaget, *The Child's Conception of the World*, trans. by Joan and Andrew Tomlinson (Totowa, NJ: Little-field, Adams, 1975), especially "The Concept of Life," pp. 194-206.

5. For a discussion of psychoanalytic "stage theory" recast in a social as well as a psychological perspective, see Erik Erikson, *Childhood and Society* (New York: Norton, 1963), and "Identity and the Life Cycle," *Psychological Issues* 1 (1959). Erikson refers to the school age as dominated by "industry."

6. Erikson's writing on adolescence has become the classic presentation of the concept of "identity." See *Childhood and Society* (New York: Norton, 1963), and "Identity and the Life Cycle," *Psychological Issues* 1 (1959). Erikson refers to the school age as dominated by "industry."

7. See, for example, Max Weber, "The Social Psychology of World Religions," in H.H. Gerth and C.W. Mills, eds., *From Max Weber: Essays in Sociology* (New York: Oxford University Press, 1946), p. 24.

8. An example of the "determinist" view is expressed by anthropologist Leslie White: "Social systems are functions of technologies and philosophies express technological forces and reflect social systems. The technological factor is therefore the determinant for the cultural system as a whole." See Leslie White, *The Science of Culture* (New York: Farrar, Straus, and Giroux, 1949), p. 336. An example of the nondeterminist view is expressed by historian Lynn White: "As our understanding of history increases, it becomes clear that a new device merely opens a door, it does not command one to enter," See Lynn White, *Medieval Technology and Social Change* (New York: Oxford University Press, 1966), p. 28. Not all positions are as polarized. Although sociologist Daniel Bell gives a privileged status to technology as a motor of change, he describes a complex relationship between technical and social factors. See Daniel Bell, *The Coming of Post-Industrial Society* (New York: Basic Books, 1973). But in the popular culture and in the popular literature on technology and its effects, the "pure" technology-driven position is rampant. See, for example, Marshall McLuhan *Understanding Media* (New York: New American Library, 1973), John Naisbitt, *Megatrends* (New York: Warner Books, 1982), and Alvin Toffler, *Future Shock* (New York: Random House, 1970). The question of technological determinism, characterized as a debate over "engines of change," is discussed in Langdon Winner, *Autonomous Technology* (Cambridge, MA: MIT Press, 1977), pp. 44-106. Marshall Sahlins makes a distinction related to the debate on technological determinism when he contrasts materialist/rationalist explanations and explanations that look to the centrality of symbols. See Marshall Sahlins, *Culture and Practical Reason* (Chicago: University of Chicago Press, 1976).

9. My analysis of the computer as an "object-to-think-with" grew out of my appreciation of the way several other authors discussed the relation between artifacts and thought. In particular, I was influenced by Claude Lévi Strauss' discussion of *bricolage* in *The Savage Mind* (Chicago: University of Chicago Pres, 1968), Mary Douglas' discussion of objects in *Purity and Danger* (London: Routledge and Kegan Paul, 1966), and Seymour Papert's description of a relationship to gears as crucial to his development as a mathematician. See Seymour Papert, "The Gears of My Childhood," in *Mindstorms*. Sharon Traweek's recent work on the culture of high-energy physicists in the United States and Japan includes a fascinating discussion of the relationship of physicists to their tools; see *Uptime, Downtime, Spacetime, and Power: An Ethnography of the Particle Physics Community in Japan and the United States*, unpublished Ph.D. dissertation, University of California at Santa Cruz, 1982.

10. For a discussion of the role of psychological theories as they enter into everyday life and become materials for the construction of personal biography, see Peter L. Berger and Thomas Luckmann, *The Social Construction of Reality: A Treatise in the*

Sociology of Knowledge (New York: Doubleday, 1967), Peter L. Berger, "Towards a Sociological Understanding of Psychoanalysis," *Social Research* 32 (Spring 1965), pp. 26-41, Peter L. Berger, *Invitation to Sociology: A Humanistic Perspective* (New York: Anchor, 1963). See also Jerome Bruner, "Freud and the Image of Man," in Jerome Bruner, *On Knowing: Essays For the Left Hand* (Cambridge, MA: Belknap, 1962). For one of the first essays sensitive to the computer as metaphor, see Ulrich Neisser, "Computers as Tools and as Metaphors," in Charles Dechert, ed., *The Social Impact of Cybernetics* (Notre Dame, Indiana: The University of Notre Dame Press, 1966). For a more extended discussion of my use of the term "psychoanalytic culture" see Sherry Turkle, *Psychoanalytic Politics: Freud's French Revolution* (New York: Basic Books, 1978).

Reprinted from The Second Self: Computers and the Human Spirit, 1984 pp. 11-25 by permission.

Coleman McCarthy forces us to consider the value of teaching and studying peace as a way of "arming" ourselves as peacemakers. We are accustomed to viewing peace as "absence of war" rather than a presence. He challenges us to look with new eyes at this term called peace.

Why We Must Teach Peace

Colman McCarthy

A question settled in my mind a few years ago and refused to leave until I not only answered it but also acted on the answer.

If peace is what every government says it seeks, and peace is the yearning of every heart, why aren't we studying it and teaching it in schools?

Governments and citizens proclaim that mathematics, languages, and science are their goals, and students are required to take those and other courses, as if the future of the species depended on them. At commencements, graduates are told to go into the world as peacemakers. Yet in most schools, peace is so unimportant that no place is found for it in the curriculum.

Rather than whine about this, which is what too many in the syndicated column trade are content to do most of the time, I decided to go into the schools myself.

Peace Can Be Taught and Learned

In 1982, I began teaching courses in alternatives to violence. After being with some 3,000 students in three universities and two high schools, I can give the preliminary report that, contrary to what some might say, with opened minds and receptive hearts, peace can be taught and learned.

I used the qualification "preliminary" because *peace*, like *love*, is a cheapened word. Nuclear missiles are now called "peacekeepers" and are presumably equipped with multiple "peaceheads." We are told repeatedly that the way to ensure peace is to be ready for war. Nearly all world governments, with an annual global arms budget of $900 billion, preach peace through strength rather than strength through peace.

The military does what it is intended to do: deal with conflicts through fists, guns, armies, or nukes. Militarists believe wholeheartedly—and deserve credit for the intensity of their beliefs—that violence is the way to stop violence. But is obvious that history proves that approach wrong—if war were effective, all our problems would have been solved thousands of years ago. More people might embrace that fact, however, if the alternatives to fists, guns, armies, and nukes were taught and learned. If the alternatives aren't made available, how can they be applied?

As a pacifist, I am uneasy with the term "peace studies." It will do for now, but a more exact description will eventually be needed. What I have been teaching is peace through nonviolence. That, too, is somewhat imprecise. The sharpest phrase is peace through soul force or, to rely on Gandhi's favorite word, *satyagraha*. Nonviolence isn't just about ending wars. It's about creating peace in our own hearts, often the last place many people ever find it.

Between 1950 and 1978, the suicide rate among teenagers in the United States rose by more than 170 percent. Some 20,000 murders are committed annually in the United States. Violent sports like football, boxing, and hockey are glorified. About 25 millions abortions are preformed in the world every year, 1.5 million in the United States alone. The leading cause of injury among American women is being beaten by a man at home.

The Philosophy of Nonviolent Force

Studying peace through nonviolence is as much about getting the bombs out of our hearts as it is about getting them out of the Pentagon budget. Every problem we have, every conflict, whether among our family or friends, or among governments, will be addressed either through violent force or nonviolent force. No third option exists. I teach my classes because I believe in nonviolent force—the

force of justice, the force of love the force of sharing wealth, the force of ideas, the force of organized resistance to corrupt power. Fighting with those kinds of forces is the essence of nonviolence.

The first class of every semester I ask my students, "Is anyone here armed?" No one has ever raised a hand. "You are all armed," I reply. "You're armed with ideas, and you're in school to become armed with more ideas."

Occasionally a student will come back with the charge that I asked a trick question. Of course I did. Nonviolence is a tricky subject. The beauty and sanity of it doesn't get into our head easily or automatically. It takes years and years of study. Why do we dismiss nonviolence so quickly by saying that it's a wonderful theory but unreal, yet we are willing to go slowly with other complex subjects?

After I ask the question about arms, I pose a second one by listing 10 names to be identified: U.S. Grant, Robert E. Lee, Dwight Eisenhower, George Patton, William Westmoreland, Jane Addams, Jeannette Rankin, A.J. Muste, Adin Ballou, and Dorothy Day. Everyone can routinely identify the first five: all are generals. It is rare that anyone knows the second five: all believers or practitioners of nonviolence. A few take a guess that the last person was an actress and singer, as in Doris Day.

The students aren't to blame for knowing only the first five names. In elementary school and high school, and continuing through college, they are taught the history of America's seven declared wars and a fair portion of the 137 undeclared wars. Violence is taught as lore—the Alamo, Custer's Last Stand, the

ride of Paul Revere, Lexington and Concord, Gettysburg. If SAT scores were based on high schoolers' knowledge of bloodshed and militarism, we would have a nation of young geniuses.

The Choice Is Ours

To teach peace through nonviolence is to give the young a chance to develop a philosophy of force. It's to expose them to the history, techniques, and practitioners of nonviolence. I often think that college is too late. Courses on nonviolence should begin in kindergarten and 1st grade, and continue through elementary school, junior high, and senior high school.

To choose to live by a philosophy of nonviolent force is to choose Jesus over Caesar, Vincent de Paul over Napoleon, William Penn over George Washington, Jeannette Rankin over Franklin Roosevelt, Dorothy Day over Lyndon Johnson, Daniel Berrigan over Ronald Reagan.

Students, or at least the wary ones, often say they are glad former flower children like me occasionally turn up on college faculties, but in the real world nonviolence won't work and hasn't worked. Look what happened, they say, to Jesus, Gandhi, King, and a lot of other pacifists. I answer with the only honest reply available. Nonviolence is a risky philosophy to live by. It is no guarantee of safety. It's a failure. All that can be said of it is that it's less of a failure than violence.

Those who prefer violent force, I tell my students, must justify the deaths of this century's 78 million war victims. (The number is a 500 percent increase over the last century.) Those who choose the handgun as the most effective way to control or persuade the next person need to talk to the 10,000 people who will be killed by gunshot in the next year. Those who prefer violent force must explain the more than 40 wars or conflicts raging in the world today, killing an estimated 41,000 people a month—most of them poor boys slaughtered by other poor boys. Those who believe America is a generous nation must account for the 38,000 children who die in the Third World every day from diseases that could be prevented by vaccinations that cost $10 per child. The Congressional Research Office reports that since 1977, U.S. development and food aid to Third World nations has decreased by 16 percent while military aid has increased 53 percent.

A Transformation in Thinking

Courses on nonviolence are easily designed. What isn't easy is shifting people's thinking. More than 1,200 U.S. campuses allow the Pentagon into their classrooms with ROTC programs, with some 108,000 students enrolled. At the same time, only 50 colleges offer a degree in peace studies, though others do offer concentrations, like the University of Portland's Certificate Program.

Only rarely though does a school promote itself for its peace program. How often do college presidents tell prospective students, "Come to my school because we have an excellent program in nonviolent studies?" Instead, they recruit students by talking of the new computer center, or the business school, or the new gym.

The militarists aren't to blame. I'm to blame for not doing more to get peace courses into the schools. The peace movement is to blame for the same reason. Liberal arts professors have to answer for their laziness in not fighting for courses in nonviolence.

But in the end, it is students themselves who must supply the moral pressure to get those courses. It's their tuition, their world, and their future. Peter Kropotkin, the Russian pacifist and communitarian, advised the young: "Think about the kind of world you want to live and work in. What do you need to build that world? Demand that your teachers teach you that!" It's advice that students—and their teachers—should take to heart.

To Embrace a Life of Peacemaking

This year I am teaching a daily class in nonviolence at Bethesda-Chevy Chase High School in Bethesda, Maryland, from 7:40 to 8:30 A.M. I have courses also at Georgetown University Law Center and the University of Maryland.

Few students have ever taken a class in nonviolence. Because of that, I often think to myself that I would do better to be teaching a course in linear physics and speaking Swahili. The student would understand it sooner. Yet, here is what students have written in their course evaluations:

The ability to look beyond the fear and self-interest of everyone, to me, is the noblest trait a person can acquire. I am amazed, not that the movement has gained strength, although that is remarkable, but that the idea was able to find

one follower in the first place. . . . If nonviolence could be compared to grade school, I would say that I am still in kindergarten. I can't wait for 1st grade to start.—Third-year student, Georgetown University Law Center

This course dispelled a lot of myths I had about peace and pacifists and introduced me to a completely new way of seeing the world. And I believe I have changed—even my friends want to know what's been "brainwashing" me!—Sophomore, University of Maryland

I had an argument with my brother. I lost my cool and hit him. Unlike in the past when this happened, I felt disappointed with myself. If one wants to contribute to making the world a place of nonviolence, one must begin by eliminating the violence in oneself.—Senior, Gorgetown Day School, Washington, DC

This course has been planting seeds in me. I cannot currently list what I have learned. I expect, rather, that after the seeds have had a few years to grow in my heart and mind, I will recognize how this course has changed me. I was here for my long-term good, not the short-term.—Junior, Wilson High School, Washington, D.C.

None of my teaching interferes with my full-time work at *The Washington Post*, where I have been privileged to be writing since 1968. If anything, my journalism and teaching are mutually reinforcing. Writing is thinking in solitude; teaching is thinking in public. Both places, an audience is there to challenge whatever is false and endorse whatever is true.

My students are a bracing mix of intellectuals, skeptics, and seekers of peace whose company is unimaginably uplifting. Whether they are in third year law or third year high school, I try to create a class atmosphere in which the study and discussion of nonviolence is directed toward giving everyone a chance to embrace a life of both personal and political peacemaking. What other empowerment, save love, is as needed or liberating?

For some students, the embracing comes quickly. They are amazed at the breadth of the literature on nonviolence. Others hang back, wanting more evidence that nonviolence isn't just a philosophy for hugging trees at high tide and full moon. It doesn't matter when the assent occurs. In all journeys, someone is first on board the train, someone else is the 50th, 100th, or 10 millionth. That we get on, when we get on, is what's crucial.

I had a letter from a former student who confessed that, when in my class, she definitely had not understood the theories of nonviolence. She wrote from Morocco, where she was in the Peace Corps. The gist of her letter touched me deeply: now that she was out of school and overseas doing the works of peace and justice in a small way, the ideas and ideals of nonviolence were all coming back to her. They did make sense. A little time was needed to put them into practice, that's all.

Teaching nonviolence is an act of faith: the belief that students will dig deep into their reserves of inner courage and love to embrace the highest calling we know, peacemaking.

Colman McCarthy, a columnist for the Washington Post is also Director for the Center for Teaching Peace in Washington, D.C.

Index

Article Assessment Form

Article Title:

Author Name:

1. How strong a reaction (positive or negative) did you have to the article?
   - [ ] quite strong
   - [ ] fairly strong
   - [ ] not very strong
   - [ ] negligible

2. Has reading the article caused you to think differently in any way about the issue(s) it treats?
   - [ ] Yes
   - [ ] No

3. How useful did you find the article in terms of the objective(s) of the course for which you read it?
   - [ ] quite useful
   - [ ] fairly useful
   - [ ] not very useful
   - [ ] negligible

4. How interesting did you find the article?
   - [ ] quite interesting
   - [ ] fairly interesting
   - [ ] not very interesting
   - [ ] boring

5. How glad are you that you read the article?
   - [ ] quite glad
   - [ ] fairly glad
   - [ ] not very glad
   - [ ] not at all glad

6. How important is it that other people read this article?
   - [ ] quite important
   - [ ] fairly important
   - [ ] not very important
   - [ ] not at all

7. Writing Style:
   - [ ] clear
   - [ ] fairly clear
   - [ ] fairly confusing
   - [ ] quite confusing

8. How familiar was the vocabulary?
   - [ ] very familiar
   - [ ] fairly familiar
   - [ ] fairly unfamiliar
   - [ ] quite unfamiliar

9. In terms of length, did you find the article
   - [ ] about right
   - [ ] too short
   - [ ] too long

Your instructor may ask you to complete this form and hand it in. Use the back of this form to record additional reactions to the article or for other purposes specified by your instructor.

Article Title

Author Name